PENGUIN  CLASSICS

PENGUIN ENGLISH POETS
GENERAL EDITOR: CHRISTOPHER RICKS

# ARTHUR GOLDING: OVID'S METAMORPHOSES

PUBLIUS OVIDIUS NASO was born in 43 BC at Sulmo (Sulmona) in central Italy. Coming from a wealthy Roman family and seemingly destined for a career in politics, he held some minor official posts before leaving public service to write, becoming the most distinguished poet of his time. His published works include *Amores*, a collection of short love poems; *Heroides*, verse-letters written by mythological heroines to their lovers; *Ars Amatoria*, a satirical handbook on love; *Remedia Amoris*, a sequel to the *Ars*; and *Metamorphoses*, his epic work on change. He was working on *Fasti*, a poem on the Roman calendar, when, in AD 8, the emperor Augustus exiled him to Tomis on the Black Sea, far from Rome and the literary life he loved. The reason for this is unclear; the pretext was the immorality of *Ars Amatoria*, but there was probably a political aspect to the affair. He continued to write, notably *Tristia* and *Epistulae ex Ponto*, and revised *Fasti*. He never returned to Rome and died, in exile, in AD 17 or 18.

ARTHUR GOLDING was born in 1536 and entered Jesus College, Cambridge, in 1552. He married Ursula Roydon, who bore him eight children. His first translation was published in 1562; the first edition of his translation of Ovid's *Metamorphoses* was published in four books in 1565. The complete fifteen-book edition appeared in 1567. It was highly praised by writers of the time, such as Thomas Nashe and William Webbe, and is known to have influenced the works of Shakespeare and Spenser. Golding is also known for his translation of Calvin's *Commentaries on the Psalms*, Caesar's *Gallic War* and for completing the translation of Philippe de Mornay's *A Work Concerning the Trueness of the Christian Religion*. He died in 1606.

MADELEINE FOREY read English at St John's College, Oxford. She was a Lecturer at Royal Holloway College, London University, between 1993 and 1998, and is currently Lecturer at Exeter College, Oxford. She has been a Fellow of All Souls College, Oxford, since 1988. She has published articles on Golding, Shakespeare, Henry Vaughan, Spenser and Milton.

# OVID'S *METAMORPHOSES*

*Translated by Arthur Golding*

*Edited with an Introduction and Notes by*
MADELEINE FOREY

PENGUIN BOOKS

PENGUIN BOOKS

Published by the Penguin Group
Penguin Books Ltd, 80 Strand, London WC2R ORL, England
Penguin Putnam Inc., 375 Hudson Street, New York, New York 10014, USA
Penguin Books Australia Ltd, 250 Camberwell Road, Camberwell, Victoria 3124, Australia
Penguin Books Canada Ltd, 10 Alcorn Avenue, Toronto, Ontario, Canada M4V 3B2
Penguin Books India (P) Ltd, 11, Community Centre, Panchsheel Park, New Delhi – 110 017, India
Penguin Books (NZ) Ltd, Cnr Rosedale and Airborne Roads, Albany, Auckland, New Zealand
Penguin Books (South Africa) (Pty) Ltd, 24 Sturdee Avenue, Rosebank 21961, South Africa

Penguin Books Ltd, Registered Offices: 80 Strand, London WC2R ORL, England

This edition first published in Penguin Books 2002

027

Introduction and Notes copyright © Madeleine Forey, 2002
All rights reserved

Set in 9.5/12 pt PostScript Monotype Bembo
Typeset by Rowland Phototypesetting Ltd, Bury St Edmunds, Suffolk
Printed and bound in Great Britain by Clays Ltd, Elcograf S.p.A.

ISBN 978-0-140-42230-6

www.greenpenguin.co.uk

# CONTENTS

## GOLDING'S *METAMORPHOSIS*

*The Poet's introduction — The creation — The golden age —
The decline of the world — Crimes of giants and men — Jove
summons parliament — Lycaon — The flood — Deucalion and
Pyrrha — The rebirth of animal life — Apollo and the Python —
Daphne and Apollo — The transformation of Io — Pan and
Syrinx — The death of Argus and the story of Io concluded —
Epaphus and Phaëton*

*Phaëton and Apollo — Phaëton begs Apollo's chariot — Phaëton
drives Apollo's chariot — The burning of the world — The earth's
plea — The death of Phaëton — The transformation of Phaëton's*

# ACKNOWLEDGEMENTS

I should like to thank Monica Tweddell for patient and meticulous copy-editing, and Christopher Ricks for valuable suggestions and support. For advice and information I am grateful to Kate Bennett, Robert Carver, Mark Edwards, Stephen Harrison and Jane Lightfoot. My greatest debt is to my husband, Chris Miller, and to my parents, without whose support the work would never have been finished.

# INTRODUCTION

## I

The classics were the raw material of the English Renaissance; to write in the sixteenth century meant to engage in dialogue with the great writers of ancient Greece and Rome. The art of translation was central to that relationship. It was part of the training of every schoolboy. It was part of the culture of imitation, which believed that the self was best expressed when other voices resonated within one's own. It was a means through which the modern vernaculars could claim the riches of the classics as their own, thus simultaneously marking their deference to the classical texts and signalling their confidence in the capacities of their native tongue. It was a central part of the Renaissance's relationship with the classical past; it constituted a claim to inheritance which was at the same time humble – both the stylistic and moral greatness of the classics was constantly felt – and superior, for the modern writer approached the classics with the advantage of Christian revelation.

England, a little later than its European fellows, established its vernacular versions of the texts central to its learning and culture, validating the language as it did so. A tendency to denigrate the English language at the beginning of the sixteenth century can be seen to give way to a growing patriotic confidence over the second half of the century. Richard Mulcaster, Spenser's old headmaster, expressed this passionately in 1582:

I love Rome but London better; I favour Italy but England more; I honour the Latin but I worship the English ... It is our accident which restrains our tongue and not the tongue itself, which will strain with the strongest and stretch to the furthest, for either government if we were conquerers or for cunning if we were treasurers, not any whit behind either the subtle Greek for couching close or the stately Latin for spreading fair. Our tongue is capable if our people would be painful.[1]

It was a period of linguistic expansion. Dictionaries and grammars of English, such as William Bullokar's *Bref Grammar of English* (1586), appeared in the later part of the century. So, too, rhetorical handbooks and mythological handbooks became newly available in English: George Puttenham's *Art of English Poesie* in 1589, Thomas Cooper's frequently reprinted *Thesaurus* (derived from continental mythographers such as Natalis Comes and Vincenzo Cartari) in 1565. And translations came thick and fast. It was, of course, also the period in which an English bible became an established concept. Coverdale's Great Bible, which followed on from Tyndale's, was officially installed in every English church in 1539. It was succeeded by the Geneva Bible (1560), the Bishop's Bible (1568) and the King James (1611).

Translations of both classics and Renaissance masterpieces proliferated. This was essentially a Christian humanist enterprise. Translation necessarily draws a text into a new context, and writers translated into the spirit and language of their own creed. Abraham Fleming translated Virgil's *Eclogues* (1575) and *Georgics* (1589); Thomas Phaer's complete *Aeneid* was printed in 1573. William Adlington's Apuleius appeared in 1566, Thomas North's Plutarch in 1579. Philemon Holland translated Livy (1600), Pliny (1601), Plutarch (1603) and others. George Chapman's first seven books of the *Iliad* came out in 1598; the complete *Iliad* followed in 1611, the *Odyssey* in 1614-15. As for Ovid, George Turbervile produced the *Heroides* in 1567, Thomas Churchyard the *Tristia* in 1572; Christopher Marlowe's version of the *Amores* was published c. 1599, his *Elegies* c. 1595; Thomas Heywood produced the *Ars Amatoria* in 1625. Arthur Golding, who published the complete *Metamorphosis*[2] in 1567, stands at the forefront of this movement. His translations, both of Ovid and others, are among those texts that both illustrate and intensify the absorption of classical culture into English. And on that success rests the explosion of literary talent in the 1590s: of Marlowe, Donne, Spenser, Jonson and Shakespeare.

In the twentieth century Ezra Pound was eloquent in Golding's praise. 'Golding's "Metamorphoses" . . . is the most beautiful book in the language (my opinion and I suspect it was Shakespeare's)', he wrote in 'The New Classics'.[3] Pound's high opinion of Golding was shared in Golding's own lifetime. In his *Discourse of English Poetry* (1586), William Webbe praised 'Master Arthur Golding, for his labor in Englishing Ovid's *Metamorphoses* for which gentleman, surely our country hath for many respects greatly to give God thanks'.[4] But after the early seventeenth century, when Golding's translation was displaced by George Sandys' more refined version, Webbe's recommendation fell on deaf ears for a long time. Interest in Golding's work was almost exclusively confined to those studying the major authors whom he influenced. This neglect is unjust, on historical as well as aesthetic grounds; the Englishing of the classical was at the very heart of the English Renaissance.

For this purpose, Ovid's *Metamorphoses* was a central text. Erasmus's *De Copia* (1512), one of the most important rhetorical works used in Elizabethan grammar schools, drew heavily on Ovid as the foremost example of classical copiousness or eloquence; in the upper school, pupils were required to read and memorize sections of the *Metamorphoses*, along with other major Latin poetic texts. The *Metamorphoses* provided both a stylistic model for the young Latinist and moral topics for his consideration. T. W. Baldwin's study of Shakespeare's education, *William Shakspere's Small Latine and Lesse Greeke*,[5] specifies the extensive acquaintance that the child at grammar school would necessarily gain with Ovid's tales.

Golding's part in the Englishing process was a significant one. Though extracts from Ovid's works were widely used in sixteenth-century grammar schools, there appears to have been no publication of a complete text of the *Metamorphoses* in England, either in Latin or in translation, before Golding's. Pollard and Redgrave's *Short-Title Catalogue*[6] records only a handful of translations published before 1567. No complete Latin edition was published in England until 1570, three years after Golding's complete English text had appeared. There had, in fact, been one complete English version of the *Metamorphoses* before that of Golding: William Caxton completed a translation in 1480.[7] But it remained in manuscript, and there is no evidence that Golding was aware of Caxton's work. Indeed, his presentation of his own work in the 1565 Epistle as one of those 'painful exercises attempted of a zeal and desire to enrich [England's] native language with things not heretofore published in the same' (p. 3) indicates his sense of the novelty of his enterprise.

II

In order to assess the nature of that enterprise in more detail, let us turn to the text itself, taking a passage that displays Golding neither at his best nor at his worst, but perhaps at his most influential. It is the passage from Book 7 (lines 244–89) in which Medea invokes the powers of magic to help her restore Jason's aged father from near death to fresh new life. I choose this famous and much imitated episode for examination because we know that it was one that Shakespeare also looked at in detail and, in the continuing process of textual appropriation and reshaping, himself reused in *The Tempest* (V.i: 'Ye elves and hills . . .'). It is his most sustained Ovidian borrowing, and one of Golding's most significant moments of influence.

Golding's passage does not match up to Shakespeare's. His attempt to use alliteration as a shortcut to an imposing tone ('O trusty time of night . . . the beams that blaze by day') is the sort of rhetorical ploy that, as Shakepeare's Bottom showed in the mechanicals' interlude, can be counterproductive; indeed, Golding's 'lightsome moon', expanding Ovid's 'Luna', is uncomfortably close to Bottom's own lines as Pyramus. But there is more to it than this. Like Bottom's notion of the actor – 'half his face must be seen through the lion's neck' – Golding's text freezes the English language at a moment of transition, part awkwardness, part new-found grace.

The most lyrical moments are achieved when he overcomes the confines of the form; when, instead of being tied by the rather plodding rhythm of the 'fourteener', he uses enjambement, works against the natural pause of the caesura and counterpoints the underlying iambic rhythm with a more varied and expressive one:

> Both man and beast and bird
> Were fast asleep. The serpents sly in trailing forward stirred
> So softly as ye would have thought they still asleep had been.
> The moisting air was whist.

There is a confidence and a lightness in his handling of the metre here; he holds onto the moment of 'stirred / So softly' that enhances the sense of a lull before the action. There is a verbal confidence too. The Latin from which Golding was working was corrupt at this point and offered some heavy-handed repetition:

> Nullo cum murmure serpens,
> Sopitae similis, nullo cum murmure serpit. (7. 186–186a)

[Without a murmur the snake crawls like one asleep, without a murmur.]

Golding's elaboration ('as ye would have thought . . .') both extends the moment and prefigures the ease with which the observer is unprepared or misled in his understanding of Medea. That she is about to perform some wonder we sense. Ovid's 'mediae noctis' becomes more potently 'the dead time of the night', out of which Medea will bring new life. And the air is 'whist', with the sort of silence that suggests a magical moment in which one holds one's breath in anticipation or awe, as in Milton's 'Nativity Ode' (1629; line 64: 'The winds with wonder whist') or Shakespeare's sole use of the word, again in *The Tempest* (I.ii: 'The wild waves whist').

The scene is thus set for the invocation of magical powers. And again, the invocation itself is subtly different from Ovid's. Golding's Medea is a more dependent figure. For her, Hecate 'know[s] best the way / To compass this our great attempt' whereas Ovid's Hecate is in part mere observer and simply 'knows what I [Medea] have begun' ('coeptis conscia nostris'). Ovid's Medea speaks of the incantations and arts possessed by sorcerers such as herself ('cantusque artisque magorum'), whereas Golding's Medea invokes them, as being separate from herself: 'Ye charms and witchcrafts'. She speaks of her doings as 'privities', a rather toned-down version of Ovid's 'arcanis' – her doings are secret, private, but the word does not really carry the power of the occult. Golding's Medea seems more aware that, without aid, she is powerless.

Classical allusions, mythological and geographical, are toned down. Instead, the moment acquires echoes of a fallen Christian state: Ovid's 'serpens' is expanded by Golding to 'serpents sly'. But it is also a moment of potential. 'I make the calm seas rough and make the rough seas plain'. Ovid's words are 'concussaque sisto, / stantia concutio cantu freta' ('and with my incantation I make the shaken seas stand still and the still seas I shake up'). Golding has taken the pattern of the sentence from Ovid, but his vocabulary is, if anything, biblical: 'Every valley shall be exalted, and every mountain and hill shall be made low; and the crooked shall be straight, and the rough places plain' (Geneva Bible, Isaiah 40: 4). If I am right in hearing an echo here, then there is an irony in the allusion to the Old Testament promise of restoration in the midst of Medea's speech, understood in the Renaissance as a set piece of the black arts, an irony parallel to, and as great as, the irony in Shakespeare's decision to put Medea's words into Prospero's mouth. Prospero alludes to her black magic at the moment of rejecting it; Golding's Medea seems to have tinges of redemption even as she proclaims her dubious powers. It is worth remembering that 'wizard' is not automatically a negative term, as indicated by Milton's later use of it for the Magi ('The star-led Wizards', line 23 in his 'Nativity Ode').

Shades of a Christian rendition are heard also in her claim to 'call up dead men from their graves' (in Shakespeare, 'graves at my command / Have waked their sleepers, oped and let them forth'). In Ovid, Medea makes 'manes . . . exire sepulcris' ('spirits to come out of their tombs'). In Golding and, following him, Shakespeare, the suggestion is clearly of bodily resurrection, not of the walking of spirits abroad implied in Ovid. Golding offers a magus who either has something of the redemptive about her (she is, after all, currently engaged in an enterprise to give new life) or is doubly damned for the divine mimesis in her witchcraft. If we look back to Golding's prefatory comments, we find confirmation of his ambivalent reading of her. Shakespeare's Prospero inherits that ambivalence.

Prospero, as we have observed, evokes Ovid's and Golding's Medea only to signal his rejection of her: 'But this rough magic I abjure'. The rough magic is, among other things, Golding's art. Rough, certainly; even at times comical when it would wish to impress, homely where Ovid's is full of grandeur (albeit often with an ironic twist). But it *is* magic. It is a transformation; classical myth is intertwined with Christian culture, and Ovidian wit is turned into native vitality and English lyricism. It has a potent charm.

## III

The Christian element in this scene may not strike the reader on first perusal, but it is worth dwelling on; for besides stylistic transformations, the most significant and pervasive act of modernization and anglicization is (appropriately, given that Golding was also a major translator of Calvin) his rewriting of the work's theology. Ovid's mythological world is overlaid with sixteenth-century Christianity. Temples become churches with spires and are occupied by priests, chaplains and mitred bishops; *pietas* is replaced by godliness; the afterlife promises heaven and hell rather than Elysium and Tartarus; and the many gods become one God. On occasion, Golding's Christian perspective prompts comments unconnected with Ovid's Latin: at 11. 473–4 he condemns oracles as 'toys to food / Fond fancies and not councillors in peril to do good'. But, as his prefatory material indicates, Golding finds Christian morality everywhere confirmed in the narrative; when its 'darkened truth' is brought to light, the 'mystery and secret meaning' turn out to be those of Christian revelation. It is therefore fitting

for Golding that the work should draw towards its close with the Romans'
search for God the Saviour, who, as they learn, is God the Son who is to
come among them. Apollo says:

> 'Not I,
> Apollo, but Apollo's son is he that must redress
> Your sorrows. Take your journey with good handsel of success
> And fetch my son among you.' (15. 715–18)

It is perhaps the aptness of this myth to the story of Christian redemption
that inspires Golding to introduce an altered vocabulary, a dialect speech
otherwise restricted to rustic scenes, at the moment of the Son's appearance
among men:

> But the wifeless priest . . .
> . . . did know the god was there
> And said, 'Behold, 'tiz God, 'tiz God!' (15. 754–6)

Significantly, William Caxton had translated this passage in language that
evoked the Eucharist, referring to 'the mysterye of the signe'.[8] In Golding's
translation the vocabulary is similarly heightened at the moment of revela-
tion. For here the revelation is double: Aesculapius is revealed to the priest,
and the Christian mystery to the reader, whose neoplatonist understanding
of pagan writings allowed him to look upon Ovid's myths and say, with
Golding, ''Tiz God, 'tiz God!' Just as Renaissance readers were used to
finding Christianity revealed in the literature of pastoral, so for Golding
Christian mystery is to be found in Ovid's classical landscape. The height-
ened language used here is a rural and unsophisticated one, and reflects the
religious ignorance and blindness of that classical world, 'blind / Through
unbelief and led astray through error even of kind' (1567 Epistle, 310–11).
Hence the characters of pagan myth become, metaphorically, the rustics
through whom, as Sidney pointed out in his *Defence of Poetry* (1579–80),
greater things may be shadowed forth.

Reference to Sidney is appropriate, for it goes hand in hand with a
specific literary connection.[9] Golding claimed that his translation of *The
Trueness of the Christian Religion* (1587) by Philippe de Mornay was a
completion of Sidney's translation, following instructions left by Sidney
himself. If this is the case, Sidney must have found in Golding, if not a
model of artistic merit, at least a writer who combined a dedication to
Calvinistic Christianity with a delight in classical mythology. Golding is

not a significant source for Sidney's works, but talents such as his helped
to form the literary environment in which Sidney's genius could flourish.
Certainly, the popular esteem that Golding's *Metamorphosis* enjoyed in his
own day is evident. The complete fifteen-book *Metamorphosis* ran through
seven editions in the sixteenth and early seventeenth centuries. It was praised
by George Peele, Thomas Nashe, Francis Meres, Thomas Blundeville and
(as already mentioned) by William Webbe. George Puttenham, too, in his
*Art of English Poesy* (1589), praised Golding along with Phaer, the translator
of Virgil, 'for a learned and well-corrected verse, specially in translation
clear and very faithfully answering their authors' intent'.[10]

Of the authors whom Golding influenced, Spenser and Shakespeare are
the most significant. Shakespeare's use of the *Metamorphosis* in his plays has
been one of the primary causes of the critical attention paid to Golding's
work in the twentieth century. While the extent of Shakespeare's familiarity
with Ovid's Latin text remains a subject for debate, borrowings clearly
establish his familiarity with the English translation. Borrowings from
Golding may be found from the earliest of Shakespeare's plays and poetry
onwards. Modern critical interest has focused on those in *A Midsummer
Night's Dream*, which relies in part upon Golding's rendition of the story
of Pyramus and Thisbe in Book 4. It has been argued that the language
and prosody of the mechanicals parody Golding's diction and verse, and
that their interlude constitutes an amused commentary on a manner of
writing now (in the mid-1590s) distinctly outmoded. Spenser's use of
Golding is more flattering to Golding.[11] Spenser's is the more sophisticated
literary sensibility, but the two writers have much in common: a preference
for allegory, appropriation of rustic or out-dated diction, and a neoplatonist
tendency to interpret pagan mysteries in the light of Christian revelation.
These factors help to explain why Spenser, the Earl of Leicester's later
protégé, might have been attracted to the Englished Ovid of Golding's
*Metamorphosis*.

## IV

The Ovid familiar to Golding was, of course, at some remove from the
Ovid of the first century AD. The mid fourteenth-century Latin commen-
tary, *Ovidius moralizatur*, by Pierre Bersuire, read the poem in the medieval
tradition of four-fold allegory – physical, historical, moral and spiritual; the

same century also produced the vast allegorized French poem *Ovide moralisé*. The end of the fifteenth century saw the publication of the first humanist commentary on the *Metamorphoses*, that of the Italian Raphael Regius. First published in Venice in 1493 and thereafter in countless editions throughout the sixteenth century, Regius's commentary (unlike Bersuire's) was accompanied by the Latin text of the *Metamorphoses*. It presented Ovid's poem as an encyclopaedia of ancient knowledge, a morally improving work that could form the basis of a sound liberal education. From as early as 1510, Regius's *Metamorphoses* started to incorporate further annotation and commentaries by other scholars. It was, to judge by surviving library holdings, the most influential version in sixteenth-century England, and was the source for Golding's translation.

For Regius, the stories were *exempla*; his preface illustrated how the myths provided general moral truths from which edifying lessons might be learnt. The moralizing is, however, confined to the prefatory material. The annotations surrounding the text itself comprise scholarly explanation of Ovid's language and allusions, often with reference to other classical and immediately post-classical writings. Further commentary added to the 1510 edition of Regius's text by Petrus Lavinius reinforces the moral interpretation, and from this date the Regius edition is called *Metamorphoseos libri moralizati*. Lavinius seeks to establish parallels between the *Metamorphoses* and the Old Testament; he explains these parallels by arguing that Ovid was either directly inspired by the Holy Spirit or knew the books of Moses indirectly via Plato and Pythagoras and the Egyptian philosophers before them. It is a reading of Ovid which brings Lavinius, consciously or not, in line with the syncretist interpretations of classical mythology by the fifteenth-century Italian neoplatonists, who found hermetic affinities between pagan and biblical revelations.

The moral interpretations to be found in the sixteenth-century editions of the *Metamorphoses* and reinforced in the grammar school lie behind Golding's own presentation of the poem. It is, he insists, a morally uplifting work, albeit one which requires careful interpretation. 'With skill, heede, and judgement, this worke must be read, / For else to the Reader it standes in small stead', he warns on his title-page, and he proceeds to discuss the moral and spiritual applications of the text at length in his Epistle and Preface to the Reader. Strange as it seems to the modern reader, the sixteenth-century reader of Ovid was practised in finding in each tale, as Golding puts it, 'pithy, apt and plain / Instructions which import the praise of virtues and the shame / Of vices' (1567 Epistle, lines 64–6). In his Preface for the general reader, Golding is prepared to leave his interpretation at the (elementary) level of *exempla*, though even here he offers more than one level of interpretation. Thus, Jove is presented both, in moral terms, as an image of 'fleshly lust' (Preface, line 53) and, in terms of social allegory, as an image of 'all states of princely port' (line 59). Golding justifies Ovid's presentation along Horatian lines of teaching and delighting; but he also uses phrases which point more specifically to a neoplatonic reading of the myths. His references to Ovid's 'dark and secret mysteries' (line 187), 'So hid that (saving unto few) they are not to be seen' (line 138), fit into the neoplatonic tradition. Golding here echoes thinkers like Pico della Mirandola, who knew that the truths hidden in pagan mysteries could be accessible only to the few: 'Hinc appellata mysteria: nec mysteria quae non occulta' ('Hence they are called mysteries; nor are those things mysteries which are not hidden').[12] These hints are expanded in the 1567 Epistle to Leicester. Golding presumably felt that, in his address to a patron of the arts, greater erudition was appropriate. He therefore pointed out the connections between Ovid's myths and the stories of the Old Testament made by commentators such as Lavinius:

> there are (and those not of the rude and vulgar sort,
> But such as have of godliness and learning good report)
> That think the poets took their first occasion of these things
> From Holy Writ, as from the well from whence all wisdom springs.
> What man is he but would suppose the author of this book
> The first foundation of his work from Moses' writings took? (338–43)

However, Golding's views do not necessarily derive from Lavinius (indeed, he seems to have no time for the theory of Ovid's direct inspiration by the Holy Spirit). He explains Ovid's 'dark philosophy' (line 7) by reference to the theories of Philo Judaeus, a first-century exegete whose allegorical reading of the Old Testament allowed him to discover much of classical philosophy in Judaic Scripture. Philo's philosophy, which in certain respects foreshadowed the syncretist ideas of the fifteenth-century neoplatonists and of Lavinius, was available to Golding in various mid sixteenth-century editions of Philo's works. Yet even in the Epistle Golding is also happy to read the myths more straightforwardly as simple moral *exempla* which import 'the praise of virtues, and the shame / Of vices' (lines 65–6).

Golding's quest for moral *exempla* was not confined to the *Metamorphoses*. In a preface to his translation of Calvin's *Commentaries on the Psalms* (1571) he wrote, 'He turneth himself into more shapes than ever did Proteus',[13] and historical narrative provided ample illustration of moral types to be imitated or avoided. So Golding's reading of history, whether classical, biblical or contemporary, was very much in line with his reading of mythology. His third publication, a translation of Justine's *Trogus Pompeius* (1564), was dedicated to the Earl of Oxford, with an exhortation that the example of the classical heroes might encourage him 'to proceed in learning and virtue'. In the providential history of the Book of Revelation he found comparable moral instruction. Of the many Protestant commentaries upon Revelation then available, Golding chose in 1574 to translate Augustine Marlorat's *Catholic Exposition upon the Revelation of Saint John*; this combined a conventional Protestant assault upon the papacy with a less usual insistence that the calamities of the Apocalypse provide moral lessons useful in daily life.

Even contemporary events offered Golding God-given signs to be read in a morally improving fashion. Gabriel Harvey, in his correspondence with Edmund Spenser concerning the earthquake of April 1580, acknowledged that certain earthquakes might be intended 'to testifie and denounce the secrete wrathe, and indignation of God'; like any other calamitous event, earthquakes served to remind mankind of 'the great latter day'. None the less, he attributed the 1580 quake to natural causes and derided those who 'without any justifyable certificate, or warrant . . . definitively . . . give sentence of his Majesties secret and inscrutable purposes . . . [as] some of the simpler and unskilfuller sort, will goe nye to doe upon the present sight . . .'.[14] Golding, writing about the same earthquake, showed no such qualms. His *Discourse upon the Earthquake* (another anti-Catholic piece) presents the earthquake as a call to repentance, a forewarning of wrath to come: 'We have signs and tokens enough at home, if we can use them to our benefit . . . forsaking the lusts and the wicked imaginations and devices of our own hearts, let us turn to the Lord our God with hearty repentance and unfeigned amendment of life.'[15] His account of the murder of one George Saunders (1573) considered this event too a God-given *exemplum*: 'His purpose is, that the execution of his judgements, should by the terror of the outward sight of the example, drive us to the inward consideration of our selves.'[16] These original works are entirely consistent with the teaching of Golding's *Moral Fabletalk*, a translation of Arnold Freitag's emblem book *Mythologia Ethica*,[17] which consists of 125 Aesopic fables in prose.

Clearly, Golding the translator of the *Metamorphoses* was not at odds with the Golding who translated a large number of works by Calvin, and the Golding who completed Philip Sidney's translation of Philippe de Mornay's *A Work Concerning the Trueness of the Christian Religion*. Both his choice of religious texts and the prefatory remarks to these translations show a strong and persistent anti-Catholicism, together with a concern for the moral improvement and repentance of his Protestant readers that is at times charged with an apocalyptic awareness.

<h1 style="text-align:center">VI</h1>

Grundy Steiner, following in the wake of T. W. Baldwin, has demonstrated Golding's use of a *Metamorphoses* text that included the Regius commentary. Steiner argues that Golding's edition also contained the supplementary notes by Jacobus Micyllus, which were incorporated into the Regius commentary in the 1543 printing.[18] He illustrates Golding's dependence on Regius at points where Golding's translation differs slightly from the exact sense of the Latin and where he inserts material completely absent from Ovid's text, but supplied by Regius. The use of Micyllus's comments is much smaller – and, of course, many passages in Golding do not show the influence of either commentator. Steiner suggests that Golding became more adept at translation and used the annotation less and less as he progressed through the text; the later books are much less heavily dependent on Regius. He concludes, 'When the tangled evidence has finally been assembled and brought into order, Golding may be found to have used not one, or two, but actually several editions.'

For the present edition I have primarily used a text of the Regius *Metamorphoses* in the Codrington Library, All Souls College, Oxford, *P. Ovidii Nasonis Metamorphoseon Libri XV*,[19] which incorporates the annotations of Micyllus and other commentators. I have also made use of the Bodleian Library's 1499 edition, *P. Ovidii Metamorphosis [sic] cum integris ac emendatissimis Raphaelis Regii enarrationibus*.[20] Quotation of Ovid's Latin and

of Regius and Micyllus's commentary in my notes to the current edition
are taken from the former, except in the few instances where the 1586
edition contains misprints not registered in Golding's use of the text; in
these cases I have silently adopted the reading of the 1499 text. The reader
needs to be aware that Regius's Latin text deviates regularly from the
one established in modern editions; this deviation accounts for much of
Golding's apparent straying from the Latin. Alterations to the Latin of
modern editions not remarked on in my notes are cases where Golding is
being faithful to the Regius Ovid. Golding's major deviations from Regius's
Latin text are indicated in the notes; where he is making use of the Regius/
Micyllus commentary, this too is indicated. The many minor changes –
and there is something in every other line, even if only a line-padder such
as 'iwis' – are not, however, annotated. A copy of the Regius Ovid remains
an essential tool for any scholar working on Golding's *Metamorphosis*.

For general purposes, however, the main areas of deviation in the
translation may easily be pointed out. In the first place, Golding at times
introduces material into the text from the Regius commentary, often to
elaborate and explain references in Ovid's Latin; he adopts the role of
commentator upon his own text. Thus Rhamnusia is described (3. 507);
the Pygmy woman's challenge to Juno is explained (6. 110); and Atalanta's
background is mentioned (8. 427–9). Deviations independent of the annota-
tions to the Latin text contribute to the Englishing of the *Metamorphoses*,
which extends beyond the mere fact of translation. The overlaying of
Chrisitanity upon Ovid's text has already been discussed. Besides this, we
should mention aspects of both the natural and social worlds of the poem.
The countryside that Golding depicts is more familiar to the English reader
than that of Ovid: it is a world of raspberries, hips and haws rather than
mountain strawberries (1. 119), crabs rather than octopuses (4. 454), lapwings
rather than hoopoes (6. 853). One encounters witches, pucks, elves and
fairies not nymphs (*passim*). Weapons include guns not Balearic slings (2.
904), cannon-shot not catapults (3. 696), bullets not rocks (8. 480). People
wear buskins and hose not sandals (3. 197), kerchiefs not fillets (9. 905),
and nightcaps not turbans (11. 204); they sit at table instead of reclining on
couches (8. 726 et al.), and have books rather than tablets (9. 626). Music
is provided by pots and pans not clashing cymbals (3. 673 et al.), viols not
lyres (5. 139 et al.), and shawms not flutes (14. 612). The dead are placed
in coffins not urns (12. 682).

This Englishing of the material aspects of Ovid's world is paralleled by a shift into English idiom and metre. In place of the Ovidian hexameters, Golding chooses rhyming 'fourteeners' (rhyming heptametric couplets) which were a popular verse form at the time he was writing. The expansive nature of the metre calls for a certain amount of padding, which often takes the form of clichéd narrative formulae and the use of multiple synonyms. He eschews Latinate diction and syntax in favour of a diction that often looks back to medieval romance. There is a heavy use of intensives ('right', 'full', 'so') and clichéd rhyme, again inherited from medieval poetry ('of yore . . . so sore'; 'every wight . . . I will recite'). Linguistically, Golding's text is robust and homely, not without comic vitality, and expansive rather than concise; it is at a considerable remove from the elegance and sophistication of Ovid's verse. Modern criticism has often derided Golding for this. But Golding's 1565 Epistle indicates his interest not simply in providing a translation of the Latin but, more specifically, in establishing Ovid's work within the English language. His hope to enrich his native language suggests that his sense of his task was not dissimilar to Spenser's when Spenser sought to establish a significant English poetics in his *Shepheardes Calender* and *The Faerie Queene*. Spenser, too, deliberately chose a backward-looking and native diction, whose value his editor 'E.K.' was at pains to point out in his prefatory epistle to *The Shepheardes Calender*: 'But whether he vseth them by such casualtye and custome, or of set purpose and choyse . . . sure I think, and think I think not amisse, that they bring great grace and, as one would say, auctoritie to the verse.'[21] Golding manages to combine modesty and assertion when, in the 1567 Epistle, he describes his completed *Metamorphosis* as 'This plenteous horn of Acheloy', and the four-book *Metamorphosis* of 1565 as 'a member rent / Or parted from the residue of the body'. Suggestions of rough handling, damage and mutilation of the text are there; but so also is an assurance of its fruitful transformation into something of great literary worth. For the horn of Achelous, which was torn from his brow but then filled with fruits and fragrant flowers and hallowed, was a major Renaissance image of copiousness: the cornucopia. And the Epistle argues that just such a blessed transformation takes place as Golding completes his work. If Golding's 'rudeness' at times predominates, his is, none the less, a deliberate poetic strategy: the English language can, it implies, accommodate the greatest works of Latin poetry, and do so without loss of its native identity.

Golding's *Metamorphosis* belongs to its own period. The seventeenth century turned for preference to Sandys' translation of 1626 (enlarged 1632);

the eighteenth century had the translation of Dryden and others in Samuel Garth's collaborative *Metamorphoses* of 1717. Ovid's work is a malleable text; it is, appropriately, one whose appearance changes in the hands of each new translator and adapter. Golding's version is essential reading for anyone with an interest in the English Renaissance. No other text so aptly encapsulates the desire of sixteenth-century writers to appropriate Latin culture and yet remain themselves.

## NOTES

1. Richard Mulcaster, *The First Part of the Elementary, which entreateth chiefly of the right writing of our English tongue* (1582), *The Peroration*, pp. 254, 259; 'painful' here means 'painstaking'.
2. It is conventional to call Golding's English translation *Metamorphosis*, following the spelling of the early editions, and to reserve the title *Metamorphoses* for Ovid's text. This convention is followed in the current edition.
3. Ezra Pound, 'The New Classis', in his *ABC of Reading* (London: 1934), p. 42.
4. In *Elizabethan Critical Essays*, 2 vols, ed. Gregory Smith (1904; reprinted London: 1950), vol. 2, p. 243.
5. T. W. Baldwin, *William Shakspere's Small Latine and Lesse Greeke* (Urbana, Ill.: 1944).
6. A. W. Pollard and G. R. Redgrave, *A Short-Title Catalogue of Books Printed in England, Scotland, and Ireland, and of English Books Printed Abroad, 1475–1640* (London: 1926; 2nd edition revised and enlarged: 1976–91). Thomas Hedley, *c.* 1552, published a verse translation of the judgement of Midas entitled *Of such as on fantesye decree & discuss: on other mens works, lo Ovids tale thus*; Thomas Howell in 1560 produced *The fable of Ovid treting of Narcissus, translated into Englysh mytre*; and in 1565/66 Thomas de la Peend's *Pleasant fable of Hermaphroditus and Salmacis* was published, also in verse.
7. Now published in facsimile in two volumes as *The Metamorphoses of Ovid translated by William Caxton* (New York: 1968). Part of the MS has been in Magdalene College, Cambridge since 1703, and part was rediscovered only in 1964. Caxton's translation offers interpretations of the 'sens allegoryqE' and the 'sens hystoryal', though these interpretations become slighter as the tales proceed, and fade out about halfway through.
8. *The Metamorphoses of Ovid translated by William Caxton*, vol. 2, Book 15.
9. For Katherine Duncan-Jones's doubts about this connection, see *Miscellaneous Prose of Sir Philip Sidney*, ed. K. Duncan-Jones and J. Van Dorsten (Oxford: 1973), pp. 155–7.
10. George Puttenham, *Art of English Poesy*, ed. G. D. Willcock and A. Walker (Cambridge: 1936), p. 63.

11. See works by A. B. Taylor in the Further Reading.

12. Pico della Mirandola, *Heptaplus*, prooemium, cited in Edgar Wind, *Pagan Mysteries in the Renaissance* (revised edition, Oxford: 1980), p. 11.

13. John Calvin, *Commentaries on the Psalms*, dedicatory epistle, sig* iii r.

14. *Discourse upon the* Earthquake, in E. Spenser, *Poetical Works*, ed. J. C. Smith and E. de Sélincourt (Oxford: 1912), p. 617.

15. In L. T. Golding, *An Elizabethan Puritan* (New York: 1937), pp. 187, 197.

16. *Ibid.*, p. 178.

17. Antwerp: 1579.

18. Grundy Steiner, 'Golding's Use of the Regius–Micyllus Commentary upon Ovid', *Journal of English and Germanic Philology*, 49 (1950), pp. 317–23.

19. Venice: 1586.

20. Venice: 1499.

21. *Edmund Spenser: The Shorter Poems*, ed. Richard A. McCabe (Harmondsworth, Penguin Classics: 1999), p. 26.

# LIST OF GOLDING'S WORKS

## ORIGINAL PUBLICATIONS

*A Brief Discourse of the Late Murder of Master G. Saunders* (1573).
*A Discourse upon the Earthquake That Happened the Sixth of April 1580* (1580).
Verses prefixed to Baret's *Alveary* (1580).

## TRANSLATIONS

*A Brief Treatise Concerning the Burning of Bucer and Fagius at Cambridge,* Translated [from C. Hubertus] by A. Golding (1562).

*The History of Leonardo Aretino Concerning the Wars between the Imperials and the Goths for the Possession of Italy,* Translated out of Latin by A. Golding (1563).

*The Abridgement of the Histories of Trogus Pompeius,* Collected by Justine and Translated by A. Golding (1564).

*The First Four Books of P. Ovidius Naso's work Entitled Metamorphosis,* Translated into English Metre by A. Golding (1565).

*The Eight Books of Caius Julius Caesar Containing His Martial Exploits in Gallia,* Translated out of Latin by A. Golding (1565).

*The Fifteen Books of P. Ovidius Naso Entitled Metamorphosis,* Translated into English Metre by A. Golding (1567).

*A Little Book* [by John Calvin] ... *Concerning Offenses,* Translated out of Latin by A. Golding (1567).

*A Postil or Exposition of the Gospels Usually Read upon the Sundays and Feast Days* [by Niels Hemmingsen] (1569).

*A Postil or Orderly Disposing of Certain Epistles Usually Read in the Church of God,* Written in Latin [by David Chytraeus] and Translated by A. Golding (1570).

*The Psalms of David and Others, with J. Calvin's Commentaries* (1571).

*A Book of Christian Questions and Answers, Written in Latin by T. Beza and Translated by A. Golding* (1572).

*A Confutation of the Pope's Bull against Elizabeth, Queen of England* [by Heinrich Bullinger] (1572).

*The Benefit That Christians Receive by Jesus Christ Crucified* [by Benedetto da Mantora], *Translated out of French by A. G.* [= Golding?] (1573).

*Sermons . . . upon the Epistle to the Galatians* [by John Calvin] (1574).

*Sermons . . . upon the Book of Job* [by John Calvin], *Translated out of French by A. Golding* (1574).

*A Catholic Exposition upon the Revelation of Saint John* [by Augustine Marlorat] (1574).

*A Justification or Clearing of the Prince of Orange against the False Slanders* [some copies add: *Translated out of French by Arthur Golding*] (1575).

*The Warfare of Christians Concerning the Conflict against the Flesh, the World, and the Devil, Translated out of Latin by A. Golding* (1576).

*The Life of the Most Godly, Valiant, and Noble Captain J. Colignie Shatilim* [by Jean de Serres], *Translated A. Golding* (1576).

*The Edict or Proclamation Set Forth upon the Pacifying of the Troubles in France, the Fourteenth Day of May, 1576, Translated out of French by A. Golding* (1576).

*A Tragedy of Abraham's Sacrifice, Written in French and Translated by A. G.* (1577).

*The Sermons of Master John Calvin upon the Epistle to the Ephesians, Translated out of French by A. Golding* (1577).

*The Work of the Excellent Philosopher Lucius Annaeus Seneca Concerning Benefiting, Translated A. Golding* (1578).

*The Joyful and Royal Entertainment of Prince Francis into Antwerp, Translated out of French by A. Golding According to the Copy Printed by Plantine* (1582).

*A Godly Prayer Written by A. Fleming, Translated out of Latin by A. Golding* (1582).

*The Sermons of Master John Calvin upon Deuteronomy, Gathered as He Preached Them, Translated out of French by A. Golding* (1583).

*The Work of P. Mela, the Cosmographer, Concerning the Situation of the World, Translated A. Golding* (1585).

*The Worthy Work of Julius Solinus, Polyhistorian, Containing Many Noble Actions of Human Creatures, Translated out of Latin by A. Golding* (1587).

*A Work Concerning the Trueness of the Christian Religion* [by Philippe de Mornay], *Begun to Be Translated by Sir P. Sidney and Finished by A. Golding* (1587).

*Politic, Moral, and Martial Discourses, Written in French* [by Jacques Hurault], *Translated by A. Golding* (1595).

*An Epitome of Frossard; or, A Summary Collection . . . Compiled in Latin by J. Sleidan and Translated by P.* [or rather A.] *Golding* (1608).

*A Most Excellent and Profitable Dialogue of the Powerful Justifying Faith, Translated out of Latin by A. Golding* (1610).

*A Moral Fabletalk* [translated after 1579 from Arnold Freitag], edited with critical commentary by Nora Rooche Field as 'Arthur Golding's *A Morall Fabletalke*: An Annotated Edition' (PhD dissertation, Columbia University: 1979).

## EDITIONS OF GOLDING'S *METAMORPHOSIS*

Golding's *Metamorphosis* went through eight early editions, seven of which appeared during his lifetime and the eighth a few years after his death. The first edition of 1565 consists of the first four books of Ovid's text, preceded by a prose epistle to the Earl of Leicester and a Preface to the Reader. In 1567 the full fifteen-book work appeared, in which a verse epistle to Leicester was substituted for the prose epistle. Further editions of this complete translation were published in 1575, 1584, 1587, 1593, 1603 and 1612.

The *Metamorphosis* was then not published again for nearly three hundred years. The 1567 text was republished in 1904 under the title *'Shakespeare's Ovid': being Arthur Golding's Translation of the Metamorphoses*, edited by W. H. D. Rouse (1904; reprinted 1961); and as *Ovid's Metamorphoses: The Arthur Golding Translation 1567*, edited by John Frederick Nims (New York and London: 1965). A facsimile reprint of the 1567 edition has also been published (Amsterdam: 1977).

# TABLE OF DATES

Philip Sidney and completed by Golding; this was one of his last publications.

1606   Golding dies intestate and deeply in debt; he is buried 13 May 1606 in the parish church of Belchamp St Paul's.

# FURTHER READING

## THE TEXT: EDITIONS, TRANSLATIONS AND COMMENTARIES

Anderson, W. S. (ed.), *P. Ovidii Nasonis metamorphoses* (Leipzig: BSB Teubner, 1977).

Bömer, Franz, *P. Ovidius Naso Metamorphosen: Kommentar* (Heidelberg: 1969–86), 7 vols.

Garth, Samuel and Dryden, John, *et al.*, *Metamorphoses*, ed. Garth Tissol (Ware: 1998).

Hoffman, Michael and Lasdun, James (ed.), *After Ovid: New Metamorphoses* (London: 1994).

Hughes, Ted, *Tales from Ovid* (London: 1997).

Martin, Christopher (ed.), *Ovid in English* (London: 1998).

Miller, F. J. (ed.), Ovid: *Metamorphoses*, Loeb Classical Library (2 vols., 1916; revised by G. P. Gould, Cambridge, MA: 1977 [1st vol., 4th imp.] and 1984 [2nd vol., 3rd imp.].

Nims, John Frederick (ed.), *Ovid's Metamorphoses: The Arthur Golding Translation 1567* (New York and London: 1965).

Rouse, W. H. D. (ed.), '*Shakespeare's Ovid*': *being Arthur Golding's Translation of the Metamorphoses* (1904; reprinted London: 1961).

Sandys, George, *Ovid's Metamorphosis Englished, Mythologized, and Represented in Figures*, ed. Karl K. Hulley and Stanley T. Vandersall (Lincoln, NE: 1970).

## BIOGRAPHY

Golding, Louis Thorn, *An Elizabethan Puritan: Arthur Golding* (New York: 1937).

## SECONDARY READING: ARTICLES

Bate, Jonathan, 'Ovid and the Sonnets: or, Did Shakespeare Feel the Anxiety of Influence?', *Shakespeare Survey*, 42 (1989), 65–76.

Celoria, Francis, 'Arthur Golding's Translation of the Names of Actaeon's Hounds in *Ovid's Metamorphosis* III. 206–224, 232–233', *Notes and Queries*, 39 (1992), 289–92.

Forey, Madeleine, ' "Bless thee, Bottom, bless thee! Thou art translated!": Ovid, Golding and *A Midsummer Night's Dream*', *Modern Language Review*, 93, no. 2 (April 1998), 321–9.

Lyne, Ralph, 'Golding's Englished *Metamorphoses*', *Translation and Literature*, 5 (1996), 183–200.

Mahon, John W., 'Perdita's Reference to Proserpina in Act IV of *The Winter's Tale*', *Notes and Queries*, 31 (1984), 214–15.

Martindale, Charles and Brown, Sarah Anne, 'A Complementary Response to Anthony Brian Taylor', *Connotations*, 2 (1992), 58–68.

Steiner, Grundy, 'Golding's Use of the Regius–Micyllus Commentary upon Ovid', *Journal of English and Germanic Philology*, 49 (1950), 317–23.

Taylor, A. B., 'Abraham Fraunce's Debts to Arthur Golding in *Amintas Dale*', *Notes and Queries*, 33 (1986), 333–6.

—, 'Arthur Golding and George Peele's *Polyhymnia*', *Notes and Queries*, 32 (1985), 17–18.

—, 'Arthur Golding and the Elizabethan Progress of Actaeon's Dogs', *Connotations*, 1 (1991), 207–23.

—, 'Debts to Golding in Spenser's Minor Poems', *Notes and Queries*, 33 (1986), 345–7.

—, 'Echoes of Golding's Ovid in John Studley's Translations of Seneca', *Notes and Queries*, 34 (1987), 185–7.

—, 'George Sandys and Arthur Golding', *Notes and Queries*, 33 (1986), 387–91.

—, 'Golding's Ovid, Shakespeare's "Small Latin", and the Real Object of Mockery in "Pyramus and Thisbe" ', *Shakespeare Survey*, 42 (1989), 53–64.

—, 'Lively, Dynamic, but Hardly a Thing of "rhythmic beauty": Arthur Golding's Fourteeners', *Connotations*, 2 (1992), 205–22.

—, 'Melting Earth and Leaping Bulls: Shakespeare's Ovid and Arthur Golding', *Connotations*, 4 (1994–5), 192–206.

—, 'Notes on Marlowe and Golding', *Notes and Queries*, 34 (1987), 191–3.

—, 'Shakespeare and Golding', *Notes and Queries*, 38 (1991), 492–9.

—, 'Shakespeare's Use of Golding's Ovid as a Source for *Titus Andronicus*', *Notes and Queries*, 35 (1988), 449–51.

—, 'Spenser and Arthur Golding', *Notes and Queries*, 32 (1985), 18–21.

—, 'Spenser and Golding: Further Debts in *The Faerie Queene*', *Notes and Queries*, 33 (1986), 342–4.

—, '*The Faerie Queene* Book I and Golding's Translation of *Metamorphoses*', *Notes and Queries*, 34 (1987), 197–9.

—, 'The Fellies, Spokes, and Nave of Fortune's Wheel: A Debt to Arthur Golding in *Hamlet*', *English Language Notes*, 25 (1987), 18–20.

—, 'The Non-Existent Carbuncles: Shakespeare, Golding and Raphael Regius', *Notes and Queries*, 32 (1985), 54–5.

—, '"Wash they his wounds with tears?": Shakespeare's Discriminate Reading of Golding', *Notes and Queries*, 35 (1988), 52.

—, 'When did Spenser read Golding?', *Notes and Queries*, 35 (1988), 38–40.

Willson, Robert F., 'Golding's *Metamorphosis* and Shakespeare's Burlesque Method in *A Midsummer Night's Dream*', *English Language Notes*, 7 (1969), 18–25.

## SECONDARY READING: BOOKS

Anderson, W. S. (ed.), *Ovid: The Classical Heritage* (New York and London: 1995).

Baldwin, T. W., *William Shakspere's Small Latine and Lesse Greeke*, 2 vols (Urbana, Ill.: 1944).

Barkan, Leonard, *The Gods Made Flesh: Metamorphosis and the Pursuit of Paganism* (New Haven and London: 1986).

Bate, Jonathan, *Shakespeare and Ovid* (Oxford: 1993).

Binns, J. W., *Ovid* (London and Boston: 1973).

Bolgar, R. R., *The Classical Heritage and its Beneficiaries* (Cambridge: 1954).

Braden, Gordon, *The Classics and English Renaissance Poetry: Three Case Studies* (New Haven and London: 1978).

Brown, Sarah Annes, *The Metamorphosis of Ovid: From Chaucer to Ted Hughes* (London: 1999).

Hulse, Clark, *Metamorphic Verse: The Elizabethan Minor Epic* (Princeton: 1981).

Keach, William, *Elizabethan Erotic Narratives: Irony and Pathos in the Ovidian Poetry of Shakespeare, Marlowe and their Contemporaries* (New Brunswick, NJ: 1977).

Martin, Christopher (ed.), *Ovid in English* (Penguin Classics, Harmondsworth: 1998).

Martindale, Charles (ed.), *Ovid Renewed: Ovidian Influences on Literature and Art from the Middle Ages to the Twentieth Century* (Cambridge: 1988).

Moss, Ann (tr. and ed.), *Latin Commentaries on Ovid from the Renaissance*, Library of Renaissance Humanism, 5 (Signal Mountain, Tenn.: 1998).

—, 'Ovid in Renaissance France', Warburg Institute Surveys, 8 (London: 1982).

Otis, Brooks, *Ovid as an Epic Poet* (2nd edn London: 1970. 1st edn 1966).

Pearcy, Lee T., *The Mediated Muse: English Translations of Ovid, 1560–1600* (Hamden, Conn.: 1984).

Seznec, Jean, *The Survival of the Pagan Gods: The Mythological Tradition and its Place in Renaissance Humanism and Art*, tr. Barbara F. Sessions (New York: 1953).

Solodow, Joseph B., *The World of Ovid's Metamorphoses* (Chapel Hill and London: 1988).

Wilkinson, L. P., *Ovid Recalled* (Cambridge: 1955).

Wind, Edgar, *Pagan Mysteries in the Renaissance* (1958; revised edition, London: 1980).

# NOTE ON THE TEXT

The first four books of Golding's *Metamorphosis* were published in 1565. The complete translation appeared in 1567, and subsequent editions were published in 1575, 1584, 1587, 1593, 1603 and 1612. This edition is based on two copies of the 1567 edition (STC no. 18956) in the Bodleian Library, Oxford (cat. nos. Douce O. 159 and Malone 321). I have also, where necessary, referred to other editions, using copies in the Bodleian Library and copies on University Microfilms reels as follows: 1565 edition (STC no. 18955, University Microfilms reel 347) from the Huntington Library, San Marino, California; 1575 edition (STC no. 18957) in the Bodleian Library, cat. no. 90 d. 25; 1584 edition (STC no. 18958, University Microfilms reel 1525) from the University of Illinois Library, Urbana, Illinois; 1587 edition (STC no. 18959, University Microfilms reel 330) from the Huntington Library; 1593 edition (STC no. 18960, University Microfilms reel 259) from the Huntington Library; 1603 edition (STC no. 18961, University Microfilms reel 1491) from the University of Illinois Library; 1612 edition (STC no. 18962) in the Bodleian Library, cat. no. Vet. A2 e. 196.

Few textual problems arise in the 1567 edition. Typographical errors and uncertainties in the text have been checked against the later editions. Clear typographical errors corrected in later editions have been silently corrected here; other alterations, including errors corrected for the first time in this edition, cases where the intended text remains unclear, and lines in which later editions have corrected a faulty metre are discussed in the Notes. Spelling and punctuation have been modernized throughout, including all the quotations from Golding's other works that appear in the Introduction and the Notes.

Pronunciation is not easy to clarify without excessive marking of the text. Accents are used to indicate syllables voiced by Golding but unvoiced in modern English. In a very few cases the spelling of the original text calls for a syllable which is wholly absent from the modern version of the word ('mushrommes' as a three-syllable word); such cases are discussed in the Notes. The metre also requires that some syllables normally voiced in modern English be omitted or swallowed. In some cases the original text supplies these in full (e.g. 'even', pronounced 'e'en'), leaving it to the reader to adjust pronunciation according to the metre; in other cases the spelling clearly indicates which syllable is omitted (e.g. 'neighbrod' for 'neighbourhood'). In the present edition the general rule has been to retain the normal spelling, so that the reader must use the metre to determine which syllables are left unvoiced. Only where there seems a possibility of confusion is the pronunciation indicated in the text or discussed in the Notes.

Golding's proper names are still more difficult. Where the spelling of proper names could be modernized without affecting the pronunciation, this has been done. However, Golding's proper names often differ from standard modern forms and may vary to accommodate the needs of metre and rhyme (e.g. 'Galat', 'Galate' and 'Galatea'; 'Caen', 'Caeney' and 'Caeneus'); in this edition, minor variations in spelling have been standardized but variant forms have been retained. Golding also regularly drops the final 's' of names ending '-eus' to indicate a change in pronunciation; thus 'Proteus' will normally be three syllables, but 'Proteu' only two. This distinction, too, is observed. The variants are given in the Index. In some instances, spelling and metre together determine the pronunciation. Golding uses 'Niob' (two syllables) and 'Niobe' (two or three syllables). 'Niob' denotes that the final 'e' is silent; 'Niobe' (two syllables) leaves the 'o' unvoiced; and 'Niobe' (three syllables) voices all three vowels separately. In such cases the reader will be able to establish the pronunciation according to the metre of the line; in a few cases that seem particularly likely to confuse, accents have been added to clarify pronunciation.

Modernization of Golding's punctuation is not straightforward; his sentence structures do not always conform to modern expectations. I have attempted to punctuate in a way that makes the syntactical progression of the sentence as clear as possible. One construction that Golding regularly uses, in which the subordinate clause is divided up and interspersed with the main clause, is particularly problematic. For example: 'The secret flames of fire / He haling inward still, did say, "O happy man . . ." ' (8. 440–41). Adding commas on either side of 'He' would serve to mark off the subordinate clause, but the sentence would remain awkward; the difficulty of splitting-up and inversion cannot be removed, and a proliferation of commas is visually off-putting. In such cases, I have punctuated as above; it is an imperfect compromise.

Headings have been added in the margins to make the text more negotiable. Footnotes represent marginal notes in the original.

This is not a critical edition and does not set out definitively to establish the relationship between the early editions. However, from the textual crux at 10. 830 it is possible to deduce that 1575 corrects 1567, and that subsequent editions up to 1593 follow 1575, making some further corrections in the process. The 1603 edition goes back to a 1567 text different from that on which 1575 is based, and is followed by 1612, which offers a few further corrections. A fuller discussion is given in the note to 10. 830.

This edition reprints the Preface to the Reader and the Epistle of 1567, along with the 1565 Epistle, which has never been reprinted.

# The. xv. Bookes

of P. Ouidius Naso, entytuled
Metamorphosis, translated oute of
*Latin into English meeter, by Ar-*
*thur Golding Gentleman,*
A worke very pleasaunt
and delectable.

With skill, heede, and iudgement, this worke must be read,
For else to the Reader it standes in small stead.

1567

Imprynted at London, by
*Willyam Seres.*

To the right honourable and his singular good Lord,
Robert, Earl of Leicester; Baron of Denbeigh,
Knight of the most noble Order of the
Garter, &c. Arthur Golding Gent.
wisheth continuance of health,
with prosperous estate
and felicity.

If this work were fully performed with like eloquence and cunning
of inditing by me in English as it was written by th'author thereof
in his mother tongue, it might perchance delight your Honour to
bestow some vacant time in the reading of it, for the number of
excellent devices and fine inventions contrived in the same, pur-
porting outwardly most pleasant tales and delectable histories, and
fraughted inwardly with most pithy instructions and wholesome
examples, and containing both ways most exquisite cunning and
deep knowledge. Wherefore to countervail my default, I request
most humbly the benefit of your L[ordship's] favour, whereby you          10
are wont not only to bear with the want of skill and rudeness of such
as commit their doings to your protection, but also are wont to
encourage them to proceed in their painful exercises attempted of a
zeal and desire to enrich their native language with things not
heretofore published in the same. Th'assured hope and confidence
whereof (furthered by the privilege of the new year, which of an
ancient and laudable custom licenceth men to testify their good wills,
not only to their friends and acquaintance, but also to their betters
and superiors by presents though never so simple) giveth me boldness
to dedicate this my maimed and unperfect translation of the first          20
four books of Ovid's *Metamorphoses* unto your Honour, and to
offer it unto you for a poor new year's gift, I confess, not corres-
pondent to your worthiness or my desire, but yet agreeable to
the state of the giver. The which if it may please you to take in good
part, I account my former travail herein sufficiently recompensed
and think myself greatly enforced to persevere in the full accom-
plishment of all the whole work. And thus beseeching God to send
your Honour many prosperous and joyful new years, I cease to

trouble you any further at this time. At Cecil House, the 23 of
December, Anno 1564.

Your good L[ordship's] most humbly to command,

Arthur Golding.

To the right honourable and his singular good Lord,
Robert, Earl of Leicester; Baron of Denbeigh,
Knight of the most noble Order of the
Garter, &c. Arthur Golding Gent.
wisheth continuance of health,
with prosperous estate
and felicity.

At length my chariot wheel about the mark hath found the way,
And at their weary race's end my breathless horses stay.
The work is brought to end by which the author did account
(And rightly) with eternal fame above the stars to mount.
For whatsoever hath been writ of ancient time in Greek
By sundry men dispersedly, and in the Latin eke,
Of this same dark philosophy of turnèd shapes, the same
Hath Ovid into one whole mass in this book brought in frame.
Four kind of things in this his work the poet doth contain.
That nothing under heaven doth aye in steadfast state remain.      10
And next, that nothing perisheth, but that each substance takes
Another shape than that it had. Of these two points he makes
The proof by showing through his work the wonderful exchange
Of gods, men, beasts and elements to sundry shapes right strange,
Beginning with creation of the world and man of slime
And so proceeding with the turns that happened till his time.
Then showeth he the soul of man from dying to be free
By samples of the noblemen who for their virtues be
Accounted and canonizèd for gods by heathen men,
And by the pains of Limbo lake and blissful state again      20
Of spirits in th'Elysian fields. And though that of these three
He make discourse dispersedly, yet specially they be
Discussèd in the latter book, in that oration where
He bringeth in Pythagoras dissuading men from fear
Of death and preaching abstinence from flesh of living things.
But as for that opinion which Pythagoras there brings
Of souls removing out of beasts to men, and out of men
To birds and beasts both wild and tame, both to and fro again,

It is not to be understood of that same soul whereby
30    We are endued with reason and discretion from on high,
But of that soul or life the which brute beasts, as well as we,
Enjoy. Three sorts of life or soul (for so they termèd be)
Are found in things. The first gives power to thrive, increase and
          grow;
And this in senseless herbs and trees and shrubs itself doth show.
The second giveth power to move and use of senses five;
And this remains in brutish beasts, and keepeth them alive.
Both these are mortal, as the which, receivèd of the air
By force of Phoebus, after death do thither eft repair.
The third gives understanding, wit and reason; and the same
40    Is it alonely which with us of soul doth bear the name.
And as the second doth contain the first, even so the third
Containeth both the other twain. And neither beast, nor bird,
Nor fish, nor herb, nor tree, nor shrub, nor any earthly wight
Save only man can of the same partake the heavenly might.
I grant that when our breath doth from our bodies go away,
It doth eftsoons return to air; and of that air there may
Both bird and beast participate, and we of theirs likewise.
For while we live – the thing itself appeareth to our eyes –
Both they and we draw all one breath. But for to deem or say
50    Our noble soul (which is divine and permanent for aye)
Is common to us with the beasts, I think it nothing less
Than for to be a point of him that wisdom doth profess.
Of this I am right well assured there is no Christian wight
That can by fondness be so far seducèd from the right.
And finally he doth proceed in showing that not all
That bear the name of men (how strong, fierce, stout, bold, hardy,
          tall,
How wise, fair, rich or highly born, how much renowned by
          fame
So e'er they be, although on earth of gods they bear the name)
Are for to be accounted men, but such as under awe
60    Of reason's rule continually do live in virtue's law;
And that the rest do differ nought from beasts, but rather be
Much worse than beasts, because they do abase their own degree.

To natural philosophy the formest three pertain,
The fourth to moral; and in all are pithy, apt and plain
Instructions which import the praise of virtues and the shame
Of vices, with the due rewards of either of the same.
As, for example, in the tale of Daphne turned to bay          *Out of the*
A mirror of virginity appear unto us may;                     *first book*
Which, yielding neither unto fear, nor force, nor flattery,
Doth purchase everlasting fame and immortality.          70
In Phaeton's fable unto sight the poet doth express          *Out of*
The natures of ambition blind and youthful wilfullness,      *the second*
The end whereof is misery, and bringeth at the last
Repentance when it is too late, that all redress is past;
And how the weakness and the want of wit in magistrate
Confoundeth both his commonweal and eke his own estate.
This fable also doth advise all parents, and all such
As bring up youth, to take good heed of cockering them too
    much.
It further doth commend the mean and willeth to beware
Of rash and hasty promises, which most pernicious are       80
And not to be performèd. And in fine it plainly shows
What sorrow to the parents and to all the kindred grows
By disobedience of the child; and in the child is meant
The disobedient subject that against his prince is bent.
The transformations of the crow and raven do declare
That claw-backs and coal-carriers ought wisely to beware
Of whom, to whom, and what they speak. For sore against his
    will
Can any friendly heart abide to hear reported ill
The party whom he favoureth. This tale doth eke bewray
The rage of wrath and jealousy to have no kind of stay;     90
And that light credit to reports should in no wise be given,
For fear that men too late to just repentance should be driven.
The fable of Ocyrhoë by all such folk is told
As are in searching things to come too curious and too bold.
A very good example is described in Battus' tale
For covetous people which for gain do set their tongues to sale.
All such as do in flattering frekes and hawks and hounds delight,   *Out of*
And dice and cards, and for to spend the time both day and night    *the third*

In foul excess of chamberwork, or too much meat and drink,
100    Upon the piteous story of Actaeon ought to think.
For these and their adherents, used excessive, are indeed
The dogs that daily do devour their followers-on with speed.
Tiresias wills inferior folk in any wise to shun
To judge between their betters, lest in peril they do run.
Narcissus is of scornfulness and pride a mirror clear
Where beauty's fading vanity most plainly may appear.
And Echo in the selfsame tale doth kindly represent
The lewd behaviour of a bawd and his due punishment.

*Out of the fourth*   110    The piteous tale of Pyramus and Thisbe doth contain
The heady force of frantic love, whose end is woe and pain.
The snares of Mars and Venus show that time will bring to light
The secret sins that folk commit in corners or by night.
Hermaphrodite and Salmacis declare that idleness
Is chiefest nurse and cherisher of all voluptuousness,
And that voluptuous life breeds sin; which, linking all together,
Make men to be effeminate, unwieldy, weak and lither.

*Out of the fifth*   Rich Pier's daughters turned to pies do openly declare
That none so bold to vaunt themselves as blindest bayards are.
The Muses plainly do declare again at other side
120    That whereas chiefest wisdom is, most mildness doth abide.

*Out of the sixth*   Arachne may example be that folk should not contend
Against their betters, nor persist in error to the end.
So doth the tale of Niobe and of her children, and
The transformation of the carls that dwelt in Lycy land,
Together with the flaying off of piper Marsyas' skin.
The first do also show that long it is ere God begin
To pay us for our faults and that he warns us oft before
To leave our folly, but at length his vengeance striketh sore;
And therefore that no wight should strive with God in word nor
        thought
130    Nor deed. But pride and fond desire of praise have ever wrought
Confusion to the parties which account of them do make.
For some of such a nature be that, if they once do take
Opinion (be it right or wrong), they rather will agree
To die, than seem to take a foil; so obstinate they be.

The tale of Tereus, Philomel and Procne doth contain
That folk are blind in things that to their proper weal pertain,
And that the man in whom the fire of furious lust doth reign
Doth run to mischief like a horse that getteth loose the rein.
It also shows the cruel wreak of women in their wrath,
And that no heinous mischief long delay of vengeance hath,            140
And, lastly, that distress doth drive a man to look about
And seek all corners of his wits, what way to wind him out.
The good success of Jason in the land of Colchos and                  *Out of*
The doings of Medea since, do give to understand                      *the seventh*
That nothing is so hard but pain and travail do it win,
For fortune ever favoureth such as boldly do begin;
That women both in helping and in hurting have no match
When they to either bend their wits; and how that for to catch
An honest meaner under fair pretence of friendship is
An easy matter. Also there is warning given of this:                  150
That men should never hastily give ear to fugitives,
Nor into hands of sorcerers commit their state or lives.
It shows, in fine, of stepmothers the deadly hate in part,
And vengeance most unnatural that was in mother's heart.
The deeds of Theseus are a spur to prowess and a glass
How princes' sons and noblemen their youthful years should pass.
King Minos shows that kings in hand no wrongful wars should
         take,
And what provision for the same they should beforehand make.
King Aeacus gives also there example how that kings
Should keep their promise and their leagues above all other things.   160
His grave description of the plague and end thereof express
The wrath of God on man for sin; and how that, ne'ertheless,
He doth us spare and multiply again for good men's sakes.
The whole discourse of Cephalus and Procris mention makes
That married folk should warily shun the vice of jealousy
And of suspicion should avoid all causes utterly,
Reproving by the way all such as causeless do misdeem
The chaste and guiltless for the deeds of those that faulty seem.
The story of the daughter of King Nisus setteth out                   *Out of the*
What wicked lust drives folk unto to bring their wills about.   170   *eighth*

And of a righteous judge is given example in the same,
Who for no meed nor friendship will consent to any blame.
We may perceive in Daedalus how every man by kind
Desires to be at liberty and with an earnest mind
Doth seek to see his native soil; and how that straight distress
Doth make men wise and sharps their wits to find their own
         redress.
We also learn by Icarus how good it is to be
In mean estate and not to climb too high, but to agree
To wholesome counsel; for the hire of disobedience is
180    Repentance when it is too late for thinking things amiss.
And Partridge tells that excellence in anything procures
Men envy, even among those friends whom nature most assures.
Philemon and his fere are rules of godly patient life,
Of sparing thrift and mutual love between the man and wife,
Of due obedience, of the fear of God, and of reward
For good or evil usage showed to wandering strangersward.
In Erisycthon doth appear a lively image both
Of wickedness and cruelty which any wight may loathe,
And of the hire that longs thereto. He showeth also plain
190    That, whereas prodigality and gluttony doth reign,
A world of riches and of goods are ever with the least
To satisfy the appetite and eye of such a beast.

*Out of
the ninth*

In Hercules' and Acheloy's encounters is set out
The nature and behaviour of two wooers that be stout.
Wherein the poet covertly taunts such as, being base,
Do seek by forgèd pedigrees to seem of noble race;
Who, when they do perceive no truth upon their side to stand,
Instead of reason and of right use force and might of hand.
This fable also signifies that valiantness of heart
200    Consisteth not in words, but deeds; and that all sleight and art
Give place to prowess. Furthermore, in Nessus we may see
What breach of promise cometh to, and how that such as be
Unable for to wreak their harms by force do oft devise
To wreak themselves by policy in far more cruel wise.
And Deianira doth declare the force of jealousy
Deceivèd through too light belief and fond simplicity.

The process following painteth out true manliness of heart
Which yieldeth neither unto death, to sorrow, grief nor smart;
And, finally, it shows that such as live in true renown
Of virtue here have after death an everlasting crown                   210
Of glory. Caun and Byblis are examples contrary:
The maid of most outrageous lust, the man of chastity.
The tenth book clearly doth contain one kind of argument,              *Out of*
Reproving most prodigious lusts of such as have been bent             *the tenth*
To incest most unnatural. And in the latter end
It showth in Hippomenes how greatly folk offend
That are ingrate for benefits which God or man bestow
Upon them in the time of need. Moreover it doth show
That beauty, will they, nill they, aye doth men in danger throw;
And that it is a foolishness to strive against the thing               220
Which God before determineth to pass in time to bring.
And last of all Adonis' death doth show that manhood strives
Against forewarning, though men see the peril of their lives.
The death of Orphey showeth God's just vengeance on the vile          *Out of the*
And wicked sort which horribly with incest them defile.               *eleventh*
In Midas of a covetous wretch the image we may see,
Whose riches justly to himself a hellish torment be;
And of a fool, whom neither proof nor warning can amend
Until he feel the shame and smart that folly doth him send.
His barber represents all blabs which seem with child to be            230
Until that they have blazed abroad the things they hear or see.
In Ceyx and Alcyone appears most constant love,
Such as between the man and wife to be it doth behove.
This Ceyx also is a light of princely courtesy
And bounty toward such whom need compelleth for to fly.
His voyage also doth declare how vainly men are led
To utter peril through fond toys and fancies in their head.
For idols' doubtful oracles and soothsayers' prophecies
Do nothing else but make fools fain and blind their bleared eyes.
Daedalion's daughter warns to use the tongue with modesty             240
And not to vaunt with such as are their betters in degree.
The siege of Troy, the death of men, the razing of the city           *Out of the*
And slaughter of King Priam's stock without remorse of pity,         *twelfth*

Which in the twelfth and thirteenth books be written, do declare
How heinous wilful perjury and filthy whoredom are
In sight of God. The frantic fray between the Lapiths and
The Centaurs is a note whereby is given to understand

*Out of the thirteenth*

The beastly rage of drunkenness. Ulysses doth express
The image of discretion, wit and great advisèdness;

250
And Ajax on the other side doth represent a man
Stout, heady, ireful, haught of mind, and such a one as can
Abide to suffer no repulse. And both of them declare
How covetous of glory and reward men's natures are.
And finally, it showeth plain that wisdom doth prevail
In all attempts and purposes when strength of hand doth fail.
The death of fair Polyxena doth show a princely mind
And firm regard of honour rare engraft in womankind.
And Polymnestor, King of Thrace, doth show himself to be
A glass for wretched covetous folk wherein themselves to see.

260
This story further witnesseth that murder crieth aye
For vengeance, and itself one time or other doth bewray.
The tale of giant Polypheme doth evidently prove
That nothing is so fierce and wild, which yieldeth not to love.
And in the person of the selfsame giant is set out
The rude and homely wooing of a country clown and lout.

*Out of the fourteenth*

The tale of apes reproves the vice of wilful perjury
And willeth people to beware they use not for to lie.
Aeneas, going down to hell, doth show that virtue may
In safety travel where it will, and nothing can it stay.

270
The length of life in Sibyl doth declare it is but vain
To wish long life, sith length of life is also length of pain.
The Grecian Achaemenides doth learn us how we ought
Be thankful for the benefits that any man hath wrought.
And in this Achaemenides the poet doth express
The image of exceeding fear in danger and distress.
What else are Circe's witchcrafts and enchantments than the vile
And filthy pleasures of the flesh, which do our souls defile?
And what is else herb moly than the gift of steadfastness
And temperance, which doth all foul concupiscence repress?

280
The tale of Anaxarete wills dames of high degree
To use their lovers courteously, how mean so e'er they be.

And Iphis learns inferior folk too fondly not to set
Their love on such as are too high for their estate to get.
Alemon's son declares that men should willingly obey
What God commands, and not upon exceptions seem to stay.
For he will find the means to bring the purpose well about
And in their most necessity dispatch them safely out
Of danger. The oration of Pythagoras implies
A sum of all the former work. What person can devise
A notabler example of true love and godliness
To one's own native countryward than Cipus doth express?
The turning to a blazing star of Julius Caesar shows
That fame and immortality of virtuous doing grows.
And lastly, by examples of Augustus and a few
Of other noble princes' sons, the author there doth show
That noblemen and gentlemen should strive to pass the fame
And virtues of their ancestors, or else to match the same.
   These fables out of every book I have interpreted
   To show how they and all the rest may stand a man in stead,
Not adding overcuriously the meaning of them all,
For that were labour infinite, and tediousness not small
Both unto your good Lordship and the rest that should them read,
Who well might think I did the bounds of modesty exceed
If I this one epistle should with matters overcharge
Which scarce a book of many quires can well contain at large.
And whereas in interpreting these few I attribute
The things to one, which heathen men to many gods impute,
Concerning mercy, wrath for sin and other gifts of grace,
Describèd for example's sake in proper time and place,
Let no man marvel at the same. For though that they, as blind
Through unbelief and led astray through error even of kind,
Knew not the true eternal God – or if they did him know,
Yet did they not acknowledge him, but vainly did bestow
The honour of the maker on the creature – yet it doth
Behove all us (who rightly are instructed in the sooth)
To think and say that God alone is he that rules all things
And worketh all in all, as lord of lords and king of kings;
With whom there are none other gods that any sway may bear,
No fatal law to bind him by, no Fortune for to fear.

*Out of the*
*fifteenth*

290

300

310

320 For gods and Fate and Fortune are the terms of heathenness,
If men usurp them in the sense that paynims do express.
But if we will reduce their sense to right of Christian law,
To signify three other things these terms we well may draw.
By gods we understand all such as God hath placed in chief
Estate to punish sin, and for the godly folk's relief;
By Fate, the order which is set and stablishèd in things
By God's eternal will and word, which in due season brings
All matters to their falling out; which falling out or end
(Because our curious reason is too weak to comprehend

330 The cause and order of the same, and doth behold it fall
Unwares to us), by name of Chance or Fortune we it call.
If any man will say these things may better learnèd be
Out of divine philosophy or scripture, I agree
That nothing may in worthiness with Holy Writ compare.
Howbeit, so far forth as things no whit impeachment are
To virtue and to godliness but furtherers of the same,
I trust we may them safely use without desert of blame.
And yet there are (and those not of the rude and vulgar sort,
But such as have of godliness and learning good report)

340 That think the poets took their first occasion of these things
From Holy Writ, as from the well from whence all wisdom
        springs.
What man is he but would suppose the author of this book
The first foundation of his work from Moses' writings took?
Not only in effect he doth with Genesis agree,
But also in the order of creation, save that he
Makes no distinction of the days. For what is else at all
That shapeless, rude and pestered heap, which Chaos he doth call,
Than even that universal mass of things which God did make
In one whole lump before that each their proper place did take?

350 Of which the Bible saith that in the first beginning God
Made heaven and earth; the earth was waste, and darkness yet
        abode
Upon the deep. Which holy words declare unto us plain
That fire, air, water and the earth did undistinct remain
In one gross body at the first. *For God the Father that*
*Made all things, framing out the world according to the plat*

Conceivèd everlastingly in mind, made first of all
Both heaven and earth uncorporal, and such as could not fall
As objects under sense of sight; and also air likewise,
And emptiness. And for these twain apt terms he did devise.
He callèd air darkness, for the air by kind is dark;                    360
And emptiness by name of depth full aptly he did mark,
For emptiness is deep and waste by nature. Overmore,
He formèd also bodiless (as other things before)
The natures both of water and of spirit and, in fine,
The light; which, being made to be a pattern most divine
Whereby to form the fixèd stars and wandering planets seven
With all the lights that afterward should beautify the heaven,
Was made by God both bodiless and of so pure a kind
As that it could alonely be perceivèd by the mind.
To this effect are Philo's words. And certainly this same          370
Is it that poets in their work confusèd Chaos name.
Not that God's works at any time were packed confusedly
Together; but because no place nor outward shape whereby
To show them to the feeble sense of man's deceitful sight
Was yet appointed unto things, until that by his might
And wondrous wisdom God in time set open to the eye
The things that he before all time had everlastingly
Decreèd by his providence. But let us further see
How Ovid's scantlings with the whole true pattern do agree.
The first day by his mighty word (saith Moses) God made light;     380
The second day the firmament, which heaven or welkin hight.
The third day he did part the earth from sea and made it dry,
Commanding it to bear all kind of fruits abundantly.
The fourth day he did make the lights of heaven to shine from
        high
And stablishèd a law in them to rule their courses by.
The fifth day he did make the whales and fishes of the deep,
With all the birds and feathered fowls that in the air do keep.
The sixth day God made every beast both wild and tame and
        worms
That creep on ground, according to their several kinds and forms.
And in the image of himself he formèd man of clay               390
To be the lord of all his works the very selfsame day.

This is the sum of Moses' words. And Ovid (whether it were
By following of the text aright, or that his mind did bear
Him witness that there are no gods but one) doth plain behold
That God (although he knew him not) was he that did unfold
The former Chaos, putting it in form and fashion new,
As may appear by these his words which underneath ensue:
*This strife did God and nature break and set in order due.*
*The earth from heaven, the sea from earth he parted orderly,*
400 *And from the thick and foggy air he took the lightsome sky.*
In these few lines he comprehends the whole effect of that
Which God did work the first three days about this noble plat.
And then by distributions he entreateth by and by
More largely of the selfsame things, and paints them out to eye
With all their bounds and furniture. And whereas we do find
The term of Nature joined with God, according to the mind
Of learnèd men, by joining so is meant none other thing
But God, the lord of nature, who did all in order bring.
The distributions being done right learnedly, anon
410 To show the other three days' works he thus proceedeth on:
*The heavenly soil to gods and stars and planets first he gave;*
*The waters next both fresh and salt he let the fishes have;*
*The subtle air to flickering fowls and birds he hath assigned;*
*The earth to beasts both wild and tame of sundry sorts and kind.*
Thus partly in the outward phrase, but more in very deed,
He seems according to the sense of scripture to proceed.
And when he comes to speak of man, he doth not vainly say
(As some have written) that he was before all time for aye,
Ne mentioneth mo gods than one in making him. But thus
420 He both in sentence and in sense his meaning doth discuss:
*Howbeit, yet of all this while the creature wanting was*
*Far more divine, of nobler mind, which should the residue pass*
*In depth of knowledge, reason, wit and high capacity,*
*And which of all the residue should the lord and ruler be.*
*Then either he that made the world and things in order set*
*Of heavenly seed engendered man; or else the earth, as yet*
*Young, lusty, fresh and in her flower, and parted from the sky*
*But late before, the seeds thereof as yet held inwardly,*

*The which Prometheus, tempering straight with water of the spring,*
*Did make in likeness to the gods that govern everything.*                               430
What other thing means Ovid here by term of heavenly seed
Than man's immortal soul, which is divine and comes indeed
From heaven and was inspired by God, as Moses showeth plain?
And whereas of Prometheus he seems to add a vain
Device, as though he meant that he had formèd man of clay,
Although it be a tale put in for pleasure by the way,
Yet by th'interpretation of the name we well may gather
He did include a mystery and secret meaning rather.
This word 'Prometheus' signifies a person sage and wise,
Of great foresight, who headily will nothing enterprise.                                 440
It was the name of one that first did images invent;
Of whom the poets do report that he to heaven up went
And there stole fire, through which he made his images alive;
And therefore that he formèd men the paynims did contrive.
Now when the poet read, perchance, that God Almighty by
His providence and by his word (which everlastingly
Is aye his wisdom) made the world, and also man to bear
His image and to be the lord of all the things that were
Erst made, and that he shapèd him of earth or slimy clay,
He took occasion, in the way of fabling, for to say                                      450
That wise Prometheus, tempering earth with water of the spring,
Did form it like the gods above that govern everything.
Thus may Prometheus seem to be th'eternal word of God,
His wisdom and his providence, which formèd man of clod.
*And where all other things behold the ground with grovelling eye,*
*He gave to man a stately look replete with majesty*
*And willed him to behold the heaven with count'nance cast on high,*
*To mark and understand what things are in the starry sky.*
In these same words both parts of man the poet doth express
As in a glass, and giveth us instruction to address                                      460
Ourselves to know our own estate; as that we be not born
To follow lust, or serve the paunch like brutish beasts forlorn,
But for to lift our eyes, as well of body as of mind,
To heaven as to our native soil, from whence we have by kind
Our better part; and by the sight thereof to learn to know
And knowledge him that dwelleth there; and wholly to bestow

Our care and travail to the praise and glory of his name,
Who for the sakes of mortal men created first the same.
Moreover, by the golden age what other thing is meant
470 Than Adam's time in Paradise, who, being innocent,
Did lead a blest and happy life until that thorough sin
He fell from God? From which time forth all sorrow did begin.
The earth, accursèd for his sake, did never after more
Yield food without great toil. Both heat and cold did vex him
            sore;
Disease of body, care of mind, with hunger, thirst and need,
Fear, hope, joy, grief and trouble fell on him and on his seed.
And this is termed the silver age. Next which there did succeed
The brazen age, when malice first in people's hearts did breed,
Which never ceasèd growing till it did so far outrage
480 That nothing but destruction could the heat thereof assuage;
For why men's stomachs, waxing hard as steel against their God,
Provokèd him from day to day to strike them with his rod.
Proud giants also did arise that with presumptuous wills
Heaped wrong on wrong, and sin on sin, like huge and lofty hills
Whereby they strove to climb to heaven and God from thence to
            draw,
In scorning of his holy word and breaking nature's law.
For which anon ensued the flood, which overflowèd all
The whole round earth and drownèd quite all creatures great and
            small,
Excepting few that God did save, as seed whereof should grow
490 Another offspring. All these things the poet here doth show
In colour, altering both the names of persons, time and place.
For where, according to the truth of scripture in this case,
The universal flood did fall but sixteen-hundred years
And six-and-sixty after the creation (as appears
By reckoning of the ages of the fathers) under Noy,
With whom seven other persons mo like safeguard did enjoy
Within the ark, which at the end of one whole year did stay
Upon the hills of Armeny; the poet, following aye
The fables of the glorying Greeks (who shamelessly did take
500 The praise of all things to themselves), in fabling wise doth make

It happen in Deucalion's time, who reigned in Thessaly
Eight-hundred winters since Noy's flood or thereupon well nigh,
Because that in the reign of him a mighty flood did fall
That drowned the greater part of Greece, towns, cattle, folk and
    all,
Save few that by the help of boats attainèd unto him
And to the highest of the forked Parnassus top did swim.
And for because that he and his were driven awhile to dwell
Among the stony hills and rocks until the water fell,
The poets hereupon did take occasion for to feign
That he and Pyrrha did repair mankind of stones again.                    510
So in the sixth book, afterward, Amphion's harp is said
The first foundation of the walls of Thebe to have laid,
Because that by his eloquence and justice (which are meant
By true accord of harmony and musical consent)
He gathered unto Thebe town and in due order knit
The people that dispersed and rude in hills and rocks did sit.
So Orphey in the tenth book is reported to delight
The savage beasts and for to hold the fleeting birds from flight,
To move the senseless stones and stay swift rivers, and to make
The trees to follow after him and for his music sake                      520
To yield him shadow where he went; by which is signified
That in his doctrine such a force and sweetness was implied
That such as were most wild, stour, fierce, hard, witless, rude and
    bent
Against good order, were by him persuaded to relent
And for to be conformable to live in reverent awe
Like neighbours in a commonweal by justice under law.
Considering, then, of things before rehearsed the whole effect,
I trust there is already showed sufficient to detect
That poets took the ground of all their chiefest fables out
Of scripture; which they shadowing with their glosses, went about        530
To turn the truth to toys and lies. And of the selfsame rate
Are also these: their Phlegeton, their Styx, their blissful state
Of spirits in th'Elysian fields; of which the former twain
Seem counterfeited of the place where damnèd souls remain,
Which we call hell; the third doth seem to fetch his pedigree
From Paradise, which scripture shows a place of bliss to be.

If poets, then, with leasings and with fables shadowed so
The certain truth, what letteth us to pluck those visors fro
Their doings, and to bring again the darkened truth to light,
540 That all men may behold thereof the clearness shining bright?
The readers, therefore, earnestly admonished are to be
To seek a further meaning than the letter gives to see.
The travail ta'en in that behalf, although it have some pain,
Yet makes it double recompence with pleasure and with gain.
With pleasure, for variety and strangeness of the things;
With gain, for good instruction which the understanding brings.
And if they, happening for to meet with any wanton word
Or matter lewd (according as the person doth afford
In whom the evil is described), do feel their minds thereby
550 Provoked to vice and wantonness (as nature commonly
Is prone to evil), let them thus imagine in their mind:
'Behold, by scent of reason and by perfect sight I find
A panther here, whose painted coat with yellow spots like gold
And pleasant smell allure mine eyes and senses to behold.
But well I know his face is grim and fierce, which he doth hide
To this intent: that, while I thus stand gazing on his hide,
He may devour me unbewares.' Ne let them more offend
At vices in this present work in lively colours penned
Than if that in a crystal glass foul images they found,
560 Resembling folk's foul visages that stand about it round.
For sure these fables are not put in writing to th'intent
To further or allure to vice; but rather this is meant:
That men, beholding what they be when vice doth reign instead
Of virtue, should not let their lewd affections have the head.
For as there is no creature more divine than man as long
As reason hath the sovereignty and standeth firm and strong,
So is there none more beastly, vile and devilish than is he
If reason, giving over, by affection mated be.
The use of this same book therefore is this: that every man
570 (Endeavouring for to know himself as nearly as he can),
As though he in a chariot sat well ordered, should direct
His mind by reason in the way of virtue and correct
His fierce affections with the bit of temperance, lest perchance
They, taking bridle in the teeth, like wilful jades do prance

Away and headlong carry him to every filthy pit
Of vice and, drinking of the same, defile his soul with it;
Or else do headlong harry him upon the rocks of sin
And, overthrowing forcibly the chariot he sits in,
Do tear him worse than ever was Hippolytus, the son
Of Theseus, when he went about his father's wrath to shun.          580
This worthy work in which of good examples are so many,
This orchard of Alcinous in which there wants not any
Herb, tree or fruit that may man's use for health or pleasure serve,
This plenteous horn of Acheloy which justly doth deserve
To bear the name of treasury of knowledge, I present
To your good Lordship once again, not as a member rent
Or parted from the residue of the body any more,
But fully now accomplishèd; desiring you therefore
To let your noble courtesy and favour countervail
My faults, where art or eloquence on my behalf doth fail.          590
For, sure, the mark whereat I shoot is neither wreaths of bay,
Nor name of poet, no, nor meed; but chiefly that it may
Be likèd well of you and all the wise and learnèd sort,
And next that every wight that shall have pleasure for to sport
Him in this garden may as well bear wholesome fruit away
As only on the pleasant flowers his reckless senses stay.
But why seem I these doubts to cast, as if that he who took
With favour and with gentleness a parcel of the book
Would not likewise accept the whole? Or even as if that they
Who do excel in wisdom and in learning would not weigh          600
A wise and learned work aright? Or else as if that I
Ought aye to have a special care how all men do apply
My doing to their own behoof? As of the former twain
I have great hope and confidence, so would I also fain
The other should, according to good meaning, find success.
If otherwise, the fault is theirs, not mine, they must confess.
And, therefore, briefly to conclude, I turn again to thee,
O noble Earl of Leicester, whose life God grant may be
As long in honour, health and wealth as ancient Nestor's was,
Or rather as Tithonus's; that all such students as          610
Do travail to enrich our tongue with knowledge heretofore
Not common to our vulgar speech may daily more and more

Proceed through thy good furtherance and favour in the same,
To all men's profit and delight and thy eternal fame;
And that (which is a greater thing) our native country may
Long time enjoy thy counsel and thy travail to her stay.

At Barwicke the 20 of April 1567.

Your good L[ordship's] most humbly to command,
Arthur Golding.

# To the Reader

I would not wish the simple sort offended for to be
When in this book the heathen names of feignèd gods they see.
The true and everliving God the paynims did not know,
Which causèd them the name of gods on creatures to bestow.
For nature being once corrupt and knowledge blinded quite
By Adam's fall, those little seeds and sparks of heavenly light
That did as yet remain in man, endeavouring forth to burst
And wanting grace and power to grow to that they were at first,
To superstition did decline and drave the fearful mind
Strange worships of the living God in creatures for to find.          10
The which, by custom taking root and growing so to strength,
Through Satan's help possessed the hearts of all the world at
     length.
Some worshipped all the host of heaven; some dead men's ghosts
     and bones;
Some wicked fiends; some worms and fowls, herbs, fishes, trees
     and stones.
The fire, the air, the sea, the land and every running brook,
Each queachy grove, each craggèd cliff the name of godhead took.
The night and day, the fleeting hours, the seasons of the year
And every strange and monstrous thing for gods mistaken were.
There was no virtue, no, nor vice, there was no gift of mind
Or body, but some god thereto or goddess was assigned.               20
Of health and sickness, life and death, of neediness and wealth,
Of peace and war, of love and hate, of murder, craft and stealth,
Of bread and wine, of slothful sleep and of their solemn games
And every other trifling toy their gods did bear the names.
And look how every man was bent to goodness or to ill,
He did surmise his foolish gods inclining to his will.

For God, perceiving man's perverse and wicked will to sin,
Did give him over to his lust to sink or swim therein.
By means whereof it came to pass (as in this book ye see)
That all their gods with whoredom, theft or murder blotted be;
Which argues them to be no gods, but worser in effect
Than they whose open punishment their doings doth detect.
Who, seeing Jove, whom heathen folk do arm with triple fire,
In shape of eagle, bull or swan to win his foul desire;
Or grisly Mars, their god of war, entangled in a net
By Venus' husband purposely to trap him warily set;
Who, seeing Saturn eating up the children he begat;
Or Venus dallying wantonly with every lusty mate;
Who, seeing Juno play the scold; Or Phoebus mourn and rue
For loss of her whom, in his rage, through jealous mood he slew;
Or else the subtle Mercury that bears the charmèd rod
Conveying neat and hiding them, would take him for a god?
For if these faults in mortal men do justly merit blame,
What greater madness can there be than to impute the same
To gods, whose natures ought to be most perfect, pure and bright,
Most virtuous, holy, chaste and wise, most full of grace and light?
But as there is no Christian man that can surmise in mind
That these or other such are gods, which are no gods by kind,
So would to God there were not now of Christian men professed
That worshipped in their deeds these gods whose names they do
        detest.
Whose laws we keep, his thralls we be, and he our god indeed.
So long is Christ our god as we in Christian life proceed;
But if we yield to fleshly lust, to lucre or to wrath,
Or if that envy, gluttony or pride the mastery hath,
Or any other kind of sin, the thing the which we serve
To be accounted for our god most justly doth deserve.
Then must we think the learnèd men that did these names
        frequent
Some further things and purposes by those devices meant.
By Jove and Juno understand all states of princely port;
By Ops and Saturn, ancient folk that are of elder sort;
By Phoebus, young and lusty brutes of hand and courage stout;
By Mars, the valiant men of war that love to fight it out;

By Pallas and the famous troop of all the Muses nine,
Such folk as in the sciences and virtuous arts do shine;
By Mercury, the subtle sort that use to filch and lie,
With thieves and merchants who to gain their travail do apply;
By Bacchus, all the meaner trades and handicrafts are meant;
By Venus, such as of the flesh to filthy lust are bent;
By Neptune, such as keep the seas; by Phoebe, maidens chaste
And pilgrims such as wanderingly their time in travel waste;          70
By Pluto, such as delve in mines and ghosts of persons dead;
By Vulcan, smiths and such as work in iron, tin or lead;
By Hecate, witches, conjurors and necromancers read,
With all such vain and devilish arts as superstition breed;
By satyrs, sylvans, nymphs and fauns with other such beside,
The plain and simple country folk that everywhere abide.
I know these names to other things oft may, and must, agree,
In declaration of the which I will not tedious be,
But leave them to the reader's will to take in sundry wise,
As matter rising giveth cause constructions to devise.                80
Now when thou read'st of god or man, in stone, in beast or tree,
It is a mirror for thyself thine own estate to see.
For under feignèd names of gods it was the poet's guise
The vice and faults of all estates to taunt in covert wise,
And likewise to extol with praise such things as do deserve,
Observing always comeliness from which they do not swerve.
And as the person greater is of birth, renown or fame,
The greater ever is his laud, or fouler is his shame.
For if the states that on the earth the room of God supply
Decline from virtue unto vice and live disorderly,                    90
To eagles, tigers, bulls and bears and other figures strange,
Both to their people and themselves most hurtful, do they change.
And when the people give themselves to filthy life and sin,
What other kind of shape thereby than filthy can they win?
So was Lycaon made a wolf, and Jove became a bull;
The t'one for using cruelty, the t'other for his trull.
So was Elpenor and his mates transformèd into swine
For following of their filthy lust in women and in wine;
Not that they lost their manly shape as to the outward show,
But for that in their brutish breasts most beastly lusts did grow.    100

For why, this lump of flesh and bones, this body, is not we;
We are a thing which earthly eyes denièd are to see.
Our soul is we, endued by God with reason from above;
Our body is but as our house, in which we work and move.
T'one part is common to us all, with God of heaven himself;
The t'other common with the beasts, a vile and stinking pelf.
The t'one bedecked with heavenly gifts and endless; t'other gross,
Frail, filthy, weak and born to die, as made of earthly dross.
Now look how long this clod of clay to reason doth obey,
So long for men by just desert account ourselves we may.
But if we suffer fleshly lusts as lawless lords to reign,
Then are we beasts; we are no men; we have our name in vain.
And if we be so drowned in vice that feeling once be gone,
Then may it well of us be said, we are a block or stone.
This surely did the poets mean when in such sundry wise
The pleasant tales of turnèd shapes they studied to devise.
Their purpose was to profit men and also to delight,
And so to handle everything as best might like the sight.
For as the image portrayed out in simple white and black
(Though well proportioned, true and fair), if comely colours lack,
Delighteth not the eye so much, nor yet contents the mind
So much as that that shadowed is with colours in his kind;
Even so a plain and naked tale or story simply told
(Although the matter be indeed of value more than gold)
Makes not the hearer so attent to print it in his heart
As when the thing is well declared, with pleasant terms and art.
All which the poets knew right well; and for the greater grace,
As Persian kings did never go abroad with open face,
But with some lawn or silken scarf, for reverence of their state,
Even so they, following in their works the selfsame trade and rate,
Did under covert names and terms their doctrines so imply
As that it is right dark and hard their meaning to espy;
But being found, it is more sweet and makes the mind more glad
Than if a man of trièd gold a treasure gainèd had.
For, as the body hath his joy in pleasant smells and sights,
Even so in knowledge and in arts the mind as much delights.
Whereof abundant hoards and heaps in poets packèd been,
So hid that (saving unto few) they are not to be seen.

And therefore, whoso doth attempt the poets' works to read
Must bring with him a staïd head and judgement to proceed.    140
For as there be most wholesome hests and precepts to be found,
So are there rocks and shallow shelves to run the ship aground.
Some naughty person, seeing vice showed lively in his hue,
Doth take occasion by and by like vices to ensue;
Another, being more severe than wisdom doth require,
Beholding vice (to outward show) exalted in desire,
Condemneth by and by the book and him that did it make
And wills it to be burnt with fire for lewd example sake.
These persons overshoot themselves and other folks deceive,
Not able of the author's mind the meaning to conceive.    150
The author's purpose is to paint and set before our eyes
The lively image of the thoughts that in our stomachs rise.
Each vice and virtue seems to speak and argue to our face,
With such persuasions as they have, their doings to embrace.
And if a wicked person seem his vices to exalt,
Esteem not him that wrate the work in such defaults to halt.
But rather with an upright eye consider well thy thought;
See if corrupted nature have the like within thee wrought.
Mark what affection doth persuade in every kind of matter;
Judge if that even in heinous crimes thy fancy do not flatter.    160
And were it not for dread of law or dread of God above,
Most men (I fear) would do the things that fond affections move.
Then take these works as fragrant flowers most full of pleasant
        juice,
The which the bee, conveying home, may put to wholesome use
And which the spider, sucking on, to poison may convert
Through venom spread in all her limbs and native in her heart.
For to the pure and godly mind are all things pure and clean,
And unto such as are corrupt the best corrupted been;
Like as the finest meats and drinks that can be made by art
In sickly folks to nourishment of sickness do convert.    170
And therefore, not regarding such whose diet is so fine
That nothing can digest with them unless it be divine,
Nor such as to their proper harm do wrest and wring awry
The things that to a good intent are written pleasantly,

Through Ovid's work of turnèd shapes I have with painful pace
Passed on, until I had attained the end of all my race.
And now I have him made so well acquainted with our tongue
As that he may in English verse, as in his own, be sung.
Wherein, although for pleasant style I cannot make account
180 To match mine author, who in that all other doth surmount,
Yet (gentle reader) do I trust my travail in this case
May purchase favour in thy sight my doings to embrace;
Considering what a sea of goods and jewels thou shalt find,
Not more delightful to the ear than fruitful to the mind.
For this do learnèd persons deem of Ovid's present work:
That in no one of all his books, the which he wrate, do lurk
Mo dark and secret mysteries, mo counsels wise and sage,
Mo good ensamples, mo reproofs of vice in youth and age,
Mo fine inventions to delight, mo matters clerkly knit,
190 No, nor more strange variety to show a learnèd wit.
The high, the low, the rich, the poor, the master and the slave,
The maid, the wife, the man, the child, the simple and the brave,
The young, the old, the good, the bad, the warrior strong and
        stout,
The wise, the fool, the country clown, the learnèd and the lout,
And every other living wight shall in this mirror see
His whole estate, thoughts, words and deeds expressly showed to
        be.
Whereof, if more particular examples thou do crave,
In reading the Epistle through thou shalt thy longing have.
Moreover, thou may'st find herein descriptions of the times,
200 With constellations of the stars and planets in their climes,
The sites of countries, cities, hills, seas, forests, plains and floods,
The natures both of fowls, beasts, worms, herbs, metals, stones and
        woods.
And finally, whatever thing is strange and delectable,
The same conveyèd shall you find most featly in some fable.
And even as in a chain each link within another winds,
And both with that that went before and that that follows binds,
So every tale within this book doth seem to take his ground
Of that that was rehearsed before, and enters in the bound

Of that that follows after it; and every one gives light
To other; so that whoso means to understand them right                210
Must have a care as well to know the thing that went before
As that the which he presently desires to see so sore.
Now to th'intent that none have cause hereafter to complain
Of me as setter out of things that are but light and vain,
If any stomach be so weak as that it cannot brook
The lively setting forth of things describèd in this book,
I give him counsel to abstain until he be more strong,
And for to use Ulysses' feat against the mermaids' song.
Or if he needs will hear and see and wilfully agree
(Through cause misconstrued) unto vice allurèd for to be,                220
Then let him also mark the pain that doth thereof ensue,
And hold himself content with that that to his fault is due.


FINIS.

# The First Book of Ovid's Metamorphoses, translated into English metre

Of shapes transformed to bodies strange I purpose to entreat.  
Ye gods, vouchsafe (for you are they that wrought this wondrous  
feat)  
To further this mine enterprise, and from the world begun  
Grant that my verse may to my time his course directly run.  
  Before the sea and land were made, and heaven that all doth  
hide,  
In all the world one only face of nature did abide  
Which Chaos hight; a huge, rude heap, and nothing else but even  
A heavy lump and clottered clod of seeds together driven  
Of things at strife among themselves for want of order due.  
No sun as yet with lightsome beams the shapeless world did view;  
No moon in growing did repair her horns with borrowed light.  
Nor yet the earth amidst the air did hang by wondrous flight,  
Just peisèd by her proper weight; nor, winding in and out,  
Did Amphitrite with her arms embrace the earth about.  
For where was earth, was sea and air; so was the earth unstable,  
The air all dark, the sea likewise to bear a ship unable.  
No kind of thing had proper shape, but each confounded other;  
For in one selfsame body strove the hot and cold together,  
The moist with dry, the soft with hard, the light with things of  
weight.  
This strife did God and nature break and set in order straight.  
The earth from heaven, the sea from earth he parted orderly,  
And from the thick and foggy air he took the lightsome sky;  
Which when he once unfolded had and severed from the blind  
And clodded heap, he, setting each from other, did them bind  
In endless friendship to agree. The fire most pure and bright,  
The substance of the heaven itself, because it was so light  

*The Poet's introduction*

*The creation*

10

20

Did mount aloft and set itself in highest place of all.
The second room of right to air for lightness did befall.
The earth, more gross, drew down with it each weighty kind of
    matter
30 And set itself in lowest place. Again, the waving water
Did lastly challenge for his place the utmost coast and bound
Of all the compass of the earth, to close the steadfast ground.
Now when he in this foresaid wise (what god so e'er he was)
Had broke and into members put this rude confusèd mass,
Then first, because in every part the earth should equal be,
He made it like a mighty ball in compass, as we see.
And here and there he cast in seas, to whom he gave a law:
To swell with every blast of wind and every stormy flaw,
And with their waves continually to beat upon the shore
40 Of all the earth within their bounds enclosed by them afore.
Moreover, springs and mighty meres and lakes he did augment,
And flowing streams of crooked brooks in winding banks he pent.
Of which the earth doth drink up some, and some with restless
    race
Do seek the sea, where, finding scope of larger room and space,
Instead of banks they beat on shores. He did command the plain
And champaign grounds to stretch out wide, and valleys to remain
Aye underneath, and eke the woods to hide them decently
With tender leaves, and stony hills to lift themselves on high.
And as two zones do cut the heaven upon the righter side
50 And other twain upon the left likewise the same divide,
The middle in outrageous heat exceeding all the rest;
Even so likewise through great foresight to God it seemèd best
The earth included in the same should so divided be,
As with the number of the heaven her zones might full agree.
Of which the middle zone in heat, the utmost twain in cold,
Exceed so far that there to dwell no creature dare be bold.
Between these two so great extremes two other zones are fixed
Where temperature of heat and cold indifferently is mixed.
Now over this doth hang the air which, as it is more slighty
60 Than earth or water, so again than fire it is more weighty.

There hath he placèd mist and clouds and, for to fear men's minds,
The thunder and the lightning eke, with cold and blustering
        winds.
And yet the maker of the world permitteth not alway
The winds to use the air at will. For at this present day,
Though each from other placèd be in sundry coasts aside,
The violence of their boisterous blasts things scarcely can abide.
They so turmoil as though they would the world in pieces rend;
So cruel is those brothers' wrath when that they do contend.
And therefore to the morning grey, the realm of Nabathy,
To Persis and to other lands and countries that do lie                    70
Far underneath the morning star did Eurus take his flight.
Likewise the setting of the sun and shutting in of night
Belong to Zephyr. And the blasts of blustereing Boreas reign
In Scythia and in other lands set under Charles his wain.
And unto Auster doth belong the coast of all the south,
Who beareth showers and rotten mists continual in his mouth.
Above all these he set aloft the clear and lightsome sky
Without all dregs of earthly filth or grossness utterly.
The bounds of things were scarcely yet by him thus pointed out
But that appearèd in the heaven stars glistering all about            80
Which in the said confusèd heap had hidden been before.
And to th'intent with lively things each region for to store,
The heavenly soil to gods and stars and planets first he gave;
The waters next both fresh and salt he let the fishes have;
The subtle air to flickering fowls and birds he hath assigned;
The earth to beasts both wild and tame of sundry sort and kind.
Howbeit, yet of all this while the creature wanting was
Far more divine, of nobler mind, which should the residue pass
In depth of knowledge, reason, wit and high capacity,
And which of all the residue should the lord and ruler be.             90
Then either he that made the world and things in order set
Of heavenly seed engendered man; or else the earth, as yet
Young, lusty, fresh and in her flowers, and parted from the sky
But late before, the seed thereof as yet held inwardly,
The which Prometheus, tempering straight with water of the
        spring,
Did make in likeness to the gods that govern everything.

And where all other beasts behold the ground with grovelling eye,
He gave to man a stately look replete with majesty
And willed him to behold the heaven with count'nance cast on
     high,
100 To mark and understand what things were in the starry sky.
And thus the earth, which late before had neither shape nor hue,
Did take the noble shape of man and was transformèd new.

*The*
*golden*
*age*
    Then sprang up first the golden age, which of itself maintained
    The truth and right of everything unforced and unconstrained.
There was no fear of punishment; there was no threatening law
In brazen tables nailèd up to keep the folk in awe.
There was no man would crouch or creep to judge with cap in
     hand;
They livèd safe without a judge in every realm and land.
The lofty pine-tree was not hewn from mountains, where it
     stood,
110 In seeking strange and foreign lands to rove upon the flood;
Men knew none other countries yet than where themselves did
     keep.
There was no town enclosèd yet with walls and ditches deep.
No horn nor trumpet was in use, no sword nor helmet worn;
The world was such that soldiers' help might easily be forborne.
The fertile earth as yet was free, untouched of spade or plough;
And yet it yielded of itself of everything enough.
And men themselves contented well with plain and simple food
That on the earth of nature's gift without their travail stood;
Did live by raspis, hips and haws, by cornels, plums and cherries,
120 By sloes and apples, nuts and pears and loathsome brambleberries,
And by the acorns dropped on ground by Jove's broad tree in
     field.
The springtime lasted all the year, and Zephyr with his mild
And gentle blast did cherish things that grew of own accord.
The ground, untilled, all kind of fruits did plenteously afford.
No muck nor tillage was bestowed on lean and barren land
To make the corn of better head and ranker for to stand.
Then streams ran milk, then streams ran wine; and yellow honey
     flowed
From each green tree whereon the rays of fiery Phoebus glowed.

But when that, into Limbo once Saturnus being thrust,
The rule and charge of all the world was under Jove unjust      130
And that the silver age came in, more somewhat base than gold,
More precious yet than freckled brass, immediately the old
And ancient spring did Jove abridge and made thereof anon
Four seasons: winter, summer, spring and autumn off and on.
Then first of all began the air with fervent heat to swelt;
Then icicles hung roping down; then, for the cold was felt,
Men gan to shroud themselves in house. Their houses were the
    thicks
And bushy queaches, hollow caves or hurdles made of sticks.
Then first of all were furrows drawn and corn was cast in ground;
The simple ox with sorry sighs to heavy yoke was bound.      140
  Next after this succeeded straight the third and brazen age,
  More hard of nature, somewhat bent to cruel wars and rage,
But yet not wholly past all grace. Of iron is the last,
In no part good and tractable as former ages past.
For when that of this wicked age once opened was the vein,
Therein all mischief rushèd forth. Then faith and truth were fain,
And honest shame, to hide their heads; for whom stepped stoutly
    in
Craft, treason, violence, envy, pride and wicked lust to win.
The shipman hoist his sails to wind whose names he did not
    know;
And ships that erst in tops of hills and mountains had ygrow      150
Did leap and dance on uncouth waves. And men began to bound
With dowels and ditches drawn in length the free and fertile
    ground
Which was as common as the air and light of sun before.
Not only corn and other fruits for sust'nance and for store
Were now exacted of the earth, but eft they gan to dig
And in the bowels of the ground unsatiably to rig
For riches couched and hidden deep in places near to hell,
The spurs and stirrers unto vice, and foes to doing well.
Then hurtful iron came abroad; then came forth yellow gold,
More hurtful than the iron far; then came forth battle bold      160

That fights with both and shakes his sword in cruel bloody hand.
Men live by ravine and by stealth. The wandering guest doth
     stand
In danger of his host, the host in danger of his guest,
And fathers of their son-in-laws; yea, seldom time doth rest
Between born brothers such accord and love as ought to be.
The goodman seeks the goodwife's death, and his again seeks she;
The stepdames fell their husbands' sons with poison do assail;
To see their fathers live so long the children do bewail.
All godliness lies underfoot. And Lady Astrey, last
170  Of heavenly virtues, from this earth in slaughter drownèd passed.

*Crimes of*           And to th'intent the earth alone thus should not be oppressed
*giants and*          And heaven above in slothful ease and careless quiet rest,
*men*           Men say that giants went about the realm of heaven to win,
To place themselves to reign as gods and lawless lords therein.
And hill on hill they heapèd up aloft unto the sky
Till God Almighty from the heaven did let his thunder fly.
The dint whereof the airy tops of high Olympus brake
And pressèd Pelion violently from under Ossa strake.
When whelmèd in their wicked work those cursèd caitiffs lay,
The earth, their mother, took their blood yet warm and (as they
180           say)
Did give it life. And for because some imps should still remain
Of that same stock, she gave it shape and limbs of men again.
This offspring eke against the gods did bear a native spite;
In slaughter and in doing wrong was all their whole delight.
Their deeds declarèd them of blood engendered for to be.

*Jove*           The which as soon as Saturn's son from heaven aloft did see,
*summons*        He fetched a sigh and therewithal, revolving in his thought
*parliament*     The shameful act which at a feast Lycaon late had wrought,
As yet unknown or blown abroad, he gan thereat to storm
190  And stomach like an angry Jove. And therefore, to reform
Such heinous acts, he summoned straight his Court of Parliament
Whereto resorted all the gods that had their summons sent.
High in the welkin is a way apparent to the sight
In starry nights, which of his passing whiteness Milky hight.
It is the street that to the court and princely palace leads
Of mighty Jove, whose thunderclaps each living creature dreads.

On both the sides of this same way do stand in stately port
The sumptuous houses of the peers (for all the common sort
Dwell scattering here and there abroad); the face of all the sky
The houses of the chief estates and princes do supply.                           200
And sure and if I may be bold to speak my fancy free,
I take this place of all the heaven the palace for to be.
Now when the gods assembled were and each had ta'en his place,
Jove, standing up aloft and leaning on his ivory mace,
Right dreadfully his bushy locks did thrice or four times shake,
Wherewith he made both sea and land and heaven itself to quake,
And afterward in wrathful words his angry mind thus brake:
    'I never was in greater care nor more perplexity
    How to maintain my sovereign state and princely royalty
When with their hundred hands apiece the adder-footed rout              210
Did practise for to conquer heaven and for to cast us out.
For though it were a cruel foe, yet did that war depend
Upon one ground, and in one stock it had his final end.
But now, as far as any sea about the world doth wind,
I must destroy both man and beast and all the mortal kind.
I swear by Styx's hideous streams that run within the ground,
All other means must first be sought; but when there can be found
No help to heal a festered sore, it must away be cut
Lest that the parts that yet are sound in danger should be put.
We have a number in the world that man's estate surmount              220
Of such whom for their private gods the country folks account,
As satyrs, fauns and sundry nymphs, with silvans eke beside,
That in the woods and hilly grounds continually abide.
Whom into heaven since that as yet we vouch not safe to take
And of the honour of this place co-partners for to make,
Such lands as to inhabit in we erst to them assigned.
That they should still enjoy the same, it is my will and mind.
But can you think that they in rest and safety shall remain
When proud Lycaon lay in wait by secret means and train
To have confounded me, your lord, who in my hand do bear              230
The dreadful thunder, and of whom even you do stand in fear?'
    The House was movèd at his words and earnestly required
    The man that had so traitorously against their lord conspired.

Even so when rebels did arise to stroy the Roman name
By shedding of our Caesar's blood, the horror of the same
Did pierce the hearts of all mankind and made the world to quake;
Whose fervent zeal in thy behalf, O August, thou did take
As thankfully as Jove doth hear the loving care of his.
Who, beckoning to them with his hand, forbiddeth them to hiss;
240    And therewithal through all the House attentive silence is.
As soon as that his majesty all muttering had allayed,
He brake the silence once again and thus unto them said:

Lycaon    'Let pass this careful thought of yours; for he that did offend
Hath dearly bought the wicked act the which he did intend.
Yet shall you hear what was his fault and vengeance for the same.
A foul report and infamy unto our hearing came
Of mischief usèd in those times; which wishing all untrue,
I did descend in shape of man th'infamèd earth to view.
It were a process overlong to tell you of the sin
250    That did abound in every place whereas I entered in;
The bruit was lesser than the truth and partial in report.
The dreadful dens of Maenalus, where savage beasts resort,
And Cyllen had I overpassed, with all the pine-trees high
Of cold Lycaeus, and from thence I entered by and by
The harbourless and cruel house of late th'Arcadian king
Such time as twilight on the earth dim darkness gan to bring.
I gave a sign that god was come, and straight the common sort
Devoutly prayed; whereat Lycaon first did make a sport
And after said, "By open proof ere long I mind to see
260    If that this wight a mighty god or mortal creature be.
The truth shall try itself." He meant (the sequel did declare)
To steal upon me in the night and kill me unbeware.
And yet he was not so content, but went and cut the throat
Of one that lay in hostage there which was an Epirot.
And part of him he did to roast and part he did to stew;
Which when it came upon the board, forthwith I overthrew
The house with just revenging fire upon the owner's head.
Who, seeing that, slipped out of doors amazed for fear and fled
Into the wild and desert woods where, being all alone,
270    As he endeavoured (but in vain) to speak and make his moan,

He fell a-howling. Wherewithal for very rage and mood
He ran me quite out of his wits and waxèd furious wood,
Still practising his wonted lust of slaughter on the poor
And silly cattle, thirsting still for blood as heretofore.
His garments turned to shaggy hair, his arms to rugged paws;
So is he made a ravening wolf whose shape expressly draws
To that the which he was before. His skin is hoary grey,
His look still grim with glaring eyes; and every kind of way
His cruel heart in outward shape doth well itself bewray.
Thus was one house destroyèd quite. But that one house alone          280
Deserveth not to be destroyed; in all the earth is none
But that such vice doth reign therein as that ye would believe
That all had sworn and sold themselves to mischief, us to grieve.
And therefore, as they all offend, so am I fully bent
That all forthwith (as they deserve) shall have due punishment.'
    These words of Jove some of the gods did openly approve
    And with their sayings more to wrath his angry courage move;
And some did give assent by signs. Yet did it grieve them all
That such destruction utterly on all mankind should fall,
Demanding what he purposèd with all the earth to do          290
When that he had all mortal men so clean destroyed, and who
On holy altars afterward should offer frankincense,
And whether that he were in mind to leave the earth fro thence
To savage beasts to waste and spoil because of man's offence.
    The king of gods bade cease their thoughts and questions in that          *The flood*
        case
    And cast the care thereof on him. Within a little space
He promised for to frame anew another kind of men
By wondrous means, unlike the first, to fill the world again.
And now his lightning had he thought on all the earth to throw,
But that he fearèd lest the flames perhaps so high should grow          300
As for to set the heaven on fire and burn up all the sky.
He did remember furthermore how that by destiny
A certain time should one day come wherein both sea and land
And heaven itself should feel the force of Vulcan's scorching
        brand,
So that the huge and goodly work of all the world so wide
Should go to wreck; for doubt whereof forthwith he laid aside

His weapons that the Cyclopes made, intending to correct
Man's trespass by a punishment contrary in effect.
And namely with incessant showers from heaven ypourèd down
310    He did determine with himself the mortal kind to drown.
    In Aeolus' prison by and by he fettered Boreas fast
    With all such winds as chase the clouds or break them with
        their blast,
And set at large the southern wind; who straight with watery
        wings
And dreadful face as black as pitch forth out of prison flings.
His beard hung full of hideous storms; all dankish was his head,
With water streaming down his hair that on his shoulders shed.
His ugly forehead wrinkled was with foggy mists full thick,
And on his feathers and his breast a stilling dew did stick.
As soon as he between his hands the hanging clouds had crushed,
320    With rattling noise a-down from heaven the rain full sadly gushed.
The rainbow, Juno's messenger, bedecked in sundry hue,
To maintain moisture in the clouds great waters thither drew.
The corn was beaten to the ground; the tillman's hope of gain
For which he toilèd all the year lay drownèd in the rain.
Jove's indignation and his wrath began to grow so hot
That for to quench the rage thereof his heaven sufficèd not;
His brother Neptune with his waves was fain to do him ease.
Who, straight assembling all the streams that fall into the seas,
Said to them, standing in his house: 'Sirs, get you home apace;
330    You must not look to have me use long preaching in this case.
Pour out your force (for so is need), your heads each one unpend,
And from your open springs your streams with flowing waters send.'
He had no sooner said the word but that, returning back,
Each one of them unloosed his spring and let his waters slack.
And to the sea with flowing streams yswollen above their banks,
One rolling in another's neck, they rushèd forth by ranks.
Himself with his three-tinèd mace did lend the earth a blow
That made it shake and open ways for waters forth to flow.
The floods at random where they list through all the fields did
        stray;
Men, beasts, trees, corn and with their gods were churches washed
340        away.

If any house were built so strong against their force to stand,
Yet did the water hide the top; and turrets in that pond
Were overwhelmed. No difference was between the sea and
      ground,
For all was sea. There was no shore nor landing to be found.
Some climbèd up to tops of hills, and some rowed to and fro
In boats where they, not long before, to plough and cart did go.
One over corn and tops of towns whom waves did overwhelm
Doth sail in ship; another sits a-fishing in an elm.
In meadows green were anchors cast (so fortune did provide),
And crooked ships did shadow vines, the which the flood did
      hide.                                                                                          350
And where but t'other day before did feed the hungry goat,
The ugly seals and porpoises now to and fro did float.
The seanymphs wondered under waves the towns and groves to
      see;
And dolphins played among the tops and boughs of every tree.
The grim and greedy wolf did swim among the silly sheep;
The lion and the tiger fierce were borne upon the deep.
It booted not the foaming boar his crooked tusks to whet;
The running hart could in the stream by swiftness nothing get.
The fleeting fowls, long having sought for land to rest upon,
Into the sea with weary wings were driven to fall anon.                          360
Th'outrageous swelling of the sea the lesser hillocks drowned;
Unwonted waves on highest tops of mountains did rebound.
The greatest part of men were drowned; and such as scaped the
      flood,
Forlorn with fasting overlong, did die for want of food.
Against the fields of Aony and Attic lies a land                                        *Deucalion*
That Phocis hight, a fertile ground while that it was a land,              *and Pyrrha*
But at that time a part of sea and even a champaign field
Of sudden waters, which the flood by forcèd rage did yield;
Whereas a hill with forkèd top, the which Parnassus hight,
Doth pierce the clouds and to the stars doth raise his head upright.       370
When at this hill (for yet the sea had whelmèd all beside)
Deucalion and his bedfellow, without all other guide,
Arrivèd in a little bark, immediately they went
And to the nymphs of Corycus with full devout intent

Did honour due, and to the gods to whom that famous hill
Was sacred, and to Themis eke in whose most holy will
Consisted then the oracles. In all the world so round
A better nor more righteous man could never yet be found
Than was Deucalion, nor again a woman, maid nor wife,
380   That fearèd God so much as she nor led so good a life.
      When Jove beheld how all the world stood like a plash of rain
      And of so many thousand men and women did remain
But one of each, howbeit those both just and both devout,
He brake the clouds and did command that Boreas with his stout
And sturdy blasts should chase the flood, that earth might see the
      sky
And heaven the earth. The seas also began immediately
Their raging fury for to cease. Their ruler laid away
His dreadful mace and with his words their woodness did allay.
He callèd Triton to him straight, his trumpeter, who stood
390   In purple robe on shoulder cast aloft upon the flood,
And bade him take his sounding trump and out of hand to blow
Retreat, that all the streams might hear and cease from thence to
      flow.
He took his trumpet in his hand; his trumpet was a shell
Of some great whelk or other fish, in fashion like a bell
That gathered narrow to the mouth and, as it did descend,
Did wax more wide and writhen still down to the nether end.
When that this trump amid the sea was set to Triton's mouth,
He blew so loud that all the streams both east, west, north and
      south
Might easily hear him blow retreat, and all that heard the sound
400   Immediately began to ebb and draw within their bound.
Then gan the sea to have a shore and brooks to find a bank,
And swelling streams of flowing floods within her channels sank.
Then hills did rise above the waves that had them overflow.
And, as the waters did decrease, the ground did seem to grow.
And after long and tedious time the trees did show their tops
All bare, save that upon the boughs the mud did hang in knops.
The world restorèd was again, which though Deucalion joyed
Then to behold, yet for because he saw the earth was void

And silent like a wilderness, with sad and weeping eyes
And ruthful voice he then did speak to Pyrrha in this wise:      410
   'O sister, O my loving spouse, O silly woman left
   As only remnant of thy sex that water hath bereft,
Whom nature first by right of birth hath linkèd to me fast,
In that we brothers' children been, and secondly the chaste
And steadfast bond of lawful bed, and lastly now of all
The present perils of the time that lately did befall:
On all the earth from east to west where Phoebus shows his face
There is no mo but thou and I of all the mortal race.
The sea hath swallowed all the rest. And scarcely are we sure
That our two lives from dreadful death in safety shall endure;      420
For even as yet the dusky clouds do make my heart adrad.
Alas, poor wretched silly soul, what heart would'st thou have had
To bear these heavy haps if chance had let thee scape alone?
Who should have been thy consort then? Who should have rued
       thy moan?
Now trust me truly, loving wife, had thou as now been drowned,
I would have followed after thee and in the sea been found.
Would God I could my father's art of clay to fashion men
And give them life, that people might frequent the world again.
Mankind, alas, doth only now within us two consist
As moulds whereby to fashion men; for so the gods do list.'      430
   And with these words the bitter tears did trickle down their
      cheek
   Until at length between themselves they did agree to seek
To God by prayer for his grace and to demand his aid
By answer of his oracle; wherein they nothing stayed,
But to Cephisus sadly went, whose stream as at that time
Began to run within his banks, though thick with muddy slime.
Whose sacred liquor straight they took and sprinkled with the
      same
Their heads and clothes, and afterward to Themis' chapel came,
The roof whereof with cindery moss was almost overgrown;
For since the time the raging flood the world had overflown,      440
No creature came within the church, so that the altars stood
Without one spark of holy fire or any stick of wood.

As soon as that this couple came within the chapel door,
They fell down flat upon the ground and, trembling, kissed the
     floor
And said: 'If prayer that proceeds from humble heart and mind
May in the presence of the gods such grace and favour find
As to appease their worthy wrath, then vouch thou safe to tell,
O gentle Themis, how the loss that on our kind befell
May now eftsoons recovered be, and help us to repair
450  The world, which drownèd under waves doth lie in great despair.'
The goddess, movèd with their suit, this answer did them make:
'Depart you hence. Go hill your heads and let your garments slake
And both of you your grandam's bones behind your shoulders
     cast.'
They stood amazèd at these words till Pyrrha at the last,
Refusing to obey the hest the which the goddess gave,
Brake silence and with trembling cheer did meekly pardon crave;
For sure, she said, she was afraid her grandam's ghost to hurt
By taking up her buried bones to throw them in the dirt.
And with the answer hereupon eftsoons in hand they go,
460  The doubtful words whereof they scan and canvas to and fro.
Which done, Prometheus' son began by counsel wise and sage
His cousin-german's fearfulness thus gently to assuage:
'Well, either in these doubtful words is hid some mystery
Whereof the gods permit us not the meaning to espy,
Or, questionless, and if the sense of inward sentence deem
Like as the tenor of the words apparently do seem,
It is no breach of godliness to do as God doth bid.
I take our grandam for the earth; the stones within her hid
I take for bones; these are the bones the which are meanèd here.'
470  Though Titan's daughter at this wise conjecture of her fere
Were somewhat moved, yet none of both did steadfast credit give,
So hardly could they in their hearts the heavenly hests believe.
But what and if they made a proof? What harm could come
     thereby?
They went their ways and veiled their heads and did their coats
     untie

And at their backs did throw the stones by name of bones
    foretold.
The stones (who would believe the thing, but that the time of old
Reports it for a steadfast truth?), of nature tough and hard,
Began to wax both soft and smooth and shortly afterward
To win therewith a better shape; and, as they did increase,
A milder nature in them grew and rudeness gan to cease.       480
For at the first their shape was such as in a certain sort
Resembled man, but of the right and perfect shape came short;
Even like to marble images new drawn and roughly wrought
Before the carver by his art to purpose hath them brought.
Such parts of them where any juice or moisture did abound
Or else were earthy turned to flesh; and such as were so sound
And hard as would not bow nor bend did turn to bones; again,
The part that was a vein before doth still his name retain.
Thus by the mighty power of God ere lenger time was passed
The mankind was restored by stones the which a man did cast;    490
And likewise also by the stones the which a woman threw
The womankind repairèd was and made again of new.
Of these are we the crooked imps and stony race indeed,
Bewraying by our toiling life from whence we do proceed.
    The lusty earth of own accord soon after forth did bring,    *The rebirth*
    According to their sundry shapes, each other living thing.    *of animal life*
As soon as that the moisture once caught heat against the sun,
And that the fat and slimy mud in moorish grounds begun
To swell through warmth of Phoebus' beams, and that the fruitful
    seed
Of things well cherished in the fat and lively soil indeed,    500
As in their mother's womb, began in length of time to grow
To one or other kind of shape wherein themselves to show,
Even so, when that seven-mouthèd Nile the watery fields forsook
And to his ancient channel eft his bridled streams betook,
So that the sun did heat the mud the which he left behind,
The husbandmen that tilled the ground among the clods did find
Of sundry creatures sundry shapes. Of which they spièd some
Even in the instant of their birth but newly then begun;
And some unperfect, wanting breast or shoulders in such wise
That in one body oftentimes appearèd to the eyes    510

One half thereof alive to be, and all the rest beside,
Both void of life and seemly shape, stark earth to still abide.
For when that moisture with the heat is tempered equally,
They do conceive and of them twain engender by and by
All kind of things. For though that fire with water aye debateth,
Yet moisture mixed with equal heat all living things createth.
And so those discords in their kind, one striving with the other,
In generation do agree and make one perfect mother.
And therefore when the miry earth, bespread with slimy mud

520    Brought over all but late before by violence of the flood,
Caught heat by warmness of the sun and calmness of the sky,
Things out of number in the world forthwith it did supply.
Whereof in part the like before in former times had been,
And some so strange and ugly shapes as never erst were seen.

*Apollo and*    In that she did such monsters breed was greatly to her woe;
*the Python*    But yet thou, ugly Python, wert engendered by her tho,
A terror to the new-made folk which never erst had known
So foul a dragon in their life, so monstrously forgrown,
So great a ground thy poison-paunch did underneath thee hide.

530    The god of shooting, who nowhere before that present tide,
Those kind of weapons put in use but at the speckled deer
Or at the roes so wight of foot, a thousand shafts well near
Did on that hideous serpent spend, of which there was not one
But forcèd forth the venomed blood along his sides to gon;
So that, his quiver almost void, he nailed him to the ground
And did him nobly at the last by force of shot confound.
And lest that time might of this work deface the worthy fame,
He did ordain in mind thereof a great and solemn game
Which of the serpent that he slew of Pythians bare the name;

540    Where whoso could the mastery win in feats of strength or sleight
Of hand or foot or rolling wheel might claim to have of right
An oaken garland fresh and brave. There was not anywhere
As yet a bay; by means whereof was Phoebus fain to wear
The leaves of every pleasant tree about his golden hair.

*Daphne*    Peneian Daphne was the first where Phoebus set his love,
*and Apollo*    Which not blind chance but Cupid's fierce and cruel wrath did
move.

The Delian god, but late before surprised with passing pride
For killing of the monstrous worm, the god of love espied
With bow in hand already bent and letting arrows go.
To whom he said, 'And what hast thou, thou wanton baby, so          550
With warlike weapons for to toy? It were a better sight
To see this kind of furniture on our two shoulders bright,
Who, when we list, with steadfast hand both man and beast can
     wound,
Who t'other day with arrows keen have nailèd to the ground
The serpent Python so forswollen, whose filthy womb did hide
So many acres of the ground in which he did abide.
Content thyself, son, sorry loves to kindle with thy brand;
For these our praises to attain thou must not take in hand.'
To him quoth Venus' son again, 'Well, Phoebus, I agree
Thy bow to shoot at every beast, and so shall mine at thee.          560
And look how far that under god each beast is put by kind,
So much thy glory less than ours in shooting shalt thou find.'
This said, with drift of feathered wings in broken air he flew
And to the forked and shady top of Mount Parnassus drew.
There from his quiver full of shafts two arrows did he take
Of sundry works: t'one causeth love, the t'other doth it slake.
That causeth love is all of gold with point full sharp and bright;
That chaseth love is blunt, whose steal with leaden head is dight.
The god this fixèd in the nymph Peneis for the nonce;
The t'other pierced Apollo's heart and overraught his bones.          570
Immediately in smouldering heat of love the t'one did swelt;
Again, the t'other in her heart no spark nor motion felt.
In woods and forests is her joy the savage beasts to chase
And as the prize of all her pain to take the skin and case.
Unwedded Phoebe doth she haunt and follow as her guide;
Unordered do her tresses wave, scarce in a fillet tied.
Full many a wooer sought her love; she, loathing all the rout,
Impatient and without a man walks all the woods about.
And as for Hymen or for love and wedlock, often sought,
She took no care; they were the furthest end of all her thought.          580
Her father many a time and oft would say, 'My daughter dear,
Thou owest me a son-in-law to be thy lawful fere.'

Her father many a time and oft would say, 'My daughter dear,
Of nephews thou my debtor art, their grandsire's heart to cheer.'
She, hating as a heinous crime the bond of bridely bed,
Demurely casting down her eyes and blushing somewhat red,
Did fold about her father's neck with fawning arms and said,
'Dear father, grant me while I live my maidenhead for to have,
As to Diana heretofore her father freely gave.'

590   Thy father, Daphne, could consent to that thou dost require
But that thy beauty and thy form impugn thy chaste desire,
So that thy will and his consent are nothing in this case
By reason of the beauty bright that shineth in thy face.
Apollo loves and longs to have this Daphne to his fere,
And as he longs, he hopes; but his foredooms do fail him there.
And as light hain when corn is reaped, or hedges burn with brands
That passers-by when day draws near throw loosely fro their
          hands,
So into flames the god is gone and burneth in his breast
And feeds his vain and barren love in hoping for the best.

600   Her hair unkembed about her neck down flaring did he see;
'O Lord, and were they trimmed,' quoth he, 'how seemly would
          she be!'
He sees her eyes as bright as fire the stars to represent;
He sees her mouth, which to have seen he holds him not content.
Her lily arms mid part and more above the elbow bare,
Her hands, her fingers and her wrists him thought of beauty rare.
And sure he thought such other parts as garments then did hide
Excellèd greatly all the rest the which he had espied.
But swifter than the whirling wind she flees and will not stay
To give the hearing to these words the which he had to say:
      'I pray thee, nymph Peneis, stay! I chase not as a foe.
      Stay, nymph! The lambs so flee the wolves, the stags the lions

610   so;
With flittering feathers silly doves so from the goshawk fly,
And every creature from his foe. Love is the cause that I
Do follow thee; alas, alas, how would it grieve my heart
To see thee fall among the briars, and that the blood should start
Out of thy tender legs, I – wretch – the causer of thy smart.

The place is rough to which thou run'st; take leisure, I thee pray;
Abate thy flight and I myself my running pace will stay.
Yet would I wish thee take advice and wisely for to view
What one he is that for thy grace in humble wise doth sue.                    620
I am not one that dwells among the hills and stony rocks;
I am no shepherd with a cur attending on the flocks;
I am no carl nor country clown, nor neatherd taking charge
Of cattle grazing here and there within this forest large.
Thou dost not know, poor simple soul, God wot thou dost not
          know
From whom thou flee'st. For if thou knew, thou would'st not flee
          me so.
In Delphos is my chief abode; my temples also stand
At Claros and at Patara within the Lycian land,
And in the Isle of Tenedos the people honour me.
The king of gods himself is known my father for to be.                        630
By me is known that was, that is and that that shall ensue.
By me men learn to sundry tunes to frame sweet ditties true.
In shooting have I steadfast hand; but surer hand had he
That made this wound within my heart that heretofore was free.
Of physic and of surgery I found the arts for need;
The power of every herb and plant doth of my gift proceed.
Now woe is me that ne'er an herb can heal the hurt of love
And that the arts that others help their lord doth helpless prove!'
     As Phoebus would have spoken more, away Peneis stale
     With fearful steps and left him in the midst of all his tale.            640
And as she ran, the meeting winds her garments backward blew
So that her naked skin appeared behind her as she flew;
Her goodly yellow golden hair that hangèd loose and slack
With every puff of air did wave and toss behind her back.
Her running made her seem more fair. The youthful god
          therefore
Could not abide to waste his words in dalliance anymore
But, as his love advisèd him, he gan to mend his pace
And with the better foot before the fleeing nymph to chase.
And even as, when the greedy grew'nd doth course the silly hare
Amidst the plain and champaign field without all covert bare,                 650

Both twain of them do strain themselves and lay on footmanship
Who may best run with all his force the t'other to outstrip,
The t'one for safety of his life, the t'other for his prey
(The grew'nd, aye pressed with open mouth to bear the hare
    away,
Thrusts forth his snout and girdeth out and at her loins doth
    snatch
As though he would at every stride between his teeth her latch;
Again, in doubt of being caught, the hare aye shrinking slips
Upon the sudden from his jaws and from between his lips);
So fared Apollo and the maid. Hope made Apollo swift,
660   And fear did make the maiden fleet, devising how to shift.
Howbeit, he that did pursue of both the swifter went,
As furthered by the feathered wings that Cupid had him lent;
So that he would not let her rest, but pressèd at her heel
So near that through her scattered hair she might his breathing
    feel.
But when she saw her breath was gone and strength began to fail,
The colour faded in her cheeks and, ginning for to quail,
She lookèd to Peneus' stream and said, 'Now, father dear,
And if you streams have power of gods, then help your daughter
    here.
O let the earth devour me quick on which I seem too fair,
670   Or else this shape which is my harm by changing straight appair.'
This piteous prayer scarce said, her sinews waxèd stark,
And therewithal about her breast did grow a tender bark.
Her hair was turnèd into leaves, her arms in boughs did grow;
Her feet that were erewhile so swift now rooted were as slow.
Her crown became the top; and thus of that she erst had been
Remainèd nothing in the world but beauty fresh and green.
Which when that Phoebus did behold, affection did so move,
The tree to which his love was turned he could no less but love.
And as he softly laid his hand upon the tender plant,
680   Within the bark new overgrown he felt her heart yet pant.
And, in his arms embracing fast her boughs and branches lithe,
He proffered kisses to the tree; the tree did from him writhe.
'Well,' quoth Apollo, 'though my fere and spouse thou cannot be,
Assurèdly from this time forth yet shalt thou be my tree.

Thou shalt adorn my golden locks and eke my pleasant harp;
Thou shalt adorn my quiver full of shafts and arrows sharp.
Thou shalt adorn the valiant knights and royal emperors
When for their noble feats of arms like mighty conquerors
Triumphantly with stately pomp up to the Capitol
They shall ascend with solemn train that do their deeds extol.          690
Before Augustus' palace door full duly shalt thou ward,
The oak amid the palace yard aye faithfully to guard.
And as my head is never pulled nor never more without
A seemly bush of youthful hair that spreadeth round about,
Even so this honour give I thee: continually to have
Thy branches clad from time to time with leaves both fresh and
          brave.'
Now when that Paean of this talk had fully made an end,
The laurel to his just request did seem to condescend
By bowing of her new-made boughs and tender branches down
And wagging of her seemly top as if it were her crown.                  700

                                                               *The
                                                          transformation
                                                                of Io*

    There is a land in Thessaly, enclosed on every side
    With woody hills, that Tempe hight, through mid whereof
       doth glide
Peneus gushing full of froth from foot of Pindus high;
Which with his headlong falling down doth cast up violently
A misty stream like flakes of smoke, besprinkling all about
The tops of trees on either side, and makes a roaring-out
That may be heard a great way off. This is the fixèd seat,
This is the house and dwelling-place and chamber of the great
And mighty river. Here he sits in court of pebble stone
And ministers justice to the waves and to the nymphs each one          710
That in the brooks and waters dwell. Now hither did resort
(Not knowing if they might rejoice and unto mirth exhort
Or comfort him) his country brooks: Spercheus, well-beseen
With sedgy head and shady banks of poplars fresh and green;
Enipeus, restless, swift and quick; old father Apidane;
Amphrysus with his gentle stream; and Aeas clad with cane;
With divers other rivers mo which, having run their race,
Into the sea their weary waves do lead with restless pace.
From hence the careful Inachus absents himself alone,
Who in a corner of his cave with doleful tears and moan                 720

Augments the waters of his stream, bewailing piteously
His daughter Io, lately lost. He knew not certainly
And if she were alive or dead. But for he had her sought
And could not find her anywhere, assuredly he thought
She did not live above the mould ne drew the vital breath,
Misgiving worser in his mind, if aught be worse than death.
  It fortuned on a certain day that Jove espied this maid
  Come running from her father's stream alone; to whom he said,
'O damsel worthy Jove himself, like one day for to make
730  Some happy person whom thou list unto thy bed to take,
I pray thee, let us shroud ourselves in shadow here together –
Of this or that' (he pointed both) 'it makes no matter whether –
Until the hottest of the day and noon be overpast.
And if for fear of savage beasts perchance thou be aghast
To wander in the woods alone, thou shalt not need to fear;
A god shall be thy guide to save thee harmless everywhere,
And not a god of meaner sort, but even the same that hath
The heavenly sceptre in his hand, who in my dreadful wrath
Do dart down thunder wanderingly. And therefore make no haste
740  To run away.' She ran apace and had already passed
The fen of Lerna and the field of Lyrcey set with trees
When Jove, intending now in vain no lenger time to leese,
Upon the country all about did bring a foggy mist
And caught the maiden whom, poor fool, he usèd as he list.
  Queen Juno, looking down that while upon the open field,
  When in so fair a day such mists and darkness she beheld,
Did marvel much, for well she knew those mists ascended not
From any river, moorish ground or other dankish plot.
She looked about her for her Jove, as one that was acquainted
750  With such escapes and with the deed had often him attainted.
Whom when she found not in the heaven, 'Unless I guess amiss,
Some wrong against me', quoth she, 'now my husband working
      is.'
And with that word she left the heaven and down to earth she
      came,
Commanding all the mists away. But Jove foresees the same,
And to a cow as white as milk his leman he conveys.
She was a goodly heifer, sure; and Juno did her praise

Although, God wot, she thought it not, and curiously she sought
Where she was bred, whose cow she was, who had her thither
      brought –
As though she had not known the truth. Her husband by and by,
Because she should not search too near, devised a cleanly lie     760
And told her that the cow was bred even now out of the ground.
Then Juno, who her husband's shift at fingers' ends had found,
Desired to have the cow of gift. What should he do as tho?
Great cruelness it were to yield his lover to her foe;
And not to give would breed mistrust. As fast as shame provoked,
So fast again at other side his love his mind revoked,
So much that love was at the point to put all shame to flight,
But that he fearèd if he should deny a gift so light
As was a cow to her that was his sister and his wife
Might make her think it was no cow and breed perchance some
      strife.     770

   Now when that Juno had by gift her husband's leman got,
    Yet altogether out of fear and careless was she not.
She had him in a jealousy and thoughtful was she still
For doubt he should invent some means to steal her from her, till
To Argus, old Arestor's son, she put her for to keep.
This Argus had an hundred eyes, of which by turn did sleep
Always a couple, and the rest did duly watch and ward
And of the charge they took in hand had ever good regard.
What way so ever Argus stood, with face, with back or side
To Io ward, before his eyes did Io still abide.     780
All day he let her graze abroad; the sun once underground,
He shut her up and by the neck with writhen withe her bound.
With crops of trees and bitter weeds now was she daily fed;
And in the stead of costly couch and good soft featherbed
She sat a-nights upon the ground, and on such ground whereas
Was not sometime so much as grass; and oftentimes she was
Compelled to drink of muddy pits. And when she did devise
To Argus for to lift her hands in meek and humble wise,
She saw she had no hands at all; and when she did assay
To make complaint, she lowèd out, which did her so affray     790
That oft she started at the noise and would have run away.

54    METAMORPHOSES

Unto her father Inach's banks she also did resort,
Where many a time and oft before she had been wont to sport.
Now, when she lookèd in the stream and saw her hornèd head,
She was aghast and from herself would all in haste have fled.
The nymphs her sisters knew her not, nor yet her own dear father;
Yet followed she both him and them and suffered them the rather
To touch and stroke her where they list, as one that pressèd still
To set herself to wonder at and gaze upon their fill.

800    The good old Inach pulls up grass and to her straight it bears;
She, as she kissed and licked his hands, did shed forth dreary tears.
And, had she had her speech at will to utter forth her thought,
She would have told her name and chance and him of help
        besought.
But for because she could not speak, she printed in the sand
Two letters with her foot whereby was given to understand
The sorrowful changing of her shape. Which seen, straight crièd
        out
Her father Inach, 'Woe is me!' And clasping her about
Her white and seemly heifer's neck and crystal horns both twain,
He shriekèd out full piteously, 'Now woe is me!' again.
'Alas, art thou my daughter dear, whom through the world I
810        sought
And could not find? And now by chance art to my presence
        brought?
My sorrow, certes, lesser far a thousand fold had been
If never had I seen thee more than thus to have thee seen.
Thou stand'st as dumb and to my words no answer can thou give,
But from the bottom of thy heart full sorry sighs dost drive
As tokens of thine inward grief and dolefully dost moo
Unto my talk – the only thing left in thy power to do.
But I, mistrusting nothing less than this so great mischance,
By some great marriage earnestly did seek thee to advance
820    In hope some issue to have seen between my son and thee.
But now thou must a husband have among the herds, I see,
And eke thine issue must be such as other cattles be.
O that I were a mortal wight, as other creatures are,
For then might death in length of time quite rid me of this care!

But now, because I am a god and fate doth death deny,
There is no help but that my grief must last eternally.'
     As Inach made this piteous moan, quick-sighted Argus drave
     His daughter into further fields to which he could not have
Access, and he himself aloof did get him to a hill
From whence he, sitting at his ease, viewed every way at will.          830
Now could no lenger Jove abide his lover so forlorn,
And thereupon he called his son that Maia had him borne,
Commanding Argus should be killed. He made no long abode,
But tied his feathers to his feet and took his charmèd rod,
With which he bringeth things asleep and fetcheth souls from hell,
And put his hat upon his head. And when that all was well,
He leapèd from his father's towers and down to earth he flew,
And there both hat and wings also he lightly from him threw,
Retaining nothing but his staff, the which he closely held
Between his elbow and his side, and through the common field          840
Went plodding like some good plain soul that had some flock to
          feed;
And as he went, he pipèd still upon an oaten reed.
Queen Juno's herdman, far in love with this strange melody,
Bespake him thus: 'Good fellow mine, I pray thee heartily,
Come sit down by me on this hill, for better feed I know
Thou shalt not find in all these fields, and (as the thing doth show)
It is a cool and shadowy plot, for shepherds very fit.'
Down by his elbow by and by did Atlas' nephew sit.
And, for to pass the time withal for seeming overlong,
He held him talk of this and that; and now and then among          850
He played upon his merry pipe to cause his watching eyes
To fall asleep. Poor Argus did the best he could devise
To overcome the pleasant naps; and though that some did sleep,
Yet of his eyes the greater part he made their watch to keep.
And after other talk, he asked (for lately was it found)
Who was the founder of that pipe that did so sweetly sound.
     Then said the god, 'There dwelt sometime a nymph of noble          *Pan and*
          fame          *Syrinx*
     Among the hills of Arcady, that Syrinx had to name.
Of all the nymphs of Nonacris and fairy far and near
In beauty and in personage this lady had no peer.          860

Full often had she given the slip both to the satyrs quick
And other gods that dwell in woods and in the forests thick
Or in the fruitful fields abroad. It was her whole desire
To follow chaste Diana's guise in maidenhead and attire.
Whom she did counterfeit so nigh that such as did her see
Might at a blush have taken her Diana for to be,
But that the nymph did in her hand a bow of cornel hold,
Whereas Diana evermore did bear a bow of gold;
And yet she did deceive folk so. Upon a certain day
870  God Pan, with garland on his head of pine-tree, saw her stray
From Mount Lycaeus all alone and thus to her did say:
"Unto a god's request, O nymph, vouchsafe thou to agree,
That doth desire thy wedded spouse and husband for to be." '
    There was yet more behind to tell: as how that Syrinx fled
    Through wayless woods and gave no ear to that that Pan had
        said,
Until she to the gentle stream of sandy Ladon came
Where, for because it was so deep she could not pass the same,
She piteously to change her shape the waternymphs besought;
And how, when Pan between his arms to catch the nymph had
        thought,
880  Instead of her he caught the reeds new grown upon the brook,
And as he sighèd with his breath the reeds he softly shook
Which made a still and mourning noise, with strangeness of the
        which
And sweetness of the feeble sound the god, delighted much,
Said, 'Certes, Syrinx, for thy sake it is my full intent
To make my comfort of these reeds wherein thou dost lament;'
And how that there of sundry reeds with wax together knit
He made the pipe which of her name the Greeks call Syrinx yet.
    But as Cyllenius would have told this tale, he cast his sight
    On Argus. And behold, his eyes had bid him all good-night.
There was not one that did not sleep, and fast he gan to nod.
Immediately he ceased his talk and with his charmèd rod
So strokèd all his heavy eyes that earnestly they slept.
Then with his woodknife by and by he lightly to him stepped
And lent him such a perilous blow whereas the shoulders grew
Unto the neck that straight his head quite from the body flew.

*The death of*
*Argus and the*
*story of Io*
*concluded*

Then tumbling down the headlong hill his bloody corse he sent,
That all the way by which he rolled was stainèd and besprent.
There li'st thou, Argus, underfoot with all thy hundred lights,
And all the light is clean extinct that was within those sights;
One endless night thy hundred èyes hath now bereft for aye.                    900
Yet would not Juno suffer so her herdsman's eyes decay,
But in her painted peacock's tail and feathers did them set,
Where they remain like precious stones and glaring eyes as yet.
    She took his death in great despite and, as her rage did move,
    Determined for to wreak her wrath upon her husband's love.
Forthwith she cast before her eyes right strange and ugly sights,
Compelling her to think she saw some fiends or wicked sprites.
And in her heart such secret pricks and piercing stings she gave her
As though the world from place to place with restless sorrow
        drave her.
Thou, Nilus, wert assigned to stay her pains and travels past;           910
To which as soon as Io came with much ado at last,
With weary knuckles on thy brim she kneelèd sadly down
And, stretching forth her fair long neck and crystal hornèd crown,
Such kind of count'nance as she had she lifted to the sky
And there with sighing sobs and tears and lowing dolefully
Did seem to make her moan to Jove, desiring him to make
Some end of those her troublous storms endurèd for his sake.
He took his wife about the neck and, sweetly kissing, prayed
That Io's penance yet at length might by her grant be stayed.
'Thou shalt not need to fear', quoth he, 'that ever she shall grieve
        thee                                                              920
From this day forth. And in this case the better to believe me,
The Stygian waters of my words unpartial witness been.'
    As soon as Juno was appeased, immediately was seen
    That Io took her native shape in which she first was born
    And eke became the selfsame thing the which she was beforn.
For by and by she cast away her rough and hairy hide,
Instead whereof a soft smooth skin with tender flesh did bide.
Her horns sank down; her eyes and mouth were brought in lesser
        room;
Her hands, her shoulders and her arms in place again did come.

930 Her cloven clees to fingers five again reducèd were,
On which the nails like polished gems did shine full bright and
        clear.
In fine, no likeness of a cow save whiteness did remain,
So pure and perfect as no snow was able it to stain.
She vaunced herself upon her feet, which then was brought to
        two;
And though she gladly would have spoke, yet durst she not so do
Without good heed, for fear she should have lowèd like a cow.
And therefore softly with herself she gan to practise how
Distinctly to pronounce her words that intermitted were.
Now as a goddess is she had in honour everywhere
940 Among the folk that dwell by Nile yclad in linen weed.
Of her in time came Epaphus, begotten of the seed
Of mighty Jove. This noble imp now jointly with his mother
Through all the cities of that land have temples, t'one with
        t'other.

*Epaphus and*
*Phaëton*
                There was his match in heart and years, the lusty Phaëton,
        A stalworth stripling strong and stout, the golden Phoebus' son.
Whom, making proud and stately vaunts of his so noble race
And unto him in that respect in nothing giving place,
The son of Io could not bear, but said unto him thus:
'No marvel though thou be so proud and full of words, iwis;
950 For every fond and trifling tale the which thy mother makes
Thy giddy wit and hare-brained head forthwith for gospel takes.
Well, vaunt thyself of Phoebus still; for when the truth is seen,
Thou shalt perceive that father's name a forgèd thing to been.'
At this reproach did Phaeton wax as red as any fire;
Howbeit for the present time did shame repress his ire.
Unto his mother Clymen straight he goeth to detect
The spiteful words that Epaphus against him did object.
'Yea, mother,' quoth he, 'and which ought your greater grief to
        be,
I, who at other times of talk was wont to be so free
960 And stout, had ne'er a word to say; I was ashamed to take
So foul a foil – the more because I could none answer make.
But if I be of heavenly race exacted, as ye say,
Then show some token of that high and noble birth, I pray,

And vouch me for to be of heaven.' With that he gently cast
His arms about his mother's neck and, clasping her full fast,
Besought her, as she loved his life and as she loved the life
Of Merops and had kept herself as undefilèd wife
And as she wishèd wealthily his sisters to bestow,
She would some token give whereby his rightful sire to know.
It is a doubtful matter whether Clymen, movèd more                970
With this her Phaeton's earnest suit exacting it so sore
Or with the slander of the bruit laid to her charge before,
Did hold up both her hands to heaven and, looking on the sun,
'My right dear child, I safely swear', quoth she to Phaëton,
'That of this star, the which so bright doth glister in thine eye,
Of this same sun that cheers the world with light indifferently
Wert thou begot. And if I feign, then with my heart I pray
That never may I see him more unto my dying day.
But if thou have so great desire thy father for to know,
Thou shalt not need in that behalf much labour to bestow.            980
The place from whence he doth arise adjoineth to our land;
And if thou think thy heart will serve, then go and understand
The truth of him.' When Phaeton heard his mother saying so,
He gan to leap and skip for joy. He fed his fancy tho
Upon the heaven and heavenly things; and so with willing mind
From Ethiope first, his native home, and afterward through Inde,
Set underneath the morning star, he went so long till as
He found me where his father's house and daily rising was.

FINIS PRIMI LIBRI.

# The Second Book of Ovid's
# Metamorphoses

The princely palace of the sun stood gorgeous to behold
On stately pillars builded high of yellow burnished gold
Beset with sparkling carbuncles that like to fire did shine.
The roof was framèd curiously of ivory pure and fine;
The two door-leaves of silver clear a radiant light did cast.
But yet the cunning workmanship of things therein far passed
The stuff whereof the doors were made. For there a perfect plat
Had Vulcan drawn of all the world: both of the surges that
Embrace the earth with winding waves, and of the steadfast
      ground,
And of the heaven itself also that both encloseth round.          10
And first and foremost in the sea the gods thereof did stand:
Loud sounding Triton with his shirl and writhen trump in hand;
Unstable Proteu, changing aye his figure and his hue
From shape to shape a thousand sithes, as list him to renew;
Aegaeon, leaning boistrously on backs of mighty whales;
And Doris with her daughters all, of which some cut the wales
With splayèd arms, some sat on rocks and dried their goodly hair,
And some did ride upon the backs of fishes here and there.
Not one in all points fully like another could ye see,
Nor very far unlike, but such as sisters ought to be.            20
The earth had towns, men, beasts and woods with sundry trees
      and rods,
And running rivers with their nymphs and other country gods.
Directly over all these same the plat of heaven was pight
Upon the two door-leaves: the signs of all the zodiac bright,
Indifferently six on the left and six upon the right.
When Clymen's son had climbèd up at length with weary pace
And set his foot within his doubted father's dwelling place,

Immediately he pressèd forth to put himself in sight
And stood aloof; for near at hand he could not bide the light.
30    In purple robe and royal throne of emeralds fresh and green
Did Phoebus sit, and on each hand stood waiting well beseen
Days, months, years, ages, seasons, times and eke the equal hours.
There stood the Springtime with a crown of fresh and fragrant
            flowers;
There waited Summer, naked stark all save a wheaten hat;
And Autumn smeared with treading grapes late at the pressing fat;
And lastly, quaking for the cold, stood Winter all forlorn
With rugged head as white as dove and garments all to torn,
Forladen with the icicles that dangled up and down
Upon his grey and hoary beard and snowy frozen crown.
40    The sun, thus sitting in the midst, did cast his piercing eye
(With which full lightly when he list he all things doth espy)
Upon his child that stood aloof, aghast and trembling sore
At sight of such unwonted things, and thus bespake him there:
'O noble imp, O Phaëton, which art not such, I see,
Of whom thy father should have cause ashamèd for to be,
Why hast thou travellèd to my court? What is thy will with me?'
Then answered he, 'Of all the world O only perfect light,
O father Phoebus – if I may usurp that name of right
And that my mother for to save herself from worldly shame
50    Hide not her fault with false pretence and colour of thy name –
Some sign apparent grant whereby I may be known thy son
And let me hang no more in doubt.' He had no sooner done
But that his father, putting off the bright and fiery beams
That glistered round about his head like clear and golden streams,
Commanded him to draw him near and, him embracing, said,
'To take me for thy rightful sire thou need not be afraid;
Thy mother Clymen of a truth from falsehood standeth free.
And for to put thee out of doubt, ask what thou wilt of me
And I will give thee thy desire. The lake whereby of old
60    We gods do swear (the which mine eyes did never yet behold)
*Phaëton*    Bear witness with thee of my grant.' He scarce this tale had told
*begs Apollo's*    But that the foolish Phaëton straight for a day did crave
*chariot*    The guiding of his wingèd steeds and chariot for to have.

Then did his father by and by forthink him of his oath
And, shaking twenty times his head as one that was full wroth,
Bespake him thus: 'Thy words have made me rashly to consent
To that which shortly both of us, I fear me, shall repent.
O, that I might retract my grant! My son, I do protest
I would deny thee nothing else save this thy fond request.
I may dissuade. There lies herein more peril than thou ween;     70
The things the which thou dost desire of great importance been,
More than thy weakness well can wield, a charge (as well appears)
Of greater weight than may agree with these thy tender years.
Thy state is mortal, weak and frail; the thing thou dost desire
Is such whereto no mortal man is able to aspire.
Yea, foolish boy, thou dost desire – and all for want of wit –
A greater charge than any god could ever have as yet.
For were there any of them all so overseen and blind
To take upon him this my charge, full quickly should he find
That none but I could sit upon the fiery axle-tree.             80
No, not even he that rules this waste and endless space we see,
Not he that darts with dreadful hand the thunder from the sky
Shall drive this chair. And yet what thing in all the world, perdie,
Is able to compare with Jove? Now first the morning way
Lies steep upright, so that the steeds in coolest of the day
And being fresh have much ado to climb against the hill.
Amidst the heaven the ghastly height augmenteth terror still;
My heart doth wax as cold as ice full many a time and oft
For fear to see the sea and land from that same place aloft.
The evening way doth fall plump down, requiring strength to
          guide,                                               90
That Tethys, who doth harbour me within her surges wide,
Doth stand in fear lest from the heaven I headlong down should
          slide.
Besides all this, the heaven aye swims and wheels about full swift
And with his rolling drives the stars their proper course to shift.
Yet do I keep my native course against this brunt so stout,
Not giving place as others do, but boldly bearing out
The force and swiftness of that heaven that whirleth so about.
Admit thou had my wingèd steeds and chariot in thine hand;
What could'st thou do? Dost think thyself well able to withstand

100   The swiftness of the whirlèd pools, but that their brunt and sway
     (Yea, do the best and worst thou can) shall bear thee quite away?
     Perchance thou dost imagine there some towns of gods to find
     With groves and temples riched with gifts, as is among mankind.
     Thou art deceivèd utterly; thou shalt not find it so.
     By blind by-ways and ugly shapes of monsters must thou go.
     And though thou knew the way so well as that thou could not
          stray,
     Between the dreadful Bull's sharp horns yet must thou make thy
          way;
     Against the cruel bow the which th'Aemonian Archer draws;
     Against the ramping Lion armed with greedy teeth and paws;
110   Against the Scorpion stretching far his fell and venomed claws;
     And eke the Crab that casteth forth his crooked clees awry,
     Not in such sort as th'other doth, and yet as dreadfully.
     Again, thou neither hast the power nor yet the skill, I know,
     My lusty coursers for to guide, that from their nostrils throw
     And from their mouths the fiery breath that breedeth in their
          breast.
     For scarcely will they suffer me, who knows their nature best,
     When that their cruel courages begin to catch a heat;
     That hardly should I deal with them, but that I know the feat.
     But lest my gift should to thy grief and utter peril tend,
120   My son, beware and (while thou may'st) thy fond request amend.
     Because thou would be known to be my child, thou seem'st to
          crave
     A certain sign. What surer sign, I pray thee, canst thou have
     Than this my fear so fatherly the which I have of thee,
     Which proveth me most certainly thy father for to be?
     Behold and mark my countenance. O, would to God thy sight
     Could pierce within my woeful breast, to see the heavy plight
     And heaps of cares within my heart. Look through the world so
          round;
     Of all the wealth and goods therein, if aught there may be found
     In heaven or earth or in the sea, ask what thou likest best
130   And sure it shall not be denied. This only one request
     That thou hast made I heartily beseech thee to relent,
     Which, for to term the thing aright, is even a punishment

And not an honour as thou think'st. My Phaeton, thou dost crave
Instead of honour even a scourge and punishment for to have.
Thou fondling, thou, what dost thou mean with fawning arms
        about
My neck thus flatteringly to hang? Thou needest not to doubt.
I have already sworn by Styx: ask what thou wilt of me
And thou shalt have. Yet let thy next wish somewhat wiser be.'
    Thus ended his advertisement. And yet the wilful lad
        Withstood his counsel, urging still the promise that he had,         140
        Desiring for to have the chair as if he had been mad.
His father, having made delay as long as he could shift,
Did lead him where his chariot stood which was of Vulcan's gift.
The axle-tree was massy gold; the buck was massy gold;
The utmost fellies of the wheels, and where the tree was rolled.
The spokes were all of silver bright. The chrysolites and gems
That stood upon the collars, trace and hounces in their hems
Did cast a sheer and glimmering light as Phoebus shone thereon.
Now while the lusty Phaëton stood gazing hereupon
And wondered at the workmanship of everything, behold,         150
The early Morning in the east began me to unfold
Her purple gates and showed her house bedecked with roses red.
The twinkling stars withdrew which by the morning star are led,
Who, as the captain of that host that hath no peer or match,
Doth leave his standing last of all within that heavenly watch.
Now when his father saw the world thus glister red and trim
And that his waning sister's horns began to waxen dim,
He bade the feather-footed hours go harness in his horse.
The goddesses with might and main themselves thereto enforce.
His fiery-foaming steeds full fed with juice of ambrosy         160
They take from manger trimly dight and to their heads do tie
Strong reinèd bits and to the chariot do them well appoint.
Then Phoebus did with heavenly salve his Phaeton's head anoint,
That scorching fire could nothing hurt; which done, upon his hair
He put the fresh and golden rays himself was wont to wear.
And then, as one whose heart misgave the sorrows drawing fast,
With sorry sighs he thus bespake his reckless son at last:
    'And if thou canst, at least yet this thy father's lore obey:
        Son, spare the whip and rein them hard; they run so swift away

170    As that thou shalt have much ado their fleeing course to stay.
Directly through the zones all five beware thou do not ride.
A broad by-way cut out askew that bendeth on the side
Contained within the bonds of three the midmost zones doth lie,
Which from the grisly northern Bear and southern pole doth fly;
Keep on this way. My chariot rakes thou plainly shalt espy.
And to th'intent that heaven and earth may well the heat endure,
Drive neither overhigh nor yet too low. For be thou sure,
And if thou mount above thy bounds, the stars thou burnest clean.
Again, beneath, thou burn'st the earth. Most safety is the mean.
And lest perchance thou overmuch the right hand way should
180        take
And so misfortune should thee drive upon the writhen Snake,
Or else by taking overmuch upon the lefter hand
Unto the Altar thou be driven that doth against it stand,
Indifferently between them both I wish thee for to ride.
The rest I put to Fortune's will, who be thy friendly guide
And better for thee than thyself as in this case provide!
Whiles that I prattle here with thee, behold, the dankish night
Beyond all Spain, her utmost bound, is passèd out of sight.
We may no lenger tarriance make; my wonted light is called;
The morning with her count'nance clear the darkness hath
190        appalled.
Take rein in hand – or if thy mind by counsel altered be,
Refuse to meddle with my wain and, while thou yet art free
And dost at ease within my house in safeguard well remain,
Of this thine unadvisèd wish not feeling yet the pain,
Let me alone with giving still the world his wonted light
And thou thereof as heretofore enjoy the harmless sight.'

*Phaëton*
*drives*
*Apollo's*
*chariot*

         Thus much in vain. For Phaëton, both young in years and wit,
      Into the chariot lightly leapt and, vauncing him in it,
Was not a little proud that he the bridle gotten had.
200    He thanked his father, whom it grieved to see his child so mad.
While Phoebus and his reckless son were intertalking this,
Eoüs, Aethon, Phlegon and the fiery Pyrois,
The restless horses of the sun, began to neigh so high
With flaming breath that all the heaven might hear them perfectly.

And with their hoofs they mainly beat upon the latticed grate,
The which when Tethys (knowing nought of this her cousin's
    fate)
Had put aside and given the steeds the free and open scope
Of all the compass of the sky within the heavenly cope,
They girded forth and, cutting through the clouds that let their
    race,
With splayèd wings they overflew the eastern wind apace.    210
The burden was so light as that the jennets felt it not;
The wonted weight was from the wain, the which they well did
    wot.
For like as ships amidst the seas that scant of ballast have
Do reel and totter with the wind and yield to every wave,
Even so the wain for want of weight it erst was wont to bear
Did hoise aloft and scale and reel, as though it empty were.
Which when the cartware did perceive, they left the beaten way
And, taking bridle in the teeth, began to run astray.
The rider was so sore aghast he knew no use of rein
Nor yet his way; and though he had, yet had it been in vain    220
Because he wanted power to rule the horses and the wain.
   Then first did sweat cold Charles his wain through force of
      Phoebus' rays
   And in the sea forbidden him to dive in vain assays.
The Serpent at the frozen pole, both cold and slow by kind,
Through heat waxed wroth and stirred about a cooler place to
    find.
And thou, Boötes, though thou be but slow of footmanship,
Yet wert thou fain (as fame reports) about thy wain to skip.
Now when unhappy Phaëton from top of all the sky
Beheld the earth that underneath a great way off did lie,
He waxèd pale for sudden fear; his joints and sinews quook;    230
The greatness of the glistering light his eyesight from him took.
Now wished he that he never had his father's horses see;
It irked him that he thus had sought to learn his pedigree.
It grieved him that he had prevailed in gaining his request;
To have been counted Merops' son he thought it now the best.
Thus thinking was he headlong driven, as when a ship is borne
By blustering winds, her sailcloths rent, her stern in pieces torn

And tackling brust, the which the pilot, trusting all to prayer,
Abandons wholly to the sea and fortune of the air.

240 What should he do? Much of the heaven he passèd had behind
And more he saw before; both which he measured in his mind,
Eft looking forward to the west, which to approach as then
Might not betide, and to the east eft looking back again.
He wist not what was best to do, his wits were ravished so.
For neither could he hold the reins, nor yet durst let them go;
And of his horses' names was none that he remembered tho.
Strange, uncouth monsters did he see dispersèd here and there
And dreadful shapes of ugly beasts that in the welkin were.
There is a certain place in which the hideous Scorpion throws

250 His arms in compass far abroad, much like a couple of bows,
With writhen tail and clasping clees, whose poison limbs do
    stretch
On every side, that of two signs they full the room do reach.
Whom when the lad beheld all moist with black and loathly
    sweat,
With sharp and needle-pointed sting as though he seemed to
    threat,
He was so sore astraught for fear, he let the bridles slack.
Which when the horses felt lie loose upon their sweating back,
At rovers straight throughout the air by ways unknown they ran
Whereas they never came before since that the world began.
For look what way their lawless rage by chance and fortune drew,

260 Without controlment or restraint that way they freely flew.
Among the stars that fixèd are within the firmament
They snatched the chariot here and there. One while they
    coursing went
Upon the top of all the sky; anon again full round
They troll me down to lower ways and nearer to the ground
So that the moon was in a maze to see her brother's wain
Run under hers. The singèd clouds began to smoke amain.
Each ground, the higher that it was and nearer to the sky,
The sooner was it set on fire and made therewith so dry
That everywhere it gan to chink. The meads and pastures green

270 Did sear away, and with the leaves the trees were burnèd clean;

The parchèd corn did yield wherewith to work his own decay.

Tush, these are trifles! Mighty towns did perish that same day

Whose countries with their folk were burnt; and forests full of wood

Were turned to ashes with the rocks and mountains where they stood.

*The burning of the world*

Then Athe, Cilician Taure and Tmole and Oeta flamèd high;

And Ide, erst full of flowing springs, was then made utter dry.

The learnèd virgins' daily haunt, the sacred Helicon,

And Thracian Haemus (not as yet surnamed Oeagrion)

Did smoke both twain. And Etna, hot of nature aye before,

Increased by force of Phoebus' flame, now ragèd ten times more.    280

The forked Parnassus, Eryx, Cynth and Othrys then did swelt,

And all the snow of Rhodope did at that present melt.

The like outrage Mount Dindymus and Mime and Mycale felt.

Cithaeron, born to sacred use, with Oss and Pindus high

And Olymp, greater than them both, did burn excessively.

The passing cold that Scythy had defended not the same,

But that the barren Caucasus was partner of this flame.

And so were eke the airy Alps and Appenine beside,

For all the clouds continually their snowy tops do hide.

Then wheresoever Phaëton did chance to cast his view,    290

The world was all on flaming fire. The breath the which he drew

Came smoking from his scalding mouth as from a seething pot;

His chariot also under him began to wax red-hot.

He could no lenger dure the sparks and cinder flying out.

Again, the culm and smouldering smoke did wrap him round about,

The pitchy darkness of the which so wholly had him hent

As that he wist not where he was nor yet which way he went.

The wingèd horses forcibly did draw him where they would.

The Ethiopians at that time (as men for truth uphold),

The blood by force of that same heat drawn to the outer part    300

And there adust from that time forth, became so black and swart.

The moisture was so drièd up in Liby land that time

That altogether dry and scorched continueth yet that clime.

The nymphs with hair about their ears bewailed their springs and
    lakes.
Boeotia for her Dirce's loss great lamentation makes;
For Amymone Argos wept; and Corinth for the spring
Pyrene, at whose sacred stream the Muses used to sing.
The rivers further from the place were not in better case.
For Tanais in his deepest stream did boil and steam apace;
Old Peneu and Caïcus, of the country Teuthrany,
And swift Ismenus in their banks by like misfortune fry.
Then burned the Psophian Erymanth and (which should burn
    again)
The Trojan Xanthus and Lycormas with his yellow vein.
Maeander, playing in his banks aye winding to and fro,
Migdonian Melas, with his waves as black as any sloe,
Eurotas, running by the foot of Tenare, boilèd tho.
Then sod Euphrates, cutting through the midst of Babylon;
Then sod Orontes and the Scythian swift Thermodoön.
Then Ganges, Colchian Phasis and the noble Ister,
Alpheus' and Sperchin's banks with flaming fire did glister.
The gold that Tagus' stream did bear did in the channel melt;
Amid Caïster of this fire the raging heat was felt
Among the choirs of singing swans that with their pleasant lay
Along the banks of Lydian brakes from place to place did stray.
And Nile for fear did run away into the furthest clime
Of all the world and hid his head, which to this present time
Is yet unfound; his mouths all seven clean void of water been
Like seven great valleys where, save dust, could nothing else be
    seen.
By like misfortune Hebrus dried and Strymon, both of Thrace;
The western rivers Rhine and Rhone and Po were in like case,
And Tiber, unto whom the gods a faithful promise gave
Of all the world the monarchy and sovereign state to have.
The ground did cranny everywhere, and light did pierce to hell
And made afraid the king and queen that in that realm do dwell.
The sea did shrink, and whereas waves did late before remain
Became a champaign field of dust and even a sandy plain.
The hills, erst hid far under waves, like islands did appear
So that the scattered Cyclads for the time augmented were.

310
320
330

The fishes drew them to the deeps; the dolphins durst not play
Above the water as before; the seals and porpoise lay                   340
With bellies upward on the waves stark dead; and fame doth go
That Nereus with his wife and daughters all were fain as tho
To dive within the scalding waves. Thrice Neptune did advance
His arms above the scalding sea with sturdy countenance
And thrice for hotness of the air was fain himself to hide.
But yet the earth, the nurse of things, enclosed on every side
Between the waters of the sea and springs that now had hidden
Themselves within their mother's womb, for all the pains abidden
Up to the neck put forth her head and, casting up her hand
Between her forehead and the sun as panting she did stand,             350
With dreadful quaking all that was she fearfully did shake
And, shrinking somewhat lower down, with sacred voice thus
     spake:
  'O king of gods, and if this be thy will and my desert,          *The earth's*
    Why dost thou stay with deadly dint thy thunder down to dart?   *plea*
And if that needs I perish must through force of fiery flame,
Let thy celestial fire, O God, I pray thee, do the same.
A comfort shall it be to have thee author of my death.
I scarce have power to speak these words' – the smoke had
    stopped her breath –
'Behold my singèd hair; behold my dim and bleared eye;
See how about my scorchèd face the scalding embers fly.                360
Is this the guerdon wherewithal ye quite my fruitfulness?
Is this the honour that ye gave me for my plenteousness
And duty done with true intent? For suffering of the plough
To draw deep wounds upon my back and rakes to rend me
    through?
For that I over all the year continually am wrought?
For giving fodder to the beasts and cattle, all for nought?
For yielding corn and other food wherewith to keep mankind?
And that to honour you withal sweet frankincense I find?
But put the case that my desert destruction duly crave;
What hath thy brother, what the seas deservèd for to have?            370
Why do the seas, his lotted part, thus ebb and fall so low,
Withdrawing from thy sky to which it ought most near to grow?

But if thou neither dost regard thy brother, neither me,
At least have mercy on thy heaven. Look round about and see
How both the poles begin to smoke; which if the fire appal,
To utter ruin (be thou sure) thy palace needs must fall.
Behold how Atlas gins to faint; his shoulders, though full strong,
Uneath are able to uphold the sparkling ax-tree long.
If sea and land do go to wreck and heaven itself do burn,
380   To old confusèd Chaos then of force we must return.
Put to thy helping hand therefore to save the little left,
If aught remain, before that all be quite and clean bereft.'

*The death of*   When ended was this piteous plaint, the earth did hold her
*Phaëton*            peace;
She could no lenger dure the heat, but was compelled to cease.
Into her bosom by and by she shrunk her singèd head
More nearer to the Stygian caves and ghosts of persons dead.
The sire of heaven, protesting all the gods – and him also
That lent the chariot to his child – that all of force must go
To havoc if he helpèd not, went to the highest part
390   And top of all the heaven from whence his custom was to dart
His thunder and his lightning down. But neither did remain
A cloud wherewith to shade the earth, nor yet a shower of rain.
Then with a dreadful thunderclap up to his ear he bent
His fist and at the waggoner a flash of lightning sent
Which strake his body from the life and threw it over wheel;
And so with fire he quenchèd fire. The steeds did also reel
Upon their knees and, starting up, sprang violently, one here
And there another, that they brast in pieces all their gear.
They threw the collars from their necks and, breaking quite
            asunder,
400   The trace and harness flang away. Here lay the bridles; yonder
The ax-tree pluckèd from the naves; and in another place
The shivered spokes of broken wheels. And so at every pace
The pieces of the chariot torn lay strewèd here and there.
But Phaëton, fire yet blasting still among his yellow hair,
Shot headlong down and glid along the region of the air
Like to a star in winter nights (the weather clear and fair)
Which, though it do not fall indeed, yet falleth to our sight;
Whom, almost in another world and from his country quite,

The river Padus did receive and quenched his burning head.
The waternymphs of Italy did take his carcass dead
And buried it, yet smoking still with Jove's three-forkèd flame,
And wrate this epitaph in the stone that lay upon the same:
*Here lies the lusty Phaëton, which took in hand to guide*
*His father's chariot; from the which although he chanced to slide,*
*Yet that he gave a proud attempt it cannot be denied.*

   With ruthful cheer and heavy heart his father made great moan
And would not show himself abroad, but mourned at home
   alone.
And if it be to be believed, as bruited is by fame,
A day did pass without the sun. The brightness of the flame
Gave light; and so unto some kind of use that mischief came.
But Clymen, having spoke as much as mothers usually
Are wonted in such wretched case discomfortably
And half beside herself for woe, with torn and scratchèd breast,
Searched through the universal world from east to furthest west,
First seeking for her son's dead corse and after for his bones.
She found them by a foreign stream, entumbled under stones.
There fell she grovelling on his grave and, reading there his name,
Shed tears thereon and laid her breast all bare upon the same.
The daughters also of the sun, no less than did their mother,
Bewailed in vain with floods of tears the fortune of their brother
And, beating piteously their breasts, incessantly did call
The buried Phaeton day and night, who heard them not at all,
About whose tomb they prostrate lay. Four times the moon had
   filled
The circle of her joinèd horns, and yet the sisters held
Their custom of lamenting still (for now continual use
Had made it custom). Of the which the eldest, Phaëtuse,
About to kneel upon the ground, complained her feet were
   numb;
To whom as faïr Lampety was rising for to come,
Her feet were held with sudden roots. The third, about to tear
Her ruffled locks, filled both her hands with leaves instead of hair.
One wept to see her legs made wood; another did repine
To see her arms become long boughs. And, shortly to define,

410

*The*
*transformation*
*of Phaëton's*
*sisters*

420

430

440

While thus they wondered at themselves, a tender bark began
To grow about their thighs and loins, which shortly overran
Their bellies, breasts and shoulders eke and hands successively,
That nothing save their mouths remained, aye calling piteously
Upon the woeful mother's help. What could the mother do
But run, now here, now there, as force of nature drew her to,
And deal her kisses while she might? She was not so content,
450 But tare their tender branches down; and from the slivers went
Red drops of blood, as from a wound. The daughter that was rent
Cried, 'Spare us, mother! Spare, I pray! For in the shape of tree
The bodies and the flesh of us, your daughters, wounded be.
And now farewell!' That word once said, the bark grew over all.
Now from these trees flow gummy tears that amber men do call,
Which, hardened with the heat of sun as from the boughs they
        fall,
The trickling river doth receive and sends as things of price
To deck the dainty dames of Rome and make them fine and nice.

*The*
*transformation*
*of Cygnus*

        Now present at this monstrous hap was Cygnus, Stenel's son,
        Who, being by the mother's side akin to Phaëton,
Was in condition more akin. He, leaving up his charge
(For in the land of Ligury his kingdom stretchèd large),
Went mourning all along the banks and pleasant stream of Po
Among the trees increasèd by the sisters late ago.
Anon his voice became more small and shrill than for a man;
Grey feathers muffled in his face; his neck in length began
Far from his shoulders for to stretch; and, furthermore, there goes
A fine red string across the joints in knitting of his toes.
With feathers closèd are his sides, and on his mouth there grew
470 A broad blunt bill; and, finally, was Cygnus made a new
And uncouth fowl that hight a swan, who neither to the wind,
The air, nor Jove betakes himself, as one that bare in mind
The wrongful fire sent late against his cousin Phaëton.
In lakes and rivers is his joy; the fire he aye doth shun
And chooseth him the contrary continually to wone.

*Apollo mourns*
*for Phaëton*

        Forlorn and altogether void of that same beauty sheen
        Was Phaeton's father in that while which erst had in him been,
Like as he looketh in th'eclipse. He hates the irksome light,
He hates himself, he hates the day and sets his whole delight

In making sorrow for his son, and in his grief doth storm          480
And chafe, denying to the world his duty to perform.
'My lot', quoth he, 'hath had enough of this unquiet state
From first beginning of the world. It irks me, though too late,
Of restless toils and thankless pains. Let whoso will for me
Go drive the chariot in the which the light should carried be.
If none dare take the charge in hand and all the gods persist
As insufficient, he himself go drive it if he list,
That at the least, by venturing our bridles for to guide,
His lightning, making childless sires, he once may lay aside.
By that time that he hath assayed the unappallèd force          490
That doth remain and rest within my fiery-footed horse,
I trow he shall by trièd proof be able for to tell
How that he did not merit death that could not rule them well.'
The gods stood all about the sun thus storming in his rage,
Beseeching him in humble wise his sorrow to assuage
And that he would not on the world continual darkness bring.
Jove eke excused him of the fire the which he chanced to fling
And with entreatance mingled threats, as did become a king.
Then Phoebus gathered up his steeds, that yet for fear did run
Like flighted fiends, and in his mood without respect begun          500
To beat his whipstock on their pates and lash them on the sides.
It was no need to bid him chafe; for ever as he rides
He still upbraids them with his son and lays them on the hides.

  And Jove almighty went about the walls of heaven to try          *Jupiter and*
  If aught were perished with the fire, which when he did espy          *Callisto*
Continuing in their former state all strong and safe and sound,
He went to view the works of men and things upon the ground.
Yet for his land of Arcady he took most care and charge.
The springs and streams that durst not run he set again at large;
He clad the earth with grass, the trees with leaves both fresh and
    green,          510
Commanding woods to spring again that erst had burnèd been.
Now as he often went and came, it was his chance to light
Upon a nymph of Nonacris, whose form and beauty bright
Did set his heart on flaming fire. She usèd not to spin
Nor yet to curl her frizzled hair with bodkin or with pin;

A garment with a buckled belt fast girded did she wear,
And in a white and slender caul slight trussèd was her hair.
Sometime a dart, sometime a bow she usèd for to bear;
She was a knight of Phoebe's troop. There came not at the Mount
520 Of Maenalus of whom Diana made so great account.
But favour never lasteth long. The sun had gone that day
A good way past the point of noon when, weary of her way,
She drew to shadow in a wood that never had been cut.
Here off her shoulder by and by her quiver did she put
And hung her bow unbent aside and couched her on the ground,
Her quiver underneath her head. Whom when that Jove had
      found
Alone and weary, 'Sure', he said, 'my wife shall never know
Of this escape; and if she do, I know the worst, I trow.
She can but chide. Shall fear of chiding make me to forslow?'
530 He counterfeiteth Phoebe straight in count'nance and array
And says, 'O virgin of my troop, where did'st thou hunt today?'
The damsel started from the ground and said, 'Hail, goddess dear,
Of greater worth than Jove, I think, though Jove himself did ·
      hear.'
Jove heard her well, and smiled thereat; it made his heart rejoice
To hear the nymph prefer him thus before himself in choice.
He fell to kissing, which was such as out of square might seem
And in such sort as that a maid could nothing less beseem.
And as she would have told what woods she rangèd had for game,
He took her fast between his arms and, not without his shame,
540 Bewrayèd plainly what he was and wherefore that he came.
The wench against him strove as much as any woman could.
I would that Juno had it seen, for then I know thou would
Not take the deed so heinously. With all her might she strove.
But what poor wench or who alive could vanquish mighty Jove?
Jove, having sped, flew straight to heaven. She hateth in her heart
The guiltless fields and wood where Jove had played that naughty
      part.
Away she goes in such a grief as that she had well nigh
Forgot her quiver with her shafts and bow that hangèd by.
Dictynna, guarded with her train and proud of killing deer
550 In ranging over Maenalus, espying, called her near.

The damsel, hearing Phoebe call, did run away amain;
She fearèd lest in Phoebe's shape that Jove had come again.
But when she saw the troop of nymphs that guarded her about,
She thought there was no more deceit and came among the rout.
O Lord, how hard a matter is't for guilty hearts to shift
And keep their count'nance! From the ground her eyes scarce
    durst she lift.
She pranks not by her mistress' side; she presses not to be
The foremost of the company, as when she erst was free.
She standeth mute, and by changing of her colour aye
The treading of her shoe awry she plainly doth bewray;       560
Diana might have found the fault, but that she was a may.
A thousand tokens did appear apparent to the eye
By which the nymphs themselves, they say, her fault did well
    espy.
Nine times the moon full to the world had showed her hornèd
    face
When, fainting through her brother's flames and hunting in the
    chase,
She found a cool and shady lawn through midst whereof she spied
A shallow brook with trickling stream on gravel bottom glide.
And, liking well the pleasant place, upon the upper brim
She dipped her foot; and finding there the water cool and trim,
'Away', she said 'with standers-by, and let us bathe us here.'     570
Then Parrhasis cast down her head with sad and bashful cheer.
The rest did strip them to their skins; she only sought delay
Until that, would or would she not, her clothes were plucked
    away.
Then with her naked body straight her crime was brought to light,
Which ill, ashamed, as with her hands she would have hid from
    sight,
'Fie, beast!' quoth Cynthia, 'Get thee hence! Thou shalt not here
    defile
This sacred spring.' And from her train she did her quite exile.    *The*
  The matron of the thundering Jove had inkling of the fact,    *transformation*
  Delaying till convenient time the punishment to exact.    *of Callisto*
There is no cause of further stay. To spite her heart withal    580
Her husband's leman bare a boy that Arcas men did call.

On whom she casting lowering look with fell and cruel mind,
Said, 'Was there, arrant strumpet thou, none other shift to find
But that thou needs must be with bairn, that all the world must
          see
My husband's open shame and thine in doing wrong to me?
But neither unto heaven nor hell this trespass shalt thou bear;
I will bereave thee of thy shape, through pride whereof thou were
So hardy to entice my fere.' Immediately with that
She raught her by the foretop fast and fiercely threw her flat
Against the ground. The wretched wench her arms up meekly
590          cast;
Her arms began with grisly hair to wax all rugged fast.
Her hands gan warp and into paws ill-favouredly to grow
And for to serve instead of feet. The lips that late ago
Did like the mighty Jove so well with side and flaring flaps
Became a wide deformèd mouth. And further, lest perhaps
Her prayers and her humble words might cause her to relent,
She did bereave her of her speech; instead whereof there went
An ireful, hoarse and dreadful voice out from a threatening throat.
But yet the selfsame mind that was before she turned her coat
600    Was in her still in shape of bear; the grief whereof she shows
By thrusting forth continual sighs, and up she ghastly throws
Such kind of hands as then remained unto the starry sky.
And for because she could not speak, she thought Jove inwardly
To be unthankful. O, how oft she, daring not abide
Alone among the desert woods, full many a time and tide
Would stalk before her house in grounds that were her own
          erewhile!
How oft, O, did she in the hills the barking hounds beguile
And in the lawns, where she herself had chasèd erst her game,
Now fly herself to save her life when hunters sought the same!
610    Full oft at sight of other beasts she hid her head for fear,
Forgetting what she was herself. For though she were a bear,
Yet when she spièd other bears she quook for very pain
And fearèd wolves, although her sire among them did remain.
   Behold, Lycaon's daughter's son that Arcas had to name,
About the age of fifteen years within the forest came

Of Erymanth, not knowing aught of this his mother's case.
There, after pitching of his toils, as he the stags did chase,
Upon his mother suddenly it was his chance to light;
Who for desire to see her son did stay herself from flight
And wistly on him cast her look, as one that did him know.          620
But he, not knowing what she was, began his heels to show.
And when he saw her still persist in staring on his face,
He was afraid and from her sight withdrew himself apace.
But when he could not so be rid, he took an armèd pike
In full intent her through the heart with deadly wound to strike.
But God Almighty held his hand and, lifting both away,
Did disappoint the wicked act. For straight he did convey
Them through the air with whirling winds to top of all the sky
And there did make them neighbour stars about the pole on high.
    When Juno shining in the heaven her husband's minion found,     630
    She swelled for spite; and down she comes to watery Tethys
        round
And unto old Oceanus, whom even the gods aloft
Did reverence for their just deserts full many a time and oft.
To whom, demanding her the cause, 'And ask ye', quoth she,
        'why
That I which am the queen of gods come hither from the sky?
Good cause there is, I warrant you. Another holds my room.
For never trust me while I live if, when the night is come
And overcasteth all the world with shady darkness whole,
Ye see not in the height of heaven (hard by the northern pole
Whereas the utmost circle runs about the axle-tree               640
In shortest circuit) gloriously installèd for to be
In shape of stars the stinging wounds that make me ill apaid.
Now is there, trow ye, any cause why folk should be afraid
To do to Juno what they list or dread her wrathful mood,
Which only by my working harm do turn my foes to good?
O, what a mighty act is done! How passing is my power!
I have bereft her woman's shape, and at this present hour
She is become a goddess! Lo, this is the scourge so sore
Wherewith I strike mine enemies! Lo, here is all the spite
That I can do; this is the end of all my wondrous might!           650

No force. I would he should, for me, her native shape restore
And take away her brutish shape like as he hath before
Done by his paramour, that fine and proper piece
Of Argos whom he made a cow – I mean Phoroneu's niece.
Why makes he not a full divorce from me and in my stead
Straight take his sweetheart to his wife and coll her in my bed?
He cannot do a better deed, I think, than for to take
Lycaon to his father-in-law. But if that you do make
Account of me, your foster-child, then grant that for my sake
660 The oxen and the wicked wain of stars in number seven,
For whoredom sake but late ago receivèd into heaven,
May never dive within your waves. Ne let that strumpet vile
By bathing of her filthy limbs your waters pure defile.'

*The raven*
*becomes black*

The gods did grant her her request; and straight to heaven she
    flew
    In handsome chariot through the air which painted peacocks
        drew,
As well beset with blazing eyes late ta'en from Argus' head
As thou, thou prating raven, white by nature being bred,
Had'st on thy feathers justly late a colly colour spread.
For this same bird in ancient time had feathers fair and white
670 As ever was the driven snow, or silver clear and bright.
He might have well compared himself in beauty with the doves
That have no blemish, or the swan that running water loves,
Or with the geese that afterward should with their gaggling out
Preserve the Roman Capitol beset with foes about.
His tongue was cause of all his harm; his tattling tongue did make
His colour, which before was white, become so foul and black.
Coronis of Larissa was the fairest maid of face
In all the land of Thessaly. She stood in Phoebus' grace
As long as that she kept her chaste, or at the least as long
680 As that she scapèd unespied in doing Phoebus wrong.
But at the last Apollo's bird her privy packing spied,
Whom no entreatance could persuade but that he swiftly hied
Him to his master to bewray the doings of his love.
Now as he flew, the prattling crow her wings apace did move
And, overtaking, fell in talk and was inquisitive
For what intent and to what place he did so swiftly drive.

And when she heard the cause thereof, she said, 'Now trust me,
    sure,
This message on the which thou go'st no goodness will procure.
And therefore hearken what I say; disdain thou not at all
To take some warning by thy friend in things that may befall.
Consider what I erst have been and what thou seest me now,
And what hath been the ground hereof. I boldly dare avow
That thou shalt find my faithfulness imputed for a crime.
For Pallas in a wicker chest had hid upon a time
A child called Ericthonius, whom never woman bare,
And took it unto maidens three that Cecrops' daughters were,
Not telling them what was within, but gave them charge to keep
The casket shut and for no cause within the same to peep.
I, standing close among the leaves upon an elm on high,
Did mark their doings and their words. And there I did espy
How Pandrosos and Herse kept their promise faithfully;
Aglauros calls them cowards both and makes no more ado
But takes the casket in her hand and doth the knots undo.
And there they saw a child whose parts beneath were like a snake.
Straight to the goddess of this deed a just report I make,
For which she gave me this reward: that never might I more
Account her for my lady and my mistress as before.
And in my room she put the fowl that flies not but by night.
A warning unto other birds my luck should be of right
To hold their tongues for being shent. But you will say,
    perchance,
I came unsent for of myself; she did me not advance.
I dare well say, though Pallas now my heavy mistress stand,
Yet if perhaps ye should demand the question at her hand,
As sore displeasèd as she is, she would not this deny,
But that she chose me first herself to bear her company.
For, well I know, my father was a prince of noble fame,
Of Phocis king by long descent; Coroneu was his name.
I was his darling and his joy, and many a wealthy peer
(I would not have you think disdain) did seek me for their fere.
My form and beauty did me hurt. For as I leisurely
Went jetting up and down the shore upon the gravel dry,

*The crow's*
690 *story*

700

710

720

As yet I customably do, the god that rules the seas,
Espying me, fell straight in love. And when he saw none ease
In suit but loss of words and time, he offered violence
And after me he runs apace. I scud as fast fro thence
From sand to shore, from shore to sand, still playing fox to hole,
Until I was so tired that he had almost got the goal.
Then called I out on god and man. But, as it did appear,
There was no man so near at hand that could my crying hear.
730  A virgin goddess pitied me because I was a maid
And at the utter plunge and pinch did send me present aid.
I cast mine arms to heaven; mine arms waxed light with feathers
           black.
I went about to cast in haste my garments from my back,
And all was feathers; in my skin the rooted feathers stack.
I was about with violent hand to strike my naked breast;
But neither had I hand nor breast that naked more did rest.
I ran, but of my feet as erst remainèd not the print;
Methought I glided on the ground. Anon with sudden dint
I rose and hovered in the air and from that instant time
740  Did wait on Pallas faithfully without offence or crime.
But what avails all this to me, and if that in my place
The wicked wretch Nyctimene, who late for lack of grace
Was turnèd to an odious bird, to honour callèd be?
I pray thee, did'st thou never hear how false Nyctimene
(A thing all over Lesbos known) defiled her father's couch?
The beast is now become a bird whose lewdness doth so touch
And prick her guilty conscience that she dares not come in sight
Nor show herself abroad a-days, but fleeteth in the night
For shame lest folk should see her fault. And every other bird
750  Doth in the air and ivy-tods with wondering at her gird.'
'A mischief take thy tattling tongue,' the raven answered tho.
'Thy vain forespeaking moves me not.' And so he forth did go
And tells his lord Apollo how he saw Coronis lie
With Isthyis, a gentleman that dwelt in Thessaly.

*The raven*          When Phoebus heard his lover's fault, he fiercely gan to frown
*becomes black*      And cast his garland from his head and threw his viol down.
*(conclusion)*       His colour changed, his face looked pale; and, as the rage of ire
                     That boilèd in his belking breast had set his heart on fire,

He caught me up his wonted tools and bent his golden bow
And by and by with deadly stripe of unavoided blow                          760
Strake through the breast the which his own had touched so oft
    afore.
She, wounded, gave a piteous shriek and (drawing from the sore
The deadly dart the which, the blood pursuing after fast,
Upon her white and tender limbs a scarlet colour cast)
Said, 'Phoebus, well, thou might have wreaked this trespass on my
    head
And yet forborne me till the time I had been brought abed.
Now in one body by thy means a couple shall be dead.'
Thus much she said; and with the blood her life did fade away.
The body, being void of soul, became as cold as clay.
Then all too late, alas, too late gan Phoebus to repent                     770
That of his lover he had ta'en so cruel punishment.
He blames himself for giving ear so unadvisedly;
He blames himself in that he took it so outrageously.
He hates and bans his faithful bird because he did inform
Him of his lover's naughtiness that made him so to storm.
He hates his bow, he hates his shaft that rashly from it went,
And eke he hates his hasty hands by whom the bow was bent.
He takes her up between his arms, endeavouring all too late
By plaster made of precious herbs to stay her helpless fate.
But when he saw there was no shift but that she needs must burn             780
And that the solemn sacred fire was pressed to serve the turn,
Then from the bottom of his heart full sorry sighs he fet
(For heavenly powers with watery tears their cheeks may never
    wet),
In case as when a cow beholds the cruel butcher stand
With lancing axe imbrued with blood and lifting up his hand
Aloft to snatch her sucking calf that hangeth by the heels
And of the axe the deadly dint upon his forehead feels.
Howbeit after sweet perfumes bestowed upon her corse
And much embracing, having sore bewailed her wrong divorce,
He followed to the place assigned her body for to burn.                     790
There could he not abide to see his seed to ashes turn,
But took the baby from her womb and from the fiery flame
And unto double Chiron's den conveyèd straight the same.

The raven, hoping for his truth to be rewarded well,
He maketh black, forbidding him with whiter birds to dwell.

*The
transformation
of Ocyrhoë*

    The centaur Chiron in the while was glad of Phoebus' boy;
    And as the burden brought some care, the honour brought him
        joy.
Upon a time with golden locks about her shoulders spread
A daughter of the centaur's (whom a certain nymph had bred

800    About the brook Caïcus' banks) that hight Ocyrhoë
Came thither. This same fair young nymph could not contented
        be
To learn the craft of surgery as perfect as her sire
But that to learn the secret dooms of fate she must aspire.
And therefore, when the furious rage of frenzy had her caught
And that the sprite of prophecy enflamèd had her thought,
She looked upon the child and said, 'Sweet babe, the gods thee
        make
A man. For all the world shall fare the better for thy sake;
All sores and sickness shalt thou cure. Thy power shall eke be such
To make the dead alive again; for doing of the which

810    Against the pleasure of the gods thy grandsire shall thee strike
So with his fire that never more thou shalt perform the like.
And of a god a bloodless corse, and of a corse (full strange!)
Thou shalt become a god again, and twice thy nature change.
And thou, my father lief and dear, who now by destiny
Art born to live for evermore and never for to die,
Shalt suffer such outrageous pain throughout thy members all
By wounding of a venomed dart that on thy foot shall fall
That oft thou shalt desire to die, and in the latter end
The fatal dames shall break thy thread and thy desire thee send.'

820    There was yet more behind to tell when suddenly she fet
A sore deep sigh and down her cheeks the tears did trickle wet.
'Mine own misfortune', quoth she, 'now hath overtake me sure.
I cannot utter any more, for words wax out of ure.
My cunning was not worth so much as that it should procure
The wrath of God; I feel by proof far better had it been
If that the chance of things to come I never had foreseen.
For now my native shape withdraws. Methinks I have delight
To feed on grass and fling in fields, I feel myself so light.

I am transformèd to a mare like other of my kin.
But wherefore should this brutish shape all over wholly win,                    830
Considering that, although both horse and man my father be,
Yet is his better part a man as plainly is to see?'
The latter end of this complaint was fumbled in such wise
As what she meant the standers-by could scarcely well devise.
Anon she neither seemed to speak nor fully for to neigh,
But like to one that counterfeits in sport the mare to play.
Within a while she neighèd plain, and down her arms were pight
Upon the ground all clad with hair and bare her body right.
Her fingers joinèd all in one, at end whereof did grow
Instead of nails a round tough hoof of whelkèd horn below.                      840
Her head and neck shot forth in length; her kirtle train became
A fair long tail; her flaring hair was made a hanging mane.
And as her native shape and voice most monstrously did pass,
So by the uncouth name of mare she after termèd was.
    The centaur Chiron wept hereat and, piteously dismayed,                     *Mercury*
    Did call on thee, although in vain, thou Delphian god, for aid.             *and Battus*
For neither lay it in thy hand to break Jove's mighty hest,
And thought it had, yet in thy state as then thou did not rest.
In Elis did thou then abide and in Messene land;
It was the time when under shape of shepherd with a wand                        850
Of olive and a pipe of reeds thou kept Admetus' sheep.
Now in this time that, save of love, thou took none other keep
And mad'st thee merry with thy pipe, the glistering Maia's son
By chance abroad the fields of Pyle spied certain cattle run
Without a herd, the which he stole and closely did them hide
Among the woods. This pretty sleight no earthly creature spied
Save one old churl that Battus hight. This Battus had the charge
Of wealthy Neleus' feeding grounds and all his pastures large
And kept a race of goodly mares. Of him he was afraid
And, lest by him his privy theft should chance to be bewrayed,                  860
He took a bribe to stop his mouth and thus unto him said:
'My friend, I pray thee, if perchance that any man enquire
This cattle, say thou saw them not. And take thou for thy hire
This fair young bullock.' T'other took the bullock at his hand
And, showing him a certain stone that lay upon the land,

Said, 'Go thy way. As soon this stone thy doings shall bewray
As I shall do.' So Mercury did seem to go his way.
Anon he comes me back again and, altered both in speech
And outward shape, said, 'Countryman, Ich heartily bezeech
And if thou zawest any kie come roiling through this ground
Or driven away, tell what he was and where they may be vound.
And I chill githee vor thy pain an heifer an' her match.'
The carl, perceiving double gain and greedy for to catch,
Said, 'Under yon same hill they were and under yon same hill
Cham zure they are,' and with his hand he pointed thereuntil.
At that Mercurius, laughing, said, 'False knave, and dost bewray
Me to myself? Dost thou bewray me to myself, I say?'
And with that word straight to a stone he turned his double heart
In which the slander yet remains without the stone's desert.

*Mercury*      The bearer of the charmèd rod, the subtle Mercury,
*and Herse*    This done, arose with waving wings and from that place did fly.
And as he hovered in the air, he viewed the fields below
Of Attic and the town itself with all the trees that grow
In Lycy where the learnèd clerks did wholesome precepts show.
By chance the very selfsame day the virgins of the town
Of old and ancient custom bare in baskets on their crown
Beset with garlands fresh and gay and strewed with flowers sweet
To Pallas' tower such sacrifice as was of custom meet.
The wingèd god, beholding them returning in a troop,
Continued not directly forth but gan me down to stoop
And fetched a windlass round about. And as the hungry kite,
Beholding unto sacrifice a bullock ready dight,
Doth soar about his wishèd prey, desirous for to snatch
But that he dareth not for such as stand about and watch;
So Mercury with nimble wings doth keep a lower gait
About Minerva's lofty towers in round and wheeling rate.
    As far as doth the morning star in clear and streaming light
    Excel all other stars in heaven; as far also as bright
Dame Phoebe dims the morning star; so far did Herse's face
Stain all the ladies of her troop. She was the very grace
And beauty of that solemn pomp and all that train so fair.
Jove's son was ravished with the sight and, hanging in the air,

870

890

900

Began to swelt within himself; in case as, when the powder
Hath driven the pellet from the gun, the pellet gins to smoulder
And in his flying wax more hot. In smoking breast he shrouds
His flames not brought from heaven above but caught beneath the
    clouds.
He leaves his journey toward heaven and takes another race,
Not minding any lenger time to hide his present case,
So great a trust and confidence his beauty to him gave.
Which though it seemèd of itself sufficient force to have,       910
Yet was he curious for to make himself more fine and brave.
He kembed his hair and stroked his beard and pried on every side
To see that in his furniture no wrinkle might be spied;
And for because his cloak was fringed and guarded broad with
    gold,
He cast it on his shoulder up most seemly to behold.
He takes in hand his charmèd rod that bringeth things asleep
And wakes them when he list again, and lastly taketh keep
That on his fair well-formèd feet his golden shoes sit clean
And that all other things thereto well correspondent been.
   In Cecrops' court were chambers three set far from all resort    920
   With ivory beds all furnishèd in far most royal sort,
Of which Aglauros had the left and Pandrose had the right
And Herse had the middlemost. She that Aglauros hight
First marked the coming of the god and, asking him his name,
Demanded him for what intent and cause he thither came.
Pleione's nephew, Maia's son, did make her answer thus:
'I am my father's messenger his pleasure to discuss
To mortal folk and hellish fiends as list him to command.
My father is the mighty Jove. To that thou dost demand
I will not feign a false excuse; I ask no more but grant    930
To keep thy sister's counsel close and for to be the aunt
Of such the issue as on her my chance shall be to get.
Thy sister Herse is the cause that hath me hither fet;
I pray thee, bear thou with my love that is so firmly set.'
Aglauros cast on Mercury her scornful eyes aside
With which against Minerva's will her secrets late she spied,
Demanding him in recompense a mighty mass of gold,
And would not let him enter in until the same were told.

The warlike goddess cast on her a stern and cruel look
940 And fetchèd such a cutting sigh that forcibly it shook
Both breast and breastplate, wherewithal it came unto her thought
How that Aglauros late ago against her will had wrought
In looking on the leman child, contrary to her oath,
The which she took her in the chest, for which she waxèd wroth.
Again she saw her cankered heart maliciously repine
Against her sister and the god and furthermore, in fine,
How that the gold which Mercury had given her for her meed
Would make her both in wealth and pride all others to exceed.

*The*
*punishment*
*of Aglauros*

She goes me straight to Envy's house, a foul and irksome cave
Replete with black and loathly filth and stinking like a grave.
It standeth in a hollow dale where neither light of sun
Nor blast of any wind or air may for the deepness come;
A dreary, sad and doleful den aye full of slothful cold
As which, aye dimmed with smouldering smoke, doth never fire
    behold.
When Pallas, that same manly maid, approachèd near this plot,
She stayed without (for to the house in enter might she not)
And with her javelin point did give a push against the door.
The door flew open by and by and fell me in the floor.
There saw she Envy sit within fast gnawing on the flesh
960 Of snakes and toads, the filthy food that keeps her vices fresh.
It loathed her to behold the sight. Anon the elf arose
And left the gnawèd adder's flesh, and slothfully she goes
With lumpish leisure like a snail; and when she saw the face
Of Pallas and her fair attire adorned with heavenly grace
She gave a sigh, a sorry sigh, from bottom of her heart.
Her lips were pale, her cheeks were wan, and all her face was
    swart,
Her body lean as any rake; she lookèd eke askew.
Her teeth were furred with filth and dross; her gums were waryish
    blue.
The working of her festered gall had made her stomach green,
970 And all bevenomed was her tongue. No sleep her eyes had seen;
Continual cark and cankered care did keep her waking still.
Of laughter (save at others' harms) the hellhound can no skill;

It is against her will that men have any good success.
And if they have, she frets and fumes within her mind no less
Than if herself had taken harm. In seeking to annoy
And work distress to other folk herself she doth destroy.
Thus is she torment to herself. Though Pallas did her hate,
Yet spake she briefly these few words to her without her gate:
'Infect thou with thy venom one of Cecrops' daughters three.
It is Aglauros whom I mean, for so it needs must be.'                    980
This said, she pight her spear in ground and took her rise thereon
And, winding from that wicked wight, did take her flight anon.
  The caitiff cast her eye aside and, seeing Pallas gone,
  Began to mumble with herself the devil's Paternoster
  And, fretting at her good success, began to blow and bluster.
She takes a crookèd staff in hand bewreathed with knobbèd pricks
And, covered with a colly cloud, wherever that she sticks
Her filthy feet she tramples down and sears both grass and corn,
That all the fresh and fragrant fields seem utterly forlorn;
And with her staff she tippeth off the highest poppy heads.              990
Such poison also everywhere ungraciously she sheds
That every cottage where she comes and every town and city
Do take infection at her breath. At length (the more is pity)
She found the fair Athenian town that flowèd freshly then
In feastful peace and joyful wealth and learnèd wits of men.
And for because she nothing saw that might provoke to weep,
It was a corsie to her heart her hateful tears to keep.
Now when she came within the court, she went without delay
Directly to the lodgings where King Cecrops' daughters lay.
There did she as Minerva bade. She laid her scurvy fist                 1000
Besmeared with venom and with filth upon Aglauros' breast,
The which she filled with hookèd thorns, and, breathing on her
            face,
Did shed the poison in her bones which spread itself apace
As black as ever virgin pitch through lungs and lights and all.
And to th'intent that cause of grief abundantly should fall,
She placèd aye before her eyes her sister's happy chance
In being wedded to the god and made the god to glance
Continually in heavenly shape before her wounded thought.
And all these things she painted out; which in conclusion wrought

1010 Such corsies in Aglauros' breast that, sighing day and night,
She gnawed and fretted in herself for very cankered spite.
And like a wretch she wastes herself with restless care and pine,
Like as the ice whereon the sun with glimmering light doth shine.
Her sister Herse's good success doth make her heart to yearn,
In case as when that fire is put to green-felled wood or fern
Which giveth neither light nor heat, but smoulders quite away.
Sometime she minded to her sire her sister to bewray
Who, well she knew, would ill abide so lewd a part to play.
And oft she thought with wilful hand to brust her fatal thread
1020 Because she would not see the thing that made her heart to bleed.
At last she sat her in the door and leanèd to a post
To let the god from entering in. To whom, now having lost
Much talk and gentle words in vain, she said, 'Sir, leave, I pray;
For hence I will not (be you sure) unless you go away.'
'I take thee at thy word,' quoth he, and therewithal he pushed
His rod against the barrèd door, and wide it open rushed.
She, making proffer for to rise, did feel so great a weight
Through all her limbs that for her life she could not stretch her
      straight.
She strove to set herself upright; but striving booted not.
1030 Her hamstrings and her knees were stiff; a chilling cold had got
In at her nails through all her limbs; and eke her veins began
For want of blood and lively heat to wax both pale and wan.
And as the fretting fistula, forgrown and past all cure,
Runs in the flesh from place to place and makes the sound and
      pure
As bad or worser than the rest, even so the cold of death
Strake to her heart and closed her veins and lastly stopped her
      breath.
She made no proffer for to speak, and though she had done so
It had been vain. For way was none for language forth to go.
Her throat congealèd into stone, her mouth became hard stone,
1040 And like an image sat she still. Her blood was clearly gone,
The which the venom of her heart so fouly did infect
That ever after all the stone with freckled spots was specked.

*Jupiter and*          When Mercury had punished thus Aglauros' spiteful tongue
*Europa*               And cankered heart, immediately from Pallas' town he flung

And, flying up with flittering wings, did pierce to heaven above.
His father called him straight aside but, showing not his love,
Said, 'Son, my trusty messenger and worker of my will,
Make no delay but out of hand fly down in haste until
The land that on the left side looks upon thy mother's light,
Yon same where standeth on the coast the town that Sidon hight.      1050
The king hath there a herd of neat that on the mountains feed;
Go, take and drive them to the sea with all convenient speed.'
He had no sooner said the word but that the herd begun,
Driven from the mountain to the shore appointed, for to run
Whereas the daughter of the king was wonted to resort
With other ladies of the court, there for to play and sport.
Between the state of majesty and love is set such odds
As that they cannot dwell in one. The sire and king of gods
Whose hand is armed with triple fire, who only with his frown
Makes sea and land and heaven to quake, doth lay his sceptre
      down                                                           1060
With all the grave and stately port belonging thereunto
And, putting on the shape of bull, as other cattle do
Goes lowing gently up and down among them in the field –
The fairest beast to look upon that ever man beheld.
For why his colour was as white as any winter's snow
Before that either trampling feet or southern wind it thaw.
His neck was brawned with rolls of flesh, and from his chest
      before
A dangling dewlap hung me down good half a foot and more.
His horns were small, but yet so fine as that ye would have
      thought
They had been made by cunning hand or out of wax been
      wrought.                                                       1070
More clear they were a hundredfold than is the crystal stone.
In all his forehead fearful frown or wrinkle there was none,
No fierce, no grim nor grisly look, as other cattle have,
But altogether so demure as friendship seemed to crave.
Agenor's daughter marvelled much so tame a beast to see,
But yet to touch him at the first too bold she durst not be.
Anon she reaches to his mouth her hand with herbs and flowers;
The loving beast was glad thereof and neither frowns nor lowers,

But till the hopèd joy might come with glad and fawning cheer
1080   He licks her hands and scarce, ah, scarce, the residue he forbear.
Sometime he frisks and skips about and shows her sport at hand;
Anon he lays his snowy side against the golden sand.
So fear by little driven away, he offered eft his breast
To stroke and coy and eft his horns with flowers to be dressed.
At last Europa, knowing not (for so the maid was called)
On whom she ventured for to ride, was ne'er a whit appalled
To set herself upon his back. Then by and by the god
From main dry land to main moist sea gan leisurely to plod.
At first he did but dip his feet within the outmost wave
1090   And back again; then further in another plunge he gave,
And so still further, till at the last he had his wishèd prey
Amid the deep where was no means to scape with life away.
The lady, quaking all for fear, with rueful count'nance cast
Aye toward shore from whence she came, held with her right
         hand fast
One of his horns and with the left did stay upon his back.
The weather flasked and whiskèd up her garments, being slack.

FINIS SECUNDI LIBRI.

# The Third Book of Ovid's Metamorphoses

The god, now having laid aside his borrowed shape of bull,
Had in his likeness showed himself and with his pretty trull
Ta'en landing in the Isle of Crete, when in that while her sire,
Not knowing where she was become, sent after to enquire
Her brother Cadmus, charging him his sister home to bring
Or never for to come again; wherein he did a thing
For which he might both justly kind and cruel callèd be.
When Cadmus over all the world had sought (for who is he
That can detect the thefts of Jove?) and nowhere could her see,
Then as an outlaw to avoid his father's wrongful ire                    10
He went to Phoebus' oracle most humbly to desire
His heavenly counsel, where he would assign him place to dwell.
'An heifer all alone in field', quoth Phoebus, '– mark her well –
Which never bare the pinching yoke nor drew the plough as yet
Shall meet thee. Follow after her; and where thou see'st her sit,
There build a town and let thereof Boeötia be the name.'
Down from Parnassus' stately top scarce fully Cadmus came
When, roiling softly in the vale before the herd alone,
He saw an heifer on whose neck of servage print was none.
He followed after leisurely as her that was his guide                    20
And thankèd Phoebus in his heart that did so well provide.
Now had he passed Cephisus' ford and eke the pleasant grounds
About the city Panope contained within those bounds.
The heifer stayed and, lifting up her forehead to the sky
Full seemly for to look upon with horns like branches high,
Did with her lowing fill the air and, casting back her eye
Upon the rest that came aloof, as softly as she could
Kneeled down and laid her hairy side against the grassy mould.

Then Cadmus gave Apollo thanks and, falling flat below,
30    Did kiss the ground and hail the fields which yet he did not know.
He was about to sacrifice to Jove, the heavenly king,
And bade his servants go and fetch him water of the spring.
    An old, forgrown, unfellèd wood stood near at hand thereby
    And in the midst a queachy plot with sedge and osiers high
Where, curbed about with pebble stone in likeness of a bow,
There was a spring with silver streams that forth thereof did flow.
Here lurkèd in his lowering den god Mars his grisly snake
With golden scales and fiery eyes, beswollen with poison black;
Three spurting tongues, three rows of teeth within his head did
    stick.
40    No sooner had the Tyrian folk set foot within this thick
And queachy plot and dippèd down their bucket in the well,
But that to bustle in his den began this serpent fell
And, peering with a marble head, right horribly to hiss.
The Tyrians let their pitchers slip for sudden fear of this
And, waxing pale as any clay, like folk amazed and flight
Stood trembling like an aspen leaf. The speckled serpent straight
Comes trailing out in waving links and knotty rolls of scales
And, bending into bunchy boughts, his body forth he hales.
And, lifting up above the waist himself unto the sky,
50    He overlooketh all the wood, as huge and big well nigh
As is the Snake that in the heaven about the northern pole
Divides the Bears. He makes no stay, but deals his dreadful dole
Among the Tyrians. Whether they did take them to their tools
Or to their heels, or that their fear did make them stand like fools
And help themselves by none of both, he snapped up some alive
And swept in others with his tail; and some he did deprive
Of life with rankness of his breath; and other some again
He stings and poisons unto death till all at last were slain.
    Now when the sun was at his height and shadows waxèd short
60    And Cadmus saw his company make tarriance in that sort,
He marvelled what should be their let and went to seek them out.
His harness was a lion's skin that wrappèd him about;
His weapons were a long strong spear with head of iron tried
And eke a light and piercing dart, and thereunto beside –

Worth all the weapons in the world – a stout and valiant heart.
When Cadmus came within the wood and saw about that part
His men lie slain upon the ground, and eke their cruel foe
Of body huge stand over them and licking with his blo
And blasting tongue their sorry wounds, 'Well, trusty friends,'
      quoth he,
'I either of your piteous deaths will straight revenger be      70
Or else will die myself therefore.' With that he, raughting fast
A mighty millstone, at the snake with all his might it cast.
The stone with such exceeding force and violence forth was
      driven
As of a fort the bulwarks strong and walls it would have riven.
And yet it did the snake no harm; his scales, as hard and tough
As if they had been plates of mail, did fence him well enough,
So that the stone rebounded back against his freckled slough.
But yet his hardness saved him not against the piercing dart;
For, hitting right between the scales that yielded in that part
Whereas the joints do knit the back, it thirlèd through the skin    80
And piercèd to his filthy maw and greedy guts within.
He, fierce with wrath, wrings back his head and, looking on the
      stripe,
The javelin steal that stickèd out between his teeth doth gripe.
The which with wresting to and fro at length he forth did wind,
Save that he left the head thereof among his bones behind.
When of his courage through the wound more kindled was the
      ire,
His throat-boll swelled with puffèd veins, his eyes gan sparkle fire;
There stood about his smearèd chaps a loathly foaming froth.
His scalèd breast ploughs up the ground; the stinking breath that
      go'th
Out from his black and hellish mouth infects the herbs full foul.    90
Sometime he winds himself in knots as round as any bowl;
Sometime he stretcheth out in length as straight as any beam;
Anon again with violent brunt he rusheth like a stream
Increased by rage of late-fall'n rain, and with his mighty sway
Bears down the wood before his breast that standeth in his way.
Agenor's son, retiring back, doth with his lion's spoil
Defend him from his fierce assaults and makes him to recoil,

Aye holding at the weapon's point. The serpent, waxing wood,
Doth crash the steel between his teeth and bites it till the blood
Dropped, mixed with poison from his mouth, did dye the green
100      grass black.
But yet the wound was very light because he writhèd back
And pulled his head still from the stroke and made the stripe to die
By giving way, until that Cadmus, following irefully
The stroke, with all his power and might did through the throat
         him rive
And nailed him to an oak behind the which he eke did cleave.
The serpent's weight did make the tree to bend; it grieved the tree
His body of the serpent's tail thus scourgèd for to be.

*Cadmus sows*
*the serpent's*
*teeth*

While Cadmus wondered at the hugeness of the vanquished
         foe,
Upon the sudden came a voice – from whence he could not
         know,
110  But sure he was he heard the voice – which said, 'Agenor's son,
What gazest thus upon this snake? The time will one day come
That thou thyself shalt be a snake.' He, pale and wan for fear,
Had lost his speech, and ruffled up stiff staring stood his hair.
Behold, man's helper at his need, Dame Pallas, gliding through
The vacant air, was straight at hand, and bade him take a plough
And cast the serpent's teeth in ground, as of the which would
         spring
Another people out of hand. He did in everything
As Pallas bade: he took a plough and eared a furrow low
And sowed the serpent's teeth whereof the foresaid folk should
         grow.
120  Anon (a wondrous thing to tell) the clods began to move,
And from the furrow first of all the pikes appeared above;
Next rose up helms with feathered crests, and then the pouldrons
         bright;
Successively the curats whole, and all the armour right.
Thus grew up men like corn in field in ranks of battle ray
With shields and weapons in their hands to fight the field that day.
Even so, when stages are attired against some solemn game
With cloths of arras gorgeously, in drawing up the same

The faces of the images do first of all them show;
And then by piecemeal all the rest in order seems to grow
Until at last they stand out full upon their feet below.                    130
  Affrighted at these new-found foes, gan Cadmus for to take
  Him to his weapons by and by resistence for to make.
'Stay, stay thyself,' cried one of them that late before were bred
Out of the ground, 'and meddle not with civil wars.' This said,
One of the brothers of that brood with lancing sword he slew;
Another sent a dart at him, the which him overthrew.
The third did straight as much for him and made him yield the
        breath,
The which he had received but now, by stroke of forcèd death.
Likewise outragèd all the rest until that, one by one,
By mutual stroke of civil war dispatchèd everych one,                    140
This brood of brothers all behewn and weltered in their blood
Lay sprawling on their mother's womb, the ground where erst
        they stood,
Save only five that did remain. Of whom Echion, led
By Pallas' counsel, threw away the helmet from his head
And with his brothers gan to treat, atonement for to make.
The which at length, by Pallas' help, so good success did take
That faithful friendship was confirmed and hand in hand was
        plight.
These afterward did well assist the noble Tyrian knight
In building of the famous town that Phoebus had behight.
  Now Thebes stood in good estate; now, Cadmus, might thou
        say
  That when thy father banished thee it was a lucky day.
To join alliance both with Mars and Venus was thy chance,
Whose daughter thou had'st ta'en to wife, who did thee much
        advance
Not only through her high renown but through a noble race
Of sons and daughters that she bare; whose children in like case
It was thy fortune for to see all men and women grown.
But aye the end of everything must markèd be and known;
For none the name of blessedness deserveth for to have
Unless the tenor of his life last blessèd to his grave.

*The
transformation
of Actaeon*

160 Among so many prosperous haps that flowed with good success
Thine eldest nephew was a cause of care and sore distress,
Whose head was armed with palmèd horns, whose own hounds in
      the wood
Did pull their master to the ground and fill them with his blood.
But if you sift the matter well, ye shall not find desert
But cruel fortune to have been the cause of this his smart.
For who could do with oversight? Great slaughter had been made
Of sundry sorts of savage beasts one morning, and the shade
Of things was waxèd very short. It was the time of day
That mid between the east and west the sun doth seem to stay,
170 Whenas the Theban stripling thus bespake his company,
Still ranging in the wayless woods some further game to spy:
'Our weapons and our toils are moist and stained with blood of
      deer;
This day hath done enough, as by our quarry may appear.
As soon as with her scarlet wheels next morning bringeth light,
We will about our work again. But now Hyperion bright
Is in the midst of heaven and sears the fields with fiery rays.
Take up your toils and cease your work, and let us go our ways.'
They did even so, and ceased their work. There was a valley thick
With pineapple and cypress trees that armèd be with prick.
180 Gargaphy hight this shady plot; it was a sacred place
To chaste Diana and the nymphs that waited on her grace.
Within the furthest end thereof there was a pleasant bower
So vaulted with the leafy trees the sun had there no power,
Not made by hand nor man's device; and yet no man alive
A trimmer piece of work than that could for his life contrive.
With flint and pommy was it walled by nature half about,
And on the right side of the same full freshly flowèd out
A lively spring with crystal stream, whereof the upper brim
Was green with grass and matted herbs that smellèd very trim.
190 When Phoebe felt herself wax faint of following of her game,
It was her custom for to come and bathe her in the same.
That day she, having timely left her hunting in the chase,
Was entered with her troop of nymphs within this pleasant place.
She took her quiver and her bow, the which she had unbent,
And eke her javelin to a nymph that servèd that intent.

Another nymph to take her clothes among her train she chose;
Two loosed her buskins from her legs and pullèd off her hose.
The Theban lady Crocale, more cunning than the rest,
Did truss her tresses handsomely which hung behind undressed;
And yet her own hung waving still. Then Niphe, neat and clean,          200
With Hyale, glistering like the grass in beauty fresh and sheen,
And Rhanis, clearer of her skin than are the rainy drops,
And little bibbling Phiale, and Psece, that pretty mops,
Poured water into vessels large to wash their lady with.
Now while she keeps this wont, behold, by wandering in the frith
He wist not wither (having stayed his pastime till the morrow),
Comes Cadmus' nephew to this thick and, entering in with
                    sorrow
(Such was his cursèd cruel fate), saw Phoebe where she washed.
The damsels, at the sight of man quite out of count'nance dashed
Because they everych one were bare and naked to the quick,             210
Did beat their hands against their breasts and cast out such a shriek
That all the wood did ring thereof and, clinging to their dame,
Did all they could to hide both her and eke themselves fro shame.
But Phoebe was of personage so comely and so tall
That by the middle of her neck she overpeered them all.
Such colour as appears in heaven by Phoebus' broken rays
Directly shining on the clouds, or such as is always
The colour of the morning clouds before the sun doth show,
Such sanguine colour in the face of Phoebe gan to glow,
There standing naked in his sight. Who, though she had her guard       220
Of nymphs about her, yet she turned her body from himward.
And, casting back an angry look, like as she would have sent
An arrow at him had she had her bow there ready bent,
So raught she water in her hand and for to wreak the spite
Besprinkled all the head and face of this unlucky knight
And thus forespake the heavy lot that should upon him light:
'Now make thy vaunt among thy mates, thou saw'st Diana bare.
Tell if thou can; I give thee leave. Tell hardly; do not spare.'
This done, she makes no further threats but by and by doth spread
A pair of lively old hart's horns upon his sprinkled head.             230

She sharps his ears; she makes his neck both slender, long and
     lank;
She turns his fingers into feet, his arms to spindle-shank.
She wraps him in a hairy hide beset with speckled spots
And planteth in him fearfulness. And so away he trots,
Full greatly wondering to himself what made him in that case
To be so wight and swift of foot. But when he saw his face
And hornèd temples in the brook, he would have cried, 'Alas!'
But as for then no kind of speech out of his lips could pass,
He sighed and brayed; for that was then the speech that did
     remain.

240    And down the eyes that were not his his bitter tears did rain.
No part remainèd (save his mind) of that he erst had been.
What should he do? Turn home again to Cadmus and the queen?
Or hide himself among the woods? Of this he was afraid,
And of the t'other ill ashamed. While doubting thus he stayed,
   His hounds espied him where he was. And Blackfoot first of all
   And Stalker, special good of scent, began aloud to call.
This latter was a hound of Crete, the other was of Spart.
Then all the kennel fell in round, and every for his part
Did follow freshly in the chase more swifter than the wind:

250    Spy, Eatall, Scalecliff, three good hounds come all of Arcas' kind;
Strong Killbuck, currish Savage, Spring and Hunter fresh of smell,
And Lightfoot, who to lead a chase did bear away the bell;
Fierce Woodman, hurt not long ago in hunting of a boar,
And Shepherd, wont to follow sheep and neat to field afore,
And Laund, a fell and eager bitch that had a wolf to sire;
Another bratch called Greedygut with two her puppies by her,
And Ladon, gaunt as any grew'nd, a hound in Sycion bred;
Blab, Fleetwood, Patch, whose fleckèd skin with sundry spots was
     spread;

    Wight, Bowman, Roister, Beauty, fair and white as winter's snow,
260    And Tawny, full of dusky hairs that over all did grow;
With lusty Ruffler, passing all the residue there in strength,
And Tempest, best of footmanship in holding out at length;
And Coal and Swift and little Wolf, as wight as any other,
Accompanied with a Cyprian hound that was his native brother;

And Snatch, amid whose forehead stood a star as white as snow,
The residue being all as black and sleek as any crow;
And shaggy Rug, with other twain that had a sire of Crete
And dam of Sparta – t'one of them called Jollyboy, a great
And large-flewed hound, the t'other Churl, who ever gnarring
      went;
And Ringwood with a shirl loud mouth, the which he freely
      spent;                                 270
With divers mo whose names to tell it were but loss of time.
These fellows over hill and dale in hope of prey do climb,
Through thick and thin and craggy cliffs where was no way to go.
He flies through grounds where oftentimes he chasèd had ere tho;
Even from his own folk is he fain, alas, to flee away.
He strainèd oftentimes to speak, and was about to say,
'I am Actaeon. Know your lord and master, sirs, I pray.'
But use of words and speech did want to utter forth his mind.
Their cry did ring through all the wood, redoubled with the
      wind.
First Slow did pinch him by the haunch, and next came Killdeer
      in,                                   280
And Hillbred fastened on his shoulder, bote him through the skin.
These came forth later than the rest but, coasting thwart a hill,
They did gaincope him as he came and held their master still
Until that all the rest came in and fastened on him too.
No part of him was free from wound. He could none other do
But sigh and in the shape of hart with voice as harts are wont
(For voice of man was none now left to help him at the brunt)
By braying show his secret grief among the mountains high
And, kneeling sadly on his knees with dreary tears in eye,
As one by humbling of himself that mercy seemed to crave,     290
With piteous look instead of hands his head about to wave.
Not knowing that it was their lord, the huntsmen cheer their
      hounds
With wonted noise and for Actaeon look about the grounds.
They halloo, who could loudest cry, still calling him by name
As though he were not there; and much his absence they do
      blame
In that he came not to the fall, but slacked to see the game.

As often as they namèd him, he sadly shook his head;
And fain he would have been away thence in some other stead.
But there he was. And well he could have found in heart to see
His dogs' fell deeds, so that to feel in place he had not be.        300
They hem him in on every side and, in the shape of stag,
With greedy teeth and griping paws their lord in pieces drag.
So fierce was cruel Phoebe's wrath, it could not be allayed
Till of his fault by bitter death the ransom he had paid.

*Juno and*
*Semele*

Much muttering was upon this fact. Some thought there was
        extended
A great deal more extremity than needed; some commended
Diana's doing, saying that it was but worthily
For safeguard of her womanhood. Each party did apply
Good reasons to defend their case. Alone the wife of Jove
Of liking or misliking it not all so greatly strove,        310
As secretly rejoiced in heart that such a plague was light
On Cadmus' image, turning all the malice and the spite
Conceivèd erst against the wench that Jove had fet fro Tyre
Upon the kindred of the wench. And for to fierce her ire
Another thing clean overthwart there cometh in the nick:
The Lady Semel great with child by Jove as then was quick.
Hereat she gan to fret and fume and, for to ease her heart
Which else would burst, she fell in hand with scolding out her
        part.
'And what a goodyear have I won by scolding erst?' she said.
'It is that arrant quean herself against whose wicked head        320
I must assay to give assault. And if, as men me call,
I be that Juno who in heaven bear greatest swing of all,
If in my hand I worthy be to hold the royal mace,
And if I be the queen of heaven and sovereign of this place,
Or wife and sister unto Jove (his sister well I know;
But as for wife, that name is vain – I serve but for a show
To cover other private scapes), I will confound that whore.
Now with a mischief is she bagged and beareth out before
Her open shame to all the world and shortly hopes to be
The mother of a son by Jove, the which hath happed to me        330
Not passing once in all my time, so sore she doth presume
Upon her beauty! But, I trow, her hope shall soon consume;

For never let me counted be for Saturn's daughter more
If by her own dear darling Jove, on whom she trusts so sore,
I send her not to Styx's stream.' This ended, up she rose
And, coverèd in golden cloud, to Semel's house she goes.
And ere she sent away the cloud, she takes an old wife's shape
With hoary hair and rivelled skin, with slow and crooked gait;
As though she had the palsy had her feeble limbs did shake,
And eke she faltered in the mouth as often as she spake.                340
She seemed old beldame Beroë of Epidaur to be,
This lady Semel's nurse, as right as though it had been she.
    So when that after mickle talk of purpose ministered
    Jove's name was opened, by and by she gave a sigh and said,
'I wish with all my heart that Jove be cause to thee of this.
But, daughter dear, I dread the worst; I fear it be amiss.
For many varlets under name of gods to serve their lust
Have into undefilèd beds themselves full often thrust.
And though it been the mighty Jove, yet doth not that suffice
Unless he also make the same apparent to our eyes;                      350
And if it be even very he, I say, it doth behove
He prove it by some open sign and token of his love.
And therefore pray him for to grant that look in what degree,
What order, fashion, sort and state he use to company
With mighty Juno, in the same in every point and case
To all intents and purposes he thee likewise embrace;
And that he also bring with him his bright three-forkèd mace.'
    With such instructions Juno had infòrmèd Cadmus' niece,
    And she, poor silly simple soul, immediately on this
Requested Jove to grant a boon the which she did not name.              360
'Ask what thou wilt, sweetheart,' quoth he, 'thou shalt not miss
        the same.
And for to make thee sure hereof, the grisly Stygian lake
Which is the fear and god of gods bear witness for thy sake.'
She, joying in her own mischance, not having any power
To rule herself but making speed to haste her fatal hour
In which she through her lover's help should work her own
        decay,
Said, 'Such as Juno findeth you when you and she do play

The games of Venus, such, I pray thee, show thyself to me
In every case.' The god would fain have stopped her mouth, but
    she
Had made such haste that out it was; which made him sigh full
370        sore,
For neither she could then unwish the thing she wished before
Nor he revoke his solemn oath. Wherefore with sorry heart
And heavy count'nance by and by to heaven he doth depart
And makes to follow after him with look full grim and stour
The slaky clouds all grisly black, as when they threat a shower;
To which he added mixed with wind a fierce and flashing flame
With dry and dreadful thunderclaps and lightning to the same
Of deadly unavoided dint. And yet, as much as may,
He goes about his vehement force and fierceness to allay.
380    He doth not arm him with the fire with which he did remove
The giant with the hundred hands, Typhoeus, from above;
It was too cruel and too sore to use against his love.
The Cyclopes made another kind of lightning far more light
Wherein they put much less of fire, less fierceness, lesser might;
It hight in heaven the second mace. Jove arms himself with this
And enters into Cadmus' house where Semel's chamber is.
She, being mortal, was too weak and feeble to withstand
Such troublous tumults of the heavens, and therefore out of hand
Was burnèd in her lover's arms. But yet he took away
390    His infant from the mother's womb, unperfect as it lay,
And (if a man may credit it) did in his thigh it sow,
Where, biding out the mother's time, it did to ripeness grow.
And when the time of birth was come, his aunt, the Lady Ine,
Did nurse him for a while by stealth and kept him trim and fine.
The nymphs of Nysa afterward did in their bowers him hide
And brought him up with milk till time he might abroad be spied.

*The*
*judgement of*
*Tiresias*

    Now while these things were done on earth and that by fatal
        doom
    The twice-born Bacchus had a time to man's estate to come,
They say that Jove, disposed to mirth, as he and Juno sat
400    A-drinking nectar after meat, in sport and pleasant rate
Did fall a-jesting with his wife and said, 'A greater pleasure
In Venus' games ye women have than men beyond all measure.'

She answered, 'No.' To try the truth they both of them agree
The wise Tiresias in this case indifferent judge to be,
Who both the man and woman's joys by trial understood.
For finding once two mighty snakes engendering in a wood,
He strake them overthwart the backs; by means whereof, behold,
(As strange a thing to be of truth as ever yet was told)
He, being made a woman straight, seven winters livèd so.
The eighth he, finding them again, did say unto them tho,     410
'And if to strike ye have such power as for to turn their shape
That are the givers of the stripe, before you hence escape
One stripe now will I lend you more.' He strake them as beforn,
And straight returned his former shape in which he first was born.
Tiresias, therefore being ta'en to judge this jesting strife,
Gave sentence on the side of Jove. The which the queen, his wife,
Did take a great deal more to heart than needed and in spite,
To wreak her teen upon her judge, bereft him of his sight.
But Jove (for to the gods it is unleeful to undo
The things which other of the gods by any means have do)     420
Did give him sight in things to come for loss of sight of eye
And so his grievous punishment with honour did supply.
By means whereof within a while in city, field and town
Through all the coast of Aony was bruited his renown.
And folk to have their fortunes read that daily did resort
Were answered so as none of them could give him misreport.

    The first that of his soothfast words had proof in all the realm     *Echo and*
    Was freckled Liriope whom sometime, surprisèd in his stream,     *Narcissus*
The flood Cephisus did enforce. This lady bare a son
Whose beauty at his very birth might justly love have won;     430
Narcissus did she call his name. Of whom the prophet sage,
Demanded if the child should live to many years of age,
Made answer, 'Yea, full long, so that himself he do not know.'
The soothsayer's words seemed long but vain, until the end did
    show
His saying to be true indeed by strangeness of the rage
And strangeness of the kind of death that did abridge his age.
For when years three times five and one he fully livèd had,
So that he seemed to stand between the state of man and lad,

The hearts of divers trim young men his beauty gan to move,
440    And many a lady fresh and fair was taken in his love.
But in that grace of Nature's gift such passing pride did reign
That to be touched of man or maid he wholly did disdain.
A babbling nymph that Echo hight (who, hearing others talk,
By no means can restrain her tongue but that it needs must walk,
Nor of herself hath power to gin to speak to any wight)
Espied him driving into toils the fearful stags of flight.
This Echo was a body then and not an only voice,
Yet of her speech she had that time no more than now the choice,
That is to say, of many words the latter to repeat.
450    The cause thereof was Juno's wrath. For when that with the feat
She might have often taken Jove in dalliance with his dames,
And that by stealth and unbewares in midst of all his games,
This elf would with her tattling talk detain her by the way
Until that Jove had wrought his will and they were fled away.
The which when Juno did perceive, she said with wrathful mood,
'This tongue that hath deluded me shall do thee little good;
For of thy speech but simple use hereafter shalt thou have.'
The deed itself did straight confirm the threatenings that she gave;
Yet Echo of the former talk doth double oft the end
460    And back again with just report the words erst spoken send.
    Now when she saw Narcissus stray about the forest wide,
    She waxèd warm, and step for step fast after him she hied.
The more she followed after him and nearer that she came,
The hotter ever did she wax, as nearer to her flame;
Like as the lively brimstone doth which, dipped about a match
And put but softly to the fire, the flame doth lightly catch.
O Lord, how often would she fain, if nature would have let,
Entreated him with gentle words some favour for to get!
But nature would not suffer her nor give her leave to gin.
470    Yet, so far forth as she by grant at nature's hand could win,
Aye ready with attentive ear she hearkens for some sound
Whereto she might reply her words, from which she is not bound.
By chance the stripling, being strayed from all his company,
Said, 'Is there anybody nigh?' Straight Echo answered, 'I.'
Amazed, he casts his eye aside and looketh round about,
And 'Come!', that all the forest rung, aloud he calleth out.

And 'Come!' saith she. He looketh back and, seeing no man follow,
'Why fly'st?' he crieth once again; and she the same doth halloo.
He still persists and, wondering much what kind of thing it was
From which that answering voice by turn so duly seemed to pass,     480
Said, 'Let us join.' She, by her will desirous to have said,
'In faith, with none more willingly at any time or stead,'
Said, 'Let us join.' And, standing somewhat in her own conceit,
Upon these words she left the wood and forth she yedeth straight
To coll the lovely neck for which she longèd had so much.
He runs his way and will not be embracèd of no such
And saith, 'I first will die ere thou shalt take of me thy pleasure.'
She answered nothing else thereto but, 'Take of me thy pleasure.'
Now when she saw herself thus mocked, she gat her to the woods
And hid her head for very shame among the leaves and buds;     490
And ever since she lives alone in dens and hollow caves.
Yet stack her love still to her heart, through which she daily raves
The more for sorrow of repulse. Through restless cark and care
Her body pines to skin and bone and waxeth wondrous bare.
The blood doth vanish into air from out of all her veins,
And nought is left but voice and bones. The voice yet still remains;
Her bones, they say, were turned to stones. From thence she, lurking still
In woods, will never show her head in field nor yet on hill.
Yet is she heard of every man; it is her only sound
And nothing else that doth remain alive above the ground.     500
Thus had he mocked this wretched nymph and many mo beside
That in the waters, woods and groves or mountains did abide.
Thus had he mockèd many men; of which one, miscontent
To see himself deluded so, his hands to heaven up bent
And said, 'I pray to God he may once feel fierce Cupid's fire,
As I do now, and yet not joy the things he doth desire.'
The goddess Rhamnuse, who doth wreak on wicked people take,
Assented to his just request for ruth and pity's sake.

   There was a spring withouten mud as silver clear and still,
   Which neither shepherds, nor the goats that fed upon the hill,

*The death of Narcissus*

Nor other cattle troubled had, nor savage beast had stirred,
Nor branch, nor stick, nor leaf of tree, nor any fowl nor bird.
The moisture fed and kept aye fresh the grass that grew about,
And with their leaves the trees did keep the heat of Phoebus out.
The stripling, weary with the heat and hunting in the chase
And much delighted with the spring and coolness of the place,
Did lay him down upon the brim; and as he stoopèd low
To staunch his thirst, another thirst of worse effect did grow.
For, as he drank, he chanced to spy the image of his face,
520 The which he did immediately with fervent love embrace.
He feeds a hope without cause why. For, like a foolish noddy,
He thinks the shadow that he sees to be a lively body.
Astraughted, like an image made of marble stone he lies,
There gazing on his shadow still with fixèd staring eyes.
Stretched all along upon the ground, it doth him good to see
His ardent eyes, which like two stars full bright and shining be,
And eke his fingers, fingers such as Bacchus might beseem,
And hair that one might worthily Apollo's hair it deem,
His beardless chin and ivory neck, and eke the perfect grace
530 Of white and red indifferently bepainted in his face.
All these he wond'reth to behold, for which (as I do gather)
Himself was to be wondered at or to be pitied rather.
He is enamoured of himself for want of taking heed;
And where he likes another thing, he likes himself indeed.
He is the party whom he woos, and suitor that doth woo;
He is the flame that sets on fire, and thing that burneth too.
O Lord, how often did he kiss that false, deceitful thing!
How often did he thrust his arms midway into the spring
To have embraced the neck he saw, and could not catch himself!
540 He knows not what it was he saw. And yet the foolish elf
Doth burn in ardent love thereof. The very selfsame thing
That doth bewitch and blind his eyes increaseth all his sting.
Thou fondling, thou, why dost thou raught the fickle image so?
The thing thou seekest is not there. And if aside thou go,
The thing thou lovest straight is gone. It is none other matter
That thou dost see than of thyself the shadow in the water.
The thing is nothing of itself. With thee it doth abide;
With thee it would depart if thou withdrew thyself aside.

No care of meat could draw him thence nor yet desire of rest
But, lying flat against the ground and leaning on his breast,     550
With greedy eyes he gazeth still upon the falsèd face;
And through his sight is wrought his bane. Yet for a little space
He turns and sets himself upright and, holding up his hands,
With piteous voice unto the wood that round about him stands
Cries out and says, 'Alas, ye woods, and was there ever any
That loved so cruelly as I? You know; for unto many
A place of harbour have you been and fort of refuge strong.
Can you remember anyone in all your time so long
That hath so pined away as I? I see and am full fain;
Howbeit, that I like and see I cannot yet attain,     560
So great a blindness in my heart through doting love doth reign!
And, for to spite me more withal, it is no journey far,
No drenching sea, no mountain high, no wall, no lock, no bar;
It is but even a little drop that keeps us two asunder.
He would be had. For look how oft I kiss the water under,
So oft again with upward mouth he riseth toward me.
A man would think to touch at least I should yet able be;
It is a trifle in respect that lets us of our love.
What wight so ever that thou art, come hither up above!
O peerless piece, why dost thou me, thy lover, thus delude?     570
Or whither fli'st thou, of thy friend thus earnestly pursued?
Iwis, I neither am so foul nor yet so grown in years
That in this wise thou should'st me shun. To have me to their
     feres
The nymphs themselves have sued ere this. And yet, as should
     appear,
Thou dost pretend some kind of hope of friendship by thy cheer.
For when I stretch mine arms to thee, thou stretchest thine
     likewise;
And if I smile, thou smilest too. And when that from mine eyes
The tears do drop, I well perceive the water stands in thine.
Like gesture also dost thou make to every beck of mine.
And, as by moving of thy sweet and lovely lips I ween,     580
Thou speakest words, although mine ears conceive not what they
     been.

It is myself, I well perceive! It is mine image sure
That, in this sort deluding me, this fury doth procure!
I am enamoured of myself; I do both set on fire
And am the same that swelteth too through impotent desire.
What shall I do? Be wooed or woo? Whom shall I woo therefore?
The thing I seek is in myself; my plenty makes me poor.
O would to God I for a while might from my body part!
This wish is strange to hear – a lover wrappèd all in smart
590   To wish away the thing the which he loveth as his heart!
My sorrow takes away my strength. I have not long to live
But in the flower of youth must die. To die it doth not grieve,
For that by death shall come the end of all my grief and pain.
I would this youngling whom I love might lenger life obtain,
For in one soul shall now decay we steadfast lovers twain.'
      This said, in rage he turns again unto the foresaid shade
      And rores the water with the tears and slobbering that he made,
      That through his troubling of the well his image gan to fade.
Which when he saw to vanish so, 'O whither dost thou fly?
600   Abide, I pray thee heartily,' aloud he gan to cry.
'Forsake me not so cruelly that loveth thee so dear,
But give me leave a little while my dazzled eyes to cheer
With sight of that which for to touch is utterly denied,
Thereby to feed my wretched rage and fury for a tide.'
As in this wise he made his moan, he strippèd off his coat
And with his fist outrageously his naked stomach smote.
A ruddy colour where he smote rose on his stomach sheer,
Like apples which do partly white and stripèd red appear
Or as the clusters, ere the grapes to ripeness fully come,
610   An orient purple here and there begins to grow on some.
Which things as soon as in the spring he did behold again,
He could no longer bear it out but, fainting straight for pain,
As lithe and supple wax doth melt against the burning flame
Or morning dew against the sun that glareth on the same,
Even so by piecemeal, being spent and wasted through desire,
Did he consume and melt away with Cupid's secret fire.
His lively hue of white and red, his cheerfulness and strength
And all the things that likèd him did wanze away at length,

So that in fine remainèd not the body which of late
The wretched Echo lovèd so. Who, when she saw his state,    620
Although in heart she angry were and mindful of his pride,
Yet ruing his unhappy case, as often as he cried,
'Alas!' she cried, 'Alas!' likewise with shirl redoubled sound.
And when he beat his breast or strake his feet against the ground
She made like noise of clapping too. These are the words that last
Out of his lips, beholding still his wonted image, passed:
'Alas, sweet boy, beloved in vain, farewell!' And by and by
With sighing sound the selfsame words the Echo did reply.
With that he laid his weary head against the grassy place,
And death did close his gazing eyes that wondered at the grace    630
And beauty which did late adorn their master's heavenly face.
And afterward, when into hell receivèd was his sprite,
He goes me to the well of Styx and there both day and night
Stands tooting on his shadow still as fondly as before.
The waternymphs, his sisters, wept and wailèd for him sore
And on his body strewed their hair clipped off and shorn
        therefore.
The woodnymphs also did lament, and Echo did rebound
To every sorrowful noise of theirs with like lamenting sound.
The fire was made to burn the corse and waxen tapers light;
A hearse to lay the body on with solemn pomp was dight.    640
But as for body, none remained. Instead thereof they found
A yellow flower with milk-white leaves new sprung upon the
        ground.
  This matter all Achaia through did spread the prophet's fame,    *Pentheus*
  That everywhere of just desert renownèd was his name.    *scorns*
But Penthey, old Echion's son, who proudly did disdain    *Bacchus*
Both god and man, did laugh to scorn the prophet's words as vain,
Upbraiding him most spitefully with losing of his sight
And with the fact for which he lost fruition of this light.
The good old father (for these words his patience much did move)
Said, 'O, how happy should'st thou be and blessed from above    650
If thou wert blind as well as I, so that thou might not see
The sacred rites of Bacchus' band! For sure the time will be,
And that full shortly, as I guess, that hither shall resort
Another Bacchus, Semel's son, whom if thou not support

With pomp and honour like a god, thy carcass shall be tattered
And in a thousand places eke about the woods be scattered.
And for to read thee what they are that shall perform the deed,
It is thy mother and thine aunts that thus shall make thee bleed.
I know it shall so come to pass, for why thou shalt disdain
660    To honour Bacchus as a god; and then thou shalt with pain
Feel how that, blinded as I am, I saw for thee too much.'
As old Tiresias did pronounce these words and other such,
Echion's son did trouble him. His words prove true indeed,
For, as the prophet did forespeak, so fell it out with speed.
Anon this new-found Bacchus comes. The woods and fields
        rebound
With noise of shouts and howling out and such confusèd sound.
The folk run flocking out by heaps, men, maids and wives
        together;
The noblemen and rascal sort ran gadding also thither
The orgies of this unknown god full fondly to perform.
670    The which when Penthey did perceive, he gan to rage and storm
    And said unto them, 'O ye imps of Mars his snake by kind,
    What aileth you? What fiend of hell doth thus enrage your
        mind?
Hath tinking sound of pots and pans, hath noise of crookèd horn,
Have fond illusions such a force that them whom heretoforn
No arming sword, no bloody trump, no men in battle ray
Could cause to shrink, now sheepish shrieks of simple women fray
And drunken woodness wrought by wine and routs of filthy frekes
And sound of toying tympans daunts and quite their courage
        breaks?
Shall I at you, ye ancient men which from the town of Tyre
680    To bring your household gods by sea in safety did aspire
And settled them within this place, the which ye now do yield
In bondage quite without all force and fighting in the field?
Or wonder at you younger sort, approaching unto me
More near in courage and in years, whom meet it were to see
With spear and not with thyrse in hand, with glittering helm on
        head
And not with leaves? Now call to mind of whom ye all are bred

And take the stomachs of that snake which, being one alone,
Right stoutly in his own defence confounded many one.
He for his harbour and his spring his life did nobly spend;
Do you no more but take a heart your country to defend.                690
He put to death right valiant knights; your battle is with such
As are but meacocks in effect. And yet ye do so much
In conquering them that by the deed the old renown ye save
Which from your fathers by descent this present time ye have.
If fatal Destinies do forbid that Thebe long shall stand,
Would God that men with cannon-shot might raze it out of hand!
Would God the noise of fire and sword did in our hearing sound,
For then in this our wretchedness there could no fault be found!
Then might we justly wail our case that all the world might see;
We should not need of shedding tears ashamèd for to be.                700
But now our town is taken by a naked beardless boy
Who doth not in the feats of arms nor horse nor armour joy,
But for to moist his hair with myrrh and put on garlands gay
And in soft purple silk and gold his body to array.
But put to you your helping hand, and straight without delay
I will compel him point by point his lewdness to bewray,
Both in usurping Jove's high name in making him his son
And forging of these ceremonies lately now begun.
Hath King Acrisius heart enough this fondling for to hate
That makes himself to be a god, and for to shut the gate             710
Of Argos at his coming there? And shall this rover make
King Penthey and the noble town of Thebe thus to quake?
Go quickly, sirs' – these words he spake unto his servants – 'Go
And bring the captain hither bound with speed. Why stay ye so?'
   His grandsire, Cadmus, Athamas and others of his kin
   Reprovèd him by gentle means, but nothing could they win.
The more entreatance that they made, the fiercer was he still;
The more his friends did go about to break him of his will,
The more they did provoke his wrath and set his rage on fire.
They made him worse in that they sought to bridle his desire.        720
So have I seen a brook ere this, where nothing let the stream,
Run smooth with little noise or none; but whereas any beam
Or craggèd stones did let his course and make him for to stay,
It went more fiercely from the stop with foamy wrath away.

Behold, all bloody come his men, and straight he them demanded
Where Bacchus was and why they had not done as he
        commanded.
'Sir,' answered they, 'we saw him not; but this same fellow here,
A chief companion in his train and worker in this gear,
We took by force,' and therewithal presented to their lord
730 A certain man of Tyrrhene land, his hands fast bound with cord
Whom they frequenting Bacchus' rites had found but late before.
A grim and cruel look, which ire did make to seem more sore,
Did Penthey cast upon the man. And though he scarcely stayed
From putting him to torments straight, 'O wretched man,' he said,
'Who by thy worthy death shalt be a sample unto other,
Declare to me the names of thee, thy father and thy mother,
And in what country thou wert born, and what hath causèd thee
Of these strange rites and sacrifice a follower for to be.'

*The story*     He, void of fear, made answer thus: 'Acoetes is my name.
*of Acoetes*     Of parents but of low degree in Lydy land I came.
No ground for painful ox to till, no sheep to bear me wool
My father left me; no, nor horse, nor ass, nor cow, nor bull.
God wot, he was but poor himself. With line and baited hook
The frisking fishes in the pools upon his reed he took.
His hands did serve instead of lands; his substance was his craft.
Now have I made you true account of all that he me left
As well of riches as of trades, in which I was his heir
And successor. For when that death bereft him use of air,
Save water he me nothing left. It is the thing alone
750 Which for my lawful heritage I claim, and other none.
Soon after, I (because that loath I was to aye abide
In that poor state) did learn a ship by cunning hand to guide
And for to know the rainy sign that hight th'Olenian Goat
Which with her milk did nourish Jove. And also I did note
The Pleiads and the Hyads moist and eke the silly Plough
With all the dwellings of the winds that make the seas so rough,
And eke such havens as are meet to harbour vessels in
With every star and heavenly sign that guides to shipmen been.
Now as by chance I late ago did toward Delos sail,
760 I came on coast of Scios Isle and, seeing day to fail,

Took harbour there and went a-land. As soon as that the night
Was spent and morning gan to peer with ruddy glaring light,
I rose and bade my company fresh water fetch aboard.
And, pointing them the way that led directly to the ford,
I went me to a little hill and viewèd round about
To see what weather we were like to have ere setting out.
Which done, I called my watermen and all my mates together
And willed them all to go aboard, myself first going thither.
"Lo, here we are!" Opheltes said (he was the master's mate)
And, as he thought, a booty found in desert fields alate,                     770
He dragged a boy upon his hand that for his beauty sheen
A maiden rather than a boy appearèd for to been.
This child, as one forlaid with wine and dreint with drowsy sleep,
Did reel as though he scarcely could himself from falling keep.
I marked his count'nance, weed and pace; no inkling could I see
By which I might conjecture him a mortal wight to be.
I thought, and to my fellows said, "What god I cannot tell,
But in this body that we see some godhead sure doth dwell.
What god so ever that thou art, thy favour to us show
And in our labours us assist and pardon these also."                          780
"Pray for thyself and not for us," quoth Dictys by and by.
(A nimbler fellow for to climb upon the mast on high
And by the cable down to slide there was not in our keel).
Swart Melanth, patron of the ship, did like his saying well;
So also did Alcimedon, and so did Libys too,
And black Epopeus eke, whose charge it did belong unto
To see the rowers at their times their duties duly do.
And so did all the rest of them; so sore men's eyes were blinded
Where covetousness of filthy gain is more than reason minded.
"Well, sirs," quoth I, "but by your leave ye shall not have it so;            790
I will not suffer sacrilege within this ship to go,
For I have here the most to do." And with that word I stepped
Upon the hatches, all the rest from entrance to have kept.
The rankest ruffian of the rout that Lycab had to name
(Who, for a murder being late driven out of Tuscan, came
To me for succour) waxèd wood and with his sturdy fist
Did give me such a churlish blow because I did resist

That overboard he had me sent, but that with much ado
I caught the tackling in my hand and held me fast thereto.
800   The wicked varlets had a sport to see me handled so.
Then Bacchus (for it Bacchus was), as though he had but tho
Been wakèd with their noise from sleep and that his drowsy brain,
Dischargèd of the wine, begun to gather sense again,
Said, "What ado? What noise is this? How came I here, I pray?
Sirs, tell me whither you do mean to carry me away."
"Fear not, my boy," the patron said. "No more but tell me where
Thou dost desire to go a-land, and we will set thee there."
"To Naxosward," quoth Bacchus tho, "set ship upon the foam.
There would I have harbour take, for Naxos is my home."
810   Like perjured caitiffs by the sea and all the gods thereof
They falsely sware it should be so, and therewithal in scoff
They bade me hoise up sail and go. Upon the righter hand
I cast about to fetch the wind, for so did Naxos stand.
"What mean'st? Art mad?" Opheltes cried, and therewithal begun
A fear of losing of their prey through every man to run.
The greater part with head and hand a sign did to me make,
And some did whisper in mine ear the left hand way to take.
I was amazed and said, "Take charge henceforth who will for me;
For of your craft and wickedness I will no furtherer be."
820   Then fell they to reviling me, and all the rout gan grudge,
Of which Aethalion said in scorn, "Belike in you, Sir Snudge,
Consists the safeguard of us all." And with that word he takes
My room and, leaving Naxos quite, to other countries makes.
The god then, dallying with these mates, as though he had at last
Begun to smell their subtle craft, out of the foredeck cast
His eye upon the sea; and then, as though he seemed to weep,
Said, "Sirs, to bring me on this coast ye do not promise keep.
I see that this is not the land the which I did request.
For what occasion in this sort deserve I to be dressed?
830   What commendation can you win or praise thereby receive
If men a lad, if many one ye compass to deceive?"
I wept and sobbèd all this while; the wicked villains laughed
And rowèd forth with might and main as though they had been
          straught.

Now even by him (for sure than he in all the world so wide
There is no god more near at hand at every time and tide)
I swear unto you that the things the which I shall declare,
Like as they seem incredible, even so most true they are.
The ship stood still amid the sea as in a dusty dock.
They, wondering at this miracle and making but a mock,
Persist in beating with their oars and on with all their sails;                840
To make their galley to remove no art nor labour fails.
But ivy troubled so their oars that forth they could not row,
And both with berries and with leaves their sails did overgrow.
And he himself with clustered grapes about his temple round
Did shake a javelin in his hand that round about was bound
With leaves of vines; and at his feet there seemèd for to couch
Of tigers, lynx and panthers shapes most ugly for to touch.
I cannot tell you whether fear or woodness were the cause,
But every person leapeth up and from his labour draws.
And there one Medon first of all began to waxen black                        850
And, having lost his former shape, did take a curbèd back.
"What monster shall we have of thee?" quoth Lycab. And with
        that
This Lycab's chaps did waxen wide, his nostrils waxèd flat,
His skin waxed tough and scales thereon began anon to grow.
And Libys, as he went about the oars away to throw,
Perceivèd how his hands did shrink and were become so short
That now for fins and not for hands he might them well report.
Another, as he would have clasped his arm about the cord,
Had ne'er an arm. And so, bemaimed in body, overboard
He leapeth down among the waves; and forkèd is his tail,                      860
As are the horns of Phoebe's face when half her light doth fail.
They leap about and sprinkle up much water on the ship;
One while they swim above, and down again anon they slip.
They fetch their frisks as in a dance, and wantonly they writhe
Now here, now there, among the waves their bodies bain and
        lithe.
And with their wide and hollow nose the water in they snuff,
And by their noses out again as fast they do it puff.
Of twenty persons (for our ship so many men did bear)
I only did remain, nigh straught and trembling still for fear.

870  The god could scarce recomfort me, and yet he said, "Go to,
Fear not, but sail to Diaward." His will I gladly do.
And so as soon as I came there, with right devout intent
His chaplain I became; and thus his orgies I frequent.'

*The death of
Pentheus*

'Thou mak'st a process very long', quoth Penthey, 'to th'intent
That, choler being cooled by time, mine anger might relent.
But, sirs' (he spake it to his men), 'go take him by and by;
With cruel torments out of hand go cause him for to die.'
Immediately they led away Acoetes out of sight
And put him into prison strong from which there was no flight.

880  But while the cruel instruments of death, as sword and fire,
Were in preparing wherewithal t'accomplish Penthey's ire,
It is reported that the doors did of their own accord
Burst open and his chains fall off. And yet this cruel lord
Persisteth fiercer than before, not bidding others go,
But goes himself unto the hill Cithaeron, which as tho,
To Bacchus being consecrate, did ring of chanted songs
And other loud confusèd sounds of Bacchus' drunken throngs.
And even as, when the bloody trump doth to the battle sound,
The lusty horse, straight neighing out, bestirs him on the ground

890  And taketh courage thereupon t'assail his enemy proud;
Even so, when Penthey heard afar the noise and howling loud
That Bacchus' frantic folk did make, it set his heart on fire
And kindled fiercer than before the sparks of settled ire.

There is a goodly plain about the middle of the hill,
Environed in with woods, where men may view each way at
will.
Here looking on these holy rites with lewd profanèd eyes
King Penthey's mother first of all her foresaid son espies,
And like a bedlam first of all she doth upon him run,
And with her javelin furiously she first doth wound her son.

900  'Come hither, sisters, come!' she cries, 'Here is that mighty boar;
Here is the boar that stroys our fields; him will I strike therefore.'
With that they fall upon him all as though they had been mad
And, clustering all upon a heap, fast after him they gad.
He quakes and shakes; his words are now become more meek and
cold;
He now condemns his own default and says he was too bold.

And, wounded as he was, he cries, 'Help, Aunt Autonoë!
Now for Actaeon's blessèd soul some mercy show to me!'
She wist not who Actaeon was, but rent without delay
His right hand off; and Ino tare his t'other hand away.
To lift unto his mother tho the wretch had ne'er an arm;                910
But, showing her his maimèd corse and wounds yet bleeding
    warm,
'O mother, see!' he says. With that Agave howleth out
And writhèd with her neck awry and shook her hair about
And, holding (from his body torn) his head in bloody hands,
She cries, 'O fellows, in this deed our noble conquest stands.'
No sooner could the wind have blown the rotten leaves fro trees
When winter's frost hath bitten them, than did the hands of these
Most wicked women Penthey's limbs from one another tear.
The Thebans, being now by this example brought in fear,
Frequent this new-found sacrifice and with sweet frankincense        920
God Bacchus' altars load with gifts in every place do cense.

FINIS TERTII LIBRI.

# The Fourth Book of Ovid's
## Metamorphoses

*The daughters*
*of Minyas*

Yet would not stout Alcithoë, Duke Minyas' daughter, bow
The orgies of this new-found god in conscience to allow.
But still she stiffly doth deny that Bacchus is the son
Of Jove; and in this heresy her sisters with her run.
The priest had bidden holiday, and that as well the maid
As mistress (for the time aside all other business laid)
In buckskin coats with tresses loose and garlands on their hair
Should in their hands the leafy spears surnamèd thyrses bear,
Foretelling them that, if they did the god's commandment break,
He would with sore and grievous plagues his wrath upon them
    wreak.                            10
The women straight, both young and old, do thereunto obey.
Their yarn, their baskets and their flax unspun aside they lay
And burn to Bacchus frankincense, whom solemnly they call
By all the names and titles high that may to him befall:
As Bromius and Lyaeus eke, begotten of the flame,
Twice born, the sole and only child that of two mothers came;
Unshorn Thyony, Nyseus, Lenaeus and the setter
Of vines whose pleasant liquor makes all tables fare the better;
Nyctelius and th'Elelean sire, Iacchus, Euhan eke,
With divers other glorious names that through the land of Greek   20
To thee, O Liber, wonted are to attributed be.
Thy youthful years can never waste; there dwelleth aye in thee
A childhood tender, fresh and fair. In heaven we do thee see
Surmounting every other thing in beauty and in grace;
And when thou stand'st without thy horns, thou hast a maiden's
    face.
To thee obeyeth all the east as far as Ganges goes,
Which doth the scorchèd land of Inde with tawny folk enclose.

Lycurgus with his twibill sharp and Penthey, who of pride
Thy godhead and thy mighty power rebelliously denied,
30   Thou, right redoubted, did'st confound; thou into sea did'st send
The Tyrrhene shipmen. Thou with bits the sturdy necks dost
          bend
Of spotted lynxes; throngs of frows and satyrs on thee tend,
And that old hag that with a staff his staggering limbs doth stay,
Scarce able on his ass to sit for reeling every way.
Thou comest not in any place but that is heard the noise
Of gaggling women's tattling tongues and shouting out of boys,
With sound of timbrels, tabors, pipes and brazen pans and pots
Confusèdly among the rout that in thine orgies trots.
The Theban women for thy grace and favour humbly sue
40   And, as the priest did bid, frequent thy rites with reverence due.
Alonely Minyas' daughters, bent of wilfulness with working
Quite out of time to break the feast, are in their houses lurking
And there do fall to spinning yarn or weaving in the frame
And keep their maidens to their work. Of which one pleasant
          dame,
As she with nimble hand did draw her slender thread and fine,
Said, 'While that others idly do serve the god of wine,
Let us that serve a better saint, Minerva, find some talk
To ease our labour while our hands about our profit walk.
And for to make the time seem short, let each of us recite
50   (As everybody's turn shall come) some tale that may delight.'
Her saying liked the rest so well that all consent therein,
And thereupon they pray that first the eldest would begin.
She had such store and choice of tales she wist not which to tell.
She doubted if she might declare the fortune that befell
To Dercetis of Babylon, whom now with scaly hide
In altered shape the Philistine believeth to abide
In watery pools; or rather how her daughter, taking wings,
In shape of dove on tops of towers in age now sadly sings;
Or how a certain waternymph by witchcraft and by charms
60   Converted into fishes dumb of young men many swarms
Until that of the selfsame sauce herself did taste at last;
Or how the tree that used to bear fruit white in ages past

Doth now bear fruit in manner black, by sprinkling up of blood.
This tale, because it was not stale nor common, seemèd good
To her to tell; and thereupon she in this wise begun,
Her busy hand still drawing out the flaxen thread she spun:
   'Within the town of whose huge walls so monstrous high and    *Pyramus and*
       thick                                                                 *Thisbe*
The fame is given Semiramis for making them of brick,
Dwelt hard together two young folk in houses joined so near
That under all one roof well nigh both twain conveyèd were.        70
The name of him was Pyramus, and Thisbe called was she.
So fair a man in all the east was none alive as he,
Nor ne'er a woman, maid nor wife in beauty like to her.
This neighbourhood bred acquaintance first; this neighbourhood
       first did stir
The secret sparks; this neighbourhood first an entrance in did
       show
For love to come to that to which it afterward did grow.
And if that right had taken place they had been man and wife,
But still their parents went about to let which for their life
They could not let; for both their hearts with equal flame did
       burn.
No man was privy to their thoughts and, for to serve their turn,    80
Instead of talk they usèd signs. The closelier they suppressed
The fire of love, the fiercer still it ragèd in their breast.
The wall that parted house from house had riven therein a cranny
Which shrunk at making of the wall. This fault, not marked of any
Of many hundred years before (what doth not love espy?),
These lovers first of all found out and made a way whereby
To talk together secretly; and through the same did go
Their loving whisperings very light and safely to and fro.
Now as at one side Pyramus and Thisbe on the t'other
Stood often drawing one of them the pleasant breath from other,    90
"O thou envious wall," they said, "why let'st thou lovers thus?
What matter were it if that thou permitted both of us
In arms each other to embrace? Or if thou think that this
Were overmuch, yet mightest thou at least make room to kiss.
And yet thou shalt not find us churls; we think ourselves in debt
For this same piece of courtesy in vouching safe to let

Our sayings to our friendly ears thus freely come and go."
Thus having where they stood in vain complainèd of their woe,
When night drew near they bade adieu and each gave kisses sweet
100  Unto the parget on their side, the which did never meet.
Next morning with her cheerful light had driven the stars aside,
And Phoebus with his burning beams the dewy grass had dried.
These lovers at their wonted place by fore-appointment met
Where, after much complaint and moan, they covenanted to get
Away from such as watchèd them and in the evening late
To steal out of their fathers' house and eke the city gate.
And to th'intent that in the fields they strayed not up and down,
They did agree at Ninus' tomb to meet without the town
And tarry underneath a tree that by the same did grow,
110  Which was a fair high mulberry with fruit as white as snow
Hard by a cool and trickling spring. This bargain pleased them
          both.
And so daylight, which to their thought away but slowly go'th,
Did in the ocean fall to rest; and night from thence doth rise.
As soon as darkness once was come, straight Thisbe did devise
A shift to wind her out of doors, that none that were within
Perceivèd her. And, muffling her with clothes about her chin
That no man might discern her face, to Ninus' tomb she came
Unto that tree and sat her down there underneath the same.
Love made her bold. But see the chance: there comes besmeared
          with blood
120  About the chaps a lioness all foaming from the wood
From slaughter lately made of kine, to staunch her bloody thirst
With water of the foresaid spring. Whom Thisbe spying first
Afar by moonlight, thereupon with fearful steps gan fly
And in a dark and irksome cave did hide herself thereby.
And as she fled away for haste, she let her mantle fall,
The which for fear she left behind, not looking back at all.
Now when the cruel lioness her thirst had staunchèd well,
In going to the wood she found the slender weed that fell
From Thisbe, which with bloody teeth in pieces she did tear.
130  The night was somewhat further spent ere Pyramus came there;
Who, seeing in the subtle sand the print of lion's paw,
Waxed pale for fear. But when also the bloody cloak he saw

All rent and torn, "One night", he said, "shall lovers two
    confound,
Of which long life deservèd she of all that live on ground.
My soul deserves of this mischance the peril for to bear;
I, wretch, have been the death of thee, which to this place of fear
Did cause thee in the night to come and came not here before.
My wicked limbs and wretched guts with cruel teeth therefore
Devour ye, O ye lions all that in this rock do dwell!
But cowards use to wish for death." The slender weed that fell    140
From Thisbe up he takes and straight doth bear it to the tree
Which was appointed erst the place of meeting for to be.
And when he had bewept and kissed the garment which he knew,
"Receive thou my blood too," quoth he. And therewithal he
    drew
His sword, the which among his guts he thrust, and by and by
Did draw it from the bleeding wound, beginning for to die,
And cast himself upon his back. The blood did spin on high
As, when a conduit pipe is cracked, the water, bursting out,
Doth shoot itself a great way off and pierce the air about.
The leaves that were upon the tree, besprinkled with his blood,    150
Were dyèd black. The root also, bestainèd as it stood,
A deep dark purple colour straight upon the berries cast.
Anon, scarce ridded of her fear with which she was aghast,
For doubt of disappointing him comes Thisbe forth in haste
And for her lover looks about, rejoicing for to tell
How hardly she had scaped that night the danger that befell.
And as she knew right well the place and fashion of the tree
(As which she saw so late before), even so when she did see
The colour of the berries turned, she was uncertain whether
It were the tree at which they both agreed to meet together.    160
While in this doubtful stound she stood, she cast her eye aside
And there beweltered in his blood her lover she espied
Lie sprawling with his dying limbs. At which she started back
And lookèd pale as any box; a shuddering through her strake,
Even like the sea which suddenly with whizzing noise doth move
When with a little blast of wind it is but touched above.
But when, approaching nearer him, she knew it was her love,

She beat her breast, she shriekèd out, she tare her golden hairs
And, taking him between her arms, did wash his wounds with
     tears.
170  She ment her weeping with his blood and, kissing all his face
(Which now became as cold as ice), she cried in woeful case,
"Alas! What chance, my Pyramus, hath parted thee and me?
Make answer, O my Pyramus! It is thy Thisb, even she
Whom thou dost love most heartily that speaketh unto thee.
Give ear and raise thy heavy head." He, hearing Thisbe's name,
Lift up his dying eyes and, having seen her, closed the same.
But when she knew her mantle there and saw his scabbard lie
Without the sword, "Unhappy man, thy love hath made thee die.
Thy love", she said, "hath made thee slay thyself. This hand of
     mine
180  Is strong enough to do the like. My love no less than thine
Shall give me force to work my wound. I will pursue the dead
And, wretched woman as I am, it shall of me be said
That like as of thy death I was the only cause and blame,
So am I thy companion eke and partner in the same.
For death which only could, alas, asunder part us twain
Shall never so dissever us but we will meet again.
And you, the parents of us both, most wretched folk alive,
Let this request that I shall make in both our names belive
Entreat you to permit that we, whom chaste and steadfast love
190  And whom even death hath joined in one, may as it doth behove
In one grave be together laid. And thou, unhappy tree,
Which shroudest now the corse of one and shalt anon through me
Shroud two, of this same slaughter hold the sicker signs for aye:
Black be the colour of thy fruit and mourning-like alway,
Such as the murder of us twain may evermore bewray."
This said, she took the sword yet warm with slaughter of her love
And, setting it beneath her breast, did to her heart it shove.
Her prayer with the gods and with their parents took effect.
For when the fruit is throughly ripe, the berry is bespecked
200  With colour tending to a black; and that which after fire
·Remainèd rested in one tomb, as Thisbe did desire.'

*Venus and*
*Mars*
      This tale thus told, a little space of pausing was betwixt
      And then began Leuconoe thus, her sisters being whist:

'This sun that with his streaming light all worldly things doth
    cheer
Was ta'en in love. Of Phoebus' loves now list and you shall hear.
It is reported that this god did first of all espy
(For everything in heaven and earth is open to his eye)
How Venus with the warlike Mars advoutery did commit.
It grievèd him to see the fact and so discovered it.
He showed her husband, Juno's son, th'advoutery and the place    210
In which this privy scape was done; who was in such a case
That heart and hand and all did fail in working for a space.
Anon he featly forged a net of wire so fine and slight
That neither knot nor noose therein apparent was to sight.
This piece of work was much more fine than any handwarp woof
Or that whereby the spider hangs in sliding from the roof;
And, furthermore, the subtleness and sleight thereof was such,
It followed every little pull and closed with every touch.
And so he set it handsomely about the haunted couch.
Now when that Venus and her mate were met in bed together,    220
Her husband by his new-found snare, before conveyèd thither,
Did snarl them both together fast in midst of all their play
And, setting ope the ivory doors, called all the gods straightway
To see them. They with shame enough fast locked together lay.
A certain god among the rest, disposèd for to sport,
Did wish that he himself also were shamèd in that sort;
The residue laughed. And so in heaven there was no talk awhile
But of this pageant, how the smith the lovers did beguile.

*Phoebus and
Leucothoë*

   'Dame Venus, highly stomaching this great displeasure, thought
To be revengèd on the part by whom the spite was wrought.    230
And like as he her secret loves and meetings had bewrayed,
So she with wound of raging love his guerdon to him paid.
What now avails, Hyperion's son, thy form and beauty bright?
What now avail thy glistering eyes with clear and piercing sight?
For thou that with thy gleams art wont all countries for to burn
Art burnt thyself with other gleams that serve not for thy turn.
And thou that ought'st thy cheerful look on all things for to show
Alonely on Leucothoë dost now the same bestow.
Thou fast'nest on that maid alone the eyes that thou dost owe

240   To all the world. Sometime more rathe thou risest in the east;
     Sometime again thou mak'st it late before thou fall to rest.
     And for desire to look on her, thou often dost prolong
     Our winter nights, and in thy light thou failest eke among.
     The fancy of thy faulty mind infects thy feeble sight,
     And so thou mak'st men's hearts afraid by daunting of thy light.
     Thou look'st not pale because the globe of Phoebe is between
     The earth and thee, but love doth cause this colour to be seen.
     Thou lovest this Leucothoë so far above all other
     That neither now for Clymene, for Rhodos, nor the mother
250   Of Circe, nor for Clytië (who at that present tide,
     Rejected from thy company, did for thy love abide
     Most grievous torments in her heart) thou seemest for to care.
     Thou mindest her so much that all the rest forgotten are.
     Her mother was Eurynome, of all the fragrant clime
     Of Araby esteemed the flower of beauty in her time.
     But when her daughter came to age, the daughter passed the
          mother
     As far in beauty as before the mother passed all other.
     Her father was King Orchamus and ruled the public weal
     Of Persey, counted by descent the seventh from ancient Bele.
260   Far underneath the western clime of Hesperus do run
     The pastures of the fiery steeds that draw the golden sun.
     There are they fed with ambrosy instead of grass all night,
     Which doth refresh their weary limbs and keepeth them in plight
     To bear their daily labour out. Now while the steeds there take
     Their heavenly food and night by turn his timely course doth
          make,
     The god, disguisèd in the shape of Queen Eurynome,
     Doth press within the chamber door of fair Leucothoë,
     His lover, whom amid twelve maids he found by candlelight
     Yet spinning on her little rock, and went me to her right
270   And, kissing her as mothers use to kiss their daughters dear,
     Said, "Maids, withdraw youselves a while and sit not listening
          here.
     I have a secret thing to talk." The maids avoid each one.
     The god then, being with his love in chamber all alone,

Said, "I am he that metes the year, that all things do behold,
By whom the earth doth all things see, the eye of all the world.
Trust me, I am in love with thee." The lady was so nipped
With sudden fear that from her hands both rock and spindle
    slipped.
Her fear became her wondrous well. He made no mo delays
But turnèd to his proper shape and took his glistering rays.
The damsel, being sore abashed at this so strange a sight        280
And overcome with sudden fear to see the god so bright,
Did make no outcry nor no noise, but held her patience still
And suffered him by forcèd power his pleasure to fulfil.
   'Hereat did Clytie sore repine, for she beyond all measure
   Was then enamoured of the sun. And stung with this
      displeasure
That he another leman had, for very spite and ire
She plays the blab and doth defame Leucothoe to her sire.
He, cruel and unmerciful, would no excuse accept,
But holding up her hands to heaven when tenderly she wept
And said it was the sun that did the deed against her will,      290
Yet like a savage beast full bent his daughter for to spill
He put her deep in delvèd ground and on her body laid
A huge great heap of heavy sand. The sun, full ill apaid,
Did with his beams disperse the sand and made an open way
To bring thy buried face to light; but such a weight there lay
Upon thee that thou could'st not raise thine hand aloft again,
And so a corse both void of blood and life thou did'st remain.
There never chanced since Phaeton's fire a thing that grieved so
      sore
The ruler of the wingèd steeds as this did. And therefore
He did attempt if by the force and virtue of his ray      300
He might again to lively heat her frozen limbs convey.
But for as much as destiny so great attempts denies,
He sprinkles both the corse itself and place wherein it lies
With fragrant nectar and therewith, bewailing much his chance,
Said, "Yet above the starry sky thou shalt thyself advance."
Anon the body, in this heavenly liquor steepèd well,
Did melt and moisted all the earth with sweet and pleasant smell.

And by and by, first taking root among the clods within,
By little and by little did with growing top begin
A pretty spirk of frankincense above the tomb to win.

*The
transformation
of Clytie*

'Although that Clytie might excuse her sorrow by her love
And seem that so to play the blab her sorrow did her move,
Yet would the author of the light resort to her no more,
But did withhold the pleasant sports of Venus used before.
The nymph, not able of herself the frantic fume to stay,
With restless care and pensiveness did pine herself away.
Bare-headed, on the bare, cold ground with flaring hair unkempt
She sat abroad both night and day and clearly did exempt
Herself by space of thrice three days from sustenance and repast,
Save only dew and save her tears with which she brake her fast.
And in that while she never rose, but starèd on the sun
And ever turned her face to his as he his course did run.
Her limbs stack fast within the ground, and all her upper part
Did to a pale ash-coloured herb clean void of blood convert,
The flower whereof, part red, part white, beshadowed with a
            blue,
Most like a violet in the shape, her count'nance overgrew.
And now, though fastened with a root, she turns her to the sun
And keeps in shape of herb the love with which she first begun.'

She made an end; and at her tale all wondered. Some denied
Her saying to be possible, and other some replied
That such as are indeed true gods may all things work at will,
But Bacchus is not any such. This arguing once made still,
To tell her tale as others had Alcithoe's turn was come
Who, with her shuttle shooting through her web within the
            loom,
Said, 'Of the shepherd Daphnis' love of Ida, whom erewhile
A jealous nymph, because he did with lemans her beguile,
For anger turnèd to a stone (such fury love doth send!),
I will not speak; it is to know. Ne yet I do intend
To tell how Scithon, variably digressing from his kind,
Was sometime woman, sometime man, as likèd best his mind.
And Celmis also will I pass, who for because he clung
Most faithfully to Jupiter when Jupiter was young

Is now become an adamant. So will I pass this hour
To show you how the Curets were engendered of a shower;
Or how that Crocus and his love, fair Smilax, turnèd were
To little flowers. With pleasant news your minds now will I cheer.
Learn why the fountain Salmacis diffamèd is of yore,
Why with his waters overstrong it weakeneth men so sore
That whoso bathes him there comes thence a perfect man no
     more.
The operation of this well is known to every wight,          350
But few can tell the cause thereof, the which I will recite.
   'The waternymphs did nurse a son of Mercury's in Ide    *Salmacis and*
   Begot on Venus, in whose face such beauty did abide    *Hermaphroditus*
As well therein his father both and mother might be known,
Of whom he also took his name. As soon as he was grown
To fifteen years of age, he left the country where he dwelt
And Ida that had fostered him. The pleasure that he felt
To travel countries and to see strange rivers with the state
Of foreign lands all painfulness of travel did abate.
Through Lycy land he travellèd to Cary, that doth bound     360
Next unto Lycia. There he saw a pool which to the ground
Was crystal clear. No fenny sedge, no barren reek, no reed
Nor rush with pricking point was there, nor other moorish weed.
The water was so pure and sheer, a man might well have seen
And numbered all the gravel stones that in the bottom been.
The utmost borders from the brim environed were with clowres
Beclad with herbs aye fresh and green and pleasant smelling
     flowers.
A nymph did haunt this goodly pool, but such a nymph as neither
To hunt, to run, nor yet to shoot had any kind of pleasure.
Of all the waterfairies she alonely was unknown         370
To swift Diana. As the bruit of fame abroad hath blown,
Her sisters oftentimes would say, "Take lightsome dart or bow
And in some painful exercise thine idle time bestow."
But never could they her persuade to run, to shoot or hunt
Or any other exercise, as Phoebe's knights are wont.
Sometime her fair, well-formèd limbs she batheth in her spring;
Sometime she down her golden hair with boxen comb doth
     bring.

And at the water as a glass she taketh counsel aye
How everything becometh her. Erewhile in fine array
380   On soft sweet herbs or soft green leaves herself she nicely lays;
Erewhile again a-gathering flowers from place to place she strays.
And, as it chanced, the selfsame time she was a-sorting gays
To make a posy when she first the young man did espy
And, in beholding him, desired to have his company.
But though she thought she stood on thorns until she went to
   him,
Yet went she not before she had bedecked her neat and trim
And pried and peered upon her clothes that nothing sat awry
And framed her count'nance as might seem most amorous to the
   eye.
 'Which done, she thus begun: "O child most worthy for to be
390   Esteemed and taken for a god, if (as thou seem'st to me)
Thou be a god, to Cupid's name thy beauty doth agree.
Or if thou be a mortal wight, right happy folk are they
By whom thou cam'st into this world; right happy is, I say,
Thy mother and thy sister too, if any be; good hap
That woman had that was thy nurse and gave thy mouth her pap.
But far above all other, far more blest than these is she
Whom thou vouchsafest for thy wife and bedfellow for to be.
Now, if thou have already one, let me by stealth obtain
That which shall pleasure both of us. Or if thou do remain
400   A maiden free from wedlock bond, let me then be thy spouse
And let us in the bridely bed ourselves together rouse."
 'This said, the nymph did hold her peace, and therewithal the
   boy
Waxed red; he wist not what love was. And sure it was a joy
To see it, how exceeding well his blushing him became.
For in his face the colour fresh appearèd like the same
That is in apples which do hang upon the sunny side;
Or ivory shadowed with a red; or such as is espied
Of white and scarlet colours mixed appearing in the moon
When folk in vain with sounding brass would ease unto her doon.
410   When at the last the nymph desired most instantly but this,
As to his sister brotherly to give her there a kiss,

And therewithal was clasping him about the ivory neck,
"Leave off", quoth he, "or I am gone and leave thee at a beck
With all thy tricks." Then Salmacis began to be afraid
And, "To your pleasure leave I free this place, my friend," she
    said.
With that she turns her back as though she would have gone her
    way;
But evermore she looketh back and, closely as she may,
She hides her in a bushy queach where, kneeling on her knee,
She always hath her eye on him. He, as a child and free
And thinking not that any wight had watchèd what he did,                420
Roams up and down the pleasant mead. And by and by amid
The flattering waves he dips his feet, no more but first the sole,
And to the ankles afterward both feet he plungeth whole.
And, for to make the matter short, he took so great delight
In coolness of the pleasant spring that straight he strippèd quite
His garments from his tender skin. When Salmacis beheld
His naked beauty, such strong pangs so ardently her held
That utterly she was astraught; and even as Phoebus' beams
Against a mirror pure and clear rebound with broken gleams,
Even so her eyes did sparkle fire. Scarce could she tarriance make;    430
Scarce could she any time delay her pleasure for to take.
She would have run and in her arms embracèd him straightway;
She was so far beside herself that scarcely could she stay.
He, clapping with his hollow hands against his naked sides,
Into the water lithe and bain with arms displayèd glides
And, rowing with his hands and legs, swims in the water clear
Through which his body fair and white doth glisteringly appear,
As if a man an ivory image or a lily white
Should overlay or close with glass that were most pure and bright.
  "The prize is won," cried Salmacis aloud; "he is mine own."         440
  And therewithal in all post haste she, having lightly thrown
Her garments off, flew to the pool and cast her thereinto
And caught him fast between her arms for aught that he could do.
Yea, maugre all his wrestling and his struggling to and fro,
She held him still and kissèd him a hundred times and mo

And, willed he, nilled he, with her hands she touched his naked
        breast.
And now on this side, now on that, for all he did resist
And strive to wrest him from her gripes, she clung unto him fast
And wound about him like a snake which, snatchèd up in haste
450    And being by the prince of birds borne lightly up aloft,
Doth writhe herself about his neck and griping talons oft
And cast her tail about his wings displayèd in the wind;
Or like as ivy runs on trees about the utter rind;
Or as the crabfish, having caught his enemy in the seas,
Doth clasp him in on every side with all his crookèd clees.
    'But Atlas' nephew still persists and utterly denies
    The nymph to have her hopèd sport; she urges him likewise
And, pressing him with all her weight, fast cleaving to him still,
"Strive, struggle, wrest and writhe," she said, "thou froward boy,
        thy fill;
Do what thou canst, thou shalt not scape. Ye gods of heaven,
460        agree
That this same wilful boy and I may never parted be."
The gods were pliant to her boon. The bodies of them twain
Were mixed and joinèd both in one; to both them did remain
One count'nance. Like as if a man should in one bark behold
Two twigs both growing into one and still together hold,
Even so, when through her hugging and her grasping of the
        t'other
The members of them mingled were and fastened both together,
They were not any lenger two but, as it were, a toy
Of double shape. Ye could not say it was a perfect boy
470    Nor perfect wench; it seemèd both and none of both to been.
Now when Hermaphroditus saw how in the water sheen,
To which he entered in a man, his limbs were weakened so
That out fro thence but half a man he was compelled to go,
He lifteth up his hands and said (but not with manly rere),
"O noble father Mercury and Venus mother dear,
This one petition grant your son which both your names doth
        bear,
That whoso comes within this well may so be weakened there

That of a man but half a man he may fro thence retire."
Both parents, movèd with the chance, did stablish this desire
The which their double-shapèd son had made, and thereupon          480
Infected with an unknown strength the sacred spring anon.'
    Their tales did end, and Minyas' daughters still their business ply
    In spite of Bacchus, whose high feast they break
        contemptuously,
When on the sudden, seeing nought, they heard about them
        round
Of tubbish timbrels perfectly a hoarse and jarring sound
With shreaming shawms and jingling bells; and furthermore they
        felt
A scent of saffron and of myrrh that very hotly smelt.
And (which a man would ill believe) the web they had begun
Immediately waxed fresh and green; the flax the which they spun
Did flourish full of ivy leaves, and part thereof did run          490
Abroad in vines. The thread itself in branches forth did spring;
Young burgeons full of clustered grapes their distaffs forth did
        bring.
And as the web they wrought was dyed a deep dark purple hue,
Even so upon the painted grapes the self same colour grew.
The day was spent, and now was come the time which neither
        night
Nor day, but even the bound of both a man may term of right.
The house at sudden seemed to shake, and all about it shine
With burning lamps, and glittering fires to flash before their eyen,
And likenesses of ugly beasts with ghastful noises yelled.
For fear whereof in smoky holes the sisters were compelled          500
To hide their heads, one here and there another, for to shun
The glistering light. And while they thus in corners blindly run,
Upon their little pretty limbs a fine crisp film there goes,
And slender fins instead of hands their shortened arms enclose.
But how they lost their former shape, of certainty to know
The darkness would not suffer them. No feathers on them grow,
And yet with sheer and vellum wings they hover from the ground.
And when they go about to speak they make but little sound,
According as their bodies give, bewailing their despite
By chirping shrilly to themselves. In houses they delight          510

*The
transformation
of Minyas'
daughters*

And not in woods. Detesting day, they flitter towards night;
Wherethrough they of the evening late in Latin take their name,
And we in English language bats or rearmice call the same.

Juno visits
the Furies

Then Bacchus' name was reverenced through all the Theban
    coast,
And Ino of her nephew's power made everywhere great boast.
Of Cadmus' daughters she alone no sorrows tasted had,
Save only that her sisters' haps perchance had made her sad.
Now Juno, noting how she waxed both proud and full of scorn,
As well by reason of the sons and daughters she had borne
520 As also that she was advanced by marriage in that town
To Athamas, King Aeolus' son, a prince of great renown,
But chiefly that her sister's son who nursèd was by her
Was then exalted for a god, began thereat to stir
And, fretting at it in herself, said, 'Could this harlot's burd
Transform the Lydian watermen and drown them in the ford?
And make the mother tear the guts in pieces of her son?
And Minyas' all three daughters clad with wings, because they
    spun
Whiles others, howling, up and down like frantic folk did run?
And can I, Juno, nothing else save sundry woes bewail?
530 Is that sufficient? Can my power no more than so avail?
He teaches me what way to work. A man may take, I see,
Example at his enemy's hand the wiser for to be.
He shows enough and overmuch the force of furious wrath
By Penthey's death. Why should not Ine be taught to tread the
    path
The which her sisters heretofore and kindred trodden hath?'
   There is a steep and irksome way, obscure with shadow fell
   Of baleful yew, all sad and still, that leadeth down to hell.
The foggy Styx doth breathe up mists, and down this way do
    wave
The ghosts of persons lately dead and buried in the grave.
540 Continual cold and ghastly fear possess this queachy plot
On either side; the silly ghost, new parted, knoweth not
The way that doth directly lead him to the Stygian city
Or where black Pluto keeps his court that never showeth pity.

A thousand ways, a thousand gates that always open stand
This city hath. And as the sea the streams of all the land
Doth swallow in his greedy gulf and yet is never full,
Even so that place devoureth still and hideth in his gull
The souls and ghosts of all the world. And though that ne'er so
    many
Come thither, yet the place is void as if there were not any.
The ghosts, without flesh, blood or bones, there wander to and
    fro,                                    550
Of which some haunt the judgement place; and other come and
    go
To Pluto's court; and some frequent the former trades and arts
The which they used in their life; and some abide the smarts
And torments for their wickedness and other ill deserts.
  So cruel hate and spiteful wrath did boil in Juno's breast
  That in the high and noble court of heaven she could not rest,
But that she needs must hither come; whose feet no sooner
    touched
The threshold but it gan to quake, and Cerberus, erst couched,
Start sternly up with three fell heads which barkèd all together.
She called the daughters of the night, the cruel Furies, thither.    560
They sat a-kembing foul black snakes from off their filthy hair
Before the dungeon door, the place where caitiffs punished were,
The which was made of adamant. When in the dark in part
They knew Queen Juno, by and by upon their feet they start.
There Tityus, stretchèd out at least nine acres full in length,
Did with his bowels feed a gripe that tare them out by strength.
The water fled from Tantalus that touched his nether lip,
And apples hanging over him did ever from him slip.
There also laboured Sisyphus that drave against the hill
A rolling stone that from the top came tumbling downward still.    570
Ixion on his restless wheel, to which his limbs were bound,
Did fly and follow both at once in turning ever round.
And Danaus' daughters, for because they did their cousins kill,
Drew water into running tubs which evermore did spill.
  When Juno with a lowering look had viewed them all
    throughout
  And on Ixion specially before the other rout,

She turns from him to Sisyphus and with an angry cheer
Says, 'Wherefore should this man endure continual penance here
And Athamas, his brother, reign in wealth and pleasure free,
Who through his pride hath aye disdained my husband, Jove, and
580                 me?'
And therewithal she pourèd out th'occasion of her hate
And why she came and what she would. She would that Cadmus'
                 state
Should with the ruin of his house be brought to swift decay,
And that to mischief Athamas the fiends should force some way.
She bids, she prays, she promises – and all is with a breath –
And moves the Furies earnestly. And as these things she saith,
The hateful hag Tisiphone with hoary ruffled hair,
Removing from her face the snakes that loosely dangled there,
Said thus: 'Madam, there is no need long circumstance to make.
590  Suppose your will already done. This loathsome place forsake
And to the wholesome air of heaven yourself again retire.'
Queen Juno went right glad away with grant of her desire;
And as she would have entered heaven, the Lady Iris came
And purgèd her with streaming drops. Anon upon the same
The furious fiend Tisiphone doth clothe her out of hand
In garment streaming gory blood and taketh in her hand
A burning cresset steeped in blood and girdeth her about
With wreathèd snakes, and so goes forth. And at her going out
Fear, Terror, Grief and Pensiveness for company she took,
600  And also Madness with his slight and ghastly staring look.

*Ino and*         Within the house of Athamas no sooner foot she set
*Athamas*         But that the posts began to quake and doors look black as jet;
The sun withdrew him. Athamas and eke his wife were cast
With ugly sights in such a fear that out of doors aghast
They would have fled. There stood the fiend and stopped their
                 passage out
And, splaying forth her filthy arms beknit with snakes about,
Did toss and wave her hateful head. The swarm of scalèd snakes
Did make an irksome noise to hear as she her tresses shakes.
About her shoulders some did crawl; some, trailing down her
                 breast,
610  Did hiss and spit out poison green and spurt with tongues infest.

Then from amid her hair two snakes with venomed hand she
    drew,
  Of which she one at Athamas and one at Ino threw.
The snakes did crawl about their breasts, inspiring in their heart
Most grievous motions of the mind. The body had no smart
Of any wound; it was the mind that felt the cruel stings.
A poison made in syrup wise she also with her brings:
The filthy foam of Cerberus, the casting of the snake
Echidna bred among the fens about the Stygian lake,
Desire of gadding forth abroad, forgetfulness of mind,
Delight in mischief, woodness, tears, and purpose whole inclined    620
To cruel murder; all the which she did together grind
And, mingling them with new-shed blood, had boilèd them in
    brass
And stirred them with a hemlock stalk. Now while that Athamas
And Ino stood and quaked for fear, this poison rank and fell
She turnèd into both their breasts and made their hearts to swell.
Then, whisking often round about her head her baleful brand,
She made it soon by gathering wind to kindle in her hand.
Thus as it were in triumph wise accomplishing her hest,
To dusky Pluto's empty realm she gets her home to rest
And putteth off the snarlèd snakes that girded in her breast.    630
  Immediately King Aeolus' son, stark mad, comes crying out
    Through all the court, 'What mean ye, sirs? Why go ye not
      about
To pitch our toils within this chase? I saw even now here ran
A lion with her two young whelps.' And therewithal he gan
To chase his wife as if indeed she had a lion been.
And like a bedlam boisterously he snatcheth from between
The mother's arms his little babe, Learchus, smiling on him
And reaching forth his pretty arms, and flung him fiercely from
    him
A twice or thrice as from a sling, and dashed his tender head
Against a hard and rugged stone until he saw him dead.    640
The wretched mother (whether grief did move her thereunto
Or that the poison spread within did force her so to do)
Howled out and frantically, with scattered hair about her ears
And with her little Melicert whom hastily she bears

In naked arms, she crieth out, 'Ho, Bacchus!' At the name
Of Bacchus Juno gan to laugh and, scorning, said in game,
'This guerdon, lo, thy foster-child requiteth for the same.'
There hangs a rock about the sea, the foot whereof is eat
So hollow with the saltish waves which on the same do beat
650   That like a house it keepeth off the moisting showers of rain;
The top is rough and shoots his front amidst the open main.
Dame Ino – madness made her strong – did climb this cliff anon
And headlong down, without regard of hurt that hung thereon,
Did throw her burden and herself. The water where she dashed
In sprinkling upward glistered red. But Venus, sore abashed
At this her niece's great mischance without offence or fault,
Her uncle gently thus bespake: 'O ruler of the haught
And swelling seas, O noble Neptune, whose dominion large
Extendeth to the heaven whereof the mighty Jove hath charge,
660   The thing is great for which I sue; but show thou for my sake
Some mercy on my wretched friends whom in thine endless lake
Thou seest tossèd to and fro. Admit thou them among
Thy gods. Of right even here to me some favour doth belong,
At least wise if amid the sea engendered erst I were
Of froth, as of the which yet still my pleasant name I bear.'
Neptunus granted her request and by and by bereft them
Of all that ever mortal was, instead whereof he left them
A haught and stately majesty; and, altering them in hue,
With shape and names most meet for gods he did them both
              endue.
670   Leucothoe was the mother's name; Palaemon was the son.
    The Theban ladies, following her as fast as they could run,
    Did of her feet perceive the print upon the utter stone.
And, taking it for certain sign that both were dead and gone,
In making moan for Cadmus' house they wrang their hands and
              tare
Their hair and rent their clothes and railed on Juno out of square
As nothing just, but more outrageous far than did behove
In so revenging of herself upon her husband's love.
The goddess Juno could not bear their railing and, 'In faith,
You also will I make to be as witnesses', she saith,

'Of my outrageous cruelty.' And so she did indeed.                          680
For she that lovèd Ino best was following her with speed
Into the sea; but as she would herself have downward cast,
She could not stir, but to the rock, as nailèd, stickèd fast.
The second, as she knocked her breast, did feel her arms wax stiff.
Another, as she stretchèd out her hands upon the cliff,
Was made a stone and there stood still, aye stretching forth her
          hands
Into the water as before. And as another stands
A-tearing of her ruffled locks, her fingers hardened were
And fastened to her frizzled top, still tearing of her hair.
And look, what gesture each of them was taken in that tide,        690
Even in the same, transformed to stones, they fastened did abide.
And some were altered into birds which Cadmies callèd be
And in that gulf with flittering wings still to and fro do flee.
     Nought knoweth Cadmus that his daughter and her little child      *The
     Admitted were among the gods that rule the surges wild.     *transformation
Compelled with grief and great mishaps that had ensued together     *of Cadmus*
And strange foretokens, often seen since first his coming thither,
He utterly forsakes his town the which he builded had,
As though the fortune of the place so hardly him bested
And not his own. And, fleeting long like pilgrims, at the last      700
Upon the coast of Illiry his wife and he were cast
Where, nigh forpined with cares and years, while of the chances
          passed
Upon their house and of their toils and former travails ta'en
They sadly talked between themselves, 'Was my spearhead the
          bane
Of that same ugly snake of Mars', quoth Cadmus, 'when I fled
From Sidon, or did I his teeth in ploughèd pasture spread?
If for the death of him the gods so cruel vengeance take,
Drawn out in length upon my womb then trail I like a snake.'
He had no sooner said the word but that he gan to glide
Upon his belly like a snake; and on his hardened side            710
He felt the scales new budding out, the which was wholly fret
With speckled drops of black and grey as thick as could be set.
He falleth grovelling on his breast, and both his shanks do grow
In one round spindle bodkin-wise with sharpened point below.

His arms as yet remainèd still; his arms that did remain
He stretchèd out and said with tears that plenteously did rain
A-down his face, which yet did keep the native fashion sound,
'Come hither, wife, come hither, wight most wretched on the
      ground,
And while that aught of me remains, vouchsafe to touch the same.

720    Come, take me by the hand as long as hand may have his name,
Before this snakish shape do whole my body overrun.'
He would have spoken more, when suddenly his tongue begun
To split in two and speech did fail. And as he did attempt
To make his moan, he hissed; for nature now had clean exempt
All other speech. His wretched wife her naked stomach beat
And cried, 'What meaneth this? Dear Cadmus, where are now thy
      feet?
Where are thy shoulders and thy hands, thy hue and manly face
With all the other things that did thy princely person grace
Which now I overpass? But why, ye gods, do ye delay

730    My body into like misshape of serpent to convey?'
When this was spoken, Cadmus licked his wife about the lips
And (as a place with which he was acquainted well) he slips
Into her bosom, lovingly embracing her, and cast
Himself about her neck as oft he had in time forepast.
Such as were there (their folk were there) were flighted at the
      sight;
For by and by they saw their necks did glister slick and bright
And on their snakish heads grew crests, and finally they both
Were into very dragons turned and forth together go'th,
T'one trailing by the t'other's side, until they gained a wood

740    The which direct against the place where as they were then stood.
And now, remembering what they were themselves in times
      forepast,
They neither shun nor hurten men with stinging nor with blast.

*Perseus and*     But yet a comfort to them both in this their altered hue
*Atlas*         Became that noble imp of theirs that Indy did subdue,
       Whom all Achaia worshippèd with temples builded new.
     All only Acrise, Abas' son (though of the selfsame stock),
     Remained who out of Argos' walls unkindly did him lock

And movèd wilful war against his godhead, thinking that
There was not any race of gods; for he believèd not
That Persey was the son of Jove or that he was conceived          750
By Danaë of golden shower through which she was deceived.
But yet ere long (such present force hath truth) he doth repent
As well his great impiety against god Bacchus meant
As also that he did disdain his nephew for to know.
But Bacchus now full gloriously himself in heaven doth show;
And Persey, bearing in his hand the monster Gorgon's head,
That famous spoil which here and there with snakish hair was
          spread,
Doth beat the air with waving wings. And as he overflew
The Lybic sands, the drops of blood that from the head did sue
Of Gorgon (being new cut off) upon the ground did fall;          760
Which, taking them and, as it were, conceiving therewithal,
Engendered sundry snakes and worms. By means whereof that
          clime
Did swarm with serpents ever since even to this present time.
     From thence he like a watery cloud was carried with the
          weather
     Through all the heaven, now here, now there, as light as any
          feather.
And from aloft he views the earth that underneath doth lie
And swiftly over all the world doth in conclusion fly.
Three times the chilling Bears, three times the Crab's fell clees he
          saw;
Ofttimes to west, ofttimes to east did drive him many a flaw.
Now at such time as unto rest the sun began to draw,          770
Because he did not think it good to be abroad all night,
Within King Atlas' western realm he ceasèd from his flight,
Requesting that a little space of rest enjoy he might
Until such time as Lucifer should bring the morning grey
And morning bring the lightsome sun that guides the cheerful day.
This Atlas, Iapet's nephew, was a man that did excel
In stature every other wight that in the world did dwell.
The utmost coast of all the earth and all that sea wherein
The tirèd steeds and wearied wain of Phoebus divèd been

780   Were in subjection to this king. A thousand flocks of sheep,
      A thousand herds of rother-beasts he in his fields did keep,
      And not a neighbour did annoy his ground by dwelling nigh.
      To him the wandering Persey thus his language did apply:
      'If high renown of royal race thy noble heart may move,
      I am the son of Jove himself; or if thou more approve
      The valiant deeds and haught exploits, thou shalt perceive in
            me
      Such doings as deserve with praise extollèd for to be.
      I pray thee of thy courtesy, receive me as thy guest
      And let me only for this night within thy palace rest.'
790   King Atlas callèd straight to mind an ancient prophecy
      Made by Parnassian Themis, which this sentence did imply:
      'The time shall one day, Atlas, come in which thy golden tree
      Shall of her fair and precious fruit despoiled and robbèd be;
      And he shall be the son of Jove that shall enjoy the prey.'
      For fear hereof he did enclose his orchard every way
      With mighty hills and put an ugly dragon in the same
      To keep it. Further he forbade that any stranger came
      Within his realm. And to this knight he said presumptuously,
      'Avoid my land, unless thou wilt by utter peril try
800   That all thy glorious acts whereof thou dost so loudly lie
      And Jove thy father be too far to help thee at thy need.'
      To these his words he added force and went about indeed
      To drive him out by strength of hand. To speak was loss of wind,
      For neither could entreating fair nor stoutness turn his mind.
      'Well then,' quoth Persey, 'sith thou dost mine honour set so
            light,
      Take here a present.' And with that he turns away his sight
      And from his left side drew me out Medusa's loathly head.
      As huge and big as Atlas was, he turnèd in that stead
      Into a mountain. Into trees his beard and locks did pass;
810   His hands and shoulders made the ridge; that part which lately was
      His head became the highest top of all the hill; his bones
      Were turned to stones; and therewithal he grew me all at once
      Beyond all measure up in height (for so God thought it best)
      So far that heaven with all the stars did on his shoulders rest.

In endless prison by that time had Aeolus locked the wind,
  And now the cheerly morning star that putteth folk in mind
To rise about their daily work shone brightly in the sky.
Then Persey unto both his feet did straight his feathers tie
And girt his woodknife to his side and from the earth did sty.
And, leaving nations numberless beneath him every way,      820
At last upon King Cephey's fields in Ethiope did he stay,
Where clean against all right and law by Jove's commandment
Andromed for her mother's tongue did suffer punishment.
Whom to a rock by both the arms when fastened he had seen,
He would have thought of marble stone she had some image been
But that her tresses to and fro the whisking wind did blow
And trickling tears warm from her eyes a-down her cheeks did
     flow.
Unwares hereat gan secret sparks within his breast to glow;
His wits were straught at sight thereof and ravished in such wise
That how to hover with his wings he scarcely could devise.      830
As soon as he had stayed himself, 'O lady fair,' quoth he,
'Not worthy of such bands as these but such wherewith we see
Together knit in lawful bed the earnest lovers be,
I pray thee, tell me what thyself and what this land is named
And wherefore thou dost wear these chains.' The lady, ill
     ashamed,
Was at the sudden stricken dumb, and like a fearful maid
She durst not speak unto a man. Had not her hands been stayed,
She would have hid her bashful face; howbeit, as she might
With great abundance of her tears she stopped up her sight.
But when that Persey oftentimes was earnestly in hand      840
To learn the matter, for because she would not seem to stand
In stubborn silence of her faults, she told him what the land
And what she hight and how her mother for her beauty's sake
Through pride did unadvisedly too much upon her take.
And ere she full had made an end, the water gan to roar;
An ugly monster from the deep was making to the shore
Which bare the sea before his breast. The virgin shrieked out.
Her father and her mother both stood mourning thereabout
In wretched case both twain, but not so wretched as the maid
Who wrongly for her mother's fault the bitter ransom paid.      850

*Perseus and the sea monster*

They brought not with them any help but, as the time and case
Required, they wept and wrang their hands and straightly did
         embrace
Her body fastened to the rock. Then Persey them bespake
And said, 'The time may serve too long this sorrow for to make,
But time of help must either now or never else be take.
Now if I, Persey, son of her whom in her father's tower
The mighty Jove begat with child in shape of golden shower,
Who cut off ugly Gorgon's head bespread with snakish hair
And in the air durst trust these wings my body for to bear,
Perchance should save your daughter's life, I think ye should as
860        then
Accept me for your son-in-law before all other men.
To these great thews (by the help of God) I purpose for to add
A just desert in helping her that is so hard bested.
I covenant with you by my force and manhood for to save her,
Conditionally that to my wife in recompense I have her.'
     Her parents took his offer straight (for who would stick
         thereat?)
     And prayed him fair and promised him that for performing that
They would endow him with the right of all their realm beside.
Like as a galley with her nose doth cut the waters wide,
870  Enforcèd by the sweating arms of rowers with the tide,
Even so the monster with his breast did bear the waves aside
And was now come as near the rock as well a man might fling
Amid the pure and vacant air a pellet from a sling;
When on the sudden Persey pushed his foot against the ground
And stièd upward to the clouds. His shadow did rebound
Upon the sea; the beast ran fierce upon the passing shade.
And as an eagle, when he sees a dragon in a glade
Lie beaking of his bluish back against the sunny rays,
Doth seize upon him unbeware and with his talons lays
880  Sure hold upon his scaly neck, lest writhing back his head
His cruel teeth might do him harm; so Persey in that stead,
Descending down the air amain, with all his force and might
Did seize upon the monster's back. And underneath the right
Fin hard unto the very hilt his hookèd sword did smite.

The monster, being wounded sore, did sometime leap aloft
And sometime under water dive, bestirring him full oft
As doth a chafèd boar beset with barking dogs about.
But Persey with his lightsome wings, still keeping him without
The monster's reach, with hookèd sword doth sometime hew his
    back
Whereas the hollow scales give way, and sometime he doth hack    890
The ribs on both his mailèd sides, and sometime he doth wound
His spindle-tail where into fish it grows most small and round.
The whale at Persey from his mouth such waves of water cast
Bemixèd with the purple blood that, all bedreint at last,
His feathers very heavy were. And doubting any more
To trust his wings now waxing wet, he straight began to soar
Up to a rock which in the calm above the water stood
But in the tempest evermore was hidden with the flood.
And leaning thereunto and with his left hand holding just
The top thereof, a dozen times his weapon he did thrust    900
Among his guts. The joyful noise and clapping of their hands,
The which were made for loosening of Andromed from her
    bands,
Filled all the coast and heaven itself. The parents of the maid,
Cassiope and Cepheus, were glad and well apaid
And, calling him their son-in-law, confessèd him to be
The help and safeguard of their house. Andromede, the fee
And cause of Persey's enterprise, from bonds now being free,
He washèd his victorious hands. And lest the snaky head
With lying on the gravel hard should catch some harm, he spread
Soft leaves and certain tender twigs that in the water grew    910
And laid Medusa's head thereon. The twigs, yet being new
And quick and full of juicy pith, full lightly to them drew
The nature of this monstrous head; for both the leaf and bough
Full strangely at the touch thereof became both hard and tough.
The seanymphs tried this wondrous fact in divers other rods
And were full glad to see the change, because there was no odds
Of leaves or twigs or of the seeds new shaken from the cods.
For still like nature ever since is in our coral found
That, look how soon it toucheth air, it waxeth hard and sound.

920  And that which under water was a stick, above is stone.
     Three altars to as many gods he makes of turf anon.
     Upon the left hand Mercury's; Minerva's on the right;
     And in the middle Jupiter's. To Pallas he did dight
     A cow; a calf to Mercury; a bull to royal Jove.
     Forthwith he took Andromede, the prize for which he strove,
     Endowèd with her father's realm. For now the god of love
     And Hymen unto marriage his mind in haste did move.
     Great fires were made of sweet perfumes, and curious garlands
            hung
     About the house which everywhere of mirthful music rung,
930  The gladsome sign of merry minds. The palace gates were set
     Wide open; none from coming in were by the porters let.
     All noblemen and gentlemen that were of any port
     To this same great and royal feast of Cephey did resort.

*The head of*
*Medusa*    When, having taken their repast as well of meat as wine,
            Their hearts began to pleasant mirth by leisure to incline,
     The valiant Persey of the folk and fashions of the land
     Began to be inquisitive. One Lyncid out of hand
     The rites and manners of the folk did do him t'understand.
     Which done, he said, 'O worthy knight, I pray thee tell us by
940  What force or wile thou got'st the head with hairs of adders sly.'
     Then Persey told how underneath cold Atlas lay a plain
     So fencèd in on every side with mountains high that vain
     Were any force to win the same. In entrance of the which
     Two daughters of King Phorcys dwelt, whose chance and hap was
            such
     That one eye servèd both their turns; whereof by wily sleight
     And stealth in putting forth his hand he did bereave them quite
     As they from t'one to t'other were delivering of the same.
     From whence by long blind crooked ways unhandsomely he came
     Through ghastly groves by ragged cliffs unto the dreary place
950  Whereas the Gorgons dwelt. And there he saw (a wretched case!)
     The shapes as well of men as beasts lie scattered everywhere
     In open fields and common ways, the which transformèd were
     From living things to stones at sight of foul Medusa's hair;
     But yet that he through brightness of his monstrous brazen shield,
     The which he in his left hand bare, Medusa's face beheld.

And while that in a sound dead sleep were all her snakes and she,
He softly parèd off her head; and how that he did see
Swift Pegasus, the wingèd horse, and eke his brother grow
Out of their mother's new-shed blood. Moreover he did show
A long discourse of all his haps, and not so long as true:                  960
As namely of what seas and lands the coasts he overflew;
And eke what stars with stying wings he in the while did view.
But yet his tale was at an end ere any looked therefore.
   Upon occasion by and by of words rehearsed before
   There was a certain nobleman demanded him wherefore
   She only of the sisters three hair mixed with adders bore.
'Sir,' answered Persey, 'sith you ask a matter worth report,
I grant to tell you your demand. She both in comely port
And beauty every other wight surmounted in such sort
That many suitors unto her did earnestly resort.                            970
And though that whole from top to toe most beautiful she were,
In all her body was no part more goodly than her hair.
I know some parties yet alive that say they did her see.
It is reported how she should abused by Neptune be
In Pallas' church; from which foul fact Jove's daughter turned her
    eye
And with her target hid her face from such a villainy.
And lest it should unpunished be, she turned her seemly hair
To loathly snakes, the which (the more to put her foes in fear)
Before her breast continually she in her shield doth bear.'

FINIS QUARTI LIBRI.

# The Fifth Book of Ovid's
# Metamorphoses

Now while that Danae's noble son was telling of these things    *The fight in*
Amid a throng of Cephey's lords, through all the palace rings     *Cepheus'*
A noise of people nothing like the sound of such as sing       *palace*
At wedding feasts, but like the roar of such as tidings bring
Of cruel war. This sudden change from feasting unto fray
Might well be likened to the sea which, standing at a stay,
The woodness of the winds makes rough by raising of the wave.
King Cephey's brother, Phiney, was the man that rashly gave
The first occasion of this fray; who, shaking in his hand
A dart of ash with head of steel, said, 'Lo, lo, here I stand    10
To challenge thee that wrongfully my ravished spouse dost hold.
Thy wings nor yet thy forgèd dad in shape of feignèd gold
Shall now not save thee from my hands.' As with that word he
       bent
His arm aloft the foresaid dart at Persey to have sent,
'What dost thou, brother?' Cephey cried, 'What madness moves
       thy mind
To do so foul a deed? Is this the friendship he shall find
Among us for his good deserts? And wilt thou needs requite
The saving of thy niece's life with such a foul despite?
Whom Persey hath not from thee ta'en, but (if thou be advised)
But Neptune's heavy wrath because his seanymphs were despised,   20
But hornèd Hammon, but the beast which from the sea arrived
On my dear bowels for to feed. That time wert thou deprived
Of thy betrothèd, when her life upon the losing stood.
Unless perchance to see her lost it would have done thee good
And eased thy heart to see me sad? And may it not suffice
That thou did'st see her to the rock fast bound before thine eyes

And did'st not help her, being both her husband and her eme?
Unless thou grudge that any man should come within my realm
To save her life, and seek to rob him of his just reward?

30 Which if thou think to be so great, thou should'st have had regard
Before to fetch it from the rock to which thou saw'st it bound.
I pray thee, brother, seeing that by him the means is found
That in mine age without my child I go not to the ground,
Permit him to enjoy the prize for which we did compound
And which he hath by due desert of purchase dearly bought.
For, brother, never let it sink nor enter in thy thought
That I set more by him than thee; but this may well be said,
I rather had to give her him than see my daughter dead.'
He gave him not a word again, but lookèd eft on him

40 And eft on Persey irefully, with count'nance stour and grim,
Not knowing which were best to hit. And after little stay
He shook his dart and flung it forth with all the power and sway
That anger gave at Persey's head. But harm it did him none;
It stickèd in the bedstead's head that Persey sat upon.

  Then Persey, sternly starting up and pulling out the dart,
  Did throw it at his foe again; and therewithal his heart
Had cliven asunder, had he not behind an altar start.
The altar (more the pity was) did save the wickèd wight.
Yet threw he not the dart in vain; it hit one Rhoetus right
Amid the forehead, who therewith sank down. And when the

50    steal
Was pluckèd out, he sprawled about and spurnèd with his heel
And all berayed the board with blood. Then all the other rout
As fierce as fire flang darts, and some there were that crièd out
That Cephey with his son-in-law was worthy for to die.
But he had wound him out of doors, protesting solemnly,
As he was just and faithful prince, and swearing eke by all
The gods of hospitality that that same broil did fall
Full sore against his will. At hand was warlike Pallas straight
And shadowed Persey with her shield and gave him heart in fight.

60 There was one Atis, born in Inde (of fair Limniace,
The river Ganges' daughter, thought the issue for to be),
Of passing beauty, which with rich array he did augment.
He ware that day a scarlet cloak, about the which there went

A guard of gold; a chain of gold he ware about his neck;
And eke his hair, perfumed with myrrh, a costly crown did deck.
Full sixteen years he was of age. Such cunning skill he could
In darting as to hit his mark far distant when he would;
Yet how to handle bow and shafts much better did he know.
Now as he was about that time to bend his hornèd bow,
   A firebrand Persey raught that did upon the altar smoke          70
   And dashed him overthwart the face with such a violent stroke
   That all bebattered was his head, the bones asunder broke.
When Lycabas of Assur land, his most assurèd friend
And dear companion, being no dissembler of his mind,
Which most entirely did him love, beheld him on the ground
Lie weltering with disfigured face and through that grievous
            wound
Now gasping out his parting ghost, his death he did lament;
And, taking hastily up the bow that Atis erst had bent,
'Encounter thou with me,' he said. 'Thou shalt not long enjoy
Thy triumphing in bravery thus for killing of this boy,            80
By which thou get'st more spite than praise.' All this was scarcely
            said
But that the arrow from the string went strainèd to the head.
Howbeit Persey, as it happed, so warily did it shun
As that it in his coat-plights hung. Then to him did he run
With Harpe in his hand, bestained with grim Medusa's blood,
And thrust him through the breast therewith. He, cothing as he
            stood,
Did look about where Atis lay with dim and dazzling eyes
Now waving under endless night, and down by him he lies
And, for to comfort him withal, together with him dies.
Behold, through greedy haste to fight one Phorbas, Methion's
            son,                                                    90
A Swevite, and of Lyby land one called Amphimedon,
By fortune sliding in the blood with which the ground was wet,
Fell down; and as they would have rose, Perseus' falchion met
With both of them. Amphimedon upon the ribs he smote,
And with the like celerity he cut me Phorbas' throat.
But unto Eryth, Actor's son, that in his hand did hold
A broad brown bill, with his short sword he durst not be too bold

To make approach. With both his hands a great and massy cup
Embossed with cunning portraiture aloft he taketh up
100   And sends it at him. He spews up red blood and, falling down
Upon his back, against the ground doth knock his dying crown.
Then down he Polydaemon throws, extract of royal race,
And Abaris, the Scythian, and Clytus in like case
And Elice with his unshorn locks and also Phlegyas
And Lycet, old Sperchesy's son, with divers others mo,
That on the heaps of corses slain he treads as he doth go.
      And Phiney, daring not presume to meet his foe at hand,
      Did cast a dart which happed to light on Idas, who did stand
Aloof as neuter (though in vain), not meddling with the fray.
110   Who, casting back a frowning look at Phiney, thus did say:
'Sith, whether that I will or no, compelled I am perforce
To take a part, have, Phiney, here him whom thou dost enforce
To be thy foe and with this wound my wrongful wound requite.'
But as he from his body pulled the dart with all his might
To throw it at his foe again, his limbs so feebled were
With loss of blood that down he fell and could not after stir.
There also lay Odites slain, the chief in all the land
Next to King Cephey, put to death by force of Clymen's hand.
Protoenor was by Hypsey killed, and Lyncide did as much
120   For Hypsey. In the throng there was an ancient man and such
A one as lovèd righteousness and greatly fearèd God;
Emathion callèd was his name. Whom sith his years forbode
To put on arms, he fights with tongue, inveighing earnestly
Against that wicked war, the which he bannèd bitterly.
As on the altar he himself with quivering hands did stay,
One Chromis tippèd off his head. His head, cut off, straightway
Upon the altar fell, and there his tongue, not fully dead,
Did babble still the banning words the which it erst had said
And breathèd forth his fainting ghost among the burning brands.
      Then Brote and Hammon, brothers, twins, stout champions of
130         their hands,
      In wrestling peerless (if so be that wrestling could sustain
The furious force of slicing swords), were both by Phiney slain.
And so was Alphit, Ceres' priest, that ware upon his crown
A stately mitre fair and white with tables hanging down.

Thou also, Iapet's son, for such affairs as these unmeet
But meet to tune thine instrument with voice and ditty sweet,
The work of peace, wert thither called th'assembly to rejoice
And for to set the marriage forth with pleasant singing voice.
As with his viol in his hand he stood a good way off,
There cometh to him Pettalus and says in way of scoff,                    140
'Go, sing the residue to the ghosts about the Stygian lake,'
And in the left side of his head his dagger point he strake.
He sank down dead with fingers still yet warbling on the string,
And so mischance knit up with woe the song that he did sing.
But fierce Lycormas could not bear to see him murdered so
Without revengement. Up he caught a mighty lever tho
That wonted was to bar the door a-right side of the house,
And therewithal to Pettalus he lendeth such a souse
Full in the noddle of the neck that, like a snetchèd ox
Straight tumbling down, against the ground his grovelling face he
          knocks.                                                        150
And Pelates, a Garamant, attempted to have caught
The left door bar; but as thereat with stretchèd hand he raught,
One Coryt, son of Marmarus, did with a javelin strike
Him through the hand, that to the wood fast nailèd did it stick.
As Pelates stood fastened thus, one Abas goared his side;
He could not fall but, hanging still upon the post, there died
Fast nailèd by the hand. And there was overthrown a knight
Of Persey's band called Melaney, and one that Doryl hight,
A man of greatest lands in all the realm of Nasamone.
That occupied so large a ground as Doryl was there none,                 160
Nor none that had such store of corn. There came a dart askew
And lighted in his cods, the place where present death doth sue.
When Alcyon of Barcey, he that gave this deadly wound,
Beheld him yesking forth his ghost and falling to the ground
With watery eyes, the white turned up, 'Content thyself', he said,
'With that same little plot of ground whereon thy corse is laid
Instead of all the large fat fields which late thou did'st possess.'
And with that word he left him dead. Perseus, to redress
This slaughter and this spiteful taunt, straight snatchèd out the dart
That stickèd in the fresh warm wound and with an angry heart            170

Did send it at the thrower's head. The dart did split his nose
Even in the midst, and at his neck again the head out goes,
So that it peerèd both the ways. Whiles fortune doth support
And further Persey thus, he kills (but yet in sundry sort)
Two brothers by the mother, t'one called Clytie, t'other Dane.
For on a dart through both his thighs did Clytie take his bane,
And Danus with another dart was stricken in the mouth.
There dièd also Celadon, a gypsy of the south;
And so did bastard Astrey too, whose mother was a Jew;
180   And sage Aethion, well foreseen in things that should ensue,
But utterly beguiled as then by birds that awkly flew.
King Cephey's harness-bearer, called Thoäctes, lost his life,
And Agyrt, whom for murdering late his father with a knife
The world spake shame of. Natheless, much more remained
            behind
Than was dispatchèd off of hand. For all were full in mind
To murder one; the wicked throng had sworn to spend their
            blood
Against the right and such a man as had deservèd good.
At other side (although in vain) of mere affection stood
The father and the mother-in-law and eke the heavy bride,
190   Who fillèd with their piteous plaint the court on every side.
But now the clattering of the swords and harness at that tide
With grievous groans and sighs of such as wounded were or died
Did raise up such a cruel roar that nothing could be heard.
For fierce Bellona so renewed the battle afterward
That all the house did swim in blood. Duke Phiney with a rout
Of mo than a thousand men environed round about
The valiant Persey all alone. The darts of Phiney's band
Came thicker than the winter's hail doth fall upon the land
By both his sides, his eyes and ears. He warily thereupon
200   Withdraws and leans his back against a huge great arch of stone;
And, being safe behind, he sets his face against his foe,
Withstanding all their fierce assaults. There did assail him tho
Upon the left side Molpheus, a prince of Choany,
And on the right Ethemon, born hard by in Araby.
Like as the tiger, when he hears the lowing out of neat
In sundry meads, enforcèd sore through abstinence from meat,

Would fain be doing with them both and cannot tell at which
Were best to give adventure first, so Persey (who did itch
To be at host with both of them and doubtful whether side
To turn him on, the right or left), upon advantage spied,        210
Did wound me Molphey on the leg and from him quite him
    drave.
He was contented with his flight; for why Ethemon gave
No respite to him to pursue but, like a frantic man,
Through eagerness to wound his neck, without regarding when
Or how to strike for haste, he burst his brittle sword in twain
Against the arch; the point whereof, rebounding back again,
Did hit himself upon the throat. Howbeit, that same wound
Was unsufficient for to send Ethemon to the ground.
He trembled, holding up his hands for mercy; but in vain.
For Persey thrust him through the heart with Hermes' hookèd
    skene.                                                          220
    But when he saw that valiantness no lenger could avail
    By reason of the multitude that did him still assail,
'Sith you yourselves me force to call mine enemy to mine aid,
I will do so. If any friend of mine be here,' he said,
'Sirs, turn your faces all away.' And therewithal he drew
Out Gorgon's head. One Thessalus straight, raging, to him flew
And said, 'Go, seek some other man whom thou may'st make
    abashed
With these thy foolish juggling toys.' And as he would have
    dashed
His javelin in him with that word to kill him out of hand,
With gesture throwing forth his dart all marble did he stand.      230
His sword through Lyncid's noble heart had Amphyx thought to
    shove;
His hand was stone and neither one nor other way could move.
But Niley, who did vaunt himself to be the river's son
That through the bounds of Egypt land in channels seven doth
    run
And in his shield had graven part of silver, part of gold,
The said seven channels of the Nile, said, 'Persey, here behold
From whence we fetch our pedigree. It may rejoice thy heart
To die of such a noble hand as mine.' The latter part

Of these his words could scarce be heard; the dint thereof was
    drowned.
Ye would have thought him speaking still with open mouth, but
240        sound
Did none forth pass. There was for speech no passage to be found.
Rebuking them cries Eryx, 'Sirs, it is not Gorgon's face,
It is your own faint hearts that make you stony in this case.
Come, let us on this fellow run and to the ground him bear
That fights by witchcraft.' As with that his feet forth stepping
    were,
They stack still fastened to the floor. He could not move aside;
An armèd image all of stone he speechless did abide.
All these were justly punishèd. But one there was a knight
Of Persey's band, in whose defence as Acont stood to fight,
250  He waxèd overgrown with stone at ugly Gorgon's sight.
Whom still as yet Astyages supposing for to live,
Did with a long sharp arming sword a washing blow him give;
The sword did clink against the stone and out the sparkles drive.
While all amazed Astyages stood wondering at the thing,
The selfsame nature on himself the Gorgon's head did bring;
And in his visage which was stone a count'nance did remain
Of wondering still. A weary work it were to tell you plain
The names of all the common sort. Two hundred from that fray
Did scape unslain, but none of them did go alive away.
260  The whole two hundred, every one, at sight of Gorgon's hair
Were turnèd into stocks of stone. Then, at the length, for fear
Did Phiney of his wrongful war forthink himself full sore.
But now, alas, what remedy? He saw there stand before
His face his men like images in sundry shapes all stone.
He knew them well and by their names did call them everych
    one,
Desiring them to succour him, and, trusting not his sight,
He feels the bodies that were next; and all were marble quite.
He turns himself from Perseyward, and humbly as he stands
He wries his arms behind his back. And, holding up his hands,
270  'O noble Persey, thou hast got the upper hand,' he said.
'Put up that monstrous shield of thine; put up that Gorgon's head

That into stones transformeth men. Put up, I thee desire.
Not hatred, nor because to reign as king I did aspire,
Have movèd me to make this fray. The only force of love
In seeking my betrothèd spouse did hereunto me move.
The better title seemeth thine because of thy desert,
And mine by former promise made. It irks me at the heart
In that I did not give thee place. None other thing I crave,
O worthy knight, but that thou grant this life of mine to save.
Let all things else beside be thine.' As thus he humbly spake,          280
Not daring look at him to whom he did entreatence make,
'The thing', quoth Persey, 'which to grant both I can find in heart
And is no little courtesy to show without desert
Upon a coward, I will grant, O fearful duke, to thee.
Set fear aside. Thou shalt not hurt with any weapon be.
I will, moreover, so provide as that thou shalt remain
An everlasting monument of this day's toil and pain.
The palace of my father-in-law shall henceforth be thy shrine
Where thou shalt stand continually before my spouse's eyen,
That, of her husband having aye the image in her sight,                 290
She may from time to time receive some comfort and delight.'
He had no sooner said these words but that he turned his shield
With Gorgon's head to that same part where Phiney with a mild
And fearful count'nance set his face. Then also, as he wried
His eyes away, his neck waxed stiff, his tears to stone were dried.
A count'nance in the stony stock of fear did still appear
With humble look and yielding hands and ghastly ruthful cheer.
    With conquest and a noble wife doth Persey home repair,
    And in revengement of the right against the wrongful heir,
As in his grandsire's just defence, he falls in hand with Proete.       300
Who, like no brother but a foe, did late before defeat
King Acrise of his towns by war and of his royal seat;
But neither could his men of war nor fortress won by wrong
Defend him from the grisly look of grim Medusa long.
And yet thee, foolish Polydect, of little Seriph king,
Such rooted rancour inwardly continually did sting
That neither Persey's prowess tried in such a sort of broils
Nor yet the perils he endured nor all his troublous toils

Could cause thy stomach to relent. Within thy stony breast
310 Works such a kind of festered hate as cannot be repressed.
Thy wrongful malice hath none end. Moreover, thou, of spite
Repining at his worthy praise, his doings dost backbite,
Upholding that Medusa's death was but a forgèd lie
So long till Persey, for to show the truth apparently,
Desiring such as were his friends to turn away their eye,
Drew out Medusa's ugly head. At sight whereof anon
The hateful tyrant Polydect was turnèd to a stone.

*Minerva visits*      The goddess Pallas all this while did keep continually
*Helicon*             Her brother Persey company till now that she did sty
320 From Seriph in a hollow cloud. And, leaving on the right
The isles of Scyre and Gyarus, she made from thence her flight
Directly over that same sea as near as eye could aim
To Thebe and Mount Helicon. And when she thither came,
She stayed herself and thus bespake the learnèd sisters nine:
'A rumour of an uncouth spring did pierce these ears of mine,
The which the wingèd steed should make by stamping with his
      hoof.
This is the cause of my repair: I would for certain proof
Be glad to see the wondrous thing. For present there I stood
And saw the selfsame Pegasus spring of his mother's blood.'
330 Dame Urany did entertain and answer Pallas thus:
'What cause so ever moves your grace to come and visit us,
Most heartily you welcome are. And certain is the fame
Of this our spring, that Pegasus was causer of the same.'
And with that word she led her forth to see the sacred spring.
Who, musing greatly with herself at strangeness of the thing,
Surveyed the woods and groves about of ancient stately port.
And when she saw the bowers to which the Muses did resort
And pleasant fields beclad with herbs of sundry hue and sort,
She said that for their studies' sake they were in happy case
340 And also that to serve their turn they had so trim a place.
*The story of*        Then one of them replièd thus: 'O noble lady, who
*Pyreneus*            (But that your virtue greater works than these are calls you to)
Should else have been of this our troop, your saying is full true.
To this our trade of life and place is commendation due.

And sure we have a lucky lot and if the world were such
As that we might in safety live; but lewdness reigns so much
That all things make us maids afraid. Methinks I yet do see
The wicked tyrant Pyren still; my heart is yet scarce free
From that same fear with which it happed us flighted for to be.
This cruel Pyren was of Thrace and with his men of war          350
The land of Phocis had subdued, and from this place not far
Within the city Daulis reigned by force of wrongful hand.
One day to Phoebus' templesward that on Parnassus stand
As we were going, in our way he met us courteously
And, by the name of goddesses saluting reverently,
Said, "O ye dames of Meony" – for why he knew us well –
"I pray you, stay and take my house until this storm" – there fell
That time a tempest and a shower – "be passed; the gods aloft
Have entered smaller sheds than mine full many a time and oft."
The rainy weather and his words so movèd us that we          360
To go into an outer house of his did all agree.
As soon as that the shower was passed and heaven was voided
          clear
Of all the clouds which late before did everywhere appear
Until that Boreas had subdued the rainy southern wind,
We would have by and by been gone. He shut the doors, in mind
To ravish us; but we with wings escapèd from his hands.
He, purposing to follow us, upon a turret stands
And saith he needs will after us the same way we did fly.
And with that word full frantically he leapeth down from high
And, pitching evelong on his face, the bones asunder crashed          370
And, dying, all abroad the ground his wicked blood bedashed.'
     Now as the Muse was telling this, they heard a noise of wings,
     And from the leafy boughs aloft a sound of greeting rings.
Minerva, looking up thereat, demanded whence the sound
Of tongues that so distinctly spake did come so plain and round.
She thought some woman or some man had greeted her that
          stound.
It was a flight of birds. Nine pies, bewailing their mischance,
In counterfeiting everything from bough to bough did dance.
As Pallas wondered at the sight, the Muse thus spake in sum:
'These also, being late ago in challenge overcome,          380

*Pierus'*
*daughters*
*challenge the*
*Muses*

Made one kind more of birds than was of ancient time beforn.
In Macedon they were about the city Pella born
Of Piërus, a great rich chuff, and Euïp, who, by aid
Of strong Lucina travailing nine times, nine times was laid
Of daughters in her childbed safe. This fond and foolish rout
Of doltish sisters, taking pride and waxing very stout
Because they were in number nine, came flocking all together
Through all the towns of Thessaly and all Achaia hither
And us with these or suchlike words to combat did provoke:
390 "Cease off, ye Thespian goddesses, to mock the simple folk
With fondness of your melody. And if ye think indeed
Ye can do aught, contend with us and see how ye shall speed.
I warrant you, ye pass us not in cunning nor in voice.
Ye are here nine and so are we. We put you to the choice
That either we will vanquish you and set you quite beside
Your fountain made by Pegasus, which is your chiefest pride,
And Aganippe too; or else confound you us, and we
Of all the woods of Macedon will dispossessèd be
So far as snowy Paeony. And let the nymphs be judges."
400 Now in good sooth it was a shame to cope with suchy drudges,
But yet more shame it was to yield. The chosen nymphs did swear
By Styx and sat them down on seats of stone that growèd there.
Then straight without commission or election of the rest
The foremost of them, pressing forth undecently, professed
The challenge to perform and sung the battles of the gods.
She gave the giants all the praise, the honour and the odds,
Abasing sore the worthy deeds of all the gods. She tells
How Typhon, issuing from the earth and from the deepest hells,
Made all the gods above afraid so greatly that they fled
410 And never stayed till Egypt land and Nile, whose stream is shed
In channels seven, receivèd them forwearied altogether;
And how the hellhound Typhon did pursue them also thither,
By means whereof the gods each one were fain themselves to hide
In forgèd shapes. She said that Jove, the prince of gods, was wried
In shape of ram, which is the cause that at this present tide
Jove's image which the Lybian folk by name of Hammon serve
Is made with crooked whelkèd horns that inward still do curve;

That Phoebus in a raven lurked, and Bacchus in a geat,
And Phoebus' sister in a cat, and Juno in a neat,
And Venus in the shape of fish, and how that last of all                420
Mercurius hid him in a bird which ibis men do call.
This was the sum of all the tale which she with rolling tongue
And yelling throat-boll to her harp before us rudely sung.

  'Our turn is also come to speak, but that perchance your grace
    To give the hearing to our song hath now no time nor space.'
'Yes, yes,' quoth Pallas, 'tell on forth in order all your tale,'
And down she sat among the trees which gave a pleasant swale.
The Muse made answer thus: 'To one Calliope here by name
This challenge we committed have and ordering of the same.
Then rose up fair Calliope with goodly bush of hair                    430
Trim wreathèd up with ivy leaves, and with her thumb gan stir
The quivering strings to try them, if they were in tune or no.
Which done, she played upon her lute and sung her ditty so:

  ' "Dame Ceres first to break the earth with plough the                *The rape of*
    manner found;                                                       *Proserpine*
  She first made corn and stover soft to grow upon the ground;
She first made laws. For all these things we are to Ceres bound.
Of her must I as now entreat. Would God I could resound
Her worthy laud; she, doubtless, is a goddess worthy praise.
Because the giant Typhon gave presumptuously assays
To conquer heaven, the hugy isle of Trinacris is laid                  440
Upon his limbs, by weight whereof perforce he down is weighed.
He strives and struggles for to rise full many a time and oft.
But on his right hand toward Rome Pelorus stands aloft;
Pachynus stands upon his left; his legs with Lilyby
Are pressèd down; his monstrous head doth under Etna lie.
From whence he, lying bolt upright, with wrathful mouth doth
    spit
Out flames of fire. He wrestleth oft and walloweth for to wit
And if he can remove the weight of all that mighty land
Or tumble down the towns and hills that on his body stand.
By means whereof it comes to pass that oft the earth doth shake,      450
And even the king of ghosts himself for very fear doth quake,
Misdoubting lest the earth should cleave so wide that light of day
Might by the same pierce down to hell and there the ghosts affray.

Forecasting this, the prince of fiends forsook his darksome hole
And, in a chariot drawn with steeds as black as any coal,
The whole foundation of the Isle of Sicil warily viewed.
When throughly he had searched each place that harm had none
      ensued,
As carelessly he ranged abroad, he chancèd to be seen
Of Venus sitting on her hill; who, taking straight between

460   Her arms her wingèd Cupid, said, 'My son, mine only stay,
My hand, mine honour and my might, go, take without delay
Those tools which all wights do subdue and strike them in the
      heart
Of that same god that of the world enjoys the lowest part.
The gods of heaven and Jove himself, the power of sea and land
And he that rules the powers on earth, obey thy mighty hand;
And wherefore, then, should only hell still unsubduèd stand?
Thy mother's empire and thine own why dost thou not advance?
The third part now of all the world now hangs in doubtful
      chance.
And yet in heaven, too, now their deeds thou see'st me fain to
      bear.

470   We are despised; the strength of love with me away doth wear.
See'st not the darter, Dian, and Dame Pallas have already
Exempted them from my behests? And now of late so heady
Is Ceres' daughter too, that if we let her have her will
She will continue all her life a maid unwedded still;
For that is all her hope and mark whereat she minds to shoot.
But thou, if aught thy gracious turn our honour may promote
Or aught our empire beautify which jointly we do hold,
This damsel to her uncle join.' No sooner had she told
These words but Cupid, opening straight his quiver, chose
      therefro

480   One arrow, as his mother bade, among a thousand mo.
But such a one it was as none more sharper was than it,
Nor none went straighter from the bow the aimèd mark to hit.
He set his knee against his bow and bent it out of hand
And made his forkèd arrow's steal in Pluto's heart to stand.
   ' "Near Enna walls there stands a lake; Pergusa is the name.
Caïster heareth not mo songs of swans than doth the same.

A wood environs every side the water round about
And with his leaves as with a veil doth keep the sun-heat out.
The boughs do yield a cool fresh air; the moistness of the ground
Yields sundry flowers; continual spring is all the year there found.    490
While in this garden Proserpine was taking her pastime
In gathering either violets blue or lilies white as lime,
And while of maidenly desire she filled her maund and lap,
Endeavouring to outgather her companions there, by hap
Dis spied her; loved her; caught her up – and all at once, well
        near.
So hasty, hot and swift a thing is love, as may appear.
The lady with a wailing voice, affright, did often call
Her mother and her waiting maids, but mother most of all.
And as she from the upper part her garment would have rent,
By chance she let her lap slip down, and out her flowers went.    500
And such a silly simpleness her childish age yet bears
That even the very loss of them did move her more to tears.
The catcher drives his chariot forth and, calling every horse
By name, to make away apace he doth them still enforce
And shakes about their necks and manes their rusty bridle reins;
And through the deepest of the lake perforce he them constrains,
And through the Palick pools, the which from broken ground do
        boil
And smell of brimstone very rank, and also by the soil
Whereas the Bacchies, folk of Corinth with the double seas,
Between unequal havens twain did rear a town for ease.    510
  '"Between the fountains of Cyan and Arethuse of Pise,
    An arm of sea that meets enclosed with narrow horns there lies.
Of this the pool called Cyane, which beareth greatest fame
Among the nymphs of Sicily, did algates take the name.
Who, vauncing her unto the waist amid her pool, did know
Dame Proserpine and said to Dis, 'Ye shall no further go;
You cannot Ceres' son-in-law be, will she so or no.
You should have sought her courteously and not enforced her so.
And if I may with great estates my simple things compare,
Anapus was in love with me; but yet he did not fare    520
As you do now with Proserpine. He was content to woo,
And I, unforced and unconstrained, consented him unto.'

This said, she spreaded forth her arms and stopped him of his way.
His hasty wrath Saturnus' son no lenger then could stay
But, cheering up his dreadful steeds, did smite his royal mace
With violence in the bottom of the pool in that same place.
The ground straight yielded to his stroke and made him way to
     hell,
And down the open gap both horse and chariot headlong fell.
Dame Cyan, taking sore to heart as well the ravishment
530  Of Proserpine against her will as also the contempt
Against her fountain's privilege, did shroud in secret heart
An inward corsie comfortless, which never did depart
Until she, melting into tears, consumed away with smart.
The selfsame waters of the which she was but late ago
The mighty goddess now she pines and wastes herself into.
Ye might have seen her limbs wax lithe; ye might have bent her
     bones;
Her nails waxed soft. And first of all did melt the smallest ones,
As hair and fingers, legs and feet (for these same slender parts
Do quickly into water turn), and afterward converts
540  To water shoulder, back, breast, side. And finally, instead
Of lively blood within her veins corrupted there was spread
Thin water, so that nothing now remainèd whereupon
Ye might take hold. To water all consumèd was anon.

*Ceres searches*    '"The careful mother in the while did seek her daughter dear
*for her*       Through all the world, both sea and land, and yet was ne'er the
*daughter*          near.
The morning with her dewy hair her slugging never found,
Nor yet the evening star that brings the night upon the ground.
Two seasoned pine-trees at the mount of Etna did she light
And bare them restless in her hands through all the dankish night.
550  Again as soon as cheerful day did dim the stars, she sought
Her daughter still from east to west. And, being overwrought,
She caught a thirst. No liquor yet had come within her throat.
By chance she spièd near at hand a pelting thatchèd cote
With peevish doors. She knocked thereat, and out there comes a
     trot.
The goddess askèd her some drink, and she denied it not,

But out she brought her by and by a draught of merry-go-down
And therewithal a hotchpotch made of steepèd barley brown
And flax and coriander seed and other simples more,
The which she in an earthen pot together sod before.
While Ceres was a-eating this, before her gazing stood                    560
A hard fast boy, a shrewd pert wag that could no manners good;
He laughèd at her and in scorn did call her greedy gut.
The goddess, being wroth therewith, did on the hotchpotch put
The liquor ere that all was eat and in his face it threw.
Immediately the skin thereof became of speckled hue
And into legs his arms did turn. And in his altered hide
A wriggling tail straight to his limbs was added more beside.
And to th'intent he should not have much power to worken
          scathe,
His body in a little room together knit she hath.
For as with pretty lizards he in fashion doth agree,                       570
So than the lizard somewhat less in every point is he.
The poor old woman was amazed, and bitterly she wept.
She durst not touch the uncouth worm who into corners crept.
And of the fleckèd spots like stars that on his hide are set
A name agreeing thereunto in Latin doth he get;
It is our swift, whose skin with grey and yellow specks is fret.
  ' "What lands and seas the goddess sought it were too long to
          sayen.
    The world did want. And so she went to Sicil back again
And, as in going everywhere she searchèd busily,
She also came to Cyane, who would assuredly                                580
Have told her all things had she not transformèd been before.
But mouth and tongue for utterance now would serve her turn no
          more.
Howbeit, a token manifest she gave her for to know
What was become of Proserpine. Her girdle she did show
Still hovering on her holy pool, which slightly from her fell
As she that way did pass; and that her mother knew too well.
For when she saw it, by and by, as though she had but then
Been new advertised of her chance, she piteously began
To rend her ruffled hair and beat her hands against her breast.
As yet she knew not where she was, but yet with rage oppressed            590

She cursed all lands and said they were unthankful everych one,
Yea, and unworthy of the fruits bestowèd them upon.
But bitterly above the rest she bannèd Sicily,
In which the mention of her loss she plainly did espy.
And therefore there with cruel hand the earing ploughs she brake
And man and beast that tilled the ground to death in anger strake.
She marred the seed and eke forbade the fields to yield their fruit.
The plenteousness of that same isle, of which there went such
    bruit
Through all the world, lay dead. The corn was killèd in the blade;
Now too much drought, now too much wet did make it for to
600    fade.
The stars and blasting winds did hurt, the hungry fowls did eat
The corn in ground. The tines and briars did overgrow the wheat,
And other wicked weeds the corn continually annoy,
Which neither tilth nor toil of man was able to destroy.
   '"Then Arethuse, flood Alphey's love, lifts from her Elian
    waves
  Her head and, shedding to her ears her dewy hair that waves
About her forehead, said, 'O thou that art the mother dear
Both of the maiden sought through all the world both far and near
And eke of all the earthly fruits, forbear thine endless toil
610 And be not wroth without a cause with this thy faithful soil.
The land deserves no punishment. Unwillingly, God wot,
She opened to the ravisher that violently her smote.
It is not, sure, my native soil for which I thus entreat;
I am but here a sojourner. My native soil and seat
Is Pisa, and from Ely town I fetch my first descent.
I dwell but as a stranger here. But, sure, to my intent
This country likes me better far than any other land.
Here now I, Arethusa, dwell; here am I settled. And
I humbly you beseech, extend your favour to the same.
620 A time will one day come when you to mirth may better frame
And have your heart more free from care, which better serve me
    may
To tell you why I from my place so great a space do stray
And unto Ortygy am brought through so great seas and waves.
The ground doth give me passage free, and by the lowest caves

Of all the earth I make my way. And here I raise my head
And look upon the stars again, near out of knowledge fled.
Now while I underneath the earth the lake of Styx did pass,
I saw your daughter Proserpine with these same eyes. She was
Not merry, neither rid of fear as seemèd by her cheer,
But yet a queen, but yet of great god Dis the stately fere,     630
But yet of that same droopy realm the chief and sovereign peer.'
   '"Her mother stood as stark as stone when she these news did
       hear,
  And long she was like one that in another world had been.
But when her great amazèdness by greatness of her teen
Was put aside, she gets her to her chariot by and by
And up to heaven in all post haste immediately doth sty
And there beslubbered all her face. Her hair about her ears,
To royal Jove in way of plaint this spiteful tale she bears:
'As well for thy blood as for mine, a suitor unto thee
I hither come. If no regard may of the mother be,     640
Yet let the child her father move, and have not lesser care
Of her, I pray, because that I her in my body bare.
Behold, our daughter, whom I sought so long, is found at last –
If finding you it term when of recovery means is past,
Or if you finding do it call to have a knowledge where
She is become. Her ravishment we might consent to bear,
So restitution might be made. And though there were to me
No interest in her at all, yet, for as much as she
Is yours, it is unmeet she be bestowed upon a thief.'
Jove answered thus: 'My daughter is a jewel dear and lief,     650
A collop of mine own flesh cut as well as out of thine.
But if we in our hearts can find things rightly to define,
This is not spite but love. And yet, madam, in faith I see
No cause of such a son-in-law ashamèd for to be,
So you contented were therewith. For put the case that he
Were destitute of all things else, how great a matter is't
Jove's brother for to be? But sure in him is nothing missed,
Nor he inferior is to me save only that by lot
The heavens to me, the hells to him the Destinies did allot.
But if you have so sore desire your daughter to divorce,     660
Though she again to heaven repair, I do not greatly force,

But yet conditionally that she have tasted there no food;
For so the Destinies have decreed.' He ceased, and Ceres stood
Full bent to fetch her daughter out; but Destinies her withstood,
Because the maid had broke her fast. For as she happed one day
In Pluto's orchard recklessly from place to place to stray,
She, gathering from a bowing tree a ripe pomegranate, took
Seven kernels out and suckèd them. None chanced hereon to
    look
Save only one Ascalaphus, whom Orphne (erst a dame
670  Among the other elves of hell not of the basest fame)
Bare to her husband Acheron within her dusky den.
He saw it and, by blabbing it ungraciously as then,
Did let her from returning thence. A grievous sigh the queen
Of hell did fetch, and of that wight that had a witness been
Against her made a cursèd bird. Upon his face she shed
The water of the Phlegeton; and by and by his head
Was nothing else but beak and down and mighty glaring eyes.
Quite altered from himself between two yellow wings he flies.
He groweth chiefly into head and hookèd talons long,
680  And much ado he hath to flask his lazy wings among.
The messenger of mourning was he made, a filthy fowl,
A sign of mischief unto men, the sluggish screeching owl.
    ' "This person for his lavish tongue and telling tales might seem
      To have deservèd punishment. But what should men esteem
To be the very cause why you, Acheloy's daughters, wear
Both feet and feathers like to birds, considering that you bear
The upper parts of maidens still? And comes it so to pass
Because, when Lady Proserpine a-gathering flowers was,
Ye mermaids kept her company? Whom after you had sought
690  Through all the earth in vain, anon, of purpose that your thought
Might also to the seas be known, ye wishèd that ye might
Upon the waves with hovering wings at pleasure rule your flight
And had the gods to your request so pliant that ye found
With yellow feathers out of hand your bodies clothèd round.
Yet lest that pleasant tune of yours, ordainèd to delight
The hearing, and so high a gift of music perish might
For want of utterance, human voice to utter things at will
And count'nance of virginity remainèd to you still.

But mean between his brother and his heavy sister go'th
God Jove and parteth equally the year between them both.    700
And now the goddess Proserpine indifferently doth reign
Above and underneath the earth, and so doth she remain
One half year with her mother and the residue with her fere.
Immediately she altered is as well in outward cheer
As inward mind; for where her look might late before appear
Sad even to Dis, her count'nance now is full of mirth and grace,
Even like as Phoebus, having put the watery clouds to chase,
Doth show himself a conqueror with bright and shining face.
   '"Then fruitful Ceres, void of care in that she did recover
Her daughter, prayed thee, Arethuse, the story to discover    710
What causèd thee to fleet so far and wherefore thou became
A sacred spring. The waters whist. The goddess of the same
Did from the bottom of the well her goodly head up rear
And, having drièd with her hand her fair green hanging hair,
The river Alphey's ancient loves she thus began to tell:
   '"'I was', quoth she, 'a nymph of them that in Achaia dwell.

*The transformation of Arethusa*

There was not one that earnester the lawns and forests sought
Or pitched her toils more handsomely. And though that of my
        thought
It was no part to seek the fame of beauty, though I were
All courage, yet the prick and prize of beauty I did bear.    720
My overmuch commended face was unto me a spite.
This gift of body, in the which another would delight,
I, rudesby, was ashamèd of. Methought it was a crime
To be beliked. I bear it well in mind that on a time,
In coming weary from the chase of Stymphalus, the heat
Was fervent and my travailing had made it twice as great.
I found a water neither deep nor shallow which did glide
Without all noise, so calm that scarce the moving might be spied.
And throughly to the very ground it was so crisp and clear
That every little stone therein did plain aloft appear.    730
The hoary sallows and the poplars, growing on the brim
Unset, upon the shoring banks did cast a shadow trim.
I entered in and first of all I dippèd but my feet,
And after to my knees. And, not content to wade so fleet,

I put off all my clothes and hung them on a sallow by
And threw myself amid the stream; which as I dallyingly
Did beat and draw and with myself a thousand masteries try ·
In casting of mine arms abroad and swimming wantonly,
I felt a bubbling in the stream, I wist not how nor what,
740   And on the river's nearest brim I stepped for fear. With that,
"O Arethusa, whither run'st?" and "Whither run'st thou?" cried
Flood Alphey from his waves again with hollow voice. I hied
Away, unclothèd as I was (for on the further side
My clothes hung still). So much more hot and eager then was he,
And, for I naked was, I seemed the readier for to be.
My running and his fierce pursuit was like as when ye see
The silly doves with quivering wings before the goshawk sty,
The goshawk sweeping after them as fast as he can fly.
To Orchomen and Psophey land and Cyllen I did hold
750   Out well, and thence to Maenalus and Erymanth the cold,
And so to Ely. All this way no ground of me he won.
But, being not so strong as he, this restless race to run
I could not long endure, and he could hold it out at length.
Yet over plains and woody hills, as long as lasted strength,
And stones and rocks and desert grounds I still maintained my
      race.
The sun was full upon my back. I saw before my face
A lazy shadow, were it not that fear did make me see't.
But certainly he fearèd me with trampling of his feet,
And of his mouth the boistrous breath upon my hairlace blew.
760   Forwearied with the toil of flight, "Help, Dian, I, thy true
And trusty squire," I said, "who oft have carried after thee
Thy bow and arrows, now am like attachèd for to be."
The goddess, movèd, took a cloud of such as scattered were
And cast upon me. Hidden thus in misty darkness there,
The river poured upon me still and hunted round about
The hollow cloud, for fear perchance I should have scapèd out.
And twice, not knowing what to do, he stalked about the cloud
When Dian had me hid, and twice he callèd out aloud,
"Ho, Arethuse, ho, Arethuse." What heart had I, poor wretch,
      then?
770   Even such as hath the silly lamb that dares not stir nor quetch when

He hears the howling of the wolf about or near the folds;
Or such as hath the squatted hare that in her form beholds
The hunting hounds on every side and dares not move a whit.
He would not thence, for why he saw no footing out as yet;
And therefore watched he narrowly the cloud and eke the place.
A chill cold sweat my siegèd limbs oppressed, and down apace
From all my body steaming drops did fall of watery hue.
Which way so e'er I stirred my foot, the place was like a stew.
The dew ran trickling from my hair. In half the while I then
Was turned to water that I now have told the tale again.                    780
His lovèd waters Alphey knew and, putting off the shape
Of man, the which he took before because I should not scape,
Returnèd to his proper shape of water by and by
Of purpose for to join with me and have my company.
But Delia brake the ground at which I, sinking into blind
By-corners, up again myself at Ortygy do wind,
Right dear to me because it doth Diana's surname bear
And for because to light again I first was raisèd there.'
    ' "Thus far did Arethusa speak. And then the fruitful dame                790
    Two dragons to her chariot put. And, reining hard the same,
Midway between the heaven and earth she in the air went
And unto Prince Triptolemus her lightsome chariot sent
To Pallas' city load with corn, commanding him to sow
Some part in ground new broken up, and some thereof to strew
In ground long tilled before. Anon the young man up did sty
And, flying over Europe and the realm of Asias high,
Alighted in the Scythian land. There reignèd in that coast
A king called Lyncus, to whose house he entered for to host.
And being there demanded how and why he thither came
And also of his native soil and of his proper name,                          800
'I hight', quoth he, 'Triptolemus and born was in the town
Of Athens in the land of Greece, that place of high renown.
I neither came by sea nor land but through the open air.
I bring with me Dame Ceres' gifts which, being sown in fair
And fertile fields, may fruitful harvests yield and finer fare.'
The savage king had spite and, to th'intent that of so rare
And gracious gifts himself might seem first founder for to be,
He entertained him in his house and, when asleep was he,

He came upon him with a sword. But as he would have killed
                                                          him,
810    Dame Ceres turned him to a lynx and, waking t'other, willed him
His sacred team-ware through the air to drive abroad again.''

*The
punishment
of Pireus'
daughters*

'The chief of us had ended this her learnèd song, and then
The nymphs with one consent did judge that we, the goddesses
Of Helicon, had won the day. But when I saw that these
Unnurtured damsels overcome began to fall a-scolding,
I said, "So little sith to us you think yourselves beholding
For bearing with your malapertness in making challenge, that
Besides your former fault ye eke do fall to railing flat,
Abusing thus our gentleness, we will from hence proceed
820    The punishment and of our wrath the rightful humour feed.''
Euippy's daughters grinned and jeered and set our threatenings
                                                          light;
But as they were about to prate and bent their fists to smite
Their wicked hands with hideous noise, they saw the stumps of
                                                          quills
New budding at their nails, and how their arms soft feather hills.
Each saw how other's mouth did purse and harden into bill,
And so, becoming uncouth birds, to haunt the woods at will.
For as they would have clapped their hands, their wings did up
                                                          them heave
And, hanging in the air, the scolds of woods, did pies them leave.
Now also, being turned to birds, they are as eloquent
830    As e'er they were, as chattering still, as much to babbling bent.'

**FINIS QUINTI LIBRI.**

# The Sixth Book of Ovid's Metamorphoses

Tritonia unto all these words attentive hearing bends,
And both the Muses' learnèd song and rightful wrath commends.
And thereupon within herself this fancy did arise:
'It is no matter for to praise; but let our self devise
Some thing to be commended for, and let us not permit
Our majesty to be despised without revenging it.'
And therewithal she purposèd to put the Lydian maid
Arachne to her neckverse, who (as had to her been said)
Presumèd to prefer herself before her noble grace
In making cloth. This damsel was not famous for the place    10
In which she dwelt, nor for her stock, but for her art. Her sire
Was Idmon, one of Colophon, a pelting purple-dyer.
Her mother was deceased; but she was of the baser sort
And egal to her make in birth, in living and in port.
But though this maid were meanly born and dwelt but in a shed
At little Hypaep, yet her trade her fame abroad did spread
Even all the Lydian cities through. To see her wondrous work
The nymphs that underneath the vines of shady Tmolus lurk
Their vineyards oftentimes forsook. So did the nymphs also
About Pactolus oftentimes their golden streams forgo.    20
And evermore it did them good not only for to see
Her cloths already made, but while they eke a-making be,
Such grace was in her workmanship. For were it so that she
The new-shorn fleeces from the sheep in bundles deftly makes,
Or afterward doth kemb the same and draws it out in flakes
Along like clouds, or on the rock doth spin the handwarp woof,
Or else embroidereth, certainly ye might perceive by proof
She was of Pallas' bringing up. Which thing she, natheless,
Denieth and, disdaining such a mistress to confess,

Minerva and
Arachne

30   'Let her contend with me,' she said. 'And if she me amend,
     I will refuse no punishment the which she shall extend.'
          Minerva took an old wife's shape and made her hair seem grey
          And with a staff her feebled limbs pretended for to stay.
     Which done, she thus began to speak: 'Not all that age doth bring
     We ought to shun. Experience doth of long continuance spring.
     Despise not mine admonishment. Seek fame and chief report
     For making cloth and arras work among the mortal sort,
     But humbly give the goddess place and pardon of her crave
     For these thine unadvisèd words. I warrant thou shalt have
40   Forgiveness if thou ask it her.' Arachne bent her brows
     And, lowering on her, left her work. And hardly she eschews
     From flying in the lady's face. Her count'nance did bewray
     Her moody mind; which bursting forth in words, she thus did say:
     'Thou comest like a doting fool; thy wit is spent with years.
     Thy life hath lasted overlong, as by thy talk appears.
     And if thou any daughter have or any daughter-in-law,
     I would she heard these words of mine. I am not such a daw
     But that without thy teaching I can well enough advise
     Myself. And lest thou shouldest think thy words in any wise
50   Avail, the selfsame mind I keep with which I first begun.
     Why comes she not herself, I say? This match why doth she
          shun?'
     Then said the goddess, 'Here she is.' And therewithal she cast
     Her old wife's rivelled shape away and showed herself at last
     Minerva-like. The nymphs did straight adore her majesty;
     So did the young new-married wives that were of Mygdony.
     The maiden only, unabashed, would nought at all relent;
     But yet she blushed, and suddenly a ruddiness besprent
     Her cheeks which wanzed away again, even like as doth the sky
     Look sanguine at the break of day and turneth by and by
60   To white at rising of the sun. As hot as any fire
     She sticketh to her tackling still; and, through a fond desire
     Of glory, to her own decay all headlong forth she runs.
     For Pallas now no lenger warns, ne now no lenger shuns,
     Ne seeks the challenge to delay. Immediately they came
     And took their places severally, and in a several frame

Each strained a web, the warp whereof was fine. The web was
    tied
Upon a beam. Between the warp a sleigh of reed did slide.
The woof on sharpened pins was put betwixt the warp and
    wrought
With fingers. And as oft as they had through the warp it brought,
They strake it with a boxen comb. Both twain of them made haste     70
And, girding close for handsomeness their garments to their waist,
Bestirred their cunning hands apace. Their earnestness was such
As made them never think of pain. They weavèd very much
Fine purple that was dyed in Tyre and colours set so trim
That each in shadowing other seemed the very same with him.
Even like as after showers of rain, when Phoebus' broken beams
Do strike upon the clouds, appears a compassed bow of gleams
Which bendeth over all the heaven, wherein although there shine
A thousand sundry colours, yet the shadowing is so fine
That, look men ne'er so wistly, yet beguileth it their eyes;     80
So like and even the selfsame thing each colour seems to rise
Whereas they meet, which further off do differ more and more.
Of glittering gold with silken thread was weavèd there good store,
And stories put in portraiture of things done long afore.
    Minerva painted Athens town and Mars's rock therein
    And all the strife between herself and Neptune, who should win
The honour for to give the name to that same noble town.
In lofty thrones on either side of Jove were settled down
Six peers of heaven with count'nance grave and full of majesty,
And every of them by his face discernèd well might be.     90
The image of the mighty Jove was king-like. She had made
Neptunus standing, striking with his long three-tinèd blade
Upon the ragged rock; and from the middle of the clift
She portrayed issuing out a horse, which was the noble gift
For which he challenged to himself the naming of the town.
She pictured out herself with shield and morion on her crown,
With curat on her breast and spear in hand with sharpened end.
She makes the earth (the which her spear doth seem to strike) to
    send
An olive-tree with fruit thereon, and that the gods thereat
Did wonder. And with victory she finished up that plat.     100

Yet to th'intent examples old might make it to be known
    To her that for desire of praise so stoutly held her own
What guerdon she should hope to have for her attempt so mad,
Four like contentions in the four last corners she did add.
The Thracians Haeme and Rhodope the foremost corner had,
Who, being sometime mortal folk, usurped to them the name
Of Jove and Juno and were turned to mountains for the same.
A Pigmy woman's piteous chance the second corner showed,
Whom Juno turnèd to a crane because she was so lewd
110   As for to stand at strife with her for beauty, charging her
Against her native countryfolk continual war to stir.
The third had proud Antigone, who durst of pride contend
In beauty with the wife of Jove, by whom she in the end
Was turnèd to a stork. No whit availèd her the town
Of Troy or that Laomedon, her father, ware a crown,
But that she clad in feathers white her lazy wings must flap
And with a bobbèd bill bewail the cause of her mishap.
The last had childless Cinyras, who, being turned to stone,
Was pictured prostrate on the ground and weeping all alone
120   And culling fast between his arms a temple's greces fine
To which his daughters' bodies were transformed by wrath divine.
The utmost borders had a wreath of olive round about,
And this is all the work the which Minerva portrayed out.
For with the tree that she herself had made but late afore
She bounded in her arras cloth, and then did work no more.
    The Lydian maiden in her web did portray to the full
    How Europe was by royal Jove beguiled in shape of bull.
A swimming bull, a swelling sea so lively had she wrought
That bull and sea in very deed ye might them well have thought.
130   The lady seemèd looking back to landward and to cry
Upon her women and to fear the water sprinkling high
And shrinking up her fearful feet. She portrayed also there
Astery struggling with an erne, which did away her bear;
And over Leda she had made a swan his wings to splay.
She added also how by Jove in shape of satyr gay
The fair Antiope with a pair of children was besped;
And how he took Amphitryo's shape when in Alcmena's bed

He gat the worthy Hercules; and how he also came
To Danae like a shower of gold, to Aegine like a flame,
A shepherd to Mnemosyne, and like a serpent sly                    140
To Proserpine. She also made Neptunus leaping by
Upon a maid of Aeolus' race in likeness of a bull,
And in the stream Enipeus' shape begetting on a trull
The giants Othe and Ephialt, and in the shape of ram
Begetting one Theophane, Bisalty's imp, with lamb.
And in a lusty stallion's shape she made him hovering there
Dame Ceres with the yellow locks, and her whose golden hair
Was turned to crawling snakes on whom he gat the wingèd horse;
She made him in a dolphin's shape Melantho to enforce.
Of all these things she missèd not their proper shapes, nor yet    150
The full and just resemblance of their places for to hit.
In likeness of a country clown was Phoebus pictured there,
And how he now ware goshawk's wings, and now a lion's hair,
And how he in a shepherd's shape was practising a wile
The daughter of one Macary, Dame Issa, to beguile;
And how the fair Erigone by chance did suffer rape
By Bacchus, who deceivèd her in likeness of a grape;
And how that Saturn in the shape of jennet did beget
The double Chiron. Round about the utmost verge was set
A narrow trail of pretty flowers with leaves of ivy fret.          160
    Not Pallas, no, nor spite itself could any quarrel pick
    To this her work. And that did touch Minerva to the quick,
Who thereupon did rend the cloth in pieces every whit
Because the lewdness of the gods was blazèd so in it.
And with an arras weaver's comb of box she fiercely smit
Arachne on the forehead full a dozen times and more.
The maid, impatient in her heart, did stomach this so sore
That by and by she hung herself. Howbeit, as she hing
Dame Pallas, pitying her estate, did stay her in the string
From death and said, 'Lewd callet, live; but hang thou still for me. 170
And lest hereafter from this curse that time may set thee free,
I will that this same punishment enacted firmly be
As well on thy posterity for ever as on thee.'
And after, when she should depart, with juice of Hecate's flower
She sprinkled her. And by and by the poison had such power

That with the touch thereof her hair, her ears and nose did fade,
And very small it both her head and all her body made.
Instead of legs to both her sides stick fingers long and fine;
The rest is belly. From the which she ne'ertheless doth twine
A slender thread and practiseth in shape of spider still
The spinner's and the webster's crafts of which she erst had skill.

     All Lydia did repine hereat and of this deed the fame
     Through Phrygie ran, and through the world was talking of the
        same.
Before her marriage Niobe had known her very well,
When yet a maid in Maeony* and Sipyle she did dwell.
And yet Arachne's punishment at home before her eyes
To use discreeter kind of talk it could her not advise
Nor (as behoveth) to the gods to yield in humble wise.
For many things did make her proud. But neither did the town
The which her husband builded had, nor houses of renown
Of which they both descended were, nor yet the puissance
Of that great realm wherein they reigned so much her mind
       enhance
(Although the liking of them all did greatly her delight)
As did the offspring of herself. And certainly she might
Have been of mothers counted well most happy, had she not
So thought herself. For she whom sage Tiresias had begot,
The prophet Manto, through instinct of heavenly power did say
These kind of words in open street: 'Ye Thebans, go your way
Apace; and unto Laton and to Laton's children pray
And offer godly frankincense and wreathe your hair with bay.
Latona by the mouth of me commands you so to do.'
The Theban women, by and by obeying thereunto,
Decked all their heads with laurel leaves as Manto did require
And, praying with devout intent, threw incense in the fire.
    Behold, out cometh Niobe environed with a guard
    Of servants and a solemn train that followed afterward.
She was herself in raiment made of costly cloth of gold
Of Phrygia fashion, very brave and gorgeous to behold.

*\*Lydia*

And of herself she was right fair and beautiful of face,
But that her wrathful stomach then did somewhat stain her grace.        210
She, moving with her portly head her hair (the which as then
Did hang on both her shoulders loose), did pause a while. And
    when
With lofty look her stately eyes she rollèd had about,
  'What madness is it', quoth she, 'to prefer the heavenly rout
  Of whom ye do but hear, to such as daily are in sight?
Or why should Laton honoured be with altars? Never wight
To my most sacred majesty did offer incense. Yet
My father was that Tantalus whom only as most fit
The gods among them at their boards admitted for to sit.
A sister of the Pleiads is my mother. Finally,        220
My grandsire on the mother's side is that same Atlas high
That on his shoulders beareth up the heavenly axle-tree.
Again, my other grandfather is Jove and, as you see,
He also is my father-in-law, wherein I glory may.
The realm of Phrygia here at hand doth unto me obey.
In Cadmus' palace I thereof the lady do remain,
And jointly with my husband I as peerless princess reign
Both over this same town whose walls my husband's harp did
    frame
And also over all the folk and people in the same.
In whatsoever corner of my house I cast mine eye,        230
A world of riches and of goods I everywhere espy.
Moreover, for the beauty, shape and favour grown in me
Right well I know I do deserve a goddess for to be.
Besides all this, seven sons I have and daughters seven likewise,
By whom shall shortly son-in-laws and daughter-in-laws arise.
Judge you now if that I have cause of stateliness or no.
How dare ye, then, prefer to me Latona, that same fro
The Titan, Coeus' imp, to whom (then ready down to lie)
The hugy earth a little plot to child on did deny?
From heaven, from earth and from the sea your goddess banished
    was        240
And, as an outcast, through the world from place to place did pass
Until that Delos, pitying her, said, "Thou dost fleet on land
And I on sea," and thereupon did lend her out of hand

A place unstable. Of two twins there brought abed was she;
And this is but the seventh part of the issue borne by me.
Right happy am I. Who can this deny? And shall so still
Continue. Who doth doubt of that? Abundance hath and will
Preserve me. I am greater than the froward Fortune may
Impeach me. For although she should pull many things away,
250   Yet should she leave me many more. My state is out of fear.
Of this my huge and populous race surmise you that it were
Possible some of them should miss; yet can I never be
So spoilèd that no mo than two shall tarry still with me.
Leave quickly this lewd sacrifice and put me off this bay
That on your heads is wreathèd thus.' They laid it straight away
And left their holy rites undone, and closely as they may
With secret whispering to themselves to Laton they did pray.
    How much from utter barrenness the goddess was, so much
    Disdained she more, and in the top of Cynthus framèd such
260   Complaint as this to both her twins: 'Lo, I, your mother dear,
Who in my body once you twain with painful travail bare,
Lo, I, whose courage is so stout as for to yield to none
Of all the other goddesses except Jove's wife alone,
Am lately doubted whether I a goddess be or no.
And if you help not, children mine, the case now standeth so
That I the honour must from hence of altars quite forgo.
But this is not mine only grief. Besides her wicked fact,
Most railing words hath Niobe to my defacing raked.
She durst prefer her bairns to you. And as for me, she named
270   Me barren in respect of her, and was no whit ashamed
To show her father's wicked tongue which she by birth doth
        take.'
This said, Latona was about entreatance for to make;
'Cease off,' quoth Phoebus. 'Long complaint is nothing but delay
Of punishment.' And the selfsame words did Phoebe also say.
And by and by they, through the air both gliding swiftly down,
On Cadmus' palace hid in clouds did light in Thebe town.
    A field was underneath the wall both level, large and wide,
    Betrampled every day with horse that men therein did ride,
Where store of cars and horses' hoofs the clods to dust had trod.
280   A couple of Amphion's sons on lusty coursers rode

In this same place. Their horses fair caparisons did wear
Of scarlet, and their bridles brave with gold bedeckèd were.
Of whom as Niob's eldest son, Ismenus, happed to bring
His horse about and reined him in to make him keep the ring,
He cried, 'Alas!' and in his breast with that an arrow stack.
And by and by his dying hand did let the bridle slack,
And on the right side of the horse he slippèd to the ground.
The second brother, Sipylus, did chance to hear the sound
Of quivers clattering in the air and, giving straight the rein
And spur together to his horse, began to fly amain                         290
As doth the master of a ship who, when he sees a shower
Approaching by some misty cloud that gins to gloom and lower,
Doth clap on all his sails because no wind should scape him by,
Though ne'er so small. Howbeit, as he turnèd for to fly,
He was not able for to scape the arrow which did strike
Him through the neck. The nock thereof did shaking upward
          stick;
The head appearèd at his throat. And as he forward gave
Himself in flying, so to ground he grovelling also drave
And toppled by the horse's mane and feet amid his race
And with his warm new-shedded blood berayèd all the place.                 300
But Phaedimus and Tantalus, the heir of the name
Of Tantalus his grandfather, who customably came
From other daily exercise to wrestling, had begun
To close and each at other now with breast to breast to run,
When Phoebus' arrow, being sent with force from strainèd string,
Did strike through both of them as they did fast together cling.
And so they sighèd both at once, and both at once for pain
Fell down to ground, and both of them at once their eyes did
          strain
To see their latest light, and both at once their ghosts did yield.
Alphenor this mischance of theirs with heavy heart beheld,                 310
And scratched and beat his woeful breast; and therewith, flying
          out
To take them up between his arms, was, as he went about
This work of kindly pity, killed. For Phoebus with a dart
Of deadly dint did rive him through the bulk and brake his heart.

And when the steal was pluckèd out, a parcel of his liver
Did hang upon the hookèd head. And so he did deliver
His life and blood into the air, departing both together.
But Damasicthon, on whose head came never scissor, felt
Mo wounds than one. It was his chance to have a grievous pelt
320    Upon the very place at which the leg is first begun
And where the hamstrings by the joint with supple sinews run.
And while to draw this arrow out he with his hand assayed,
Another through his weasand went, and at the feathers stayed.
The blood did drive out this again and, spinning high, did spout
A great way off and pierced the air with sprinkling all about.
The last of all, Iliony, with stretchèd hands and speech
Most humble (but in vain) did say, 'O gods, I you beseech
Of mercy all in general.' He wist not what he said
Ne how that unto all of them he ought not to have prayed.
330    The god that held the bow in hand was movèd; but as then
The arrow was already gone so far that back again
He could not call it. Ne'ertheless, the wound was very small
Of which he died, for why his heart it did but lightly gall.

    The rumour of the mischief self and moan of people and
    The weeping of her servants gave the mother t'understand
The sudden stroke of this mischance. She wondered very much
And stormèd also that the gods were able to do such
A deed or durst attempt it; yea, she thought it more than right
That any of them over her should have so mickle might.
340    Amphion had fordone himself already with a knife
And ended all his sorrows quite together with his life.
Alas, alas, how greatly doth this Niobe differ here
From t'other Niobe who a-late, disdaining any peer,
Did from Latona's altars drive her folk and through the town
With haughty look and stately gait went pranking up and down!
Then spited at among her own, but piteous now to those
That heretofore for her deserts had been her greatest foes.
She falleth on the corses cold and, taking no regard,
Bestowed her kisses on her sons as whom she afterward
Did know she never more should kiss. From whom she, lifting
350    tho
Her blue and bruisèd arms to heaven, said, 'O thou cruel foe,

Latona, feed, yea, feed thyself, I say, upon my woe
And overgorge thy stomach, yea, and glut thy cruel heart
With these my present painful pangs of bitter griping smart.
In corses seven I seven times dead am carried to my grave.
Rejoice, thou foe, and triumph now in that thou seem'st to have
The upper hand. What? Upper hand? No, no, it is not so.
As wretched as my case doth seem, yet have I left me mo
Than thou for all thy happiness canst of thine own account.
Even after all these corses yet I still do thee surmount.'                    360
Upon the end of these same words the twanging of the string
In letting of the arrow fly was clearly heard. Which thing
Made everyone save Niobe afraid; her heart was so
With sorrow hardened that she grew more bold. Her daughters
        tho
Were standing all with mourning weed and hanging hair before
Their brothers' coffins. One of them, in pulling from the sore
An arrow sticking in his heart, sank down upon her brother
With mouth to mouth, and so did yield her fleeting ghost.
        Another,
In comforting the wretched case and sorrow of her mother,
Upon the sudden held her peace. She stricken was within             370
With double wound, which causèd her her talking for to blin
And shut her mouth; but first her ghost was gone. One, all in vain
Attempting for to scape by flight, was in her flying slain.
Another on her sister's corse doth tumble down stark dead.
This quakes and trembles piteously; and she doth hide her head.
And when that six with sundry wounds dispatchèd were and gone,
At last as yet remainèd one. And for to save that one
Her mother with her body whole did cling about her fast
And, wrying her, did over her her garments wholly cast
And crièd out, 'O, leave me one! This little one yet save!             380
Of many but this only one, the least of all, I crave.'
But while she prayed, for whom she prayed was killed. Then
        down she sat,
Bereft of all her children quite and drawing to her fate
Among her daughters and her sons and husband newly dead.
Her cheeks waxed hard; the air could stir no hair upon her head;

The colour of her face was dim and clearly void of blood;
And sadly under open lids her eyes unmovèd stood.
In all her body was no life. For even her very tongue
And palate of her mouth was hard, and each to other clung.

390 Her pulses ceasèd for to beat; her neck did cease to bow,
Her arms to stir, her feet to go. All power forwent as now,
And into stone her very womb and bowels also bind.
But yet she wept and, being hoist by force of whirling wind,
Was carried into Phrygie. There upon a mountain's top
She weepeth still in stone; from stone the dreary tears do drop.

Then all, both men and women, feared Latona's open ire
And far with greater sumptuousness and earnester desire
Did worship the great majesty of this their goddess, who
Did bear at once both Phoebus and his sister Phoebe too.

400 And through occasion of this chance (as men are wont to do
In cases like) the people fell to telling things of old,
Of whom a man among the rest this tale ensuing told:

*Diana and the Lycian peasants*

'The ancient folk that in the fields of fruitful Lycia dwelt
Due penance also for their spite to this same goddess felt.
The baseness of the parties makes the thing itself obscure,
Yet is the matter wonderful. Myself, I you assure,
Did presently behold the pond and saw the very place
In which this wondrous thing was done. My father then in case,
Not able for to travel well by reason of his age,

410 To fetch home certain oxen thence made me to be his page,
Appointing me a countryman of Lycia to my guide.
With whom as I went plodding in the pasture grounds, I spied
Amidst a certain pond an old square altar coloured black
With cinder of the sacrifice that still upon it stack.
About it round grew wavering reeds. My guide anon did stay
And softly, "O be good to me," he in himself did say.
And I with like soft whispering did say, "Be good to me."
And then I asked him whether that the altar we did see
Belongèd to the waternymphs or fauns or other god

420 Peculiar to the place itself upon the which we yode.
He made me answer thus: "My guest, no god of country race
Is in this altar worshippèd. That goddess claims this place

From whom the wife of mighty Jove did all the world forfend
When, wandering restless here and there, full hardly in the end
Unsettled Delos did receive, then floating on the wave,
As tide and weather to and fro the swimming island drave.
There, maugre Juno, who with might and main against her strave,
Latona, staying by a date and olive-tree that stead
In travail, of a pair of twins was safely brought abed.
And after her deliverance folk report that she for fear        430
Of Juno's wrath did fly from hence and in her arms did bear
Her babes, which afterward became two gods. In which her travel
In summer, when the scorching sun is wont to burn the gravel
Of Lycy country, where the fell Chimaera hath his place,
The goddess, weary with the long continuance of her race,
Waxed thirsty by the means of drought with going in the sun.
Her babes had also sucked her breasts as long as milk would run.
By chance she spied this little pond of water here below.
And country carls were gathering there these osier twigs that grow
So thick upon a shrubby stalk, and of these rushes green        440
And flags that in these moorish plots so rife of growing been.
She, coming hither, kneelèd down the water up to take
To cool her thirst. The churlish clowns forfended her the lake.
Then gently said the goddess, 'Sirs, why do you me forfend
The water? Nature doth to all in common water send.
For neither sun, nor air, nor yet the water private be;
I seek but that which Nature's gift hath made to all things free.
And yet I humbly crave of you to grant it unto me.
I did not go about to wash my weary limbs and skin;
I would but only quench my thirst. My throat is scalt within    450
For want of moisture, and my chaps and lips are parching dry,
And scarcely is there way for words to issue out thereby.
A draught of water will to me be heavenly nectar now,
And sure I will confess I have receivèd life of you.
Yea, in your giving of a drop of water unto me
The case so standeth as you shall preserve the lives of three.
Alas, let these same silly souls that in my bosom stretch
Their little arms' – by chance her babes their pretty dolls did
        reach –

'To pity move you.' What is he so hard that would not yield
460 To this, the gentle goddess's entreatance meek and mild?
Yet they, for all the humble words she could devise to say,
Continued in their wilful mood of churlish saying nay
And threatened for to send her thence unless she went away,
Reviling her most spitefully. And not contented so,
With hands and feet the standing pool they troubled to and fro
Until, with trampling up and down maliciously, the soft
And slimy mud that lay beneath was raisèd up aloft.
With that the goddess was so wroth that thirst was quite forgot.
And unto such unworthy carls herself she humbleth not
470 Ne speaketh meaner words than might beseem a goddess well
But, holding up her hands to heaven, 'For ever mought you dwell
In this same pond,' she said. Her wish did take effect with speed,
For underneath the water they delight to be indeed.
Now dive they to the bottom down, now up their heads they
pop;
Another while with sprawling legs they swim upon the top.
And oftentimes upon the banks they have a mind to stand,
And oftentimes from thence again to leap into the pond.
And there they now do practise still their filthy tongues to scold,
And shamelessly (though underneath the water) they do hold
480 Their former wont of brawling still amid the water cold.
Their voices still are hoarse and harsh, their throats have puffèd
gowls,
Their chaps with brawling widened are, their hammer-headed
jowls
Are joinèd to their shoulders just, the necks of them do seem
Cut off, the ridgebone of their back sticks up of colour green,
Their paunch – which is the greatest part of all their trunch – is
grey;
And so they up and down the pond, made newly frogs, do play."'

*The flaying*
*of Marsyas*
When one of Lyce (I wot not who) had spoken in this sort,
Another of a satyr straight began to make report
Whom Phoebus, overcoming on a pipe (made late ago
490 By Pallas), put to punishment. 'Why flayest thou me so?
Alas!' he cried, 'It irketh me. Alas, a sorry pipe
Deserveth not so cruelly my skin from me to strip.'

For all his crying, o'er his ears quite pullèd was his skin.
Nought else he was than one whole wound. The grisly blood did
   spin
From every part; the sinews lay discovered to the eye;
The quivering veins without a skin lay beating nakedly.
The panting bowels in his bulk ye might have numbered well,
And in his breast the sheer small strings a man might easily tell.
The country fauns, the gods of woods, the satyrs of his kin,
The Mount Olympus, whose renown did ere that time begin,     500
And all the nymphs and all that in those mountains kept their
   sheep
Or grazèd cattle thereabouts, did for this satyr weep.
The fruitful earth waxed moist therewith and, moisted, did receive
Their tears and in her bowels deep did of the same conceive.
And when that she had turnèd them to water, by and by
She sent them forth again aloft to see the open sky.
The river that doth rise thereof, beginning there his race,
In very deep and shoring banks to seaward runs apace
Through Phrygie; and according as the satyr, so the stream
Is callèd Marsyas, of the brooks the clearest in that realm.    510
   With such examples as these same the common folk returned
    To present things, and every man through all the city mourned
For that Amphion was destroyed with all his issue so.
But all the fault and blame was laid upon the mother tho.
For her alonely Pelops mourned, as men report, and he
In opening of his clothes did show, that every man might see,
His shoulder on the left side bare of ivory for to be.
This shoulder at his birth was like his t'other, both in hue
And flesh, until his father's hands most wickedly him slew
And that the gods, when they his limbs again together drew    520
To join them in their proper place and form by nature due,
Did find out all the other parts save only that which grew
Between the throat-boll and the arm. Which when they could not
   get,
This other made of ivory white in place thereof they set;
And by that means was Pelops made again both whole and sound.
   The neighbour princes thither came, and all the cities round

*Mourning for
the house of
Amphion*

About besought their kings to go and comfort Thebe: as Arge.
And Sparta and Mycene, which was under Pelops' charge,
And Calydon, unhated of the frowning Phoebe yet,
530  The wealthy town Orchomenos and Corinth, which in it
Had famous men for workmanship in metals, and the stout
Messene, which full twenty years did hold besiegers out,
And Patrae and the lowly town Cleona, Neley's Pyle
And Troezen, not surnamèd yet Pittheia for a while,
And all the other borough towns and cities which do stand
Within the narrow balk at which two seas do meet at hand
Or which do bound upon the balk without in main firm land.

*Tereus and*  Alonely Athens (who would think?) did neither come nor send.
*Philomel*  War barrèd them from courtesy, the which they did intend.
540  The king of Pontus with an host of savage people lay
In siege before their famous walls and curstly did them fray
Until that Tereus, king of Thrace, approaching to their aid,
Did vanquish him and with renown was for his labour paid.
And sith he was so puissant in men and ready coin
And came of mighty Mars's race, Pandion sought to join
Alliance with him by and by and gave him to his fere
His daughter Procne. At this match (as after will appear)
Was neither Juno, president of marriage wont to be,
Nor Hymen, no, nor any one of all the Graces three.
550  The Furies, snatching tapers up that on some hearse did stand,
Did light them and before the bride did bear them in their hand.
The Furies made the bridegroom's bed. And on the house did
ruck
A cursèd owl, the messenger of ill success and luck.
And all the night-time, while that they were lying in their beds,
She sat upon the bedstead's top right over both their heads.
Such handsel Procne had the day that Tereus did her wed;
Such handsel had they when that she was brought of child abed.
All Thracia did rejoice at them and thanked their gods and willed
That both the day of Procne's match with Tereus should be held
560  For feastful and the day likewise that Itys first was born;
So little know we what behoves. The sun had now outworn
Five harvests and by course five times had run his yearly race
When Procne, flattering Tereus, said, 'If any love or grace

Between us be, send either me my sister for to see
Or find the means that hither she may come to visit me.
You may assure your father-in-law she shall again return
Within a while. Ye do to me the highest great good turn
That can be, if you bring to pass I may my sister see.'
Immediately the king commands his ships afloat to be,
And shortly after, what with sail and what with force of oars,   570
In Athens' haven he arrives and lands at Pirey shores.
As soon as of his father-in-law the presence he obtained
And had of him been courteously and friendly entertained,
Unhappy handsel entered with their talking first together.
The errands of his wife, the cause of his then coming thither,
He had but new begun to tell and promisèd that when
She had her sister seen she should with speed be sent again,
When (see the chance) came Philomel in raiment very rich
And yet in beauty far more rich, even like the fairies which
Reported are the pleasant woods and water springs to haunt,   580
So that the like apparel and attire to them you grant.
King Tereus at the sight of her did burn in his desire,
As if a man should chance to set a gulf of corn on fire
Or burn a stack of hay. Her face indeed deservèd love.
But as for him, to fleshly lust even nature did him move;
For of those countries commonly the people are above
All measure prone to lechery. And therefore both by kind
His flame increased and by his own default of vicious mind.
He purposed fully to corrupt her servants with reward
Or for to bribe her nurse, that she should slenderly regard   590
Her duty to her mistressward. And rather than to fail,
The lady even herself with gifts he minded to assail
And all his kingdom for to spend, or else by force of hand
To take her and in maintenance thereof by sword to stand.
There was not under heaven the thing but that he durst it prove,
So far unable was he now to stay his lawless love.
Delay was deadly. Back again with greedy mind he came
Of Procne's errands for to talk, and underneath the same
He works his own ungraciousness. Love gave him power to frame
His talk at will. As oft as he demanded out of square,   600
Upon his wife's importunate desire himself he bare.

He also wept, as though his wife had willèd that likewise.
O God, what blindness doth the hearts of mortal men disguise!
By working mischief Tereus gets him credit for to seem
A loving man and winneth praise by wickedness extreme.
Yea, and the foolish Philomel the selfsame thing desires
Who, hanging on her father's neck with flattering arms, requires
Against her life and for her life his licence for to go
To see her sister. Tereus beholds her wistly tho

610 And, in beholding, handles her with heart. For when he saw
Her kiss her father and about his neck her arms to draw,
They all were spurs to prick him forth and wood to feed his fire
And food of forcing nourishment to further his desire.
As oft as she her father did between her arms embrace,
So often wishèd he himself her father in that case.
For nought at all should that in him have wrought the greater
        grace.
Her father could not say them nay, they lay at him so sore.
Right glad thereof was Philomel and thankèd him therefore;
And, wretched wench, she thinks she had obtainèd such a thing

620 As both to Procne and herself should joy and comfort bring,
When both of them in very deed should afterward it rue.
To endward of his daily race and travel Phoebus drew,
And on the shoring side of heaven his horses downward flew.
A princely supper was prepared and wine in gold was set,
And after meat to take their rest the princes did them get.
But though the king of Thrace that while were absent from her
        sight,
Yet swelted he and, in his mind revolving all the night
Her face, her gesture and her hands, imagined all the rest
(The which as yet he had not seen) as liked his fancy best.

630 He feeds his flames himself. No wink could come within his eyes
For thinking aye on her. As soon as day was in the skies,
Pandion, holding in his hand the hand of Tereus pressed
To go his way and shedding tears, betook him thus his guest:
'Dear son-in-law, I give thee here, sith godly cause constrains,
This damsel. By the faith that in thy princely heart remains
And for our late alliance sake and by the gods above,
I humbly thee beseech that as a father thou do love

And maintain her, and that as soon as may be (all delay
Will unto me seem overlong) thou let her come away,
The comfort of my careful age on whom my life doth stay.          640
And thou, my daughter Philomel, it is enough, iwis,
That from her father set so far thy sister Procne is;
If any spark of nature do within thy heart remain,
With all the haste and speed thou canst return to me again.'
In giving charge, he kissèd her; and down his cheeks did rain
The tender tears. And as a pledge of faith he took the right
Hands of them both and, joining them, did each to other plight,
Desiring them to bear in mind his commendations to
His daughter and her little son. And then with much ado
For sobbing, at the last he bade adieu as one dismayed;          650
The foremisgiving of his mind did make him sore afraid.
   As soon as Tereus and the maid together were aboard
   And that their ship from land with oars was halèd on the ford,
'The field is ours!' he cried aloud; 'I have the thing I sought.'
And up he skipped; so barbarous and so beastly was his thought
That scarce even there he could forbear his pleasure to have
      wrought.
His eye went never off of her, as when the scareful erne,
With hookèd talons trussing up a hare among the fern,
Hath laid her in his nest from whence the prisoner cannot scape;
The ravening fowl with greedy eyes upon his prey doth gape.      660
Now was their journey come to end; now were they gone a-land
In Thracia, when that Tereus took the lady by the hand
And led her to a pelting grange that peakishly did stand
In woods forgrown. There, waxing pale and trembling sore for
      fear
And dreading all things and with tears demanding sadly where
Her sister was, he shut her up, and therewithal bewrayed
His wicked lust; and so by force, because she was a maid
And all alone, he vanquished her. It booted nought at all
That she on sister, or on sire or on the gods did call.
She quaketh like the wounded lamb which, from the wolf's hoar
      teeth                                                      670
New shaken, thinks herself not safe; or as the dove that see'th

Her feathers with her own blood stained who, shuddering still,
    doth fear
The greedy hawk that did her late with griping talons tear.
    Anon, when that this mazèdness was somewhat overpassed,
    She rent her hair and beat her breast and up to heavenward cast
Her hands in mourning wise and said, 'O cankered carl, O fell
And cruel tryant, neither could the godly tears that fell
A-down my father's cheeks when he did give thee charge of me,
Ne of my sister that regard that ought to be in thee,
680    Nor yet my chaste virginity, nor conscience of the law
Of wedlock from this villainy thy barbarous heart withdraw!
Behold, thou hast confounded all! My sister thorough me
Is made a cuckquean; and thyself through this offence of thee
Art made a husband to us both, and unto me a foe:
A just deservèd punishment for lewdly doing so.
But to th'intent, O perjured wretch, no mischief may remain
Unwrought by thee, why doest thou from murdering me refrain?
Would God thou had it done before this wicked rape. From
        hence
Then should my soul most blessèdly have gone without offence.
690    But if the gods do see this deed and if the gods, I say,
Be aught and in this wicked world bear any kind of sway,
And if with me all other things decay not, sure the day
Will come that for this wickedness full dearly thou shalt pay.
Yea, I myself, rejecting shame, thy doings will bewray.
And if I may have power to come abroad, them blaze I will
In open face of all the world. Or if thou keep me still
As prisoner in these woods, my voice the very woods shall fill
And make the stones to understand. Let heaven to this give ear,
And all the gods and powers therein, if any god be there.'
700    The cruel tyrant, being chafed and also put in fear
    With these and other such her words, both causes so him stung
That, drawing out his naked sword that at his girdle hung,
He took her rudely by the hair and wrung her hands behind her,
Compelling her to hold them there while he himself did bind her.
When Philomela saw the sword, she hoped she should have died
And for the same her naked throat she gladly did provide.

But as she yearned and callèd aye upon her father's name
And strivèd to have spoken still, the cruel tyrant came
And with a pair of pinions fast did catch her by the tongue
And with his sword did cut it off. The stump whereon it hung    710
Did patter still. The tip fell down and, quivering on the ground,
As though that it had murmurèd it made a certain sound.
And as an adder's tail cut off doth skip a while, even so
The tip of Philomela's tongue did wriggle to and fro
And nearer to her mistressward in dying still did go.
And after this most cruel act, for certain men report
That he (I scarcely dare believe) did oftentimes resort
To maimèd Philomela and abused her at his will.
Yet after all this wickedness he, keeping count'nance still,
Durst unto Procne home repair; and she immediately           720
Demanded where her sister was. He, sighing feignèdly,
Did tell her falsely she was dead, and with his subtle tears
He maketh all his tale to seem of credit in her ears.
Her garments glittering all with gold she from her shoulders tears
And puts on black and setteth up an empty hearse and keeps
A solemn obit for her soul; and piteously she weeps
And waileth for her sister's fate who was not in such wise
As that was for to be bewailed. The sun had in the skies
Passed through the twelve celestial signs and finished full a year.
But what should Philomela do? She watchèd was so near         730
That start she could not for her life. The walls of that same grange
Were made so high of main hard stone that out she could not
        range.
Again, her tongueless mouth did want the utterance of the fact.
Great is the wit of pensiveness, and when the head is racked
With hard misfortune sharp forecast of practice entereth in.
A warp of white upon a frame of Thracia she did pin
And weavèd purple letters in between it, which bewrayed
The wicked deed of Tereus. And having done, she prayed
A certain woman by her signs to bear them to her mistress.
She bare them and delivered them, not knowing ne'ertheless     740
What was in them. The tyrant's wife unfolded all the clout
And of her wretched fortune read the process whole throughout.

She held her peace. A wondrous thing it is she should so do,
But sorrow tied her tongue and words agreeable unto
Her great displeasure were not at commandment at that stound,
And weep she could not. Right and wrong she reckoneth to
      confound,
And on revengement of the deed her heart doth wholly ground.

*Procne's*
*revenge*

    It was the time that wives of Thrace were wont to celebrate
    The three year rites of Bacchus which were done a-night-times
      late.

750 A-night-times soundeth Rhodope of tinkling pans and pots;
A-night-times, giving up her house, abroad Queen Procne trots
Disguised like Bacchus' other frows and armèd to the proof
With all the frantic furniture that serves for that behoof.
Her head was covered with a vine; about her loose was tucked
A red deer's skin; a lightsome lance upon her shoulder rucked.
In post gads terrible Procne through the woods, and at her heels
A flock of frows; and where the sting of sorrow which she feels
Enforceth her to furiousness, she feigns it to proceed
Of Bacchus' motion. At the length she, finding out indeed
The outset grange, howled out and cried, 'Now, well!' and open
760       brake
The gates and straight her sister thence by force of hand did take
And, veiling her in like attire of Bacchus, hid her head
With ivy leaves and home to court her sore amazèd led.

    As soon as Philomela wist she set her foot within
    That cursèd house, the wretched soul to shudder did begin,
And all her face waxed pale. Anon her sister, getting place,
Did pull off Bacchus' mad attire and, making bare her face,
Embracèd her between her arms. But she, considering that
Queen Procne was a cuckquean made by means of her, durst nat
770 Once raise her eyes, but on the ground fast fixèd held the same.
And where she would have taken God to witness that the shame
And villainy was wrought to her by violence, she was fain
To use her hand instead of speech. Then Procne chafed amain
And was not able in herself her choler to restrain
But, blaming Philomela for her weeping, said these words:
'Thou must not deal in this behalf with weeping but with swords,

Or with some thing of greater force than swords. For my part, I
Am ready, yea, and fully bent all mischief for to try.
This palace will I either set on fire and in the same
Bestow the cursèd Tereus, the worker of our shame,                    780
Or pull away his tongue or put out both his eyes, or cut
Away those members which have thee to such dishonour put,
Or with a thousand wounds expulse that sinful soul of his.
The thing that I do purpose on is great, whate're it is.
I know not what it may be yet.' While Procne hereunto
Did set her mind, came Itys in, who taught her what to do.
She, staring on him cruelly, said, 'Ah, how like thou art
Thy wicked father,' and without mo words a sorrowful part
She purposèd, such inward ire was boiling in her heart.
But notwithstanding, when her son approachèd to her near            790
And lovingly had greeted her by name of mother dear
And with his pretty arms about the neck had hugged her fast
And flattering words with childish toys in kissing forth had cast,
The mother's heart of hers was then constrainèd to relent;
Assuagèd wholly was the rage to which she erst was bent,
And from her eyes against her will the tears enforcèd went.
But when she saw how pity did compel her heart to yield,
She turnèd to her sister's face from Itys and beheld
Now t'one, now t'other earnestly, and said, 'Why tattles he
And she sits dumb, bereft of tongue? As well why calls not she       800
Me sister as this boy doth call me mother? See'st thou not,
Thou daughter of Pandion, what a husband thou hast got?
Thou growest wholly out of kind. To such a husband as
Is Tereus, pity is a sin.' No more delay there was.
She draggèd Itys after her, as when it haps in Inde
A tiger gets a little calf that sucks upon a hind
And drags him through the shady woods. And when that they had
            found
A place within the house far off and far above the ground,
Then Procne strake him with a sword, now plainly seeing whither
He should and holding up his hands and crying, 'Mother,
            mother,'                                                     810
And flying to her neck, even where the breast and side do bound,
And never turned away her face. Enough had been that wound

Alone to bring him to his end. The t'other sister slit
His throat. And while some life and soul was in his members yet,
In gobbets they them rent; whereof were some in pipkins boiled
And other some on hissing spits against the fire were broiled.
And with the jellied blood of him was all the chamber foiled.
   To this same banquet Procne bade her husband, knowing
      nought
   Nor nought mistrusting of the harm and lewdness she had
      wrought.

820 And feigning a solemnity according to the guise
Of Athens, at the which there might be none in any wise
Besides her husband and herself, she banished from the same
Her household folk and sojourners and such as guestwise came.
King Tereus, sitting in the throne of his forefathers, fed
And swallowed down the selfsame flesh that of his bowels bred.
And he, so blinded was his heart, 'Fetch Itys hither,' said.
No lenger her most cruel joy dissemble could the queen
But, of her murder coveting the messenger to been,
She said, 'The thing thou askest for thou hast within.' About

830 He lookèd round and askèd, 'Where?' To put him out of doubt,
As he was yet demanding, 'Where?' and calling for him, out
Leapt Philomel with scattered hair aflight, like one that fled
Had from some fray where slaughter was, and threw the bloody
      head
Of Itys in his father's face. And never more was she
Desirous to have had her speech that able she might be
Her inward joy with worthy words to witness frank and free.
The tyrant with a hideous noise away the table shoves
And rears the fiends from hell. One while with yawning mouth he
      proves
To perbrake up his meat again and cast his bowels out.

840 Another while with wringing hands he weeping goes about
And of his son he terms himself the wretched grave. Anon
With naked sword and furious heart he followeth fierce upon
Pandion's daughters. He that had been present would have
      deemed
Their bodies to have hovered up with feathers. As they seemed,

So hovered they with wings indeed. Of whom the one away
To woodward flies, the other still about the house doth stay.
And of their murder from their breasts not yet the token go'th,
For even still yet are stained with blood the feathers of them both.
And he, through sorrow and desire of vengeance waxing wight,
Became a bird upon whose top a tuft of feathers light 850
In likeness of a helmet's crest doth trimly stand upright.
Instead of his long sword, his bill shoots out a passing space.
A lapwing namèd is this bird; all armèd seems his face.

 The sorrow of this great mischance did stop Pandion's breath   *Boreas and*
 Before his time and long ere age determined had his death.    *Orithyia*
Erecthey, reigning after him, the government did take,
A prince of such a worthiness as no man well can make
Resolution if he more in arms or justice did excel.
Four sons and daughters four he had, of which a couple well
Did each in beauty other match. The one of these whose name 860
Was Procris unto Cephalus, King Aeolus' son, became
A happy wife. The Thracians and King Tereus were a let
To Boreas, so that long it was before the god could get
His dear-belov'd Orithyia while trifling he did stand
With fair entreatance rather than did use the force of hand.
But when he saw he no relief by gentle means could find,
Then, turning unto boisterous wrath (which unto that same wind
Is too familiar and too much accustomèd by kind),
He said, 'I servèd am but well; for why laid I apart
My proper weapons, fierceness, force and ire and cruel heart, 870
And fell to fawning like a fool, which did me but disgrace?
For me is violence meet. Through this the pestered clouds I chase;
Through this I toss the seas; through this I turn up knotty oaks
And harden snow and beat the ground in hail with sturdy strokes.
When I my brothers chance to get in open air and sky
(For that is my field in the which my masteries I do try),
I charge upon them with such brunt that of our meeting smart
The heaven between us sounds and from the hollow clouds doth
  start
Enforcèd fire. And when I come in holes of hollow ground
And fiercely in those empty caves do rouse my back up round, 880

I trouble even the ghosts and make the very world to quake.
This help in wooing of my wife to speed I should have take.
Erecthey should not have been prayed my father-in-law to be;
He should have been compelled thereto by stout extremity.'
    In speaking these or other words as sturdy, Boreas gan
    To flask his wings, with waving of the which he raisèd then
So great a gale that all the earth was blasted therewithal
And troubled was the main broad sea. And as he trailed his pall
Bedusted over highest tops of things, he swept the ground.
890  And having now in smoky clouds himself enclosèd round,
Between his dusky wings he caught Orithyia, straught for fear,
And like a lover very soft and easily did her bear.
And as he flew, the flames of love enkindled more and more
By means of stirring. Neither did he stay his flight before
He came within the land and town of Cicones with his prey.
And there soon after, being made his wife, she happed to lay
Her belly; and a pair of boys she at a burden brings,
Who else in all resembled full their mother, save in wings
The which they of their father took. Howbeit (by report)
900  They were not born with wings upon their bodies in this sort.
While Calaïs and Zetes had no beard upon their chin,
They both were callow. But as soon as hair did once begin
In likeness of a yellow down upon their cheeks to sprout,
Then (even as comes to pass in birds) the feathers budded out
Together on their pinions too and spreadèd round about
On both their sides. And finally, when childhood once was spent
And youth come on, together they with other Minies went
To Colchos in the galley that was first devised in Greece
Upon a sea as then unknown, to fetch the golden fleece.

**FINIS SEXTI LIBRI.**

# The Seventh Book of Ovid's
## Metamorphoses

And now in ship of Pagasa the Minies cut the seas;        *Jason and*
And leading under endless night his age in great disease        *Medea*
Of scarcity was Phiney seen, and Boreas' sons had chased
Away the maiden-facèd fowls that did his victuals waste.
And after suffering many things in noble Jason's band,
In muddy Phasis' gushing stream at last they went a-land.
There, while they, going to the king, demand the golden fleece
(Brought thither certain years before by Phrixus out of Greece)
And of their dreadful labours wait an answer to receive,
Aeëtes' daughter in her heart doth mighty flames conceive.   10
And after struggling very long, when reason could not win
The upper hand of rage, she thus did in herself begin:
   'In vain, Medea, dost thou strive. Some god, whate'er he is,
   Against thee bends his force. For what a wondrous thing is this!
Is anything like this which men do term by name of love?
For why should I my father's hests esteem so hard above
All measure? Sure, in very deed they are too hard and sore.
Why fear I lest yon stranger, whom I never saw before,
Should perish? What should be the cause of this my fear so great?
Unhappy wench, and if thou canst, suppress this uncouth heat   20
That burneth in thy tender breast. And if so be I could,
A happy turn it were, and more at ease then be I should.
But now an uncouth malady perforce against my will
Doth hale me. Love persuades me one, another thing my skill.
The best I see and like; the worst I follow headlong still.
Why, being of the royal blood, so fondly dost thou rave
Upon a stranger thus to dote, desiring for to have
An husband of another world? At home thou mightest find
A lover meet for thine estate on whom to set thy mind.

30      And yet it is but even a chance if he shall live or no.
        God grant him for to live! I may without offence pray so,
        Although I loved him not; for what hath Jason trespassed me?
        Who would not pity Jason's youth unless they cruel be?
        What creature is there but his birth and prowess might him move?
        And, setting all the rest aside, who would not be in love
        With Jason's goodly personage? My heart, assuredly,
        Is touched therewith. But if that I provide not remedy,
        With burning breath of blasting bulls needs singèd must he be.
        Of seeds that he himself must sow a harvest shall he see
40      Of armèd men in battle ray upon the ground up grow,
        Against the which it hoveth him his manhood for to show.
        And as a prey he must be set against the dragon fell.
        If I these things let come to pass, I may confess right well
        That of a tiger I was bred and that within my breast
        A heart more hard than any steel or stony rock doth rest.
        Why, rather, do I not his death with wrathful eyes behold
        And joy with others, seeing him to utter peril sold?
        Why do I not enforce the bulls against him? Why, I say,
        Exhort I not the cruel men which shall in battle ray
50      Arise against him from the ground, and that same dragon too
        Within whose eyes came never sleep? God shield I so should do!
        But prayer smally boots, except I put to helping hand.
        And shall I like a caitiff then betray my father's land?
        Shall I a stranger save whom we nor none of ours doth know
        That he, by me preservèd, may without me homeward row
        And take another to his wife and leave me, wretched wight,
        To torments? If I wist that he could work me such a spite
        Or could in any other's love than only mine delight,
        The churl should die for me. But sure he beareth not the face
60      Like one that would do so. His birth, his courage and his grace
        Do put me clearly out of doubt he will not me deceive;
        No, nor forget the great good turns he shall by me receive.
        Yet shall he to me first his faith for more assurance plight,
        And solemnly he shall be sworn to keep the covenant right.
        Why fear'st thou now without a cause? Step to it out of hand
        And do not any lenger time thus lingering fondly stand.

For aye shall Jason think himself beholding unto thee
And shall thee marry solemnly; yea, honoured shalt thou be
Of all the mothers great and small throughout the towns of
    Greece
For saving of their sons that come to fetch the golden fleece.    70
And shall I then leave brother, sister, father, kith and kin
And household gods and native soil and all that is therein
And sail I know not whither with a stranger? Yea. Why not?
My father surely cruel is, my country rude, God wot,
My brother yet a very babe; my sister, I dare say,
Contented is with all her heart that I should go away.
The greatest god is in myself; the things I do forsake
Are trifles in comparison of those that I shall take.
For saving of the Greekish ship renownèd shall I be.
A better place I shall enjoy, with cities rich and free    80
Whose fame doth flourish fresh even here and people that excel
In civil life and all good arts and, whom I would not sell
For all the goods within the world, Duke Aeson's noble son;
Whom had I to my lawful fere assuredly once won,
Most happy, yea, and blest of God I might myself account,
And with my head above the stars to heaven I should surmount.
But men report that certain rocks (I know not what) do meet
Amid the waves and monstrously again asunder fleet;
And how Charybdis, utter foe to ships that pass thereby,
Now sowpeth in, now speweth out the sea incessantly;    90
And ravening Scylla, being hemmed with cruel dogs about,
Amidst the gulf of Sicily doth make a barking out.
What skilleth that? As long as I enjoy the thing I love
And hang about my Jason's neck, it shall no whit me move
To sail the dangerous seas; as long as him I may embrace,
I cannot, surely, be afraid in any kind of case.
Or if I chance to be afraid, my fear shall only tend
But for my husband. Call'st thou him thy husband? Dost pretend
Gay titles to thy foul offence, Medea? Nay, not so.
But rather look about how great a lewdness thou dost go    100
And shun the mischief while thou may'st.' She had no sooner said
These words but right and godliness and shamefastness were stayed
Before her eyes, and frantic love did fly away dismayed.

She went me to an altar that was dedicate of old
To Persey's daughter, Hecate (of whom the witches hold
As of their goddess), standing in a thick and secret wood
So close it could not well be spied. And now the raging mood
Of furious love was well allayed and clearly put to flight,
When, spying Aeson's son, the flame that seemèd quenchèd quite
Did kindle out of hand again. Her cheeks began to glow,
And flushing over all her face the scarlet blood did flow.
And even as, when a little spark that was in ashes hid,
Uncovered with the whisking winds, is from the ashes rid,
Eftsoons it taketh nourishment and kindleth in such wise
That to his former strength again and flaming it doth rise;
Even so her quailèd love, which late ye would have thought had
          quite
Been vanished out of mind, as soon as Jason came in sight,
Did kindle to his former force in viewing of the grace
With which he did avaunce himself, then coming there in place.
And, as it chancèd, far more fair and beautiful of face
She thought him then than ever erst. But sure it doth behove
Her judgement should be borne withal because she was in love.
She gaped and gazèd in his face with fixèd staring eyen,
As though she never had him seen before that instant time.
So far she was beside herself, she thought it should not be
The face of any worldly wight the which she then did see.
She was not able for her life to turn her eyes away.
But when he took her by the hand and, speaking, gan to pray
Her softly for to succour him and promised faithfully
To take her to his wedded wife, she, falling by and by
A-weeping, said, 'Sir, what I do I see apparently.
Not want of knowledge of the truth but love shall me deceive.
You shall be savèd by my means. And now I must receive
A faithful promise at your hand for saving of your life.'
He made a solemn vow and sware to take her to his wife
By triple Hecate's holy rites, and by what other power
So ever else had residence within that secret bower,
And by the sire of him that should his father-in-law become
Who all things doth behold, and as he hoped to overcome

110

120

130

The dreadful dangers which he had soon after to assay.                    140
Duke Jason, being credited, received of her straightway
Enchanted herbs and, having learnt the usage of the same,
Departed thence with merry heart and to his lodging came.
   Next morn had chased the streaming stars, and folk by heaps
      did flock
   To Mars's sacred field and there stood thronging in a shock
To see the strange pastimes. The king, most stately to behold,
With ivory mace above them all did sit in throne of gold.
Anon the brazen-hoofèd bulls from stony nostrils cast
Out flakes of fire; their scalding breath the growing grass did blast.
And look what noise a chimney full of burning fuel makes,                 150
Or flint in softening in the kell when first the fire it takes
By sprinkling water thereupon; such noise their boiling breasts,
Turmoiling with the fiery flames enclosèd in their chests,
Such noise their scorchèd throat-bolls make. Yet stoutly Jason
     went
To meet them. They their dreadful eyes against him grimly bent
And eke their horns with iron tipped, and strake the dust about
In stamping with their cloven clees, and with their bellowing out
Set all the field upon a smoke. The Minies, seeing that,
Were past their wits with sudden fear. But Jason feelèd nat
So much as any breath of theirs; such strength hath sorcery.              160
Their dangling dewlaps with his hand he coyed unfearfully
And, putting yokes upon their necks, he forcèd them to draw
The heavy burden of the plough which erst they never saw
And for to break the field which erst had never felt the share.
The men of Colchos, seeing this, like men amazèd fare.
The Minies with their shouting out their mazèdness augment
And unto Jason therewithal give more encouragement.
Then in a soldier's cap of steel a viper's teeth he takes
And sows them in the new-ploughed field. The ground, them
     soaking, makes
The seed foresteeped in poison strong both supple, lithe and soft,        170
And of these teeth a right strange grain there grows anon aloft.
For even as in the mother's womb an infant doth begin
To take the lively shape of man and formèd is within

To due proportion piece by piece in every limb, and when
Full ripe he is he takes the use of air with other men;
So when that of the viper's teeth the perfect shape of man
Within the bowels of the earth was formèd, they began
To rise together orderly upon the fruitful field.
And (which a greater wonder is) immediately they wield
Their weapons growing up with them. Whom when the Greeks beheld
180   Preparing for to push their pikes, which sharply headed were,
In Jason's face, down went their heads, their hearts did faint for
        fear.
And also she that made him safe began abashed to be;
For when against one naked man so huge an army she
Beheld of armèd enemies bent, her colour did abate
And suddenly both void of blood and lively heat she sat.
And lest the chanted weeds the which she had him given before
Should fail at need, a helping charm she whispered overmore
And practised other secret arts the which she kept in store.
190   He, casting straight a mighty stone amid his thickest foes,
Doth void the battle from himself and turns it unto those.
These earth-bred brothers by and by did one another wound
And never ceasèd till that all lay dead upon the ground.
The Greeks were glad and in their arms did clasp their champion
        stout
And, clinging to him, earnestly embracèd him about.
And thou, O fond Medea, too, could'st well have found in heart
The champion for to have embraced, but that withheld thou wert
By shamefastness. And yet thou had'st embracèd him, if dread
Of staining of thine honour had not stayed thee in that stead.
200   But yet, as far forth as thou may'st, thou dost in heart rejoice
And secretly (although without expressing it in voice)
Dost thank thy charms and eke the gods as authors of the same.
        Now was remaining as the last conclusion of this game
        By force of chanted herbs to make the watchful dragon sleep
        Within whose eyes came never wink, who had in charge to
            keep
The goodly tree upon the which the golden fleeces hung.
With crested head and hookèd paws and triple spurting tongue

Right ugly was he to behold. When Jason had besprent
Him with the juice of certain herbs from Lethey river sent
And thrice had mumbled certain words which are of force to cast            210
So sound a sleep on things that even as dead a time they last,
Which make the raging surges calm and flowing rivers stay,
The dreadful dragon by and by, whose eyes before that day
Wist never erst what sleeping meant, did fall so fast asleep
That Jason safely took the fleece of gold that he did keep.
Of which his booty being proud, he led with him away
The author of his good success, another fairer prey.
And so with conquest and a wife he loosed from Colchos strand
And in Larissa haven safe did go again a-land.

    The ancient men of Thessaly together with their wives            *Medea*
     To church with offering gon for saving of their children's lives.   *rejuvenates*
Great heaps of fuming frankincense were fried in the flame,             *Aeson*
And vowèd bulls to sacrifice with horns fair gilded came.
But from this great solemnity Duke Aeson was away,
Now at death's door and spent with years. Then Jason thus gan
    say:
'O wife, to whom, I do confess, I owe my life indeed,
Though all things thou to me hast given and thy deserts exceed
Belief, yet if enchantment can (for what so hard appears
Which strong enchantment cannot do?), abate thou from my years
And add them to my father's life.' As he these words did speak,         230
The tears were standing in his eyes. His godly suit did break
Medea's heart, who therewithal bethought her of her sire,
In leaving whom she had expressed a far unlike desire.
But yet, bewraying not her thoughts, she said, 'O husband, fie,
What wickedness hath scaped your mouth! Suppose you then
    that I
Am able of your life the term where I will to bestow?
Let Hecate never suffer that! Your suit, as well you know,
Against all right and reason is. But I will put in proof
A greater gift than you require and more for your behoof.
I will assay your father's life by cunning to prolong,                  240
And not with your years for to make him young again and strong,
So our three-formèd goddess grant with present help to stand
A furtherer of the great attempt the which I take in hand.'

Before the moon should circlewise close both her horns in one,
　Three nights were yet as then to come. As soon as that she
　　shone
Most full of light and did behold the earth with fulsome face,
Medea, with her hair not trussed so much as in a lace
But flaring on her shoulders twain and barefoot, with her gown
Ungirded, gat her out of doors and wandered up and down

250　Alone the dead time of the night. Both man and beast and bird
Were fast asleep. The serpents sly in trailing forward stirred
So softly as ye would have thought they still asleep had been.
The moisting air was whist; no leaf ye could have moving seen.
The stars alonely fair and bright did in the welkin shine,
To which she, lifting up her hands, did thrice herself incline;
And thrice with water of the brook her hair besprinkled she;
And, gasping thrice, she oped her mouth. And, bowing down her
　　knee
Upon the bare hard ground, she said, 'O trusty time of night
Most faithful unto privities, O golden stars, whose light

260　Doth jointly with the moon succeed the beams that blaze by day,
And thou, three-headed Hecate, who knowest best the way
To compass this our great attempt and art our chiefest stay,
Ye charms and witchcrafts and thou earth, which both with herb
　　and weed
Of mighty working furnishest the wizards at their need,
Ye airs and winds, ye elves of hills, of brooks, of woods alone,
Of standing lakes and of the night, approach ye everych one.
Through help of whom (the crookèd banks much wondering at
　　the thing)
I have compellèd streams to run clean backward to their spring.
By charms I make the calm seas rough and make the rough seas
　　plain

270　And cover all the sky with clouds and chase them thence again;
By charms I raise and lay the winds and burst the viper's jaw
And from the bowels of the earth both stones and trees do draw.
Whole woods and forests I remove; I make the mountains shake
And even the earth itself to groan and fearfully to quake;
I call up dead men from their graves; and thee, O lightsome moon,
I darken oft, though beaten brass abate thy peril soon.

Our sorcery dims the morning fair and darks the sun at noon.
The flaming breath of fiery bulls ye quenchèd for my sake
And causèd their unwieldy necks the bended yoke to take.
Among the earth-bred brothers you a mortal war did set 280
And brought asleep the dragon fell, whose eyes were never shut.
By means whereof deceiving him that had the golden fleece
In charge to keep, you sent it thence by Jason into Greece.
Now have I need of herbs that can by virtue of their juice
To flowering prime of lusty youth old withered age reduce.
I am assured ye will it grant. For not in vain have shone
These twinkling stars, ne yet in vain this chariot all alone
By draught of dragons hither comes.' With that was fro the sky
A chariot softly glancèd down and stayèd hard thereby.
    As soon as she had gotten up and with her hand had coyed 290
    The dragons' reinèd necks and with their bridles somewhat
        toyed,
They mounted with her in the air whence, looking down, she saw
The pleasant Temp of Thessaly and made her dragons draw
To places further from resort. And there she took the view
What herbs on high Mount Pelion and what on Ossa grew,
And what on Mountain Othrys and on Pindus growing were,
And what Olympus (greater than Mount Pindus far) did bear.
Such herbs of them as likèd her she pulled up root and rind,
Or cropped them with a hookèd knife. And many she did find
Upon the banks of Apidane agreeing to her mind 300
And many at Amphrysus' fords. And thou, Enipeus, eke
Did'st yield her many pretty weeds of which she well did like.
Peneus' and Spercheus' streams contributory were,
And so were Boebe's rushy banks of such as growèd there.
About Anthedon, which against the Isle Euboea stands,
A certain kind of lively grass she gathered with her hands,
The name whereof was scarcely known or what the herb could do
Until that Glaucus afterward was changèd thereinto.
Nine days with wingèd dragons drawn, nine nights in chariot swift
She, searching every field and frith, from place to place did shift. 310
She was no sooner home returned but that the dragons fell,
Which lightly of her gathered herbs had taken but the smell,

Did cast their sloughs and with their sloughs their rivelled age
    forgo.
She would none other house than heaven to hide her head as tho,
But kept her still without the doors. And as for man, was none
That once might touch her. Altars twain of turf she builded; one
Upon her left hand unto Youth, another on the right
To triple Hecate. Both the which as soon as she had dight
With vervain and with other shrubs that on the fields do rise,
320.   Not far from thence she digged two pits and, making sacrifice,
Did cut a couple of black rams' throats and fillèd with their blood
The open pits, on which she poured of warm milk pure and good
A bowlful and another bowl of honey clarified.
And, babbling to herself, therewith full bitterly she cried
On Pluto and his ravished wife, the sovereign states of hell,
And all the elves and gods that on or in the earth do dwell
To spare old Aeson's life a while and not in haste deprive
His limbs of that same agèd soul which kept them yet alive.
Whom when she had sufficiently with mumbling long besought,
She bade that Aeson's feebled corse should out of doors be
330        brought
Before the altars. Then with charms she cast him in so deep
A slumber that upon the herbs he lay for dead asleep.
Which done, she willèd Jason thence a great way off to go,
And likewise all the ministers that servèd her as tho,
And not presume those secrets with unhallowed eyes to see.
They did as she commanded them. When all were voided, she,
With scattered hair about her ears like one of Bacchus' frows,
Devoutly by and by about the burning altars goes
And, dipping in the pits of blood a sort of clifted brands,
340   Upon the altars kindled them that were on both her hands.
And thrice with brimstone, thrice with fire and thrice with water
    pure
She purgèd Aeson's aged corse that slept and slumbered sure.
    The medicine, seething all the while a-wallop in a pan
Of brass, to spurt and leap aloft and gather froth began.
There boilèd she the roots, seeds, flowers, leaves, stalks and juice
       together
Which from the fields of Thessaly she late had gathered thither.

She cast in also precious stones fetched from the furthest east
And, which the ebbing ocean washed, fine gravel from the west.
She put thereto the dew that fell upon a Monday night;
And flesh and feathers of a witch, a cursèd odious wight                    350
Which in the likeness of an owl abroad a-nights did fly
And infants in their cradles change or suck them that they die;
The singles also of a wolf* which, when he list, could take
The shape of man and, when he list, the same again forsake.
And from the River Cyniphis, which is in Lyby land,
She had the fine sheer-scalèd films of watersnails at hand.
And of an endless-livèd hart the liver had she got,
To which she added of a crow that then had livèd not
So little as nine hundred years the head and bill also.
    Now when Medea had with these and with a thousand mo           360
    Such other kind of nameless things bested her purpose through
For lengthening of the old man's life, she took a withered bough
Cut lately from an olive-tree and, jumbling all together,
Did raise the bottom to the brim. And as she stirrèd hither
And thither with the withered stick, behold, it waxèd green!
Anon the leaves came budding out, and suddenly were seen
As many berries dangling down as well the bough could bear.
And where the fire had from the pan the scumming cast, or where
The scalding drops did fall, the ground did spring-like flourish
    there
And flowers with fodder fine and soft immediately arose.                    370
    Which when Medea did behold, with naked knife she goes
    And cuts the old man's throat and, letting all his old blood go,
Supplies it with the boilèd juice; the which when Aeson tho
Had at his mouth or at his wound receivèd in, his hair
As well of head as beard from grey to coal-black turnèd were.
His lean, pale, hoar and withered corse grew fulsome, fair and
    fresh;
His furrowed wrinkles were fulfilled with young and lusty flesh.
His limbs waxed frolic, bain and lithe. At which he wondering
    much,
Remembered that at forty years he was the same or such.

*A werewolf

380 And as from dull unwieldsome age to youth he backward drew,
Even so a lively youthful sprite did in his heart renew.

*Medea's plot*
*to kill Pelias*

The wonder of this monstrous act had Bacchus seen from high
And, finding that to youthful years his nurses might thereby
Restorèd be, did at her hand receive it as a gift.
And lest deceitful guile should cease, Medea found a shift
To feign that Jason and herself were fallen at odds in wrath.
And thereupon in humble wise to Pelias' court she go'th
Where, for because the king himself was feebled sore with age,
His daughters entertained her; whom Medea, being sage,
Within a while through false pretence of feignèd friendship

390        brought

To take her bait. For as she told what pleasures she had wrought
For Jason, and among the rest as greatest sadly told
How she had made his father young that withered was and old
And tarried long upon that point, they hopèd glad and fain
That their old father might likewise his youthful years regain.
And this they craving instantly, did proffer for her pain
What recompense she would desire. She held her peace a while
As though she doubted what to do, and with her subtle guile
Of counterfeited gravity more eager did them make.

400 As soon as she had promised them to do it for their sake,
'For more assurance of my grant, yourselves', quoth she, 'shall see
The oldest ram in all your flock a lamb straight made to be
By force of my confections strong.' Immediately a ram
So old that no man thereabouts remembered him a lamb
Was thither by his warpèd horns which turnèd inward to
His hollow temples drawn, whose withered throat she slit in two.
And when she clean had drainèd out that little blood that was,
Upon the fire with herbs of strength she set a pan of brass
And cast his carcass thereinto. The medicine did abate

410 The largeness of his limbs and seared his dossers from his pate
And with his horns abridged his years. Anon was plainly heard
The bleating of a new-yeaned lamb from mid the kettleward.
And as they wondered for to hear the bleating, straight the lamb
Leaped out and, frisking, ran to find the udder of some dam.
King Pelias' daughters were amazed; and when they did behold
Her promise come to such effect, they were a thousandfold

More earnest at her than before. Thrice Phoebus, having plucked
The collars from his horses' necks, in Iber had them ducked.
And now in heaven the streaming stars the fourth night shinèd
    clear,
When false Medea on the fire had hangèd water sheer         420
With herbs that had no power at all. The king and all his guard
Which had the charge that night about his person for to ward
Were through her nightspells and her charms in deadly sleep all
    cast,
And Pelias' daughters with the witch, which egged them forward,
    passed
Into his chamber by the watch and compassed in his bed.
Then, 'Wherefore stand ye doubting thus like fools?' Medea said.
'On! Draw your swords and let ye out his old blood, that I may
Fill up his empty veins again with youthful blood straightway.
Your father's life is in your hands. It lieth now in you
To have him old and withered still or young and lusty. Now     430
If any nature in ye be, and that ye do not feed
A fruitless hope, your duty to your father do with speed.
Expulse his age by sword and let the filthy matter out.'
Through these persuasions which of them so ever went about
To show herself most natural became the first that wrought
Against all nature. And for fear she should be wicked thought,
She executes the wickedness which most to shun she sought.
Yet was not any one of them so bold that durst abide
To look upon their father when she strake, but wried aside
Her eyes; and so their cruel hands, not marking where they hit,     440
With faces turned another way at all adventure smit.
He, all beweltered in his blood, awakèd with the smart
And, maimed and mangled as he was, did give a sudden start,
Endeavouring to have risen up. But when he did behold
Himself among so many swords, he, lifting up his old
Pale waryish arms, said, 'Daughters mine, what do ye? Who hath
    put
These wicked weapons in your hands your father's throat to cut?'
With that their hearts and hands did faint; and as he talkèd yet,
Medea, breaking of his words, his windpipe quickly slit

450    And in the scalding liquor torn did drown him by and by.

*Medea's flight*        But had she not with wingèd worms straight mounted in the
        sky,
       She had not scapèd punishment. But, stying up on high,
       She over shady Pelion flew, where Chiron erst did dwell,
       And over Othrys and the grounds renowned for that befell
       To ancient Ceramb, who, such time as old Deucalion's flood
       Upon the face of all the earth like one main water stood,
       By help of nymphs with feathered wings was in the aïr lift
       And so escapèd from the flood undrownèd by the shift.
       She left Aeolian Pitany upon her left hand and

460    The serpent that became a stone upon the Lesbian sand;
       And Ida woods where Bacchus hid a bullock (as is said)
       In shape of stag, the which his son had thievishly conveyed;
       And where the sire of Corytus lies buried in the dust;
       The fields which Maeras (when he first did into barking brust)
       Affrayed with strangeness of the noise; and eke Eurypyl's town,
       In which the wives of Cos had horns like oxen on their crown
       Such time as Herc'les with his host departed from the isle;
       And Rhodes to Phoebus consecrate; and Ialyse, where erewhile
       The Telchines with their noisome sight did everything bewitch,

470    At which their heinous wickedness Jove taking rightful pritch,
       Did drown them in his brother's waves. Moreover she did pass
       By Ceos and old Carthey walls, where Sir Alcidamas
       Did wonder how his daughter should be turnèd to a dove.
       The swanny Temp and Hyrie's pool she viewèd from above,
       The which a sudden swan did haunt. For Phylly there for love
       Of Hyrie's son did at his bidding birds and lions tame
       And, being willed to break a bull, performèd straight the same,
       Till, wrathful that his love so oft so straitly should him use,
       When for his last reward he asked the bull, he did refuse

480    To give it him. The boy, displeased, said, 'Well, thou wilt anon
       Repent thou gave it not,' and leapt down headlong from a stone.
       They all supposed he had been fallen; but, being made a swan,
       With snowy feathers in the air to flacker he began.
       His mother Hyrie, knowing not he was preservèd so,
       Resolvèd into melting tears for pensiveness and woe

And made the pool that bears her name. Not far from hence doth
  stand
The city Brauron where sometime, by mounting from the land
With waving pinions, Ophy's imp, Dame Combe, did eschew
Her children which with naked swords to slay her did pursue.
Anon she kenned Calaury fields, which did sometime pertain   490
To chaste Diana, where a king and eke his wife both twain
Were turned to birds. Cyllene hill upon her right hand stood
In which Menephron like a beast of wild and savage mood
To force his mother did attempt. Far thence she spied where sad
Cephisus mournèd for his niece whom Phoebus turnèd had
To ugly shape of swelling seal, and Eumel's palace fair,
Lamenting for his son's mischance with whewling in the air.
At Corinth with her wingèd snakes at length she did arrive.
Here men (so ancient fathers said that were as then alive)
Did breed of dewy mushrooms. But after that her teen   500
With burning of her husband's bride by witchcraft wreaked had
  been
And that King Creon's palace she on blazing fire had seen
And in her own dear children's blood had bathed her wicked
  knife,
Not like a mother but a beast bereaving them of life,
Lest Jason should have punished her, she took her wingèd snakes
And, flying thence again, in haste to Pallas' city makes,
Which saw the ancient Periphas and righteous Pheney too
Together flying, and the niece of Polypemon, who
Was fastened to a pair of wings as well as t'other two.
 Aegeus entertainèd her, wherein he was to blame   510 *The*
 Although he had no further gone but stayed upon the same;   *arrival of*
He thought it not to be enough to use her as his guest   *Theseus*
Unless he took her to his wife. And now was Thesey pressed,
Unknown unto his father yet, who by his knightly force
Had set from robbers clear the balk that makes the straight divorce
Between the seas Ionian and Aegean. To have killed
This worthy knight Medea had a goblet ready filled
With juice of flintwort venomous, the which she long ago
Had out of Scythy with her brought. The common bruit is so

520    That of the teeth of Cerberus this flintwort first did grow.
There is a cave that gapeth wide with darksome entry low;
There goes a way slope down by which, with triple chain made
    new
Of strong and sturdy adamant, the valiant Herc'le drew
The currish hellhound Cerberus, who, dragging arseward still
And writhing back his scowling eyes because he had no skill
To see the sun and open day, for very moody wrath
Three barkings yellèd out at once and spit his slavering froth
Upon the greenish grass. This froth (as men suppose) took root
And, thriving in the battling soil, in burgeons forth did shoot
530    To bane and mischief men withal. And for because the same
Did grow upon the bare hard flints, folk gave the foresaid name
Of flintwort thereunto. The king by egging of his queen
Did reach his son this bane as if he had his enemy been.
And Thesey, of this treason wrought not knowing aught, had
    ta'en
The goblet at his father's hand which held his deadly bane,
When suddenly by the ivory hilts that were upon his sword
Aegeus knew he was his son and, rising from the board,
Did strike the mischief from his mouth. Medea with a charm
Did cast a mist and so scaped death deservèd for the harm
540    Intended. Now albeit that Aegeus were right glad
That in the saving of his son so happy chance he had,
Yet grievèd it his heart full sore that such a wicked wight
With treason wrought against his son should scape so clear and
    quite.
    Then fell he unto kindling fire on altars everywhere
    And glutted all the gods with gifts. The thick-necked oxen
        were
With garlands wreathed about their horns knocked down for
    sacrifice.
A day of more solemnity than this did never rise
Before on Athens, by report. The ancients of the town
Made feasts; so did the meaner sort and every common clown.
And as the wine did sharp their wits, they sung this song: 'O
550    knight
Of peerless prowess, Theseus, thy manhood and thy might

Through all the coast of Marathon with worthy honour sounds
For killing of the Cretish bull that wasted those same grounds.
The folk of Cremyon think themselves beholden unto thee,
For that without disquieting their fields may tillèd be.
By thee the land of Epidaur beheld the clubbish son
Of Vulcan dead. By thee likewise the country that doth run
Along Cephisus' banks beheld the fell Procrustes slain.
The dwelling-place of Ceres, our Eleusis, glad and fain
Beheld the death of Cercyon. That orpèd Sinis, who          560
Abused his strength in bending trees and tying folk thereto
Their limbs asunder for to tear when, loosened from the stops,
The trees unto their proper place did trice their strainèd tops,
Was killed by thee. Thou made the way that leadeth to the town
Alcathoe in Boeotia clear by putting Sciron down.
To this same outlaw's scattered bones the land denièd rest,
And likewise did the sea refuse to harbour such a guest
Till, after floating to and fro long while, as men do say,
At length they hardened into stones. And at this present day
The stones are callèd Sciron's cliffs. Now if we should account   570
Thy deeds together with thy years, thy deeds would far surmount
Thy years. For thee, most valiant prince, these public vows we
        keep;
For thee with cheerful hearts we quaff these bowls of wine so
        deep.'
The palace also of the noise and shouting did resound,
The which the people made for joy. There was not to be found
In all the city any place of sadness. Natheless
(So hard it is of perfect joy to find so great excess
But that some sorrow therewithal is meddled more or less)
Aegeus had not in his son's recovery such delight
But that there followed in the neck a piece of Fortune's spite.   580
    King Minos was preparing war; who, though he had great store          *Minos*
    Of ships and soldiers, yet the wrath the which he had before          *threatens war*
Conceivèd in his father's breast for murdering of his son,
Androgeus, made him far more strong and fiercer for to run
To rightful battle to revenge the great displeasure done.
Howbeit, he thought it best ere he his warfare did begin
To find the means of foreign aids some friendship for to win.

And thereupon with flying fleet, where passage did permit,
He went to visit all the isles that in those seas do sit.
590 Anon the isles Astypaley and Anaphe both twain,
The first constrained for fear of war, the last in hope of gain,
Took part with him. Low Mycony did also with him hold;
So did the chalky Cimoly; and Siphney, which of old
Was very rich with veins of gold; and Scyros, full of bold
And valiant men; and Seriphy, the smooth or rather fell;
And Parey, which for marblestone doth bear away the bell;
And Sithney, which a wicked wench called Arne did betray
For money, who upon receipt thereof without delay
Was turnèd to a bird which yet of gold is gripple still
600 And is as black as any coal, both feathers, feet and bill:
A caddow is the name of her. But yet Oliary
And Didymy and Andrey eke, and Tene and Gyary
And Pepareth, where olive-trees most plenteously do grow,
In no wise would agree their help on Minos to bestow.
   Then Minos, turning lefthandwise, did sail to Oenope
   Where reigned that time King Aeacus. This isle had callèd be
Of old by name of Oenope; but Aeacus turned the name
And after of his mother's name Aegina called the same.
The common folk ran out by heaps, desirous for to see
610 A man of such renown as Minos bruited was to be.
The king's three sons, Duke Telamon, Duke Peley and the young
Duke Phocus, went to meet with him. Old Aeacus also, clung
With age, came after leisurely and askèd him the cause
Of his repair. The ruler of the hundred shires gan pause
And, musing on the inward grief that nipped him at the heart,
Did shape him answer thus: 'O prince, vouchsafe to take my part
In this same godly war of mine; assist me in the just
Revengement of my murdered son that sleepeth in the dust.
I crave your comfort for his death.' Aegina's son replied,
620 'Thy suit is vain and of my realm perforce must be denied.
For unto Athens is no land more sure than this allied;
Such leagues between us are which shall infringed for me abide.'
Away went Minos sad and said, 'Full dearly shalt thou buy
Thy leagues.' He thought it for to be a better policy

To threaten war than war to make and there to spend his store
And strength, which in his other needs might much avail him
    more.
  As yet might from Oenopia walls the Cretish fleet be kenned
  When thitherward with puffèd sails and wind at will did tend
A ship from Athens, which anon, arriving at the strand,
Set Cephal with ambassade from his countrymen a-land.     630
The king's three sons, though long it were since last they had him
    seen,
Yet knew they him. And after old acquaintance eft had been
Renewed by shaking hands, to court they did him straight
    convey.
This prince, which did allure the eyes of all men by the way,
As in whose stately person still remainèd to be seen
The marks of beauty which in flower of former years had been,
Went holding out an olive branch that grew in Attic land.
And for the reverence of his age there went on either hand
A nobleman of younger years: Sir Clytus on the right
And Butes on the left, the sons of one that Pallas hight.    640
When greeting first had passed between these nobles and the king,
Then Cephal, setting straight abroach the message he did bring,
Desirèd aid and showed what leagues stood then in force between
His country and the Aeginites and also what had been
Decreed betwixt their ancestors, concluding in the end
That under colour of this war, which Minos did pretend
To only Athens, he indeed the conquest did intend
Of all Achaia. When he thus by help of learnèd skill
His country message furthered had, King Aeacus, leaning still
His left hand on his sceptre, said, 'My lords, I would not have    650
Your state of Athens seem so strange as succour here to crave.
I pray, command. For be ye sure that what this isle can make
Is yours. Yea, all that e'er I have shall hazard for your sake.
I want no strength; I have such store of soldiers that I may
Both vex my foes and also keep my realm in quiet stay.
And now I think me blest of God that time doth serve to show
Without excuse the great good will that I to Athens owe.'
'God hold it, sir,' quoth Cephalus, 'God make the number grow

Of people in this town of yours; it did me good a-late
660   When such a goodly sort of youth of all one age and rate
Did meet me in the street. But yet methinks that many miss
Which at my former being here I have beheld ere this.'

*The plague at*       At that the king did sigh and thus with plaintful voice did say:
*Aegina*                 'A sad beginning afterward in better luck did stay.
I would I plainly could the same before your faces lay.
Howbeit, I will disorderly repeat it as I may.
And lest I seem to weary you with overlong delay,
The men that you so mindfully enquire for lie in ground
And nought of them save bones and dust remaineth to be found.
670   But as it happed, what loss thereby did unto me redound!
A cruel plague through Juno's wrath, who dreadfully did hate
This land that of her husband's love did take the name a-late,
Upon my people fell. As long as that the malady
None other seemed than such as haunts man's nature usually
And of so great mortality the hurtful cause was hid,
We strove by physic of the same the patients for to rid.
The mischief overmastered art; yea, physic was to seek
To do itself good. First the air with foggy stinking reek
Did daily overdrip the earth and close calm clouds did make
The weather faint; and while the moon four times her light did
680       take
And filled her empty horns therewith and did as often slake,
The warm south winds with deadly heat continually did blow.
Infected were the springs and ponds and streams that ebb and
          flow.
And swarms of serpents crawled about the fields that lay untilled,
Which with their poison even the brooks and running waters
          filled.
   'In sudden dropping down of dogs, of horses, sheep and kine,
      Of birds and beasts both wild and tame as oxen, wolves and
          swine,
The mischief of this secret sore first outwardly appears.
The wretched ploughman was amazed to see his sturdy steers
690   Amid the furrow sinking down ere half his work was done.
Whole flocks of sheep did faintly bleat, and therewithal begun

Their fleeces for to fall away and leave the naked skin,
And all their bodies with the rot attaintèd were within.
The lusty horse, that erst was fierce in field renown to win
Against his kind, grew cowardly and, now forgetting quite
The ancient honour which he pressed so oft to get in fight,
Stood sighing sadly at the rack as waiting for to yield
His weary life without renown of combat in the field.
The boar to chafe, the hind to run, the cruel bear to fall
Upon the herds of rother-beasts had now no lust at all.                    700
A languishing was fallen on all. In ways, in woods, in plains
The filthy carrions lay, whose stench the air itself disdains.
A wondrous thing to tell, not dogs, not ravening fowls, nor yet
Hoar-coated wolves would once attempt to taste of them a bit.
Look where they fell, there rotted they and with their savour bred
More harm and further still abroad the foul infection spread.
  'With loss that touchèd yet more near, on husbandmen it crept
  And ragingly within the walls of this great city stepped.
It took men first with swelting heat that scalt their guts within,
The signs whereof were steaming breath and fiery-coloured skin.          710
The tongue was harsh and swollen, the mouth through drought of
        burning veins
Lay gaping up to hale in breath, and as the patient strains
To draw it in, he sucks therewith corrupted air beside.
No bed, no clothes, though ne'er so thin, the patients could abide,
But laid their hardened stomachs flat against the bare cold ground.
Yet no abatement of the heat therein their bodies found,
But heat the earth. And as for leech, was none that help could
        hight;
The surgeons and physicians too were in the selfsame plight.
Their cureless cunning hurt themselves. The nearer any man
Approacheth his diseasèd friend and doth the best he can               720
To succour him most faithfully, the sooner did he catch
His bane. All hope of health was gone. No easement nor dispatch
Of this disease except in death and burial did they find.
Look, whereunto that each man's mind and fancy was inclined,
That followed he. He never passed what was for his behoof.
For why, that nought could do them good was felt too much by
        proof.

In every place without respect of shame or honesty,
At wells, at brooks, at ponds, at pits by swarms they thronging lie.
But sooner might they quench their life than staunch their thirst
    thereby.
730 And therewithal so heavy and unwieldy they become
That, wanting power to rise again, they dièd there. Yet some
The selfsame waters guzzled still without regard of fear.
So weary of their loathsome beds the wretched people were
That out they leapt. Or if to stand their feeble force denied,
They wallowed down and out of doors immediately them hied.
It was a death to every man his own house to abide.
And for they did not know the cause whereof the sickness came,
The place (because they did it know) was blamèd for the same.
Ye should have seen some, half fordead, go plundering here and
    there
740 By highways' sides while that their legs were able them to bear,
And some lie weeping on the ground or rolling piteously
Their weary eyes which afterwards should never see the sky,
Or stretching out their limbs to heaven that overhangs on high;
Some here, some there, and yonder some, in whatsoever coast
Death, finding them, enforcèd them to yield their fainting ghost.
    'What heart had I, suppose you, then, or ought I then to have?
In faith, I might have loathed my life and wished me in my
    grave
As other of my people were. I could not cast mine eye
In any place, but that dead folk there strewèd I did spy
750 Even like as from a shaken twig when rotten apples drop,
Or mast from beeches, holms or oaks when poles do scar their
    top.
Yon stately church with greces long against our court you see;
It is the shrine of Jupiter. What wight was he or she
That on those altars burnèd not their frankincense in vain?
How oft, yea, even with frankincense that partly did remain
Still unconsumèd in their hands did die both man and wife
As each of them with mutual care did pray for other's life!
How often died the mother there in suing for her son
Unheard upon the altarstone, her prayer scarce begun!

How often at the temple door, even while the priest did bid          760
His beads and pour pure wine between their horns, at sudden slid
The oxen down without stroke given! Yea, once when I had
          thought
Myself by offering sacrifice Jove's favour to have sought
For me, my realm and these three imps, the ox with grievous
          groan
Upon the sudden sunk me down, and little blood or none
Did issue scarce to stain the knife with which they slit his throat.
The sickly inwards eke had lost the signs whereby we note
What things the gods for certainty would warn us of before;
For even the very bowels were attainted with the sore.
Before the holy temple doors and (that the death might be          770
The more despiteful) even before the altars did I see
The stinking corses scattered. Some with halters stopped their
          wind,
By death expulsing fear of death, and of a wilful mind
Did haste their end, which of itself was coming on apace.
The bodies which the plague had slain were (O most wretched
          case!)
Not carried forth to burial now. For why, such store there was
That scarce the gates were wide enough for coffins forth to pass.
So either loathly on the ground unburied did they lie
Or else without solemnity were burnt in bonfires high.
No reverence nor regard was had. Men fell together by          780
The ears for firing. In the fire that was prepared for one
Another stranger's corse was burnt. And lastly, few or none
Were left to mourn. The silly souls of mothers with their small
And tender babes and age with youth, as fortune did befall,
Went wandering ghastly up and down unmournèd for at all.
In fine, so far outrageously this helpless murrain raves,
There was not wood enough for fire nor ground enough for
          graves.
    'Astonied at the stourness of so stout a storm of ills,
    I said, "O father Jupiter, whose mighty power fulfils
Both heaven and earth, if flying fame report thee not amiss          790
In vouching that thou did'st embrace in way of love ere this

The river Asop's daughter, fair Aegina even by name,
And that to take me for thy son thou count it not a shame,
Restore thou me my folk again or kill thou me likewise."
He gave a sign by sudden flash of lightning from the skies
And double peal of thundercracks. "I take this same," quoth I,
"And as I take it for a true and certain sign whereby
Thou dost confirm me for thy son, so also let it be
A hansel of some happy luck thou mindest unto me."
800  Hard by us, as it happed that time, there was an oaken tree
With spreaded arms as bare of boughs as lightly one shall see.
This tree (as all the rest of oaks) was sacred unto Jove,
And sprouted of an acorn which was fet from Dodon grove.
Here marked we how the pretty ants, the gatherers-up of grain,
One following other all along in order of a train,
Great burdens in their little mouths did painfully sustain
And nimbly up the rugged bark their beaten path maintain.
As wondering at the swarm I stood, I said, "O father dear,
As many people give thou me as ants are creeping here
810  And fill mine empty walls again." Anon the oak did quake
And, unconstrained of any blast, his lofty branches shake,
The which did yield a certain sound. With that for dreadful fear
A shuddering through my body strake and up stood stiff my hair.
But yet I kissèd reverently the ground and eke the tree.
Howbeit, I durst not be so bold of hope acknown to be.
Yet hopèd I and in my heart did shroud my secret hope.
Anon came night, and sleep upon my careful carcass crope.
Methought I saw the selfsame oak with all his boughs and twigs
And all the pismires creeping still upon his taunts and sprigs.
Which, trembling with a sudden braid, these harvest folk off
820           threw
And shed them on the ground about, who on the sudden grew
In bigness more and more and from the earth themselves did lift
And stood upright against the tree and therewithal did shift
Their meagreness and coal-black hue and number of their feet
And clad their limbs with shape of man. Away my sleep did fleet.
And when I woke, misliking of my dream, I made my moan
That in the gods I did perceive but slender help or none.

But straight much trampling up and down and shuffling did I hear,
And (which to me that present time did very strange appear)
Of people talking in my house methought I heard the rere.                    830
Now while I, musing on the same, supposed it to have been
Some fancy of the foolish dream which lately I had seen,
Behold, in comes me Telamon in haste and, thrusting ope
My chamber door, said, "Sir, a sight of things surmounting hope
And credit shall you have; come forth!" Forth came I by and by,
And even such men for all the world there standing did I spy
As in my sleep I dreamèd of and knew them for the same.
They, coming to me, greeted me their sovereign lord by name.
And I, my vows to Jove performed, my city did divide
Among my new inhabiters and gave them land beside                           840
Which by decease of such as were late owners of the same
Lay waste. And in remembrance of the race whereof they came
The name of Emmets I them gave. Their persons you have seen;
Their disposition is the same that erst in them hath been.
They are a sparing kind of folk, on labour wholly set,
A gatherer and an horder-up of such as they do get.
These fellows, being like in years and courage of the mind,
Shall go a warfare way as soon as that the eastern wind
Which brought you hither luckily' – the eastern wind was it
That brought them hither – 'turning, to the southern coast do flit.'        850
     With this and other suchlike talk they brought the day to end.                   *Cephalus'*
     The even in feasting and the night in sleeping they did spend.                        *javelin*
The sun next morrow in the heaven with golden beams did burn,
And still the eastern wind did blow and hold them from return.
Sir Pallas' sons to Cephal came (for he their elder was),
And he and they to Aeacus' court together forth did pass.
The king as yet was fast asleep. Duke Phocus at the gate
Did meet them and receivèd them according to their state,
For Telamon and Peleus already forth were gone
To muster soldiers for the wars. So Phocus all alone                        860
Did lead them to an inner room where goodly parlours were
And causèd them to sit them down. As he was also there
Now sitting with them, he beheld a dart in Cephal's hand
With golden head, the steal whereof he well might understand

Was of some strange and unknown tree. When certain talk had
    passed
A while of other matters there, 'I am', quoth he at last,
'A man that hath delight in woods and loves to follow game,
And yet I am not able, sure, by any means to aim
What wood your javelin steal is of. Of ash it cannot be,
870 For then the colour should be brown. And if of cornel tree,
It would be full of knobbèd knots. I know not what it is,
But sure mine eyes did never see a fairer dart than this.'

*Cephalus*     The one of those same brethren twain, replying to him, said,
*and Procris*     'Nay then, the special property will make you more dismayed
Than doth the beauty of this dart. It hitteth whatsoever
He throws it at. The stroke thereof by chance is rulèd never.
For having done his feat, it flies all bloody back again
Without the help of any hand.' The prince was earnest then
To know the truth of all: as whence so rich a present came,
880 Who gave it him, and whereupon the party gave the same.
Duke Cephal answered his demand in all points, one except,
The which (as known apparently) for shame he overleapt:
His beauty, namely, for the which he did receive the dart.
And, for the loss of his dear wife right pensive at the heart,
He thus began with weeping eyes: 'This dart, O goddess' son,
(Ye ill would think it) makes me yearn and long shall make me
    doon
If long the gods do give me life. This weapon hath undone
My dear beloved wife and me. Oh, would to God this same
Had never unto me been given. There was a noble dame
That Procris hight. But you, perchance, have oftener heard the
890     name
Of great Orithyia, whose renown was bruited so by fame
That blustering Boreas ravished her. To this Orithyia she
Was sister. If a body should compare in each degree
The face and natures of them both, he could none other deem
But Procris worthier of the twain of ravishment should seem.
Her father and our mutual love did make us man and wife.
Men said I had (and so I had indeed) a happy life.
Howbeit God's will was otherwise. For had it pleasèd him,
Of all this while and even still yet in pleasure should I swim.

The second month that she and I by band of lawful bed           900
Had joined together been, as I my masking toils did spread
To overthrow the hornèd stags, the early Morning grey,
Then newly having chasèd night and gun to break the day
From Mount Hymettus' highest tops that freshly flourish aye,
Espied me and against my will conveyed me quite away.
I trust the goddess will not be offended that I say
The truth of her. Although it would delight one to behold
Her ruddy cheeks, although of day and night the bounds she hold,
Although on juice of ambrosy continually she feed,
Yet Procris was the only wight that I did love indeed.          910
On Procris only was my heart; none other word had I
But Procris only in my mouth; still "Procris" did I cry.
I op'nèd what a holy thing was wedlock, and how late
It was ago since she and I were coupled in that state;
Which band (and specially so soon) it were a shame to break.
The goddess, being movèd at the words that I did speak,
Said, "Cease thy plaint, thou carl, and keep thy Procris still for
      me.
But, if my mind deceive me not, the tune will shortly be
That wish thou wilt thou had her not." And so in anger she
To Procris sent me back again. In going homeward as            920
Upon the goddess' sayings with myself I musing was,
I gan to dread bad measures lest my wife had made some scape.
Her youthful years begarnishèd with beauty, grace and shape
In manner made me to believe the deed already done.
Again, her manners did forbid mistrusting oversoon.
But I had been away; but even the same from whom I came
A shrewd example gave how lightly wives do run in blame;
But we poor lovers are afraid of all things. Hereupon
I thought to practise feats, which thing repented me anon
And shall repent me while I live. The purpose of my drifts      930
Was for t'assault her honesty with great rewards and gifts.
The Morning, fooding this my fear, to further my device
My shape (which thing methought I felt) had altered with a trice;
By means whereof anon unknown to Pallas' town I came
And entered so my house. The house was clearly void of blame

And showèd signs of chastity in mourning ever sith
Their master had been rapt away. A thousand means wherewith
To come to Procris' speech had I devised, and scarce at last
Obtained I it. As soon as I mine eye upon her cast,
940 My wits were ravished in such wise that nigh I had forgot
The purposed trial of her troth. Right much ado, God wot,
I had to hold mine own, that I the truth bewrayèd not.
To keep myself from kissing her full much ado I had,
As reason was I should have done. She lookèd very sad;
And yet as sadly as she looked, no wight alive can show
A better count'nance than did she. Her heart did inward glow
In longing for her absent spouse. How beautiful a face,
Think you, Sir Phocus, was in her whom sorrow so did grace?
What should I make report how oft her chaste behaviour strave
950 And overcame most constantly the great assaults I gave?
Or tell how oft she shut me up with these same words: "To one
(Where'er he is) I keep myself, and none but he alone
Shall sure enjoy the use of me"? What creature, having his
Wits perfect, would not be content with such a proof as this
Of her most steadfast chastity? I could not be content,
But still to purchase to myself more woe I further went.
At last, by proffering endless wealth and heaping gifts on gifts,
In overlading her with words I drave her to her shifts.
Then cried I out, "Thine evil heart myself I tardy take.
960 Where of a strange advouterer the count'nance I did make,
I am indeed thy husband. O unfaithful woman thou,
Even I myself can testify thy lewd behaviour now."
She made none answer to my words but, being stricken dumb
And with the sorrow of her heart alonely overcome,
Forsaketh her entangling house and naughty husband quite
And, hating all the sort of men by reason of the spite
That I had wrought her, strayed abroad among the mountains
high
And exercised Diana's feats. Then kindled by and by
A fiercer fire within my bones than ever was before
970 When she had thus forsaken me by whom I set such store.
I prayed her she would pardon me and did confess my fault,
Affirming that myself likewise with such a great assault

Of richesse might right well have been enforced to yield to blame,
The rather if performance had ensuèd of the same.
When I had this submission made and she sufficiently
Revenged her wrongèd chastity, she then immediately
Was reconciled; and afterward we livèd many a year
In joy, and never any jar between us did appear.
Besides all this – as though her love had been too small a gift –
She gave me eke a goodly grew'nd which was of foot so swift      980
That, when Diana gave him her, she said he should outgo
All others. And with this same grew'nd she gave this dart also,
The which you see I hold in hand. Perchance ye fain would know
What fortune to the grew'nd befell. I will unto you show
A wondrous case. The strangeness of the matter will you move.
The crinks of certain prophesies, surmounting far above
The reach of ancient wits to read, the brooknymphs did expound;
And mindless of her own dark doubts Dame Themis being found,
Was as a reckless prophetess thrown flat against the ground;
For which presumptuous deed of theirs she took just punishment.      990
  'To Thebes in Boeotia straight a cruel beast she sent
    Which wrought the bane of many a wight. The countryfolk did
        feed
Him with their cattle and themselves until (as was agreed)
That all we youthful gentlemen that dwellèd thereabout,
Assembling, pitched our corded toils the champaign fields
        throughout.
But net ne toil was none so high that could his wightness stop;
He mounted over at his ease the highest of the top.
Then every man let slip their grew'nds, but he them all
        outstripped
And even as nimbly as a bird in dalliance from them whipped.
Then all the field desirèd me to let my Laelaps go      1000
(The grew'nd that Procris unto me did give was namèd so)
Who, struggling for to wrest his neck already from the band,
Did stretch his collar. Scarcely had we let him out of hand
But that where Laelaps was become we could not understand.
The print remainèd of his feet upon the parchèd sand,
But he was clearly out of sight. Was never dart, I trow,
Nor pellet from enforcèd sling, nor shaft from Cretish bow

That flew more swift than he did run. There was not far fro
    thence
About the middle of the lawn a rising ground, from whence
1010  A man might overlook the fields. I gat me to the knap
Of this same hill and there beheld of this strange course the hap
In which the beast seems one while caught and, ere a man would
    think,
Doth quickly give the grew'nd the slip and from his biting shrink.
And like a wily fox he runs not forth directly out
Nor makes a windlass over all the champaign fields about
But, doubling and indenting still, avoids his enemy's lips
And, turning short, as swift about as spinning wheel he whips
To disappoint the snatch. The grew'nd, pursuing at an inch,
Doth cote him, never losing ground, but, likely still to pinch,
1020  Is at the sudden shifted of. Continually he snatches
In vain; for nothing in his mouth save only air he latches.
Then thought I for to try what help my dart at need could show.
Which as I chargèd in my hand by level aim to throw
And set my fingers to the thongs, I, lifting from below
Mine eyes, did look right forth again; and straight amidst the field
(A wondrous thing!) two images of marble I beheld,
Of which ye would have thought the t'one had fled on still apace
And that with open barking mouth the t'other did him chase.
In faith it was the will of God (at least, if any gods
Had care of them) that in their pace there should be found none
1030      odds.'
     Thus far; and then he held his peace. 'But tell us ere we part',
     Quoth Phocus, 'what offence or fault committed hath your
      dart?'
His dart's offence he thus declared: 'My lord, the ground of all
My grief was joy. Those joys of mine remember first I shall.
It doth me good even yet to think upon that blissful time
(I mean the fresh and lusty years of pleasant youthful prime)
When I, a happy man, enjoyed so fair and good a wife
And she with such a loving make did lead a happy life.
The care was like of both of us, the mutual love all one.
1040  She would not to have lain with Jove my presence have forgone;

Ne was there any wight that could of me have won the love,
No, though Dame Venus had herself descended from above.
The glowing brands of love did burn in both our breasts alike.
Such time as first with crazèd beams the sun is wont to strike
The tops of towers and mountains high, according to the wont
Of youthful men, in woody parks I went abroad to hunt.
But neither horse nor hounds to make pursuit upon the scent
Nor servingman nor knotty toil before or after went.
For I was safe with this same dart. When weary waxed mine arm
With striking deer and that the day did make me somewhat warm,    1050
Withdrawing for to cool myself, I sought among the shades
For air that from the valleys cold came breathing in at glades.
The more excessive was my heat, the more for air I sought.
I waited for the gentle air; the air was that that brought
Refreshing to my weary limbs. And (well I bear't in thought),
"Come, air!" I wonted was to sing, "Come, ease the pain of me!
Within my bosom lodge thyself most welcome unto me,
And, as thou heretofore art wont, abate my burning heat."
By chance (such was my destiny) proceeding to repeat
Mo words of dalliance like to these, I usèd for to say,    1060
"Great pleasure do I take in thee; for thou from day to day
Dost both refresh and nourish me. Thou makest me delight
In woods and solitary grounds. Now would to God I might
Receive continual at my mouth this pleasant breath of thine."
Some man (I wot not who) did hear these doubtful words of mine
And, taking them amiss, supposed that this same name of "air",
The which I called so oft upon, had been some lady fair.
He thought that I had loved some nymph. And thereupon
      straightway
He runs me like a hare-brained blab to Procris to bewray
This fault, as he surmisèd it, and there with lavish tongue    1070
Reported all the wanton words that he had heard me sung.
A thing of light belief is love. She (as I since have heard)
For sudden sorrow swounded down. And when long afterward
She came again unto herself, she said she was accursed
And born to cruel destiny; and me she blamèd worst
For breaking faith. And, fretting at a vain surmisèd shame,
She dreaded that which nothing was; she feared a headless name.

She wist not what to say or think. The wretch did greatly fear
Deceit; yet could she not believe the tales that talkèd were.
1080 Unless she saw her husband's fault apparent to her eye
She thought she would not him condemn of any villainy.
Next day, as soon as morning light had driven the night away,
I went abroad to hunt again. And speeding, as I lay
Upon the grass, I said, "Come, air, and ease my painful heat."
And on the sudden as I spake there seemèd for to beat
A certain sighing in mine ears, of what I could not guess.
But ceasing not for that, I still proceeded natheless
And said, "O come, most pleasant air." With that I heard a sound
Of rustling softly in the leaves that lay upon the ground;
1090 And, thinking it had been some beast, I threw my flying dart.
It was my wife, who, being now sore wounded at the heart,
Cried out, "Alas!" As soon as I perceivèd by the shriek
It was my faithful spouse, I ran me to the voiceward like
A madman that had lost his wits. There found I her half dead,
Her scattered garments staining in the blood that she had bled,
And (wretched creature as I am!) yet drawing from the wound
The gift that she herself had given. Then softly from the ground
I lifted up that body of hers of which I was more chare
Than of mine own, and from her breast her clothes in haste I tare.
1100 And, binding up her cruel wound, I strivèd for to stay
The blood and prayed she would not thus by passing so away
Forsake me as a murderer. She, waxing weak at length
And drawing to her death apace, enforcèd all her strength
To utter these few words at last: "I pray thee humbly by
Our bond of wedlock, by the gods as well above the sky
As those to whom I now must pass, as ever I have aught
Deservèd well by thee, and by the love which, having brought
Me to my death, doth even in death unfaded still remain,
To nestle in thy bed and mine let never Air obtain."
1110 This said, she held her peace, and I perceivèd by the same
And told her also how she was beguilèd in the name.
But what availèd telling then? She cothed, and with her blood
Her little strength did fade. Howbeit, as long as that she could
See aught, she starèd in my face and, gasping still on me,
Even in my mouth she breathèd forth her wretched ghost. But she

Did seem with better cheer to die for that her conscience was
Dischargèd quite and clear of doubts.' Now in conclusion, as
Duke Cephal, weeping, told this tale to Phocus and the rest,
Whose eyes were also moist with tears to hear the piteous gest,
Behold, King Aeacus and with him his eldest sons both twain          1120
Did enter in, and after them there followed in a train
Of well-appointed men of war new levied, which the king
Delivered unto Cephalus to Athens town to bring.

FINIS SEPTIMI LIBRI.

# The Eighth Book of Ovid's Metamorphoses

The daystar now beginning to disclose the morning bright
And for to cleanse the droopy sky from darkness of the night,
The eastern wind went down, and flakes of foggy clouds gan
  show.
And from the south a merry gale on Cephal's sails did blow,
The which did hold so fresh and large that he and all his men
Before that he was lookèd for arrivèd safe again
In wishèd haven. In that while King Minos with his fleet
Did waste the coast of Megara. And first he thought it meet
To make a trial of the force and courage of his men
Against the town Alcathoë, where Nisus reignèd then;                    10
Among whose honourable hair that was of colour grey
One scarlet hair did grow upon his crown, whereon the stay
Of all his kingdom did depend. Six times did Phoebe fill
Her horns with borrowed light, and yet the war hung wavering
  still
In fickle Fortune's doubtful scales; and long with fleeting wings
Between them both flew Victory. A turret of the king's
Stood hard adjoining to the wall which, being touchèd, rings;
For Phoebus (so men say) did lay his golden viol there,
And so the stones the sound thereof did ever after bear.
King Nisus' daughter oftentimes resorted to this wall                   20
And strake it with a little stone to raise the sound withal
In time of peace. And in the war she many a time and oft
Beheld the sturdy storms of Mars from that same place aloft.
And by continuance of the siege the captains' names she knew,
Their arms, horse, armour and array in every band and crew.
But specially above the rest she noted Minos' face.
She knew enough, and more than was enough as stood the case.

For were it that he hid his head in helm with feathered crest,
To her opinion in his helm he stainèd all the rest;
30  Or were it that he took in hand of steel his target bright,
She thought in wielding of his shield he was a comely knight;
Or were it that he raised his arm to throw the piercing dart,
The lady did commend his force and manhood joined with art;
Or drew he with his arrow nocked his bended bow in hand,
She sware that so in all respects was Phoebus wont to stand.
But when he showed his visage bare, his helmet laid aside,
And on a milk-white steed brave trapped in purple robe did ride,
She scarce was mistress of herself; her wits were almost straught.
A happy dart she thought it was that he in fingers caught;
40  And happy callèd she those reins that he in hand had raught.
And if she might have had her will, she could have found in heart
Among the enemies to have gone; she could have found in heart
From down the highest turret there her body to have thrown
Among the thickest of the tents of Gnossus to have flown,
Or for to ope the brazen gates and let the enemy in,
Or whatsoever else she thought might Minos' favour win.
And as she sat beholding still the king of Candy's tent,
    She said, 'I doubt me whether that I rather may lament
    Or of this woeful war be glad. It grieves me at the heart
50  That thou, O Minos, unto me, thy lover, enemy art.
But had not this same warfare been, I never had him known.
Yet might he leave this cruel war and take me as his own.
A wife, a fere, a pledge for peace he might receive of me.
O flower of beauty, O thou prince most peerless, if that she
That bare thee in her womb were like in beauty unto thee,
A right good cause had Jove on her enamoured for to be.
O, happy were I if with wings I through the air might glide
And safely to King Minos' tent from this same turret slide.
Then would I utter who I am and how the fiery flame
60  Of Cupid burnèd in my breast, desiring him to name
What dowry he would ask with me in loän of his love –
Save only of my father's realm no question he should move.
For rather than by traitorous means my purpose should take place,
Adieu, desire of hopèd love! Yet oftentimes such grace

Hath from the gentle conqueror proceeded erst, that they
Which took the foil have found the same their profit and their
     stay.
Assuredly, the war is just that Minos takes in hand
As in revengement of his son late murdered in this land.
And as his quarrel seemeth just, even so it cannot fail;
But rightful war against the wrong must, I believe, prevail.      70
Now if this city in the end must needs be taken, why
Should his own sword and not my love be means to win it by?
It were yet better he should speed by gentle means without
The slaughter of his people, yea, and (as it may fall out)
With spending of his own blood too. For sure I have a care,
O Minos, lest some soldier wound thee ere he be aware.
For who is he in all the world that hath so hard a heart
That wittingly against thy head would aim his cruel dart?
I like well this device, and on this purpose will I stand:
To yield myself, endowèd with this city, to the hand      80
Of Minos, and in doing so to bring this war to end.
But smally it availeth me the matter to intend;
The gates and issues of this town are kept with watch and ward,
And of the keys continually my father hath the guard.
My father only is the man of whom I stand in dread;
My father only hindereth me of my desirèd speed.
Would God that I were fatherless! Tush, every wight may be
A god as in their own behalf and if their hearts be free
From fearfulness. For fortune works against the fond desire
Of such as through faint-heartedness attempt not to aspire.      90
Some other, feeling in her heart such flames of Cupid's fire,
Already would have put in proof some practice to destroy
What thing so ever of her love the furtherance might annoy.
And why should any woman have a bolder heart than I?
Through fire and sword I boldly durst adventure for to fly.
And yet in this behalf at all there needs no sword nor fire;
There needeth but my father's hair to accomplish my desire.
That purple hair of his to me more precious were than gold;
That purple hair of his would make me blest a thousandfold;

100 That hair would compass my desire and set my heart at rest.'
    Night, chiefest nurse of thoughts to such as are with care
        oppressed,
    Approachèd while she spake these words, and darkness did
        increase
Her boldness. At such time as folk are wont to find release
Of cares that all the day before were working in their heads
By sleep, which falleth first of all upon them in their beds,
Her father's chamber secretly she entered, where (alas
That ever maiden should so far the bounds of nature pass!)
She robbed her father of the hair upon the which the fate
Depended both of life and death and of his royal state.
110 And, joying in her wicked prey, she bears it with her so
As if it were some lawful spoil acquirèd of the foe.
    And, passing through a postern gate, she marchèd through the mid
Of all her enemies (such a trust she had in that she did)
Until she came before the king; whom, troubled with the sight,
She thus bespake: 'Enforced, O king, by love against all right,
I, Scylla, Nisus' daughter, do present unto thee here
My native soil, my household gods and all that else is dear.
For this my gift none other thing in recompense I crave
Than of thy person, which I love, fruition for to have.
120 And in assurance of my love, receive thou here of me
My father's purple hair; and think I give not unto thee
A hair, but even my father's head.' And, as these words she spake,
The cursèd gift with wicked hand she proffered him to take.
But Minos did abhor her gift and, troubled in his mind
With strangeness of the heinous act so sore against her kind,
He answered, 'O thou slander of our age, the gods expel
Thee out of all this world of theirs and let thee nowhere dwell!
Let rest on neither sea nor land be granted unto thee!
Assure thyself that, as for me, I never will agree
130 That Candy, Jove's own foster place, as long as I there reign
Shall unto such a monstrous wight a harbour place remain.'
    This said, he, like a righteous judge, among his vanquished foes
    Set order under pain of death. Which done, he willèd those
That servèd him to go aboard and anchors up to weigh.
When Scylla saw the Candian fleet afloat to go away

And that the captain yielded not so good reward as she
Had for her lewdness lookèd for, and when in fine she see
That no entreatance could prevail, then, bursting out in ire,
With stretchèd hands and scattered hair as furious as the fire
She, shreaming, crièd out aloud, 'And whither dost thou fly,    140
Rejecting me, the only means that thou hast conquered by?
O cankered churl, preferred before my native soil, preferred
Before my father, whither fly'st, O carl of heart most hard?
Whose conquest, as it is my sin, so doth it well deserve
Reward of thee, for that my fault so well thy turn did serve.
Doth neither thee the gift I gave, nor yet my faithful love,
Nor yet that all my hope on thee alonely rested, move?
For whither shall I now resort, forsaken thus of thee?
To Megara, the wretched soil of my nativity?
Behold, it lieth vanquishèd and trodden underfoot.    150
But put the case it flourished still; yet could it nothing boot.
I have foreclosed it to myself through treason when I gave
My father's head to thee, whereby my countryfolk I drave
To hate me justly for my crime. And all the realms about
My lewd example do abhor. Thus have I shut me out
Of all the world, that only Crete might take me in. Which if
Thou like a churl deny and cast me up without relief,
The Lady Europe surely was not mother unto thee,
But one of Afric Syrts where none but serpents fostered be,
But even some cruel tiger bred in Armen or in Inde,    160
Or else the gulf Charybdis raised with rage of southern wind.
Thou wert not got by Jove, ne yet thy mother was beguiled
In shape of bull; of this thy birth the tale is false compiled.
But rather some unwieldy bull even altogether wild
That never lowèd after cow was, out of doubt, thy sire.
O father Nisus, put thou me to penance for my hire.
Rejoice thou in my punishment, thou town by me betrayed.
I have deservèd, I confess, most justly to be paid
With death. But let some one of them that through my lewdness
        smart
Destroy me. Why dost thou, that by my crime a gainer art,    170
Commit like crime thyself? Admit this wicked act of me
As to my land and fatherward indeed most heinous be;

Yet oughtest thou to take it as a friendship unto thee.
But she was meet to be thy wife that in a cow of tree
Could play the harlot with a bull and in her womb could bear
A bairn in whom the shapes of man and beasts confounded were.
How say'st thou, carl? Compel not these my words thine ears to
    glow?
Or do the winds that drive thy ships in vain my sayings blow?
In faith, it is no wonder though thy wife, Pasiphaë,
180   Preferred a bull to thee, for thou more cruel wert than he.
Now woe is me! To make more haste it standeth me in hand.
The water sounds with oars and hales from me and from my land.
In vain thou strivest, O thou churl, forgetful quite of my
Deserts; for even in spite of thee pursue thee still will I.
Upon thy curbèd keel will I take hold and, hanging so,
Be drawn along the sea with thee wherever thou do go.'
    She scarce had said these words but that she leapèd on the
        wave;
    And, getting to the ships by force of strength that love her gave,
Upon the king of Candy's keel in spite of him she clave.
190   Whom when her father spied (for now he hovered in the air
And, being made a hobby-hawk, did soar between a pair
Of nimble wings of iron mail), he sousèd down amain
To seize upon her as she hung and would have torn her fain
With bowing beak. But she for fear did let the carrack go.
And as she was about to fall, the lightsome air did so
Uphold her that she could not touch the sea, as seemèd tho.
Anon all feathers she became and forth away did fly,
Transformèd to a pretty bird that stieth to the sky.
And for because like clippèd hair her head doth bear a mark,
200   The Greeks it 'ciris' call, and we do name the same a lark.

*Theseus and*
*the Minotaur*
    As soon as Minos came a-land in Crete, he by and by
    Performed his vows to Jupiter in causing for to die
A hundred bulls for sacrifice; and then he did adorn
His palace with the enemy's spoils by conquest won beforn.
The slander of his house increased, and now appearèd more
The mother's filthy whoredom by the monster that she bore
Of double shape, an ugly thing. This shameful infamy,
This monster borne him by his wife, he minds by policy

To put away; and in a house with many nooks and crinks
From all men's sights and speech of folk to shut it up he thinks.          210
Immediately one Daedalus, renownèd in that land
For fine device and workmanship in building, went in hand
To make it. He confounds his work with sudden stops and stays
And with the great uncertainty of sundry winding ways
Leads in and out and to and fro at divers doors astray.
And as with trickling stream the brook Maeander seems to play
In Phrygia and with doubtful race runs counter to and fro
And, meeting with himself, doth look if all his streams or no
Come after and, retiring eft clean backward to his spring
And marching eft to open sea as straight as any string,          220
Indenteth with reversèd stream; even so of winding ways
Unnumerable Daedalus within his work conveys.
Yea, scarce himself could find the means to wind himself well out,
So busy and so intricate the house was all about.
    Within this maze did Minos shut the monster that did bear
    The shape of man and bull. And when he twice had fed him
        there
With blood of Attic princes' sons that given for tribute were,
The third time, at the ninth year's end, the lot did chance to light
On Theseus, King Aegeus' son; who like a valiant knight
Did overcome the Minotaur and by the policy          230
Of Minos' eldest daughter (who had taught him for to tie
A clew of linen at the door to guide himself thereby),
As busy as the turnings were, his way he out did find;
Which never man had done before. And straight he, having wind,
With Minos' daughter sailed away to Dia, where, unkind
And cruel creature that he was, he left her post alone
Upon the shore. Thus desolate and making doleful moan,
God Bacchus did both comfort her and take her to his bed.
And with an everlasting star, the more her fame to spread,
He took the chaplet from her head and up to heaven it threw.          240
The chaplet thirlèd through the air; and, as it gliding flew,
The precious stones were turned to stars which blazèd clear and
        bright
And took their place (continuing like a chaplet still to sight)

Amid between the Kneeler-down and him that gripes the snake.

    Now in this while gan Daedalus a weariness to take
    Of living like a banished man and prisoner such a time
In Crete, and longèd in his heart to see his native clime.
But seas enclosèd him as if he had in prison be.
Then thought he, 'Though both sea and land King Minos stop fro
      me,

250   I am assured he cannot stop the air and open sky.
To make my passage that way, then, my cunning will I try.
Although that Minos like a lord held all the world beside,
Yet doth the air from Minos' yoke for all men free abide.'
This said, to uncouth arts he bent the force of all his wits
To alter nature's course by craft. And orderly he knits
A row of feathers one by one, beginning with the short
And overmatching still each quill with one of longer sort,
That on the shoring of a hill a man would think them grow.
Even so the country organ-pipes of oaten reeds in row

260   Each higher than another rise. Then fastened he with flax
The middle quills and joinèd in the lowest sort with wax.
And when he thus had finished them, a little he them bent
In compass, that the very birds they full might represent.
There stood me by him Icarus, his son, a pretty lad,
Who, knowing not that he in hands his own destruction had,
With smiling mouth did one while blow the feathers to and fro
Which in the air on wings of birds did flask not long ago,
And with his thumbs another while he chafes the yellow wax
And lets his father's wondrous work with childish toys and knacks.

270   As soon as that the work was done, the workman by and by
Did peise his body on his wings and in the air on high
Hung wavering and did teach his son how he should also fly.
'I warn thee,' quoth he, 'Icarus, a middle race to keep.
For if thou hold too low a gait, the dankness of the deep
Will overlade thy wings with wet. And if thou mount too high,
The sun will singe them. Therefore see between them both thou
      fly.
I bid thee not behold the star Boötes in the sky,
Nor look upon the bigger Bear to make thy course thereby,
Nor yet on Orion's naked sword. But ever have an eye

To keep the race that I do keep, and I will guide thee right.'          280
In giving counsel to his son to order well his flight,
He fastened to his shoulders twain a pair of uncouth wings;
And as he was in doing it and warning him of things,
His agèd cheeks were wet, his hands did quake. In fine he gave
His son a kiss, the last that he alive should ever have.
And then he, mounting up aloft, before him took his way,
Right fearful for his follower's sake, as is the bird the day
That first she tolleth from her nest among the branches high
Her tender young ones in the air to teach them for to fly.
So heartens he his little son to follow, teaching him          290
A hurtful art. His own two wings he waveth very trim
And looketh backward still upon his son's. The fishermen
Then standing angling by the sea and shepherds leaning then
On sheephooks and the ploughmen on the handles of their
          plough,
Beholding them, amazèd were and thought that they that through
The air could fly were gods. And now did on their left side stand
The isles of Paros and of Dele and Samos, Juno's land,
And on their right Lebinthus and the fair Calydna, fraught
With store of honey, when the boy a frolic courage caught
To fly at random. Whereupon, forsaking quite his guide,          300
Of fond desire to fly to heaven above his bounds he stied.
And there the nearness of the sun, which burned more hot aloft,
Did make the wax, with which his wings were gluèd, lithe and
          soft.
As soon as that the wax was molt, his naked arms he shakes;
And, wanting wherewithal to wave, no help of air he takes.
But, calling on his father loud, he drownèd in the wave;
And by this chance of his those seas his name forever have.
His wretched father (but as then no father) cried in fear,
'O Icarus, O Icarus, where art thou? Tell me where
That I may find thee, Icarus.' He saw the feathers swim          310
Upon the waves, and cursed his art that had so spited him.
At last he took his body up and laid it in a grave
And to the isle the name of him then buried in it gave.

And as he of his wretched son the corse in ground did hide,          *Daedalus and*
The cackling partridge from a thick and leafy thorn him spied          *Partridge*

And, clapping with his wings, for joy aloud to call began.
There was of that same kind of bird no mo but he as then.
In times forepast had none been seen. It was but late anew
Since he was made a bird; and that thou, Daedalus, may'st rue,
320    For while the world doth last, thy shame shall thereupon ensue.
For why thy sister, ignorant of that which after happed,
Did put him to thee to be taught, full twelve years old and apt
To take instruction. He did mark the middle bone that goes
Through fishes, and according to the pattern ta'en of those
He filèd teeth upon a piece of iron one by one
And so devisèd first the saw, where erst was never none.
Moreover, he two iron shanks so joined in one round head
That, opening an indifferent space, the one point down shall tread
And t'other draw a circle round. The finding of these things
330    The spiteful heart of Daedalus with such a malice stings
That headlong from the holy tower of Pallas down he threw
His nephew, feigning him to fall by chance, which was not true.
But Pallas, who doth favour wits, did stay him in his fall
And, changing him into a bird, did clad him over all
With feathers soft amid the air. The quickness of his wit
(Which erst was swift) did shed itself among his wings and feet.
And as he Partridge hight before, so hights he partridge still.
Yet mounteth not this bird aloft, ne seems to have a will
To build her nest in tops of trees among the boughs on high,
340    But flecketh near the ground and lays her eggs in hedges dry.
And for because her former fall she aye in mind doth bear,
She ever since all lofty things doth warily shun for fear.

*The
Calydonian
boar-hunt*

        And now, forwearied, Daedalus alighted in the land
    Within the which the burning hills of fiery Etna stand;
To save whose life King Cocalus did weapon take in hand,
For which men thought him merciful. And now with high
            renown
Had Theseus ceasèd the woeful pay of tribute in the town
Of Athens. Temples deckèd were with garlands everywhere,
And supplications made to Jove and warlike Pallas were
350    And all the other gods. To whom, more honour for to show,
Gifts, blood of beasts and frankincense the people did bestow

As in performance of their vows. The right redoubted name
Of Theseus through the land of Greece was spread by flying fame.
And now the folk that in the land of rich Achaia dwelt
Prayed him of succour in the harms and perils that they felt.
Although the land of Calydon had then Meleäger,
Yet was it fain in humble wise to Theseus to prefer
A supplication for the aid of him. The cause wherefore
They made such humble suit to him was this: there was a boar
The which Diana, for to wreak her wrath conceived before,                360
Had thither as her servant sent the country for to waste.
For men report that Oeney, when he had in storehouse placed
The full increase of former year, to Ceres did assign
The firstlings of his corn and fruits; to Bacchus, of the vine;
And unto Pallas olive oil. This honouring of the gods
Of grain and fruits who put their help to toiling in the clods
Ambitiously to all, even those that dwell in heaven, did climb.
Diana's altars, as it happed, alonely at that time
Without reward of frankincense were overskipped, they say.
Even gods are subject unto wrath. 'He shall not scape away                370
Unpunished. Though unworshippèd he passèd me with spite,
He shall not make his vaunt he scaped me unrevengèd quite,'
Quoth Phoebe. And anon she sent a boar to Oeney's ground
Of such a hugeness as no bull could ever yet be found
In Epire; but in Sicily are bulls much less than he.
His eyes did glister blood and fire. Right dreadful was to see
His brawnèd neck; right dreadful was his hair which grew as thick
With pricking points as one of them could well by other stick.
And like a front of armèd pikes set close in battle ray
The sturdy bristles on his back stood staring up alway.                380
The scalding foam with gnashing hoarse which he did cast aside
Upon his large and brawnèd shield did white as curds abide.
Among the greatest elephants in all the land of Inde
A greater tush than had this boar ye shall not lightly find.
Such lightning flashèd from his chaps as searèd up the grass.
Now trampled he the spindling corn to ground where he did pass;
Now, ramping up their ripèd hope, he made the ploughmen weep
And chanked the kernel in the ear. In vain their floors they sweep;
In vain their barns for harvest long the likely store they keep.

390 The spreaded vines with clustered grapes to ground he rudely sent,
'And, full of berries, loaden boughs from olive-trees he rent.
On cattle also did he rage; the shepherd nor his dog
Nor yet the bulls could save the herds from outrage of this hog.
The folk themselves were fain to fly. And yet they thought them
        not
In safety when they had themselves within the city got
Until their prince, Meleäger, and with their prince a knot
Of lords and lusty gentlemen of hand and courage stout
With chosen fellows for the nonce of all the lands about
Enflamèd were to win renown. The chief that thither came

400 Were both the twins of Tyndarus★ of great renown and fame,
The one in all activity of manhood, strength and force,
The other for his cunning skill in handling of a horse;
And Jason, he that first of all the galley did invent;
And Theseus with Pirithous, between which two there went
A happy league of amity; and two of Thesty's race†;
And Lynce, the son of AphaVy; and Idas, swift of pace;
And fierce Leucippus; and the brave Acastus with his dart,
In handling of the which he had the perfect skill and art;
And Caeney who, by birth a wench, the shape of man had won;

410 And Dryas and Hippothoüs; and Phoenix eke, the son
Of old Amyntor; and a pair of Actor's imps‡; and Phyle,
Who came from Elis. Telamon was also there that while;
And so was also Peleus, the great Achilles' sire;
And Pheret's son§; and Iolay the Theban, who with fire
Helped Hercules the monstrous heads of Hydra off to sear.
The lively lad Eurytion and Echion, who did bear
The prick and prize for footmanship, were present also there;
And Lexel of Narytium, too; and Panopey beside;
And Hyle and cruel Hippasus; and Nestor, who that tide

420 Was in the prime of lusty youth. Moreover, thither went
Three children of Hippocoön¶ from old Amyclae sent;
And he that of Penelope the father-in-law became‖;
And eke the son of Parrhasus, Ancaeus called by name.

There was the son of Ampycus\*, of great forecasting wit;
And Oecley's son†, who of his wife was unbetrayèd yet.
And from the city Tegea there came the paragon
Of Lycy forest, Atalant, a goodly lady, one
Of Schoeney's daughters, then a maid. The garment she did wear
A braided button fastened at her gorget. All her hair
Untrimmèd in one only knot was trussèd. From her left          430
Side hanging on her shoulder was an ivory quiver deft
Which, being full of arrows, made a clattering as she went;
And in her right hand she did bear a bow already bent.
Her furniture was such as this. Her count'nance and her grace
Was such as in a boy might well be called a wench's face
And in a wench be called a boy's. The prince of Calydon
No sooner cast his eye on her but, being caught anon
In love, he wished her to his wife. But unto this desire
God Cupid gave not his consent. The secret flames of fire
He haling inward still, did say, 'O happy man is he          440
Whom this same lady shall vouchsafe her husband for to be.'
The shortness of the time and shame would give him leave to say
No more; a work of greater weight did draw him then away.
    A wood thick grown with trees which stood unfellèd to that
        day,
    Beginning from a plain, had thence a large prospect throughout
The falling grounds that every way did muster round about.
As soon as that the men came there, some pitchèd up the toils,
Some took the couples from the dogs and some pursued the foils
In places where the swine had tracked, desiring for to spy
Their own destruction. Now there was a hollow bottom by          450
To which the watershoots of rain from all the high grounds drew.
Within the compass of this pond great store of osiers grew
And sallows lithe and flackering flags and moorish rushes eke,
And lazy reeds on little shanks and other baggage like.
From hence the boar was rousèd out. And fiercely forth he flies
Among the thickest of his foes, like thunder from the skies
When clouds in meeting force the fire to burst by violence out.
He bears the trees before him down, and all the wood about

\*Mopsus          †Amphiaraus

Doth sound of crashing. All the youth with hideous noise and
      shout
Against him bend their boar-spear points with hand and courage
460      stout.
He rushes forth among the dogs that held him at a bay
And, now on this side, now on that, as any come in way
He rips their skins and splitteth them and chaseth them away.
Echion first of all the rout a dart at him did throw,
Which missed and in a maple-tree did give a little blow.
The next (if he that threw the same had usèd lesser might)
The back at which he aimèd it was likely for to smite.
It overflew him. Jason was the man that cast the dart.
With that the son of Ampycus* said, 'Phoebus, if with heart
470 I have and still do worship thee, now grant me for to hit
The thing that I do level at.' Apollo grants him it
As much as lay in him to grant. He hit the swine indeed,
But neither entered he his hide nor causèd him to bleed.
For why Diana, as the dart was flying, took away
The head of it; and so the dart could headless bear no sway.
But yet the moody beast thereby was set the more on fire
And, chafing like the lightning swift, he uttereth forth his ire.
The fire did sparkle from his eyes, and from his boiling breast
He breathèd flaming flakes of fire conceivèd in his chest.
480 And look with what a violent brunt a mighty bullet goes
From engines bent against a wall or bulwarks full of foes,
With even such violence rushed the swine among the hunts
      amain
And overthrew Eupalamon and Pelagon both twain
That in the right wing placèd were. Their fellows, stepping to
And drawing them away, did save their lives with much ado.
But as for poor Enaesimus, Hippocoon's son had not
The luck to scape the deadly dint. He would away have got
And, trembling, turned his back for fear; the swine him overtook
And cut his hamstrings, so that straight his going him forsook.
490 And Nestor to have lost his life was like by fortune ere
The siege of Troy, but that he took his rist upon his spear

*Mopsus

And, leaping quickly up upon a tree that stood hard by,
Did safely from the place behold his foe whom he did fly.
The boar then, whetting sharp his tusks against the oaken wood,
To mischief did prepare himself with fierce and cruel mood.
And, trusting to his weapons which he sharpened had anew,
In great Orithyia's thigh a wound with hookèd groin he drew.
The valiant brothers, those same twins of Tyndarus* (not yet
Celestial signs), did both of them on goodly coursers sit
As white as snow; and each of them had shaking in his fist          500
A lightsome dart with head of steel to throw it where he list.
And for to wound the bristled boar they surely had not missed,
But that he still recovered so the coverts of the wood
That neither horse could follow him nor dart do any good.
Still after followed Telamon whom, taking to his feet
No heed at all for eagerness, a maple root did meet
Which trippèd up his heels and flat against the ground him laid.
And while his brother Peleus relievèd him, the maid
Of Tegea took an arrow swift and shot it from her bow.
The arrow, lighting underneath the aver's ear below                 510
And somewhat razing of the skin, did make the blood to show.
The maid herself not gladder was to see that lucky blow
Than was the prince Meleäger. He was the first that saw
And first that showèd to his mates the blood that she did draw
And said, 'For this thy valiant act due honour shalt thou have.'
The men did blush and, cheering up each other, courage gave
With shouting; and disorderly their darts by heaps they threw.
The number of them hindered them, not suffering to ensue
That any lighted on the mark at which they all did aim.
Behold, enraged against his end the hardy knight that came          520
From Arcady rushed rashly with a poleaxe in his fist
And said, 'You younglings, learn of me what difference is betwixt
A wench's weapons and a man's, and all of you give place
To my redoubted force. For though Diana in this chase
Should with her own shield him defend, yet should this hand of
        mine
Even maugre Dame Diana's heart confound this orpèd swine.'

*Castor & Pollux

Such boasting words as these through pride presumptuously he
        crakes
And, straining out himself upon his tiptoes, straight he takes
His poleaxe up with both his hands. But as this bragger meant
530   To fetch his blow, the cruel beast his malice did prevent
And in his cods, the speeding place of death, his tushes puts
And rippeth up his paunch. Down falls Ancaeus, and his guts
Come tumbling out besmeared with blood and foilèd all the plot.
Pirithoüs, Ixion's son, at that abashèd not
But, shaking in his valiant hand his hunting staff, did go
Still stoutly forward face to face t'encounter with his foe;
To whom Duke Theseus cried afar, 'O dearer unto me
Than is myself, my soul, I say, stay! Lawful we it see
For valiant men to keep aloof. The overhardy heart
540   In rash adventuring of himself hath made Ancaeus smart.'
This said, he threw a weighty dart of cornel with a head
Of brass which, being levelled well, was likely to have sped,
But that a bough of chestnut-tree thick-leavèd by the way
Did latch it and by means thereof the dint of it did stay.
Another dart that Jason threw by fortune missed the boar
And light between a mastiff's chaps and through his guts did gore
And nailed him to the earth. The hand of Prince Meleäger
Played hitty-missy. Of two darts his first did fly too far
And lighted in the ground; the next amid his back sticked fast.
550   And while the boar did play the fiend and turnèd round aghast
And, grunting, flang his foam about together mixed with blood,
The giver of the wound (the more to stir his enemy's mood)
Stepped in and underneath the shield did thrust his boar-spear
        through.
Then all the hunters, shouting out, demeanèd joy enough,
And glad was he that first might come to take him by the hand.
About the ugly beast they all with gladness gazing stand
And, wondering what a field of ground his carcass did possess,
There durst not any be so bold to touch him. Ne'ertheless,
They every of them with his blood their hunting staves made red.
560   Then steppèd forth Meleäger and, treading on his head,
Said thus: 'O lady Atalant, receive thou here my fee
And of my glory vouch thou safe partaker for to be.'

Immediately the ugly head with both the tushes brave
And eke the skin with bristles stour right grisly he her gave.
The lady for the giver's sake was in her heart as glad
As for the gift; the rest repined that she such honour had.
Through all the rout was murmuring. Of whom with roaring rere
And arms displayed that all the field might easily see and hear,
The Thesties cried, 'Dame, come off and lay us down this gear.
And thou, a woman, offer not us men so great a shame                    570
As we to toil and thou to take the honour of our game.
Ne let that fair smooth face of thine beguile thee, lest that he
That, being doted in thy love, did give thee this our fee
Be overfar to rescue thee.' And with that word they took
The gift from her, and right of gift from him. He could not brook
This wrong but, gnashing with his teeth for anger that did boil
Within, said fiercely, 'Learn ye, you that other folks despoil
Of honour given, what difference is between your threats and
          deeds.'
And therewithal Plexippus' breast, who no such matter dreads,
With wicked weapon he did pierce. As Toxey doubting stood             580
What way to take, desiring both t'avenge his brother's blood
And fearing to be murdered as his brother was before,
Meleager (to dispatch all doubts of musing any more)
Did heat his sword for company in blood of him again
Before Plexippus' blood was cold that did thereon remain.
     Althaea, going toward church with presents for to yield          *Althaea's*
     Due thanks and worship to the gods that for her son had killed   *revenge*
The boar, beheld her brothers brought home dead; and by and by
She beat her breast and filled the town with shrieking piteously
And, shifting all her rich array, did put on mourning weed.            590
But when she understood what man was doer of the deed,
She left all mourning and from tears to vengeance did proceed.
There was a certain firebrand which, when Oeney's wife did lie
In childbed of Meleager, she chancèd to espy
The Destinies putting in the fire. And in the putting in
She heard them speak these words as they his fatal thread did spin:
'O lately born, like time we give to thee and to this brand.'
And when they so had spoken, they departed out of hand.

Immediately the mother caught the blazing bough away
600 And quenchèd it. This bough she kept full charily many a day,
And in the keeping of the same she kept her son alive.
But now, intending of his life him clearly to deprive,
She brought it forth and, causing all the coals and shivers to
Be laïd by, she like a foe did kindle fire thereto.
Four times she was about to cast the firebrand in the flame;
Four times she pullèd back her hand from doing of the same.
As mother and as sister both she strove what way to go;
The divers names drew diversely her stomach to and fro.
Her face waxed often pale for fear of mischief to ensue;
610 And often red about the eyes through heat of ire she grew.
One while her look resembled one that threatened cruelness;
Another while ye would have thought she minded piteousness.
And though the cruel burning of her heart did dry her tears,
Yet burst out some. And as a boat, which tide contrary bears
Against the wind, feels double force and is compelled to yield
To both, so Thesty's daughter now, unable for to wield
Her doubtful passions, diversely is carried off and on,
And changeably she waxes calm and storms again anon.
But better sister ginneth she than mother for to be
620 And, to th'intent her brothers' ghosts with blood to honour, she
In meaning to be one way kind doth work another way
Against kind. When the plaguey fire waxed strong, she thus did
        say:
'Let this same fire my bowels burn.' And as, in cursed hands
The fatal wood she holding, at the hellish altar stands,
She said, 'Ye triple goddesses of wreak, ye hellhounds three,
Behold ye all this furious fact and sacrifice of me.
I wreak, and do against all right. With death must death be paid;
On mischief mischief must be heaped; on corse must corse be laid.
Confounded let this wicked house with heapèd sorrows be.
630 Shall Oeney joy his happy son in honour for to see
And Thesty mourn, bereft of his? Nay; better yet it were
That each with other company in mourning you should bear.
Ye brothers' ghosts and souls new dead, I wish no more but you
To feel the solemn obsequies which I prepare as now,

And that mine offering you accept which dearly I have bought,
The issue of my wretched womb. Alas, alas, what thought
I for to do? O brothers, I beseech you bear with me!
I am his mother; so to do my hands unable be!
His trespass, I confess, deserves the stopping of his breath,
But yet I do not like that I be author of his death.                    640
And shall he then with life and limb and honour, too, scape free
And, vaunting in his good success, the king of Calydon be;
And you, dear souls, lie rakèd up but in a little dust?
I will not surely suffer it. But let the villain trust
That he shall die and draw with him to ruin and decay
His kingdom, country and his sire that doth upon him stay.
Why, where is now the mother's heart and pity that should reign
In parents and the ten months' pains that once I did sustain?
O, would to God thou burnèd had a baby in this brand
And that I had not ta'en it out and quenched it with my hand!      650
That all this while thou livèd hast, my goodness is the cause.
And now most justly unto death thine own desert thee draws.
Receive the guerdon of thy deed, and render thou again
Thy twice-given life – by bearing first and secondarily when
I caught this firebrand from the flame – or else come deal with me
As with my brothers, and with them let me entombèd be.
I would, and cannot. What, then, shall I stand to in this case?
One while my brothers' corses seem to press before my face
With lively image of their deaths; another while my mind
Doth yield to pity, and the name of mother doth me blind.          660
Now woe is me! To let you have the upper hand is sin,
But ne'ertheless the upper hand, O brothers, do you win,
Conditionally that, when that I to comfort you withal
Have wrought this feat, myself to you resort in person shall.'
    This said, she turned away her face and with a trembling hand
    Did cast the deathful brand amid the burning fire. The brand
Did either sigh or seem to sigh in burning in the flame,
Which sorry and unwilling was to fasten on the same.
Meleager, being absent and not knowing aught at all,
Was burnèd with this flame and felt his bowels to appal           670
With secret fire. He bare out long the pain with courage stout,
But yet it grievèd him to die so cowardly without

The shedding of his blood. He thought Ancaeus for to be
A happy man that died of wound. With sighing callèd he
Upon his agèd father and his sisters and his brother
And lastly on his wife too, and by chance upon his mother.
His pain increasèd with the fire and fell therewith again,
And at the selfsame instant quite extinguished werè both twain.
And as the ashes soft and hoar by leisure overgrew
680    The glowing coals, so leisurely his spirit from him drew.
    Then droopèd stately Calydon. Both young and old did mourn;
    The Lords and Commons did lament; and married wives with
        torn
And tattered hair did cry, 'Alas!' His father did beray
His hoary head and face with dust and on the earth flat lay,
Lamenting that he livèd had to see that woeful day.
For now his mother's guilty hand had for that cursèd crime
Done execution on herself by sword before her time.
If God to me a hundred mouths with sounding tongues should
        send
And reason able to conceive, and thereunto should lend
690    Me all the grace of eloquence that e'er the Muses had,
I could not show the woe wherewith his sisters were bested.
Unmindful of their high estate, their naked breasts they smit
Until they made them black and blue. And while his body yet
Remainèd, they did cherish it and cherish it again.
They kissed his body; yea, they kissed the chest that did contain
His corse. And after that the corse was burnt to ashes, they
Did press his ashes with their breasts, and down along they lay
Upon his tomb and there embraced his name upon the stone
And filled the letters of the same with tears that from them gon.
700    At length Diana, satisfied with slaughter brought upon
The house of Oeney, lifts them up with feathers everych one
(Save Gorge and the daughter-in-law of noble Alcmene) and
Makes wings to stretch along their sides and hornèd nebs to stand
Upon their mouths. And finally she, altering quite their fair
And native shape, in shape of birds doth send them through the
        air.

*Acheloüs and*
*the nymphs*

The noble Theseus in this while, with others having done
His part in killing of the boar, to Athensward begun

To take his way. But Acheloy, then being swollen with rain,
Did stay him of his journey and from passage him restrain.
'Of Athens valiant knight,' quoth he, 'come underneath my roof      710
And for to pass my raging stream as yet attempt no proof.
This brook is wont whole trees to bear and evelong stones to carry
With hideous roaring down his stream. I oft have seen him harry
Whole sheepcotes standing near his banks with flocks of sheep
    therein.
Nought booted bulls their strength; nought steeds by swiftness
    there could win.
Yea, many lusty men this brook hath swallowed when the snow
From mountains molten causèd him his banks to overflow.
The best is for you for to rest until the river fall
Within his bounds and run again within his channel small.'
'Content', quoth Theseus, 'Acheloy, I will not sure refuse      720
Thy counsel nor thy house.' And so he both of them did use.
Of pommy hollowed diversely and ragged pebble stone
The walls were made. The floor with moss was soft to tread upon.
The roof thereof was checkerwise with shells of purple wrought
And pearl. The sun then full two parts of day to end had brought,
And Theseus down to table sat with such as late before
Had friendly borne him company at killing of the boar.
At one side sat Ixion's son, and on the other sat
The Prince of Troezen, Lelex, with a thin-haired hoary pate,
And then such other as the brook of Acarnania did      730
Vouchsafe the honour to his board and table for to bid,
Who was right glad of such a guest. Immediately there came
Barefooted nymphs who brought in meat. And when that of the
    same
The lords had taken their repast, the meat away they took
And set down wine in precious stones. Then Theseus, who did
    look
Upon the sea that underneath did lie within their sight,
Said, 'Tell us what is yon same place,' and with his finger right
He pointed thereunto, 'I pray, and what that island hight –
Although it seemeth mo than one.' The river answered thus:
'It is not one main land alone that kennèd is of us.      740

There are upon a five of them. The distance of the place
Doth hinder to discern between each isle the perfect space.
And that the less ye wonder may at Phoebe's act alate
To such as had neglected her upon contempt or hate,
These isles were sometime waternymphs who, having killèd neat
Twice five and callèd to their feast the country gods to eat,
Forgetting me, kept frolic cheer. At that I gan to swell
And ran more large than ever erst; and being overfell
In stomach and in stream, I rent the wood from wood and field
From field, and with the ground the nymphs (as then with
           stomachs mild
750  Remembering me) I tumbled to the sea. The waves of me
And of the sea the ground, that erst all whole was wont to be,
Did rend asunder into all the isles you yonder see
And made a way for waters now to pass between them free.
They now of Urchins have their name. But of these islands, one
A great way off – behold ye – stands, a great way off alone,
As you may see. The mariners do call it Perimele.
With her (she was as then a nymph) so far in love I fell
That of her maidenhood I her spoiled; which thing displeased so
           sore
760  Her father, Sir Hippodamas, that from the craggy shore
He threw her headlong down to drown her in the sea. But I
Did latch her straight and, bearing her afloat, did loud thus cry:
"O Neptune with thy three-tined mace, who hast by lot the
           charge
Of all the waters wild that bound upon the earth at large,
To whom we holy streams do run, in whom we take our end,
Draw near and gently to my boon effectually attend.
This lady whom I bear afloat myself hath hurt. Be meek
And upright. If Hippodamas perchance were fatherlike
Or if that he extremity through outrage did not seek,
770  He oughted to have pitied her and for to bear with me.
Now help us, Neptune, I thee pray, and condescend that she
Whom from the land her father's wrath and cruelness doth chase,
Who through her father's cruelness is drowned, may find the
           grace
To have a place; or rather let herself become a place,

And I will still embrace the same." The king of seas did move
His head and, as a token that he did my suit approve,
He made his surges all to shake. The nymph was sore afraid.
Howbeit she swam, and as she swam my hand I softly laid
Upon her breast which quivered still. And while I touched the
    same
I sensibly did feel how all her body hard became          780
And how the earth did overgrow her bulk. And, as I spake,
New earth enclosed her swimming limbs, which by and by did
    take
Another shape and grew into a mighty isle.' With that
The river ceased, and all men there did wonder much thereat.
    Pirithous, being over haught of mind and such a one
  As did despise both god and man, did laugh them everych one
To scorn for giving credit and said thus: 'The words thou spak'st
Are feignèd fancies, Acheloy; and overstrong thou mak'st
The gods to say that they can give and take 'way shapes.' This
    scoff
Did make the hearers all amazed, for none did like thereof.      790
And Lelex, of them all the man most ripe in years and wit,
Said thus: 'Unmeasurable is the power of heaven, and it
Can have none end. And look what God doth mind to bring
    about
Must take effect. And in this case to put ye out of doubt,
  'Upon the hills of Phrygie near a teil there stands a tree       *Baucis and*
  Of oak enclosèd with a wall. Myself the place did see,         *Philemon*
For Pitthey unto Pelops' fields did send me, where his father
Did sometime reign. Not far fro thence there is a pool which
    rather
Had been dry ground inhabited; but now it is a mere
And moorcocks, coots and cormorants do breed and nestle there.   800
The mighty Jove and Mercury, his son, in shape of men
Resorted thither on a time. A thousand houses when
For room to lodge in they had sought, a thousand houses barred
Their doors against them. Ne'ertheless one cottage afterward
Receivèd them, and that was but a pelting one indeed.
The roof thereof was thatchèd all with straw and fennish reed.

Howbeit, two honest ancient folk, of whom she Baucis hight
And he Philemon, in that cote their faith in youth had plight
And in that cote had spent their age. And for they patiently
810   Did bear their simple poverty, they made it light thereby
And showèd it nothing to be repinèd at at all.
It skills not whether there for hinds or master you do call;
For all the household were but two, and both of them obeyed
And both commanded. When the gods at this same cottage stayed
And, ducking down their heads, within the low-made wicket
        came,
Philemon, bringing each a stool, bade rest upon the same
Their limbs, and busy Baucis brought them cushions, homely
        gear.
Which done, the embers on the hearth she gan abroad to stir
And laid the coals together that were raked up overnight
820   And with the brands and drièd leaves did make them gather might
And with the blowing of her mouth did make them kindle bright.
Then from an inner house she fetched sear sticks and clifted brands
And put them broken underneath a skillet with her hands.
Her husband from their gardenplot fetched coleworts, of the
        which
She shredded small the leaves, and with a fork took down a flitch
Of resty bacon from the balk made black with smoke, and cut
A piece thereof and in the pan to boiling did it put.
And while this meat a-seething was, the time in talk they spent,
By means whereof away without much tediousness it went.
830   There hung a bowl of beech upon a spirget by a ring;
The same with warmèd water filled the two old folk did bring
To bathe their guests' foul feet therein. Amid the house there
        stood
A couch whose bottom, sides and feet were all of sallow wood
And on the same a mat of sedge. They cast upon this bed
A covering which was never wont upon it to be spread
Except it were at solemn feasts; and yet the same was old
And of the coarsest, with a bed of sallow meet to hold.
The gods sat down. The agèd wife, right chare and busy as
A bee, set out a table of the which the third foot was

A little shorter than the rest. A tile-sherd made it even          840
And took away the shoringness. And when they had it driven
To stand up level, with green mints they by and by it wiped.
Then set they on it Pallas' fruit* with double colour striped
And cornels kept in pickle moist and endive and a root
Of radish and a jolly lump of butter fresh and soot
And eggs rear-roasted. All these cates in earthen dishes came.
Then set they down a graven cup made also of the same
Self kind of plate and mazers made of beech, whose inner side
Was rubbed with yellow wax. And when they pausèd had a tide,
Hot meat came piping from the fire. And shortly thereupon          850
A cup of green hedge wine was brought. This ta'en away, anon
Came in the latter course which was of nuts, dates, drièd figs,
Sweet smelling apples in a maund made flat of osier twigs,
And prunes and plums and purple grapes cut newly from the tree,
And in the midst a honeycomb new taken from the bee.
Besides all this there did ensue good count'nance overmore
With will not poor nor niggardly. Now all the while before
As often as Philemon and Dame Baucis did perceive
The empty cup to fill alone and wine to still receive,
Amazèd at the strangeness of the thing, they gan straightway       860
With fearful hearts and hands held up to frame themselves to pray,
Desiring for their slender cheer and fare to pardoned be.
They had but one poor goose which kept their little tenantry,
And this to offer to the gods, their guests, they did intend.
The gander, wight of wing, did make the slow old folk to spend
Their pains in vain and mocked them long. At length he seemed
          to fly
For succour to the gods themselves, who bade he should not die.
"For we be gods," quoth they, "and all this wicked township shall
Abye their guilt. On you alone this mischief shall not fall.
No more but give you up your house and follow up this hill         870
Together, and upon the top thereof abide our will."
They both obeyed. And as the gods did lead the way before,
They laggèd slowly after with their staves and laboured sore
Against the rising of the hill. They were not mickle more

*Olives

Than full a flight-shot from the top when, looking back, they saw
How all the town was drownèd save their little shed of straw.
And as they wondered at the thing and did bewail the case
Of those that had their neighbours been, the old poor cote so base
Whereof they had been owners erst became a church. The props
880    Were turnèd into pillars huge; the straw upon the tops
Was yellow, so that all the roof did seem of burnished gold;
The floor with marble pavèd was; the doors on either fold
Were graven. At the sight hereof Philemon and his make
Began to pray in fear. Then Jove thus gently them bespake:
"Declare, thou righteous man, and thou, O woman meet to have
A righteous husband, what ye would most chiefly wish or crave."
Philemon, taking conference a little with his wife,
Declarèd both their meanings thus: "We covet during life
Your chaplains for to be to keep your temple. And because
890    Our years in concord we have spent, I pray, when death near draws
Let both of us together leave our lives, that neither I
Behold my wife's decease nor she see mine when I do die."
Their wish had sequel to their will. As long as life did last
They kept the church; and being spent with age of years forepast,
By chance as standing on a time without the temple door
They told the fortune of the place, Philemon old and poor
Saw Baucis flourish green with leaves, and Baucis saw likewise
Philemon branching out in boughs and twigs before her eyes.
And as the bark did overgrow the heads of both, each spake
900    To other while they might. At last they each of them did take
Their leave of other both at once, and therewithal the bark
Did hide their faces both at once. The Phrygians in that park
Do at this present day still show the trees that shapèd were
Of their two bodies, growing yet together jointly there.
These things did ancient men report of credit very good;
For why there was no cause why they should lie. As I there stood
I saw the garlands hanging on the boughs and, adding new,
I said, "Let them whom God doth love be gods, and honour due
Be given to such as honour him with fear and reverence true." '

*The sacrilege*     He held his peace, and both the thing and he that did it tell
*of Erysicthon*     Did move them all, but Theseus most. Whom, being minded
                well

To hear of wondrous things, the brook of Calydon thus bespake:
'There are, O valiant knight, some folk that had the power to take
Strange shape for once and all their lives continued in the same;
And other some to sundry shapes have power themselves to frame,
As thou, O Proteu, dwelling in the sea that clips the land.
For now a younker, now a boar, anon a lion, and
Straightway thou did'st become a snake and by and by a bull,
That people were afraid of thee to see thy hornèd skull.
And oftentimes thou seemed a stone, and now and then a tree,                    920
And counterfeiting water sheer thou seemèdst oft to be
A river, and another while contrary thereunto
Thou wert a fire. No lesser power than also thus to do
Had Erysicthon's daughter, whom Autolychus took to wife.
Her father was a person that despisèd all his life
The power of gods and never did vouchsafe them sacrifice.
He also is reported to have hewn in wicked wise
The grove of Ceres and to fell her holy woods, which aye
Had undiminished and unhacked continued to that day.
There stood in it a warry oak which was a wood alone.                           930
Upon it round hung fillets, crowns and tables many one,
The vows of such as had obtained their heart's desire. Full oft
The woodnymphs underneath this tree did fetch their frisks aloft,
And oftentimes with hand in hand they dancèd in a round
About the trunk, whose bigness was of timber good and sound
Full fifteen fathom. All the trees within the wood beside
Were unto this as weeds to them, so far it did them hide.
Yet could not this move Triop's son his axe therefro to hold,
But bade his servants cut it down. And when he did behold
Them stinting at his hest, he snatched an axe with furious mood                 940
From one of them and wickedly said thus: "Although this wood
Not only were the darling of the goddess but also
The goddess even herself, yet would I make it ere I go
To kiss the clowres with her top that pranks with branches so."
This spoken, as he sweaked his axe aside to fetch his blow,
The menaced oak did quake and sigh, the acorns that did grow
Thereon together with the leaves to wax full pale began
And, shrinking in for fear, the boughs and branches lookèd wan.

As soon as that his cursèd hand had wounded once the tree,
950 The blood came spinning from the carf as freshly as ye see
It issue from a bullock's neck whose throat is newly cut
Before the altar, when his flesh to sacrifice is put.
They were amazèd everych one. And one among them all
To let the wicked act durst from the tree his hatchet call.
The lewd Thessalian, facing him, said, "Take thou here to thee
The guerdon of thy godliness," and, turning from the tree,
He choppèd off the fellow's head. Which done, he went again
And hewèd on the oak. Straight from amid the tree as then
There issued such a sound as this: "Within this tree dwell I,
960 A nymph to Ceres very dear, who now before I die
In comfort of my death do give thee warning thou shalt buy
Thy doing dear within a while." He goeth wilfully
Still thorough with his wickedness, until at length the oak,
Pulled partly by the force of ropes and cut with axe's stroke,
Did fall and with his weight bare down of underwood great store.
The woodnymphs, with the losses of the wood's and theirs right
   sore
Amazèd, gathered on a knot and all in mourning weed
Went sad to Ceres, praying her to wreak that wicked deed
Of Erysicthon's. Ceres was content it should be so,
970 And with the moving of her head in nodding to and fro
She shook the fields, which laden were with fruitful harvest tho.
And therewithal a punishment most piteous she proceeds
To put in practice, were it not that his most heinous deeds
No pity did deserve to have at anybody's hand.
With helpless hunger him to pine in purpose she did stand.
And for as much as she herself and Famine might not meet
(For Fate forbiddeth Famine to abide within the leet
Where Plenty is), she thus bespake a fairy of the hill:
"There lieth in the utmost bounds of Tartary the chill
980 A dreary place, a wretched soil, a barren plot; no grain,
No fruit, no tree is growing there, but there doth aye remain
Unwieldsome Cold with trembling Fear and Paleness white as
   clout
And foodless Famine. Will thou her immediately without

Delay to shed herself into the stomach of the wretch
And let no plenty staunch her force, but let her working stretch
Above the power of me. And lest the longness of the way
May make thee weary, take thou here my chariot; take, I say,
My dragons for to bear thee through the air." In saying so,
She gave her them. The nymph mounts up and, flying thence as
    tho,
Alights in Scythy land and up the craggèd top of high        990
Mount Caucasus did cause her snakes with much ado to sty;
Where, seeking long for Famine, she the gap-toothed elf did spy
Amid a barren stony field a-ramping up the grass
With ugly nails and chanking it. Her face pale-coloured was;
Her hair was harsh and shirl; her eyes were sunken in her head;
Her lips were hoar with filth; her teeth were furred and rusty red.
Her skin was starchèd and so sheer a man might well espy
The very bowels in her bulk how every one did lie.
And eke above her curbèd loins her withered hips were seen;
Instead of belly was a space where belly should have been.    1000
Her breast did hang so sagging down as that a man would ween
That scarcely to her ridge-bone had her ribs been fastened well.
Her leanness made her joints bollen big and knee-pans for to
    swell,
And with exceeding mighty knobs her heels behind boined out.
Now when the nymph beheld this elf afar (she was in doubt
To come too near her) she declared her lady's message. And
In that same little while, although the nymph aloof did stand
And though she were but newly come, yet seemèd she to feel
The force of Famine. Whereupon she, turning back her wheel,
Did rein her dragons up aloft, who straight with courage free    1010
Conveyed her into Thessaly. Although that Famine be
Aye contrary to Ceres' work, yet did she then agree
To do her will and, gliding through the air supported by
The wind, she found th'appointed house. And, entering by and by
The caitiff's chamber where he slept (it was in time of night),
She huggèd him between her arms there snorting bolt upright
And, breathing her into him, blew upon his face and breast,
That hunger in his empty veins might work as he did rest.

And when she had accomplishèd her charge, she then forsook
1020   The fruitful climates of the world and home again betook
Herself unto her fruitless fields and former dwelling place.
The gentle sleep did all this while with feathers soft embrace
The wretched Erysicthon's corse who, dreaming straight of meat,
Did stir his hungry jaws in vain as though he had to eat.
And, chanking tooth on tooth apace, he grinds them in his head
And occupies his empty throat with swallowing, and instead
Of food devours the lither air. But when that sleep with night
Was shaken off, immediately a furious appetite
Of feeding gan to rage in him which in his greedy gums
And in his meatless maw doth reign unstaunched. Anon there
1030        comes
Before him whatsoever lives on sea, in air or land.
And yet he crieth still for more. And though the platters stand
Before his face full furnishèd, yet doth he still complain
Of hunger, craving meat at meal. The food that would sustain
Whole households, townships, shires and realms suffice not him
        alone.
The more his pampered paunch consumes, the more it maketh
        moan.
And as the sea receives the brooks of all the worldly realms
And yet is never satisfied for all the foreign streams,
And as the fell and ravening fire refuseth never wood
1040   But burneth faggots numberless and with a furious mood
The more it hath, the more it still desireth evermore,
Increasing in devouring through increasement of the store;
So wicked Erysicthon's mouth in swallowing of his meat
Was ever hungry more and more and longèd aye to eat.
Meat tolled in meat; and as he ate the place was empty still.
The hunger of his brinkless maw, the gulf that nought might fill,
Had brought his father's goods to nought. But yet continued aye
His cursèd hunger unappeased, and nothing could allay
The flaming of his starvèd throat. At length, when all was spent
1050   And into his unfillèd maw both goods and lands were sent,
*Erysicthon's*   An only daughter did remain, unworthy to have had
*daughter*   So lewd a father. Her he sold, so hard he was bested.

But she of gentle courage could no bondage well abide
And therefore, stretching out her hands to seaward there beside,
"Now save me", quoth she, "from the yoke of bondage, I thee
      pray,
O thou that my virginity enjoyest as a prey."
Neptunus had it, who to this her prayer did consent.
And though her master, looking back (for after him she went),
Had newly seen her, yet he turned her shape and made her man
And gave her look of fisherman. Her master, looking then     1060
Upon her, said, "Good fellow, thou that on the shore dost stand
With angling rod and baited hook and hanging line in hand,
I pray thee, as thou dost desire the sea aye calm to thee
And fishes for to bite thy bait and stricken still to be,
Tell where the frizzle-toppèd wench in coarse and sluttish gear
That stood right now upon this shore – for well I wot that here
I saw her standing – is become. For further than this place
No footstep is appearing." She, perceiving by the case
That Neptune's gift made well with her and being glad to see
Herself enquired for of herself, said thus: "Whoe'er you be,     1070
I pray you for to pardon me. I turnèd not mine eye
At one side ne at other from this place, but did apply
My labour hard. And that you may the lesser stand in doubt,
So Neptune further still the art and craft I go about,
As now a while no living wight upon this level sand
(Myself excepted), neither man nor woman, here did stand."
Her master did believe her words and, turning backward, went
His way beguiled; and straight to her her native shape was sent.
But when her father did perceive his daughter for to have
A body so transformable, he oftentimes her gave     1080
For money. But the damsel still escapèd, now a mare
And now a cow and now a bird, a hart, a hind or hare,
And ever fed her hungry sire with undeservèd fare.
But after that the malady had wasted all the meats
As well of store as that which she had purchased by her feats,
Most cursèd caitiff as he was, with biting he did rend
His flesh and by diminishing his body did intend
To feed his body till that death did speed his fatal end.

But what mean I to busy me in foreign matters thus?
1090 To alter shapes within precinct is lawful even to us,
My lords. For sometime I am such as you do now me see;
Sometime I wind me in a snake; and oft I seem to be
A captain of the herd with horns. For taking horns on me
I lost a tine which heretofore did arm me, as the print
Doth plainly show.' With that same word he sighèd and did stint.

**FINIS OCTAVI LIBRI.**

# The Ninth Book of Ovid's
## Metamorphoses

'What aileth thee', quoth Theseus, 'to sigh so sore? And how *Acheloüs and*
Befell it thee to get this maim that is upon thy brow?' *Hercules*
The noble stream of Calydon made answer, who did wear
A garland made of reeds and flags upon his sedgy hair,
'A grievous penance you enjoin. For who would gladly show
The combats in the which himself did take the overthrow?
Yet will I make a just report in order of the same.
For why to have the worser hand was not so great a shame
As was the honour such a match to undertake. And much
It comforts me that he who did me overcome was such          10
A valiant champion. If perchance you erst have heard the name
Of Deianire, the fairest maid that ever God did frame
She was, in mine opinion. And the hope to win her love
Did mickle envy and debate among her wooers move.
With whom I entering to the house of him that should have be
My father-i'-law, "Parthaon's son," I said, "accept thou me
Thy son-i'-law;" and Hercules in selfsame sort did woo.
And all the other suitors straight gave place unto us two.
He vaunted of his father Jove and of his famous deeds
And how against his stepdame's spite his prowess still proceeds.   20
And I again at other side said thus: "It is a shame
That god should yield to man." (This strife was long ere he
          became
A god.) "Thou seest me a lord of waters in thy realm,
Where I in wide and winding banks do bear my flowing stream.
No stranger shalt thou have of me sent far from foreign land,
But one of household, or at least a neighbour here at hand.
Alonely let it be to me no hindrance that the wife
Of Jove abhors me not, ne that upon the pain of life

She sets me not to task. For where thou boastest thee to be
30　Alcmena's son, Jove either is not father unto thee
Or, if he be, it is by sin. In making Jove thy father
Thou mak'st thy mother but a whore. Now choose thee whether rather
Thou had to grant this tale of Jove surmisèd for to be,
Or else thyself begot in shame and born in bastardy."
　　'At that he grimly bends his brows, and much ado he hath
　　To hold his hands, so sore his heart enflamèd is with wrath.
He said no more but thus: "My hand doth serve me better than
My tongue. Content I am, so I in fighting vanquish can,
That thou shalt overcome in words." And therewithal he gan
40　Me fiercely to assail. Methought it was a shame for me,
That had even now so stoutly talked, in doings faint to be.
I, casting off my greenish cloak, thrust stiffly out at length
Mine arms and strained my pawing arms to hold him out by strength
And framèd every limb to cope. With both his hollow hands
He caught up dust and sprinkled me; and I likewise with sands
Made him all yellow too. One while he at my neck doth snatch;
Another while my clear crisp legs he striveth for to catch
Or trips at me; and everywhere the vantage he doth watch.
My weightiness defended me and clearly did defeat
50　His stout assaults as, when a wave with hideous noise doth beat
Against a rock, the rock doth still both safe and sound abide
By reason of his massiness. We drew a while aside.
And then, encountering fresh again, we kept our places stout,
Full minded not to yield an inch, but for to hold it out.
Now were we standing foot to foot; and I with all my breast
Was leaning forward and with head against his head did rest,
And with my griping fingers I against his fingers thrust.
So have I seen two mighty bulls together fiercely joust
In seeking as their prize to have the fairest cow in all
60　The field to be their make, and all the herd both great and small
Stand gazing on them fearfully, not knowing unto which
The conquest of so great a gain shall fall. Three times a twitch
Gave Hercules and could not wrench my leaning breast him fro,
But at the fourth he shook me off and made me to let go

My hold. And with a push (I will tell truth) he had a knack
To turn me off, and heavily he hung upon my back.
And if I may believèd be (as sure I mean not, I,
To vaunt myself vaingloriously by telling of a lie),
Methought a mountain whelmèd me. But yet with much ado
I wrested in my sweating arms and hardly did undo                    70
His griping hands. He, following still his vantage, suffered not
Me once to breathe or gather strength, but by and by he got
Me by the neck. Then was I fain to sink with knee to ground
And kiss the dust. Now when in strength too weak myself I
        found,
I took me to my sleights and slipped in shape of snake away
Of wondrous length. And when that I of purpose him to fray
Did bend myself in swelling rolls and made a hideous noise
Of hissing with my forkèd tongue, he, smiling at my toys
And laughing them to scorn, said thus: "It is my cradle game
To vanquish snakes, O Acheloy. Admit thou overcame                   80
All other snakes, yet what art thou comparèd to the snake
Of Lerna, who by cutting off did still increasement take?
For of a hundred heads not one so soon was parèd away
But that upon the stump thereof there budded other tway.
This sprouting snake, whose branching heads by slaughter did
        revive
And grow by cropping, I subdued and made it could not thrive.
And thinkest thou, who, being none, would'st seem a snake, to
        scape?
Who dost with forgèd weapons fight and under borrowed shape?"
This said, his fingers of my neck he fastened in the nape;
Methought he gripped my throat as though he did with pinions
        nip.                                                         90
I struggled from his churlish thumbs my pinchèd chaps to slip;
But, do the best and worst I could, he overcame me so.
Then thirdly did remain the shape of bull. And quickly tho
I, turning to the shape of bull, rebelled against my foe.
He, stepping to my left side close, did fold his arms about
My wattled neck and, following me then running mainly out,

Did drag me back and made me pitch my horns against the
                                    ground,
And in the deepest of the sand he overthrew me round.
And yet not so content, such hold his cruel hand did take
100 Upon my whelkèd horn that he asunder quite it brake
And pulled it from my maimèd brow. The waterfairies came
And, filling it with fruit and flowers, did consecrate the same;
And so my horn the treasury of plenteousness became.'
       As soon as Acheloy had told this tale, a waiting maid
       With flaring hair that lay on both her shoulders and arrayed
Like one of Dame Diana's nymphs with solemn grace forth came
And brought that rich and precious horn and heapèd in the same
All kind of fruits that harvest sends, and specially such fruit
As serves for latter course at meals of every sort and suit.
110       As soon as daylight came again and that the sunny rays
       Did shine upon the tops of things, the princes went their ways.
They would not tarry till the flood were altogether fallen
And that the river in his banks ran low again and calm.
Then Acheloy amid his waves his crab-tree face did hide
And head, disarmèd of a horn. And though he did abide
In all parts else both safe and sound, yet this deformity
Did cut his comb. And for to hide this blemish from the eye,
He hides his hurt with sallow leaves or else with sedge and reed.

*The shirt*       But of the selfsame maid the love killed thee, fierce Ness,
*of Nessus* .             indeed
       When, piercing swiftly through thy back, an arrow made thee
120             bleed.
For as Jove's issue with his wife was onward on his way
In going to his countryward, enforced he was to stay
At swift Euenus' bank because the stream was risen sore
Above his bounds through rage of rain that fell but late before.
Again, so full of whirlpools and of gulls the channel was
That scarce a man could anywhere find place of passage. As,
Not caring for himself but for his wife, he there did stand,
This Nessus came unto him (who was strong of body and
Knew well the fords) and said, 'Use thou thy strength, O
                                    Hercules,
130 In swimming. I will find the means this lady shall with ease

Be set upon the further bank.' So Hercules betook
His wife to Nessus. She for fear of him and of the brook
Looked pale. Her husband, as he had his quiver by his side
Of arrows full and on his back his heavy lion's hide
(For to the further bank he erst his club and bow had cast),
Said, 'Sith I have begun, this brook both must and shall be passed.'
He never casteth further doubts nor seeks the calmest place,
But through the roughest of the stream he cuts his way apace.
Now as he on the further side was taking up his bow,
He heard his wedlock shrieking out and did her calling know          140
And cried to Ness (who went about to deal unfaithfully
In running with his charge away), 'Ho, whither dost thou fly,
Thou roister, thou, upon vain hope by swiftness to escape
My hands? I say, give ear, thou Ness, for all thy double shape,
And meddle not with that that's mine. Though no regard of me
Might move thee to refrain from rape, thy father yet might be
A warning, who for offering shame to Juno now doth feel
Continual torment in his limbs by turning on a wheel.
For all that thou hast horse's feet which do so bold thee make,
Yet shalt thou not escape my hands. I will thee overtake          150
With wound and not with feet:' He did according as he spake.
For with an arrow as he fled he strake him through the back,
And out before his breast again the hookèd iron stack.
And when the same was pullèd out, the blood amain ensued
At both the holes, with poison foul of Lerna snake imbrued.
This blood did Nessus take and said within himself, 'Well, sith
I needs must die, yet will I not die unrevenged.' And with
The same he stained a shirt and gave it unto Deianire,
Assuring her it had the power to kindle Cupid's fire.

A great while after, when the deeds of worthy Hercules          160
Were such as fillèd all the world and also did appease
The hatred of his stepmother, as he upon a day
With conquest from Oechalia came and was about to pay
His vows to Jove upon the mount of Ceny, tattling Fame
(Who in reporting things of truth delights to sauce the same
With tales, and of a thing of nought doth ever greater grow
Through false and newly forgèd lies that she herself doth sow)

Told Deianire that Hercules did cast a liking to
A lady callèd Iole. And Deianira, who
170 Was jealous over Hercules, gave credit to the same.
And when that of a leman first the tidings to her came,
She, being stricken to the heart, did fall to tears alone
And in a lamentable wise did make most woeful moan.
 Anon she said, 'What mean these tears thus gushing from mine
  eyen?
 My husband's leman will rejoice at these same tears of mine.
Nay, sith she is to come, the best it were to shun delay
And for to work some new device and practice while I may
Before that in my bed her limbs the filthy strumpet lay.
And shall I then complain, or shall I hold my tongue with skill?
180 Shall I return to Calydon, or shall I tarry still?
Or shall I get me out of doors and let them have their will?
What if that I, Meleäger, remembering me to be
Thy sister, to attempt some act notorious did agree
And in a harlot's death did show, that all the world might see,
What grief can cause the womankind to enterprise among,
And specially when thereunto they forcèd are by wrong?'
 With wavering thoughts right violently her mind was tossèd
  long.
 At last she did prefer before all others for to send
The shirt bestainèd with the blood of Nessus to the end
190 To quicken up the quailing love. And so, not knowing what
She gave, she gave her own remorse and grief to Lichas that
Did know as little as herself; and, wretched woman, she
Desired him gently to her lord presented it to see.
The noble prince, receiving it without mistrust therein,
Did wear the poison of the snake of Lerna next his skin.
 To offer incense and to pray to Jove he did begin,
 And on the marble altar he full bowls of wine did shed
Whenas the poison, with the heat resolving, largely spread
Through all the limbs of Hercules. As long as e'er he could,
200 The stoutness of his heart was such that sigh no whit he would.
But when the mischief grew so great all patience to surmount,
He thrust the altar from him straight and filled all the Mount.

Of Oeta with his roaring out. He went about to tear
The deathful garment from his back; but where he pullèd, there
He pulled away the skin. And (which is loathsome to report)
It either cleavèd to his limbs and members in such sort
As that he could not pull it off, or else it tare away
The flesh, that bare his mighty bones and grisly sinews lay.
The scalding venom, boiling in his blood, did make it hiss
As when a gad of steel red hot in water quenchèd is.                    210
There was no measure of his pain. The frying venom hent
His inwards, and a purple sweat from all his body went.
His singèd sinews, shrinking, cracked; and with a secret strength
The poison even within his bones the marrow melts at length.
And, holding up his hands to heaven, he said with hideous rere,
   'O Saturn's daughter, feed thyself on my distresses here.
   Yea, feed and, cruel wight, this plague behold thou from above
And glut thy savage heart therewith. Or if thy foe may move
Thee unto pity (for to thee I am an utter foe),
Bereave me of my hateful soul, distressed with helpless woe            220
And born to endless toil. For death shall unto me be sweet,
And for a cruel stepmother is death a gift most meet.
And is it I that did destroy Busiris, who did foil
His temple floors with strangers' blood? Is't I that did despoil
Antaeus of his mother's help? Is't I that could not be
Abashèd at the Spaniard who in one had bodies three?
Nor at the triple-headed shape, O Cerberus, of thee?
Are you the hands that by the horns the bull of Candy drew?
Did you King Augy's stable cleanse, whom afterward ye slew?
Are you the same by whom the fowls were scared from
         Stymphaly?                                                    230
Caught you the stag in Maidenwood which did not run but fly?
Are you the hands whose puissance receivèd for your pay
The golden belt of Thermodoon? Did you convey away
The apples from the dragon fell that wakèd night and day?
Against the force of me defence the Centaurs could not make;
Nor yet the boar of Arcady; nor yet the ugly snake
Of Lerna, who by loss did grow and double force still take.
What! Is it I that did behold the pampered jades of Thrace
With mangers full of flesh of men on which they fed apace?

240  Is't I that down at sight thereof their greasy mangers threw
And both the fatted jades themselves and eke their master slew?
The Nemean lion by these arms lies dead upon the ground.
These arms the monstrous giant Cake by Tiber did confound.
Upon these shoulders have I borne the weight of all the sky.
Jove's cruel wife is weary of commanding me; yet I
Unweary am of doing still. But now on me is light
An uncouth plague, which neither force of hand nor virtue's
       might
Nor art is able to resist. Like wasting fire it spreads
Among mine inwards and throughout on all my body feeds.
250  But all this while Eurysthey lives in health. And some men may
Believe there be some gods indeed!' Thus much did Hercule say.

*The death*
*of Hercules*

       And, wounded, over Oeta high he, stalking, gan to stray,
       As when a bull in maimèd bulk a deadly dart doth bear
And that the doer of the deed is shrunk aside for fear.
Oft sighing might you him have seen, oft trembling, oft about
To tear the garment with his hands from top to toe throughout
And throwing down the mighty trees and chafing with the hills
Or casting up his hands to heaven, where Jove his father dwells.
Behold, as Lichas, trembling, in a hollow rock did lurk,
260  He spièd him. And as his grief did all in fury work,
He said, 'Art thou, Sir Lichas, he that broughtest unto me
This plaguey present? Of my death must thou the worker be?'
He quaked and shaked and lookèd pale and fearfully gan make
Excuse. But as with humbled hands he, kneeling to him, spake,
The furious Herc'le caught him up and, swingeing him about
His head a half a dozen times or more, he flung him out
Into th'Euboean sea with force surmounting any sling.
He hardened into pebble stone as in the air he hing.
And even as rain, congealed by wind, is laid to turn to snow
270  And of the snow, round rollèd up, a thicker mass to grow
Which falleth down in hail, so men in ancient time report
That Lichas, being swinged about by violence in that sort
(His blood then being drainèd out and having left at all
No moisture), into pebble stone was turnèd in his fall.
Now also in th'Euboean sea appears a high short rock
In shape of man, against the which the shipmen shun to knock

As though it could them feel. And they do call it by the name
Of Lichas still. But thou, Jove's imp of great renown and fame,
Did'st fell the trees of Oeta high and, making of the same
A pile, did'st give to Poean's son\* thy quiver and thy bow          280
And arrows, which should help again Troy town to overthrow.
He put to fire and, as the same was kindling in the pile,
Thyself did'st spread thy lion's skin upon the wood the while
And, leaning with thy head against thy club, thou laid'st thee
    down
As cheerfully as if with flowers and garlands on thy crown
Thou had'st been set a-banqueting among full cups of wine.
Anon on every side about those careless limbs of thine
The fire began to gather strength and crackling noise did make,
Assailing him whose noble heart for dalliance did it take.
    The gods for this defender of the earth were sore afraid;          290
    To whom with cheerful count'nance Jove, perceiving it, thus
        said:
'This fear of yours is my delight, and gladly even with all
My heart I do rejoice, O gods, that mortal folk me call
Their king and father, thinking me aye mindful of their weal,
And that mine offspring should do well yourselves do show such
        zeal.
For though that you do attribute your favour to desert,
Considering his most wondrous acts, yet I, too, for my part
Am bound unto you. Ne'ertheless, for that I would not have
Your faithful hearts without just cause in fearful passions wave,
I would not have you of the flames in Oeta make account.          300
For as he hath all other things, so shall he them surmount.
Save only on that part that he hath taken of his mother,
The fire shall have no power at all. Eternal is the t'other,
The which he takes of me, and cannot die ne yield to fire.
When this is rid from earthly dross, then will I lift it higher
And take it into heaven. And I believe this deed of mine
Will gladsome be to all the gods. If any do repine,
If any do repine, I say, that Herc'le should become
A god, repine he still for me and look he sour and glum.

\*Philoctetes

'310    But let him know that Hercules deserveth this reward
And that he shall against his will allow it afterward.'
The gods assented everych one, and Juno seemed to make
No evil count'nance to the rest, until her husband spake
The last. For then her look was such as well they might perceive
She did her husband's noting her in evil part conceive.
    While Jove was talking with the gods, as much as fire could
        waste,
    So much had fire consumed. And now, O Hercules, thou hast
No carcass for to know thee by. That part is quite bereft
Which of thy mother thou did'st take; alonely now is left

320    The likeness that thou took'st of Jove. And as the serpent sly
In casting off his withered slough renews his years thereby
And waxeth lustier than before and looketh crisp and bright
With scourèd scales, so Hercules, as soon as that his sprite
Had left his mortal limbs, gan in his better part to thrive
And for to seem a greater thing than when he was alive
And with a stately majesty right reverend to appear.
His mighty father took him up above the cloudy sphere
And in a chariot placèd him among the streaming stars.
Huge Atlas felt the weight thereof. But nothing this disbars

330    Eurysthey's malice. Cruelly he prosecutes the hate
Upon the offspring which he bare against the father late.

*The transformation of Galantis*

    But yet to make her moan unto and wail her misery
    And tell her son's great works, which all the world could testify,
Old Alcmen had Dame Iole. By Hercules' last will
In wedlock and in hearty love she joinèd was to Hyll,
By whom she then was big with child when thus Alcmena said:
'The gods at least be merciful and send thee then their aid
And short thy labour, when the fruit the which thou go'st withal,
Now being ripe, enforceth thee with fearful voice to call

340    Upon Illithyia, president of childbirths, whom the ire
Of Juno at my travailing made deaf to my desire.
For when the sun through twice five signs his course had fully run
And that the painful day of birth approachèd of my son,
My burden strainèd out my womb and that that I did bear
Became so great that of so huge a mass ye well might swear

That Jove was father. Neither was I able to endure
The travail any lenger time. Even now, I you assure,
In telling it a shuddering cold through all my limbs doth strike,
And partly it renews my pains to think upon the like.
I, being in most cruel throes nights seven and days eke seven          350
And tirèd with continual pangs, did lift my hands to heaven
And, crying out aloud, did call Lucina to mine aid
To loose the burden from my womb. She came as I had prayed,
But so corrupted long before by Juno, my most foe,
That for to martyr me to death with pain she purposed tho.
For when she heard my piteous plaints and groanings, down she
          sat
On yon same altar which you see there standing at my gate.
Upon her left knee she had pitched her right ham, and beside
She stayed the birth with fingers one within another tied
In lattice-wise. And secretly she whispered witching spells          360
Which hindered my deliverance more than all her doings else.
I laboured still and, forced by pain and torments of my fits,
I railed on Jove (although in vain) as one beside her wits,
And aye I wishèd for to die. The words that I did speak
Were such as even the hardest stones of very flint might break.
The wives of Thebe, being there, for safe deliverance prayed
And, giving cheerful words, did bid I should not be dismayed.
Among the other women there that to my labour came
There was an honest yeoman's wife; Galantis was her name.
Her hair was yellow as the gold; she was a jolly dame          370
And stoutly servèd me, and I did love her for the same.
This wife (I know not how) did smell some packing gone about
On Juno's part. And as she oft was passing in and out,
She spied Lucina set upon the altar, holding fast
Her arms together on her knees and with her fingers cast
Within each other on a knot, and said unto her thus:
"I pray you, whosoe'er you be, rejoice you now with us;
My Lady Alcmen hath her wish and safe is brought abed."
Lucina leapèd up amazed at that that she had said
And let her hands asunder slip. And I immediately          380
With loosening of the knot had safe deliverance by and by.

They say that, in deceiving Dame Lucina, Galant laughed;
And therefore by the yellow locks the goddess, wroth, her
            caught
And draggèd her. And as she would have risen from the ground,
She kept her down and into legs her arms she did confound.
Her former stoutness still remains; her back doth keep the hue
That erst was in her hair; her shape is only altered new.
And for with lying mouth she helped a woman labouring, she
Doth kindle also at her mouth. And now she haunteth free

390 Our houses as she did before, a weasel, as we see.'

*The transformation of Dryope*

        With that she sighs to think upon her servant's hap, and then
        Her daughter-in-law immediately replièd thus again:
'But mother, she whose altered shape doth move your heart so
            sore
Was neither kith nor kin to you. What will you say, therefore,
If of mine own dear sister I the wondrous fortune show
(Although my sorrow and the tears that from mine eyes do flow
Do hinder me and stop my speech)? Her mother – you must
            know
My father by another wife had me – bare never mo
But this same Lady Dryope, the fairest lady tho

400 In all the land of Oechaly. Whom, being then no maid
(For why the god of Delos and of Delphos* had her frayed),
Andraemon taketh to his wife and thinks him well apaid.
There is a certain leaning lake whose bowing banks do show
A likeness of the salt sea shore. Upon the brim do grow
All round about it myrtle-trees. My sister thither goes,
Unwares what was her destiny, and (which you may suppose
Was more to be disdainèd at) the cause of coming there
Was to the fairies of the lake fresh garlands for to bear.
And in her arms a baby, her sweet burden, she did hold

410 Who, sucking on her breast, was yet not full a twelvemonth old.
Not far from this same pond did grow a lote-tree, flourished gay
With purple flowers and berries sweet and leaves as green as bay.
Of these same flowers to please her boy my sister gathered some;
And I had thought to do so too, for I was thither come.

*Apollo

I saw how from the slivered flowers red drops of blood did fall
And how that, shuddering horribly, the branches quaked withal.
You must perceive that – as too late the countryfolk declare –
A nymph called Lotis, flying from foul Priap's filthy ware,
Was turnèd into this same tree, reserving still her name.
My sister did not know so much who, when she backward came,          420
Afraid at that that she had seen, and having sadly prayed
The nymphs of pardon, to have gone her way again assayed.
Her feet were fastened down with roots; she strivèd all she might
To pluck them up, but they so sure within the earth were pight
That nothing save her upper parts she could that present move.
A tender bark grows from beneath up leisurely above
And softly overspreads her loins. Which when she saw, she went
About to tear her hair; and full of leaves her hand she hent.
Her head was overgrown with leaves. And little Amphise (so
Had Eurytus, his grandsire, named her son not long ago)               430
Did feel his mother's dugs wax hard. And as he still them drew
In sucking, not a whit of milk nor moisture did ensue.
I, standing by thee, did behold thy cruel chance; but nought
I could relieve thee, sister mine. Yet to my power I wrought
To stay the growing of thy trunk and of thy branches by
Embracing thee. Yea, I protest, I would right willingly
Have in the selfsame bark with thee been closèd up. Behold,
Her husband, good Andraemon, and her wretched father old,
Sir Eurytus, came thither and enquired for Dryope.
And as they asked for Dryope, I showed them Lote the tree.            440
They kissed the wood which yet was warm and, falling down
        below,
Did hug the roots of that their tree. My sister now could show
No part which was not wood except her face. A dew of tears
Did stand upon the wretched leaves late formèd of her hairs.
And while she might and while her mouth did give her way to
        speak,
With such complaint as this her mind she last of all did break:
"If credit may be given to such as are in wretchedness,
I swear by God, I never yet deservèd this distress.
I suffer pain without desert. My life hath guiltless been.
And if I lie, I would these boughs of mine which now are green       450

Might withered be and I hewn down and burnèd in the fire.
This infant from his mother's womb remove you, I desire,
And put him forth to nurse and cause him underneath my tree
Ofttimes to suck and oftentimes to play. And when that he
Is able for to speak, I pray you let him greet me here
And sadly say, 'In this same trunk is hid my mother dear.'
But learn him for to shun all ponds and pulling flowers from trees,
And let him in his heart believe that all the shrubs he sees
Are bodies of the goddesses. Adieu, dear husband, now;
460 Adieu, dear father, and adieu, dear sister. And in you
If any love of me remain, defend my boughs, I pray,
From wound of cutting hook and axe and bit of beast for aye.
And for I cannot stoop to you, raise you yourselves to me
And come and kiss me while I may yet touched and kissèd be,
And lift me up my little boy. I can no lenger talk,
For now about my lily neck as if it were a stalk
The tender rind begins to creep and overgrows my top.
Remove your fingers from my face; the spreading bark doth stop
My dying eyes without your help." She had no sooner left
470 Her talking, but her life therewith together was bereft.
But yet a good while after that her native shape did fade
Her new-made boughs continued warm.' Now while that Iole
    made
Report of this same wondrous tale and while Alcmena (who
Did weep) was drying up the tears of Iole, weeping too,
By putting to her thumb, there happed a sudden thing so strange
That unto mirth from heaviness their hearts it straight did change.

*Iolaüs recovers*
*his youth*

    For at the door in manner even a very boy as then
    With short soft down about his chin, revokèd back again
To youthful years, stood Iolay with count'nance smooth and trim.
480 Dame Hebe, Juno's daughter, had bestowed this gift on him,
Entreated at his earnest suit; whom, minding fully there
The giving of like gift again to any to forswear,
Dame Themis would not suffer. 'For', quoth she, 'this present
    hour
Is cruel war in Thebe town, and none but Jove hath power
To vanquish stately Canapey. The brothers shall alike
Wound either other. And alive a prophet shall go seek

His own quick ghost among the dead, the earth him swallowing
    in.
The son, by taking vengeance for his father's death, shall win
The name of kind and wicked man in one and selfsame case.
And, flight with mischiefs, from his wits and from his native place    490
The Furies and his mother's ghost shall restlessly him chase
Until his wife demand of him the fatal gold for meed
And that his cousin Phegey's sword do make his sides to bleed.
Then shall the fair Callirhoë, Achelous' daughter, pray
The mighty Jove in humble wise to grant her children may
Retire again to youthful years and that he will not see
The death of him that did revenge unvengèd for to be.
Jove, movèd at her suit, shall cause his daughter-in-law to give
Like gift and back from age to youth Callirhoe's children drive.'
    When Themis through foresight had spoke these words of
        prophecy,    500
    The gods began among themselves vain talk to multiply.
They moiled why others might not give like gift as well as she.
First Pallant's daughter grudgèd that her husband old should be;
The gentle Ceres murmured that her Iasion's hair was hoar;
And Vulcan would have called again the years long spent before
By Ericthonius; and the nice Dame Venus, having care
Of time to come, the making young of old Anchises sware.
So every god had one to whom he special favour bare.
And through this partial love of theirs seditiously increased
A hurly-burly, till the time that Jove among them pressed    510
And said, 'So smally do you stand in awe of me this hour
As thus to rage? Thinks any of you himself to have such power
As for to alter destiny? I tell you, Iolay
Recovered hath by destiny his years erst passed away.
Callirhoe's children must return to youth by destiny
And not by force of arms or suit sustained ambitiously.
And to th'intent with milder minds ye may this matter bear,
Even I myself by Destinies am ruled. Which if I were
Of power to alter, think you that our Aeacus should stoop
By reason of his feeble age or Rhadamanth should droop?    520
Or Minos, who by reason of his age is now disdained
And lives not in so sure a state as heretofore he reigned?'

The words of Jove so moved the gods that none of them
    complained
Sith Rhadamanth and Aeacus were both with age constrained,
And Minos also who, as long as lusty youth did last,
Did even with terror of his name make mighty realms aghast.
But then was Minos weakened sore and greatly stood in fear
Of Milet, one of Deione's race, who proudly did him bear
Upon his father Phoebus and the stoutness of his youth.
530 And though he feared he would rebel, yet durst not he his mouth
Once open for to banish him his realm until at last,
Departing of his own accord, Miletus swiftly passed
The Goat Sea and did build a town upon the Asian ground
Which still retains the name of him that first the same did found.
And there the daughter of the brook Maeander, which doth go
So often backward, Cyanee, a nymph of body so
Exceeding comely as the like was seldom heard of, as
She by her father's winding banks for pleasure walking was,
Was known by Milet. Unto whom a pair of twins she brought,
540 And of the twins the names were Caun and Byblis. Byblis ought
To be a mirror unto maids in lawful wise to love.

*Caun and*
*Byblis*

    This Byblis cast a mind to Caun, but not as did behove
    A sister to her brotherward. When first of all the fire
Did kindle, she perceived it not. She thought in her desire
Of kissing him so oftentimes no sin ne yet no harm
In clipping him about the neck so often with her arm.
The glittering gloss of godliness beguiled her long. Her love
Began from evil unto worse by little to remove.
She comes to see her brother decked in brave and trim attire,
550 And for to seem exceeding fair it was her whole desire.
And if that any fairer were in all the flock than she,
It spites her. In what case she was as yet she did not see.
Her heat exceeded not so far as for to vow; and yet
She suffered in her troubled breast full many a burning fit.
Now calleth she him master; now she utter hateth all
The names of kin. She rather had he should her Byblis call
Than sister. Yet no filthy hope she durst permit to creep
Within her mind awake. But as she lay in quiet sleep,

She oft beheld her love and oft she thought her brother came
And lay with her, and (though asleep) she blushèd at the same.    560
When sleep was gone, she long lay dumb, still musing on the
    sight,
And said with wavering mind, 'Now woe is me, most wretched
    wight.
What means the image of this dream that I have seen this night?
I would not wish it should be true. Why dreamèd I, then, so?
Sure he is fair, although he should be judgèd by his foe.
He likes me well. And were he not my brother, I might set
My love on him, and he were me right worthy for to get.
But unto this same match the name of kindred is a let.
Well, so that I awake do still me undefilèd keep,
Let come as often as they will such dreamings in my sleep.    570
In sleep there is no witness by. In sleep yet may I take
As great a pleasure (in a sort) as if I were awake.
O Venus and thy tender son, Sir Cupid, what delight,
How present feeling of your sport hath touchèd me this night!
How lay I as it were resolved, both marrow, flesh and bone!
How glads it me to think thereon! Alas, too soon was gone
That pleasure, and too hasty and despiteful was the night
In breaking of my joys! O Lord, if name of kindred might
Between us two removèd be, how well it would agree,
O Caun, that of thy father I the daughter-in-law should be!    580
How fitly might my father have a son-in-law of thee!
Would God that all save ancestors were common to us twain;
I would thou were of nobler stock than I. I cannot sayen,
O pearl of beauty, what she is whom thou shalt make a mother.
Alas, how ill befalls it me that I could have none other
Than those same parents which are thine! So only still my brother
And not my husband may'st thou be. The thing that hurts us both
Is one, and that between us aye inseparably go'th.
What mean my dreams then? What effect have dreams? And may
    there be
Effect in dreams? The gods are far in better case than we,    590
For why the gods have matchèd with their sisters, as we see.
So Saturn did ally with Ops, the nearest of his blood;
So Tethys with Oceanus; so Jove did think it good

To take his sister Juno to his wife. What then? The gods
Have laws and charters by themselves. And sith there is such odds
Between the state of us and them, why should I sample take
Our worldly matters equal with the heavenly things to make?
This wicked love shall either from my heart be driven away
Or, if it cannot be expulsed, God grant I perish may
600  And that my brother kiss me laid on hearse to go to grave.
But my desire the full consent of both of us doth crave.
Admit the matter liketh me; he will for sin it take.
But yet the sons of Aeolus no scrupulousness did make
In going to their sisters' beds. And how come I to know
The feats of them? To what intent these samples do I show?
Ah, whither am I headlong driven? Avaunt, foul filthy fire!
And let me not in other wise than sister-like desire
My brother's love. Yet if that he were first in love with me,
His fondness to incline unto perchance I could agree.
610.  Shall I therefore, who would not have rejected him if he
Had sued to me, go sue to him? And canst thou speak indeed
And canst thou utter forth thy mind and tell him of thy need?
My love will make me speak. I can. Or if that shame do stay
My tongue, a sealèd letter shall my secret love bewray.'
        This likes her best. Upon this point now rests her doubtful
                mind.
        So, raising up herself, upon her left side she inclined
And, leaning on her elbow, said, 'Let him advise him what
To do, for I my frantic love will utter plain and flat.
Alas, to what ungraciousness intend I for to fall?
620  What fury raging in my heart my senses doth appal?'
In thinking so, with trembling hand she framèd her to write
The matter that her troubled mind in musing did indite.
Her right hand holds the pen; her left doth hold the empty wax.
She gins; she doubts; she writes; she in the tables findeth lacks.
She notes, she blurs, dislikes and likes, and changeth this for that.
She lays away the book, and takes it up. She wots not what
She would herself. Whatever thing she mindeth for to do
Misliketh her. A shamefastness with boldness mixed thereto
Was in her count'nance. She had once writ 'sister'; out again
630  The name of 'sister' for to raze she thought it best. And then

She snatched the tables up and did these following words engrave:
  'The health which, if thou give her not, she is not like to have
  Thy lover wisheth unto thee. I dare not, ah, for shame
I dare not tell thee who I am nor let thee hear my name.
And if thou do demand of me what thing I do desire,
Would God that nameless I might plead the matter I require
And that I were unknown to thee by name of Byblis, till
Assurance of my suit were wrought according to my will.
As tokens of my wounded heart might these to thee appear:
My colour pale, my body lean, my heavy mirthless cheer,      640
My watery eyes, my sighs without apparent causes why,
My oft embracing of thee, and such kisses (if perdie
Thou markèd them) as very well thou might have felt and found
Not for to have been sister-like. But though with grievous wound
I then were stricken to the heart, although the raging flame
Did burn within, yet take I God to witness of the same,
I did as much as lay in me this outrage for to tame.
And long I strivèd (wretched wench!) to scape the violent dart
Of Cupid. More I have endured of hardness and of smart
Than any wench, a man would think, were able to abide.      650
Force forceth me to show my case, which fain I still would hide,
And mercy at thy gentle hand in fearful wise to crave.
Thou only may'st the life of me, thy lover, spill or save.
Choose which thou wilt. No enemy craves this thing, but such a
    one
As, though she be allied so sure as surer can be none,
Yet covets she more surely yet allièd for to be
And with a nearer kind of band to link herself to thee.
Let agèd folks have skill in law; to age it doth belong
To keep the rigour of the laws and search out right from wrong.
Such youthful years as ours are yet rash folly doth beseem;      660
We know not what is lawful yet. And therefore we may deem
That all is lawful that we list, ensuing in the same
The doings of the mighty gods. Not dread of worldly shame
Nor yet our father's roughness, no, nor fearfulness should let
Our purpose. Only let all fear aside be wholly set.
We underneath the name of kin our pleasant scapes may hide.
Thou knowest I have liberty to talk with thee aside,

And openly we kiss and cull. And what is all the rest
That wants? Have mercy on me now, who plainly have expressed
670  My case; which thing I had not done, but that the utter rage
Of love constrains me thereunto, the which I cannot swage.
Deserve not on my tomb thy name subscribèd for to have,
That thou art he whose cruelness did bring me to my grave.'
     Thus much she wrate in vain, and wax did want her to indite,
     And in the margent she was fain the latter verse to write.
Immediately to seal her shame she takes a precious stone
The which she moists with tears; from tongue the moisture quite
     was gone.
She called a servant shamefastly and, after certain fair
And gentle words, 'My trusty man, I pray thee, bear this pair
680  Of tables', quoth she, 'to my' – and a great while afterward
She added, 'brother'. Now through chance or want of good
     regard
The table slippèd down to ground in reaching to himward.
The handsel troubled sore her mind; but yet she sent them. And
Her servant, spying time, did put them into Cauny's hand.
Maeander's nephew suddenly in anger flung away
The tables ere he half had read, scarce able for to stay
His fistock from the servant's face, who quaked, and thus did say:
'Avaunt, thou bawdy ribald, while thou may'st. For were it not
For shame, I should have killèd thee.' Away, afraid, he got
690  And told his mistress of the fierce and cruel answer made
By Cauny. By and by the hue of Byblis gan to fade,
And all her body was benumbed with icy cold for fear
To hear of this repulse. As soon as that her senses were
Returned again, her furious flames returnèd with her wits.
And thus she said so oft that scarce her tongue the air hits:
     'And worthily! For why was I so rash as to discover
     By hasty writing this my wound, which most I ought to cover?
I should with doubtful, glancing words have felt his humour first
And made a train to try him, if pursue or no he durst.
700  I should have viewèd first the coast to see the weather clear,
And then I might have launchèd safe and boldly from the pier.
But now I hoist up all my sails before I tried the wind,
And therefore am I driven upon the rocks against my mind

And all the sea doth overwhelm me. Neither may I find
The means to get to harbour or from danger to retire.
Why did not open tokens warn to bridle my desire,
Then when the tables, falling in delivering them, declared
My hope was vain? And ought not I then either to have spared
From sending them as that day, or have changèd whole my mind?
Nay, rather shifted of the day; for had I not been blind,                    710
Even God himself by soothfast signs the sequel seemed to hit.
Yea, rather than to writing thus my secrets to commit
I should have gone and spoke myself and presently have showed
My fervent love. He should have seen how tears had from me
     flowed.
He should have seen my piteous look right lover-like. I could
Have spoken more than into those my tablets enter would.
About his neck against his will mine arms I might have wound
And, had he shaked me off, I might have seemèd for to swound.
I humbly might have kissed his feet and, kneeling on the ground,
Besought him for to save my life. All these I might have proved             720
Whereof, although no one alone his stomach could have moved,
Yet all together might have made his hardened heart relent.
Perchance there was some fault in him that was of message sent;
He stepped unto him bluntly, I believe, and did not watch
Convenient time, in merry cue at leisure him to catch.
These are the things that hindered me. For certainly I know
No sturdy stone nor massy steel doth in his stomach grow.
He is not made of adamant. He is no tiger's whelp.
He never suckèd lioness. He might with little help
Be vanquished. Let us give fresh charge upon him. While I live,        730
Without obtaining victory I will not over give.
For firstly, if it lay in me my doings to revoke,
I should not have begun at all. But feeling that the stroke
Is given, the second point is now to give the push to win.
For neither he, although that I mine enterprise should blin,
Can ever while he lives forget my deed. And sith I shrink,
My love was light or else I meant to trap him he shall think;
Or at the least he may suppose that this my rage of love
Which broileth so within my breast proceeds not from above

740 By Cupid's stroke but of some foul and filthy lust. In fine,
    I cannot but to wickedness now more and more incline.
    By writing is my suit commenced; my meaning doth appear;
    And, though I cease, yet can I not accounted be for clear.
    Now that that doth remain behind is much as in respect
    My fond desire to satisfy and little in effect
    To aggravate my fault withal.' Thus much she said. And so
    Unconstant was her wavering mind, still floating to and fro,
    That, though it irked her for to have attempted, yet proceeds
    She in the selfsame purpose of attempting, and exceeds
750 All measure. And, unhappy wench, she takes from day to day
    Repulse upon repulse, and yet she hath not grace to stay.
       Soon after, when her brother saw there was with her no end,
       He fled his country for because he would not so offend
    And in a foreign land did build a city. Then men say
    That Byblis through despair and thought all wholly did dismay.
    She tare her garments from her breast, and furiously she wrung
    Her hands and beat her arms and, like a bedlam, with her tongue
    Confessèd her unlawful love. But, being of the same
    Dispointed, she forsook her land and hateful house for shame
760 And followed after flying Caun. And as the frows of Thrace
    In doing of the three-years rites of Bacchus, in like case
    The married wives of Bubassy saw Byblis howling out
    Through all their champaign fields. The which she leaving, ran
          about
    In Caria to the Lelegs, who are men in battle stout,
    And so to Lycia. She had passed Crag, Limyre and the brook
    Of Xanthus and the country where Chimaera, that same puck,
    Hath goatish body, lion's head and breast and dragon's tail,
    When woods did want. And Byblis now, beginning for to quail
    Through weariness in following Caun, sank down and laid her
          head
    Against the ground and kissed the leaves that wind from trees had
770       shed.
    The nymphs of Caria went about in tender arms to take
    Her often up. They oftentimes persuaded her to slake
    Her love, and words of comfort to her deaf-eared mind they
          spake.

She still lay dumb, and with her nails the greenish herbs she held
And moisted with a stream of tears the grass upon the field.
The waternymphs (so folk report) put under her a spring
Which never might be dried. And could they give a greater thing?
Immediately, even like as when ye wound a pitch-tree rind
The gum doth issue out in drops, or as the western wind
With gentle blast together with the warmth of sun unbind        780
The ice, or as the clammy kind of cement which they call
Bitumen issueth from the ground full fraughted therewithal;
So Phoebus' niece, Dame Byblis, then consuming with her tears,
Was turnèd to a fountain which in those same valleys bears
The title of the founder still and gusheth freshly out
From underneath a sugarchest as if it were a spout.

    The fame of this same wondrous thing perhaps had fillèd all        *The*
    The hundred towns of Candy, had a greater not befall        *transformation*
More nearer home by Iphis' means, transformèd late before.        *of Iphis*
For in the shire of Phaestus, hard by Gnossus, dwelt of yore        790
A yeoman of the meaner sort that Lictus had to name.
His stock was simple and his wealth according to the same;
Howbeit his life so upright was as no man could it blame.
He came unto his wife, then big and ready down to lie,
And said, 'Two things I wish thee: t'one, that, when thou out
      shalt cry,
Thou may'st dispatch with little pain; the other, that thou have
A boy. For girls to bring them up a greater cost do crave
And I have no ability. And therefore, if thou bring
A wench (it goes against my heart to think upon the thing),
Although against my will, I charge it straight destroyèd be.        800
The bond of nature needs must bear in this behalf with me.'
This said, both wept exceedingly, as well the husband who
Did give commandment as the wife that was commanded to.
Yet Telethusa earnestly at Lict her husband lay
(Although in vain) to have good hope and of himself more stay.
But he was full determinèd. Within a while the day
Approachèd that the fruit was ripe, and she did look to lay
Her belly every minute, when at midnight in her rest
Stood by her (or did seem to stand) the goddess Isis, dressed

810 And trainèd with the solemn pomp of all her rites. Two horns
Upon her forehead like the moon with ears of ripened corns
Stood glistering as the burnished gold. Moreover she did wear
A rich and stately diadem. Attendant on her were
The barking bug Anubis and the saint of Bubast and
The pied-coat Apis and the god that gives to understand
By finger holden to his lips that men should silence keep,
And Lybian worms, whose stinging doth enforce continual sleep,
And thou, Osiris, whom the folk of Egypt ever seek
And never can have sought enough, and rittle-rattles eke.
820 Then, even as though that Telethuse had fully been awake
And seen these things with open eyes, thus Isis to her spake:
'My servant Telethusa, cease this care and break the charge
Of Lict; and when Lucina shall have let thy fruit at large,
Bring up the same, whate'er it be. I am a goddess who
Delights in helping folk at need. I hither come to do
Thee good. Thou shalt not have a cause hereafter to complain
Of serving of a goddess that is thankless for thy pain.'
When Isis had this comfort given, she went her way again.
     A joyful wight rose Telethuse and, lifting to the sky
     Her hardened hands, did pray her dream might work
830          effectually.
Her throes increased and forth alone anon the burden came.
A wench was born to Lictus, who knew nothing of the same.
The mother, making him believe it was a boy, did bring
It up, and none but she and nurse were privy to the thing.
The father, thanking God, did give the child the grandsire's
          name,
The which was Iphis. Joyful was the mother of the same
Because the name did serve alike to man and woman both;
And so the lie through godly guile forth unperceivèd go'th.
The garments of it were a boy's; the face of it was such
840 As either in a boy or girl of beauty uttered much.
When Iphis was of thirteen years, her father did ensure
The brown Ianthe unto her, a wench of look demure
Commended for her favour and her person more than all
The maids of Phaestus. Telest men her father's name did call;

He dwelt in Dictis. They were both of age and favour like
And under both one schoolmaster they did for nurture seek.
And hereupon the hearts of both the dart of love did strike
And wounded both of them alike. But unlike was their hope.
Both longèd for the wedding day together for to cope.
For whom Ianthe thinks to be a man she hopes to see          850
Her husband; Iphis loves whereof she thinks she may not be
Partaker, and the selfsame thing augmenteth still her flame.
Herself, a maiden, with a maid (right strange!) in love became.
    She scarce could stay her tears. 'What end remains for me?'
        quoth she,
    'How strange a love, how uncouth, how prodigious reigns in
        me!
If that the gods did favour me, they should destroy me quite.
Or if they would not me destroy, at leastwise yet they might
Have given me such a malady as might with nature stand
Or nature were acquainted with. A cow is never fond
Upon a cow, nor mare on mare. The ram delights the ewe,          860
The stag the hind, the cock the hen. But never man could show
That female yet was ta'en in love with female kind. O would
To God I never had been born! Yet lest that Candy should
Not bring forth all that monstrous were, the daughter of the sun
Did love a bull; howbeit there was a male to dote upon.
My love is furiouser than hers, if truth confessèd be.
For she was fond of such a lust as might be compassed; she
Was servèd by a bull beguiled by art in cow of tree,
And one there was for her with whom advoutery to commit.
If all the cunning in the world and sleights of subtle wit          870
Were here, or if that Daedalus himself with uncouth wing
Of wax should hither fly again, what comfort should he bring?
Could he with all his cunning crafts now make a boy of me?
Or could he, O Ianthe, change the native shape of thee?
Nay, rather, Iphis, settle thou thy mind and call thy wits
About thee; shake thou off these flames that foolishly by fits
Without all reason reign. Thou see'st what nature hath thee made,
Unless thou wilt deceive thyself. So far forth wisely wade

As right and reason may support, and love as women ought.
Hope is the thing that breeds desire; hope feeds the amorous
880        thought.
This hope thy sex denieth thee. Not watching doth restrain
Thee from embracing of the thing whereof thou art so fain,
Nor yet the husband's jealousy, nor roughness of her sire,
Nor yet the coyness of the wench doth hinder thy desire;
And yet thou canst not her enjoy. No, though that god and man
Should labour to their uttermost and do the best they can
In thy behalf, they could not make a happy wight of thee.
I cannot wish the thing but that I have it. Frank and free
The gods have given me what they could. As I will, so wills he
890 That must become my father-in-law; so wills my father too.
But nature, stronger than them all, consenteth not thereto.
This hindereth me, and nothing else. Behold, the blissful time,
The day of marriage, is at hand. Ianthe shall be mine,
And yet I shall not her enjoy. Amid the water we
Shall thirst. O Juno, president of marriage, why with thee
Comes Hymen to this wedding where no bridegroom you shall
        see,
But both are brides that must that day together coupled be?'
    This spoken, she did hold her peace. And now the t'other maid
    Did burn as hot in love as she, and earnestly she prayed
The bridal day might come with speed. The thing for which she
900        longed
Dame Telethusa fearing sore, from day to day prolonged
The time, oft feigning sickness, oft pretending she had seen
Ill tokens of success. At length all shifts consumèd been.
The wedding day, so oft delayed, was now at hand. The day
Before it, taking from her head the kerchief quite away
And from her daughter's head likewise, with scattered hair she laid
Her hands upon the altar and with humble voice thus prayed:
    'O Isis, who dost haunt the town of Paraetony and
    The fields by Mareotis lake and Pharos, which doth stand
910 By Alexandria, and the Nile divided into seven
Great channels, comfort thou my fear and send me help from
        heaven.

Thyself, O goddess, even thyself and these thy relics I
Did once behold and knew them all, as well thy company
As eke thy sounding rattles and thy cressets burning by;
And mindfully I markèd what commandment thou did'st give.
That I escape unpunishèd, that this same wench doth live,
Thy counsel and thy hest it is. Have mercy now on twain
And help us.' With that word the tears ran down her cheeks
  amain.
 The goddess seemèd for to move her altar; and indeed
 She movèd it. The temple doors did tremble like a reed,  920
And horns in likeness to the moon about the church did shine,
And rattles made a raughtish noise. At this same lucky sign,
Although not wholly careless, yet right glad she went away.
And Iphis followed after her with larger pace than aye
She was accustomed, and her face continued not so white.
Her strength increasèd, and her look more sharper was to sight.
Her hair grew shorter, and she had a much more lively sprite
Than when she was a wench. For thou, O Iphis, who right now
A mother wert, art now a boy. With offerings, both of you,
To church retire and there rejoice with faith unfearful! They  930
With offerings went to church again and there their vows did pay.
They also set a table up, which this brief metre had:
*The vows that Iphis vowed a wench he hath performed a lad.*
Next morrow over all the world did shine with lightsome flame
When Juno and Dame Venus and Sir Hymen jointly came
To Iphis' marriage, who, as then transformèd to a boy,
Did take Ianthe to his wife and so her love enjoy.

FINIS NONI LIBRI.

# The Tenth Book of Ovid's
# Metamorphoses

*Orpheus and Eurydice*

From thence in saffron-coloured robe flew Hymen through the
air
And into Thracia, being called by Orphey, did repair.
He came indeed at Orphey's call; but neither did he sing
The words of that solemnity nor merry count'nance bring
Nor any handsel of good luck. His torch with drizzling smoke
Was dim; the same to burn out clear no stirring could provoke.
The end was worser than the sign. For as the bride did roam
Abroad accompanied with a train of nymphs to bring her home,
A serpent lurking in the grass did sting her in the ankle,
Whereof she died incontinent, so swift the bane did rankle.          10
Whom when the Thracian poet had bewailed sufficiently
On earth, the ghosts departed hence he minding for to try,
Down at the gate of Taenarus did go to Limbo lake.
And thence by ghastly folk and souls late buried he did take
His journey to Persephone and to the king of Ghosts
That like a lordly tyrant reigns in those unpleasant coasts.
And, playing on his tunèd harp, he thus began to sound:
    'O you, the sovereigns of the world set underneath the ground,
    To whom we all (whatever thing is made of mortal kind)
Repair, if by your leave I now may freely speak my mind,          20
I come not hither as a spy the shady hell to see
Nor yet the foul three-headed cur, whose hairs all adders be,
To tie in chains. The cause of this my voyage is my wife,
Whose foot a viper stinging, did abridge her youthful life.
I would have borne it patiently; and so to do I strave.
But Love surmounted power. This god is known great force to
have

Above on earth. And whether he reign here or no I doubt,
But I believe he reigns here too. If fame that flies about
Of former rape report not wrong, Love coupled also you.
30    By these same places full of fear, by this huge Chaos now
And by the stillness of this waste and empty kingdom, I
Beseech ye, of Eurydice unreel the destiny
That was so swiftly reelèd up. All things to you belong,
And though we, lingering for a while, our pageants do prolong,
Yet soon or late we all to one abiding-place do roam.
We haste us thither all; this place becomes our latest home;
And you do over humankind reign longest time. Now when
This woman shall have livèd full her time, she shall again
Become your own. The use of her but for a while I crave.
40    And if the Destinies for my wife deny me for to have
Release, I fully am resolved for ever here to dwell.
Rejoice you in the death of both.' As he this tale did tell
        And playèd on his instrument, the bloodless ghosts shed tears.
        To tire on Tityus' growing heart the greedy gripe forbears;
The shunning water Tantalus endeavoureth not to drink;
And Danaus' daughters ceased to fill their tubs that have no brink.
Ixion's wheel stood still; and down sat Sisyphus upon
His rolling stone. Then first of all (so fame for truth hath gone)
The Furies, being stricken there with pity at his song,
50    Did weep. And neither Pluto nor his lady were so strong
And hard of stomach to withhold his just petition long.
They callèd forth Eurydice, who was as yet among
The newcome ghosts and limpèd of her wound. Her husband
        took
Her with condition that he should not back upon her look
Until the time that he were past the bounds of Limbo quite,
Or else to lose his gift. They took a path that steep upright
Rose dark and full of foggy mist. And now they were within
A kenning of the upper earth, when Orphey did begin
To doubt him lest she followed not; and through an eager love,
60    Desirous for to see her, he his eyes did backward move.
Immediately she slippèd back. He, reaching out his hands,
Desirous to be caught and for to catch her grasping stands.

But nothing save the slippery air (unhappy man!) he caught.
She, dying now the second time, complained of Orphey nought.
For why, what had she to complain, unless it were of love
Which made her husband back again his eyes upon her move?
Her last farewell she spake so soft that scarce he heard the sound,
And then revolted to the place in which he had her found.

   This double dying of his wife set Orphey in a stound
    No less than him who, at the sight of Pluto's dreadful hound     70
That on the middle neck of three doth bear an iron chain,
Was stricken in a sudden fear and could it not restrain
Until the time, his former shape and nature being gone,
His body quite was overgrown and turnèd into stone;
Or than the foolish Olenus, who on himself did take
Another's fault and, guiltless, needs himself would guilty make
Together with his wretched wife Lethaea, for whose pride
They both, becoming stones, do stand even yet on watery Ide.
He would have gone to hell again and earnest suit did make;
But Charon would not suffer him to pass the Stygian lake.     80
Seven days he sat forlorn upon the bank and never ate
A bit of bread. Care, tears and thought and sorrow were his meat.
And, crying out upon the gods of hell as cruel, he
Withdrew to lofty Rhodope and Haeme which beaten be
With northern winds. Three times the sun had passèd through the
    sheer
And watery sign of Pisces and had finished full the year.
And Orphey, were it that his ill success he still did rue
Or that he vowèd so to do, did utterly eschew
The womankind. Yet many a one desirous were to match
With him; but he them with repulse did all alike dispatch.     90
He also taught the Thracian folk a stews of males to make
And of the flowering prime of boys the pleasure for to take.

   There was a hill, and on the hill a very level plot
    Fair green with grass; but as for shade or covert was there not.
As soon as that this poet born of gods in that same place
Sat down and touched his tunèd strings, a shadow came apace.
There wanted neither Chaon's tree nor yet the trees to which
Fresh Phaeton's sisters turnèd were, nor beech, nor holm, nor
    witch,

*Orpheus'*
*audience of*
*trees*

Nor gentle asp, nor wifeless bay, nor lofty chestnut-tree,
Nor hazel spalt, nor ash whereof the shafts of spears made be,
Nor knotless fir, nor cheerful plane, nor maple fleckèd grain,
Nor lote, nor sallow which delights by waters to remain,
Nor slender-twiggèd tamarisk, nor box aye green of hue,
Nor fig-trees loaden with their fruit of colours brown and blue,
Nor double-coloured myrtle-trees. Moreover thither came
The writhing ivy and the vine that runs upon a frame,
Elms clad with vines and ashes wild and pitch-trees black as coal
And, full of trees with goodly fruit red stripèd, orchards whole,
And palm-trees lithe which in reward of conquest men do bear,
And pineapple with tufted top and harsh and prickling hair,
The tree to Cybel, mother of the gods, most dear, for why
Her minion Attis, putting off the shape of man, did die
And hardened into this same tree. Among this company
Was present with a pikèd top the cypress, now a tree,
Sometime a boy belovèd of the god that with a string
Doth arm his bow and with a string in tune his viol bring.
For, hallowed to the nymphs that in the fields of Carthey were,
There was a goodly mighty stag whose horns such breadth did
           bear
As that they shadowed all his head. His horns of gold did shine;
And down his breast hung from his neck a chain with jewels fine.
Amid his front with pretty strings a tablet, being tied,
Did waver as he went; and from his ears on either side
Hung pearls of all one growth about his hollow temples bright.
This goodly spitter, being void of dread, as having quite
Forgot his native fearfulness, did haunt men's houses and
Would suffer folk (yea, though unknown) to coy him with their
           hand.
But more than unto all folk else he dearer was to thee,
O Cypariss, the fairest wight that ever man did see
In Cea. Thou to pastures, thou to water springs him led,
Thou wreathèdst sundry flowers between his horns upon his head.
Sometime a horseman, thou his back for pleasure did'st bestride
And, haltering him with silken bit, from place to place did'st ride.
In summertime about high noon, when Titan with his heat
Did make the hollow crabbèd clees of Cancer for to sweat,

100

110

120

130

Unweeting Cyparissus with a dart did strike this hart
Quite through. And when that of the wound he saw he must
    depart,
He purposed for to die himself. What words of comfort spake
Not Phoebus to him, willing him the matter light to take
And not more sorrow for it than was requisite to make?
But still the lad did sigh and sob, and as his last request    140
Desirèd God he might thenceforth from mourning never rest.
Anon through weeping overmuch his blood was drainèd quite;
His limbs waxed green; his hair which hung upon his forehead
    white
Began to be a bristled bush and, taking by and by
A stiffness, with a sharpened top did face the starry sky.
The god did sigh and sadly said, 'Myself shall mourn for thee,
And thou for others; and aye one in mourning thou shalt be.'
Such wood as this had Orphey drawn about him as among
The herds of beasts and flocks of birds he sat amidst the throng.
And when his thumb sufficiently had trièd every string    150
And found that, though they severally in sundry sounds did ring,
Yet made they all one harmony, he thus began to sing:
    'O Muse, my mother, frame my song of Jove. For everything
    Is subject unto royal Jove. Of Jove the heavenly king
I oft have showed the glorious power. I erst in graver verse
The giants slain in Phlegra fields with thunder did rehearse.
But now I need a milder style to tell of pretty boys
That were the darlings of the gods, and of unlawful joys
That burnèd in the breasts of girls, who for their wicked lust
According as they did deserve receivèd penance just.    160
The king of gods did burn erewhile in love of Ganymede,
The Phrygian, and the thing was found which Jupiter that stead
Had rather be than that he was. Yet could he not beteem
The shape of any other bird than eagle for to seem.
And so he, soaring in the air with borrowed wings, trussed up
The Trojan boy, who still in heaven even yet doth bear his cup
And brings him nectar, though against Dame Juno's will it be.
    'And thou, Amyclae's son (had not thy heavy destiny
    Abridgèd thee before thy time), had'st also placèd been
By Phoebus in the firmament. Howbeit, as is seen,

The<br>transformation<br>of Hyacinthus

Thou art eternal so far forth as may be. For as oft
As watery Pisces giveth place to Aries, that the soft
And gentle springtide doth succeed the winter sharp and stour,
So often thou renew'st thyself and on the fair green clowre
Dost shoot out flowers. My father bare a special love to thee
Above all others, so that while the god went oft to see
Eurotas and unwallèd Spart, he left his noble town
Of Delphos (which amid the world is situate in renown)
Without a sovereign. Neither harp nor bow regarded were.
180 Unmindful of his godhead, he refusèd not to bear
The nets, nor for to hold the hounds, nor as a painful mate
To travel over craggèd hills, through which continual gait
His flames augmented more and more. And now the sun did stand
Well near midway between the nights last past and next at hand.
They stripped themselves and nointed them with oil of olive fat
And fell to throwing of a sledge that was right huge and flat.
First Phoebus, peising it, did throw it from him with such strength
As that the weight drave down the clouds in flying. And at length
It fell upon substantial ground, where plainly it did show
190 As well the cunning as the force of him that did it throw.
Immediately, upon desire himself the sport to try,
The Spartan lad made haste to take up unadvisedly
The sledge before it still did lie. But as he was in hand
To catch it, it, rebounding up against the hardened land,
Did hit him full upon the face. The god himself did look
As pale as did the lad, and up his swounding body took.
Now culls he him, now wipes he from the wound the blood
          away;
Another while his fading life he strives with herbs to stay.
Nought booted leechcraft. Helpless was the wound. And like as
          one
200 Bruised violet stalks or poppy stalks or lilies growing on
Brown spindles, straight they, withering, droop with heavy heads
          and are
Not able for to hold them up, but with their tops do stare
Upon the ground; so Hyacinth, in yielding of his breath,
Chopped down his head. His neck, bereft of strength by means of
          death,

Was even a burden to itself and down did loosely writhe
On both his shoulders, now at one and now at other lithe.
"Thou fad'st away, my Hyacinth, defrauded of the prime
Of youth," quoth Phoebus, "and I see thy wound, my heinous
    crime.
Thou art my sorrow and my fault; this hand of mine hath wrought
Thy death. I like a murderer have to thy grave thee brought.    210
But what have I offended, though, unless that to have played
Or if that to have lovèd an offence it may be said?
Would God I render might my life with and instead of thee.
To which sith fatal destiny denieth to agree,
Both in my mind and in my mouth thou evermore shalt be.
My viol stricken with my hand, my songs shall sound of thee,
And in a new-made flower thou shalt with letters represent
Our sighings. And the time shall come ere many years be spent
That in thy flower a valiant prince shall join himself with thee
And leave his name upon the leaves for men to read and see."    220
While Phoebus thus did prophesy, behold, the blood of him
Which dyed the grass ceased blood to be, and up there sprang a
    trim
And goodly flower more orient than the purple cloth ingrain
In shape of lily, were it not that lilies do remain
Of silver colour, whereas these of purple hue are seen.
Although that Phoebus had the cause of this great honour been,
Yet thought he not the same enough. And therefore did he write
His sighs upon the leaves thereof. And so in colour bright
The flower hath $\alpha\iota$ writ thereon, which letters are of grief.
So small the Spartans thought the birth of Hyacinth reprieve    230
Unto them, that they worship him from that day unto this.
And as their fathers did before, so they do never miss
With solemn pomp to celebrate his feast from year to year.
  'But if perchance that Amathus, the rich in metals, were    *The Propoets*
    Demanded if it would have bred the Propoets, it would swear    *and the*
Yea, even as gladly as the folk whose brows sometime did bear    *Cerastes*
A pair of whelkèd horns, whereof they Cerasts namèd are.
Before their door an altar stood of Jove that takes the care
Of aliens and of travellers, which loathsome was to see
For lewdness wrought thereon. If one that had a stranger be    240

Had looked thereon, he would have thought there had on it been
     killed
Some sucking calves or lambs. The blood of strangers there was
     spilled.
Dame Venus, sore offended at this wicked sacrifice,
To leave her cities and the land of Cyprus did devise.
But then, bethinking her, she said, "What hath my pleasant
     ground,
What have my cities trespassèd? What fault in them is found?
Nay, rather let this wicked race by exile punished been,
Or death, or by some other thing that is a mean between
Both death and exile. What is that save only for to change
Their shape?" In musing with herself what figure were most
250          strange,
She cast her eye upon a horn. And therewithal she thought
The same to be a shape right meet upon them to be brought.
And so she from their mighty limbs their native figure took
And turned them into boisterous bulls with grim and cruel look.
Yet durst the filthy Propoets stand in stiff opinion that
Dame Venus was no goddess, till she, being wroth thereat,
To make their bodies common first compelled them everych one,
And after changed their former kind. For when that shame was
     gone
And that they waxèd brazen fast, she turnèd them to stone,
In which between their former shape was difference small or
260          none.

The story of      'Whom for because Pygmalion saw to lead their life in sin,
Pygmalion       Offended with the vice whereof great store is packed within
The nature of the womankind, he led a single life.
And long it was ere he could find in heart to take a wife.
Now in the while by wondrous art an image he did grave
Of such proportion, shape and grace as nature never gave
Nor can to any woman give. In this his work he took
A certain love. The look of it was right a maiden's look,
And such a one as that ye would believe had life and that
270   Would movèd be, if womanhood and reverence letted not.
So artificial was the work. He wond'reth at his art
And of his counterfeited corse conceiveth love in heart.

He often touched it, feeling if the work that he had made
Were very flesh or ivory still. Yet could he not persuade
Himself to think it ivory. For he oftentimes it kissed
And thought it kissèd him again. He held it by the fist
And talkèd to it. He believed his fingers made a dint
Upon her flesh, and fearèd lest some black or bruisèd print
Should come by touching overhard. Sometime with pleasant
          bourds
And wanton toys he dallyingly doth cast forth amorous words.    280
Sometime (the gifts wherein young maids are wonted to delight)
He brought her ouches, fine round stones and lilies fair and white
And pretty singing birds and flowers of thousand sorts and hue,
And painted balls and amber from the tree distillèd new.
In gorgous garments, furthermore, he did her also deck
And on her fingers put me rings and chains about her neck.
Rich pearls were hanging at her ears and tablets at her breast.
All kind of things became her well. And when she was undressed
She seemèd not less beautiful. He laid her in a bed
The which with scarlet dyed in Tyre was richly overspread          290
And, terming her his bedfellow, he couchèd down her head
Upon a pillow soft, as though she could have felt the same.
    'The feast of Venus, hallowed through the isle of Cyprus, came;
    And bullocks white with gilden horns were slain for sacrifice
And up to heaven of frankincense the smoky fume did rise
Whenas Pygmalion, having done his duty that same day,
Before the altar standing, thus with fearful heart did say:
"If that you gods can all things give, then let my wife, I pray" –
He durst not say "be yon same wench of ivory", but – "be like
My wench of ivory." Venus, who was nought at all to seek        300
What such a wish as that did mean, then present at her feast,
For handsel of her friendly help did cause three times at least
The fire to kindle and to spire thrice upward in the air.
As soon as he came home, straightway Pygmalion did repair
Unto the image of his wench and, leaning on the bed,
Did kiss her. In her body straight a warmness seemed to spread.
He put his mouth again to hers and on her breast did lay
His hand. The ivory waxèd soft and, putting quite away

All hardness, yielded underneath his fingers, as we see
310 A piece of wax made soft against the sun or drawn to be
In divers shapes by chafing it between one's hands and so
To serve to uses. He, amazed, stood wavering to and fro
'Tween joy and fear to be beguiled. Again he burnt in love,
Again with feeling he began his wishèd hope to prove.
He felt it very flesh indeed. By laying on his thumb
He felt her pulses beating. Then he stood no longer dumb
But thankèd Venus with his heart. And at the length he laid
His mouth to hers who was as then become a perfect maid.
She felt the kiss and blushed thereat and, lifting fearfully
320 Her eyelids up, her lover and the light at once did spy.
The marriage that herself had made the goddess blessèd so
That, when the moon with fulsome light nine times her course
       had go,
This lady was delivered of a son that Paphos hight,
Of whom the island takes that name. Of him was born a knight
Called Cinyras who, had he had none issue, surely might
Of all men underneath the sun been thought the happiest wight.

*Myrrha and*        'Of wicked and most cursed things to speak I now commence.
*Cinyras*      Ye daughters and ye parents all, go, get ye far from hence.
Or if ye minded be to hear my tale, believe me nought
330 In this behalf, ne think that such a thing was ever wrought.
Or if ye will believe the deed, believe the vengeance too
Which lighted on the party that the wicked act did do.
But if that it be possible that any wight so much
From nature should degenerate as for to fall to such
A heinous crime as this is, I am glad for Thracia, I
Am glad for this same world of ours, yea, glad exceedingly
I am for this my native soil, for that there is such space
Between it and the land that bred a child so void of grace.
I would the land Panchaia should of amomy be rich
340 And cinnamon and costus sweet and incense also, which
Doth issue largely out of trees, and other flowers strange,
As long as that it beareth myrrh; not worth it was the change
New trees to have of such a price. The god of love denies
His weapons to have hurted thee, O Myrrha, and he tries

Himself unguilty by thy fault. One of the Furies three
With poisoned snakes and hellish brands hath rather blasted thee.
To hate one's father is a crime as heinous as may be;
But yet more wicked is this love of thine than any hate.
The youthful lords of all the east and peers of chief estate
Desire to have thee to their wife and earnest suit do make.          350
Of all (excepting only one) thy choice, O Myrrha, take.
    'She feels her filthy love and strives against it, and within
    Herself said, "Whither runs my mind? What think I to begin?
Ye gods, I pray, and godliness, ye holy rites and awe
Of parents, from this heinous crime my vicious mind withdraw
And disappoint my wickedness — at leastwise if it be
A wickedness that I intend. As far as I can see
This love infringeth not the bonds of godliness a whit.
For every other living wight Dame Nature doth permit
To match without offence of sin. The heifer thinks no shame          360
To bear her father on her back; the horse bestrides the same
Of whom he is the sire; the goat doth buck the kid that he
Himself begat; and birds do tread the selfsame birds, we see,
Of whom they hatchèd were before. In happy case they are
That may do so without offence. But man's malicious care
Hath made a bridle for itself, and spiteful laws restrain
The things that Nature setteth free. Yet are there realms, men
            sayen,
In which the mother with the son and daughter with the father
Do match, wherethrough of godliness the bond augments the
            rather
With doubled love. Now woe is me it had not been my lot             370
In that same country to be born, and that this luckless plot
Should hinder me. Why think I thus? Avaunt, unlawful love!
I ought to love him, I confess; but so as doth behove
His daughter. Were not Cinyras my father, then, iwis,
I might obtain to lie with him. But now because he is
Mine own, he cannot be mine own. The nearness of our kin
Doth hurt me. Were I further off, perchance I more might win.
And if I wist that I thereby this wickedness might shun,
I would forsake my native soil and far from Cyprus run.

380 This evil heat doth hold me back that, being present still,
I may but talk with Cinyras and look on him my fill
And touch and kiss him, if no more may further granted be.
Why, wicked wench! And canst thou hope for further? Dost not see
How by thy fault thou dost confound the rights of name and kin?
And wilt thou make thy mother be a cuckquean by thy sin?
Wilt thou thy father's leman be? Wilt thou be both the mother
And sister of thy child? Shall he be both thy son and brother?
And stand'st thou not in fear at all of those same sisters three
Whose heads with crawling snakes instead of hair bematted be,
Which, pushing with their cruel brands folks' eyes and mouths, do
390     see
Their sinful hearts? But thou, now while thy body yet is free,
Let never such a wickedness once enter in thy mind.
Defile not mighty Nature's hest by lust against thy kind.
What though thy will were fully bent? Yet even the very thing
Is such as will not suffer thee the same to end to bring.
For why he, being well disposed and godly, mindeth aye
So much his duty that from right and truth he will not stray.
Would God like fury were in him as is in me this day!"
   'This said, her father Cinyras (who doubted what to do
400   By reason of the worthy store of suitors which did woo
His daughter), bringing all their names, did will her for to show
On which of them she had herself most fancy to bestow.
At first she held her peace awhile and, looking wistly on
Her father's face, did boil within; and scalding tears anon
Ran down her visage. Cinyras, who thought them to proceed
Of tender-hearted shamefastness, did say there was no need
Of tears, and dried her cheeks and kissed her. Myrrha took of it
Exceeding pleasure in herself. And when that he did wit
What husband she did wish to have, she said, "One like to you."
410 He, understanding not her thought, did well her words allow
And said, "In this thy godly mind continue." At the name
Of godliness she cast me down her look for very shame,
For why her guilty heart did know she well deservèd blame.
   'High midnight came, and sleep both care and carcasses
     oppressed.
But Myrrha, lying broad awake, could neither sleep nor rest.

She fries in Cupid's flames and works continually upon
Her furious love. One while she sinks in deep despair. Anon
She fully minds to give attempt, but shame doth hold her in.
She wishes and she wots not what to do, nor how to gin.
And like as when a mighty tree with axes hewèd round,          420
Now ready with a stripe or twain to lie upon the ground,
Uncertain is which way to fall and tott'reth every way;
Even so her mind with doubtful wound affeebled then did stray
Now here, now there uncertainly, and took of both increase.
No measure of her love was found, no rest nor yet release
Save only death. Death likes her best. She riseth full in mind
To hang herself. About a post her girdle she doth bind,
And said, "Farewell, dear Cinyras, and understand the cause
Of this my death." And with that word about her neck she draws
The noose. Her trusty nurse, that in another chamber lay,          430
By fortune heard the whispering sound of these her words, folk
     say.
The agèd woman, rising up, unbolts the door. And when
She saw her in that plight of death, she, shrieking out, began
To smite herself and scratched her breast and quickly to her ran
And rent the girdle from her neck. Then, weeping bitterly
And holding her between her arms, she asked the question why
She went about to hang herself so unadvisedly.
The lady held her peace as dumb and, looking on the ground
Unmovably, was sorry in her heart for being found
Before she had dispatched herself. Her nurse still at her lay          440
And, showing her her empty dugs and naked head all grey,
Besought her for the pains she took with her both night and day
In rocking and in feeding her, she would vouchsafe to say
Whate'er it were that grievèd her. The lady turned away
Displeased and fetched a sigh. The nurse was fully bent in mind
To bolt the matter out; for which not only she did bind
Her faith in secret things to keep, but also said, "Put me
In trust to find a remedy. I am not, thou shalt see,
Yet altogether dulled by age. If furiousness it be,
I have both charms and chanted herbs to help. If any wight          450
Bewitcheth thee, by witchcraft I will purge and set thee quite.

Or if it be the wrath of God, we shall with sacrifice
Appease the wrath of God right well. What may I more surmise?
No thieves have broken in upon this house and spoiled the
        wealth.
Thy mother and thy father both are living and in health."
When Myrrha heard her father named, a grievous sigh she fet
Even from the bottom of her heart. Howbeit, the nurse as yet
Misdeemed not any wickedness. But ne'ertheless she guessed
There was some love and, standing in one purpose, made request
460 To break her mind unto her. And she set her tenderly
Upon her lap. The lady wept and sobbèd bitterly.
Then, culling her in feeble arms, she said, "I well espy
Thou art in love. My diligence in this behalf I swear
Shall serviceable to thee be. Thou shalt not need to fear
That e'er thy father shall it know." At that same word she leapt
From nurse's lap like one that had been past her wits and stepped
With fury to her bed at which she, leaning down her face,
Said, "Hence, I pray thee! Force me not to show my shameful
        case."
And when the nurse did urge her still, she answered, "Either get
470 Thee hence, or cease to ask me why myself I thus do fret.
The thing that thou desir'st to know is wickedness." The old
Poor nurse gan quake and, trembling both for age and fear, did
        hold
Her hands to her. And kneeling down right humbly at her feet,
One while she fair entreated her with gentle words and sweet;
Another while, unless she made her privy of her sorrow,
She threatened her and put her in a fear she would next morrow
Bewray her, how she went about to hang herself. But if
She told her, she did plight her faith and help to her relief.
She lifted up her head and then with tears fast gushing out
480 Beslubbered all her nurse's breast. And going oft about
To speak, she often stayed and with her garments hid her face
For shame and lastly said, "O happy is my mother's case
That such a husband hath." With that a grievous sigh she gave
And held her peace. These words of hers a trembling chillness
        drave

In nurse's limbs which pierced her bones; for now she understood
The case. And all her hoary hair up stiffly staring stood,
And many things she talked to put away her cursèd love,
If that it had been possible the madness to remove.
The maid herself to be full true the counsel doth espy,
Yet if she may not have her love she fully minds to die.        490
"Live still," quoth nurse. "Thou shalt obtain" – she durst not say
    "thy father",
But stayed at that. And for because that Myrrha should the rather
Believe her, she confirmed her words by oath. The yearly feast
Of gentle Ceres came, in which the wives both most and least
Apparelled all in white are wont the firstlings of the field,
Fine garlands made of ears of corn, to Ceres for to yield.
And for the space of thrice three nights they counted it a sin
To have the use of any man, or once to touch his skin.
   'Among these women did the queen frequent the secret rites.
   Now while that of his lawful wife his bed was void a-nights,      500
The nurse was double diligent. And finding Cinyras
Well washed with wine, she did surmise there was a pretty lass
In love with him, and highly she her beauty setteth out.
And being askèd of her years, she said she was about
The age of Myrrha. "Well," quoth he, "then bring her to my
    bed."
Returning home, she said, "Be glad, my nursechild; we have
    sped."
Not all so wholly in her heart was wretched Myrrha glad
But that her fore-misgiving mind did also make her sad.
Howbeit, she also did rejoice as in a certain kind,
Such discord of affections was within her cumbered mind.      510
   'It was the time that all things rest. And now Boötes bright,
   The driver of the oxen seven about the northpole pight,
Had somewhat turned his wain aside, when wicked Myrrha sped
About her business. Out of heaven the golden Phoebe fled.
With clouds more black than any pitch the stars did hide their
    head.
The night becometh utter void of all her wonted light.
And first before all other hid their faces out of sight

Good Icar and Erigone his daughter, who for love
Most virtuous to her fatherward was taken up above
And made a star in heaven. Three times had Myrrha warning
520      given
By stumbling to retire; three times the deathful owl that even
With doleful noise prognosticates unhappy luck. Yet came
She forward still. The darkness of the night abated shame.
Her left hand held her nurse, her right the dark blind way did
    grope.
Anon she to the chamber came; anon the door was ope;
Anon she entered in. With that her faltering hams did quake,
Her colour died, her blood and heart did clearly her forsake.
The nearer she approachèd to her wickedness, the more
She trembled. Of her enterprise it irkèd her full sore,
And fain she would she might unknown have turnèd back. Nurse
530      led
Her, pausing, forward by the hand. And, putting her to bed,
"Here take this damsel, Cinyras; she is thine own," she said.
And so she laid them breast to breast. The wicked father takes
His bowels into filthy bed, and there with words aslakes
The maiden's fear and cheers her up. And lest this crime of theirs
Might want the rightful terms, by chance as in respect of years
He "daughter" did her call, and she him "father". Being sped
With cursèd seed in wicked womb, she left her father's bed;
Of which soon after she became great baggèd with her shame.
540 Next night the lewdness doubled; and no end was of the same
Until at length that Cinyras, desirous for to know
His lover that so many nights upon him did bestow,
Did fetch a light; by which he saw his own most heinous crime
And eke his daughter. Natheless, his sorrow at that time
Repressed his speech. Then hanging by he drew a rapier bright.
Away ran Myrrha, and by means of darkness of the night
She was delivered from the death. And, straying in the broad
Date-bearing fields of Araby, she through Panchaia yode
And, wandering full nine months, at length she rested, being tired,
550 In Saba land. And when the time was near at hand expired
And that uneath the burden of her womb she well could bear,
Not knowing what she might desire, distressed between the fear

Of death and tediousness of life, this prayer she did make:
"O gods, if of repentant folk you any mercy take,
Sharp vengeance, I confess, I have deservèd, and content
I am to take it patiently. Howbeit, to th'intent
That neither with my life the quick nor with my death the dead
Annoyèd be, from both of them exempt me this same stead
And, altering me, deny to me both life and death." We see
To such as do confess their faults some mercy showed to be.          560
The gods did grant her this request, the last that she should make.
The ground did overgrow her feet and ankles as she spake,
And from her bursten toes went roots which, writhing here and
          there,
Did fasten so the trunk within the ground she could not stir.
Her bones did into timber turn, whereof the marrow was
The pith, and into waterish sap the blood of her did pass.
Her arms were turned to greater boughs, her fingers into twig;
Her skin was hardened into bark. And now her belly big
The eching tree had overgrowen and overta'en her breast
And hasted for to win her neck and hide it with the rest.          570
She made no tarriance nor delay, but met the coming tree
And shrunk her face within the bark thereof. Although that she
Together with her former shape her senses all did lose,
Yet weepeth she, and from her tree warm drops do softly ooze.
The which her tears are had in price and honour, and the myrrh
That issueth from her gummy bark doth bear the name of her
   'And shall do while the world doth last. The misbegotten child
   Grew still within the tree and from his mother's womb defiled
Sought means to be deliverèd. Her burdened womb did swell
Amid the tree and stretched her out. But words wherewith to tell          580
And utter forth her grief did want. She had no use of speech
With which Lucina in her throes she might of help beseech.
Yet like a woman labouring was the tree and, bowing down,
Gave often sighs and shed forth tears as though she there should
          drown.
Lucina to this woeful tree came gently down and laid
Her hand thereon and, speaking words of ease, the midwife
          played.

The tree did cranny, and the bark, dividing, made a way
And yielded out the child alive, which cried and wailed
      straightway.
The waternymphs upon the soft sweet herbs the child did lay
590  And bathed him with his mother's tears. His face was such as spite
Must needs have praised. For such he was in all conditions right
As are the naked Cupids that in tables pictured be.
But to th'intent he may with them in every point agree,
Let either him be furnishèd with wings and quiver light
Or from the Cupids take their wings and bows and arrows quite.

*Venus and*
*Adonis*    'Away slips fleeting time unspied and mocks us to our face,
    And nothing may compare with years in swiftness of their pace.
That wretched imp whom wickedly his grandfather begat
And whom his cursèd sister bare, who hidden was alate
600  Within the tree and lately born, became immediately
The beautifulest babe on whom man ever set his eye.
Anon a stripling he became, and by and by a man,
And every day more beautiful than other he became,
That in the end Dame Venus fell in love with him, whereby
He did revenge the outrage of his mother's villainy.
For as the armèd Cupid kissed Dame Venus, unbeware
An arrow sticking out did raze her breast upon the bare.
The goddess, being wounded, thrust away her son. The wound
Appearèd not to be so deep as afterward was found;
610  It did deceive her at the first. The beauty of the lad
Enflamed her. To Cythera Isle no mind at all she had,
Nor unto Paphos where the sea beats round about the shore,
Nor fishy Gnide, nor Amathus that hath of metals store.
Yea, even from heaven she did abstain. She loved Adonis more
Than heaven. To him she clingèd aye and bare him company.
And in the shadow wont she was to rest continually
And for to set her beauty out most seemly to the eye
By trimly decking of herself. Through bushy grounds and groves
And over hills and dales and lawns and stony rocks she roves
620  Bare-kneed, with garment tuckèd up according to the wont
Of Phoebe; and she cheered the hounds with hallooing like a
      hunt,

Pursuing game of hurtless sort, as hares made low before
Or stags with lofty heads or bucks. But with the sturdy boar
And ravening wolf and bear whelps armed with ugly paws and eke
The cruel lions, which delight in blood and slaughter seek,
She meddled not. And of these same she warnèd also thee,
Adonis, for to shun them if thou would'st have warnèd be.
"Be bold on cowards," Venus said, "for whoso doth advance
Himself against the bold may hap to meet with some mischance.
Wherefore I pray thee, my sweet boy, forbear too bold to be,          630
For fear thy rashness hurt thyself and work the woe of me.
Encounter not the kind of beasts whom nature armèd hath,
For doubt thou buy thy praise too dear, procuring thee some
      scathe.
Thy tender youth, thy beauty bright, thy count'nance fair and
      brave,
Although they had the force to win the heart of Venus, have
No power against the lions nor against the bristled swine.
The eyes and hearts of savage beasts do nought to these incline.
The cruel boars bear thunder in their hookèd tushes, and
Exceeding force and fierceness is in lions to withstand.
And sure I hate them at my heart." To him demanding "Why?",          640
"A monstrous chance," quoth Venus, "I will tell thee by and by
That happened for a fault. But now unwonted toil hath made
Me weary; and behold, in time this poplar with his shade
Allureth, and the ground for couch doth serve to rest upon.
I pray thee, let us rest us here." They sat them down anon,
And, lying upward with her head upon his lap along,
She thus began, and in her tale she bussèd him among:
   '"Perchance thou hast ere this time heard of one that overcame     *Atalanta and*
      The swiftest men in footmanship; no fable was that fame.        *Hippomenes*
She overcame them, out of doubt. And hard it is to tell               650
Thee whether she in footmanship or beauty more excel.
Upon a season, as she asked of Phoebus what he was
That should her husband be, he said, 'For husband do not pass,
O Atalanta. Thou at all of husband hast no need;
Shun husbanding. But yet thou canst not shun it, I thee read.
Alive, thou shalt not be thyself.' She, being sore afraid
Of this Apollo's oracle, did keep herself a maid

And livèd in the shady woods. When wooers to her came
And were of her importunate, she drave away the same
660    With boisterous words and with sore condition of the game.
'I am not to be had', quoth she, 'unless ye able be
In running for to vanquish me. Ye must contend with me
In footmanship. And whoso wins the wager, I agree
To be his wife. But if that he be found too slow, then he
Shall lose his head. This of your game the very law shall be.'
She was indeed unmerciful. But such is beauty's power
That, though the said condition were extreme and oversour,
Yet many suitors were so rash to undertake the same.
Hippomenes as a looker-on of this uncourteous game
670    Sat by and said, 'Is any man so mad to seek a wife
With such apparent peril and the hazard of his life?'
And utterly he did condemn the young men's love. But when
He saw her face and body bare (for why the lady then
Did strip her to the naked skin) the which was like to mine
Or rather, if that thou wert made a woman, like to thine,
He was amazed. And holding up his hands to heaven he saith,
'Forgive me, you with whom I found such fault even now. In
        faith,
I did not know the wager that ye ran for.' As he praiseth
The beauty of her, in himself the fire of love he raiseth.
680    And through an envy, fearing lest she should away be won,
He wished that ne'er a one of them so swift as she might run.
'And wherefore', quoth he, 'put not I myself in press to try
The fortune of this wager? God himself continually
Doth help the bold and hardy sort.' Now while Hippomenes
Debates these things within himself and other like to these,
The damsel runs as if her feet were wings. And though that she
Did fly as swift as arrow from a Turkey bow, yet he
More wondered at her beauty than at swiftness of her pace.
Her running greatly did augment her beauty and her grace.
690    The wind, aye whisking from her feet the labels of her socks,
Upon her back as white as snow did toss her golden locks
And eke th'embroidered garters that were tied beneath her ham.
A redness mixed with white upon her tender body came,

As when a scarlet curtain strained against a plastered wall
Doth cast like shadow, making it seem ruddy therewithal.
Now while the stranger noted this, the race was fully run,
And Atalant, as she that had the wager clearly won,
Was crownèd with a garland brave. The vanquished, sighing sore,
Did lose their lives according to agreement made before.
Howbeit, nought at all dismayed with these men's luckless case, 700
He steppèd forth and, looking full upon the maiden's face,
Said, 'Wherefore dost thou seek renown in vanquishing of such
As were but dastards? Cope with me. If fortune be so much
My friend to give me victory, thou needest not hold scorn
To yield to such a noble man as I am. I am born
The son of noble Megarey, Onchesty's son, and he
Was son to Neptune. Thus am I great-grandchild by degree
In right descent of him that rules the waters. Neither do
I out of kind degenerate from virtue meet thereto.
Or if my fortune be so hard as vanquished for to be, 710
Thou shalt obtain a famous name by overcoming me.'
In saying thus, Atlanta cast a gentle look on him
And, doubting whether she rather had to lose the day or win,
  ' "Said thus: 'What god, an enemy to the beautiful, is bent
    To bring this person to his end and therefore hath him sent
To seek a wife with hazard of his life? If I should be
Myself the judge in this behalf, there is not, sure, in me
That doth deserve so dearly to be earnèd. Neither doth
His beauty move my heart at all; yet is it such, in sooth,
As well might move me. But because as yet a child he is, 720
His person moves me not so much as doth his age, iwis;
Besides that manhood is in him and mind un'fraid of death,
Besides that of the watery race from Neptune, as he saith,
He is the fourth, besides that he doth love me and doth make
So great account to win me to his wife that for my sake
He is contented for to die, if fortune be so sore
Against him to deny him me. Thou stranger, hence, therefore!
Away, I say, now while thou may'st and shun my bloody bed!
My marriage cruel is and craves the losing of thy head.
There is no wench but that would such a husband gladly catch, 730
And she that wise were might desire to meet with such a match.

But why now, after heading of so many, do I care
For thee? Look thou to that. For sith so many men as are
Already put to slaughter cannot warn thee to beware
But that thou wilt be weary of thy life, die! Do not spare!
And shall he perish then because he sought to live with me,
And for his love unworthily with death rewarded be?
All men of such a victory will speak too foul a shame.
But all the world can testify that I am not to blame.
Would God thou would'st desist. Or else, because thou art so

740        mad,
I would to God a little more thy feet of swiftness had.
Ah, what a maiden's countenance is in this childish face!
Ah, foolish boy, Hippomenes, how wretched is thy case!
I would thou never had'st me seen. Thou worthy art of life.
And if so be I happy were and that to be a wife
The cruel Destinies had not me forbidden, sure thou art
The only wight with whom I would be matched with all my
        heart.'
    ' "This spoken, she, yet raw and but new stricken with the dart
Of Cupid, being ignorant, did love and knew it nat.

750  Anon her father and the folk assembled willèd that
They should begin their wonted race. Then Neptune's issue
        prayed
With careful heart and voice to me, and thus devoutly said:
'O Venus, favour mine attempt and send me down thine aid
To compass my desirèd love which thou hast on me laid.'
His prayer moved me, I confess, and long I not delayed
Before I helped him. Now there is a certain field, the which
The Cyprian folk call Damasene, most fertile and most rich
Of all the Cyprian fields. The same was consecrate to me
In ancient time and of my church the glebeland wont to be.

760  Amid this field with golden leaves there grows a goodly tree
The crackling boughs whereof are all of yellow gold. I came
And gathered golden apples three and, bearing thence the same
Within my hand, immediately to Hippomen I gat,
Invisible to all wights else save him, and taught him what
To do with them. The trumpets blew; and, girding forward, both
Set forth and on the hovering dust with nimble feet each go'th.

A man would think they able were upon the sea to go
And never wet their feet, and on the ails of corn also
That still is growing in the field and never down them tread.
The man took courage at the shout and words of them that said,    770
'Now, now is time, Hippomenes, to ply it; hie apace!
Enforce thyself with all thy strength; lag not in any case!
Thou shalt obtain.' It is a thing right doubtful whether he
At these well-willing words of theirs rejoicèd more or she.
O Lord, how often when she might outstrip him did she stay
And gazèd long upon his face, right loath to go her way!
A weary breath proceeded from their parchèd lips, and far
They had to run. Then Neptune's imp, her swiftness to disbar,
Trolled down at one side of the way an apple of the three.
Amazed thereat and covetous of the goodly apple, she    780
Did step aside and snatchèd up the rolling fruit of gold.
With that Hippomenes coted her. The folk that did behold
Made noise with clapping of their hands. She recompensed her
        sloth
And loss of time with footmanship, and straight again outgo'th
Hippomenes, leaving him behind. And being stayed again
With taking up the second, she him overtook. And when
The race was almost at an end, he said, 'O goddess, thou
That art the author of this gift, assist me friendly now.'
And therewithal, of purpose that she might the longer be
In coming, he with all his might did bowl the last of three    790
Askew at one side of the field. The lady seemed to make
A doubt in taking of it up. I forcèd her to take
It up, and to the apple I did put a heavy weight
And made it of such massiness she could not lift it straight.
And lest that I in telling of my tale may longer be
Than they in running of their race, outstrippèd quite was she.
And he that won her, marrying her, enjoyed her for his fee.
    '"Think'st thou I was not worthy thanks, Adonis? Thinkest
        thou
    I earnèd not that he to me should frankincense allow?
But he, forgetful, neither thanks nor frankincense did give,    800
By means whereof to sudden wrath he justly did me drive.

For being grievèd with the spite, because I would not be
Despised of such as were to come, I thought it best for me
To take such vengeance of them both as others might take heed
By them. And so against them both in anger I proceed.
A temple of the mother of the gods that vowèd was
And builded by Echion in a darksome grove they pass.
There through my might Hippomenes was touched and stirrèd so
That needs he would to venery, though out of season, go.
810    Not far from this same temple was with little light a den
With pommy vaulted naturally, long consecrate ere then
For old religion, not unlike a cave, where priests of yore
Bestowèd had of images of wooden gods good store.
Hippomenes, entering hereinto, defiled the holy place
With his unlawful lust, from which the idols turned their face.
And Cybel with the towered tops, disdaining, doubted whether
She in the lake of Styx might drown the wicked folk together.
The penance seemèd overlight; and therefore she did cause
Thin yellow manes to grow upon their necks, and hookèd paws
820    Instead of fingers to succeed. Their shoulders were the same
They were before; with wondrous force deep-breasted they
        became.
Their look became fierce, cruel, grim and sour. A tufted tail,
Stretched out in length far after them, upon the ground doth trail.
Instead of speech they roar; instead of bed they haunt the wood.
And, dreadful unto others, they for all their cruel mood
With tamèd teeth chank Cybel's bits in shape of lions. Shun
These beasts, dear heart; and not from these alonely see thou run,
But also from each other beast that turns not back to flight
But offereth with his boisterous breast to try the chance of fight,
830    Lest that thine overhardiness be hurtful to us both."

*The death
of Adonis*

  'This warning given, with yokèd swans away through air she
        go'th.
  But manhood by admonishment restrainèd could not be.
By chance his hounds, in following of the track, a boar did see
And rousèd him. And as the swine was coming from the wood,
Adonis hit him with a dart askew and drew the blood.

The boar straight with his hookèd groin the hunting-staff out
    drew
Bestainèd with his blood, and on Adonis did pursue;
Who, trembling and retiring back, to place of refuge drew.
And hiding in his cods his tusks as far as he could thrust,
He laid him all along for dead upon the yellow dust.       840
Dame Venus in her chariot drawn with swans was scarce arrived
At Cyprus, when she knew afar the sigh of him deprived
Of life. She turned her cygnets back; and when she from the sky
Beheld him dead and in his blood beweltered for to lie,
She leapèd down and tore at once her garments from her breast
And rent her hair and beat upon her stomach with her fist
And, blaming sore the Destinies, said, "Yet shall they not obtain
Their will in all things. Of my grief remembrance shall remain,
Adonis, while the world doth last. From year to year shall grow
A thing that of my heaviness and of thy death shall show      850
The lively likeness. In a flower thy blood I will bestow.
Had'st thou the power, Persephone, rank-scented mints to make
Of women's limbs? And may not I like power upon me take
Without disdain and spite, to turn Adonis to a flower?"
This said, she sprinkled nectar on the blood, which through the
    power
Thereof did swell like bubbles sheer that rise in weather clear
On water. And before that full an hour expirèd were,
Of all one colour with the blood a flower she there did find
Even like the flower of that same tree whose fruit in tender rind
Have pleasant grains enclosed. Howbeit the use of them is short,      860
For why the leaves do hang so loose through lightness in such sort
As that the winds, that all things pierce, with every little blast
Do shake them off and shed them so as that they cannot last.'

FINIS DECIMI LIBRI.

# The Eleventh Book of Ovid's
## Metamorphoses

Now while the Thracian poet with this song delights the minds
Of savage beasts and draws both stones and trees against their
       kinds,
Behold, the wives of Cicony with red deer skins about
Their furious breasts, as in the field they gadded on a rout,
Espied him from a hillock's top still singing to his harp.
Of whom one shook her head at him and thus began to carp:
'Behold,' says she, 'behold, yon same is he that doth disdain
Us women.' And with that same word she sent her lance amain
At Orphey's singing mouth. The lance, armed round about with
      leaves,
Did hit him; and without a wound a mark behind it leaves.      10
Another threw a stone at him which, vanquished with his sweet
And most melodious harmony, fell humbly at his feet
As sorry for the furious act it purposèd. But rash
And heady riot out of frame all reason now did dash,
And frantic outrage reigned. Yet had the sweetness of his song
Appeased all weapons, saving that the noise, now growing strong
With blowing shawms and beating drums and bedlam howling out
And clapping hands on every side by Bacchus' drunken rout,
Did drown the sound of Orphey's harp. Then first of all stones
      were
Made ruddy with the prophet's blood and could not give him ear.      20
And first the flock of Bacchus' frows by violence brake the ring
Of serpents, birds and savage beasts that for to hear him sing
Sat gazing round about him there. And then with bloody hands
They ran upon the prophet, who among them singing stands.
They flocked about him, like as when a sort of birds have found
An owl a-daytimes in a tod and hem him in full round;

As when a stag by hungry hounds is in a morning found,
The which forestall him round about and pull him to the ground,
Even so the prophet they assail and throw their thyrses green
30    At him, which for another use than that invented been.
Some cast me clods, some boughs of trees and some threw stones.
     ·    And lest
That weapon wherewithal to wreak their woodness (which
          increased)
Should want, it chanced that oxen by were tilling of the ground
And labouring men with brawnèd arms not far fro thence were
          found
A-digging of the hardened earth and earning of their food
With sweating brows. They, seeing this same rout, no longer
          stood
But ran away and left their tools behind them. Everywhere
Through all the field their mattocks, rakes and shovels scattered
          were.
Which when the cruel fiends had caught and had asunder rent
40    The hornèd oxen, back again to Orpheyward they went
And, wicked wights, they murdered him, who never till that hour
Did utter words in vain nor sing without effectual power.
And through that mouth of his, O Lord, which even the stones
          had heard
And unto which the witless beasts had often given regard,
His ghost, then breathing into air, departed. Even the fowls
Were sad for Orphey, and the beast with sorry sighing howls.
The rugged stones did mourn for him; the woods, which many a
          time
Had followed him to hear him sing, bewailèd this same crime.
Yea, even the trees, lamenting him, did cast their leafy hair;
50    The rivers also with their tears, men say, increasèd were.
Yea, and the nymphs of brooks and woods upon their streams did
          sail
With scattered hair about their ears in boats with sable sail.
His members lay in sundry steads. His head and harp both came
To Hebrus. And (a wondrous thing) as down the stream they
          swam,

His harp did yield a mourning sound; his lifeless tongue did make
A certain lamentable noise as though it still yet spake;
And both the banks in mourning wise made answer to the same.
At length a-down their country stream to open sea they came
And lighted on Methymny shore in Lesbos land. And there
No sooner on the foreign coast now cast a-land they were,                    60
But that a cruel-natured snake did straight upon them fly
And, licking on his ruffled hair the which was dropping dry,
Did gape to tire upon those lips that had been wont to sing
Most heavenly hymns. But Phoebus, straight preventing that same
     thing,
Dispoints the serpent of his bit and turns him into stone
With gaping chaps. Already was the ghost of Orphey gone
To Pluto's realm; and there he all the places eft beheld
The which he heretofore had seen. And as he sought the field
Of fair Elysion where the souls of goodly folk do wone,
He found his wife Eurydice, to whom he straight did run                      70
And held her in embracing arms. There now he one while walks
Together with her cheek by cheek; another while he stalks
Before her; and another while he followeth her. And now
Without all kind of forfeiture he safely might avow
His looking backward at his wife. But Bacchus, grievèd at
The murder of the chaplain of his orgies, suffered not
The mischief unrevenged to be. For by and by he bound
The Thracian women by the feet with writhen root in ground,
As many as consenting to this wicked act were found.
And look how much that each of them the prophet did pursue,                  80
So much he, sharpening of their toes, within the ground them
     drew.
And as the bird, that finds her leg besnarlèd in the net
(The which the fowler subtlely hath closely for her set)
And feels she cannot get away, stands flickering with her wings
And with her fearful leaping up draws closer still the strings;
So each of these, when in the ground they fastened were, assayed,
Aflighted sore, to fly away. But every one was stayed
With winding root which held her down. Her frisking could not
     boot.
And while she looked what was become of toe, of nail and foot,

90 She saw her legs grow round in one and turning into wood.
And as her thighs with violent hand she sadly striking stood,
She felt them tree; her breast was tree; her shoulders eke were
tree.
Her arms long boughs ye might have thought and not deceivèd
be.

*Midas'*
*golden touch*

But Bacchus was not so content. He quite forsook their land
And with a better company removèd out of hand
Unto the vineyard of his own Mount Tmolus and the river
Pactolus, though as yet no streams of gold it did deliver
Ne spited was for precious sands. His old accustomed rout
Of woodwards and of frantic frows environed him about.

100 But old Silenus was away. The Phrygian ploughmen found
Him reeling both for drunkenness and age and brought him
bound
With garlands unto Midas, king of Phrygia, unto whom
The Thracian Orphey and the priest Eumolphus, coming from
The town of Athens, erst had taught the orgies. When he knew
His fellow and companion of the selfsame badge and crew,
Upon the coming of this guest he kept a feast the space
Of twice five days and twice five nights together in that place.
And now th'eleventh time Lucifer had mustered in the sky
The heavenly host, when Midas comes to Lydia jocundly

110 And yields the old Silenus to his foster-child. He, glad
That he his foster-father had eftsoons recovered, bade
King Midas ask him what he would. Right glad of that was he,
But not a whit at latter end the better should he be.
He, minding to misuse his gifts, said, 'Grant that all and some
The which my body toucheth bare may yellow gold become.'
God Bacchus, granting his request, his hurtful gift performed,
And that he had not better wished he in his stomach stormed.
Rejoicing in his harm, away full merry goes the king
And for to try his promise true he toucheth everything.

120 Scarce giving credit to himself, he pullèd young green twigs
From off an holm-tree; by and by all golden were the sprigs.
He took a flintstone from the ground; the stone likewise became
Pure gold. He touchèd next a clod of earth; and straight the same

By force of touching did become a wedge of yellow gold.
He gathered ears of ripened corn; immediately, behold,
The corn was gold. An apple then he pullèd from a tree;
Ye would have thought the Hesperids had given it him. If he
On pillars high his fingers laid, they glistered like the sun.
The water where he washed his hands did from his hands so run
As Danae might have been therewith beguiled. He scarce could
        hold                                                    130
His passing joys within his heart for making all things gold.
While he thus joyed, his officers did spread the board anon
And set down sundry sorts of meat and manchet thereupon.
Then whether his hand did touch the bread, the bread was massy
        gold;
Or whether he chewed with hungry teeth his meat, ye might
        behold
The piece of meat between his jaws a plate of gold to be.
In drinking wine and water mixed, ye might discern and see
The liquid gold run down his throat. Amazèd at the strange
Mischance and being both a wretch and rich, he wished to change
His riches for his former state. And now he did abhor           140
The thing which even but late before he chiefly longèd for.
No meat his hunger slakes; his throat is shrunken up with thirst;
And justly doth his hateful gold torment him as accurst.
Then, lifting up his sorry arms and hands to heaven, he cried,
'O father Bacchus, pardon me. My sin I will not hide.
Have mercy, I beseech thee, and vouchsafe to rid me quite
From this same harm that seems so good and glorious unto sight.'
The gentle Bacchus straight upon confession of his crime
Restorèd Midas to the state he had in former time
And, having made performance of his promise, he bereft him      150
The gift that he had granted him. And lest he should have left him
Bedaubèd with the dregs of that same gold which wickedly
He wishèd had, he willèd him to get him by and by
To that great river which doth run by Sardis town, and there
Along the channel up the stream his open arms to bear
Until he cometh to the spring, and then his head to put
Full underneath the foaming spout where greatest was the gut,

And so in washing of his limbs to wash away his crime.
The king, as was commanded him, against the stream did climb.
160 And straight the power of making gold, departing quite from him,
Infects the river, making it with golden stream to swim.
The force whereof the banks about so soakèd in their veins
That even as yet the yellow gold upon the clods remains.

*The*
*judgement*
*of Midas*

  Then Midas, hating riches, haunts the pasture grounds and
   groves
  And up and down with Pan among the lawns and mountains
   roves.
But still a head more fat than wise and doltish wit he hath,
The which, as erst, yet once again must work their master scathe.
The mountain Tmole from lofty top to seaward looketh down
And, spreading far his burly sides, extendeth to the town
170 Of Sardis with the t'one side and to Hypaep with the t'other.
There Pan among the fairy elves that dancèd round together,
In setting of his cunning out for singing and for play
Upon his pipe of reeds and wax, presuming for to say
Apollo's music was not like to his, did take in hand
A far unequal match whereof the Tmole for judge should stand.
The ancient judge sits down upon his hill and rids his ears
From trees and only on his head an oaken garland wears,
Whereof the acorns dangled down about his hollow brow.
And looking on the god of neat, he said, 'Ye need not now
180 To tarry longer for your judge.' Then Pan blew loud and strong
His country pipe of reeds and with his rude and homely song
Delighted Midas' ears (for he by chance was in the throng).
When Pan had done, the sacred Tmole to Phoebus turned his
   look,
And with the turning of his head his bushy hair he shook.
Then Phoebus with a crown of bay upon his golden hair
Did sweep the ground with scarlet robe. In left hand he did bear
His viol made of precious stones and ivory intermixed,
And in his right hand for to strike his bow was ready fixed.
He was the very pattern of a good musician right.
190 Anon he gan with cunning hand the tunèd strings to smite,
The sweetness of the which did so the judge of them delight

That Pan was willèd for to put his reedpipe in his case
And not to fiddle nor to sing where viols were in place.
   The judgement of the holy hill was likèd well of all
   Save Midas, who found fault therewith and wrongful did it call.
Apollo could not suffer well his foolish ears to keep
Their human shape, but drew them wide and made them long and
      deep
And filled them full of whitish hairs and made them down to sag
And through too much unstableness continually to wag.
His body, keeping in the rest his manly figure still,                   200
Was punished in the part that did offend for want of skill.
And so a slow-paced ass's ears his head did after bear.
This shame endeavoureth he to hide; and therefore he did wear
A purple nightcap ever since. But yet his barber who
Was wont to not him spièd it and, being eager to
Disclose it, when he neither durst to utter it nor could
It keep in secret still, he went and diggèd up the mould
And, whispering softly in the pit, declared what ears he spied
His master have and, turning down the clowre again, did hide
His blabbèd words within the ground and, closing up the pit,         210
Departed thence and never made mo words at all of it.
Soon after there began a tuft of quivering reeds to grow
Which, being ripe, bewrayed their seed and him that did them
      sow.
For when the gentle southern wind did lightly on them blow,
They uttered forth the words that had been buried in the ground
And so reproved the ass's ears of Midas with their sound.
   Apollo after this revenge from Tmolus took his flight         *The*
   And, sweeping through the air, did on the selfsame side alight    *ingratitude*
Of Hellespontus in the realm of King Laomedon.                   *of Troy*
There stood upon the right side of Sigaeum and upon                  220
The left of Rhoetey cliff that time an altar built of old
To Jove, that heareth all men's words. Here Phoebus did behold
The foresaid King Laomedon beginning for to lay
Foundation of the walls of Troy; which work from day to day
Went hard and slowly forward and required no little charge.
Then he together with the god that rules the surges large

Did put themselves in shape of men and bargained with the king
Of Phrygia for a sum of gold his work to end to bring.
Now when the work was done, the king their wages them denied
230 And falsely faced them down with oaths it was not as they said.
'Thou shalt not mock us unrevenged,' quoth Neptune. And anon
He causèd all the surges of the sea to rush upon
The shore of covetous Troy and made the country like the deep.
The goods of all the husbandmen away he quite did sweep
And overwhelmed their fields with waves. And, thinking this too
          small
A penance for the falsehood, he demanded therewithal
His daughter for a monster of the sea. Whom, being bound
Unto a rock, stout Hercules delivering safe and sound,
Required his steeds which were the hire for which he did
          compound.
240 And when that of so great desert the king denied the hire,
The twice-forsworn false town of Troy he sackèd in his ire.
And Telamon in honour of his service did enjoy
The lady Hesione, daughter of the covetous king of Troy.
For Peleus had already got a goddess to his wife
And livèd unto both their joys a right renownèd life.
And sure he was not prouder of his grandsire than of thee
That wert become his father-in-law. For many mo than he
Have had the hap of mighty Jove the nephews for to be;
But never was it heretofore the chance of any one
250 To have a goddess to his wife, save only his alone.
For unto watery Thetis thus old Proteu did foretell:
'Go, marry; thou shalt bear a son whose doings shall excel
His father's far in feats of arms, and greater he shall be
In honour, high renown and fame than ever erst was he.'
This causèd Jove the watery bed of Thetis to forbear,
Although his heart were more than warm with love of her, for
          fear
The world some other greater thing than Jove himself should
          breed,
And willed the son of Aeacus, this Peleus, to succeed
In that which he himself would fain have done, and for to take
260 The lady of the sea in arms a mother her to make.

There is a bay of Thessaly that bendeth like a bow;                    *Peleus and*
   The sides shoot forth where, if the sea of any depth did flow,    *Thetis*
It were a haven. Scarcely doth the water hide the sand.
It hath a shore so firm that if a man thereon do stand
No print of foot remains behind; it hindereth not one's pace
Ne covered is with hovering reek. Adjoining to this place
There is a grove of myrtle-trees with fruit of dual colour
And in the midst thereof a cave. I cannot tell you whether
That nature or the art of man were maker of the same.
It seemèd rather made by art. Oft Thetis hither came                   270
Stark naked, riding bravely on a bridled dolphin's back;
There Peleus as she lay asleep upon her often brake.
And for because that at her hands entreatance nothing wins,
He, folding her about the neck with both his arms, begins
To offer force. And, surely, if she had not fallen to wiles
And shifted oftentimes her shape, he had obtained erewhiles.
But she became sometimes a bird; he held her like a bird.
Anon she was a massy log; but Peleus never stirred
A whit for that. Then thirdly she of speckled tiger took
The ugly shape; for fear of whose most fierce and cruel look           280
His arms he from her body twitched. And at his going thence
In honour of the watery gods he burnèd frankincense
And pourèd wine upon the sea with fat of neat and sheep,
Until the prophet that doth dwell within Carpathian deep
Said thus: 'Thou son of Aeacus, thy wish thou sure shalt have.
Alonely when she lies asleep within her pleasant cave
Cast grins to trap her unbewares; hold fast with snarling knot.
And though she feign a hundred shapes, deceive thee let her
    not,
But stick unto't, whate'er it be, until the time that she
Returneth to the native shape she erst was wont to be.'               290
When Proteu thus had said, within the sea he ducked his head
And suffered on his latter words the water for to spread.
The lightsome Titan downward drew and with declining chair
Approachèd to the western sea, when Nerey's daughter fair,
Returning from the sea, resorts to her accustomed couch.
And Peleus scarcely had begun her naked limbs to touch

But that she changed from shape to shape, until at length she
      found
Herself surprised. Then, stretching out her arms with sighs
      profound,
She said, 'Thou overcomest me, and not without the aid
Of God.' And then she Thetis-like appeared in shape of maid.
The noble prince, embracing her, obtained her at his will
To both their joys and with the great Achilles did her fill.
   A happy wight was Peleus in his wife; a happy wight
   Was Peleus also in his son. And if ye him acquit
Of murdering Phocus, happy him in all things count ye might.
But guilty of his brother's blood and banished for the same
From both his father's house and realm, to Trachin sad he came.
The son of lightsome Lucifer, King Ceyx, who in face
Expressed the lively beauty of his father's heavenly grace,
Without all violent rigour and sharp executions reigned
In Trachin. He right sad that time, unlike himself, remained
Yet mourning for his brother's chance, transformèd late before.
When Peleus thither came, with care and travail tirèd sore,
He left his cattle and his sheep (whereof he brought great store)
Behind him in a shady vale not far from Trachin town
And with a little company himself went thither down.
As soon as leave to come to court was granted him, he bare
A branch of olive in his hand and humbly did declare
His name and lineage. Only of his crime no word he spake
But of his flight another cause pretensedly did make,
Desiring leave within his town or country to abide.
The king of Trachin gently thus to him again replied:
'Our bounty to the meanest sort, O Peleus, doth extend;
We are not wont the desolate our country to forfend.
And though I be of nature most inclinèd good to do,
Thine own renown, thy grandsire Jove are forcements thereunto.
Misspend no longer time in suit. I gladly do agree
To grant thee what thou wilt desire. These things that thou dost
      see,
I would thou should account them as thine own, such as they be;
I would they better were.' With that he weepèd. Peleus and
His friends desirèd of his grief the cause to understand.

He answered thus: 'Perchance ye think this bird that lives by
    prey
And puts all other birds in fear had wings and feathers aye.
He was a man. And as he was right fierce in feats of arms
And stout and ready both to wreak and also offer harms,
So was he of a constant mind. Daedalion men him hight.
Our father was that noble star that brings the morning bright
And in the welkin last of all gives place to Phoebus' light.
My study was to maintain peace; in peace was my delight,
And for to keep me true to her to whom my faith is plight.     340
My brother had felicity in war and bloody fight.
His prowess and his force, which now doth chase in cruel flight
The doves of Thisbe since his shape was altered thus anew,
Right puissant princes and their realms did heretofore subdue.
He had a child called Chione, whom nature did endue
With beauty so that, when to age of fourteen years she grew,
A thousand princes, liking her, did for her favour sue.
By fortune as bright Phoebus and the son of Lady May
Came t'one from Delphos, t'other from Mount Cyllen, by the
    way
They saw her both at once and both at once were ta'en in love.     350
Apollo till the time of night deferred his suit to move;
But Hermes could not bear delay. He strokèd on the face
The maiden with his charmèd rod which hath the power to chase
And bring in sleep; the touch whereof did cast her in so dead
A sleep that Hermes by and by his purpose of her sped.
As soon as night with twinkling stars the welkin had besprent,
Apollo in an old wife's shape to Chion closely went
And took the pleasure which the son of Maia had forehent.
Now when she full her time had gone, she bare by Mercury
A son that hight Autolychus, who proved a wily pie     360
And such a fellow as in theft and filching had no peer.
He was his father's own son right; he could men's eyes so blear
As for to make the black things white and white things black
    appear.
And by Apollo (for she bare a pair) was born his brother
Philammon, who in music art excellèd far all other

*The
transformation
of Daedalion*

As well in singing as in play. But what availèd it
To bear such twins and of two gods in favour to have sit
And that she to her father had a stout and valiant knight
Or that her grandsire was the son of Jove, that god of might?
370 Doth glory hurt to any folk? It surely hurted her.
For, standing in her own conceit, she did herself prefer
.Before Diana and dispraised her face; who, therewithal
Inflamed with wrath, said, "Well, with deeds we better please her
        shall."
Immediately she bent her bow and let an arrow go
Which strake her through the tongue, whose spite deservèd
        wounding so.
Her tongue waxed dumb; her speech gan fail that erst was
        overrife;
And as she strivèd for to speak, away went blood and life.
How wretched was I then, O God! How strake it to my heart!
What words of comfort did I speak to ease my brother's smart!
380 To which he gave his ear as much as doth the stony rock
To hideous roaring of the waves that do against it knock.
There was no measure nor none end in making of his moan,
Nor in bewailing comfortless his daughter that was gone.
But when he saw her body burn, four times with all his might
He rushèd forth to thrust himself amid the fire in sight.
Four times he, being thence repulsed, did put himself to flight
And ran me whereas was no way, as doth a bullock when
A hornet stings him in the neck. Methought he was as then
More wighter far than any man. Ye would have thought his feet
390 Had had some wings. So fled he quite from all and, being fleet
Through eagerness to die, he gat to Mount Parnassus' knap.
And there Apollo, pitying him and ruing his mishap,
Whenas Daedalion from the cliff himself had headlong flung,
Transformed him to a bird and on the sudden as he hung
Did give him wings and bowing beak and hookèd talons keen
And eke a courage full as fierce as ever it had been.
And, furthermore, a greater strength he lent him therewithal
Than one would think conveyed might be within a room so
        small.

And now in shape of goshawk he to none indifferent is,
But wreaks his teen on all birds. And because himself ere this          400
Did feel the force of sorrow's sting within his wounded heart,
He maketh others oftentimes to sorrow and to smart.'

    As Ceyx of his brother's chance this wondrous story saith,          *The slaughter*
     Comes running thither all in haste and almost out of breath          *of Peleus'*
Anetor the Phocian, who was Peley's herdman. He          *cattle*
Said, 'Peley, Peley, I do bring sad tidings unto thee.'
'Declare it, man,' quoth Peleus, 'whatever that it be.'
King Ceyx at his fearful words did stand in doubtful stound.
'Thiz noontide,' quoth the herdman, 'ich did drive your cattle
    down
To zea, and zome o' them did zit upon the yellow zand          410
And lookèd on the large main pool of water near at hand.
Zome roilèd zoftly up and down, and zome o' them did zwim
And bare their jolly hornèd heads above the water trim.
A church stands near the zea, not decked with gold nor marble
    stone
But made of wood and hid with trees that dreeping hang thereon.
A visherman that zat and dried hiz nets upo' the zhore
Did tell'z that Nereus and his nymphs did haunt the place of yore
And how that they been gods o' zea. There butts a plot vorgrown
With zallow trees upon the zame, the which is overblown
With tides and is a marsh. Vrom thence a wolf, an orpèd wight,          420
With hideous noise of rustling made the grounds near hand
    affright.
Anon he comes me buskling out, bezmearèd all his chaps
With blood daubaken and with voam as vierce as thunder claps.
Hiz eyen did glaster red as vire, and though he ragèd zore
Vor vamine and vor madness both, yet ragèd he much more
In madness. Vor he carèd not his hunger vor to zlake
Or i' the death of oxen two or three an end to make,
But wounded all the herd and made a havoc of them all;
And zome of us, too, in devence did happen vor to vall
In danger of his deadly chaps and lost our lives. The zhore          430
And zea is stained with blood and all the ven is on a roar.
Delay breeds loss. The case denies now doubting for to stand.
While owt remains, let all of us take weapon in our hand.

Let's arm ourzelves and let uz altogether on him vall.'
   The herdman held his peace. The loss moved Peleus not at all.
   But calling his offence to mind, he thought that Nerey's
      daughter,
The childless Lady Psamathe, determined with that slaughter
To keep an obit to her son whom he before had killed.
Immediately upon this news the king of Trachin willed

440  His men to arm them and to take their weapons in their hand,
And he addressed himself to be the leader of the band.
His wife Alcyone, by the noise admonished of the same
In dressing of her head, before she had it brought in frame
Cast down her hair and, running forth, caught Ceyx fast about
The neck, desiring him with tears to send his folk without
Himself and in the life of him to save the lives of twain.
'O princess, cease your godly fear,' quoth Peleus then again.
'Your offer doth deserve great thanks. I mind not war to make
Against strange monsters. I as now another way must take.

450  The seagods must be pacified.' There was a castle high
And in the same a lofty tower whose top doth face the sky,
A joyful mark for mariners to guide their vessels by.
To this same turret up they went and there with sighs beheld
The oxen lying everywhere stark dead upon the field
And eke the cruel stroy-good with his bloody mouth and hair.
Then Peleus, stretching forth his hands to seaward, prayed in fear
To waterish Psamath that she would her sore displeasure stay
And help him. She no whit relents to that that he did pray.
But Thetis for her husband made such earnest suit that she

460  Obtained his pardon. For anon the wolf (who would not be
Revokèd from the slaughter for the sweetness of the blood)
Persisted sharp and eager still until that, as he stood
Fast biting on a bullock's neck, she turned him into stone
As well in substance as in hue, the name of wolf alone
Reservèd. For although in shape he seemèd still yet one,
The very colour of the stone bewrayed him to be none
And that he was not to be feared. Howbeit, froward fate
Permits not Peleus in that land to have a settled state.
He wandereth like an outlaw to the Magnetes. There at last

470  Acastus the Thessalian purged him of his murder past.

In this meantime the Trachine king, sore vexèd in his thought
  With signs that both before and since his brother's death were
    wrought,
For counsel at the sacred spells (which are but toys to food
Fond fancies and not councillors in peril to do good)
Did make him ready to the god of Claros for to go.
For heathenish Phorbas and the folk of Phlegia had as tho
The way to Delphos stopped, that none could travel to or fro.
But ere he on his journey went, he made his faithful make
Alcyone privy to the thing. Immediately there strake
A chillness to her very bones, and pale was all her face    480
Like box, and down her heavy cheeks the tears did gush apace.
Three times about to speak, three times she washed her face with
    tears.
And, stinting oft, with sobs she thus complainèd in his ears:
  'What fault of mine, O husband dear, hath turned thy heart fro
    me?
  Where is that care of me that erst was wont to be in thee?
And canst thou, having left thy dear Alcyone, merry be?
Do journeys long delight thee now? Doth now mine absence
    please
Thee better than my presence doth? Think I that thou at ease
Shalt go by land? Shall I have cause but only for to mourn
And not to be afraid? And shall my care of thy return    490
Be void of fear? No, no! The sea me sore afraid doth make.
To think upon the sea doth cause my flesh for fear to quake.
I saw the broken ribs of ships alate upon the shore;
And oft on tombs I read their names whose bodies long before
The sea had swallowed. Let not fond vain hope seduce thy mind
That Aeolus is thy father-in-law, who holds the boisterous wind
In prison and can calm the seas at pleasure. When the winds
Are once let loose upon the sea, no order then them binds.
Then neither land hath privilege, nor sea exemption finds.
Yea, even the clouds of heaven they vex and with their meeting
    stout    500
Enforce the fire with hideous noise to brust in flashes out.
The more that I do know them (for right well I know their power
And saw them oft, a little wench within my father's bower),

So much the more I think them to be feared. But if thy will
By no entreatance may be turned at home to tarry still
But that thou needs wilt go, then me, dear husband, with thee
    take.
So shall the sea us equally together toss and shake.
So worser than I feel I shall be certain not to fear.
So shall we whatsoever haps together jointly bear.
510    So shall we on the broad main sea together jointly sail.'
    These words and tears wherewith the imp of Aeolus did assail
    Her husband born of heavenly race did make his heart relent.
For he loved her no less than she loved him. But fully bent
He seemèd neither for to leave the journey which he meant
To take by sea nor yet to give Alcyone leave as tho
Companion of his perilous course by water for to go.
He many words of comfort spake her fear away to chase,
But nought he could persuade therein to make her like the case.
This last assuagement of her grief he added in the end,
520    Which was the only thing that made her loving heart to bend:
'All tarriance will assuredly seem overlong to me.
And by my father's blazing beams, I make my vow to thee
That at the furthest ere the time (if God thereto agree)
The moon do fill her circle twice again I will here be.'
When in some hope of his return this promise had her set,
He willed a ship immediately from harbour to be fet
And throughly riggèd for to be, that neither mast nor sail
Nor tackling, no, nor other thing should appertaining fail.
Which when Alcyone did behold, as one whose heart misgave
530    The haps at hand, she quaked again and tears out gushing drave.
And, straining Ceyx in her arms with pale and piteous look,
Poor wretched soul, her last farewell at length she sadly took
And swounded flat upon the ground. Anon the watermen
(As Ceyx sought delays and was in doubt to turn again)
Set hand to oars, of which there were two rows on either side,
And all at once with equal stroke the swelling sea divide.
She, lifting up her watery eyes, beheld her husband stand
Upon the hatches, making signs by beckoning with his hand;
And she made signs to him again. And after that the land

Was far removèd from the ship and that the sight began                              540
To be unable to discern the face of any man,
As long as e'er she could, she looked upon the rowing keel.
And when she could no longer time for distance ken it well,
She lookèd still upon the sails that flaskèd with the wind
Upon the mast. And when she could the sails no longer find,
She gat her to her empty bed with sad and sorry heart
And laid her down. The chamber did renew afresh her smart
And of her bed did bring to mind the dear departed part.
　　From harbour now they quite were gone; and now a pleasant
　　　　gale
　　Did blow. The master made his men their oars aside to hale       550
And hoisèd up the topsail on the highest of the mast
And clapped on all his other sails, because no wind should waste.
Scarce full t'one half (or, sure, not much above) the ship had run
Upon the sea and every way the land did far them shun,
When toward night the wallowing waves began to waxen white
And eke the heady eastern wind did blow with greater might.
Anon the master crièd, 'Strike the topsail! Let the main
Sheet fly and fardel it to the yard!' Thus spake he, but in vain.
For why, so hideous was the storm upon the sudden braid
That not a man was able there to hear what other said,                            560
And loud the sea with meeting waves extremely raging roars.
Yet fell they to it of themselves. Some haled aside the oars;
Some fencèd in the galley's sides; some down the sailcloths rend;
Some pump the water out and sea to sea again do send;
Another hales the sailyards down. And while they did each thing
Disorderly, the storm increased and from each quarter fling
The winds with deadly feud and bounce the raging waves
　　　　together.
The pilot, being sore dismayed, saith plain, he knows not whither
To wend himself nor what to do or bid, nor in what state
Things stood; so huge the mischief was and did so overmate       570
All art. For why of rattling ropes, of crying men and boys,
Of flushing waves and thundering air confusèd was the noise.
The surges, mounting up aloft, did seem to mate the sky
And with their sprinkling for to wet the clouds that hang on high.

One while the sea, when from the brink it raised the yellow sand,
Was like in colour to the same. Another while did stand
A colour on it blacker than the lake of Styx. Anon
It lieth plain and loometh white with seething froth thereon.
And with the sea the Trachine ship aye alteration took:
580 One while as from a mountain's top it seemèd down to look
To valleys and the depth of hell; another while, beset
With swelling surges round about which near above it met,
It lookèd from the bottom of the whirlpool up aloft
As if it were from hell to heaven. A hideous flushing oft
The waves did make in beating full against the galley's side.
The galley, being stricken, gave as great a sound that tide
As did sometime the battleram of steel or now the gun
In making battery to a tower. And as fierce lions run
Full breast with all their force against the armèd men that stand
590 In order bent to keep them off with weapons in their hand,
Even so, as often as the waves by force of wind did rave,
So oft upon the netting of the ship they mainly drave
And mounted far above the same. Anon off fell the hoops;
And having washed the pitch away, the sea made open loops
To let the deadly water in. Behold, the clouds did melt
And showers large came pouring down. The seamen that them
    felt
Might think that all the heaven had fallen upon them that same
    time
And that the swelling sea likewise above the heaven would climb.
The sails were throughly wet with showers, and with the heavenly
    rain
600 Was mixed the waters of the sea. No lights at all remain
Of sun or moon or stars in heaven; the darkness of the night,
Augmented with the dreadful storm, takes double power and
    might.
Howbeit, the flashing lightnings oft do put the same to flight
And with their glancing now and then do give a sudden light.
The lightning sets the waves on fire. Above the netting skip
The waves and with a violent force do light within the ship.
And as a soldier stouter than the rest of all his band
That oft assails a city walls defended well by hand

At length attains his hope and, for to purchase praise withal,
Alone among a thousand men gets up upon the wall;                    610
So, when the lofty waves had long the galley's sides essayed,
At length the tenth wave, rising up with huger force and braid,
Did never cease assaulting of the weary ship till that
Upon the hatches like a foe victoriously it gat.
A part thereof did still as yet assault the ship without,
And part had gotten in. The men, all trembling, ran about
As in a city comes to pass when of the enemies some
Dig down the walls without and some already in are come.
All art and cunning was to seek; their hearts and stomachs fail.
And look how many surges came their vessel to assail,               620
So many deaths did seem to charge and break upon them all.
One weeps; another stands amazed; the third them blest doth call
Whom burial doth remain. To God another makes his vow
And, holding up his hands to heaven, the which he sees not now,
Doth pray in vain for help. The thought of this man is upon
His brother and his parents whom he clearly hath forgone;
Another calls his house and wife and children unto mind;
And every man in general the things he left behind.
Alcyone moveth Ceyx' heart; in Ceyx' mouth is none
But only one Alcyone. And though she were alone                     630
The wight that he desirèd most, yet was he very glad
She was not there. To Trachinward to look desire he had,
And homeward fain he would have turned his eyes which never
            more
Should see the land. But when he knew not which way was the
            shore
Nor where he was, the raging sea did roll about so fast
And all the heaven with clouds as black as pitch was overcast
That never night was half so dark, there came a flaw at last
That with his violence brake the mast and strake the stern away.
A billow, proudly pranking up as vaunting of his prey
By conquest gotten, walloweth whole and breaketh not asunder,       640
Beholding with a lofty look the waters working under.
And look, as if a man should from the places where they grow
Rend down the mountains Athe and Pind and whole them
            overthrow

Into the open sea, so soft the billow, tumbling down,
With weight and violent stroke did sink and in the bottom drown
The galley. And the most of them that were within the same
Went down therewith and never up to open air came
But dièd strangled in the gulf. Another sort again
Caught pieces of the broken ship. The king himself was fain
650   A shiver of the sunken ship in that same hand to hold
In which he erst a royal mace had held of yellow gold.
His father and his father-in-law he calls upon – alas,
In vain. But chiefly in his mouth his wife Alcyone was.
In heart was she; in tongue was she. He wishèd that his corse
To land where she might take it up the surges might enforce
And that by her most loving hands he might be laid in grave.
In swimming still, as often as the surges leave him gave
To ope his lips, he harpèd still upon Alcyone's name;
And when he drownèd in the waves he muttered still the same.
660   Behold, even full upon the wave a flake of water black
Did break and underneath the sea the head of Ceyx strake.
That night the lightsome Lucifer for sorrow was so dim
As scarcely could a man discern or think it to be him.
And for as much as out of heaven he might not step aside,
With thick and darksome clouds that night his count'nance he did
        hide.
    Alcyone, of so great mischance not knowing aught as yet,
    Did keep a reckoning of the nights that in the while did flit
And hasted garments both for him and for herself likewise
To wear at his homecoming, which she vainly did surmise.
670   To all the gods devoutly she did offer frankincense,
But most above them all the church of Juno she did cense.
And for her husband (who as then was none) she kneeled before
The altar, wishing health and soon arrival at the shore
And that none other woman might before her be preferred.
Of all her prayers this one piece effectually was heard.
For Juno could not find in heart entreated for to be
For him that was already dead. But to th'intent that she
From Dame Alcyone's deadly hands might keep her altars free,
She said, 'Most faithful messenger of my commandments, O
680   Thou rainbow, to the sluggish house of Slumber swiftly go

And bid him send a dream in shape of Ceyx to his wife
Alcyone for to show her plain the losing of his life.'
Dame Iris takes her pall wherein a thousand colours were
And, bowing like a stringèd bow upon the cloudy sphere,
Immediately descended to the drowsy house of Sleep
Whose court the clouds continually do closely overdreep.
   Among the dark Cimmerians is a hollow mountain\* found
   And in the hill a cave that far doth run within the ground,
The chamber and the dwelling place where slothful Sleep doth
    couch.
The light of Phoebus' golden beams this place can never touch.    690
A foggy mist with dimness mixed streams upward from the
    ground,
And glimmering twilight evermore within the same is found.
No watchful bird with barbèd bill and combèd crown doth call
The morning forth with crowing out. There is no noise at all
Of waking dog nor gaggling goose, more waker than the
    hound,
To hinder sleep. Of beast ne wild ne tame there is no sound.
No boughs are stirred with blasts of wind. No noise of tattling
    tongue
Of man or woman ever yet within that bower rung.
Dumb quiet dwelleth there. Yet from the roche's foot doth go
The River of Forgetfulness, which runneth trickling so    700
Upon the little pebble stones which in the channel lie
That unto sleep a great deal more it doth provoke thereby.
Before the entry of the cave there grows a poppy store
With seeded heads and other weeds innumerable more,
Out of the milky juice of which the night doth gather sleeps
And over all the shadowed earth with dankish dew them dreeps.
Because the craking hinges of the door no noise should make,
There is no door in all the house nor porter at the gate.
Amid the cave, of ebony a bedstead standeth high
And on the same a bed of down with coverings black doth lie    710
In which the drowsy god of sleep his lither limbs doth rest.
About him, forging sundry shapes, as many dreams lie pressed

\*The house of Sleep

As ears of corn do stand in fields in harvest time or leaves
Do grow on trees or sea to shore of sandy cinder heaves.
As soon as Iris came within this house and with her hand
Had put aside the dazzling dreams that in her way did stand,
The brightness of her robe through all the sacred house did shine.
The god of sleep, scarce able for to raise his heavy eyen,
A three or four times at the least did fall again to rest
720   And with his nodding head did knock his chin against his breast.
At length he, shaking of himself, upon his elbow leaned.
And, though he knew for what she came, he asked her what she
        meant.
'O Sleep', quoth she, 'the rest of things, O gentlest of the gods,
Sweet Sleep, the peace of mind with whom crook'd care is aye at
        odds,
Which cherishest men's weary limbs appalled with toiling sore
And makest them as fresh to work and lusty as before,
Command a dream (that in their kinds can everything express)
To Trachin, Herc'les' town, himself this instant to address;
And let him lively counterfeit to Queen Alcyona
730   The image of her husband who is drownèd in the sea
By shipwreck. Juno willeth so.' Her message being told,
Dame Iris went her way. She could her eyes no longer hold
From sleep. But when she felt it come, she fled that instant time
And by the bow that brought her down to heaven again did
        climb.
    Among a thousand sons and mo that father Slumber had
    He called up Morph, the feigner of man's shape, a crafty lad.
None other could so cunningly express man's very face,
His gesture and his sound of voice and manner of his pace
Together with his wonted weed and wonted phrase of talk.
740   But this same Morphey only in the shape of man doth walk.
There is another who the shapes of beast or bird doth take
Or else appeareth unto men in likeness of a snake.
The gods do call him Icelos, and mortal folk him name
Phobetor. There is also yet a third who from these same
Works diversely, and Phantasos he highteth; into streams
This turns himself and into stones and earth and timber beams

And into every other thing that wanteth life. These three
Great kings and captains in the night are wonted for to see.
The meaner and inferior sort of others haunted be.
Sir Slumber overpassed the rest, and of the brothers all                    750
To do Dame Iris' message he did only Morphey call.
Which done, he, waxing luskish, straight laid down his drowsy
          head
And softly shrunk his lazy limbs within his sluggish bed.
    Away flew Morphey through the air – no flickering made his
          wings –
    And came anon to Trachin. There his feathers off he flings
And in the shape of Ceyx stands before Alcyone's bed,
Pale, wan, stark nak'd and like a man that was but lately dead.
His beard seemed wet, and of his head the hair was dropping dry.
And, leaning on her bed, with tears he seemèd thus to cry:
'Most wretched woman, knowest thou thy loving Ceyx now,                     760
Or is my face by death deformed? Behold me well, and thou
Shalt know me. For thy husband, thou thy husband's ghost shalt
          see.
No good thy prayers and thy vows have done at all to me.
For I am dead. In vain of my return no reckoning make.
The cloudy south amid the sea our ship did tardy take
And, tossing it with violent blasts, asunder did it shake.
And floods have filled my mouth which called in vain upon thy
          name.
No person whom thou may'st misdeem brings tidings of the same;
Thou hearest not thereof by false report of flying fame,
But I myself, I presently my shipwreck to thee show.                        770
Arise, therefore, and woeful tears upon thy spouse bestow.
Put mourning raiment on and let me not to Limbo go
Unmournèd for.' In showing of this shipwreck, Morphey so
Did feign the voice of Ceyx that she could none other deem
But that it should be his indeed. Moreover he did seem
To weep in earnest, and his hands the very gesture had
Of Ceyx. Queen Alcyone did groan and, being sad,
Did stir her arms and thrust them forth his body to embrace,
Instead whereof she caught but air. The tears ran down her face.

780 She crièd, 'Tarry! Whither fly'st? Together let us go!'
 And all this while she was asleep. Both with her crying so
 And flighted with the image of her husband's ghastly sprite
 She started up and sought about if find him there she might
 (For why her grooms, awaking with the shriek, had brought a
   light).
 And when she nowhere could him find, she gan her face to smite
 And tare her nightclothes from her breast and strake it fiercely
   and,
 Not passing to untie her hair, she rent it with her hand.
 And when her nurse of this her grief desired to understand
 The cause, 'Alcyone is undone, undone and cast away
790 With Ceyx, her dear spouse,' she said. 'Leave comforting, I pray.
 By shipwreck he is perished; I have seen him; and I knew
 His hands. When in departing I to hold him did pursue
 I caught a ghost; but such a ghost as well discern I might
 To be my husband's. Natheless he had not to my sight
 His wonted count'nance, neither did his visage shine so bright
 As heretofore it had been wont. I saw him, wretched wight,
 Stark naked, pale and with his hair still wet; even very here
 I saw him stand.' With that she looks if any print appear
 Of footing whereas he did stand upon the floor behind.
800 'This, this is it that I did fear in far-forecasting mind
 When, flying me, I thee desired thou should'st not trust the wind.
 But sith thou wentest to thy death, I would that I had gone
 With thee; ah, meet, it meet had been thou should'st not go alone
 Without me. So it should have come to pass that neither I
 Had overlivèd thee nor yet been forcèd twice to die.
 Already absent in the waves now tossèd have I be.
 Already have I perishèd. And yet the sea hath thee
 Without me. But the cruelness were greater far of me
 Than of the sea if after thy decease I still would strive
810 In sorrow and in anguish still to pine away alive.
 But neither will I strive in care to lengthen still my life
 Nor, wretched wight, abandon thee, but like a faithful wife
 At leastwise now will come as thy companion. And the hearse
 Shall join us, though not in the selfsame coffin, yet in verse.

Although in tomb the bones of us together may not couch,
Yet in a graven epitaph my name thy name shall touch.'
Her sorrow would not suffer her to utter any more.
She sobbed and sighed at every word until her heart was sore.

   The morning came, and out she went right pensive to the shore
To that same place in which she took her leave of him before.   820
While there she musing stood and said, 'He kissed me even here,
Here weighèd he his anchors up, here loosed he from the pier,'
And while she called to mind the things there markèd with her
     eyes,
In looking on the open sea a great way off she spies
A certain thing much like a corse come hovering on the wave.
At first she doubted what it was. As tide it nearer drave,
Although it were a good way off, yet did it plainly show
To be a corse. And though that whose it was she did not know,
Yet for because it seemed a wreck her heart thereat did rise.
And as it had some stranger been, with water in her eyes   830
She said, 'Alas, poor wretch, whoe'er thou art, alas for her
That is thy wife, if any be.' And as the waves did stir,
The body floated nearer land; the which the more that she
Beheld, the less began in her of staïd wit to be.
Anon it did arrive on shore. Then plainly she did see
And know it, that it was her fere. She shriekèd, 'It is he!'
And therewithal her face, her hair and garments she did tear
And, unto Ceyx stretching out her trembling hands with fear,
Said, 'Com'st thou home in such a plight to me, O husband dear?
Return'st in such a wretched plight?' There was a certain pier   840
That builded was by hand of waves the first assaults to break
And at the haven's mouth to cause the tide to enter weak.
She leaped thereon. (A wonder sure it was she could do so.)
She flew and with her new-grown wings did beat the air as tho;
And on the waves, a wretched bird, she whiskèd to and fro.
And with her croaking neb, then grown to slender bill and round,
Like one that wailed and mournèd still she made a moaning
     sound.
Howbeit, as soon as she did touch his dumb and bloodless flesh
And had embraced his lovèd limbs with wings made new and
     fresh

850 And with her hardened neb had kissed him coldly, though in vain,
Folk doubt if Ceyx, feeling it, to raise his head did strain
Or whether that the waves did lift it up; but surely he
It felt. And through compassion of the gods both he and she
Were turned to birds. The love of them eke subject to their fate
Continued after; neither did the faithful bond abate
Of wedlock in them, being birds, but stands in steadfast state.
They tread and lay and bring forth young, and now the alcyon*
         sits
In wintertime upon her nest (which on the water flits)
A sevennight, during all which time the sea is calm and still
860 And every man may to and fro sail safely at his will.
For Aeolus for his offspring's sake the winds at home doth keep
And will not let them go abroad for troubling of the deep.

*The         An ancient father, seeing them about the broad sea fly,*
*transformation*    Did praise their love for lasting to the end so steadfastly.
*of Aesacus*
His neighbour or the selfsame man made answer (such is chance),
'Even this fowl also whom thou see'st upon the surges glance
With spindle-shanks' – he pointed to the wide-jowled
         cormorant –
'Before that he became a bird of royal race might vaunt.
And if thou covet lineally his pedigree to seek,
870 His ancestors were Ilus and Assaracus, and eke
Fair Ganymede whom Jupiter did ravish as his joy,
Laomedon and Priamus, the last that reigned in Troy.
Stout Hector's brother was this man. And had he not in prime
Of lusty youth been ta'en away, his deeds perchance in time
Had purchased him as great a name as Hector, though that he
Of Dymant's daughter Hecuba had fortune born to be.
For Aesacus reported is begotten to have been
By scape in shady Ida on a maiden fair and sheen
Whose name was Alexothoë, a poor man's daughter that
880 With spade and mattock for himself and his a living gat.
This Aesacus the city hates and gorgeous court doth shun,
And in the unambitious fields and woods alone doth wone.

*The kingfisher.

He seldom haunts the town of Troy. Yet, having not a rude
And blockish wit nor such a heart as could not be subdued
By love, he spied Eperie (whom oft he had pursued
Through all the woods) then sitting on her father Cebrius'
    brim
A-drying of her hair against the sun, which hangèd trim
Upon her back. As soon as that the nymph was ware of him
She fled, as when the grizzled wolf doth scare the fearful hind
Or when the falcon far from brooks a mallard haps to find.    890
The Trojan knight runs after her and, being swift through love,
Pursueth her whom fear doth force apace her feet to move.
Behold, an adder lurking in the grass there as she fled
Did bite her foot with hookèd tooth and in her body spread
His venom. She did cease her flight and sudden fell down dead.
Her lover, being past his wits, her carcass did embrace
And cried, "Alas, it irketh me, it irks me of this chase.
But this I feared not. Neither was the game of that I willed
Worth half so much. Now two of us thee, wretched soul, have
    killed.
The wound was given thee by the snake; the cause was given by
    me.    900
The wickeder of both am I, who, for to comfort thee,
Will make thee satisfaction with my death." With that at last
Down from a rock, the which the waves had undermined, he
    cast
Himself into the sea. Howbeit Dame Tethys, pitying him,
Received him softly; and as he upon the waves did swim,
She covered him with feathers. And though fain he would have
    died,
She would not let him. Wroth was he that death was him denied
And that his soul compelled should be against his will to bide
Within his wretched body still from which it would depart,
And that he was constrained to live perforce against his heart.    910
And as he on his shoulders now had newly taken wings,
He mounted up, and down upon the sea his body dings.
His feathers would not let him sink. In rage he diveth down,
And desperately he strives himself continually to drown.

His love did make him lean; long legs, long neck doth still remain.
His head is from his shoulders far; of sea he is most fain.
And for he underneath the waves delighteth for to drive,
A name according thereunto the Latins do him give.'

### FINIS UNDECIMI LIBRI.

# The Twelfth Book of Ovid's Metamorphoses

King Priam, being ignorant that Aesacus, his son,
Did live in shape of bird, did mourn; and at a tomb whereon
His name was written Hector and his brother solemnly
Did keep an obit. Paris was not at this obsequy.
Within a while with ravished wife he brought a lasting war
Home unto Troy. There followed him a thousand ships not far
Conspired together with the aid that all the Greeks could find.
And vengeance had been ta'en forthwith, but that the cruel wind
Did make the seas unsailable, so that their ships were fain
At road at fishy Aulis in Boeotia to remain.                          10
Here, as the Greeks according to their wont made sacrifice
To Jove and on the altar old the flame aloft did rise,
They spied a speckled snake creep up upon a plane-tree by,
Upon the top whereof there was among the branches high
A nest, and in the nest eight birds; all which and eke their dam
That flickering flew about her loss the hungry snake did cram
Within his maw. The standers by were all amazed thereat.
But Calchas, Thestor's son, who knew what meaning was in that,
Said, 'We shall win. Rejoice, ye Greeks; by us shall perish Troy.
But long the time will be before we may our will enjoy.'              20
And then he told them how the birds nine years did signify
Which they before the town of Troy, not taking it, should lie.
The serpent, as he wound about the boughs and branches green,
Became a stone; and still in stone his snakish shape is seen.

    The seas continued very rough and suffered not their host
      Embarkèd for to pass from thence to take the further coast.
Some thought that Neptune favoured Troy because himself did
      build
The walls thereof. But Calchas (who both knew and never held

His peace in time) declarèd that the goddess Phoebe must
30    Appeasèd be with virgin's blood for wrath conceivèd just.
As soon as pity yielded had to case of public weal
And reason got the upper hand of father's loving zeal,
So that the lady Iphigen before the altar stood
Among the weeping ministers to give her maiden's blood,
The goddess, taking pity, cast a mist before their eyes
And, as they prayed and stirred about to make the sacrifice,
Conveys her quite away and with a hind her room supplies.
Thus with a slaughter meet for her Diana being pleased,
The raging surges with her wrath together were appeased.
40    The thousand ships had wind at poop. And when they had abode
Much trouble, at the length all safe they gat the Phrygian road.

*The house*        Amid the world, 'tween heaven and earth and sea, there is a
*of Rumour*            place
Set from the bounds of each of them indifferently in space,
From whence is seen whatever thing is practised anywhere
Although the realm be ne'er so far, and roundly to the ear
Comes whatsoever spoken is. Fame hath his dwelling there,
Who in the top of all the house is lodgèd in a tower.
A thousand entries, glades and holes are framèd in this bower.
There are no doors to shut; the doors stand open night and day.
50    The house is all of sounding brass and roareth every way,
Reporting double every word it heareth people say.
There is no rest within; there is no silence anywhere.
Yet is there not a yelling out, but humming, as it were
The sound of surges being heard far off or like the sound
That at the end of thunderclaps long after doth redound
When Jove doth make the clouds to crack. Within the courts is
        press
Of common people which to come and go do never cease.
And millions both of truths and lies run gadding everywhere,
And words confusely fly in heaps, of which some fill the ear
60    That heard not of them erst, and some coal-carriers' part do play
To spread abroad the things they heard. And ever by the way
The thing that was invented grows much greater than before,
And everyone that gets it by the end adds somewhat more.

Light Credit dwelleth there; there dwells rash Error; there doth
    dwell
Vain Joy; there dwelleth heartless Fear and Bruit, that loves to tell
Uncertain news upon report whereof he doth not know
The author; and Sedition, who fresh rumours loves to sow.
This Fame beholdeth what is done in heaven, on sea and land,
And what is wrought in all the world he lays to understand.

> He gave the Troyans warning that the Greeks with valiant men
> And ships approachèd, that unwares they could not take them
>     then.

*Cygnet and
Achilles*

For Hector and the Trojan folk well armèd were at hand
To keep the coast and bid them base before they came a-land.
Protesilay by fatal doom was first that died in field
Of Hector's spear; and after him great numbers mo were killed
Of valiant men. That battle did the Greeks full dearly cost.
And Hector with his Phrygian folk of blood no little lost
In trying what the Greeks could do. The shore was red with
    blood.
And now King Cygnet, Neptune's son, had killèd where he stood
A thousand Greeks. And now the stout Achilles caused to stay     80
His chariot, and his lance did slay whole bands of men that day.
And, seeking Cygnet, through the field, or Hector, he did stray.
At last with Cygnet he did meet (for Hector had delay
Until the tenth year afterward). Then, hasting forth his horses
With flaxen manes, against his foe his chariot he enforces
And, brandishing his shaking dart, he said, 'O noble wight,
A comfort let it be to thee that such a valiant knight
As is Achilles killeth thee.' In saying so he threw
A mighty dart which, though it hit the mark at which it flew,
Yet pierced it not the skin at all. Now when this blunted blow     90
Had hit on Cygnet's breast and did no print of hitting show,
'Thou goddess' son', quoth Cygnet, '(for by fame we do thee
    know),
Why wond'rest at me for to see I cannot wounded be?'
(Achilles wondred much thereat.) 'This helmet which ye see
Bedecked with horses' yellow manes, this shield that I do bear,
Defend me not. For ornaments alonely I them wear.

For this same cause arms Mars himself likewise. I will disarm
Myself, and yet unrazèd will I pass without all harm.
It is to some effect not born to be of Nerey's race,
100 So that a man be born of him that with three-forkèd mace
Rules Nereus and his daughters too and all the sea beside.'
This said, he at Achilles sent a dart that should abide
Upon his shield. It piercèd through the steel and through ninefold
Of oxen hides, and stayed upon the tenth. Achilles bold
Did wrest it out and forcibly did throw the same again.
His body, being hit again, unwounded did remain
And clear from any print of wound. The third went eke in vain,
And yet did Cygnet to the same give full his naked breast.
Achilles chafèd like a bull that in the open list
110 With dreadful horns doth push against the scarlet clothes that there
Are hangèd up to make him fierce and, when he would them tear,
Doth find his wounds deluded. Then Achilles looked upon
His javelin's socket, if the head thereof were loose or gone.
The head stack fast. 'My hand, belike, is weakened then', quoth
            he,
'And all the force it had before is spent on one, I see.
For sure I am it was of strength, both when I first down threw
Lyrnessus' walls and when I did Isle Tenedos subdue
And eke Axaetion's Thebe with her proper blood embrew;
And when so many of the folk of Teuthrany I slew
120 That with their blood Caïcus' stream became of purple hue;
And when the noble Telephus did of my dart of steel
The double force of wounding and of healing also feel.
Yea, even the heaps of men slain here by me that on this strand
Are lying still to look upon do give to understand
That this same hand of mine both had and still hath strength.' This
            said
(As though he had distrusted all his doings ere that stead),
He threw a dart against a man of Lycia land that hight
Menoetes, through whose curats and his breast he strake him
            quite.
And when he saw with dying limbs him sprawling on the ground,
130 He steppèd to him straight and pulled the javelin from the wound

And said aloud, 'This is the hand, this is the selfsame dart
With which my hand did strike even now Menoetes to the heart.
Against my t'other copemate will I use the same; I pray
To God it may have like success.' This said, without delay
He sent it toward Cygnet. And the weapon did not stray
Nor was not shunnèd, in so much it lighted full upon
His shoulder; and it gave a rap as if upon some stone
It lighted had, rebounding back. Howbeit, where it hit
Achilles saw it bloody and was vainly glad of it.
For why there was no wound; it was Menoetes' blood. Then leapt    140
He hastily from his chariot down and like a madman stepped
To careless Cygnet with his sword. He saw his sword did pare
His target and his morion both. But when it touched the bare,
His body was so hard it did the edge thereof abate.
He could no lenger suffer him to triumph in that rate
But with the pommel of his sword did thump him on the pate
And bobbed him well about the brows a dozen times and more
And, pressing on him as he still gave back, amazed him sore
And troubled him with buffeting, not respiting a whit.
Then Cygnet gan to be afraid, and mists began to flit    150
Before his eyes and dimmed his sight. And as he still did yield
In giving back, by chance he met a stone amid the field
Against the which Achilles thrust him back with all his might
And, throwing him against the ground, did cast him bolt upright.
Then, bearing boistrously with both his knees against his chest
And leaning with his elbows and his target on his breast,
He shut his headpiece close and just and underneath his chin
So hard it strained that way for breath was neither out nor in
And closèd up the vent of life. And having gotten so
The upper hand, he went about to spoil his vanquished foe.    160
But nought he in his armour found. For Neptune had as tho
Transformed him to the fowl whose name he bare but late ago.
This labour, this encounter brought the rest of many days,
And either party in their strength a while from battle stays.
    Now while the Phrygians watch and ward upon the walls of
        Troy
    And Greeks likewise within their trench, there came a day of
        joy

In which Achilles for his luck in Cygnet's overthrow
A cow in way of sacrifice on Pallas did bestow.
Whose inwards when he had upon the burning altar cast
170 And that the acceptable fume had through the aïr passed
To godward and the holy rites had had their dues, the rest
Was set on boards for men to eat in dishes finely dressed.
The princes, sitting down, did feed upon the roasted flesh,
And both their thirst and present cares with wine they did refresh.
Not harps nor songs nor hollow flutes to hear did them delight;
They talkèd till they nigh had spent the greatest part of night.
And all their communication was of feats of arms in fight
That had been done by them or by their foes. And every wight
Delights to open oftentimes by turn as came about
180 The perils and the narrow brunts himself had shifted out.
For what thing should be talked before Achilles rather? Or
What kind of things than such as these could seem more meeter
       for
Achilles to be talking of? But in their talk most breme
Was then Achilles' victory of Cygnet. It did seem
A wonder that the flesh of him should be so hard and tough
As that no weapon might have power to raze or pierce it through
But that it did abate the edge of steel. It was a thing
That both Achilles and the Greeks in wondrous maze did bring.
Then Nestor said, 'This Cygnet is the person now alone
190 Of your time that defièd steel and could be pierced of none.
But I have seen now long ago one Caen of Perrheby;
I saw one Caen of Perrheby a thousand wounds defy
With unattainted body. In Mount Othrys he did dwell
And was renownèd for his deeds. And, which in him right well
A greater wonder did appear, he was a woman born.'
This uncouth made them all much more amazèd than beforn,
And every man desirèd him to tell it. And among
The rest, Achilles said, 'Declare, I pray thee – for we long
To hear it, every one of us – O eloquent old man,
200 The wisdom of our age, what was that Caen and how he won
Another than his native shape, and in what road, or in
What fight or skirmish 'tween you first acquaintance did begin,

And who in fine did vanquish him, if any vanquished him.'
  Then Nestor: 'Though the length of time have made my senses
      dim

*The story of*
*Caeney*

And divers things erst seen in youth now out of mind be gone,
Yet bear I still mo things in mind; and of them all is none
Among so many both of peace and war that yet doth take
More steadfast root in memory. And if that time may make
A man great store of things through long continuance for to
      see,
Two hundred years already of my life full passèd be,         210
And now I go upon the third. This foresaid Caeney was
The daughter of one Elaty. In beauty she did pass
The maidens all of Thessaly. From all the cities by
And from thy cities also, O Achilles, came (for why
She was thy countrywoman) store of wooers, who in vain
In hope to win her love did take great travail, suit and pain.
Thy father also had perchance attempted here to match,
But that thy mother's marriage was already then dispatched
Or she at least affiancèd. But Caeney matched with none.
Howbeit, as she on the shore was walking all alone       220
The god of sea did ravish her, so fame doth make report.
And Neptune, for the great delight he had in Venus' sport,
Said, "Caeney, ask me what thou wilt and I will give it thee."
(This also bruited is by fame.) "The wrong here done to me",
Quoth Caeney, "makes me wish great things. And therefore to
      th'intent
I may no more constrainèd be to such a thing, consent
I may no more a woman be. And if thou grant thereto,
It is even all that I desire or wish thee for to do."
In baser tune these latter words were uttered, and her voice
Did seem a man's voice, as it was indeed. For to her choice   230
The god of sea had given consent. He granted him beside
That free from wounding and from hurt he should from thence
      abide
And that he should not die of steel. Right glad of this same grant,
Away went Caeney and the fields of Thessaly did haunt

And in the feats of chivalry from that time spent his life.

'The overbold Ixion's son* had taken to his wife

Hippodame. And, covering boards in bowers of boughs of
trees,

His cloud-bred brothers one by one he placèd in degrees.

There were the lords of Thessaly. I also was among

240   The rest. A cheerful noise of feast through all the palace rung;

Some made the altars smoke, and some the bridal carols sung.

Anon comes in the maiden bride, a goodly wench of face,

With wives and maidens following her with comely gait and
grace.

We said that Sir Pirithoüs was happy in his wife,

Which handsel had deceivèd us well near through sudden strife.

For of the cruel Centaurs thou, most cruel Euryt, tho,

Like as thy stomach was with wine far overchargèd, so

As soon as thou beheld'st the bride thy heart began to frayne,

And doubled with thy drunkenness thy raging lust did reign.

250   The feast was troubled by and by with tables overthrown.

The bride was halèd by the head, so far was fury grown.

Fierce Euryt caught Hippodame, and every of the rest

Caught such as comèd next to hand or such as liked him best.

It was the lively image of a city ta'en by foes.

The house did ring of women's shrieks. We all up quickly rose,

And first said Theseus thus: "What ail'st? Art mad, O Eurytus,

That darest, seeing me alive, misuse Pirithoüs,

Not knowing that in one thou dost abuse us both?" And lest

He might have seemed to speak in vain, he thrust 'way such as
pressed

260   About the bride and took her from them, fretting sore thereat.

No answer made him Eurytus (for such a deed as that

Defended could not be with words), but with his saucy fist

He flew at gentle Theseus' face and bobbed him on the breast.

By chance hard by an ancient cup of image-work did stand

Which, being huge, himself more huge, Sir Theseus took in
hand

*Pirithoüs

And threw't at Euryt's head. He spewed as well at mouth as
    wound
Mixed clods of blood and brain and wine, and on the soilèd
    ground
Lay sprawling bolt upright. The death of him did set the rest
His double-limbèd brothers so on fire that all the quest
With one voice crièd out, "Kill! Kill!" The wine had given them
    heart.              270
Their first encounter was with cups and cans thrown overthwart
And brittle tankards and with bowls, pans, dishes, pots and trays,
Things serving late for meat and drink and then for bloody frays.
First Amycus, Ophion's son, without remorse began
To reave and rob the bridehouse of his furniture. He ran
And pullèd down a lampbeam full of lights and, lifting it
Aloft like one that with an axe doth fetch his blow to slit
An ox's neck in sacrifice, he on the forehead hit
A Lapith namèd Celadon and crushèd so his bones
That none could know him by the face. Both eyes flew out at
    once;              280
His nose was beaten back and to his palate battered flat.
One Pelates, a Macedon, exceeding wroth thereat,
Pulled out a maple trestle's foot and knapped him in the necks,
That bobbing with his chin against his breast to ground he becks.
And as he spitted out his teeth with blackish blood, he lent
Another blow to Amycus which straight to hell him sent.
Gryne, standing by and lowering with a fell grim visage at
The smoking altars, said, "Why use we not these same?" With
    that
He caught a mighty altar up with burning fire thereon
And it among the thickest of the Lapiths threw anon.      290
And two he overwhelmed therewith called Brote and Orion.
This Orion's mother, Mycale, is known of certainty
The moon, resisting, to have drawn by witchcraft from the sky.
"Full dearly shalt thou buy it", quoth Exadius, "may I get
A weapon." And with that instead of weapon he did set
His hand upon a vowed hart's horn that on a pine-tree high
Was nailed, and with two tines thereof he strake out either eye

Of Gryne; whereof some stack upon the horn and some did fly
Upon his beard and there with blood like jelly mixed did lie.

300   A flaming firebrand from amidst an altar Rhoetus snatched,
With which upon the left side of his head Charaxus latched
A blow that cracked his skull. The blaze among his yellow hair
Ran singeing up, as if dry corn with lightning blasted were.
And in his wound the searèd blood did make a grievous sound,
As, when a piece of steel red hot ta'en up with tongs is drowned
In water by the smith, it spurts and hisseth in the trough.
Charaxus from his curlèd head did shake the fire; and though
He wounded were, yet caught he up upon his shoulders twain
A stone, the jamb of either door, that well would load a wain.

310   The mass thereof was such as that it would not let him hit
His foe. It lighted short, and with the falling down of it
A mate of his that Comet hight it all in pieces smit.
Then Rhoet, restraining not his joy, said thus: "I would the rout
Of all thy mates might in the selfsame manner prove them stout."
And with his half-burnt brand the wound he searchèd new again,
Not ceasing for to lay on load upon his pate amain
Until his head was crushed and of his scalp the bones did swim
Among his brains. In jolly ruff he passèd straight from him
To Coryt and Euagrus and to Dryant on a row.
Of whom when Coryt (on whose cheeks young mossy down gan

320     grow)
Was slain, "What praise or honour", quoth Euagrus, "hast thou
    got
By killing of a boy?" Mo words him Rhoetus suffered not
To speak, but in his open mouth did thrust his burning brand
And down his throat-boll to his chest. Then, whisking in his hand
His firebrand round about his head, he fiercely did assail
The valiant Dryant. But with him he could not so prevail.
For as he triumphed in his luck, proceeding for to make
Continual slaughter of his foes, Sir Dryant with a stake
Whose point was hardened in the fire did cast at him a foin
And thrust him through the place in which the neck and shoulders

330     join.

He groaned and from his cannel-bone could scarcely pull the
    stake.
And being soilèd with his blood, to flight he did him take.
Orneus also ran away, and Lycidas likewise;
And Medon, whose right shoulderplate was also wounded, flies.
So did Pisenor, so did Caun, and so did Mermeros,
Who, late outrunning every man, now, wounded, slower goes.
And so did Phole and Menelas and Abas, who was wont
To make a spoil among wild boars as oft as he did hunt;
And eke the wizard Astylos, who counsellèd his mates
To leave that fray. But he to them in vain of leaving prates.    340
He eke to Nessus (who for fear of wounding seemèd shy)
Said, "Fly not, thou shalt scape this fray of Herc'les' bow to die."
But Lycid and Eurynomos and Imbreus and Are
Escaped not death. Sir Dryant's hand did all alike them spare.
Caenaeus also, though that he in flying were not slack,
Yet was he wounded on the face; for as he lookèd back,
A weapon's point did hit him full midway between the eyes
Whereas the nose and forehead meet. For all this din yet lies
Aphipnas snorting fast asleep, not minding for to wake,
Wrapped in a cloak of bearskins which in Ossa Mount were take.    350
And in his lither hand he held a pot of wine. Whom when
That Phorbas saw (although in vain) not meddling with them,
    then
He set his fingers to the thong; and saying, "Thou shalt drink
Thy wine with water taken from the Stygian fountain's brink,"
He threw his dart at him. The dart (as he that time by chance
Lay bolt upright upon his back) did through his throat-boll glance.
He died and felt no pain at all. The black swart blood gushed out
And on the bed and in the pot fell flushing like a spout.
I saw Petraeus go about to pull out of the ground
An oaken tree. But as he had his arms about it round    360
And shaked it to and fro to make it loose, Pirithous cast
A dart which nailèd to the tree his writhing stomach fast.
Through prowess of Pirithoüs (men say) was Lycus slain;
Through prowess of Pirithoüs died Chrome. But they both twain
Less honour to their conqueror were than Dictys was or than
Was Helops. Helops with a dart was stricken, which through ran

His head and, entering at the right ear, to the left ear went.
And Dictys, from a slippery knap down sliding, as he meant
To shun Pirithous pressing on, fell headlong down and with
His hugeness brake the greatest ash that was in all the frith
And goared his guts upon the stump. To wreak his death comes
      Phare,
And from the mount a mighty rock with both his hands he tare;
Which as he was about to throw, Duke Theseus did prevent
And with an oaken plant upon his mighty elbow leant
Him such a blow as that he brake the bones and passed no further.
For leisure would not serve him then his maimèd corse to murder.
He leapt on high Bianor's back, who none was wont to bear
Besides himself. Against his sides his knees fast nipping were;
And, with his left hand taking hold upon his foretop hair,
He cuffed him with his knobbèd plant about the frowning face
And made his wattled brows to break. And with his oaken mace
He overthrew Nedymnus; and Lycespes with his dart;
And Hippasus, whose beard did hide his breast the greater part;
And Riphey, taller than the trees; and Therey, who was wont
Among the hills of Thessaly for cruel bears to hunt
And bear them angry home alive. It did Demoleon spite
That Theseus had so good success and fortune in his fight.
An old long pine-tree rooted fast he strave with all his might
To pluck up whole, both trunk and root. Which when he could
      not bring
To pass, he brake it off and at his enemy did it fling.
But Theseus by admonishment of heavenly Pallas (so
He would have folk believe it were) start back a great way fro
The weapon as it came. Yet fell it not without some harm.
It cut from Crantor's left side bulk his shoulder, breast and arm.
This Crantor was thy father's squire, Achilles, and was given
Him by Amyntor, ruler of the Dolops, who was driven
By battle for to give him as an hostage for the peace
To be observèd faithfully. When Peleus in the press
A great way off beheld him thus fallen dead of this same wound,
"O Crantor, dearest man to me of all above the ground,
Hold here an obit-gift," he said. And both with force of heart
And hand at stout Demoleon's head he threw an ashen dart,

370

380

390

400

Which brake the wattling of his ribs and sticking in the bone
Did shake. He pullèd out the steal with much ado alone;
The head thereof stack still behind among his lungs and lights.
Enforced to courage with his pain, he riseth straight uprights
And, pawing at his enemy with his horsish feet, he smites
Upon him. Peleus bare his strokes upon his burgonet
And fenced his shoulders with his shield and evermore did set
His weapon upward with the point, which by his shoulders
    pierced                                             410
Through both his breasts at one full blow. Howbeit, your father
    erst
Had killèd Hyle and Phlegrey and Hiphinoüs aloof
And Danes, who boldly durst at hand his manhood put in proof.
To these was added Dorylas, who ware upon his head
A cap of wolf's skin; and the horns of oxen dyèd red
With blood were then his weapon. I (for then my courage gave
Me strength) said, "See how much thy horns less force than iron
    have,"
And therewithal with manly might a dart at him I drave.
Which when he could not shun, he clapped his right hand flat
    upon
His forehead where the wound should be; for why his hand anon    420
Was nailed to his forehead fast. He roarèd out amain.
And as he stood amazèd and began to faint for pain,
Your father Peleus (for he stood hard by him) strake him under
The middle belly with his sword and ripped his womb asunder.
Out girds me Doryl straight and trails his guts upon the ground
And, trampling underneath his feet, did break them; and they
    wound
About his legs so snarling that he could no further go
But fell down dead with empty womb. Nought booted Cyllar tho
His beauty in that frantic fray – at least wise if we grant
That any might in that strange shape of nature's beauty vaunt.    430
His beard began but then to bud; his beard was like the gold;
So also were his yellow locks which, goodly to behold,
Midway beneath his shoulders hung. There rested in his face
A sharp and lively cheerfulness with sweet and pleasant grace.

His neck, breast, shoulders, arms and hands, as far as he was man,
Were such as never carver's work yet stain them could or can.
His nether part likewise, which was a horse, was every whit
Full equal with his upper part, or little worse than it.
For had ye given him horse's neck and head, he was a beast
440    For Castor to have ridden on. So burly was his breast;
So handsome was his back to bear a saddle; and his hair
Was black as jet, but that his tail and feet milk-whitish were.
Full many females of his race did wish him to their make.
But only Dame Hylonome for lover he did take.
Of all the half-brutes in the woods there did not any dwell
More comely than Hylonome. She used herself so well
In dalliance and in loving and in uttering of her love
That she alone held Cyllarus. As much as did behove
In suchy limbs, she trimmèd them as most the eye might move.
With combing smooth she made her hair; she wallowed her full
450         oft
In roses and in rosemary or violets sweet and soft.
Sometime she carried lilies white. And twice a day she washed
Her visage in the spring that from the top of Pagas passed;
And in the stream she twice a day did bathe her limbs. And on
Her leftside or her shoulders came the comeliest things and none
But finest skins of choicest beasts. Alike each lovèd other.
Together they among the hills roamed up and down; together
They went to covert; and that time together they did enter
The Lapith's house and there the fray together did adventure.
460    A dart on Cyllar's left side came (I know not who it sent)
Which somewhat underneath his neck his breast asunder splint.
As lightly as his heart was razed, no sooner was the dart
Plucked out, but all his body waxed stark cold and dyèd swart.
Immediately Hylonome his dying limbs up stayed
And put her hand upon the wound to stop the blood and laid
Her mouth to his and laboured sore to stay his passing sprite.
But when she saw him throughly dead, then, speaking words
         which might
Not to my hearing come for noise, she sticked herself upon
The weapon that had gorèd him and died with him anon,

Embracing him between her arms. There also stood before 470
Mine eyes the grim Phaeocomes, both man and horse, who wore
A lion's skin upon his back fast knit with knots afore.
He, snatching up a timber log which scarcely two good team
Of oxen could have stirred, did throw the same with force
    extreme
At Phonoleny's son. The log him all in fitters strake
And of his head the brainpan in a thousand pieces brake,
That at his mouth, his ears and eyes and at his nostrils too
His crushèd brain came roping out, as cream is wont to do
From sieves or riddles made of wood or as a cullis out
From strainer or from colander. But as he went about 480
To strip him from his harness as he lay upon the ground
(Your father knoweth this full well), my sword his guts did
    wound.
Teleboas and Cthonius both were also slain by me.
Sir Cthonius for his weapon had a forkèd bough of tree;
The t'other had a dart. His dart did wound me – you may see
The scar thereof remaining yet. Then was the time that I
Should sent have been to conquer Troy. Then was the time that I
Might through my force and prowess, if not vanquish Hector
    stout,
Yet at the least have held him wag, I put you out of doubt.
But then was Hector nobody, or but a babe. And now 490
Am I forspent and worn with years. What should I tell you how
Pyraetus died by Periphas? Or wherefore should I make
Long process for to tell you of Sir Ampycus, that strake
The four-foot Oecley on the face with dart of cornel-tree,
The which had neither head nor point? Or how that Macare
Of mountain Pelethrony with a lever lent a blow
To Erigdupus on the breast which did him overthrow?
Full well I do remember that Cymelius threw a dart
Which lighted full in Nessy's flank about his privy part.
And think not you that Mops, the son of Ampycus, could do 500
No good but only prophesy. This stout Odites, who
Had both the shapes of man and horse, by Mops's dart was slain.
And, labouring for to speak his last, he did but strive in vain;

For Mops's dart together nailed his tongue and nether chap
And, piercing through his throat, did make a wide and deadly gap.
Five men had Caen already slain; their wounds I cannot say.
The names and number of them all right well I bear away.
The names of them were Styphelus and Brome and Helymus,
Pyracmon with his forest bill and stout Antimachus.
510  Out steps the biggest centaur there, huge Latreus, armèd in
Alesus of Emathia's spoil, slain late before by him.
His years were mid 'tween youth and age; his courage still was
     young;
And on his auburn head hoar hairs peered here and there among.
His furniture was then a sword, a target and a lance
Emathian-like. To both the parts he did his face advance
And, brandishing his weapon brave, in circlewise did prance
About and stoutly spake these words: "And must I bear with you,
Dame Caeney? For none other than a mother, I avow,
No better than a mother will I count thee while I live.
Rememb'rest not what shape by birth Dame Nature did thee
520      give?
Forget'st thou how thou purchasèdst this counterfeited shape
Of man? Considerest what thou art by birth, and how for rape
Thou art become the thing thou art? Go take thy distaff and
Thy spindle, and in spinning yarn go exercise thy hand.
Let men alone with feats of arms." As Latreus made this stout
And scornful taunting, in a ring still turning him about,
This Caeney with a dart did hit him full upon the side
Whereas the horse and man were joined together in a hide.
The stripe made Latreus mad, and with his lance in rage he strake
530  Upon Sir Caeney's naked ribs. The lance rebounded back
Like hailstones from a tilèd house, or as a man should pat
Small stones upon a drumslade's head. He came more near with
     that
And in his brawnèd side did strive to thrust his sword. There was
No way for sword to enter in. "Yet shalt thou not so pass
My hands," said he. "Well, sith the point is blunted, thou shalt die
Upon the edge." And with that word he fetched his blow awry
And, sidling, with a sweeping stroke along his belly smit.
The stripe did give a clink as if it had on marble hit,

And therewithal the sword did break and on his neck did light.
When Caeney had sufficiently given Latreus leave to smite          540
His flesh which was unmaimable, "Well now", quoth he, "let's
       see
If my sword able be or no to bite the flesh of thee."
In saying so, his dreadful sword as far as it would go
He underneath his shoulder thrust and, wrenching to and fro
Among his guts, made wound in wound. Behold, with hideous
       cry
The double-membered Centaurs, sore abashed, upon him fly
And throw their weapons all at him. Their weapons down did fall
As if they had rebated been, and Caeney for them all
Abides unstricken through. Yea, none was able blood to draw.
The strangeness of the case made all amazèd that it saw.          550
"Fie, fie, for shame", quoth Monychus, "that such a rabble can
Not overcome one wight alone who scarcely is a man.
Although, to say the very truth, he is the man and we
Through faintness that that he was born by nature for to be.
What profits these huge limbs of ours? What helps our double
       force?
Or what avails our double shape of man as well as horse,
By puissant nature joined in one? I cannot think that we
Of sovereign goddess Juno were begot, or that we be
Ixion's sons, who was so stout of courage and so haught
As that he durst on Juno's love attempt to give assault.          560
The enemy that doth vanquish us is scarcely half a man.
Whelm blocks and stones and mountains whole upon his hard
       brainpan
And press ye out his lively ghost with trees. Let timber choke
His chaps; let weight enforce his death instead of wounding
       stroke."
This said, by chance he gets a tree blown down by blustering
       blasts
Of southern winds and on his foe with all his might it casts
And gave example to the rest to do the like. Within
A while the shadows which did hide Mount Pelion waxèd thin,
And not a tree was left upon Mount Othrys ere they went.
Sir Caeney, underneath this great huge pile of timber pent,       570

Did chafe and on his shoulders hard the heavy logs did bear.
But when above his face and head the trees up stackèd were,
So that he had no venting place to draw his breath, one while
He fainted, and another while he heavèd at the pile
To tumble down the logs that lay so heavy on his back
And for to win the open air again above the stack,
As if the Mountain Ida, lo, which yonder we do see
So high, by earthquake at a time should chance to shaken be.
Men doubt what did become of him. Some hold opinion that
580    The burden of the woods had driven his soul to Limbo flat.
But Mopsus said it was not so. For he did see a brown
Bird flying from amid the stack and towering up and down.
It was the first time and the last that ever I beheld
That fowl. When Mopsus softly saw him soaring in the field,
He lookèd wistly after him and crièd out on high,
"Hail, peerless pearl of Lapith race; hail, Caeney, late ago
A valiant knight and now a bird of whom there is no mo."
The author causèd men believe the matter to be so.
Our sorrow set us in a rage. It was to us a grief
590    That by so many foes one knight was killed without relief.
Then ceased we not to wreck our teen till most was slain in fight
And that the rest, discomfited, were fled away by night.'
    As Nestor all the process of this battle did rehearse
    Between the valiant Lapiths and misshapen Centaurs fierce,
Tlepolemus, displeasèd sore that Hercules was passed
With silence, could not hold his peace, but out these words did cast:
'My lord, I muse you should forget my father's praise so quite.
For often unto me himself was wonted to recite
How that the cloud-bred folk by him were chiefly put to flight.'

*The death*
*of Nestor's*
*brothers*

    Right sadly Nestor answered thus: 'Why should you me
        constrain
    To call to mind forgotten griefs and for to rear again
The sorrows now outworn by time? Or force me to declare
The hatred and displeasure which I to your father bear?
In sooth, his doings greater were than might be well believed.
He filled the world with high renown, which nobly he achieved.
Which thing I would I could deny. For neither set we out
Deiphobus, Polydamas, nor Hector, that most stout

And valiant knight, the strength of Troy; for who will praise his
      foe?
Your father overthrew the walls of Messene long ago
And razèd Pyle and Ely towns, unworthy serving so.                    610
And fierce against my father's house he used both sword and fire.
And (not to speak of others whom he killèd in his ire)
Twice six we were, the sons of Nele, all lusty gentlemen.
Twice six of us, excepting me, by him were murdered then.
The death of all the rest might seem a matter not so strange,
But strange was Periclymen's death, who had the power to change
And leave and take what shape he list (by Neptune to him given,
The founder of the house of Nele). For when he had been driven
To try all shapes and none could help, he last of all became
The fowl that in his hookèd feet doth bear the flashing flame         620
Sent down from heaven by Jupiter. He, practising those birds,
With flapping wings and bowing beak and hookèd talons girds
At Herc'le and bescratched his face. Too certain, I may say,
Thy father aimed his shaft at him. For as he towering lay
Among the clouds, he hit him underneath the wing. The stroke
Was small; howbeit, because therewith – the sinews being broke –
He wanted strength to maintain flight, he fell me to the ground
Through weakness of his wing. The shaft that stickèd in the
      wound
By reason of the burden of his body pierced his side
And at the left side of his neck all bloody forth did glide.          630
Now tell me, O thou beautiful Lord Admiral of the Fleet
Of Rhodes, if me to speak the praise of Herc'le it be meet.
But lest that of my brothers' deaths men think I do desire
A further venge than silence of the prowess of thy sire,
I love thee even with all my heart and take thee for my friend.'
When Nestor of his pleasant tales had made this friendly end,
They callèd for a bowl of wine and from the table went,
And all the residue of the night in sleeping soundly spent.

   But Neptune, like a father, took the matter sore to heart          *The death*
   That Cygnet to a swan he was constrainèd to convert.              *of Achilles*
And, hating fierce Achilles, he did wreak his cruel teen
Upon him more uncourteously than had beseeming been.

For when the wars well near full twice five years had lasted, he
Unshorn Apollo thus bespake: 'O nephew unto me
Most dear of all my brother's imps, who helpèdst me to lay
Foundation of the walls of Troy for which we had no pay,
And canst thou sighs forbear to see the Asian empire fall?
And doth it not lament thy heart when thou to mind dost call
So many thousand people slain in keeping Ilion wall?
650   Or — to th'intent particularly I do not speak of all —
Rememb'rest thou not Hector's ghost, who harried was about
His town of Troy? Where ne'ertheless Achilles, that same stout
And far in fight more butcherly, who strives with all his might
To stroy the work of me and thee, lives still in healthful plight.
If ever he do come within my danger, he shall feel
What force is in my triple mace. But sith with sword of steel
I may not meet him as my foe, I pray thee, unbeware
Go kill him with a sudden shaft and rid me of my care.'
Apollo did consent, as well his uncle for to please
660   As also for a private grudge himself had for to ease.
And in a cloud he down among the host of Troy did slide
Where Paris dribbling out his shafts among the Greeks he spied.
And, telling him what god he was, said, 'Wherefore dost thou
        waste
Thine arrows on the simple sort? If any care thou hast
Of those that are thy friends, go turn against Achilles' head
And like a man revenge on him thy brothers that are dead.'
In saying this, he brought him where Achilles with his brand
Was beating down the Trojan folk, and levelled so his hand
As that Achilles tumbled down stark dead upon the land.
670       This was the only thing whereof the old king Priam might
        Take comfort after Hector's death. That stout and valiant
            knight
Achilles, who had overthrown so many men in fight,
Was by that coward carpet-knight bereavèd of his life
Who like a caitiff stale away the Spartan prince's wife.
But if of weapon womanish he had foreknown it had
His destiny been to lose his life, he would have been more glad
That Queen Penthesilea's bill had slain him out of hand.
Now was the fear of Phrygian folk, the only glory and

Defence of Greeks, that peerless prince in arms, Achilles, turned
To ashes. That same god that had him armed him also burned.           680
Now is he dust; and of that great Achilles bideth still
A thing of nought that scarcely can a little coffin fill.
Howbeit, his worthy fame doth live and spreadeth over all
The world, a measure meet for such a person to befall.
This matcheth thee, Achilles, full; and this can never die.
His target also, to th'intent that men might plainly spy
What wight's it was, did move debate, and for his armour burst
Out deadly feud. Not Diomed nor Ajax Oiley durst
Make claim or challenge to the same, nor Atreus' younger son
Nor yet his elder, though in arms much honour they had won.           690
Alone the sons of Telamon and Laërt did assay
Which of them two of that great prize should bear the bell away.
But Agamemnon from himself the burden puts and clears
His hands of envy, causing all the captains and the peers
Of Greece to meet amid the camp together in a place,
To whom he put the hearing and the judgement of the case.

FINIS DUODECIMI LIBRI.

# The Thirteenth Book of Ovid's
## Metamorphoses

The lords and captains being set together with the king
And all the soldiers standing round about them in a ring,
The owner of the sevenfold shield, to these did Ajax rise.
And as he could not bridle wrath, he cast his frowning eyes
Upon the shore and on the fleet that there at anchor lies
And, throwing up his hands, 'O God, and must we plead', quoth
    he,
'Our case before our ships? And must Ulysses stand with me?
But like a wretch he ran his way when Hector came with fire,
Which I, defending, from these ships did force him to retire.
It easier is, therefore, with words in print to maintain strife        10
Than for to fight it out with fists. But neither am I rife
In words nor he in deeds. For look, how far I him excel
In battle and in feats of arms, so far bears he the bell
From me in talking. Neither think I requisite to tell
My acts among you. You yourselves have seen them very well.
But let Ulysses tell you his, done all in hudder-mudder
And whereunto the only night is privy and none other.
The prize is great, I do confess, for which we strive. But yet
It is dishonour unto me for that in claiming it
So base a person standeth in contention for the same.        20
To think it mine already ought to counted be no shame
Nor pride in me, although the thing of right great value be
Of which Ulysses stands in hope. For now already he
Hath won the honour of this prize, in that when he shall sit
Besides the cushion, he may brag he strave with me for it.

And though I wanted valiantness, yet should nobility
Make with me. I of Telamon am known the son to be,
Who under valiant Hercules the walls of Troy did scale
And in the ship of Pagasa to Colchos land did sail.
30    His father was that Aeacus who executeth right
Among the ghosts where Sisyphus heaves up with all his might
The massy stone aye tumbling down. The highest Jove of all
Acknowledgeth this Aeacus and doth his son him call.
Thus am I, Ajax, the third from Jove. Yet let this pedigree,
O Achives, in this case of mine available not be
Unless I prove it fully with Achilles to agree.
He was my brother, and I claim that was my brother's. Why
Should'st thou, that art of Sisyph's blood and for to filch and lie
Expressest him in every point, by forgèd pedigree
40    Ally thee to the Aeacids, as though we did not see
Thee to the house of Aeacus a stranger for to be?
And is it reason that you should this armour me deny
Because I former was in arms and needed not a spy
To fetch me forth? Or think you him more worthy it to have
That came to warfare hindermost and feigned himself to rave,
Because he would have shunned the war, until a subtler head
And more unprofitable for himself, Sir Palamed,
Escried the crafty fetches of his fearful heart and drew
Him forth a warfare, which he sought so cowardly to eschew?
50    Must he now needs enjoy the best and richest armour, who
Would none at all have worn unless he forcèd were thereto,
And I with shame be put beside my cousin-german's gifts
Because to shun the foremost brunt of wars I sought no shifts?
Would God this mischief-master had in very deed been mad
Or else believèd so to be, and that we never had
Brought such a panion unto Troy. Then should not Poean's son
In Lemnos like an outlaw to the shame of all us wone.
Who, lurking now (as men report) in woods and caves, doth
        move
The very flints with sighs and groans and prayers to God above
60    To send Ulysses his desert. Which prayer, if there be
A god, must one day take effect. And now behold how he,
By oath a soldier of our camp, yea, and as well as we

A captain too, alas, who was by Hercules assigned
To have the keeping of his shafts, with pain and hunger pined,
Is clad and fed with fowls and dribs his arrows up and down
At birds, which were by destiny prepared to stroy Troy town!
Yet liveth he because he is not still in company
With sly Ulysses. Palamed, that wretched knight, perdie,
Would eke he had abandoned been. For then should still the same
Have been alive, or at the least have died without our shame.          70
But this companion, bearing, ah, too well in wicked mind
His madness which Sir Palamed by wisdom out did find,
Appeachèd him of treason, that he practised to betray
The Greekish host. And for to vouch the fact, he showed
        straightway
A mass of gold that he himself had hidden in his tent
And forgèd letters which he feigned from Priam to be sent.
Thus, either by his murdering men or else by banishment,
Abateth he the Greekish strength. This is Ulysses' fight.
This is the fear he puts men in. But though he had more might
Than Nestor hath in eloquence, he shall not compass me          80
To think his lewd abandoning of Nestor for to be
No fault; who, being cast behind by wounding of his horse
And slow with age, with calling on Ulysses waxing hoarse,
Was ne'ertheless betrayed by him. Sir Diomed knows this crime
Is unsurmised. For he himself did at that present time
Rebuke him oftentimes by name and fiercely him upbraid
With flying from his fellow so who stood in need of aid.
With rightful eyes doth God behold the deeds of mortal men.
Lo, he that helpèd not his friend wants help himself again.
And as he did forsake his friend in time of need, so he          90
Did in the selfsame peril fall forsaken for to be.
He made a rod to beat himself. He called and crièd out
Upon his fellows. Straight I came; and there I saw the lout
Both quake and shake for fear of death and look as pale as clout.
I set my shield between him and his foes and him bestrid
And saved the dastard's life. Small praise redounds of that I did.
But if thou wilt contend with me, let's to the selfsame place
Again; be wounded as thou wert and in the foresaid case

Of fear, beset about with foes; couch underneath my shield;
100    And then contend thou with me there amid the open field.
Howbeit, I had no sooner rid this champion of his foes
But, where for wounds he scarce before could totter on his toes,
He ran away apace as though he nought at all did ail.
Anon comes Hector to the field and bringeth at his tail
The gods. Not only thy heart there, Ulysses, did thee fail
But even the stoutest courages and stomachs gan to quail,
So great a terror brought he in. Yet in the midst of all
His bloody ruff, I coped with him and with a foiling fall
Did overthrow him to the ground. Another time, when he
110    Did make a challenge, you, my lords, by lot did choose out me
And I did match him hand to hand. Your wishes were not vain.
For if you asked me what success our combat did obtain,
I came away unvanquishèd. Behold, the men of Troy
Brought fire and sword and all the fiends our navy to destroy.
And where was sly Ulysses then with all his talk so smooth?
This breast of mine was fain to fence your thousand ships,
         forsooth,
The hope of your returning home. For saving that same day
So many ships, this armour give. But (if that I shall say
The truth) the greater honour now this armour bears away,
120    And our renowns together link. For, as of reason ought,
An Ajax for this armour, not an armour now is sought
For Ajax. Let Dulichius match with these the horses white
Of Rhesus, dastard Dolon, and the coward carpet-knight,
King Priam's Helen, and the stealth of Pallady by night.
Of all these things was nothing done by day nor nothing wrought
Without the help of Diömed. And therefore, if ye thought
To give them to so small deserts, divide the same and let
Sir Diomed have the greater part. But what should Ithacus get
And if he had them, who doth all his matters in the dark,
130    Who never weareth armour, who shoots aye at his own mark
To trap his foe by stealth unwares? The very headpiece may
With brightness of the glistering gold his privy feats bewray
And show him lurking. Neither well of force Dulichius were
The weight of great Achilles' helm upon his pate to wear.

It cannot but a burden be, and that right great, to bear
With whose same shrimpish arms of his Achilles' mighty spear.
Again his target, graven with the whole huge world thereon,
Agrees not with a fearful hand, and chiefly such a one
As taketh filching even by kind. Thou, losel, thou dost seek
A gift that will but weaken thee. Which if the folk of Greek            140
Shall give thee through their oversight, it will be unto thee
Occasion of thine enemies spoiled, not fearèd, for to be;
And flight (wherein, thou coward, thou all others may'st outbrag)
Will hindered be when after thee such masses thou shalt drag.
Moreover, this thy shield, that feels so seld the force of fight,
Is sound. But mine is gashed and hacked and stricken thorough
        quite
A thousand times with bearing blows. And therefore mine must
        walk
And put another in his stead. But what needs all this talk?
Let's now be seen another while what each of us can do.
The thickest of our armèd foes this armour throw into                   150
And bid us fetch the same fro thence. And which of us doth fetch
The same away, reward ye him therewith.' Thus far did stretch
The words of Ajax; at the end whereof there did ensue
A muttering of the soldiers, till Laërtes' son, the prew,
Stood up and raisèd soberly his eyelids from the ground
(On which he had a little while them pitchèd in a stound)
And, looking on the noblemen who longed his words to hear,
He thus began with comely grace and sober pleasant cheer:
    'My lords, if my desire and yours might erst have taken place,      *Ulysses claims*
    It should not at this present time have been a doubtful case        *Achilles' arms*
What person hath most right to this great prize for which we
        strive.
Achilles should his armour have, and we still him alive.
Whom sith that cruel destiny to both of us denies' –
With that same word, as though he wept, he wiped his watery
        eyes –
'What wight of reason rather ought to be Achilles' heir
Than he through whom to this your camp Achilles did repair?

Alonely let it not avail Sir Ajax here that he
Is such a dolt and grosshead as he shows himself to be,
Ne let my wit (which aye hath done you good, O Greeks) hurt
    me.
170 But suffer this mine eloquence, such as it is, which now
Doth for his master speak and oft ere this hath spoke for you,
Be undisdained. Let none refuse his own good gifts he brings.
For as for stock and ancestors and other suchlike things
Whereof ourselves no founders are, I scarcely dare them grant
To be our own. But for as much as Ajax makes his vaunt
To be the fourth from Jove, even Jove the founder is also
Of my house, and than four descents I am from him no mo.
Laërtes is my father and Arcesius his, and he
Begotten was of Jupiter. And in this pedigree
180 Is neither any damnèd soul nor outlaw, as ye see.
Moreover, by my mother's side I come of Mercury:
Another honour to my house. Thus both by father's side
And mother's, as you may perceive, I am to gods allied.
But neither for because I am a better gentleman
Than Ajax by the mother's side, nor that my father can
Avouch himself unguilty of his brother's blood, do I
This armour claim. Weigh you the case by merits uprightly,
Provided no prerogative of birthright Ajax bear
For that his father Telamon and Peleus brothers were.
190 Let only prowess in this prize the honour bear away.
Or if the case on kindred or on birthright seem to stay,
His father Peleus is alive, and Pyrrhus eke, his son;
What title then can Ajax make? This gear of right should wone
To Phthia or to Scyros Isle. And Teucer is as well
Achilles' uncle as is he. Yet doth not Teucer mell.
And if he did, should he obtain? Well, sith the case doth rest
On trial which of us can prove his doings to be best,
I needs must say my deeds are mo than well I can express;
Yet will I show them orderly as near as I can guess.
200 Foreknowing that her son should die, the lady Thetis hid
Achilles in a maid's attire; by which fine sleight she did
All men deceive and Ajax too. This armour in a pack
With other women's trifling toys I carried on my back,

A bait to train a manly heart. Apparelled like a maid,
Achilles took the spear and shield in hand and with them played.
Then said I, "O thou goddess' son, why should'st thou be afraid
To raze great Troy, whose overthrow for thee is only stayed?"
And, laying hand upon him, I did send him, as you see,
To valiant doings meet for such a valiant man as he.
And therefore all the deeds of him are my deeds. I did wound          210
King Teleph with his spear and, when he lay upon the ground,
I was entreated with the spear to heal him safe and sound.
That Thebe lieth overthrown is my deed, you must think;
I made the folk of Tenedos and Lesbos for to shrink.
Both Chryse and Cillas, Phoebus' towns, and Scyros I did take,
And my right hand Lyrnessus' walls to ground did level make.
I gave you him that should confound (besides a number mo)
The valiant Hector. Hector, that our most renownèd foe,
Is slain by me. This armour here I sue again to have;
This armour, by the which I found Achilles. I it gave          220
Achilles while he was alive and, now that he is gone,
I claim it as mine own again. What time the grief of one
Had pierced the hearts of all the Greeks and that our thousand sail
At Aulis by Euboea stayed because the winds did fail,
Continuing either none at all or clean against us long,
And that our Agamemnon was by Destinies overstrong
Commanded for to sacrifice his guiltless daughter to
Diana, which her father then refusing for to do,
Was angry with the gods themselves and, though he were a king,
Continued also father-like; by reason, I did bring          230
His gentle nature to relent for public profit's sake.
I must confess (whereat his grace shall no displeasure take),
Before a partial judge I undertook a right hard case.
Howbeit, for his brother's sake and for the royal mace
Committed and his people's weal, at length he was content
To purchase praise with blood. Then was I to the mother sent,
Who not persuaded was to be but compassed with some guile.
Had Ajax on this errand gone, our ships had all this while
Lain still there yet for want of wind. Moreover, I was sent
To Ilion as ambassador. I boldly thither went          240

And entered and beheld the court, wherein there was as then
Great store of princes, dukes, lords, knights and other valiant men.
And yet I boldly, ne'ertheless, my message did at large,
The which the whole estate of Greece had given me erst in
      charge.
I made complaint of Paris and accused him to his head,
Demanding restitution of Queen Helen that same stead
And of the booty with her ta'en. Both Priamus the king
And eke Antenor, his ally, the words of me did sting.
And Paris and his brothers and the residue of his train

250    That under him had made the spoil could hard and scarce refrain
Their wicked hands. You, Menelay, do know I do not feign.
And that day was the first in which we jointly gan sustain
A taste of perils, store whereof did then behind remain.
It would be overlong to tell each profitable thing
That during this long lasting war I well to pass did bring
By force as well as policy. For after that the first
Encounter once was overpast, our enemies never durst
Give battle in the open field, but held themselves within
Their walls and bulwarks till the time the tenth year did begin.
Now what did'st thou of all that while, that canst do nought but

260      strike?
Or to what purpose servèdst thou? For if thou my deeds seek,
I practised sundry policies to trap our foes unware;
I fortified our camp with trench which heretofore lay bare.
I heartened our companions with a quiet mind to bear
The longness of the weary war; I taught us how we were
Both to be fed and furnishèd. And to and fro I went
To places where the council thought most meet I should be sent.
Behold, the king, deceivèd in his dream by false pretence
Of Jove's commandment, bade us raise our seige and get us hence.

270    The author of his doing so may well be his defence.
Now Ajax should have letted this and called them back again
To sack the town of Troy. He should have fought with might and
      main.
Why did he not restrain them when they ready were to go?
Why took he not his sword in hand? Why gave he not as tho

Some counsel for the fleeting folk to follow at the brunt?
In faith, it had a trifle been to him that aye is wont
Such vaunting in his mouth to have. But he himself did fly
As well as others. I did see and was ashamèd, I,
To see thee when thou fled'st and did'st prepare so cowardly
To sail away. And thereupon I thus aloud did cry:                    280
"What mean ye, sirs? What madness doth you move to go to ship
And suffer Troy, as good as ta'en, thus out of hand to slip?
What else this tenth year bear ye home than shame?" With
        suchlike word
And other which the eloquence of sorrow did afford,
I brought them from their flying ships. Then Agamemnon called
Together all the captains who with fear were yet appalled.
But Ajax durst not then once creak. Yet durst Thersites be
So bold as rail upon the kings, and he was paid by me
For playing so the saucy jack. Then stood I on my toes
And to my fearful countrymen gave heart against their foes         290
And shed new courage in their minds through talk that fro me
        goes.
From that time forth whatever thing hath valiantly achieved
By this good fellow been, is mine, who him from flight reprieved.
And now to touch thee: which of all the Greeks commendeth
        thee
Or seeketh thee? But Diömed communicates with me
His doings and alloweth me, and thinks him well apaid
To have Ulysses ever as companion at the braid.
And somewhat worth you will it grant, I trow, alone for me
Out of so many thousand Greeks by Diomed picked to be.
No lot compellèd me to go, and yet I, setting light               300
As well the peril of my foes as danger of the night,
Killed Dolon, who about the selfsame feat that night did stray
That we went out for. But I first compelled him to bewray
All things concerning faithless Troy and what it went about.
When all was learned and nothing left behind to hearken out,
I might have then come home with praise. I was not so content.
Proceeding further, to the camp of Rhesus straight I went
And killèd both himself and all his men about his tent

And, taking both his chariot and his horses which were white,
310   Returnèd home in triumph like a conqueror from fight.
Deny you me the armour of the man whose steeds the foe
Requirèd for his playing of the spy a-night, and so
May Ajax be more kind to me than you are! What should I
Declare unto you how my sword did waste right valiantly
Sarpedon's host of Lycia? I by force did overthrow
Alastor, Chrome and Coeranos and Haly on a row.
Alcander and Noëmon, too, and Prytanis beside
And Thoön and Theridamas and Charops also died
By me, and so did Eunomos, enforcèd by cruel fate;
320   And many mo in sight of Troy I slew of baser state.
There also are, O countrymen, about me woundings which
The place of them make beautiful. See here' – his hand did
        twitch
His shirt aside – 'and credit not vain words. Lo, here the breast
That always to be one in your affairs hath never missed.
And yet of all this while no drop of blood hath Ajax spent
Upon his fellows. Woundless is his body and unrent.
But what skills that, as long as he is able for to vaunt
He fought against both Troy and Jove to save our fleet? I grant
He did so. For I am not of such nature as of spite
330   Well doings to deface, so that he challenge not the right
Of all men to himself alone and that he yield to me
Some share, who of the honour look a partner for to be.
Patroclus also, having on Achilles' armour, sent
The Trojans and their leader hence, to burn our navy bent.
And yet thinks he that none durst meet with Hector saving he,
Forgetting both the king and eke his brother, yea, and me,
Where he himself was but the ninth appointed by the king
And by the fortune of his lot preferred to do the thing!
But now for all your valiantness, what issue had, I pray,
340   Your combat? Shall I tell? Forsooth, that Hector went his way
And had no harm. Now woe is me, how grieveth it my heart
To think upon that season when the bulwark of our part,
Achilles, died! When neither tears nor grief nor fear could make
Me for to stay, but that upon these shoulders I did take,

I say, upon these shoulders I Achilles' body took
And this same armour clapped thereon, which now to wear I
    look.
Sufficient strength I have to bear as great a weight as this,
And eke a heart wherein regard of honour rooted is.
Think you that Thetis for her son so instantly besought
Sir Vulcan this same heavenly gift to give her, which is wrought    350
With such exceeding cunning, to th'intent a soldier that
Hath neither wit nor knowledge should it wear? He knows not
    what
The things engraven on the shield do mean. Of ocean sea,
Of land, of heaven and of the stars no skill at all hath he.
The Bear that never dives in sea he doth not understand,
The Pleiads, nor the Hyads, nor the cities that do stand
Upon the earth, nor yet the sword that Orion holds in hand.
He seeks to have an armour of the which he hath no skill.
And yet in finding fault with me, because I had no will
To follow this same painful war and sought to shun the same    360
And made it somewhat longer time before I thither came,
He sees not how he speaks reproach to stout Achilles' name.
For if to have dissembled in this case ye count a crime,
We both offenders be. Or if protracting of the time
Ye count blameworthy, yet was I the timelier of us twain.
Achilles' loving mother him, my wife did me detain.
The former time was given to them; the rest was given to you.
And therefore do I little pass although I could not now
Defend my fault, sith such a man of prowess, birth and fame
As was Achilles was with me offender in the same.    370
But yet was he espièd by Ulysses' wit, but nat
Ulysses by Sir Ajax' wit. And lest ye wonder at
The railing of this foolish dolt at me, he doth object
Reproach to you. For if that I offended to detect
Sir Palamed of forgèd fault, could you without your shame
Arraign him and condemn him eke to suffer for the same?
But neither could Sir Palamed excuse him of the crime
So heinous and so manifest; and you yourselves that time
Not only his indictment heard, but also did behold
His deed avouchèd to his face by bringing in the gold.    380

And as for Philoctetes, that he is in Lemnos, I
Deserve not to be touched therewith. Defend your crime; for why
You all consented thereunto. Yet do not I deny
But that I gave the counsel to convey him out of way
From toil of war and travail, that by rest he might assay
To ease the greatness of his pains. He did thereto obey
And by so doing is alive. Not only faithful was
This counsel that I gave the man, but also happy, as
The good success hath showèd since. Whom sith the Destinies do
390   Require in overthrowing Troy, appoint not me thereto,
But let Sir Ajax rather go. For he with eloquence
Or by some subtle policy shall bring the man fro thence
And pacify him, raging through disease and wrathful ire.
Nay, first the River Simoïs shall to his spring retire
And Mountain Ida shall thereon have standing never a tree,
Yea, and the faithless town of Troy by Greeks shall rescued be
Before that Ajax' blockish wit shall aught at all avail
When my attempts and practices in your affairs do fail.
For though thou, Philoctetes, with the king offended be
400   And with thy fellows everych one and most of all with me,
Although thou curse and ban me to the hellish pit for aye
And wishest in thy pain that I by chance might cross thy way
Of purpose for to draw my blood, yet will I give assay
To fetch thee hither once again. And (if that Fortune say
Amen) I will as well have thee and eke thine arrows as
I have the Trojan prophet who by me surprisèd was,
Or as I did the oracles and Trojan fates disclose,
Or as I from her chapel through the thickest of her foes
The Phrygian Pallad's image fetched. And yet doth Ajax still
410   Compare himself with me! Ye know it was the Destinies' will
That Troy should never taken be by any force until
This image first were got. And where was then our valiant knight
Sir Ajax? Where the stately words of such a hardy wight?
Why feareth he? Why dares Ulysses, venturing through the watch,
Commit his person to the night his business to dispatch?
And through the pikes not only for to pass the guarded wall,
But also for to enter to the strongest tower of all

And for to take the idol from her chapel and her shrine
And bear her thence amid his foes? For had this deed of mine
Been left undone, in vain his shield of oxen hides sevenfold      420
Should yet the son of Telamon have in his left hand hold.
That night subduèd I Troy town; that night did I it win
And opened it for you likewise with ease to enter in.
Cease to upbraid me by these looks and mumbling words of thine
With Diömed; his praise is in this fact as well as mine.
And thou thyself, when for our ships thou did'st in rescue stand,
Wert not alone; the multitude were helping thee at hand.
I had but only one with me, who (if he had not thought
A wise man better than a strong and that preferment ought
Not always follow force of hand) would now himself have sought      430
This armour. So would t'other Ajax better stayèd do,
And fierce Eurypyl and the son of haught Andraemon, too.
No less might eke Idomeney and eke Meriones,
His countryman, and Menelay. For every one of these
Are valiant men of hand and not inferior unto thee
In martial feats. And yet they are contented ruled to be
By mine advice. Thou hast a hand that serveth well in fight;
Thou hast a wit that stands in need of my direction right.
Thy force is witless; I have care of that that may ensue.
Thou well canst fight; the king doth choose the times for fighting
      due      440
By mine advice. Thou only with thy body canst avail;
But I with body and with mind to profit do not fail.
And look how much the master doth excel the galley-slave,
Or look how much pre-eminence the captain ought to have
Above his soldier; even so much excel I also thee.
A wit far passing strength of hand enclosèd is in me.
In wit rests chiefly all my force. My lords, I pray, bestow
This gift on him who aye hath been your watchman, as ye know.
And for my ten years' cark and care endurèd for your sake
Full recompense for my deserts with this same honour make.      450
Our labour draweth to an end; all lets are now by me
Dispatchèd. And by bringing Troy in case to taken be,
I have already taken it. Now, by the hope that ye
Conceive within a while of Troy the ruin for to see,

And by the gods of whom alate our enemies I bereft,
And as by wisdom to be done yet anything is left,
If any bold adventurous deed or any perilous thing
That asketh hazard both of life and limb to pass to bring,
Or if ye think of Trojan fates there yet doth aught remain,
460  Remember me. Or if from me this armour you restrain,
Bestow it on this same.' With that he showèd with his hand
Minerva's fatal image which hard by in sight did stand.

*Ulysses wins*
*the arms*

    The lords were movèd with his words, and then appearèd plain
    The force that is in eloquence. The learnèd man did gain
The armour of the valiant. He that did so oft sustain
Alone both fire and sword and Jove and Hector could not bide
One brunt of wrath; and whom no force could vanquish ere that
      tide,
Now only anguish overcomes. He draws his sword and says,
'Well, this is mine yet; unto this no claim Ulysses lays.
470  This must I use against myself; this blade that heretofore
Hath bathèd been in Trojan blood must now his master gore,
That none may Ajax overcome save Ajax.' With that word
Into his breast (not wounded erst) he thrust his deathful sword.
His hand to pull it out again unable was. The blood
Did spout it out. Anon the ground, bestainèd, where he stood
Did breed the pretty purple flower upon a clowre of green
Which of the wound of Hyacinth had erst engendered been.
The selfsame letters eke that for the child were written then
Were now again amid the flower new written for the man.
480  The former time complaint, the last a name did represent.

*The fall*
*of Troy*

    Ulysses, having won the prize, within a while was sent
To Thoant's and Hypsiphyle's realm, the land defamed of old
For murdering all the men therein by women overbold.
At length attaining land and luck according to his mind,
To carry Herc'les' arrows back he set his sails to wind.
Which when he with the lord of them among the Greeks had
      brought
And of the cruel war at length the utmost feat had wrought,
At once both Troy and Priam fell. And Priam's wretched wife
Lost after all her woman's shape and barkèd all her life

In foreign country. In the place that bringeth to a strait                    490
The long spread sea of Hellespont did Ilion burn in height.
The kindled fire with blazing flame continued unallayed,
And Priam with his agèd blood Jove's altar had berayed.
And Phoebus' priestess, casting up her hands to heaven on high,
Was dragged and halèd by the hair. The Grays most spitefully
(As each of them had prisoners ta'en in meed of victory)
Did draw the Trojan wives away, who, lingering while they
        mought
Among the burning temples of their gods, did hang about
Their sacred shrines and images. Astyanax down was cast
From that same turret from the which his mother in time past         500
Had showèd him his father stand oft, fighting to defend
Himself and that same famous realm of Troy that did descend
From many noble ancestors. And now the northern wind
With prosperous blasts to get them thence did put the Greeks in
        mind.
The shipmen went aboard and hoist up sails and made fro
        thence.
'Adieu, dear Troy,' the women cried. 'We halèd are from hence.'
And therewithal they kissed the ground and left, yet smoking still,
Their native houses. Last of all took ship against her will
Queen Hecub, who (a piteous case to see) was found amid
The tombs in which her sons were laid. And there, as Hecub did        510
Embrace their chests and kiss their bones, Ulysses, void of care,
Did pull her thence. Yet raught she up and in her bosom bare
Away a crumb of Hector's dust and left on Hector's grave
Her hoary hairs and tears, which for poor offerings she him gave.

Against the place where Ilion was there is another land              *The deaths of*
    Manurèd by the Biston men. In this same realm did stand          *Polydorus and*
King Polymnestor's palace rich, to whom King Priam sent                *Polyxena*
His little infant Polydore to foster, to th'intent
He might be out of danger from the wars; wherein he meant
Right wisely, had he not with him great riches sent, a bait           520
To stir a wicked covetous mind to treason and deceit.
For when the state of Troy decayed, the wicked king of Thrace
Did cut his nursechild's weasand and (as though the sinful case

Together with the body could have quite been put away)
He threw him also in the sea. It happened by the way
That Agamemnon was compelled with all his fleet to stay
Upon the coast of Thrace until the sea were waxen calm
And till the hideous storms did cease and furious winds were
    fallen.
Here, rising ghastly from the ground which far about him brake,
530 Achilles with a threatening look did like resemblance make
As when at Agamemnon he his wrongful sword did shake
And said, 'Unmindful part ye hence of me, O Greeks? And must
My merits thankless thus with me be buried in the dust?
Nay, do not so! But to th'intent my death due honour have,
Let Polyxene in sacrifice be slain upon my grave.'
Thus much he said. And shortly his companions, doing as
By vision of his cruel ghost commandment given them was,
Did fetch her from her mother's lap, whom at that time well near
In that most great adversity alonely she did cheer.
540 The haughty and unhappy maid (and rather to be thought
A man than woman) to the tomb with cruel hands was brought
To make a cursèd sacrifice. Who, minding constantly
Her honour, when she, standing at the altar pressed to die,
Perceived the savage ceremonies in making ready and
The cruel Neoptolemus with naked sword in hand
Stand staring with ungentle eyes upon her gentle face,
    She said, 'Now use thou when thou wilt my gentle blood. The
    case
    Requires no more delay. Bestow thy weapon in my chest
Or in my throat;' in saying so she proffered bare her breast
550 And eke her throat. 'Assure yourselves, it never shall be seen
That any wight shall by my will have slave of Polyxene.
Howbeit, with such a sacrifice no god ye can delight.
I would desire no more but that my wretched mother might
Be ignorant of this my death. My mother hind'reth me
And makes the pleasure of my death much lesser for to be.
Howbeit, not the death of me should justly grieve her heart
But her own life. Now to th'intent I freely may depart
To Limbo, stand ye men aloof; and sith I ask but right,
Forbear to touch me. So my blood unstainèd in his sight

Shall far more acceptable be, whatever wight he be                560
Whom ye prepare to pacify by sacrificing me.
Yet (if that these last words of mine may purchase any grace)
I, daughter of King Priam erst and now in prisoner's case,
Beseech you all unransomèd to render to my mother
My body and for burial of the same to take none other
Reward than tears; for while she could she did redeem with gold.'
This said, the tears that she forbare the people could not hold;
And even the very priest himself full sore against his will
And weeping thrust her through the breast, which she held stoutly
       still.
She, sinking softly to the ground with fainting legs, did bear       570
Even to the very latter gasp a count'nance void of fear.
And when she fell, she had a care such parts of her to hide
As womanhood and chastity forbiddeth to be spied.
   The Trojan women took her up and, mourning, reckonèd
   King Priam's children and what blood that house alone had
       shed.
They sighed for fair Polyxene; they sighèd eke for thee,
Who late wert Priam's wife, who late wert counted for to be
The flower of Asia in his flower and queen of mothers all,
But now the booty of the foe, as evil lot did fall,
And such a booty as the sly Ulysses did not pass                 580
Upon her, saving that erewhile she Hector's mother was.
So hardly for his mother could a master Hector find!
Embracing in her agèd arms the body of the mind
That was so stout, she poured thereon with sobbing sighs unsoft
The tears that for her husband and her children had so oft
And for her country shedded been. She weepèd in her wound
And kissed her pretty mouth and made her breast with strokes to
       sound
According to her wonted guise and in the jellied blood
Berayèd all her grizzled hair and in a sorrowful mood
Said these and many other words with breast bescratched and rent:   590
   'O daughter mine, the last for whom thy mother may lament
   (For what remains?), O daughter, thou art dead and gone! I see
Thy wound which at the very heart strikes me as well as thee.

And lest that any one of mine unwounded should depart,
Thou also gotten hast a wound. Howbeit, because thou wert
A woman, I believèd thee from weapon to be free.
But notwithstanding that thou art a woman, I do see
Thee slain by sword. Even he that killed thy brothers killeth thee,
Achilles, the decay of Troy and maker bare of me.

600  What time that he of Paris' shaft by Phoebus' means was slain,
I said, "Of fierce Achilles now no fear doth more remain."
But then, even then, he most of all was fearèd for to be.
The ashes of him rageth still against our race, I see;
We feel an enemy of him, dead and buried in his grave.
To feed Achilles' fury I a fruitful issue gave.
Great Troy lies underfoot, and with a right great grievous fall
The mischiefs of the commonweal are fully ended all.
But though to others Troy be gone, yet stands it still to me;
My sorrows run as fresh a race as ever and as free.

610  I, late ago a sovereign state, advancèd with such store
Of daughters, sons and son-in-laws and husband overmore
And daughter-in-laws, am carried like an outlaw bare and poor,
By force and violence halèd from my children's tombs, to be
Presented to Penelope a gift, who, showing me
In spinning my appointed task, shall say, "This same is she
That was sometime King Priam's wife; this was the famous
          mother
Of Hector." And now, after loss of such a sort of other,
Thou, who alonely in my grief my comfort did'st remain,
To pacify our enemy's wrath upon his tomb art slain.

620  Thus bare I deathgifts for my foes. To what intent am I,
Most wretched wight, remaining still? Why do I linger? Why
Doth hurtful age preserve me still alive? To what intent,
Ye cruel gods, reserve ye me that hath already spent
Too many years, unless it be new burials for to see?
And who would think that Priamus might happy counted be
Sith Troy is razèd? Happy man is he in being dead.
His life and kingdom he forwent together; and this stead
He sees not thee, his daughter, slain. But peradventure thou
Shall, like the daughter of a king, have sumptuous burial now

And with thy noble ancestors thy body laid shall be.                    630
Our lineage hath not so good luck. The most that shall to thee
Be yielded are thy mother's tears and in this foreign land,
To hide thy murdered corse withal, a little heap of sand.
For all is lost. Nay, yet remains (for whom I well can find
In heart to live a little while) an imp unto my mind
Most dear, now only left alone, sometime of many mo
The youngest, little Polydore, delivered late ago
To Polymnestor, king of Thrace, who dwells within these bounds.
But wherefore do I stay so long in washing of her wounds
And face berayed with gory blood?' In saying thus, she went        640
To seaward with an agèd pace and hoary hair berent.
And, wretched woman, as she called for pitchers for to draw
Up water, she of Polydore on shore the carcass saw
And eke the mighty wounds at which the tyrant's sword went
          thorough.
The Trojan ladies shriekèd out. But she was dumb for sorrow.
The anguish of her heart foreclosed as well her speech as eke
Her tears, devouring them within. She stood astonied, like
As if she had been stone. One while the ground she stared upon;
Another while a ghastly look she cast to heaven; anon
She lookèd on the face of him that lay before her killed.           650
Sometimes his wounds, his wounds, I say, she specially beheld.
And therewithal she armed herself and furnished her with ire,
Wherethrough, as soon as that her heart was fully set on fire,
As though she still had been a queen to vengeance she her bent,
Enforcing all her wits to find some kind of punishment.
And as a lion, robbèd of her whelps, becometh wood
And, taking on the footing of her enemy where he stood,
Pursueth him, though out of sight; even so Queen Hecube
(Now having ment her tears with wrath), forgetting quite that she
Was old but not her princely heart, to Polymnestor went,           660
The cursèd murderer, and desired his presence to th'intent
To show to him a mass of gold (so made she her pretence)
Which for her little Polydore was hid not far from thence.
The Thracian king, believing her, as eager of the prey,
Went with her to a secret place. And as they there did stay,
With flattering and deceitful tongue he thus to her did say:

'Make speed, I pray thee, Hecuba, and give thy son this gold.
I swear by God it shall be his, as well that I do hold
Already as that thou shalt give.' Upon him speaking so
670    And swearing and forswearing too, she lookèd sternly tho
And, being sore enflamed with wrath, caught hold upon him and,
Straight calling out for succour to the wives of Troy at hand,
Did in the traitor's face bestow her nails and scratchèd out
His eyes; her anger gave her heart and made her strong and stout.
She thrust her fingers in as far as could be and did bore
Not now his eyes (for why his eyes were pullèd out before)
But both the places of the eyes berayed with wicked blood.

    The Thracians, at their tyrant's harm for anger waxing wood,
    Began to scare the Trojan wives with darts and stones. Anon
680    Queen Hecub, running at a stone, with gnarring seized thereon
And worried it between her teeth. And as she oped her chap
To speak, instead of speech she barked. The place of this mishap
Remaineth still and of the thing there done bears yet the name.
Long mindful of her former ills, she sadly for the same
Went howling in the fields of Thrace. Her fortune movèd not
Her Trojans only but the Greeks, her foes, to ruth. Her lot
Did move even all the gods to ruth, and so effectually
That Hecub to deserve such end even Juno did deny.

    Although the Morning of the selfsame wars had favourer been,
    She had no leisure to lament the fortune of the queen
Nor on the slaughters and the fall of Ilion for to think.
A household care more nearer home did in her stomach sink,
For Memnon, her beloved son, whom dying she beheld
Upon the fierce Achilles' spear amid the Phrygian field.
She saw it, and her ruddy hue with which she wonted was
To dye the breaking of the day did into paleness pass,
And all the sky was hid with clouds. But when his corse was
    gone
To burningward, she could not find in heart to look thereon.
But with her hair about her ears she kneelèd down before
700    The mighty Jove and thus gan speak unto him, weeping sore:
    'Of all that have their dwelling place upon the golden sky
    The lowest (for through all the world the fewest shrines have I)

But yet a goddess, I do come, not that thou should'st decree
That altars, shrines and holidays be made to honour me;
Yet if thou mark how much that I, a woman, do for thee
In keeping night within her bounds by bringing to thee light,
Thou well may'st think me worthy some reward to claim of right.
But neither now is that the thing the Morning cares to have,
Ne yet her state is such as now due honour for to crave.
Bereft of my dear Memnon, who in fighting valiantly          710
To help his uncle (so it was your will, O gods) did die
Of stout Achilles' sturdy spear even in his flowering prime,
I sue to thee, O king of gods, to do him at this time
Some honour as a comfort of his death and ease this heart
Of mine, which greatly grievèd is with wound of piercing smart.'
  No sooner Jove had granted Dame Aurora her desire
  But that the flame of Memnon's corse, that burnèd in the fire,
Did fall; and flaky rolls of smoke did dark the day, as when
A foggy mist steams upward from a river or a fen
And suffereth not the sun to shine within it. Black as coal      720
The cinder rose and, into one round lump assembling whole,
Grew gross and took both shape and hue. The fire did life it send;
The lightness of the substance self did wings unto it lend.
And at the first it flittered like a bird, and by and by
It flew, a feathered bird indeed. And with that one gan fly
Innumerable mo of selfsame brood, who once or twice
Did soar about the fire and made a piteous shrieking thrice.
The fourth time in their flying round themselves they all
          withdrew
In battles twain, and fiercely forth of either side one flew
To fight a combat. With their bills and hookèd talons keen      730
And with their wings courageously they wreak their wrathful
          teen.
And mindful of the valiant man of whom they issued been,
They never ceasèd jobbing each upon the other's breast
Until they, falling both down dead with fighting overpressed,
Had offered up their bodies as a worthy sacrifice
Unto their cousin Memnon, who to ashes burnèd lies.
These sudden birds were namèd of the founder of their stock;
For men do call them Memnon's birds. And every year a flock

Repair to Memnon's tomb, where two do in the foresaid wise

740 In manner of a year-mind slay themselves in sacrifice.

Thus, whereas others did lament that Dymant's daughter barked,

Aurora's own grief busied her, that smally she it marked;

Which thing she to this present time with piteous tears doth show,

For through the universal world she sheddeth moisting dew.

*The flight*     Yet suffered not the Destinies all hope to perish quite
*of Aeneas*
Together with the town of Troy. That good and godly knight,

The son of Venus, bare away by night upon his back

His agèd father and his gods, an honourable pack.

Of all the riches of the town that only prey he chose,

750 So godly was his mind. And like a banished man he goes

By water with his own young son, Ascanius, from the Isle

Antandros, and he shuns the shore of Thracia, which erewhile

The wicked tyrant's treason did with Polydore's blood defile.

And, having wind and tide at will, he safely with his train

Arrivèd at Apollo's town where Anius then did reign.

Who, being both Apollo's priest and of that place the king,

Did entertain him in his house and unto church him bring

And showed him both the city and the temples known of old

And eke the sacred trees by which Latona once took hold

760 When she of childbirth travailèd. As soon as sacrifice

Was done with oxen's inwards, burnt according to the guise,

And casting incense in the fire and shedding wine thereon,

They joyful to the court returned; and there they took anon

Repast of meat and drink. Then said the good Anchises this:

'O Phoebus' sovereign priest, unless I take my marks amiss,

As I remember, when I first of all this town did see

Four daughters and a son of thine thou haddest here with thee.'

*Anius'*       King Anius shook his head, whereon he ware a mitre white,
*daughters*
And answered thus: 'O noble prince, in faith thou guessest
right.

770 Of children five a father then thou diddest me behold,

Who now (with such unconstancy are mortal matters rolled)

Am in a manner childless quite. For what avails my son

Who in the Isle of Anderland a great way hence doth wone?

Which country takes his name of him. And in the selfsaid place,

Instead of father, like a king he holds the royal mace.

Apollo gave his lot to him; and Bacchus, for to show
His love, a greater gift upon his sisters did bestow
Than could be wished or credited. For whatsoever they
Did touch was turnèd into corn and wine and oil straightway.
And so there was rich use in them. As soon as that the fame    780
Hereof to Agamemnon's ears, the scourge of Trojans, came,
Lest you might taste your storms alone and we not feel the same
In part, an host he hither sent and, whether I would or no,
Did take them from me, forcing them among the Greeks to go
To feed the Greekish army with their heavenly gift. But they
Escapèd whither they could by flight. A couple took their way
To Isle Euboea; t'other two to Anderland did fly,
Their brother's realm. An host of men pursued them by and by
And threatened war unless they were delivered. Force of fear,
Subduing nature, did constrain the brother (men must bear    790
With fearfulness) to render up his sisters to their foe.
For neither was Aeneas there nor valiant Hector (who
Did make your war last ten years long) the country to defend.
Now when they should like prisoners have been fettered, in the
    end
They, casting up their hands (which yet were free) to heaven, did
    cry
To Bacchus for to succour them; who helped them by and by —
At leastwise if it may be termed a help in wondrous wise
To alter folk. For never could I learn ne can surmise
The manner how they lost their shape. The thing itself is known.
With feathered wings as white as snow they quite away are flown,    800
Transformèd into dovehouse doves, thy wise Dame Venus' birds.'

When that the time of meat was spent with these and suchlike
    words,
The table was removèd straight and then they went to sleep.
Next morrow, rising up as soon as day began to peep,
They went to Phoebus' oracle, which willèd them to go
Unto their mother country and the coasts their stock came fro.
King Anius bare them company. And when away they should,
He gave them gifts. Anchises had a sceptre all of gold;
Ascanius had a quiver and a cloak right brave and trim;
Aeneas had a standing cup presented unto him.    810

*The flight of Aeneas (continued)*

The Theban, Therses, who had been King Anius' guest erewhile,
Did send it out of Thessaly. But Alcon, one of Myle,
Did make the cup, and he thereon a story portrayed out.
It was a city with seven gates in circuit round about
Which men might easily all discern. The gates did represent
The city's name and showèd plain what town thereby was meant.
Without the town were funerals a-doing for the dead
With hearses, tapers, fires and tombs. The wives with ruffled head
And stomachs bare pretended grief; the nymphs seemed tears to
        shed
820   And wail the drying of their wells. The leafless trees did sear;
And, licking on the parchèd stones, goats roamèd here and there.
Behold, amid this Theban town was lively portrayed out
Echion's daughters twain, of which the one with courage stout
Did proffer both her naked throat and stomach to the knife,
And t'other with a manly heart did also spend her life
For safeguard of her countryfolk; and how that thereupon
They both were carried solemnly on hearses and anon
Were burnèd in the chiefest place of all the Theban town.
Then (lest their lineage should decay, who died with such
        renown)
830   Out of the ashes of the maids there issued two young men,
And they unto their mothers' dust did obsequies again.
Thus much was gravèd curiously in ancient precious brass,
And on the brim a trail of flowers of bear-breech gilded was.
The Trojans also gave to him as costly gifts again:
Because he was Apollo's priest they gave to him as then
A chest to keep in frankincense; they gave him furthermore
A crown of gold wherein were set of precious stones great store.
    Then, calling to remembrance that the Trojans issued were
    Of Teucer's blood, they sailed to Crete. But long they could
        not there
840   Abide th'infection of the air. And so they did forsake
The hundred cities and with speed to Italyward did make.
The winter waxèd hard and rough and tossed them very sore.
And when their ships arrivèd were upon the perilous shore
Among the Strophad Isles, the bird Aëllo did them fear.
The coasts of Dulich, Ithaca and Same they passèd were

And eke the court of Neritos, where wise Ulysses reigned,
And came to Ambrace, for the which the gods strong strife
    maintained.
There saw they turnèd into stone the judge whose image yet
At Actium in Apollo's church in sign thereof doth sit.
They viewèd also Dodon grove where oaks spake, and the coast    850
Of Chaon where the sons of King Molossus scaped a most
Ungracious fire by taking wings. From thence they coasted by
The country of the Phaeacs, fraught with fruit abundantly.
Then took they land in Epire, and to Buthrotos they went,
Whereas the Trojan prophet dwelt, whose reign did represent
An image of their ancient Troy. There being certified
Of things to come by Helen (who while there they did abide
Informèd them right faithfully of all that should betide),
They passèd into Sicily. With corners three this land
Shoots out into the sea; of which Pachynus' front doth stand    860
Against the south coast, Lilyby doth face the gentle west,
And Pelore unto Charles's wain doth northward bare his breast.
The Trojans under Pelore gat with oars and prosperous tides,
And in the even by Zancle shore their fleet at anchor rides.
Upon the left side restlessly Charybdis aye doth beat them
And swalloweth ships and spews them up as fast as it doth eat
    them.
And Scylla beateth on their right, which from the navel down
Is patchèd up with cruel curs and upward to the crown
Doth keep the count'nance of a maid. And (if that all be true
That poets feign) she was sometime a maid right fair of hue.    870
To her made many wooers suit, all which she did eschew.
And, going to the salt-seanymphs (to whom she was right dear),
She vaunted to how many men she gave the slip that year.
To whom the Lady Galate in kembing of her hair
Said thus with sighs: 'But they that sought to thee, O lady, were
None other than of human kind, to whom without all fear
Of harm thou mightest, as thou dost, give nay. But as for me,
Although that I of Nereus and grey Doris daughter be
And of my sisters have with me continually a guard,
I could not scape the Cyclops' love, but to my grief full hard.'    880

With that her tears did stop her speech. As soon as that the maid
Had dried them with her marble thumb and moaned the nymph,
    she said,
'Dear goddess, tell me all your grief and hide it not from me.
For, trust me, I will unto you both true and secret be.'
Then unto Cratey's daughter thus the nymph her plaint did frame:

*Acis and*
*Galatea*

  'Of Faun and nymph Symaethis born was Acis, who became
  A joy to both his parents, but to me the greater joy.
For, being but a sixteen years of age, this fair sweet boy
Did take me to his love what time about his childish chin

890  The tender hair like mossy down to sprout did first begin.
I lovèd him beyond all God's forbode, and likewise me
The giant Cyclops. Neither, if demanded it should be,
I well were able for to tell you whether that the love
Of Acis or the Cyclops' hate did more my stomach move.
There was no odds between them. O dear goddess Venus, what
A power hast thou! Behold how even this ugly giant that
No spark of meekness in him hath, who is a terror to
The very woods, whom never guest nor stranger came unto
Without displeasure, who the heavens and all the gods despiseth,

900  Doth feel what thing is love. The love of me him so surpriseth
That Polypheme, regarding not his sheep and hollow cave
And having care to please, doth go about to make him brave.
His stour stiff hair he kembeth now with strong and sturdy rakes
And with a scythe doth marquisotte his bristled beard and takes
Delight to look upon himself in waters and to frame
His count'nance. Of his murderous heart the wildness waxeth tame.
His unastaunchèd thirst of blood is quenchèd. Ships may pass
And repass safely. In the while that he in love thus was
One Telemus, Eurymed's son, a man of passing skill

910  In birdflight, taking land that time in Sicil, went until
The orpèd giant Polypheme and said, "This one round eye
That now amid thy forehead stands shall one day ere thou die
By sly Ulysses blinded be." The giant laughed thereat
And said, "O foolish soothsayer, thou deceivèd art in that.
For why another, even a wench, already hath it blinded."
Thus scorning him that told him truth because he was high-
    minded,

He either made the ground to shake in walking on the shore
Or roused him in his shady cave. With wedgèd point before
There shoots a hill into the sea, whereof the sea doth beat
On either side. The one-eyed fiend came up and made his seat      920
Thereon, and after came his sheep undriven. As soon as he
Had at his foot laid down his staff, which was a whole pine-tree
Well able for to be a mast to any ship, he takes
His pipe compact of five-score reeds, and therewithal he makes
So loud a noise that all the hills and waters thereabout
Might easily hear the shirlness of the shepherd's whistling out.
I, lying underneath the rock and leaning in the lap
Of Acis, marked these words of his which far I heard by hap:
  ' "More white thou art than primrose leaf, my lady Galate,
    More fresh than mead, more tall and straight than lofty
            alder-tree;                                            930
More bright than glass, more wanton than the tender kid,
            forsooth;
Than cockleshells continually with water worn more smooth;
More cheerful than the winter's sun or summer's shadow cold;
More seemly and more comely than the plane-tree to behold;
Of value more than apples be, although they were of gold;
More clear than frozen ice, more sweet than grape through ripe,
      iwis;
More soft than butter newly made or down of cygnet is;
And much more fair and beautiful than garden to mine eye,
But that thou from my company continually dost fly.
And thou, the selfsame Galat, art more tettish for to frame       940
Than oxen of the wilderness whom never wight did tame;
More fleeting than the waves, more hard than warried oak to
            twine;
More tough than willow twigs, more lithe than is the wild white
            vine;
More than this rock unmovable, more violent than a stream;
More proud than peacock praised, more fierce than fire and more
            extreme;
More rough than briars, more cruel than the new-delivered bear;
More merciless than trodden snake, than sea more deaf of ear;

And – which (and if it lay in me) I chiefly would restrain –
Not only swifter pacèd than the stag in chase on plain,
950   But also swifter than the wind and flightful air. But if
Thou knew me well, it would thee irk to fly and be a grief
To tarry from me. Yea, thou would'st endeavour all thy power
To keep me wholly to thyself. The quarry is my bower
Hewn out of whole main stone. No sun in summer there can
        swelt;
No nipping cold in wintertime within the same is felt.
Gay apples weighing down the boughs have I and grapes like
        gold,
And purple grapes on spreaded vines as many as can hold.
Both which I do reserve for thee. Thyself shalt with thy hand
The soft sweet strawberries gather which in woody shadow stand.
960   The cornel berries also from the tree thyself shalt pull,
And pleasant plums, some yellow like new wax, some blue, some
        full
Of ruddy juice. Of chestnuts eke, if my wife thou wilt be,
Thou shalt have store and fruits all sorts. All trees shall serve for
        thee.
This cattle here is all mine own. And many mo beside
Do either in the bottoms feed or in the woods them hide,
And many standing at their stalls do in my cave abide.
The number of them (if a man should ask) I cannot show.
Tush, beggars of their cattle use the number for to know.
And for the goodness of the same no whit believe thou me,
970   But come thyself, and if thou wilt, the truth thereof to see.
See how their udders full do make them straddle. Lesser ware
Shut up at home in close warm pends are lambs. There also are
In other pinfolds kids of selfsame yeaning-time. Thus have
I always milk as white as snow; whereof I some do save
To drink, and of the rest is made good cheese. And, furthermore,
Not only stale and common gifts and pleasures whereof store
Is to be had at each man's hand (as leverets, kids and does,
A pair of pigeons or a nest of birds new found or roes)
Shall unto thee presented be; I found this t'other day
980   A pair of bearwhelps, each so like the other as they lay

Upon a hill, that scarce ye each discern from other may.
And when that I did find them, I did take them up and say,
'These will I for my lady keep for her therewith to play.'
Now put thou up thy fair bright head, good Galat, I thee pray,
Above the greenish waves; now come, my Galat, come away
And of my present take no scorn. I know myself to be
A jolly fellow. For even now I did behold and see
Mine image in the water sheer, and sure methought I took
Delight to see my goodly shape and favour in the brook.
Behold how big I am. Not Jove in heaven (for so you men          990
Report one Jove to reign, of whom I pass not for to ken)
Is huger than this doughty corse of mine. A bush of hair
Doth overdreep my visage grim and shadows, as it were,
A grove upon my shoulders twain. And think it not to be
A shame for that with bristled hair my body rough ye see.
A foul ill-favoured sight it is to see a leafless tree;
A loathly thing it is a horse without a mane to keep.
As feathers do become the birds and wool becometh sheep,
Even so a beard and bristled skin becometh also men.
I have but one eye which doth stand amid my front. What then?     1000
This one round eye of mine is like a mighty target. Why,
Views not the sun all things from heaven? Yet but one only eye
Hath he. Moreover in your seas my father bears the sway.
Him will I make thy father-in-law. Have mercy, I thee pray,
And hearken to mine humble suit. For only unto thee
Yield I. Even I, of whom both heaven and Jove despisèd be
And eke the piercing thunderbolt, do stand in awe and fear
Of thee, O Nerey. Thine ill will is grievouser to bear
Than is the deadly thunderclap. Yet could I better find
In heart to suffer this contempt of thine with patient mind      1010
If thou did'st shun all other folk as well as me. But why,
Rejecting Cyclops, dost thou love dwarf Acis? Why, say I,
Prefer'st thou Acis unto me? Well, let him likèd be
Both of himself and also (which I would be loath) of thee.
And if I catch him he shall feel that in my body is
The force that should be. I shall paunch him quick. Those limbs
        of his

I will in pieces tear and strew them in the fields and in
Thy waters if he do thee haunt. For I do swelt within,
And, being chafed, the flame doth burn more fierce to my unrest.
1020  Methinks Mount Etna with his force is closèd in my breast.
And yet it nothing moveth thee." As soon as he had talked
Thus much in vain (I saw well all), he rose and, fuming, stalked
Among his woods and wonted lawns, as doth a bulchin when
The cow is from him ta'en. He could him nowhere rest as then.
Anon the fiend espièd me and Acis where we lay
Before we wist or fearèd it and, crying out, gan say,
"I see ye, and confounded might I be with endless shame
But if I make this day the last agreement of your game."
These words were spoke with such a rere as very well became
1030  An angry giant. Etna shook with loudness of the same.
I, scared therewith, dopped underneath the water, and the knight
Simethus, turning straight his back, did give himself to flight
And crièd, "Help me, Galate, help, parents, I you pray,
And in your kingdom me receive, who perish must straightway."
The round-eyed devil made pursuit and, rending up a fleece
Of Etna rock, threw after him; of which a little piece
Did Acis overtake. And yet as little as it was,
It overwhelmèd Acis whole. I, wretched wight, alas,
Did that which Destinies would permit. Forthwith I brought to
       pass
1040  That Acis should receive the force his father had before.
His scarlet blood did issue from the lump, and more and more
Within a while the redness gan to vanish; and the hue
Resembled at the first a brook with rain distroubled new
Which waxeth clear by length of time. Anon the lump did cleave,
And from the hollow cliff thereof high reeds sprang up alive;
And at the hollow issue of the stone the bubbling water
Came trickling out. And by and by (which is a wondrous matter)
The stripling with a wreath of reed about his hornèd head
Avaunced his body to the waist. Who, save he was that stead
1050  Much bigger than he erst had been and altogether grey,
Was Acis still. And, being turned to water, at this day
In shape of river still he bears his former name away.'

The Lady Galat ceased her talk, and straight the company brake.

And Nerey's daughters, parting thence, swam in the gentle lake.
Dame Scylla home again returned. She durst not her betake
To open sea, and either roamed upon the sandy shore
Stark nak'd or, when for weariness she could not walk no more,
She then withdrew her out of sight and gat her to a pool
And in the water of the same her heated limbs did cool.
Behold the fortune. Glaucus, who, then being late before            1060
Transformèd in Euboea Isle upon Anthedon shore,
Was new become a dweller in the sea, as he did swim
Along the coast was ta'en in love at sight of Scylla trim
And spake such words as he did think might make her tarry still.
Yet fled she still, and swift for fear she gat her to a hill
That butted on the sea. Right steep and upward sharp did shoot
A lofty top with trees; beneath was hollow at the foot.
Here Scylla stayed and, being safe by strongness of the place
(Not knowing if he monster were or god, that did her chase),
She lookèd back. And, wondering at his colour and his hair        1070
With which his shoulders and his back all wholly covered were,
She saw his nether parts were like a fish with tail writhed round,
Who, leaning to the nearest rock, said thus with loud clear sound:
  'Fair maid, I neither monster am nor cruel savage beast,
  But of the sea a god, whose power and favour is not least.
For neither Proteu in the sea nor Triton have more might
Nor yet the son of Athamas that now Palaemon hight.
Yet once I was a mortal man. But you must know that I
Was given to seaworks and in them me only did apply.
For sometime I did draw the drag in which the fishes were,          1080
And sometime, sitting on the cliffs, I angled here and there.
There butteth on a fair green mead a bank whereof t'one half
Is closed with sea, the rest is clad with herbs which never calf
Nor hornèd ox nor silly sheep nor shag-haired goat did feed.
The busy bee did never there of flowers sweet smelling speed;
No gladsome garlands ever there were gathered for the head.
No hand those flowers ever yet with hookèd scythe did shred;

I was the first that ever set my foot upon that plot.
Now as I dried my dropping nets and laid abroad my lot
1090 To tell how many fishes had by chance to net been sent
Or through their own too light belief on baited hook been hent
(The matter seemeth like a lie, but what avails to lie?),
As soon as that my prey had touched the grass, it by and by
Began to move and flask their fins and swim upon the dry
As in the sea. And as I paused and wondered at the sight,
My draught of fishes everych one to seaward took their flight
And, leaping from the shore, forsook their newfound master quite.
I was amazèd at the thing and, standing long in doubt,
I sought the cause, if any god had brought this same about
1100 Or else some juice of herb. And as I so did musing stand,
"What herb", quoth I, "hath such a power?" And, gathering with
       my hand
The grass, I bit it with my tooth. My throat had scarcely yet
Well swallowed down the uncouth juice, when like an ague fit
I felt mine inwards suddenly to shake, and with the same
A love of other nature in my breast with violence came.
And long I could it not resist, but said, "Dear land, adieu;
For never shall I haunt thee more." And with that word I threw
My body in the sea. The gods thereof, receiving me,
Vouchsafèd in their order me installèd for to be,
1110 Desiring old Oceanus and Tethys for their sake
The rest of my mortality away from me to take.
They hallowed me and, having said nine times the holy rhyme
That purgeth all profanèdness, they chargèd me that time
To put my breastbulk underneath a hundred streams. Anon
The brooks from sundry coasts and all the seas did ride upon
My head. From whence as soon as I returnèd, by and by
I felt myself far otherwise through all my limbs than I
Had been before; and in my mind I was another man.
Thus far of all that me befell make just report I can.
1120 Thus far I bear in mind. The rest my mind perceivèd not.
Then first of all this hoary green-grey grisled beard I got
And this same bush of hair, which all along the seas I sweep,
And these same mighty shoulders and these greyish arms and feet

Confounded into finnèd fish. But what availeth me
This goodly shape and of the gods of sea to lovèd be
Or for to be a god myself, if they delight not thee?'
    As he was speaking this and still about to utter more,
    Dame Scylla him forsook; whereat he waxing angry sore
And being quickened with repulse, in rage he took his way
To Circe's, Titan's daughter's, court, which full of monsters lay.     1130

FINIS LIBRI DECIMI TERTII.

# The Fourteenth Book of Ovid's
# Metamorphoses

Now had th'Euboean fisherman, who lately was become

A god of sea to dwell in sea for aye, already swum
Past Etna, which upon the face of Giant Typho lies,
Together with the pasture of the Cyclops, which defies
Both plough and harrow and by teams of oxen sets no store,
And Zancle and cracked Rhegion, which stands at other shore,
And eke the rough and shipwreck sea which, being hemmèd in
With two main lands on either side, is as a bound between
The fruitful realms of Italy and Sicil. From that place
He, cutting through the Tyrrhene sea with both his arms apace,          10
Arrivèd at the grassy hills and at the palace high
Of Circe, Phoebus' imp, which full of sundry beasts did lie.
When Glaucus in her presence came and had her greeted and
Receivèd friendly welcoming and greeting at her hand,
He said, 'O goddess, pity me, a god, I thee desire.
Thou only (if at least thou think me worthy so great hire)
Canst ease this love of mine. No wight doth better know than I
The power of herbs, who late ago transformèd was thereby.
And now to open unto thee of this my grief the ground,
Upon th'Italian shore against Messene walls I found          20
Fair Scylla. Shame it is to tell how scornful she did take
The gentle words and promises and suit that I did make.
But if that any power at all consist in charms, then let
That sacred mouth of thine cast charms; or if more force be set
In herbs to compass things withal, then use the herbs that have
Most strength in working. Neither think I hither come to crave
A medicine for to heal myself and cure my wounded heart.
I force no end. I would have her be partner of my smart.'

But Circe – for no natures are more lightly set on fire
30      Than such as she is, whether that the cause of this desire
Were only in herself or that Dame Venus, bearing aye
In mind her father's deed in once disclosing of her play,
Did stir her hereunto – said thus: 'It were a better way
For thee to fancy such a one whose will and whole desire
Is bent to thine and who is singed with selfsame kind of fire.
Thou worthy art of suit to thee and, credit me, thou should'st
Be wooed indeed, if any hope of speeding give thou would'st.
And therefore doubt not. Only of thy beauty liking have.
Lo, I, who am a goddess and the imp of Phoebus brave,
40      Who can so much by charms, who can so much by herbs, do vow
Myself to thee. If I disdain, disdain me also thou.
And if I yield, yield thou likewise. And in one only deed
Avenge thyself of twain.' To her entreating thus to speed,
'First trees shall grow', quoth Glaucus, 'in the sea and reek shall
            thrive
On tops of hills ere I, as long as Scylla is alive,
Do change my love.' The goddess waxed right wroth; and sith she
            could
Not hurt his person, being fallen in love with him, ne would,
She spited her that was preferred before her. And upon
Displeasure ta'en of this repulse, she went her way anon.
50      And wicked weeds of grisly juice together she did bray;
And in the braying, witching charms she over them did say.
And, putting on a russet cloak, she passèd through the rout
Of savage beasts that in her court came fawning round about
And, going unto Rhegion cliff which stands against the shore
Of Zancle, entered by and by the waters that do roar
With violent tides, upon the which she stood as on firm land
And ran and never wet her feet a whit. There was at hand
A little plash that bowèd like a bow that standeth bent
Where Scylla wonted was to rest herself and thither went
60      From rage of sea and air what time the sun amid the sky
Is hottest, making shadows short by mounting up on high.
This plash did Circe then infect against that Scylla came
And with her poisons, which had power most monstrous shapes to
            frame,

Defiлèd it. She sprinkled there the juice of venomed weeds,
And thrice nine times with witching mouth she, softly mumbling,
    reads
A charm right dark of uncouth words. No sooner Scylla came
Within this plash and to the waist had waded in the same
But that she saw her hinderloins with barking bugs attaint.
And at the first, not thinking with her body they were ment
As parts thereof, she started back and rated them. And sore          70
She was afraid the eager curs should bite her. But the more
She shunnèd them, the surer still she was to have them there.
In seeking where her loins and thighs and feet and ankles were,
Chaps like the chaps of Cerberus instead of them she found.
Nought else was there than cruel curs from belly down to ground.
So underneath misshappen loins and womb remaining sound
Her mannish masties' backs were aye within the water drowned.
    Her lover Glaucus wept thereat and Circe's bed refused                   *Aeneas'*
    That had so passing cruelly her herbs on Scylla used.                    *voyaging*
But Scylla in that place abode. And for the hate she bore              80
To Circeward, as soon as meet occasion served therefore,
She spoiled Ulysses of his mates. And shortly after she
Had also drowned the Trojan fleet, but that (as yet we see)
She was transformed to rock of stone which shipmen warily shun.
When from this rock the Trojan fleet by force of oars had won
And from Charybdis' greedy gulf and were in manner ready
To have arrived in Italy, the wind did rise so heady
As that it drave them back upon the coast of Afric. There
The Tyrian queen, who afterward unpatiently should bear
The going of this Trojan prince away, did entertain                    90
Aeneas in her house and was right glad of him and fain.
Upon a pile made underneath pretence of sacrifice
She gored herself upon a sword and in most woeful wise,
As she herself had been beguiled, so she beguilèd all.
Eftsoon Aeneas, flying from the newly rearèd wall
Of Carthage in that sandy land, retirèd back again
To Sicil, where his faithful friend Acestes reigned. And when
He there had done his sacrifice and kept an obit at
Hid father's tomb, he out of hand did mend his galleys that

100 Dame Iris, Juno's messenger, had burnèd up almost.
And, sailing thence, he kept his course aloof along the coast
Of Aeoly and of Vulcan's isles, the which of brimstone smoke.
And, passing by the mermaids' rocks (his pilot by a stroke
Of tempest being drowned in sea), he sailed by Prochyte and
Inarime and, which upon a barren hill doth stand,
The land of Ape Isle, which doth take that name of people sly
There dwelling. For the sire of gods, abhorring utterly
The lewdness of the Cercops and their wilful perjury
And eke their guileful dealing, did transform them everych one
110 Into an evil-favoured kind of beast, that, being none,
They might yet still resemble men. He knit in lesser space
Their members, and he beat me flat their noses to their face,
The which he fillèd furrow-like with wrinkles everywhere.
He clad their bodies over all with fallow-coloured hair
And put them into this same isle to dwell forever there.
But first he did bereave them of the use of speech and tongue
Which they to cursèd perjury did use, both old and young.
To chatter hoarsely and to shriek, to jabber and to squeak
He hath them left, and for to mop and mow, but not to speak.

*Aeneas visits*
*the underworld*

Aeneas, having passed this isle and on his right hand left
The town of Naples and the tomb of Misene on his left
Together with the fenny grounds, at Cumey landed and
Went unto long-lived Sibyl's house, with whom he went in hand
That he to see his father's ghost might go by Averne deep.
She long upon the earth in stound her eyes did fixèd keep.
And at the length, as soon as that the sprite of prophecy
Was entered her, she, raising them, did thus again reply:
'O most renownèd wight, of whom the godliness by fire
And valiantness is tried by sword, great things thou dost require.
130 But fear not, Trojan. For thou shalt be lord of thy desire
To see the reverend image of thy dear-belovèd sire.
Among the fair Elysian fields, where godly folk abide,
And all the lowest kingdoms of the world I will thee guide.
No way to virtue is restrained.' This spoken, she did show
A golden bough that in the wood of Proserpine did grow
And willèd him to pull it from the tree. He did obey
And saw the power of dreadful hell and where his grandsires lay

And eke the agèd ghost of stout Anchises. Furthermore,
He learned the customs of the land arrived at late before
And what adventures should by war betide him in that place.          140
From thence retiring up again a slow and weary pace,
He did assuage the tediousness by talking with his guide.
For as he in the twilight dim this dreadful way did ride,
He said, 'Whether present thou thyself a goddess be
Or such a one as God doth love most dearly, I will thee
For ever as a goddess take and will acknowledge me
Thy servant for safe guiding me the place of death to see
And for thou from the place of death hast brought me safe and
        free.
For which desert, what time I shall attain to open air,
I will a temple to thee build right sumptuous, large and fair          150
And honour thee with frankincense.' The prophetess did cast
Her eye upon Aeneas back and, sighing, said at last,
'I am no goddess. Neither think thou canst with conscience right
With holy incense honour give to any mortal wight.
But to th'intent through ignorance thou err not, I had been
Eternal and of worldly life I should none end have seen
If that I would my maidenhood on Phoebus have bestowed.
Howbeit while he stood in hope to have the same and trowed
To overcome me with his gifts, "Thou maid of Cumes," quoth
        he,
"Choose what thou wilt, and of thy wish the owner thou shalt
        be."                                                           160
I, taking full my hand of dust and showing it him there,
Desirèd like a fool to live as many years as were
Small grains of cinder in that heap; I quite forgot to crave
Immediately the race of all those years in youth to have.
Yet did he grant me also that, upon condition I
Would let him have my maidenhood, which thing I did deny.
And so, rejecting Phoebus' gift, a single life I led.
But now the blissful time of youth is altogether fled,
And irksome age with trembling pace is stolen upon my head,
Which long I must endure. For now already, as you see,                 170
Seven hundred years are come and gone and, that the number be

Full matchèd of the grains of dust, three hundred harvests mo
I must, three hundred vintages, see more before I go.
The day will come that length of time shall make my body small
And little of my withered limbs shall leave or nought at all.
And none shall think that ever god was ta'en in love with me.
Even out of Phoebus' knowledge then, perchance, I grown shall
     be,
Or, at the least, that ever he me loved he shall deny,
So sore I shall be alterèd. And then shall no man's eye
180 Discern me. Only by my voice I shall be known, for why
The Fates shall leave me still my voice for folk to know me by.'

*Achaemenides'*        As Sibyl in the vaulted way such talk as this did frame,
*story*            The Trojan knight Aeneas up at Cumes fro Limbo came.
And, having done the sacrifice accustomed for the same,
He took his journey to the coast which had not yet the name
Received of his nurse. In this same place he found a mate
Of wise Ulysses, Marcare of Neritos, who late
Before had after all his long and tedious toils there stayed.
He, spying Achaemenides (whom late ago, afraid,
190 They had among Mount Etna's cliffs abandoned when they fled
From Polypheme) and wondering for to see he was not dead,
Said thus: 'O Achaemenides, what chance or rather what
Good god hath saved the life of thee? What is the reason that
A barbarous ship bears thee, a Greek? Or whither sailest thou?'

     To him thus Achaemenides, his own man freely now
And not forgrown as one forlorn nor clad in bristled hide,
Made answer: 'Yet again I would I should in peril hide
Of Polypheme and that I might those chaps of his behold
Besmearèd with the blood of men, but if that I do hold
200 This ship more dear than all the realm of wise Ulysses or
If lesser of Aeneas I do make account than for
My father. Neither (though I did as much as done might be)
I could enough be thankful for his goodness towards me.
That I still speak and breathe, that I the sun and heaven do see,
Is his gift. Can I thankless, then, or mindless of him be,
That down the round-eyed giant's throat this soul of mine went
     not
And that from henceforth, when to die it ever be my lot,

I may be laid in grave or, sure, not in the giant's maw?
What heart had I that time (at least if fear did not withdraw
Both heart and sense) when, left behind, you taking ship I saw?          210
I would have callèd after you, but that I was afraid
By making outcry to my foe myself to have bewrayed.
For even the noise that you did make did put Ulysses' ship
In danger. I did see him from a craggèd mountain strip
A mighty rock and into sea it throw midway and more.
Again, I saw his giant's paw throw huge big stones great store
As if it were a sling. And sore I fearèd lest your ship
Should drownèd by the water be that from the stones did skip
Or by the stones themselves, as if myself had been therein.
But when that flight had savèd you from death, he did begin          220
On Etna, sighing, up and down to walk, and with his paws
Went groping of the trees among the woods. And for because
He could not see, he knocked his shins against the rocks each
          where.
And, stretching out his grisly arms (which all begrimèd were
With baken blood) to seaward, he the Greekish nation banned
And said, 'O, if that some good chance might bring unto my hand
Ulysses or some mate of his on whom to wreak mine ire,
Upon whose bowels with my teeth I like a hawk might tire,
Whose living members might with these my talons tearèd been,
Whose blood might bubble down my throat, whose flesh might
          pant between          230
My jaws, how light or none at all this losing of mine eye
Would seem!' These words and many mo the cruel fiend did cry.
A shuddering horror piercèd me to see his smudgèd face
And cruel hands and in his front the foul round eyeless place
And monstrous members and his beard, beslubbered with the
          blood
Of man. Before mine eyes then death the smallest sorrow stood.
I lookèd every minute to be seizèd in his paw;
I lookèd ever when he should have crammed me in his maw.
And in my mind I of that time, methought, the image saw
When, having dinged a dozen of our fellows to the ground          240
And lying like a lion fierce or hunger-starvèd hound

Upon them, very eagerly he down his greedy gut
Their bowels and their limbs yet more than half-alive did put
And with their flesh together crashed the bones and marrow
       white.
I, trembling like an aspen leaf, stood sad and bloodless quite
And, in beholding how he fed and belkèd up again
His bloody victuals at his mouth and uttered out amain
The clotted gobbets mixed with wine, I thus surmised: like lot
Hangs over my head now, and I must also go to pot.

250    And, hiding me for many days and quaking horribly
At every noise and dreading death and wishing for to die,
Appeasing hunger with the leaves of trees and herbs and mast,
Alone and poor and footless and to death and penance cast,
A long time after I espied this ship afar at last
And, running downward to the sea, by signs did succour seek.
Where finding grace, this Trojan ship receivèd me, a Greek.
But now, I pray thee, gentle friend, declare thou unto me
Thy captain's and thy fellows' luck that took the sea with thee.'

*Macareus'*
*story* 260    He told him how that Aeolus, the son of Hippot, he
    That keeps the winds in prison close, did reign in Tuscan sea
And how Ulysses, having at his hand a noble gift,
The wind enclosed in leather bags, did sail with prosperous drift
Nine days together, in so much they came within the sight
Of home; but on the tenth day, when the morning gan give light,
His fellows, being somewhat touched with covetousness and spite,
Supposing that it had been gold, did let the winds out quite.
The which, returning whence they came, did drive them back
       amain,
That in the realm of Aeolus they went a-land again.
'From thence', quoth he, 'we came unto the ancient Lamy's town,

270    Of which the fierce Antiphates that season ware the crown.
A couple of my mates and I were sent unto him; and
A mate of mine and I could scarce by flight escape his hand.
The third of us did with his blood imbrue the wicked face
Of lewd Antiphate, who with sword us, flying thence, did chase
And, following after with a rout, threw stones and logs which
       drowned
Both men and ships. Howbeit, one by chance escapèd sound

Which bare Ulysses and myself. So having lost most part
Of all our dear companions, we with sad and sorry heart
And much complaining did arrive at yonder coast which you
May ken far hence. A great way hence, I say, we see it now;    280
But, trust me truly, overnear I saw it once. And thou,
Aeneas, goddess Venus' son, the justest knight of all
The Trojan race (for sith the war is done, I cannot call
Thee foe), I warn thee, get thee far from Circe's dwelling-place.
For when our ships arrivèd there, remembering eft the case
Of cruel King Antiphates and of that hellish wight
The round-eyed giant Polypheme, we had so small delight
To visit uncouth places that we said we would not go.
Then cast we lots. The lot fell out upon myself as tho
And Polite and Eurylochus and on Elpenor, who    290
Delighted too too much in wine, and eighteen other mo.
All we did go to Circe's house. As soon as we came thither
And in the portal of the hall had set our feet together,
A thousand lions, wolves and bears did put us in a fear
By meeting us. But none of them was to be fearèd there.
For none of them could do us harm; but with a gentle look
And following us with fawning feet their wanton tails they shook.
Anon did damsels welcome us and led us through the hall,
The which was made of marble stone, floor, arches, roof and wall,
To Circe. She sat underneath a traverse in a chair    300
Aloft right rich and stately in a chamber large and fair.
She ware a goodly long-trained gown, and all her rest attire
Was every whit of goldsmith's work. There sat me also by her
The seanymphs and her ladies, whose fine fingers never knew
What tozing wool did mean nor thread from whirlèd spindle
        drew.
They sorted herbs and, picking out the flowers that were mixed,
Did put them into maunds and with indifferent space betwixt
Did lay the leaves and stalks on heaps according to their hue.
And she herself the work of them did oversee and view.
The virtue and the use of them right perfectly she knew,    310
And in what leaf it lay and which in mixture would agree.
And so, perusing every herb by good advisement, she

Did weigh them out. As soon as she us entering in did see
And greeting had both given and ta'en, she lookèd cheerfully
And, granting all that we desired, commanded by and by
A certain potion to be made of barley parchèd dry
And wine and honey mixed with cheese. And with the same she
  sly
Had ment the juice of certain herbs, which unespied did lie
By reason of the sweetness of the drink. We took the cup
320 Delivered by her wicked hand and quaffed it clearly up
With thirsty throats. Which done and that the cursèd witch had
  smit
Our highest hair tips with her wand (it is a shame, but yet
I will declare the truth), I waxed all rough with bristled hair
And could not make complaint with words. Instead of speech I
  there
Did make a raughtish grunting and with grovelling face gan bear
My visage downward to the ground. I felt a hookèd groin
To waxen hard upon my mouth and brawnèd neck to join
My head and shoulders. And the hands with which I late ago
Had taken up the charmèd cup were turned to feet as tho.
330 Such force there is in sorcery. In fine, with other mo
That tasted of the selfsame sauce they shut me in a sty.
From this mishap Eurylochus alonely scaped, for why
He only would not taste the cup. Which had he not fled fro,
He should have been a bristled beast as well as we; and so
Should none have borne Ulysses word of our mischance, nor he
Have come to Circe to revenge our harms and set us free.
The peace-procurer, Mercury, had given to him a white
Fair flower whose root is black, and of the gods it moly hight.
Assured by this and heavenly hests, he entered Circe's bower.
340 And, being bidden for to drink the cup of baleful power,
As Circe was about to stroke her wand upon his hair,
He thrust her back and put her with his nakèd sword in fear.
Then fell they to agreement straight, and faith in hand was plight.
And, being made her bedfellow, he claimèd as in right
Of dowry for to have his men again in perfect plight.
She sprinkled us with better juice of uncouth herbs and strake
The awk end of her charmèd rod upon our heads and spake

Words to the former contrary. The more she charmed, the more
Arose we upward from the ground on which we dared before.
Our bristles fell away; the cleft our cloven clees forsook.                    350
Our shoulders did return again, and next our elbows took
Our arms and hands their former place. Then, weeping, we
    embrace
Our lord and hing about his neck, who also wept apace.
And not a word we rather spake than such as might appear
From hearts most thankful to proceed. We tarried there a year.
  'I in that while saw many things and many things did hear.
  I markèd also this one thing with store of other gear
Which one of Circe's four chief maids (whose office was alway
Upon such hallows to attend) did secretly bewray
To me. For in the while my lord with Circe kept alone,                         360
This maid a young man's image showed of fair white marble stone
Within a chancel. On the head thereof were garlands store
And eke a woodspeck. And as I demanded her wherefore
And who it was they honoured so in holy church and why
He bare that bird upon his head, she, answering by and by,
Said, "Learn hereby, Sir Macare, to understand the power
My lady hath, and mark thou well what I shall say this hour.
   '"There reigned erewhile in Italy one Picus, Saturn's son,    *The story*
    Who lovèd warlike horse and had delight to see them run.      *of Picus*
He was of feature as ye see. And by this image here                            370
The very beauty of the man doth livelily appear.
His courage matched his personage, and scarcely had he well
Seen twenty years. His count'nance did allure the nymphs that
    dwell
Among the Latian hills. The nymphs of fountains and of brooks,
As those that haunted Albula*, were ravished with his looks;
And so were they that Numic bears and Anio, too, and Alme
That runneth short, and heady Nar and Farfar cool and calm;
And all the nymphs that used to haunt Diana's shady pool
Or any lakes or meres near hand or other waters cool.
But he, disdaining all the rest, did set his love upon                         380
A lady whom Venilia bare (so fame reporteth) on

*Now called Tiber

The stately Mountain Palatine by Janus, that doth bear
The double face. As soon as that her years for marriage were
Thought able, she, preferring him before all other men,
Was wedded to this Picus, who was king of Laurents then.
She was in beauty excellent, but yet in singing much
More excellent; and thereupon they named her Singer. Such
The sweetness of her music was that she therewith delights
The savage beasts and causèd birds to cease their wandering
    flights

390  And movèd stones and trees and made the running streams to stay.
Now while that she in woman's tune records her pleasant lay
At home, her husband rode abroad upon a lusty horse
To hunt the boar and bare in hand two hunting staves of force.
His cloak was crimson, buttoned with a golden button fast.
Into the selfsame forest eke was Phoebus' daughter passed
From those same fields that of herself the name of Circe bear
To gather uncouth herbs among the fruitful hillocks there.
As soon as, lurking in the shrubs, she did the king espy,
She was astraught. Down fell her herbs to ground. And by and by

400  Through all her bones the flame of love the marrow gan to fry.
And when she from this forcèd heat had called her wits again,
She purposed to bewray her mind. But unto him as then
She could not come for swiftness of his horse and for his men
That guarded him on every side. 'Yet shalt thou not', quoth she,
'So shift thee fro my hands, although the wind should carry thee,
If I do know myself, if all the strength of herbs fail not
Or if I have not quite and clean my charms and spells forgot.'
In saying of these words she made the likeness of a boar
Without a body, causing it to swiftly pass before

410  King Picus' eyes and for to seem to get him to the wood
Where for the thickness of the trees a horse might do no good.
Immediately the king, unwares, a hot pursuit did make
Upon the shadow of his prey and quickly did forsake
His foaming horse's sweating back and, following vain wan hope,
Did run a-foot among the woods and through the bushes' crop.
Then Circe fell a-mumbling spells and, praying like a witch,
Did honour strange and uncouth gods with uncouth charms, by
    which

She used to make the moon look dark and wrap her father's head
In watery clouds. And then likewise the heaven was overspread
With darkness, and a foggy mist steamed upward from the ground.    420
And ne'er a man about the king to guard him could be found,
But every man in blind by-ways ran scattering in the chase
Through her enchantments. At the length she, getting time and
        place,
Said, 'By those lightsome eyes of thine which late have ravished
        mine
And by that goodly personage and lovely face of thine,
The which compelleth me, that am a goddess, to incline
To make this humble suit to thee that art a mortal wight,
Assuage my flame and make this sun, who by his heavenly sight
Foresees all things, thy father-in-law; and hardly hold not scorn
Of Circe, who by long descent of Titan's stock am born.'    430
Thus much said Circe. He, right fierce rejecting her request
And her, said, 'Whosoe'er thou art, go, set thy heart at rest.
I am not thine nor will not be. Another holds my heart.
And long God grant she may it hold, that I may never start
To lewdness of a foreign lust from bond of lawful bed
As long as Janus' daughter, my sweet Singer, is not dead.'
Dame Circe, having oft renewed her suit in vain before,
Said, 'Dearly shalt thou buy thy scorn. For never shalt thou more
Return to Singer. Thou shalt learn by proof what one can do
That is provokèd and in love, yea, and a woman too.    440
But Circe is both stirred to wrath and also ta'en in love,
Yea, and a woman.' Twice her face to westward she did move
And twice to eastward. Thrice she laid her rod upon his head
And therewithal three charms she cast. Away King Picus fled
And, wondering that he fled more swift than erst he had been
        wont,
He saw the feathers on his skin and at the sudden brunt
Became a bird that haunts the woods. Whereat he taking spite,
With angry bill did job upon hard oaks with all his might
And in his mood made hollow holes upon their boughs. The hue
Of crimson which was in his cloak upon his feathers grew;    450
The gold that was a clasp and did his cloak together hold
Is feathers, and about his neck goes circlewise like gold.

His servants, luring in that while oft over all the ground
In vain and finding nowhere of their king no inkling, found
Dame Circe (for by that time she had made the aïr sheer
And suffered both the sun and winds the misty steams to clear)
And, charging her with matter true, demanded for their king
And, offering force, began their darts and javelins for to fling.
She, sprinkling noisome venom straight and juice of poisoning
    might,
460  Did call together Erebus and Chaos and the night
And all the fiends of darkness and, with howling out along,
Made prayers unto Hecate. Scarce ended was her song
But that (a wondrous thing to tell) the woods leapt from their
    place,
The ground did groan, the trees near hand looked pale in all the
    chase;
The grass, besprent with drops of blood, looked red, the stones did
    seem
To roar and bellow hoarse and dogs to howl and raise extreme
And all the ground to crawl with snakes black-scaled, and ghastly
    sprites
Fly whisking up and down. The folk were flighted at these sights.
And as they, wondering, stood amazed, she stroked her witching
    wand
470  Upon their faces, at the touch whereof there out of hand
Came wondrous shapes of savage beasts upon them all. Not one
Retainèd still his native shape. The setting sun was gone
Beyond the utmost coast of Spain, and Singer longed in vain
To see her husband. Both her folk and people ran again
Through all the woods. And ever as they went, they sent their
    eyes
Before them for to find him out; but no man him espies.
Then Singer thought it not enough to weep and tear her hair
And beat herself (all which she did); she gat abroad and there
Ranged over all the broad wild fields like one besides her wits.
480  Six nights and full as many days, as fortune led by fits,
She strayed me over hills and dales, and never tasted rest
Nor meat nor drink of all the while. The seventh day, sore
    oppressed

And tirèd both with travel and with sorrow, down she sat
Upon cold Tiber's bank and there with tears in mourning rate
She, warbling on her grief in tune nor shirl nor over high,
Did make her moan as doth the swan who, ready for to die,
Doth sing his burial song before. Her marrow molt at last
With mourning, and she pined away. And finally she passed
To lither air. But yet her fame remainèd in the place;
For why the ancient husbandmen according to the case                    490
Did name it Singer of the nymph that dièd in the same."
Of such as these are, many things that year by fortune came
Both to my hearing and my sight. We, waxing resty then
And slugs by discontinuance, were commanded yet again
To go aboard and hoise up sails. And Circe told us all
That long and doubtful passage and rough seas should us befall.
I promise thee, those words of hers me throughly made afraid;
And therefore hither I me gat, and here I have me stayed.'
    This was the end of Macar's tale. And ere long time was gone,         *War in*
    Aeneas' nurse was buried in a tomb of marble stone           500 *Latium*
And this short verse was set thereon: *In this same very place*
*My nursechild, whom the world doth know to be a child of grace,*
*Delivering me, Caieta, quick from burning by the Grays,*
*Hath burnt me, dead, with such a fire as justly wins him praise.*
Their cables from the grassy strand were loosed, and by and by
From Circe's slanderous house and from her treasons far they fly.
And, making to the thick-grown groves, where through the
        yellow dust
The shady Tiber into sea his gushing stream doth thrust,
Aeneas got the realm of King Latinus, Faunus' son,
And eke his daughter, whom in fight by force of arms he won.           510
He enterprisèd war against a nation fierce and strong,
And Turn was wrath for holding of his wife away by wrong.
Against the shire of Latium met all Tyrrhene, and long
With busy care haught victory by force of arms was sought.
Each party to augment their force by foreign succour wrought;
And many sent the Rutils help, and many came to aid
The Trojans. Neither was the good Aeneas ill apaid
Of going to Euander's town. But Venulus in vain
To outcast Diomed's city went his succour to obtain.

This Diomed under Daunus, king of Calabry, did found
A mighty town and with his wife in dowry held the ground.
Now when from Turnus Venulus his message had declared
Desiring help, th'Aetolian knight said none could well be spared.
And in excuse he told him how he neither durst be bold
To prest his father's folk to war of whom he had no hold,
Nor any of his countrymen had left as then alive
To arm. 'And lest ye think', quoth he, 'I do a shift contrive,
Although by opening of the thing my bitter grief revive,
I will abide to make a new rehearsal. After that
530   The Greeks had burnèd Troy and on the ground had laid it flat
And that the Prince of Naryx by his ravishing the maid
In Pallas' temple on us all the penance had displayed
Which he himself deserved alone, then, scattered here and there
And harried over all the seas, we Greeks were fain to bear
Night, thunder, tempest, wrath of heaven and sea, and, last of all,
Sore shipwreck at Mount Capharey to mend our harms withal.
And lest that me to make too long a process ye might deem
In setting forth our heavy haps, the Greeks might that time seem
Right rueful even to Priamus. Howbeit Minerva, she
540   That weareth armour, took me from the waves and savèd me.
But from my father's realm again by violence I was driven;
For Venus, bearing still in mind the wound I had her given
Long time before, did work revenge. By means whereof such toil
Did toss me on the sea and on the land I found such broil
By wars, that in my heart I thought them blest of God whom erst
The violence of the raging sea and hideous winds had pierced
And whom the wrathful Capharey by shipwreck did confound,
Oft wishing also I had there among the rest been drowned.
My company, now having felt the worst that sea or war
550   Could work, did faint and wished an end of straying out so far.
But Acmon, hot of nature and too fierce through slaughters made,
Said, "What remaineth, sirs, through which our patience cannot
           wade?
What further spite hath Venus yet to work against us more?
When worse misfortunes may be feared than have been felt
           before,

Then prayer may advantage men and vowing may them boot.
But when the worst is passed of things, then fear is under foot.
And when that bale is highest grown, then boot must next ensue.
Although she hear me and do hate us all (which thing is true)
That serve here under Diomed, yet set we light her hate;
And dearly it should stand us on to purchase high estate."    560
With such stout words did Acmon stir Dame Venus unto ire
And raised again her settled grudge. Not many had desire
To hear him talk thus out of square; the most of us that are
His friends rebuked him for his words. And as he did prepare
To answer, both his voice and throat by which his voice should
    go
Were small; his hair to feathers turned. His neck was clad as tho
With feathers; so was breast and back. The greater feathers stack
Upon his arms, and into wings his elbows bowèd back.
The greatest portion of his feet was turnèd into toes;
A hardened bill of horn did grow upon his mouth and nose    570
And sharpened at the nether end. His fellows, Lycus, Ide,
Rethenor, Nyct and Abas, all stood wondering by his side.
And as they wondered, they received the selfsame shape and hue.
And finally, the greater part of all my band up flew
And, clapping with their new-made wings, about the oars did
    gird.
And if ye do demand the shape of this same doubtful bird*,
Even as they be not very swans, so draw they very near
The shape of cygnets white. With much ado I settled here
And with a little remnant of my people do obtain
The dry grounds of my father-in-law, King Daunus, who did
    reign    580
In Calabry.' Thus much the son of Oeney said. Anon
  Sir Venulus, returning from the king of Calydon,
   Forsook the coast of Puteol and the fields of Messapy,
In which he saw a darksome den forgrown with bushes high
And watered with a little spring. The half-goat Pan that hour
Possessèd it; but heretofore it was the fairies' bower.

*The elk

A shepherd of Apulia from that country scared them first.
But afterward, recovering heart and hardiness, they durst
Despise him when he chasèd them and with their nimble feet
590 Continued on their dancing still in time and measure meet.
The shepherd found me fault with them and with his lout-like
      leaps
Did counterfeit their minion dance and rappèd out by heaps
A rabble of unsavoury taunts even like a country clown,
To which most lewd and filthy terms of purpose he did join.
And after he had once begun, he could not hold his tongue,
Until that in the timber of a tree his throat was clung.
For now he is a tree, and by his juice discern ye may
His manners. For the olive wild doth sensibly bewray
By berries full of bitterness his railing tongue. For aye
600 The harshness of his bitter words the berries bear away.

*Turnus attacks*
*the Trojan*
*ships*

    Now when the king's ambassador returnèd home without
      The succour of th'Aetolian prince, the Rutils, being stout,
Made luckless war without their help. And much on either side
Was shed of blood. Behold, King Turn made burning brands to
      glide
Upon their ships, and they that had escapèd water stood
In fear of fire. The flame had singed the pitch, the wax and wood
And other things that nourish fire and, roaming up the mast,
Caught hold upon the sails, and all the tackling gan to waste.
The rowers' seats did almost smoke when, calling to her mind
That these same ships were pine-trees erst and shaken with the
610       wind
On Ida Mount, the mother of the gods, Dame Cybel, filled
The air with sound of bells and noise of shawms. And as she held
The reins that ruled the lions tame which drew her chariot, she
Said thus: 'O Turnus, all in vain these wicked hands of thee
Do cast this fire. For by myself dispointed it shall be.
I will not let the wasting fire consume these ships which are
A parcel of my forest Ide, of which I am most chare.'
It thundered as the goddess spake, and with the thunder came
A storm of rain and skipping hail. And sudden with the same
620 The sons of Astrey, meeting fierce and fighting very sore,
Did trouble both the sea and air and set them on a roar.

Dame Cybel, using one of them to serve her turn that tide,
Did break the cables at the which the Trojan ships did ride
And bare them prone and underneath the water did them drive.
The timber of them, softening, turned to bodies straight alive.
The stems were turned to heads, the oars to swimming feet and
        toes,
The sides to ribs; the keel that through the middle galley goes
Became the ridgebone of the back, the sails and tackling hair;
And into arms on either side the sailyards turnèd were.
Their hue is dusky as before, and now in shape of maid                    630
They play among the waves of which even now they were afraid.
And, being seanymphs, whereas they were bred in mountains
        hard,
They haunt for aye the water soft and never afterward
Had mind to see their native soil. But yet, forgetting not
How many perils they had felt on sea by luckless lot,
They often put their helping hand to ships distressed by wind
Unless that any carried Greeks. For, bearing still in mind
The burning of the town of Troy, they hate the Greeks by kind.
And therefore of Ulysses' ships right glad they were to see
The shivers; and as glad they were as any glad might be              640
To see Alcinous' ships wax hard and turnèd into stone.
   These ships thus having gotten life and being turned each one
  To nymphs, a body would have thought the miracle so great
Should into Turnus' wicked heart some godly fear have beat
And made him cease his wilful war. But he did still persist.
And either party had their gods their quarrel to assist,
And courage also, which as good as gods might well be thought.
In fine they neither for the realm nor for the sceptre sought
Nor for the Lady Lavine, but for conquest. And for shame
To seem to shrink in leaving war, they still prolonged the same.         650
At length Dame Venus saw her son obtain the upper hand.
King Turnus fell and eke the town of Ardea, which did stand
Right strong in high estate as long as Turnus livèd. But
As soon as that Aeneas' sword to death had Turnus put,
The town was set on fire; and from amid the embers flew
A fowl which till that present time no person ever knew

And beat the ashes fiercely up with flapping of his wing.
The leanness, paleness, doleful sound and every other thing
That may express a city sacked, yea, and the city's name
Remainèd still unto the bird. And now the very same
With hernsew's feathers doth bewail the town whereof it came.

*Aeneas becomes a god*

And now Aeneas' prowess had compellèd all the gods
And Juno also (who with him was most of all at odds)
To cease their old displeasure quite. And now he, having laid
Good ground whereon the growing wealth of July might be
    stayed,
Was ripe for heaven. And Venus had great suit already made
To all the gods and, clipping Jove, did thus with him persuade:
'Dear father, who hast never been uncourteous unto me,
Now show the greatest courtesy, I pray thee, that may be.
And on my son Aeneas, who a grandchild unto thee
Hath got of my blood, if thou wilt vouchsafe him aught at all,
Vouchsafe some godhead to bestow, although it be but small.
It is enough that once he hath already seen the realm
Of Pluto utter pleasureless and passèd Styx's stream.'
The gods assented; neither did Queen Juno then appear
In count'nance strange, but did consent with glad and merry
    cheer.
Then Jove: 'Aeneas worthy is a saint in heaven to be.
Thy wish for whom thou dost it wish I grant thee frank and free.'
This grant of his made Venus glad. She thanked him for the same
And, gliding through the air upon her yokèd doves, she came
To Laurent shore where, clad with reed, the River Numic deep
To seaward (which is near at hand) with stealing pace doth creep.
She bade this river wash away whatever mortal were
In good Aeneas' body and them under sea to bear.
The hornèd brook fulfilled her hest and with his water sheer
Did purge and cleanse Aeneas from his mortal body clear.
The better portion of him did remain unto him sound.
His mother, having hallowed him, did noint his body round
With heavenly odours and did touch his mouth with ambrosy,
The which was mixed with nectar sweet, and made him by and by
A god to whom the Romans give the name of Indiges,
Endeavouring with their temples and their altars him to please.

660

670

680

690

Ascanius with the double name from thence began to reign,      *Aeneas'*
  In whom the rule of Alba and of Latium did remain.      *successors*
Next him succeeded Silvius, whose son Latinus held
The ancient name and sceptre which his grandsire erst did wield.
The famous Epyt after this Latinus did succeed,
Then Capys and King Capetus. But Capys was indeed
The foremost of the two. From this the sceptre of the realm
Descended unto Tiberine, who, drowning in the stream      700
Of Tiber, left that name thereto. This Tiberine begat
Fierce Remulus and Acrota. By chance it happened that
The elder brother, Remulus, for counterfeiting oft
The thunder with a thunderbolt was killèd from aloft.
From Acrota, whose staïdness did pass his brother's skill,
The crown did come to Aventine, who in the selfsame hill
In which he reignèd buried lies and left thereto his name.
The rule of nation Palatine at length to Proca came.
  In this king's reign Pomona* lived. There was not to be found      *Pomona and*
  Among the woodnymphs anyone in all the Latian ground      *Vertumnus*
That was so cunning for to keep an orchard as was she,
Nor none so painful to preserve the fruit of every tree.
And thereupon she had her name. She passed not for the woods
Nor rivers, but the villages and boughs that bear both buds
And plenteous fruit. Instead of dart a shredding hook she bare,
With which the overlusty boughs she eft away did pare
That spreaded out too far and eft did make therewith a rift
To griffe another imp upon the stock within the cleft.
And lest her trees should die through drought, with water of the
     springs
She moisteth of their sucking roots the little crumpled strings.      720
This was her love and whole delight. And as for Venus' deeds,
She had no mind at all of them. And for because she dreads
Enforcement by the countryfolk, she walled her yards about,
Not suffering any man at all to enter in or out.
What have not those same nimble lads so apt to frisk and dance,
The satyrs, done, or what the Pans that wantonly do prance

*\*It may be interpreted Appleby*

With hornèd foreheads, and the old Silenus, who is aye
More youthful than his years, and eke the fiend that scares away
The thieves and robbers with his hook or with his privy part,
730   To win her love? But yet than these a far more constant heart
Had sly Vertumnus*, though he sped no better than the rest.
O Lord, how often, being in a mower's garment dressed,
Bare he in bundles sheaves of corn! And when he was so dight
He was the very pattern of a harvest mower right.
Oft binding new-made hay about his temples he might seem
A haymaker. Oft times in hand made hard with work extreme
He bare a goad, that men would swear he had but newly then
Unyoked his weary oxen. Had he ta'en in hand again
A shredding hook, ye would have thought he had a gardener been
740   Or pruner of some vines. Or had you him with ladder seen
Upon his neck, a gatherer of fruit ye would him deem.
With sword a soldier, with his rod an angler he did seem.
And finally in many shapes he sought to find access
To joy the beauty but by sight that did his heart oppress.
Moreover, putting on his head a woman's wimple gay
And staying by a staff, grey hairs he forth to sight did lay
Upon his forehead and did feign a beldame for to be;
By means whereof he came within her goodly orchards free
And, wondering at the fruit, said, 'Much more skill hast thou, I see,
750   Than all the nymphs of Albula. Hail, lady mine, the flower
Unspotted of pure maidenhood in all the world this hour!'
And with that word he kissèd her a little; but his kiss
Was such as true old women would have never given, iwis.
Then, sitting down upon a bank, he lookèd upward at
The branches bent with harvest's weight. Against him where he
          sat
A goodly elm with glistering grapes did grow; which after he
Had praisèd and the vine likewise that ran upon the tree,
      'But if', quoth he, 'this elm without the vine did single stand,
      It should have nothing (saving leaves) to be desirèd; and
760   Again, if that the vine which runs upon the elm had nat
The tree to lean unto, it should upon the ground lie flat.

*Turner

Yet art thou not admonished by example of this tree
To take a husband, neither dost thou pass to married be.
But would to God thou wouldest. Sure, Queen Helen never had
Mo suitors, nor the lady that did cause the battle mad
Between the half-brute Centaurs and the Lapiths, nor the wife
Of bold Ulysses who was eke aye fearful of his life
Than thou should'st have. For thousands now (even now most
     chiefly when
Thou seemest suitors to abhor) desire thee, both of men
And gods and half-gods, yea, and all the fairies that do dwell    770
In Alban hills. But if thou wilt be wise and mindest well
To match thyself and wilt give ear to this old woman here
(To whom thou more than to them all art, trust me, lief and dear
And more than thou thyself believ'st), the common matches flee
And choose Vertumnus to thy make. And take thou me to be
His pledge. For more he to himself not known is than to me.
He roves not like a runagate through all the world abroad;
This country hereabout (the which is large) is his abode.
He doth not, like a number of these common wooers, cast
His love to everyone he sees. Thou art the first and last    780
That ever he set mind upon. Alonely unto thee
He vows himself as long as life doth last. Moreover he
Is youthful and with beauty sheen endued by nature's gift,
And aptly into any shape his person he can shift.
Thou canst not bid him be the thing, though all things thou
     should'st name,
But that he fitly and with ease will straight become the same.
Besides all this, in all one thing both twain of you delight,
And of the fruits that you love best the firstlings are his right,
And gladly he receives thy gifts. But neither covets he
Thy apples, plums, nor other fruits new gathered from the tree,    790
Nor yet the herbs of pleasant scent that in thy gardens be,
Nor any other kind of thing in all the world, but thee.
Have mercy on his fervent love and think himself to crave
Here present by the mouth of me the thing that he would have.
And fear the god that may revenge, as Venus, who doth hate
Hard-hearted folks, and Rhamnuse, who doth either soon or late

Express her wrath with mindful wreak. And to th'intent thou may
The more beware, of many things which time by long delay
Hath taught me I will show thee one which over all the land
800  Of Cyprus blazèd is abroad, which, being rightly scanned,
May easily bow thy hardèned heart and make it for to yield.

*Iphis and*
*Anaxarete*

'One Iphis, born of low degree, by fortune had beheld
    The Lady Anaxarete, descended of the race
Of Teucer; and in viewing her the fire of love apace
Did spread itself through all his bones. With which he striving
            long,
When reason could not conquer rage because it was so strong,
Came humbly to the lady's house and, one while laying ope
His wretched love before her nurse, besought her by the hope
Of Lady Anaxarete her nursechild's good success
810  She would not be against him in that case of his distress.
Another while entreating fair some friend of hers, he prayed
Him earnestly with careful voice of furtherance and of aid.
Ofttimes he did prefer his suit by gentle letters sent.
Oft garlands moisted with the dew of tears that from him went
He hangèd on her posts. Ofttimes his tender sides he laid
Against the threshold hard and oft in sadness did upbraid
The lock with much ungentleness. The lady, crueller
Than are the rising narrow seas or falling Kids and far
More hard than steel of Noricum and than the stony rock
820  That in the quarry hath his root, did him despise and mock.
Beside her doings merciless of stateliness and spite,
She, adding proud and scornful words, defrauds the wretched
            wight
Of very hope. But Iphis now, unable anymore
To bear the torment of his grief, still standing there before
Her gate, spake these his latest words: "Well, Anaxarete,
Thou hast the upper hand. Henceforth thou shalt not need to be
Aggrievèd any more with me. Go, triumph hardily;
Go, vaunt thyself with joy; go, sing the song of victory;
Go, put a crown of glittering bay upon thy cruel head.
830  For why thou hast the upper hand, and I am gladly dead.
Well, steely-hearted, well, rejoice! Compelled yet shalt thou be
Of somewhat in me for to have a liking. Thou shalt see

A point wherein thou may'st me deem most thankful unto thee,
And in the end thou shalt confess the great desert of me.
But yet remember that, as long as life in me doth last,
The care of thee shall never from this heart of mine be cast.
For both the life that I do live in hope of thee and t'other
Which nature giveth shall have end and pass away together.
The tidings neither of my death shall come to thee by fame.
Myself, I do assure thee, will be bringer of the same.                                840
Myself, I say, will present be, that those same cruel eyen
Of thine may feed themselves upon this lifeless corse of mine.
But yet, O gods, if you behold men's deeds, remember me –
My tongue will serve to pray no more – and cause that I may be
Longtime hereafter spoken of; and length the life by fame
The which ye have abridged in years." In saying of this same,
He lifted up his watery eyes and arms that waxèd wán
To those same stoops which oft he had with garlands decked ere
        then
And, fastening on the top thereof a halter, thus did say:
"Thou cruel and ungodly wight, these are the wreaths that may      850
Most pleasure thee." And with that word he, thrusting in his
        head,
Even then did turn him towards her, as good as being dead,
And wretchedly did totter on the post with strangled throat.
The wicket, which his fearful feet in sprawling mainly smote,
Did make a noise and, flying ope, bewrayed his doing plain.
The servants shrieked and, lifting up his body (but in vain)
Conveyed him to his mother's house (his father erst was slain).
His mother laid him in her lap and, clipping in her arms
Her son's cold body, after that she had bewailed her harms
With words and doings mother-like, the corse with mourning
        cheer                                                                         860
To burial sadly through the town was borne upon a bier.
The house of Anaxarete by chance was near the way
By which this piteous pomp did pass, and of the doleful lay
The sound came to the ears of her whom God already gan
To strike. "Yet let us see", quoth she, "the burial of this man."
And up the high wide-windowèd house in saying so she ran.

Scarce had she well on Iphis looked that on the bier did lie
But that her eyes waxed stark and from her limbs the blood gan
    fly.
Instead thereof came paleness in. And as she backward was
870  In mind to go, her feet stack fast and could not stir. And as
She would have cast her count'nance back, she could not do it.
      And
The stony hardness which alate did in her stomach stand
Within a while did overgrow her whole from sole to crown.
And lest you think this gear surmised, even yet in Salamin town
Of Lady Anaxarete the image standeth plain.
The temple also in the which the image doth remain
Is unto Venus consecrate by name of Looker-Out.
And therefore, weighing well these things, I pray thee, look about,
Good lady, and away with pride; and be content to frame
880  Thyself to him that loveth thee and cannot quench his flame.
So neither may the Lenten's cold thy budding fruit trees kill
Nor yet the sharp and boisterous winds thy flowering gardens
    spill.'

*Pomona and*    The god that can upon him take what kind of shape he list
*Vertumnus*    Now, having said thus much in vain, omitted to persist
*(conclusion)*  In beldame's shape and showed himself a lusty gentleman,
Appearing to her cheerfully, even like as Phoebus when
He, having overcome the clouds that did withstand his might,
Doth blaze his brightsome beams again with fuller heat and light.
He offered force; but now no force was needed in the case,
890  For why she, being caught in love with beauty of his face,
Was wounded then as well as he and gan to yield apace.

*Aeneas'*    Next Proca reigned Amulius in Ausony by wrong
*successors*    Till Numitor, the rightful heir deposèd very long,
*(continued)*  Was by his daughters' sons restored. And on the feastful day
Of Pale foundation of the walls of Rome they gan to lay.
Soon after Tacy and the lords of Sabine stirred debate,
And Tarpey for her traitorous deed in opening of the gate
Of Tarpey tower was pressed to death, according to desert,
With armour heaped upon her head. Then, fierce and stout of
    heart,

The Sabines, like to tongueless wolves, without all noise of talk          900
Assailed the Romans in their sleep and to the gates gan stalk
Which Ilia's son had closèd fast with locks and bars. But yet
Dame Juno had set open one and, as she opened it,
Had made no noise of craking with the hinges, so that none
Perceived the opening of the gate but Venus all alone.
And she had shut it up, but that it is not lawful to
One god to undo anything another god hath do.
The waternymphs of Ausony held all the grounds about
The church of Janus, where was store of springs fresh flowing out.
Dame Venus prayed these nymphs of help; and they, considering
    that                                                                     910
The goddess did request no more but right, denied it nat.
They opened all their fountain veins and made them flow apace.
Howbeit, the passage was not yet to Janus' open face
Foreclosèd; neither had as yet the water stopped the way.
They put rank brimstone underneath the flowing spring that day
And eke with smoky rosin set their veins on fire for aye.
Through force of these and other things the vapour piercèd low,
Even down unto the very roots on which the springs did grow,
So that the waters which alate in coldness might compare
Even with the frozen Alps now hot as burning furnace are.          920
The two gateposts with sprinkling of the fiery water smoked,
Whereby the gate behighted to the Sabines quite was choked
With rising of this fountain strange until that Mars's knight
Had armèd him. Then Romulus did boldly offer fight.
The Roman ground with Sabines and with Romans both were
    spread,
And with the blood of father-in-laws which wicked sword had
    shed
Flowed mixed the blood of son-in-laws. Howbeit, it seemèd best
To both the parties at the length from battle for to rest
And not to fight to utterance, and that Tacy should become
Co-partner with King Romulus of sovereignty in Rome.              930
Within a while King Tacy died, and both the Sabines and
The Romans under Romulus in equal right did stand.
The god of battle, putting off his glittering helmet then,
With suchlike words as these bespake the sire of gods and men:

'The time, O father (in as much as now the Roman state
Is waxen strong upon the good foundation laid alate
Depending on the stay of one) is come for thee to make
Thy promise good which thou of me and of thy grandchild spake,
Which was to take him from the earth and in the heaven him stay.
Thou once (I marked thy gracious words and bare them well
940         away)
Before a great assembly of the gods did'st to me say,
"There shall be one whom thou shalt raise above the starry sky."
Now let thy saying take effect.' Jove granting by and by,
The air was hid with darksome clouds and thunder forth did fly
And lightning made the world aghast. Which Mars perceiving to
Be lucky tokens for himself his enterprise to do,
Did take his rist upon his spear and boldly leapt into
His bloody chariot. And he lent his horses with his whip
A yerking lash and through the air full smoothly down did slip.
950 And, staying on the woody top of mountain Palatine,
He took away King Romulus, who there did then define
The private cases of his folk, unseemly for a king.
And as a leaden pellet broad enforcèd from a sling
Is wont to die amid the sky, even so his mortal flesh
Sank from him down the subtle air. Instead whereof a fresh
And goodly shape more stately and more meet for sacred shrine
Succeeded, like our Quirin that in stately robe doth shine.

        Hersilia for her fere, as lost, of mourning made none end
        Until Queen Juno did command Dame Iris to descend
960 Upon the rainbow down and thus her message for to do:
'O of the Latian country and the Sabine nation too
Thou peerless pearl of womanhood, most worthy for to be
The wife of such a noble prince as heretofore was he
And still to be the wife of him canonizèd by name
Of Quirin, cease thy tears. And if thou have desire the same
Thy holy husband for to see, ensue me to the queach
That groweth green on Quirin's hill, whose shadows overreach
The temple of the Roman king.' Dame Iris did obey
And, sliding by her painted bow, in former words did say
970 Her errand to Hersilia. She, scarce lifting up her eyes,
With sober count'nance answered, 'O thou goddess (for surmise

I cannot who thou art, but yet I well may understand
Thou art a goddess), lead me, O dear goddess, lead me and
My husband to me show. Whom if the fatal sisters three
Will of their gracious goodness grant me leave but once to see,
I shall account me into heaven receivèd for to be.'
Immediately with Thaumant's imp to Quirin's hill she went.
There, gliding from the sky, a star straight down to ground was
    sent,
The sparks of whose bright blazing beams did burn Hersilia's hair;
And with the star the air did up her hair to heavenward bear.    980
The builder of the town of Rome, receiving straight the same
Between his old acquainted hands, did alter both her name
And eke her body, calling her Dame Ora. And by this
She jointly with her husband for a goddess worshipped is.

FINIS LIBRI DECIMI QUARTI.

# The Fifteenth Book of Ovid's Metamorphoses

A person in the while was sought sufficient to sustain
The burden of so great a charge and worthy for to reign
Instead of such a mighty prince. The noble Nume by Fame
(Who harpèd then upon the truth before to pass it came)
Appointed to the empire was. This Numa thought it not
Enough that he the knowledge of the Sabine rites had got.
The deepness of his noble wit to greater things was bent:
To search of things the natures out. The care of this intent
Did cause that he from Curey and his native country went
With painful travel to the town where Hercules did host.     10
And, asking who it was of Greece that in th'Italian coast
Had built that town, an agèd man well seen in stories old
To satisfy his mind therein the process thus him told:

  'As Hercules, enrichèd with the Spanish kine, did hold       *The story*
  His voyage from the ocean sea, men say, with lucky cut     *of Myscelus*
He came a-land on Lacine coast; and while he there did put
His beasts to grazing, he himself in Croton's house did rest,
The greatest man in all those parts and unto strangers best;
And that he there refreshed him of his tedious travel; and
That when he should depart, he said, "Where now thy house
     doth stand                                                  20
Shall in thy childer's children's time a city builded be."
Which words of his have provèd true, as plainly now we see.
For why there was one Myscelus, a Greek, Alemon's son,
A person more in favour of the gods than anyone
In those days was. The god that bears the boisterous club* did stay
Upon him, being fast asleep, and said, "Go, seek straightway

*Hercules

The stony streams of Aesary. Thy native soil for aye
Forsake." And sore he threatened him unless he did obey.
The god and sleep departed both together. Up did rise
Alemon's son and in himself did secretly devise
Upon this vision. Long his mind strove doubtful to and fro.
The god bade go; his country laws did say he should not go,
And death was made the penalty for him that would do so.
Clear Titan in the ocean sea had hid his lightsome head,
And dusky night had put up hers most thick with stars bespread.
The selfsame god by Myscelus did seem to stand eftsoon,
Commanding him the selfsame thing that he before had done
And threatening mo and greater plagues unless he did obey.
Then, being stricken sore in fear, he went about straightway
His household from his native land to foreign to convey.
A rumour hereupon did rise through all the town of Arge,
And disobedience of the law was laid to his charge.
As soon as that the case had first been pleaded and the deed
Apparently perceivèd so that witness did not need,
Arraignèd and forlorn, to heaven he cast his hands and eyes
And said, "O god whose labours twelve have purchased thee the
    skies,
Assist me, I thee pray. For thou art author of my crime."
When judgement should be given it was the guise in ancient time
With white stones to acquit the clear and eke with black to cast
The guilty. That time also so the heavy sentence passed;
The stones were cast unmerciful all black into the pot.
But when the stones were pourèd out to number, there was not
A black among them. All were white. And so through Herc'les'
    power
A gentle judgement did proceed, and he was quit that hour.
Then gave he thanks to Hercules and, having prosperous blast,
Cut over the Ionian Sea and so by Tarent passed,
Which Spartans built, and Sybaris and Neaeth Salentine
And Thurine bay and Emese and eke the pastures fine
Of Calabry. And, having scarce well sought the coasts that lie
Upon the sea, he found the mouth of fatal Aesary.
Not far from thence he also found the tomb in which the ground
Did cover Croton's holy bones and in that place did found

30
40
50
60

The city that was willèd him and gave thereto the name
Of him that there lay burièd.' Such original as this same
This city in th'Italian coast is said to have by fame.

    Here dwelt a man of Samos Isle, who, for the hate he had
      To lordliness and tyranny, though unconstrained, was glad
To make himself a banished man. And though this person were
Far distant from the gods by site of heaven, yet came he near
To them in mind. And he by sight of soul and reason clear
Beheld the things which nature doth to fleshly eyes deny.
And when with care most vigilant he had assuredly
Imprinted all things in his heart, he set them openly
Abroad for other folk to learn. He taught his silent sort
(Which wondered at the heavenly words their master did report)
The first foundation of the world; the cause of everything;
What nature was and what was God; whence snow and lightning
        spring;
And whether Jove or else the winds in breaking clouds do
        thunder;
What shakes the earth; what law the stars do keep their courses
        under;
And whatsoever other thing is hid from common sense.
He also is the first that did enjoin an abstinence
To feed of any living thing. He also first of all
Spake thus, although right learnedly, yet to effect but small:
    'Ye mortal men, forbear to frank your flesh with wicked food.
      Ye have both corn and fruits of trees and grapes and herbs right
        good;
And though that some be harsh and hard, yet fire may make them
        well
Both soft and sweet. Ye may have milk and honey which doth
        smell
Of flowers of thyme. The lavish earth doth yield you plenteously
Most gentle food and riches to content both mind and eye.
There needs no slaughter nor no blood to get your living by.
The beasts do break their fast with flesh; and yet not all beasts
        neither,
For horses, sheep and rother-beasts to live by grass had liefer.

*The teachings*
*of Pythagoras*

70

80

90

The nature of the beast that doth delight in bloody food
Is cruel and unmerciful, as lions fierce of mood,
Armenian tigers, bears and wolves. O, what a wickedness
It is to cram the maw with maw and frank up flesh with flesh
And for one living thing to live by killing of another,
As who should say that of so great abundance, which our mother
The earth doth yield most bounteously, none other might delight

100    Thy cruel teeth to chew upon than grisly wounds that might
Express the Cyclops' guise! Or else as if thou could not staunch
The hunger of thy greedy gut and evil-mannered paunch
Unless thou stroyed some other wight! But that same ancient age
Which we have named the golden world, clean void of all such
        rage,
Lived blessedly by fruit of trees and herbs that grow on ground
And stainèd not their mouths with blood. Then birds might safe
        and sound
Fly where they listed in the air. The hare, unscared of hound,
Went pricking over all the fields. No angling hook with bait
Did hang the silly fish that bote, mistrusting no deceit.

110    All things were void of guilefulness; no treason was in trust,
But all was friendship, love and peace. But after that the lust
Of one (what god so e'er he was), disdaining former fare,
To cram that cruel crop of his with fleshmeat did not spare,
He made a way for wickedness. And first of all the knife
Was stained with blood of savage beasts in ridding them of life.
And that had nothing been amiss if there had been the stay;
For why we grant without the breach of godliness we may
By death confound the things that seek to take our lives away.
But as to kill them reason was, even so again there was

120    No reason why to eat their flesh. This lewdness thence did pass
On further still. Whereas there was no sacrifice beforn,
The swine (because with hookèd groin he rooted up the corn
And did deceive the tillmen of their hope next year thereby)
Was deemèd worthy by desert in sacrifice to die.
The goat for biting vines was slain at Bacchus' altar, who
Wreaks such misdeeds. Their own offence was hurtful to these
        two.

But what have you, poor sheep, misdone, a cattle meek and mild
Created for to maintain man, whose fulsome dugs do yield
Sweet nectar, who doth clothe us with your wool in soft array,
Whose life doth more us benefit than doth your death far way?          130
What trespass have the oxen done – a beast without all guile
Or craft, unhurtful, simple, born to labour every while?
In faith, he is unmindful and unworthy of increase
Of corn that in his heart can find his tillman to release
From plough to cut his throat; that in his heart can find, I say,
Those necks with hatchets off to strike, whose skin is worn away
With labouring aye for him, who turned so oft his land most
          tough,
Who brought so many harvests home. Yet is it not enough
That such a great outrageousness committed is. They father
Their wickedness upon the gods, and falsely they do gather          140
That in the death of painful ox the highest doth delight.
A sacrifice unblemishèd and fairest unto sight
(For beauty worketh them their bane), adorned with garlands and
With glittering gold, is sited at the altar for to stand.
There hears he words (he wots not what) the which the priest
          doth pray
And on his forehead suffereth him between his horns to lay
The ears of corn that he himself hath wrought for in the clay
And staineth with his blood the knife that he himself, perchance,
Hath in the water sheer ere then beheld by sudden glance.
Immediately they, haling out his heartstrings still alive          150
And poring on them, seek therein God's secrets to retrieve.
Whence comes so greedy appetite in men of wicked meat?
And dare ye, O ye mortal men, adventure thus to eat?
Nay, do not, I beseech you, so. But give good ear and heed
To that that I shall warn you of, and trust it as your creed
That, whensoever you do eat your oxen, you devour
Your husbandmen. And for as much as God this instant hour
Doth move my tongue to speak, I will obey his heavenly power.
My god Apollo's temple I will set you open and
Disclose the wondrous heavens themselves and make you
          understand          160

The oracles and secrets of the godly majesty.
Great things and such as wit of man could never yet espy
And such as have been hidden long, I purpose to descry.
I mind to leave the earth and up among the stars to sty;
I mind to leave this grosser place and in the clouds to fly
And on stout Atlas' shoulders strong to rest myself on high
And, looking down from heaven on men that wander here and
     there
In dreadful fear of death as though they void of reason were,
To give them exhortation thus and plainly to unwind
170   The whole discourse of destiny as nature hath assigned.
O men amazed with dread of death, why fear ye Limbo, Styx
And other names of vanity, which are but poets' tricks,
And perils of another world, all false surmisèd gear?
For whether fire or length of time consume the bodies here,
Ye well may think that further harms they cannot suffer more.
For souls are free from death. Howbeit they, living evermore,
Their former dwellings are received and live again in new.
For I myself (right well in mind I bear it to be true)
Was in the time of Trojan War Euphorbus, Pantheu's son,
180   Quite through whose heart the deathful spear of Menelay did run.
I late ago in Juno's church at Argos did behold
And knew the target which I in my left hand there did hold.
All things do change. But nothing, sure, doth perish. This same
     sprite
Doth fleet and, fisking here and there, doth swiftly take his flight
From one place to another place and entereth every wight,
Removing out of man to beast and out of beast to man.
But yet it never perisheth nor never perish can.
And even as supple wax with ease receiveth figures strange
And keeps not aye one shape ne bides assurèd aye from change
190   And yet continueth always wax in substance, so, I say,
The soul is aye the selfsame thing it was, and yet astray
It fleeteth into sundry shapes. Therefore, lest godliness
Be vanquished by outrageous lust of belly beastliness,
Forbear (I speak by prophecy) your kinsfolk's ghosts to chase
By slaughter; neither nourish blood with blood in any case.
And sith on open sea the winds do blow my sails apace,

In all the world there is not that that standeth at a stay.
Things ebb and flow, and every shape is made to pass away.
The time itself continually is fleeting like a brook,
For neither brook nor lightsome time can tarry still. But look      200
As every wave drives other forth, and that that comes behind
Both thrusteth and is thrust itself; even so the times by kind
Do fly and follow both at once and evermore renew.
For that that was before is left, and straight there doth ensue
Another that was never erst. Each twinkling of an eye
Doth change. We see that after day comes night and darks the sky,
And after night the lightsome sun succeedeth orderly.
Like colour is not in the heaven when all things weary lie
At midnight sound asleep as when the daystar clear and bright
Comes forth upon his milk-white steed. Again in other plight      210
The morning, Pallant's daughter fair, the messenger of light,
Delivereth into Phoebus' hands the world of clearer hue.
The circle also of the sun, what time it riseth new
And when it setteth, looketh red; but when it mounts most high,
Then looks it white because that there the nature of the sky
Is better and from filthy dross of earth doth further fly.
The image also of the moon that shineth aye by night
Is never of one quantity. For that that giveth light
Today is lesser than the next that followeth till the full,
And then contrariwise each day her light away doth pull.      220
What! See'st thou not how that the year, as representing plain
The age of man, departs itself in quarters four? First bain
And tender in the spring it is, even like a sucking babe.
Then green and void of strength and lush and foggy is the blade
And cheers the husbandman with hope; then all things flourish
      gay.
The earth with flowers of sundry hue then seemeth for to play,
And virtue small or none to herbs there doth as yet belong.
The year, from springtide passing forth to summer, waxeth strong,
Becometh like a lusty youth. For in our life throughout
There is no time more plentiful, more lusty, hot and stout.      230
Then followeth harvest, when the heat of youth grows somewhat
      cold,
Ripe, mild, disposèd mean betwixt a young man and an old

And somewhat sprent with greyish hair. Then ugly winter, last,
Like age steals on with trembling steps, all bald or overcast
With shirl thin hair as white as snow. Our bodies also aye
Do alter still from time to time and never stand at stay.
We shall not be the same we were today or yesterday.
The day hath been we were but seed and only hope of men,
And in our mother's womb we had our dwelling-place as then.

240   Dame Nature put to cunning hand and suffered not that we
Within our mother's strainèd womb should aye distressèd be,
But brought us out to air and from our prison set us free.
The child, newborn, lies void of strength. Within a season tho
He, waxing four-footed, learns like savage beasts to go.
Then, somewhat faltering and as yet not firm of foot, he stands
By getting somewhat for to help his sinews in his hands.
From that time, growing strong and swift, he passeth forth the
      space
Of youth and also, wearing out his middle age apace,
Through droopy age's steepy path he runneth out his race.

250   This age doth undermine the strength of former years and throws
It down; which thing old Milo by example plainly shows.
For when he saw those arms of his (which heretofore had been
As strong as ever Hercules in working deadly teen
Of biggest beasts) hang flapping down and nought but empty skin,
He wept. And Helen, when she saw her agèd wrinkles in
A glass, wept also, musing in herself what men had seen
That by two noble princes' sons she twice had ravished been.
Thou Time, the eater up of things, and Age of spiteful teen
Destroy all things. And when that long continuance hath them bit,

260   You leisurely by lingering death consume them every whit.
And these that we call elements do never stand at stay.
The interchanging course of them I will before ye lay.
Give heed thereto. This endless world contains therein, I say,
Four substances of which all things are gendered. Of these four
The earth and water for their mass and weight are sunkèn lower;
The other couple, air and fire, the purer of the twain,
Mount up, and nought can keep them down. And though there
      do remain

A space between each one of them, yet everything is made
Of them same four and into them at length again do fade.
The earth, resolving leisurely, doth melt to water sheer;                  270
The water, finèd, turns to air; the air eke, purgèd clear
From grossness, spireth up aloft and there becometh fire.
From thence in order contrary they back again retire.
Fire, thickening, passeth into air; and air, waxing gross,
Returns to water; water eke, congealing into dross,
Becometh earth. No kind of thing keeps aye his shape and hue.
For nature, loving ever change, repairs one shape anew
Upon another. Neither doth there perish aught (trust me)
In all the world but, altering, takes new shape. For that which we
Do term by name of being born is for to gin to be                          280
Another thing than that it was; and likewise for to die
To cease to be the thing it was. And though that variably
Things pass perchance from place to place, yet all, from whence
        they came
Returning, do unperishèd continue still the same.
But as for in one shape, be sure that nothing long can last.
Even so the ages of the world from gold to iron passed.
Even so have places oftentimes exchangèd their estate.
For I have seen it sea which was substantial ground alate;
Again, where sea was I have seen the same become dry land.
And shells and scales of seafish far have lain from any strand,           290
And in the tops of mountains high old anchors have been found.
Deep valleys have by watershot been made of level ground,
And hills by force of gulling oft have into sea been worn.
Hard gravel ground is sometime seen where marish was beforn,
And that that erst did suffer drought becometh standing lakes.
Here nature sendeth new springs out, and there the old in takes.
Full many rivers in the world through earthquakes heretofore
Have either changed their former course or dried and run no
        more.
So Lycus, being swallowed up by gaping of the ground,
A great way off fro thence is in another channel found.                   300
Even so the River Erasine among the fields of Arge
Sinks one while and another while runs great again at large.

Caïcus also of the land of Mysia (as men say),
Misliking of his former head, runs now another way.
In Sicil, also, Amasene runs sometime full and high,
And sometime, stopping up his spring, he makes his channel dry.
Men drank the waters of the brook Anigrus heretofore
Which now is such that men abhor to touch them anymore;
Which comes to pass (unless we will discredit poets quite)
310 Because the Centaurs, vanquishèd by Hercules in fight,
Did wash their wounds in that same brook. But doth not Hypanis
That springeth in the Scythian hills, which at his fountain is
Right pleasant, afterward become of brackish bitter taste?
Antissa and Phoenician Tyre and Pharos in time past
Were compassed all about with waves; but none of all these three
Is now an isle. Again the town of Leucas once was free
From sea and in the ancient time was joinèd to the land;
But now environed round about with water it doth stand.
Men say that Sicil also hath been joined to Italy
320 Until the sea consumed the bounds between and did supply
The room with water. If ye go to seek for Helice
And Bury, which were cities of Achaia, you shall see
Them hidden under water; and the shipmen yet do show
The walls and steeples of the towns drowned under as they row.
Not far from Pitthey Troezen is a certain high ground found
All void of trees, which heretofore was plain and level ground
But now a mountain. For the winds (a wondrous thing to say),
Enclosèd in the hollow caves of ground and seeking way
To pass therefro, in struggling long to get the open sky
330 In vain (because in all the cave there was no vent whereby
To issue out), did stretch the ground and make it swell on high
As doth a bladder that is blown by mouth or as the skin
Of hornèd goat in bottlewise when wind is gotten in.
The swelling of the foresaid place remains at this day still
And, by continuance waxing hard, is grown a pretty hill.
Of many things that come to mind by hearsay and by skill
Of good experience, I a few will utter to you mo.
What! Doth not water in his shapes change strangely to and fro?
The well of hornèd Hammon is at noontide passing cold;
340 At morn and even it waxeth warm; at midnight none can hold

His hand therein for passing heat. The well of Athamane
Is said to kindle wood what time the moon is in the wane.
The Cicones have a certain stream which, being drunk, doth
    bring
Men's bowels into marble hard; and whatsoever thing
Is touched therewith it turns to stone. And by your bounds,
    behold,
The rivers Crathe and Sybaris make yellow hair like gold
And amber. There are also springs (which thing is far more
    strange)
Which not the body only but the mind do also change.
Who hath not heard of Salmacis, that foul and filthy sink?
Or of the lake of Ethiope, which if a man do drink,                          350
He either runneth mad or else with wondrous drowsiness
Forgoeth quite his memory? Whoever doth repress
His thirst with draught of Clitor well hates wine and doth delight
In only water, either for because there is a might
Contrary unto warming wine by nature in the well
Or else because (for so the folk of Arcady do tell)
Melampus, Amythaon's son, when he delivered had
King Proetus' daughters by his charms and herbs from being mad,
Cast into that same water all the baggage wherewithal
He purged the madness of their minds; and so it did befall               360
That loathsomeness of wine did in those waters aye remain.
Again, in Lyncest contrary effect to this doth reign.
For whoso drinks too much thereof, he reeleth here and there
As if by quaffing wine no whit allayed he drunken were.
There is a lake in Arcady which Pheney men did name
In ancient time, whose doubtfulness deserveth justly blame.
A'night-times take thou heed of it, for if thou taste the same
A'night-times, it will hurt. But if thou drink it in the day
It hurteth not. Thus lakes and streams, as well perceive ye may,
Have divers powers and diversely. Even so the time hath been          370
That Delos, which stands steadfast now, on waves was floating
    seen.
And galleys have been sore afraid of frushing by the isles
Symplegads, which together dashed upon the sea erewhiles

But now do stand unmovable against both wind and tide.
Mount Etna with his burning ovens of brimstone shall not bide
Aye fire; neither was it so for ever erst. For whether
The earth a living creature be and that to breathe out hither
And thither flame great store of vents it have in sundry places
And that it have the power to shift those vents in divers cases,
380   Now damming these, now opening those, in moving to and fro;
Or that the whisking winds, restrained within the earth below,
Do beat the stones against the stones and other kind of stuff
Of fiery nature which do fall on fire with every puff;
As soon as those same winds do cease, the caves shall straight be
     cold.
Or if it be a rosin mould that soon of fire takes hold,
Or brimstone mixed with clayish soil on fire doth lightly fall,
Undoubtedly, as soon as that same soil consumèd shall
No longer yield the fatty food to feed the fire withal
And ravening nature shall forgo her wonted nourishment,
390   Then, being able to abide no longer famishment,
For want of sustenance it shall cease his burning. I do find
By fame that under Charles's wain in Pallene are a kind
Of people which by diving thrice three times in Triton lake
Become all feathered and the shape of birds upon them take.
The Scythian witches also are reported for to do
The selfsame thing (but hardly I give credit thereunto)
By smearing poison over all their bodies. But (and if
A man to matters tried by proof may safely give belief)
We see how flesh by lying still a while and catching heat
400   Doth turn to little living beasts. And yet a further feat:
Go, kill an ox and bury him (the thing by proof man sees),
And of his rotten flesh will breed the flower-gathering bees
Which, as their father did before, love fields exceedingly
And unto work in hope of gain their busy limbs apply.
The hornet is engendered of a lusty buried steed.
Go, pull away the clees from crabs that in the sea do breed
And bury all the rest in mould, and of the same will spring
A scorpion which with writhen tail will threaten for to sting.
The caterpillars of the field, the which are wont to weave
410   Hoar films upon the leaves of trees, their former nature leave

(Which thing is known to husbandmen) and turn to butterflies.
The mud hath in it certain seed whereof green froshes rise.
And first it brings them footless forth; then, after, it doth frame
Legs apt to swim; and furthermore, of purpose that the same
May serve them for to leap afar, their hinder part is much
More longer than their forepart is. The bearwhelp also, which
The bear hath newly littered, is no whelp immediately,
But like an evil-favoured lump of flesh alive doth lie.
The dam by licking shapeth out his members orderly
Of such a size as such a piece is able to conceive.                    420
Or mark ye not the bees of whom our honey we receive,
How that their young ones, which do lie within the six-square
          wax,
Are limbless bodies at the first and after, as they wax,
In process take both feet and wings? What man would think it
          true
That Lady Venus' simple birds, the doves of silver hue,
Or Juno's bird that in his tail bears stars, or Jove's stout knight,
The erne, and every other fowl of whatsoever flight
Could all be hatchèd out of eggs, unless he did it know?
Some folk do hold opinion, when the backbone which doth grow
In man is rotten in the grave, the pith becomes a snake.               430
Howbeit of other things all these their first beginning take.
One bird there is that doth renew itself and, as it were,
Beget itself continually. The Syrians name it there
A phoenix. Neither corn nor herbs this phoenix liveth by
But by the juice of frankincense and gum of amomy.
And when that of his life well full five hundred years are past,
Upon a holm-tree or upon a date-tree at the last
He makes him with his talons and his hardened bill a nest.
Which when that he with casia sweet and nardus soft hath dressed
And strowèd it with cinnamon and myrrha of the best,                   440
He rucketh down upon the same and in the spices dies.
Soon after of the father's corse, men say, there doth arise
Another little phoenix, which as many years must live
As did his father. He, as soon as age doth strength him give
To bear the burden, from the tree the weighty nest doth lift
And godlily his cradle thence and father's hearse doth shift;

And, flying through the subtle air, he gets to Phoebus' town
And there before the temple door doth lay his burden down.
But if that any novelty worth wondering be in these,
450   Much rather may we wonder at the hyen, if we please:
To see how interchangeably it one while doth remain
A female, and another while becometh male again.
The creature also which doth live by only air and wind
All colours that it leaneth to doth counterfeit by kind.
The grapegod Bacchus, when he had subdued the land of Inde,
Did find a spotted beast called lynx whose urine (by report),
By touching of the open air, congealeth in such sort
As that it doth become a stone. So coral, which as long
As water hides it is a shrub and soft, becometh strong
460   And hard as soon as it doth touch the air. The day would end
And Phoebus' panting steeds should in the ocean deep descend
Before all alterations I in words could comprehend.
So see we all things changeable. One nation gathereth strength;
Another waxeth weak; and both do make exchange at length.
So Troy, which once was great and strong as well in wealth as
          men
And able ten years' space to spare such store of blood as then,
Now, being base, hath nothing left of all her wealth to show
Save ruins of the ancient works which grass doth overgrow
And tombs wherein their ancestors lie buried on a row.
470   Once Sparta was a famous town; great Mycene flourished trim;
Both Athens and Amphion's towers in honour once did swim.
A pelting plot is Sparta now; great Mycene lies on ground.
Of Thebe, the town of Oedipus, what have we more than sound?
Of Athens, King Pandion's town, what resteth more than name?
Now also of the race of Troy is rising (so saith Fame)
The city Rome, which at the bank of Tiber, that doth run
Down from the hill of Apennine, already hath begun
With great advisement for to lay foundation of her state.
This town then changeth by increase the form it had alate
480   And of the universal world in time to come shall hold
The sovereignty, so prophecies and lots (men say) have told.
And, as I do remember me, what time that Troy decayed,
The prophet Helen, Priam's son, these words ensuing said

Before Aeneas, doubting of his life in weeping plight:
"O goddess' son, believe me, if thou think I have foresight
Of things to come, Troy shall not quite decay while thou dost
     live.
Both fire and sword shall unto thee thy passage freely give.
Thou must from hence and Troy with thee convey away in haste,
Until that both thyself and Troy in foreign land be placed
More friendly than thy native soil. Moreover, I foresee          490
A city by the offspring of the Trojans built shall be,
So great as never in the world the like was seen before,
Nor is this present, neither shall be seen for evermore.
A number of most noble peers for many years afore
Shall make it strong and puïssant; but he that shall it make
The sovereign lady of the world by right descent shall take
His first beginning from thy son, the little Jule. And when
The earth hath had her time of him, the sky and welkin then
Shall have him up for evermore, and heaven shall be his end."
Thus far, I well remember me, did Helen's words extend       500
To good Aeneas. And it is a pleasure unto me
The city of my countrymen increasing thus to see,
And that the Grecians' victory becomes the Trojans' weal.
But lest, forgetting quite themselves, our horses hap to steal
Beyond the mark: the heaven and all that under heaven is found
Doth alter shape. So doth the ground and all that is in ground.
And we that of the world are part (considering how we be
Not only flesh but also souls, which may with passage free
Remove them into every kind of beast both tame and wild),
Let live in safety honestly with slaughter undefiled       510
The bodies which perchance may have the spirits of our brothers,
Our sisters or our parents or the spirits of some others
Allièd to us, either by some friendship or some kin,
Or at the least the souls of men abiding them within.
And let us not Thyestes-like thus furnish up our boards
With bloody bowels. Oh, how lewd example he affords!
How wickedly prepareth he himself to murder man
That with a cruel knife doth cut the throat of calf and can
Unmovably give hearing to the lowing of the dam,

520    Or stick the kid that waileth like the little babe, or eat
The fowl that he himself before had often fed with meat!
What wants of utter wickedness in working such a feat?
What may he after pass to do? Well, either let your steers
Wear out themselves with work or else impute their death to
        years.
Against the wind and weather cold let wethers yield ye coats,
And udders full of battling milk receive ye of the goats.
Away with springes, snares and grins; away with risp and net.
Away with guileful feats; for fowls no limetwigs see ye set.
No feared feathers pitch ye up to keep the red deer in,
530    Ne with deceitful baited hook seek fishes for to win.
If aught do harm, destroy it. But destroy't, and do no more.
Forbear the flesh, and feed your mouths with fitter food
        therefore.'

*The death*
*of Numa*

    Men say that Numa, furnishèd with such philosophy
    As this and like, returnèd to his native soil and by
Entreatance was content of Rome to take the sovereignty.
Right happy in his wife which was a nymph, right happy in
His guides which were the Muses nine, this Numa did begin
To teach religion. By the means whereof he shortly drew
That people unto peace, who erst of nought but battle knew.
540    And when through age he ended had his reign and eke his life,
Through Latium he was mournèd for of man and child and wife
As well of high as low degree. His wife, forsaking quite
The city, in Vale Aricine did hide her out of sight
Among the thickest groves and there with sighs and plaints did let
The sacrifice of Dian, whom Orestes erst had set
From Taurica in Chersonese and in that place had fet.
How oft, ah, did the woodnymphs and the waternymphs persuade
Egeria for to cease her moan! What means of comfort made
They! Ah, how often Theseus' son her, weeping, thus bespake:

*Hippolytus'*
*story*   550

    'O nymph, thy mourning moderate; thy sorrow somewhat
        slake.
    Not only thou hast cause to heart thy fortune for to take.
Behold like haps of other folks, and this mischance of thine
Shall grieve thee less. Would God examples (so they were not
        mine)

Might comfort thee. But mine, perchance, may comfort thee. If
    thou
In talk by hap hast heard of one Hippolytus ere now
That through his father's light belief and stepdame's craft was slain,
It will a wonder seem to thee, and I shall have much pain
To make thee to believe the thing. But I am very he.
The daughter of Pasiphaë, in vain oft tempting me
My father's chamber to defile, surmised me to have sought      560
The thing that she with all her heart would fain I should have
    wrought.
And whether it were for fear I should her wickedness bewray,
Or else for spite because I had so often said her nay,
She charged me with her own offence. My father, by and by
Condemning me, did banish me his realm without cause why
And at my going like a foe did ban me bitterly.
To Pitthey Troezen outlaw-like my chariot straight took I.
My way lay hard upon the shore of Corinth. Suddenly
The sea did rise, and like a mount the wave did swell on high
And seemèd huger for to grow in drawing ever nigh      570
And, roaring, cleavèd in the top. Up starts immediately
A hornèd bullock from amid the broken wave and by
The breast did raise him in the air and at his nostrils and
His platter-mouth did puff out part of sea upon the land.
My servants' hearts were sore afraid. But my heart, musing aye
Upon my wrongful banishment, did nought at all dismay.
My horses, setting up their ears and snorting, waxèd shy
And, being greatly flighted with the monster in their eye,
Turned down to sea and on the rocks my waggon drew. In vain
I, striving for to hold them back, laid hand upon the rein      580
All white with foam and, haling back, lay almost bolt upright.
And sure the fierceness of the steeds had yielded to my might,
But that the wheel that runneth aye about the ax-tree round
Did break by dashing on a stub and overthrew to ground.
Then from the chariot I was snatched, the bridles being cast
About my limbs. Ye might have seen my sinews sticking fast
Upon the stub; my guts drawn out alive; my members part
Still left upon the stump and part forth harried with the cart;

The crashing of my broken bones; and with what passing pain
590    I breathèd out my weary ghost. There did not whole remain
One piece of all my corse by which ye might discern as tho
What lump or part it was. For all was wound from top to toe.
Now canst thou, nymph, or darest thou compare thy harms with
        mine?
Moreover, I the lightless realm beheld with these same eyen
And bathed my tattered body in the River Phlegeton.
And had not bright Apollo's son his cunning showed upon
My body by his surgery, my life had quite be gone.
Which after I by force of herbs and leechcraft had again
Received by Aesculapius' means, though Pluto did disdain,
600    Then Cynthia (lest this gift of hers might work me greater spite)
Thick clouds did round about me cast. And to th'intent I might
Be safe myself and harmlessly appear to others' sight,
She made me old. And for my face, she left it in such plight
That none can know me by my look. And long she doubted
        whether
To give me Dele or Crete. At length, refusing both together,
She placed me here. And therewithal she bade me give up quite
The name that of my horses in remembrance put me might.
"For whereas erst Hippolytus★ hath been thy name," quoth she,
"I will that Virby† afterward thy name forever be."
610    From that time forth within this wood I keep my residence
As of the meaner gods a god of small magnificence;
And here I hide me underneath my sovereign lady's wing,
Obeying humbly to her hest in every kind of thing.'

*The transformation of Egeria*    But yet the harms of other folk could nothing help nor boot
Egeria's sorrows to assuage. Down at the mountain's foot
She, lying, melted into tears till Phoebus' sister sheen,
For pity of her great distress in which she had her seen,
Did turn her to a fountain clear and melted quite away
Her members into water thin that never should decay.
The strangeness of the thing did make the nymphs astonied,
620            and
The lady of Amazon's son amazed thereat did stand.

★Horse slain        †Twice man

As when the Tyrrhene tillman saw, in earing of his land,
The fatal clod first stir alone without the help of hand
And by and by, forgoing quite the earthly shape of clod,
To take the seemly shape of man and shortly like a god
To tell of things as then to come. The Tyrrhenes did him call
By name of Tages. He did teach the Tuscans first of all
To guess by searching bulks of beasts what after should befall.
Or like as did King Romulus, when suddenly he found
His lance on mountain Palatine fast rooted in the ground                630.
And bearing leaves, no longer now a weapon but a tree
Which shadowed such as wonderingly came thither for to see.
Or else as Cipus, when he in the running brook had seen                *The story*
His horns; for why he saw them and, supposing there had been           *of Cipus*
No credit to be given unto the glancing image, he
Put oft his fingers to his head and felt it so to be.
And, blaming now no more his eyes, in coming from the chase
With conquests of his foes he stayed and, lifting up his face
(And with his face, his horns) to heaven, he said, 'Whatever thing
Is by this wonder meant, O gods, if joyful news it bring,               640
I pray ye, let it joyful to my folk and country be;
But if it threaten evil, let the evil light on me.'
In saying so, an altar green of clowres he did frame
And offered fuming frankincense in fire upon the same
And poured bowls of wine thereon and searched therewithal
The quivering inwards of a sheep to know what should befall.
A Tyrrhene wizard, having sought the bowels, saw therein
Great changes and attempts of things then ready to begin
Which were not plainly manifest. But when that he at last
His eyes from inwards of the beast on Cipus' horns had cast,            650
'Hail, king!' he said. 'For unto thee, O Cipus, unto thee
And to thy horns shall this same place and Rome obedient be.
Abridge delay and make thou haste to enter at the gates
Which tarry open for thee. So command the soothfast Fates.
Thou shalt be king as soon as thou hast entered once the town,
And thou and thine for evermore shalt wear the royal crown.'
With that he, stepping back his foot, did turn his frowning face
From Romeward, saying, 'Far, Oh far, the gods such handsel
      chase.

More right it were I all my life a banished man should be
660 Than that the hóly Capitol me reigning there should see.'
Thus much he said. And by and by together he did call
The people and the senators. But yet he first of all
Did hide his horns with laurel leaves. And then without the wall
He, standing on a mount the which his men had made of sods
And having after ancient guise made prayer to the gods,
Said, 'Here is one that shall, unless ye banish him your town
Immediately, be king of Rome and wear a royal crown.
What man it is I will by sign but not by name bewray.
He hath upon his brow two horns. The wizard here doth say
670 That if he enter Rome you shall like servants him obey.
He might have entered at your gates which open for him lay,
But I did stay him thence. And yet there is not unto me
A nearer friend in all the world. Howbeit, forbid him ye,
O Romans, that he come not once within your walls. Or if
He have deservèd, bind him fast in fetters like a thief.
Or in this fatal tyrant's death of fear dispatch your mind.'
Such noise as pine-trees make what time the heady eastern wind
Doth whizz amongst them or as from the sea doth far rebound,
Even such among the folk of Rome that present was the sound.
680 Howbeit, in that confusèd roar of fearful folk did fall
Out one voice asking, 'Who is he?' And staring therewithal
Upon their foreheads, they did seek the foresaid horns. Again
Quoth Cipus, 'Lo, ye have the man for whom ye seek.' And then
He pulled (against his people's will) his garland from his head
And showèd them the two fair horns that on his brows were
            spread.
At that the people dasheth down their looks and, sighing, is
Right sorry (who would think it true?) to see that head of his
Most famous for his good deserts. Yet did they not forget
The honour of his personage, but willingly did set
690 The laurel garland on his head again. And by and by
The senate said, 'Well, Cipus, sith until the time thou die
Thou may'st not come within these walls, we give thee as much
            ground
In honour of thee as a team of steers can plough thee round

Between the dawning of the day and shutting in of night.'
Moreover, on the brazen gate at which this Cipus might
Have entered Rome, a pair of horns were graved to represent
His wondrous shape, as of his deed an endless monument.
 Ye Muses, who to poets are the present springs of grace,
  Now show (for you know, neither are you dulled by time or
     space)
How Aesculapius in the isle that is in Tiber deep
Among the sacred saints of Rome had fortune for to creep.
A cruel plague did heretofore infect the Latian air,
And people's bodies, pining pale, the murrain did appair.
When, tirèd with the burial of their friends, they did perceive
Themselves no help at man's hand nor by physic to receive,
Then, seeking help from heaven, they sent to Delphos (which
     doth stand
Amid the world) for counsel to be had at Phoebus' hand,
Beseeching him with healthful aid to succour their distress
And of the mighty city Rome the mischief to redress.
The quivers which Apollo bright himself was wont to bear,
The bay-trees and the place itself together shaken were.
And by and by the table from the furthest part of all
The chancel spake these words, which did their hearts with fear
     appal:
'The thing ye Romans seek for here ye should have sought more
     nigh
Your country. Yea, and nearer home go seek it now. Not I,
Apollo, but Apollo's son is he that must redress
Your sorrows. Take your journey with good handsel of success
And fetch my son among you.' When Apollo's hest was told
Among the prudent senators, they searched what town did hold
His son, and unto Epidaur a galley for him sent.
As soon as that th'ambassador arrivèd there, they went
Unto the council and the lords of Greekland, whom they pray
To have the god, the present plagues of Romans for to stay,
And for themselves the oracle of Phoebus forth they lay.
The council were of sundry minds and could not well agree.
Some thought that succour in such need denièd should not be;

*How
Aesculapius
came to Rome*

700

710

720

And divers did persuade to keep their help and not to send
Their gods away, sith they themselves might need them in the
          end.
While doubtfully they off and on debate this curious case,
730  The evening twilight utterly the day away did chase
And on the world the shadow of the earth had darkness brought.
That night the lord ambassador, as sleep upon him wrought,
Did dream he saw before him stand the god whose help he sought
In shape as in his chapel he was wonted for to stand,
With right hand stroking down his beard and staff in t'other hand
And meekly saying, 'Fear not, I will come and leave my shrine.
This serpent which doth wreathe with knots about this staff of
          mine
Mark well and take good heed thereof, that when thou shalt it see
Thou may'st it know. For into it transformèd will I be.
740  But bigger I will be, for I will seem of such a size
As may celestial bodies well to turn into suffice.'
Straight with the voice the god and, with the voice and god, away
Went sleep. And after sleep was gone ensuèd cheerful day.
Next morning having clearly put the fiery stars to flight,
The lords, not knowing what to do, assembled all forthright
Within the sumptuous temple of the god that was required,
And of his mind by heavenly sign some knowledge they desired.
They scarce had done their prayers, when the god in shape of
          snake
With lofty crest of gold began a hissing for to make
750  Which was a warning given. And with his presence he did shake
The altar, shrine, doors, marble floor and roof all laid with gold;
And, vauncing up his breast, he stayed right stately to behold
Amid the church, and round about his fiery eyes he rolled.
The sight did fray the people. But the wifeless priest (whose hair
Was trussèd in a fair white caul) did know the god was there
And said, 'Behold, 'tiz God, 'tiz God! As many as be here,
Pray both with mouth and mind! O thou our glorious God,
          appear
To our behoof and help thy folk that keep thy hallows right!'
The people present worshippèd his godhead there in sight,

Repeating double that the priest did say. The Romans eke          760
Devoutly did with godly voice and heart his favour seek.
The god by nodding did consent and gave assurèd sign
By shaking of his golden crest that on his head did shine
And hissèd twice with spurting tongue. Then trailed he down the
      fine
And glistering greces of his church. And, turning back his eyen,
He lookèd to his altarward and to his former shrine
And temple, as to take his leave and bid them all farewell.
From thence right huge upon the ground (which sweet of flowers
      did smell
That people strewèd in his way) he passèd stately down
And, bending into boughts, went through the heart of all the
      town                                                        770
Until that he the bowing wharf beside the haven took;
Where staying, when he had (as seemed) dismissed with gentle
      look
His train of chaplains and the folk that waited on him thither,
He laid him in the Roman ship to sail away together.
The ship did feel the burden of his godhead to the full
And for the heavy weight of him did after pass more dull.
The Romans, being glad of him and having killed a steer
Upon the shore, untied their ropes and cables from the pier.
   The lightsome wind did drive the ship. The god, avauncing
      high
   And leaning with his neck upon the galley's side, did lie      780
And look upon the greenish waves; and, cutting easily through
Th'Ionian sea with little gales of western wind not rough,
The sixth day morning came upon the coast of Italy.
And, passing forth by Juno's church that must'rth to the eye
Upon the head of Lacine, he was carried also by
The rock of Scyly. Then he left the land of Calabry
And, rowing softly by the rock Zephirion, he did draw
To Celen cliffs, the which upon the right side have a flaw.
By Romech and by Caulon and by Narice thence he passed
And from the straits of Sicily gat quite and clear at last.       790
Then ran he by th'Aeolian Isles and by the metal mine
Of Tempsa and by Leucosy and temperate Paest, where fine

And pleasant roses flourish aye. From thence by Capreas
And Atheny, the headland of Minerva, he did pass
To Surrent, where with gentle vines the hills be overclad,
And by the town of Hercules and Stabey ill bested
And Naples, born to idleness, and Cumes, where Sibyl had
Her temples, and the scalding baths and Lintern, where grows
    store
Of mastic trees, and Volturn, which bears sand apace from shore,
800  And Sinuess, whereas adders are as white as any snow,
And Minturn, of infected air because it stands so low,
And Caiety, where Aeneas did his nurse in tomb bestow,
And Formy, where Antiphates the Lestrigon did keep,
And Trache, environed with a fen, and Circe's mountain steep,
To Ancon with the boistrous shore. As soon as that the ship
Arrivèd here (for now the sea was rough), the god let slip
His circles and in bending boughts and wallowing waves did glide
Into his father's temple which was builded there beside
Upon the shore. And when the sea was calm and pacified,
810  The foresaid god of Epidaur his father's church forsook
(The lodging of his nearest friend which for a time he took)
And with his crackling scales did in the sand a furrow cut
And, taking hold upon the stern, did in the galley put
His head and rested till he came past Camp and Lavine sands
And entered Tiber's mouth, at which the city Ostia stands.
The folk of Rome came hither all by heaps, both men and wives
And eke the nuns that keep the fire of Vesta as their lives,
To meet the god and welcomed him with joyful noise. And as
The galley rowèd up the stream, great store of incense was
820  On altars burnt on both the banks, so that on either side
The fuming of the frankincense the very air did hide;
And also slain in sacrifice full many cattle died.
Anon he came to Rome, the head of all the world; and there
The serpent, lifting up himself, began his head to bear
Right up along the mast, upon the top whereof on high
He lookèd round about, a meet abiding-place to spy.
The Tiber doth divide itself in twain and doth embrace
A little pretty island (so the people term the place)
From either side whereof the banks are distant equal space.

Apollo's snake, descending from the mast, conveyed him thither      830
And, taking eft his heavenly shape, as one repairing hither
To bring our city healthfulness, did end our sorrows quite.

    Although to be a god with us admitted were this wight,      *Caesar is*
    Yet was he born a foreigner. But Caesar hath obtained      *made a god*
His godhead in his native soil and city where he reigned.
Whom, peerless both in peace and war, not more his wars up knit
With triumph nor his great exploits achievèd by his wit
Nor yet the great renown that he obtained so speedily
Have turnèd to a blazing star than did his progeny.
For of the acts of Caesar, none is greater than that he      840
Left such a son behind him as Augustus is, to be
His heir. For are they things more hard, to overcome the realm
Of Britain standing in the sea, or up the sevenfold stream
Of Nile that beareth paper reed victorious ships to row,
Or to rebellious Numidy to give an overthrow,
Or Juba, king of Moors, and Pons (which proudly did it bear
Upon the name of Mithridate) to force by sword and spear
To yield them subjects unto Rome, or by his just desert
To merit many triumphs and of some to have his part,
Than such an heir to leave behind in whom the gods do show      850
Exceeding favour unto men for that they do bestow
So great a prince upon the world? Now to th'intent that he
Should not be born of mortal seed, the other was to be
Canonized for a god. Which thing when golden Venus see
(She also saw how dreadful death was for the bishop then
Prepared and how conspiracy was wrought by wicked men),
She lookèd pale. And as the gods came any in her way,
She said unto them one by one, 'Behold and see, I pray,
With how exceeding eagerness they seek me to betray
And with what wondrous craft they strive to take my life away;      860
I mean the thing that only now remaineth unto me
Of Jule, the Trojans' race. Must I then only ever be
Thus vexed with undeservèd cares? How seemeth now the pain
Of Diomed's spear of Calydon to wound my hand again!
How seems it me that Troy again is lost through ill defence!
How seems my son Aeneas like a banished man from thence

To wander far again and on the sea to tossèd be
And war with Turnus for to make – or rather (truth to say)
With Juno! What mean I about harms passèd many a day
870    Against mine offspring thus to stand? This present fear and woe
Permit me not to think on things now passed so long ago.
Ye see how wicked swords against my head are whetted. I
Beseech ye, keep them from my throat and set the traitors by
Their purpose. Neither suffer you Dame Vesta's fire to die
By murdering of her bishop.' Thus went Venus woefully
Complaining over all the heaven and moved the gods thereby.
And for they could not break the strong decrees of destiny,
They showèd signs most manifest of sorrow to ensue.
For battles fighting in the clouds with crashing armour flew,
880    And dreadful trumpets sounded in the air and horns eke blew,
As warning men beforehand of the mischief that did brew.
And Phoebus also, looking dim, did cast a drowsy light
Upon the earth, which seemed likewise to be in sorry plight.
From underneath amid the stars brands oft seemed burning bright.
It often rainèd drops of blood. The morning star looked blue
And was bespotted here and there with specks of rusty hue.
The moon also had spots of blood. The screech owl sent from hell
Did with her tune unfortunate in every corner yell.
Salt tears from ivory images in sundry places fell.
890    And in the chapels of the gods was singing heard and words
Of threatening. Not a sacrifice one sign of good affords,
But great turmoil to be at hand their heartstrings do declare,
And when the beast is rippèd up, the inwards headless are.
About the court and every house and churches in the nights
The dogs did howl, and everywhere appearèd ghastly sprites,
And with an earthquake shaken was the town. Yet could not all
These warnings of the gods dispoint the treason that should fall
Nor overcome the Destinies. The naked swords were brought
Into the temple; for no place in all the town was thought
900    So meet to work the mischief in or for them to commit
The heinous murder as the court in which they used to sit
In council. Venus then with both her hands her stomach smit
And was about to hide him with the cloud in which she hid
Aeneas, when she from the sword of Diomed did him rid,

Or Paris, when from Menelay she did him safe convey.
But Jove, her father, staying her, did thus unto her say:
'Why, daughter mine, wilt thou alone be striving to prevent
Unvanquishable destiny? In faith, and if thou went
Thyself into the house in which the fatal sisters three
Do dwell, thou shouldest there of brass and steel substantial see          910
The registers of things so strong and massy made to be
That safe and everlasting they do neither stand in fear
Of thunder nor of lightning nor of any ruin there.
The destinies of thine offspring thou shalt there find graven deep
In adamant. I read them and in mind I do them keep.
And for because thou shalt not be quite ignorant of all,
I will declare what things I marked hereafter to befall.
The man for whom thou makest suit hath livèd full his time
And, having run his race on earth, must now to heaven up climb,
Where thou shalt make a god of him aye honoured for to be          920
With temples and with altars on the earth. Moreover, he
That is his heir and bears his name shall all alone sustain
The burden laid upon his back and shall our help obtain
His father's murder to revenge. The town of Mutiny,
Besiegèd by his power, shall yield. The fields of Pharsaly
Shall feel him, and Philippos in the realm of Macedon
Shall once again be stained with blood. The great Pompeius' son
Shall vanquished be by him upon the sea of Sicily.
The Roman captain's wife, the Queen of Egypt, through her
          high
Presumption trusting to her match too much, shall threat in vain          930
To make her canop over our high Capitol to reign.
What should I tell thee of the wild and barbarous nations that
At both the oceans dwelling be? The universal plat
Of all the earth inhabited shall all be his. The sea
Shall unto him obedient be likewise. And when that he
Hath stablished peace in all the world, then shall he set his mind
To civil matters, upright laws by justice for to find,
And by example of himself all others he shall bind.
Then, having care of time to come and of posterity,
A holy wife shall bear to him a son that may supply          940

His careful charge and bear his name. And lastly, in the end
He shall to heaven among the stars, his ancestors, ascend,
But not before his life by length to drooping age do tend.
And therefore from the murdered corse of Julius Caesar take
His soul with speed and of the same a burning cresset make,
That from our heavenly palace he may evermore look down
Upon our royal Capitol and court within Rome town.'

 He scarcely ended had these words but Venus out of hand
 Amid the senate-house of Rome invisible did stand
950 And from her Caesar's body took his new expulsèd sprite,
The which she not permitting to resolve to aïr quite,
Did place it in the sky among the stars that glister bright.
And as she bare it, she did feel it gather heavenly might
And for to waxen fiery. She no sooner let it fly
But that, a goodly shining star, it up aloft did sty
And drew a great way after it bright beams like burning hair.

*The destiny* Who, looking on his son's good deeds, confessèd that they were
*of Augustus* Far greater than his own; and glad he was to see that he
Excellèd him. Although his son in no wise would agree
960 To have his deeds preferred before his father's, yet doth Fame
(Who aye is free and bound to no command) withstand the same
And, striving in that one behalf against his hest and will,
Proceedeth to prefer his deeds before his father's still.
Even so to Agamemnon's great renown gives Atreus place;
Even so Achilles' deeds the deeds of Peleus do abase;
Even so beyond Aegeus far doth Thesey's prowess go;
And (that I may examples use full matching these) even so
Is Saturn less in fame than Jove. Jove rules the heavenly spheres
And all the triple-shapèd world; and our Augustus bears
970 Dominion over all the earth. They both are fathers; they
Are rulers both. Ye gods to whom both fire and sword gave way
What time ye with Aeneas came from Troy; ye gods that were
Of mortal men canonizèd; thou Quirin, who did'st rear
The walls of Rome; and Mars, who wert the valiant Quirin's sire;
And Vesta, of the household gods of Caesar with thy fire
Most holy; and thou, Phoebus, who with Vesta also art
Of household; and thou, Jupiter, who in the highest part

Of mountain Tarpey hast thy church; and all ye gods that may
With conscience safe by poets be appealèd to: I pray,
Let that same day be slow to come and after I am dead                    980
In which Augustus (who as now of all the world is head),
Quite giving up the care thereof, ascend to heaven for aye,
There, absent hence, to favour such as unto him shall pray.

    Now have I brought a work to end which neither Jove's fierce *The poet's*
      wrath                                                                                    *conclusion*
    Nor sword, nor fire, nor fretting age with all the force it hath
Are able to abolish quite. Let come that fatal hour
Which, saving of this brittle flesh, hath over me no power
And at his pleasure make an end of mine uncertain time.
Yet shall the better part of me assurèd be to climb
Aloft above the starry sky; and all the world shall never              990
Be able for to quench my name. For look how far so ever
The Roman empire by the right of conquest shall extend,
So far shall all folk read this work. And time without all end
(If poets as by prophecy about the truth may aim)
My life shall everlastingly be lengthened still by fame.

FINIS LIBRI DECIMI QUINTI.

*Laus & honor soli Deo.*

# NOTES

## TITLE-PAGE

The wording comes from the 1567 edition.

## EPISTLE OF 1565

**Dedication** *Robert, Earl of Leicester*: Robert Dudley, Earl of Leicester (1532–88), at that time Elizabeth's favourite, a man of Puritan sympathies and an influential patron of the arts.

**14–15** *not heretofore published*: Golding's was the first published English translation of whole books of the *Metamorphoses*. See Introduction.

**16** *the privilege of the new year*: new-year gift-giving was a common custom at this period. The gifts were typically offered to patrons whose goodwill the giver wanted to win.

**29** *Cecil House*: Golding had been appointed by William Cecil as 'receiver' for his young nephew Edward de Vere in 1562.

## EPISTLE OF 1567

**1** *mark*: finishing-post of a race.

**3–4** *the author . . . mount*: referring to Ovid's claims in 15. 989–91.

**5–8** Golding's description of Ovid's creation, which gives a structure to matter already in existence 'dispersedly', reflects Ovid's description of the creation of the world; see 1. 5 ff.

**9** *Four kind of things*: the four topics are (i) the mutability of everything under heaven (10), (ii) the continuance of all things, though altered (11–12), (iii) the immortality of the soul (17–21), and (iv) the necessity of virtue and reason in men's lives (55–62).

**20** *Limbo*: not a term which appears in Ovid's text, though frequently used in Golding's translation. Limbo was, in Roman Catholic theology, the abode of souls who were excluded from both heaven and hell.

**23** *the latter book*: i.e. Book 15.

**26** *that opinion*: Pythagoras' doctrine of the transmigration of souls, heretical to the Elizabethan mind, was widely referred to in Elizabethan literature. See Marlowe's *Doctor Faustus* (in Faustus's last speech), 'Ah, Pythagoras' metempsychosis!', and Shakespeare's *Twelfth Night* IV. ii.

**29** *understood*: all editions up to that of 1603 read 'understand'; 1612 changes this to 'understood'.

**32** *Three sorts of life or soul*: referring to the doctrine of three souls – vegetative, sensitive and rational.

**38** *By force of Phoebus*: as the sun.

**52** *a point*: i.e. a matter that distinguishes the wise from the foolish. See Feste's questions to the 'mad' Malvolio on this point in *Twelfth Night* IV. ii.

**74** *that*: i.e. with the result that.

**79** *the mean*: i.e. the middle path.

**96** *set their tongues to sale*: i.e. lie for the sake of profit. Presumably proverbial.

**101** *their adherents*: those things connected with them.

**127** *he warns us oft before*: compare Golding's views in his *Discourse upon the Earthquake*: 'God never poured out his grievous displeasure and wrath upon any nation, realm, city, kingdom, state or country, but he gave some notable forewarning thereof by some dreadful wonder' (L. T. Golding, *An Elizabethan Puritan*, p. 185).

**138** The horse used as a motif of lust is commonplace; see, e.g., Shakespeare's *Venus and Adonis* 259 ff.

**149** *an honest meaner*: a person of honest disposition.

**181** *Partridge*: Daedalus' nephew, see 8. 314 ff.

**191–2** *with the least . . . satisfy*: i.e. far from satisfying.

**219** *will they, nill they*: whether they want it or not.

**266** *apes*: into which the Cercopes were transformed. The ape is a common symbol of deceit and trickery.

**278** *herb moly*: a mythical plant with a white flower and black root, endowed with magic properties. The name was applied to various plants supposed to be identical with the mythical moly, especially wild garlic.

**338–41** Golding's comments here are in line with interpretations of Ovid which find Christian morality in the *Metamorphoses* – the allegorical reading of Ovid evident from the fourteenth-century *Ovide moralisé* onwards – and in line more broadly with the neoplatonic synthesis of classical myths with Christian revelation and the earlier syncretic philosophy of Philo Judaeus, on whom see the next note.

**354–69** *For God the Father . . .*: Golding's quotation is a translation of Philo Judaeus, *On the Discourse of the World's Creation Given by Moses* (*De Opificio Mundi*), §29. Philo Judaeus (*c.* 20 BC–*c.* 50 AD), also known as Philo of Alexandria, was a Jewish thinker and exegete who developed an allegorical interpretation of Scripture which enabled him to find much of Greek philosophy in the Old Testament; his interpretations were of huge influence on the biblical exegesis of the Christian Church.

**366** *wandering planets seven*: there are nine planets, including Earth and Pluto, which was not discovered until 1930. The seven referred to here are Mercury, Venus, Mars, Jupiter, Saturn, Uranus and Neptune.

**380** *saith Moses*: in Genesis 1.

**398–400** *Metamorphosis* 1. 20–22.

**411–14** *Metamorphosis* 1. 83–6.

**418** *As some have written*: the idea that man existed eternally could be traced to Plato (*Phaedrus* 245) or imputed to Aristotle, who believed in the eternity of the world. Belief in the pre-existence of human beings as 'pure minds' was ascribed to Origen; the doctrine of the pre-existent flesh was ascribed to the second-century Gnostic Apelles and the fourth-century heresiarch Apollinarius of Laodicea. Plato also proposed the notion that more than one god was responsible for the creation of man (*Timaeus* 41–2). There was also a Jewish tradition that the angels were the creators of the body. Although it is not clear which writers Golding has in mind here, his purpose is evidently to distance Ovid's text from beliefs which would constitute Christian heresy.

**421–30** *Metamorphosis* 1. 87–96.

**439** *Prometheus*: from Greek προμηθής, forethinking, cautious, wary.

**455–8** *Metamorphosis* 1. 97–100.

**495** *Noy*: Noah. For Noah's Flood, see Genesis 6–9.

**498** *the hills of Armeny*: Noah's ark settled on the mountains of Ararat in Armenia (Genesis 8. 4).

**501** *Deucalion*: mythical king of Phthia in Thessaly, son of Prometheus.

**532** *Phlegeton . . . Styx*: rivers of the underworld.

**533** *th'Elysian fields*: where the spirits of the blessed remain.

**544** *double recompence . . . with gain*: bringing it in line with Horace's view of poetry as something which both teaches and delights (Horace, *Art of Poetry* 343).

**573** *affections*: Golding returns to the image of the passions as horses to be kept in check.

**579** *Hippolytus*: for his story, see 15. 550–613.

**582** *orchard of Alcinous*: an image of plenty, like the following 'horn of Acheloy'. Alcinous' orchard, described in Homer's *Odyssey* 7, bore fruit all year round. Literary anthologies and miscellanies are commonly described as gardens, woods, etc., as, for example, Ben Jonson's *Timber* (printed in 1640), or the 1597 anthology *The Arbour of Amorous Devises*. Alcinous is mentioned at *Metamorphosis* 14. 641.

**584** *horn of Acheloy*: see 9. 1–103 for the fight between Acheloüs (in the form of a bull) and Hercules, in which one of the bull's horns is turned into a cornucopia. The cornucopia is commonly adopted as an image of literary wealth and eloquence.

**586** *a member rent*: Golding's four-book *Metamorphosis* of 1565 is compared to the horn torn from Acheloüs' head.

**591** *wreaths of bay*: the reward of the poet; the relevant myth is that of Daphne and Apollo, *Metamorphosis* 1. 545–700.

**598** *a parcel of the book*: the 1565 four-book *Metamorphosis*, also dedicated to Leicester.
**609** *Nestor*: famed for his age and wisdom. See *Metamorphosis* 12.
**610** *Tithonus*: granted immortality by Zeus at the request of Eos. He is referred to at 9. 503.
**617** *Barwicke*: a manor belonging to the Vere estate in White Colne, Essex.

## PREFACE TO THE READER

**33** *Jove . . . triple fire*: Jupiter was commonly depicted holding three-pronged lightning.
**40** *her*: Coronis.
**117** *Their purpose was . . . to delight*: returning to Horace's definition of the purpose of poetry (see note to line 544 of the 1567 Epistle).
**128** *As Persian kings*: compare Herodotus, *Histories* 1. 99.
**130** *they*: i.e. the poets.
**131** *covert names and terms*: returning to the neoplatonic reading of classical mythology proposed in the Epistle.
**138** *saving unto few*: since it is the nature of the pagan mysteries to remain hidden to the majority.
**142** *rocks and shallow shelves*: the image relates to the story of Ulysses and the sirens, to which Golding refers at the end of the Preface in his admonitions to the weak-stomached reader. See line 218 and note.
**156** *Esteem not . . . defaults to halt*: i.e. do not assume that the author of the work lives by these vices.
**167–8** See Titus 1. 15: 'Unto the pure all things are pure: but unto them that are defiled and unbelieving is nothing pure; but even their mind and conscience is defiled.'
**185** *For this do learnèd persons deem*: as illustrated by the quantities of annotation which accompanied sixteenth-century editions of the text.
**218** *Ulysses' feat*: Ulysses was warned by Circe about the sirens (*mermaids*), who attracted passing sailors with their singing, luring their ships to grief on the rocky coast and then devouring them. Ulysses therefore ordered his sailors to block up their ears with wax to avoid hearing the sirens' music, had himself tied to the mast and forbade his men to untie him, no matter how strongly he should plead. They thus passed the sirens safely; the sirens, in frustration at their failure, threw themselves into the sea and drowned. See Homer, *Odyssey* 12. 37–54, 154–200. Ovid alludes only indirectly to the story; see *Metamorphosis* 14. 495–6.

## THE FIRST BOOK

**14** *Amphitrite*: i.e. the sea.

**71** *Eurus*: the east wind, who is assigned to the eastern lands of the dawn (*morning grey*, line 69).

**73** *Zephyr*: the west wind.

*Boreas*: the north wind.

**74** *Charles his wain*: the constellation comprising the seven bright stars in Ursa Major, also known as the Plough; in Ovid, 'septem . . . triones' (seven ploughing oxen).

**75** *Auster*: the south wind.

**93** *in her flowers*: in her prime.

**107** *There was no man . . . in hand*: an idiomatic rendition of Ovid's 'nec supplex turba timebat / Iudicis ora sui' (nor did the suppliant crowd fear its judge's words).

**119–20** Golding's list includes fruits familiar from English hedgerows, diverging widely from Ovid's, which consists of 'Arbuteos' (arbute fruit or wild strawberries), 'montana . . . fraga' (mountain strawberries); 'Corna' (Cornelian cherries) and 'mora' (blackberries).

**129** *Limbo*: in Ovid, 'tartara'.

**143** *past all grace*: a Christianized rendering of Ovid's 'scelerata' (impious, wicked).

**148** Golding adapts Ovid's list to include *envy, pride and wicked lust*, three of the seven deadly sins.

**152** Golding's *dowels and ditches* replace and anglicize Ovid's 'limite' (boundary line).

**156** Golding's language contains implications of sexual depravity (*to rig* meaning 'to play the wanton') which will reappear in Milton's description of the fallen world in *Paradise Lost* 1. 686–8:

> [men] with impious hands
> Rifled the bowels of their mother Earth
> For treasures better hid.

The bodily metaphor is already present in Ovid's 'viscera' (entrails, womb).

**157** *hell*: in Ovid, 'stygiis . . . umbris' (the Stygian shades).

**169** *godliness*: in place of Ovid's 'Pietas'.

*Astrey*: Astraea, goddess of justice.

**177–8** *Olympus . . . Pelion . . . Ossa*: the hills heaped up by the giants; *under* should probably be understood adjectivally (i.e. lower Ossa), otherwise Golding's translation would shift Ossa from the bottom of the pile ('subiectae . . . Ossae') to the middle.

**191–8** *Court of Parliament . . . peers*: Golding offers English equivalents for Ovid's 'Concilium' (assembly) and 'deorum . . . nobilium' (gods of high rank).

**202** *the palace*: having already introduced the terminology of English government, Golding's translation falls flat here; Ovid's joke is to compare the Milky Way to the Palatine district, the home of Roman imperial power. George Sandys reproduces Ovid's humour better when he translates:

> This glorious Roofe I would not doubt to call,
> Had I but boldnesse lent mee, Heaven's *White-Hall*.

*(Metamorphoses* I. 179–80)

**210** *with their hundred hands*: see 3. 381.

*the adder-footed rout*: i.e. the giants.

**237** *August*: Caesar Augustus; apparently an allusion to one of the several conspiracies against Augustus.

**272** *He ran me*: an 'ethical dative' of informal narrative style, which introduces into the sentence a person (usually the speaker) who is only marginally interested in the fact described in that sentence. It is used frequently in Golding's translation, often, as here, to render the narrative more vivid and immediate.

**304** *Vulcan*: god of fire.

**311** *Aeolus*: appointed as steward of the winds and who, according to *Aeneid* I. 52 ff., kept them imprisoned in a huge cave on the island of Lipara.

**340** *churches*: a Christian rendition of Ovid's 'penetralia', the shrine within the house to the household gods.

**352** *porpoises*: Golding's addition, as it is at 2. 340.

**394** Golding adds the image of the bell, which somewhat confuses the description.

**433–46** Golding's translation gives a clearly Christian rendition of the episode. Golding adds *for his grace* (433) and *grace and favour* (446); compare, for example, the Common Prayer Book's general collect: 'Prevent us, O Lord, in all our doings with thy most gracious favour'. Ovid's 'delubra' (shrine) and 'templi' (temple) become a church or chapel (438, 441, 443). Where Ovid's couple appeal with the prayers of the righteous ('precibus . . . iustis'), Golding's couple offer prayers proceeding *from humble heart and mind* (445).

**463** *in these doubtful words . . . mystery*: Golding's addition, as is *if the sense . . . do seem* (465–6). Deucalion's correct understanding of the oracle is made to replicate neoplatonic readings of myth. Ovid's Deucalion states only, 'Aut fallax . . . est sollertia nobis . . .' (Unless my wit deceives me . . . ).

**539** *Pythians*: possibly a misprint for 'Pythian', but retained in all editions.

**545** *Peneian*: i.e. daughter of Peneius. 'Peneis' is used interchangeably with 'Daphne' throughout the episode.

**595** *foredooms*: Apollo was the god of prophecy.

**635** *for need*: of necessity. Golding's addition.

**692** *The oak*: the 'civic crown', a wreath of oak-leaves hung over the door to Augustus' palace.

**696** *from time to time*: at all times.

**697** *Paean*: 'the Healer'; one of Apollo's titles.

**741** *Lyrcey*: misprinted as 'Lincey' in all editions.

**762** *at fingers' ends had found*: was thoroughly familiar with.

**773** *She had him in a jealousy*: she was suspicious of him.

**784** *costly couch . . . featherbed*: Golding's expansion of Ovid's 'toro' (bed).

**831** *Now could . . . forlorn*: i.e. Jove could no longer abide the fact that his lover was so forlorn.

**832** *Maia*: one of the seven sisters who became the seven stars of the constellation known as the Pleiades.

**833** *He*: i.e. Maia's son, Mercury.

**835** *and fetcheth souls from hell*: Golding's addition, prompted by Regius's quotation from Virgil, *Aeneid* 4. 242–3: 'animas ille evocat orco Pallentes, alias sub tristia tartara mittit' (he summons pale souls from the infernal regions, others he sends down to the sorrows of Tartarus). Mercury (or Hermes) had the task of accompanying the spirits of the dead to Hades and hence was given the name 'Psychopompus' (accompanier of souls).

**859** *fairy*: Golding's addition from English folklore.

**888** *Cyllenius*: Mercury. Mount Cyllene in Arcadia was Mercury's birthplace.

**898–9** *lights . . . light . . . sights*: Golding's attempt to reproduce Ovid's wordplay on 'lumen' (light) and 'lumina' (eyes).

**907** *some fiends or wicked sprites*: in place of Ovid's 'Erinnyn' (one of the Furies).

**906** *her*: i.e. Io's.

**933** *no snow . . . stain*: i.e. no snow could make it look less white by comparison. Golding's addition.

**950–51** *For every . . . gospel takes*: a forcefully idiomatic rendition of Ovid's 'Matri . . . omnia demens / Credis' (You are a fool to believe all your mother says).

**967** *Merops*: king of Ethiopia and Clymene's husband.

## THE SECOND BOOK

**16** *Doris*: mother of the Nereids, who, according to Ovid, have green ('virides'), not *goodly* (17), hair.

**37** *all to torn*: exceedingly torn. Golding's description of Winter enlarges substantially upon Ovid's.

**59** *The lake*: i.e. the Styx.

**107–11** *the dreadful Bull . . . Aemonian Archer . . . ramping Lion . . . Scorpion . . . Crab*: Taurus, Sagittarius (formerly the centaur Chiron who lived in Haemonia or Thessaly), Leo, Scorpio and Cancer.

**117** *When that . . . catch a heat*: when their fierce spirits start to grow more excited.

**157** *his waning sister's horns*: i.e. the horns of the moon, Diana.

**158** *horse*: a collective singular, as at 2. 491.

**174** *northern Bear*: see note to 1. 74.

**181, 183** *Snake . . . Altar*: the snake is the Dragon, a northern constellation, the Altar a southern constellation in front of the forefeet of Sagittarius.

**222** *Charles*: see note to 1. 74.

**224** *Serpent*: see note to 2. 181.

**226** *Boötes*: Ursa Minor.

**237–8** *her sailcloths . . . brust*: Golding's addition, prompted by Regius's reference to 'omnia retinacula' (all the cables).

**252** *that of two signs . . . reach*: i.e. they reach across two signs of the zodiac.

**277** *The learnèd virgins*: the Muses.

**292** *as from a seething pot*: a domesticated rendition of Ovid's 'velut e fornace profunda' (as from a deep furnace).

**305** *Dirce*: a spring (named after the woman whose body was thrown into it).

**306** *Amymone*: a fountain (named after one of Danaus' daughters).

**308** *The rivers further from the place*: perhaps a misunderstanding of Ovid's 'sortita loco distantes flumina ripas' (rivers allotted banks set far apart), despite Regius's gloss, 'amnes latissimi' (very wide rivers).

**312** *(which should burn again)*: in the battle between Achilles and the river, when Hera called on the help of Hephaestus, god of fire, to set fire to it. See Homer, *Iliad* 21. 328–82.

**313** *Lycormas with his yellow vein*: Regius notes, 'fluvius est Aetoliae, flavas volvens arenas' (it is a river in Aetolia which whirls up yellow sand).

**315** *with his waves . . . sloe*: Regius points out that the Greek μέλας means 'black', but the simile is Golding's addition.

**323** *swans*: in Ovid, less specifically, 'Flumineae volucres' (river birds), although Regius glosses 'cygni' (swans). Golding perhaps overlooks the fact that when Cygnus is transformed into a swan, later in Book 2, he is described as *a new / And uncouth fowl* (2. 470–71).

**325–7** The mystery of the Nile's source is a common topic of classical poets.

**348** *for all the pains abidden*: having stood firm despite all the pains.

**370** *thy brother*: i.e. Neptune.

**390** Golding omits Ovid's 'Unde solet nubes latis inducere terris' (whence he draws the clouds over the wide lands), Ovid 2. 307, although he keeps the subsequent reference to the clouds.

**394** *the waggoner*: i.e. Phaëton.

**422** *discomfortably*: six syllables (spelt 'discomfortablely' in the 1567 edition).

**471** *a swan*: see note to 2. 323 above.

**476** *beauty sheen*: 1567 reads 'bodie shene'; later editions correct 'body' to 'beauty', except for 1603 and 1612 which retain the 1567 reading.

**477** *which erst had in him been*: referring to the *beauty sheen* of the previous line.

**482–3** *My lot . . . the world*: Golding's rendition of Ovid's 'satis, inquit, ab aevi / Sors mea principiis fuit irrequieta' ('Enough!' he said. 'My lot has been a restless one from the beginning of time').

**487** *he*: i.e. Jove.

**499–500** *that yet . . . fiends*: the religious overtones are Golding's; Ovid writes 'amentes, et adhuc terrore paventes' (frenzied and still trembling with fear).

**513** *Nonacris*: a town in Arcadia; here used to denote Arcadia more generally.

**537** *And in such sort . . . beseem*: and in a manner that could not be less fitting for a maid.

**539** *not without his shame*: with a dishonourable act.

**542** *I . . . I*: an unusual reference to the narrational persona; not in Ovid.

**549** *Dictynna*: one of Diana's names.

**551** *Phoebe*: another of Diana's names.

**555** *O Lord*: in place of Ovid's 'Heu' (alas).

**559** *mute*: two syllables; 'muĕt' in the 1567 text.

**560** *The treading of her shoe awry*: her fall from chastity. Ovid, more compassionately, speaks of 'laesi . . . signa . . . pudoris' (the signs of injured honour).

**566** *She*: i.e. Diana.

**570** *Away . . . with standers-by*: in Ovid, not a command but a statement: 'Procul est . . . arbiter omnis' (every onlooker is far away).

**571** *Parrhasis*: the Arcadian; used as a name for Callisto.

**576** *Cynthia*: another of Diana's names, from Mount Cynthus on Delos where she and Apollo were born.

**586** *But neither . . . bear*: a Christian rendition of Ovid's 'haud impune feres' (you will not get away unpunished).

**629** Callisto and Arcas become the Bears, Ursa Major and Ursa Minor.

**636** *Good cause . . . you*: Golding's addition.

**651** *No force*: no matter.

*for me*: for all I care.

**654** *Phoroneu's niece*: i.e. Io (actually Phoroneus' sister).

**659** *your foster-child*: as in Homer, *Iliad* 14. 301–3.

**660** *The oxen . . . wain . . . seven*: Ursa Major and Ursa Minor were also known respectively as the Seven Ploughing Oxen (Septentriones) and the Waggon.

**673–4** The story of the Sacred Geese, which frustrated the Gauls' attempt to storm the Citadel by their timely cackling, is told in Livy, *Ab Urbe Condita* 5. 47.

**681** *Apollo's bird*: i.e. the raven.

**695** Ericthonius was conceived from the seed of Hephaestus (Vulcan) which Athena wiped from her leg and cast on the ground. The story is told in Apollodorus, *The Library* 3. 14. 6.

**704** *a child . . . snake*: in Ovid, 'Infantem . . . aporrectumque draconem' (a child and a snake stretched out next to it), but Regius glosses 'appositum draconem sibi videre visae sunt, quia Erichthonius serpentinos habebat pedes' (it seemed to them that they saw a snake next to him, since Erichthonius had snake's feet). Cecrops, Aglauros' father, was half-snake and half-man.

**708** *the fowl . . . by night*: the owl.

**710** *for being shent*: i.e. for fear of being punished.

**722** *the god that rules the seas*: Neptune.

**726** *still playing fox to hole*: Golding's addition.

**731** *at the utter plunge and pinch*: when disaster was on the point of overwhelming me.

**742** *Nyctimene*: literally 'night one', i.e. the owl.

**749–50** *every other bird . . . gird*: in Ovid, 'a cunctis expellitur aethere toto' (she is driven off by all from the whole sky).

**754** *Isthyis*: not in Ovid. The name is established by Micyllus in his supplementary notes to Regius's commentary: 'Isthye videlicet'.

**756** *viol*: in Ovid, 'plectrum' (for his lyre). Apollo was god of music.

**762** *She*: i.e. Coronis.

**779** *plaster made of precious herbs*: Golding's rendition of Ovid's 'medicas . . . artes' (medical skills).

**786** *that hangeth by the heels*: Golding's addition.

**789** *her wrong divorce*: i.e. her death. Golding's understanding of 'iniusta' (unjust) follows Regius's note: 'nam iniuste illam peremisse sibi Apollo videbatur' (for it seemed to Apollo that he had killed her unjustly).

**792** *the baby*: Aesculapius.

**793** *double Chiron*: Chiron was one of the Centaurs, creatures with the body of a horse and the head and shoulders of a man.

**799** *a certain nymph*: Chariclo.

**809** *for doing of the which*: for Aesculapius' raising of Hippolytus, see 15. 596 ff. Aesculapius' arrival at Rome is described in 15. 698 ff.

**817** *a venomed dart*: in Ovid, 'dirae / Sanguine serpentis' (by the dreadful snake's blood). The reference is to Hercules' arrows which were smeared with the blood of the Lernaean Hydra; the story is mentioned in Regius's notes.

**832** *Yet . . . to see?*: Golding's addition.

**838** *all clad . . . right*: Golding's addition.

**844** *mare*: Golding offers an English equivalent to Ocyrhoë's new name of Hippe (mare) or, in some versions, Melanippe (black mare).

**846** *thou Delphian god*: i.e. Apollo.

**851** *thou kept Admetus' sheep*: Golding's addition, based on the story mentioned in Regius's notes. Apollo tended the flocks of Admetus for nine years when he was obliged to serve a mortal in punishment for having slain the Cyclops.

**853** *glistering Maia's son*: i.e. Mercury.

**854** *certain cattle*: according to Ovid, the cattle to which Apollo is not paying attention. Golding obscures the connection between the stories.

**858** *Neleus*: father of Nestor.

**860–61** *lest by him . . . his mouth*: Golding's rendition of Ovid's 'blanda . . . manu seduxit' (he drew him aside with a coaxing hand).

**869–75** Golding has both Mercury and Battus speak in a Somerset accent to indicate the rusticity of the scene. It would have been more consistent to give Battus this accent in lines 866–7 as well.

**872** *chill*: shall.

**875** *Cham*: I am.

**878–9** *a stone . . . desert*: Golding's comment is obscure without reference to the Latin; in Ovid, the word for the stone is 'Index', which also carries the meaning of 'informer, tell-tale'. The stone is traditionally understood to be the touchstone, which can be used to distinguish true gold from other metals.

**883** *Attic*: Golding's substitution for Ovid's 'Munychios . . . agros', an area which is 'gratam . . . Minervae' (favoured by Minerva).

**884** *Lycy*: the Lyceum, where Aristotle was to set up his school. The anachronism is Ovid's.

**903–4** Golding modernizes Ovid's image of lead thrown from a Balearic sling ('Balearica plumbum / Funda iacit').

**919** *And that . . . been*: Golding's addition.

**928** *To mortal folk and hellish fiends*: Golding's addition, perhaps owing something to Regius's gloss on 'Juppiter': 'qui rex est, & deorum, & hominum' (who is king of both gods and men).

**938** *And would not . . . told*: in place of Ovid's 'interea tectis excedere cogit' (meanwhile she compelled him to go away from the house).

**943** *the leman child*: in Ovid, 'Lemniacem stirpem' (the child of the Lemnian [i.e. Vulcan]).

**948** *and pride*: Golding's addition.

**949–69** This passage contains a number of additions by Golding: *a foul and irksome cave* (949); *and stinking like a grave* (950); *and fell me in the floor* (958); *and toads* (960); *like a snail* (963); *and all her face was swart* (966); *as any rake* (967); *her gums were waryish blue* (968). Golding also changes Envy's green breasts to a green stomach (the stomach being the seat of passion).

**968** *waryish*: *OED* uncertainly proposes 'unwholesome-looking', citing only this example and that at 7. 446.

**984** *the devil's Paternoster*: a muttered imprecation, and Golding's Christian addition.

**993** *(the more is pity)*: Golding's addition.

**1018** *Who . . . to play*: in place of Ovid's 'velut crimen' (as if it were a crime).

**1046** *showing not his love*: i.e. not revealing that his passion for Europa was the motive behind his instructions.

**1085** Golding adds the name Europa, which is given in Regius's notes.

## THE THIRD BOOK

**34** *a queachy plot*: Golding omits Ovid's description of the cave in which the snake lives.

**37** *god Mars his grisly snake*: the snake was Mars' son.

**43** *marble*: a peculiar substitution for Ovid's 'longo . . . antro' (from the deep cave).

**49** *above the waist*: the idea of the serpent's waist is Golding's; Ovid reads 'media plus parte leves erectus in auras' (raised up into the light air by more than half its length).

**81** *filthy maw and greedy guts*: in place of Ovid's 'ilia' (flank).

**126–30** Roman stage curtains were lowered, rather than raised, to reveal the stage; Golding's words *drawing up* confuse the image. His *cloths of arras* are also anachronistic; compare 6. 165.

**126** *against some solemn game*: for some ceremonial entertainment.

**166** *oversight*: Golding's meaning here is obscure, but since all editions give the same reading there is no reason to suspect a printing error. Actaeon's mistake was to oversee Diana, but it is difficult to see a connection between this and Golding's question. Ovid reads 'quod enim scelus error habebat?' (for what crime was there in a mistake?).

**175** *Hyperion*: i.e. the sun.

**197** *buskins . . . hose*: Golding's substitution for Ovid's 'Vincla' (sandals).

**200–203** Ovid gives only the names of the nymphs; Golding adds a descriptive phrase for each one based broadly on Regius's comments.

**203** *bibbling*: OED cites Golding's phrase under the definition 'drinking, tippling, dabbling with a bill like a duck drinking'. Although the description sits oddly among those of the other nymphs, it clearly derives from Regius's gloss on Phiale: 'vas est quidem hauriendis, infundendisque aquis accommodatum . . . sed hoc loco pro nympha ponitur, quae Dianae corpus aqua perfundebat' (it is indeed a vessel suitable for drinking and pouring out water; but here it is put for the nymph who pours water over Diana's body).

**245–81** *Blackfoot . . . Hillbred*: Golding supplies English names in this passage, many of which approximate to the meanings of Ovid's names.

**248** *every*: each. 'Every' is retained in all editions except for 1612 which distorts the metre by correcting it to 'every one'.

**250** *come all of Arcas' kind*: all Arcadian (Arcadia was named after Arcas, for whose story see 2. 614–29).

**252** *did bear away the bell*: won the prize.

**286** *with voice as harts are wont*: in Ovid, with a noise 'quem non . . . edere possit / Cervus' (which a deer could not produce).

**313** *the wench*: i.e. Europa.

**315** *Another thing clean overthwart*: another thing to annoy her completely.

*in the nick*: at this precise moment.

**319** *what . . . erst?*: what the hell have I gained by scolding before?

**326–7** *But . . . whore*: Golding's replacement of Ovid's words, 'at puto furto est / Contenta, et thalami brevis est iniuria nostri' (but, I suppose, she is content with her stolen love, and the wrong done to my marriage-bed is brief).

**328** *with a mischief is she bagged*: she is big (pregnant) with the outcome of her ill-doing.

**381** *Typhoeus*: on the giants, see I. 173–8 and 208–11.

**383** *The Cyclopes*: for the Cyclopes as makers of thunderbolts, see I. 307.

**428** *freckled*: in Ovid, 'Caerula' (blue, dark).

*his*: i.e. of Cephisus.

**433** *so that himself he do not know*: an ironic reversal of the famous inscription 'Know thyself' in Apollo's temple in Delphi.

**440** *was taken in his love*: fell in love with him.

**447** *an only voice*: just a voice.

**450** *with the feat*: in the act.

**452** *And that . . . games*: Golding's addition.

**459** *of the former . . . oft the end*: often repeats the end of what has just been said.

**467** *O Lord*: in Ovid, simply 'O'.

**481–3** *by her will . . . Said*: in Ovid, 'nulli . . . libentius umquam / Responsura sono . . . retulit' (never to answer other sound more willingly, she said). If Golding's *said* (481) could be understood as 'conversed', then line 482 would not be a quotation of her words, and the translation would be closer to the Latin.

**483** *standing somewhat in her own conceit*: having a rather high opinion of herself. Perhaps a misunderstanding of Ovid's 'verbis favet ipsa suis: egressaque silva / Ibat' (she helped her words along by coming out of the wood).

**507** *Rhamnuse*: Rhamnusia or Nemesis. Golding adds the explanatory clause based on Regius's lengthy note.

**521** *like . . . noddy*: Golding's addition.

**532** *or . . . rather*: Golding's addition.

**632** *hell*: in Ovid, 'inferna sede' (the infernal place).

**648** *the fact . . . light*: i.e. the cause of his loss of eyesight.

**649** The description of Tiresias is Golding's.

**670** *The which . . . storm*: Golding's addition.

**672** *What fiend of hell*: Golding's Christian elaboration of Ovid's 'Quis furor' (what frenzy).

**673** *pots and pans*: an appealingly domestic rendition of Ovid's 'Aera . . . Aere repulsa' (clashing cymbals).

**679** *Shall I at you*: the verb, 'wonder', is delayed for several lines.

**690** *your country*: in Ovid, 'fama . . . vestra' (your renown).

**695** *Destinies*: two syllables.

**696** *cannon-shot*: in Ovid, 'tormenta' (catapults, missiles).

**705** *put to you your helping hand*: i.e. don't try to help.

**707** *in making him his son*: i.e. in claiming to be Jove's son.

**709** *King Acrisius*: father of Danae; see also 4. 746–54.

**746** *Now have I made you true account*: perhaps Golding's misunderstanding of the words which, in Ovid, are spoken by his father to Acoetes: 'Accipe, quas habeo ... opes' (receive what wealth I have).

**753–5** *th'Olenian Goat . . . Pleiads and the Hyads moist . . . silly Plough*: all of the stars mentioned in this passage are associated with rain; the Hyads are a small group of stars forming part of the Bull.

**754** *Which . . . Jove*: Golding's explanatory addition, prompted by Regius's gloss, 'quae Iovem aluisse fertur' (who is said to have nourished Jove).

**814–5** *A fear . . . to run*: for Ovid's 'Pro se quisque timet' (every man fears for himself), which is elaborated by Regius: 'unusquisque, inquit, pro se est sollicitus, ne Naxon devehatur' (each one, he says, is anxious for himself, lest he sail to Naxos).

**821** *Sir Snudge*: Sir Miser; Golding's idiomatic addition.

**829** *in this sort . . . dressed*: treated in this way.

**861** *As . . . fail*: i.e. like the crescent moon.

**864** *fetch their frisks*: caper about.

**871** *to Diaward*: towards Dia, Dia being an old name for Naxos.

**873** *His chaplain I became*: for Ovid's 'Accessi sacris' (I joined the rites).

**899** *javelin*: for Ovid's 'thyrso'.

**913** *writhèd with her neck awry*: twisted her neck askew.

## THE FOURTH BOOK

**1–4** Golding gives the scene a more Christian tone, adding *conscience* and supplying *heresy* for 'Impietatis' (impiety).

**10** *with . . . plagues*: Golding's addition, again appropriate to a biblical God.

**25** *horns*: Bacchus tended to be depicted with horns in primitive representations.

**33** *that old hag*: Silenus, Bacchus' drunken (male) tutor, for whom see Virgil, Eclogue 6.

**37** *and brazen pans and pots*: Golding's homely version of Ovid's 'Concavaque aera' (and cymbals).

**39** *grace and favour*: for 'Placatus, mitisque' (gentle and mild); compare note to 1. 433–46.

**46** *idly*: three syllables; 1567 reads 'idelly', perhaps punning on 'idol'.

**47** *saint*: in place of Ovid's 'dea' (goddess). Minerva was, among other things, the goddess of spinning and weaving.

**52** *the eldest*: in Ovid, the sister who has just spoken.

**67 ff.** Ovid's story of Pyramus and Thisbe provides the source for the mechanicals' interlude in Shakespeare's *A Midsummer Night's Dream*.

**68** *Semiramis*: Semiramis and her husband Ninus were the mythical founders of the Assyrian empire. Semiramis built the city of Babylon and erected the tomb for her husband mentioned at line 108.

**74** *neighbourhood . . . neighbourhood . . . neighbourhood*: two syllables. 1567 reads 'neighbrod . . . neyghbrod . . . neighbrod'.

**164** *box*: i.e. boxwood.

**203** *Leuconoe*: all editions mistakenly reproduce 'Leucothoe', the name of the woman in the ensuing story.

**210** *her husband*: i.e. Vulcan.

**243** *in thy light . . . among*: i.e. your light also fails.

**276** *I am in love with thee*: Golding attempts to soften Ovid's blunter 'mihi . . . places' (you please me).

**323–8** Clytie is transformed into a heliotrope.

**338** *it is to know*: it is well known.

**344** *Curets*: spirits, companions of Zeus during his childhood.

**360** 1567 reads 'He travelde through the lande of Lycie to Carie that doth bound'. 1575, followed by all subsequent editions, corrects the metre of the line to that which is given here.

**364–5** *a man . . . been*: Golding's addition.

**370** *waterfairies*: for Ovid's 'Naiadum' (naiads).

**409** *When folk . . . doon*: it was believed that the clashing of bronze cymbals could restore an eclipsed moon.

**446** *willed he, nilled he*: whether he wanted to or not.

**454** *crabfish*: Golding's substitute for Ovid's 'polypus' (cuttle-fish, octopus).

**455** *clees*: for Ovid's 'flagellis' (tentacles).

**456** *nephew*: great-grandson.

**486** *shreaming shawms . . . bells*: for Ovid's 'adunco tibia cornu. / Tinnulaque aera' (flute, curving horn and tinkling cymbals).

**512** The Latin 'vespertilio' (bat) is derived from 'vesper' (evening).

**513** The line is, of course, Golding's addition; it is the first time in the translation that Golding's narrative voice distinguishes itself openly from that of the translated text.

**524** *burd*: i.e. Bacchus; the 'harlot' is Semele.

**525** *the Lydian watermen*: of Acoetes' story in Book 3.

**526** *the mother . . . her son*: Agave and Pentheus.

**537** *hell*: for Ovid's 'infernas sedes' (underworld).

**558** *Cerberus*: the three-headed dog of the underworld.

**576** *on Ixion specially*: he was being punished for attempting to rape Juno.

**594** *And purgèd her*: the ritual removes the taint of death.

*upon the same*: thereupon.

**602** *black as jet*: in Ovid, the doors become pale (pallor).

**617–18** *the snake / Echidna bred*: the Hydra.

**651** *and shoots . . . main*: i.e. the top juts out well over the sea.

**655** *red*: in Ovid, the waves become white ('recanduit').

**665** *my . . . name*: in Greek, Aphrodite. The Greek word ἀφρός means 'froth'.

**700** *pilgrims*: Golding's addition.

**704** *Was my spearhead the bane . . .*: apparently a misunderstanding of 'sacer' (sacred/detestable). Golding loses the sense of the Latin, in which Cadmus asks whether the snake that he speared was sacred, despite Regius's gloss: 'dubitat Cadmus, an ille serpens, quem ad fontem interfecit, alicui deorum fuerit consecratus, qui sibi malorum causa fuerit' (Cadmus wonders whether the serpent he killed at the fountain is consecrated to some one of the gods, who is the cause of his ills).

**706** *his teeth*: see 3. 108 ff.

**714** *In one round spindle bodkin-wise*: Golding's metaphor.

**724** Golding omits Ovid 591, 'Cadme mane, teque infelix his exue monstris' (Stay, Cadmus, unhappy man, and put off this monstrous form).

**744** *that noble imp*: i.e. Bacchus.

**746** *of the selfsame stock*: Acrisius and Bacchus were both descendants of Neptune.

**748–9** *thinking . . . gods*: in Ovid, 'genusque / Non putat esse deum' (he thought that his stock was not that of the gods).

**754** *his nephew*: i.e. his grandson. Danae, Perseus' mother, was the daughter of Acrisius.

**759** *Lybic*: of Libya.

**778–9** *that sea wherein . . . divèd been*: i.e. where the sun goes down at the end of the day.

**783** Golding omits Ovid 637–8.

**805** Golding omits Ovid 653–4.

**813** *God*: for Ovid's 'dii' (gods).

**822** *commandment*: four syllables; the spelling in 1567 is 'commaundement'.

**856** *her*: i.e. Danae.

**893** *whale*: for Ovid's 'Bellua' (monster).

**916–17** Perhaps these two lines are a misunderstanding of Ovid, although it is difficult to relate it to Ovid's 'et idem contigere gaudent: / Seminaque ex illis ut erant iactata per undas' (and they are delighted that the same thing happens. And the seeds from these, as they had been scattered on the waves).

**916** *there was no odds*: there was no difference.

**926** *Endowèd with her father's realm*: Ovid's 'indotata' (without a dowry) is glossed as 'valde dotata' (with a huge dowry) by Regius.

**927** *marriage*: three syllables.

**937** *Lyncid*: Lyncides is a name for Perseus, descendant of Lynceus. Golding's assumption that it is the name of one of the other diners is due to the corruption of the Regius text at this point.

**975** *church*: for Ovid's 'templo' (temple).

## THE FIFTH BOOK

**12** *thy forgèd dad*: in Ovid, simply 'Iupiter'. See 4. 856–7.

**18** *despite*: insulting action, injury.

**19** *if thou be advised*: if you consider the matter.

**20** *because his seanymphs were despised*: Cephey's wife, Cassiopea, claimed to surpass the Nereids in beauty.

**21** *Hammon*: the Jupiter of North Africa, who predicted that calamity would be averted if Andromeda were exposed as prey to the sea-monster.

**44** *the bedstead's head*: a typically homely rendition of Ovid's 'toro' (couch).

**85** *Harpe*: Perseus' curved sword; from the Greek ἁρπη, sickle.

**134** *stately mitre*: in Ovid, 'albenti . . . vitta' (white headband).

**139** *viol*: in Ovid, 'plectrum' (plectrum or lyre).

**151** *a Garamant*: from the region of Phazania in North Africa.

**179** *Jew*: in Ovid, 'Palaestina' (Palestinian).

**195** *Duke*: Golding's addition.

**196** *mo*: spelt 'moe' in 1567 edition, making it two syllables.

**209** *at host*: in battle.

**228** *foolish juggling toys*: a more scornful description than Ovid's 'miracula' (miracles).

**249** *in whose defence*: i.e. in Perseus' defence; the *knight* (248) is Acont.

**300** *Proete*: i.e. Proteus, who fought with his twin brother Acrisius, Perseus' grand-father.

**305** *Polydect*: Polydectus, enamoured of Danae, had sent Perseus to win the Gorgon's head to keep him out of the way. On his return, Perseus found his mother at the altar seeking sanctuary from Polydectus' violence. Perseus therefore turned him into stone.

**329** *his mother*: Medusa.

**356** *Meony*: Regius explains Ovid's 'Maeonides' as 'musas' (Muses), and takes the word to be derived from the city Maeonia. Micyllus is less certain and offers a variety of possible explanations.

**364** *Boreas*: the north wind.

**370** *evelong*: probably implying 'straight down', although this precise meaning is not offered in *OED*. See 8. 712 and note for another problematic usage of this word.

**384** *Lucina*: goddess of childbirth.

**395** *set you quite beside*: to set aside completely.

**397** *Aganippe*: another spring on Mount Helicon.

**419** *Phoebus' sister*: Diana.

**422–3** *rolling tongue . . . throat-boll*: Golding's addition.

**440** *Trinacris*: Sicily.

**486** *Caïster*: see, for example, Homer, *Iliad* 2. 459–61 for the commonplace of the swans on the Cayster.

**495** *Dis*: i.e. Pluto.

**509** *Bacchies*: the Bacchiadae were the founders of Corinth, which lies between two seas, the Adriatic and the Aegean.

**510** *a town*: Syracuse, famed for its two harbours and reputedly founded by a Corinthian.

**556–7** *merry-go-down . . . hotchpotch*: in Ovid, the woman gives Ceres 'Dulce . . . testa quod coxerat ante polenta' (something sweet which she had cooked before from barley in an earthenware pot). Merry-go-down is a strong ale; a hotchpotch is a dish containing a mixture of many ingredients; Golding adds the flax and coriander seed to Ovid's barley.

**575** *A name . . . in Latin*: 'stellio', perhaps with reference to a pun on 'stellatus' (starred).

**605** *Elian*: from Elis, in the western part of the Peloponnese. Compare *Ely town* at line 615.

**611–12** *Unwillingly . . . smote*: in Ovid, 'patuit . . . invita rapinae' (it opened unwillingly to the robbery). By using the feminine pronoun for the land and personifying 'the ravisher', Golding emphasizes the similarities between the condition of the land and the condition of Proserpine.

**623** *Ortygy*: an island off Syracuse (Sicily).

**633** *like one that . . . had been*: Golding avoids Ovid's blander 'Attonitae' (thunderstruck).

**644** *If finding you . . . past*: if you call it 'finding', when the means of recovery are gone.

**667** *pomegranate*: three syllables.

**731–2** *growing on the brim / Unset*: i.e. growing naturally, not planted by man.


## THE SIXTH BOOK

**1** *Tritonia*: Minerva.

**8** *neckverse*: Golding's addition. The genuineness of those claiming benefit of clergy to save themselves from being hanged was tested by a 'neckverse', a Latin verse (usually the opening of Psalm 51); if they could read it out, they escaped hanging. The addition is beautifully apt to the story of Arachne.

**61** *She sticketh . . . still*: she holds her ground.

**96** *morion*: anachronistic; a sixteenth-century helmet without beaver or visor.

**110** *for beauty*: Golding's addition, drawing on Regius's gloss.

**117** *And . . . mishap*: Golding substitutes *bewail the cause of her mishap* for Ovid's 'plaudat' (she claps) and *bobbèd* for Ovid's 'crepitante' (rattling). None of *OED*'s definitions of 'bobbed' make sense in this context; it seems more likely that the meaning is simply 'bobbing'.

**127** *Europe*: Europa, see 2. 1043–96.

**133** *Astery*: According to Apollodorus, *The Library* 1. 4. 1, Asteria flung herself into the sea in the form of a quail to escape Jove's advances.

**134** *Leda*: visited by Jove in the form of a swan.

**137** *Amphitryo*: Amphitryon, Alcmena's husband.

**146** Golding's *hovering* (meaning 'covering') is transitive.

**159** *double Chiron*: see note to 2. 793.

**166** *a dozen times*: Golding has multiplied Ovid's 'Ter, quater' (three or four times). Regius offers 'saepius' (often).

**218** *Tantalus*: an inauspicious reference; Tantalus killed his son Pelops, cooked him and served him up to the gods to see if they could tell that it was not animal flesh.

**220** *Pleiads*: see note to 1. 832.

**228** *my husband's harp*: when the foundations of Thebes were being laid, a huge rock followed after Amphion as he played his harp.

**238** *Coeus*: one of the Titans.

**267–8** *Besides her wicked fact . . . to my defacing raked*: on top of her wicked deed, Niobe has added railing words which defame me.

**284** *keep the ring*: keep to the circular course.

**301** *heir*: two syllables.

**315** *liver*: in place of Ovid's 'pulmonis' (lung).

**434** *Chimaera*: see 9. 766–7.

**485** *trunch*: not in *OED* except as 'truncheon' or 'post, stake'. Here the word clearly means 'trunk', and may simply be a misprint, but since it is preserved in all editions it is possible that it is a variant form not recognized by *OED*.

**515** *Pelops*: see note to 6. 218. Ceres inadvertently ate part of Pelops' shoulder at Tantalus' feast.

**529** *Calydon*: for the grudge of Diana (*Phoebe*) against Calydon, see 8. 359–94.

**534** *Pittheia*: after Pittheus, Pelops' son.

**535** *borough towns*: Golding's addition.

**536** *two seas*: the Ionian Sea and the Aegean Sea.

**540** *The king of Pontus*: the name is provided by Micyllus.

**554–5** The two lines are Golding's addition.

**579** *fairies*: in place of Ovid's 'Naiadas, et Dryadas'.

**601** *himself he bare*: i.e. he used the excuse of his wife's emotions to cover his own.

**635** Golding omits Ovid 6. 497. Ovid includes Pandion's daughters' and Tereus' wishes as reasons for letting Philomel go.

**663** *grange*: for Ovid's 'stabula' (hut, pen).

*peakishly*: the only instance of the word offered in *OED*, which hesitantly glosses 'obscurely, remotely', translating Ovid's 'obscura' (hidden).

**687** *doest*: Golding's spelling, indicating two syllables.

**689** *Then . . . offence*: a Christian rendition of Ovid's 'vacuas habuissem criminis umbras' (I would have had a shade free from guilt).

**725–6** *and keeps . . . soul*: a Christian rendition of 'falsisque piacula manibus infert' (and brings expiatory sacrifices for the false shade).

**750** *pans and pots*: for Ovid's 'aeris' (cymbals).

**752** *to the proof*: to the utmost.

**756** *In post*: in haste.

**760** *Now, well!*: in place of Ovid's Bacchic cry, 'euoe'.

**776** *in this behalf*: in this matter.

**797** *pity*: a significant shift from Ovid's 'pietate' (piety, devotion to family). Also at 804.

**803** *out of kind*: in this case both 'unnatural' and 'alien to your (family) group'.

**809–11** Golding's syntax is awkward. Procne strikes Itys *even where the breast and side do bound*; meanwhile Itys is *now plainly seeing . . . And flying to her neck*.

**815** *pipkins*: in place of Ovid's 'cavis . . . ahenis' (bronze cauldrons).

**819** The line is Golding's addition.

**838** *And rears the fiends from hell*: a Christian rendition of Ovid's 'Vipereasque ciet Stygia de valle sorores' (and summons the snaky sisters from the Stygian valley).

**845–6** *the one . . . the other*: a nightingale and a swallow respectively.

**853** *lapwing*: Ovid's bird is a hoopoe, which is not resident in Britain.

**862** *a let*: because after Tereus' behaviour no other Thracian was a welcome suitor.

**892** *very soft and easily*: Golding's rather inappropriate addition.

**896–7** *lay / Her belly*: give birth.

**897** *at a burden*: at one birth.

**907** *Minies*: i.e. Argonauts.

**908** *galley . . . first devised*: traditionally, Jason's *Argo* was the first ship to be built.


# THE SEVENTH BOOK

**3** *Phiney*: Phineus, a blind seer tormented by the Harpies until Boreas' sons, Zetes and Calaïs, chased them away.

**4** *maiden-facèd fowls*: the Harpies, fearful bird-like monsters with the head of a maiden, long claws and a face pale with hunger.

**8** The line is Golding's addition. Regius offers a long explanatory note on the golden fleece.

**32** *trespassed*: a Christian rendition of Ovid's 'commisit' (committed).

**70** *For saving . . . fleece*: expanding on Ovid's 'Servatrix' (saviour).

**77** *The greatest god*: i.e. Love.

**87** *certain rocks*: the Symplegades, which Jason had encountered on his journey to Colchos.

**89** *Charybdis*: a whirlpool.

**90** *sowpeth*: OED offers 'saturate' but here the meaning is clearly 'sucks'. Probably not a misprint; it is retained in all editions.

**102** *godliness*: for Ovid's 'pietas'.

**105–6** *(of whom . . . goddess)*: Golding's addition. Micyllus provides a long note on Hecate.

**120–22** According to Ovid, Medea's love could be forgiven her because Jason *was* particularly handsome that day.

**133–4** *And now . . . life*: for Ovid's 'Servatus promissa dato' (when you have been saved, fulfil your promise).

**136** *triple Hecat*: Hecate, Diana and Luna were regarded as three aspects of the same goddess.

**138** *the sire*: the sun, father of Aeëtes.

**147** *in throne of gold*: for Ovid's 'Agmine purpureus' (clad in purple).

**150** *a chimney*: in Ovid, 'fornace' (a furnace).

**166** *their mazèdness augment*: perhaps misunderstanding Ovid's repetitive 'augent, / Adiiciuntque animos' (boosted [Jason's] spirits).

**196** *O fond Medea*: for Ovid's 'barbara' (barbarian woman).

**211** *So sound . . . last*: in Ovid, simply 'placidos . . . somnos' (peaceful sleep).

**221** *To church*: Golding's Christianized rendition.

**231** *godly suit*: for Ovid's 'pietate'.

**242** *three-formèd goddess*: see note to 7. 136.

**263** *Ye charms and witchcrafts*: not a new invocation in Ovid, but the things sustained by Hecate.

**265** *elves*: for Ovid's 'Dii' (gods). Golding's lines lies behind Prospero's famous invocation 'Ye elves of hills, brooks, standing lakes and groves' (*The Tempest* V. i).

**308** *Glaucus*: see 13. 1060 ff.

**318** In 1567 simply 'To Hecat'. 1575 and subsequent editons correct the metre by adding 'triple'.

**321** *a couple*: only one in Ovid.

**326** *elves*: Golding's addition.

**350–52** *a witch . . . die*: expanding on Ovid's 'strigis' (screech-owl). Regius's note reads 'Vulgus autem putat striges non esse aves sed vetulas, quae se veneficio quodam in aves convertunt, infantesque dormientes aggrediuntur, ac eorum sanguinem ita exugunt, ut aut mortui inveniantur in cunis, aut diu vivere non possint' (But the common people think that screech-owls are not birds but old women who change themselves into birds through some sorcery and attack sleeping children and suck out their blood in such a way that either they are found dead in their cradles or they cannot live long).

**353** *singles*: entrails. Although the word 'prosecta' can also signify 'tail' (of deer) and 'claw' (of bird), Golding's meaning can be established by Regius's note: 'intestina a prosecando, et recidendo dicta' (intestines, derived from 'cutting out' and 'lopping off').

**356** *watersnails*: in Ovid, 'Chelydri' (watersnakes).

**379** *at forty years*: in Ovid, 'Ante quater denos . . . annos' (forty years before); Regius, however, understands the text as Golding does.

**404** *So old . . . lamb*: an endearing rendition of Ovid's 'innumeris effetus . . . annis' (worn out by countless years).

**412** *mid the kettleward*: from the middle of the pan.

**424** *the witch*: for Ovid's 'Colchide' (the Colchian woman).

**446** *waryish*: see note to 2. 968.

**450** *torn*: referring to *him* (Pelias).

**453** *Chiron*: the most famous of the Centaurs.

**455** *Ceramb*: Cerambus escaped the flood by being turned into a beetle.

**460** *The serpent*: turned into stone by Apollo because it tried to eat Orpheus' severed head. See 11. 60–66.

**461** *where Bacchus hid a bullock*: the story is not otherwise known.

**463** *the sire of Corytus*: Paris.

**464** *Maeras*: another unknown story.

**466** *the wives of Cos*: another unknown story.

**473** *turnèd to a dove*: Ovid implies that she gives birth to a dove, but Micyllus refers to 'filiam in columbam mutatam' (the daughter turned into a dove).

**478** *so straitly should him use*: should be so exacting in his demands. Golding's translation derives not from the main text of Regius's Latin but from the alternative reading offered: 'stricto . . . amore' (severe love).

**495** *niece*: in Ovid, 'nepotis' (grandson).

**500** *mushrooms*: three syllables; 1567 gives 'Mushrommes'.

**501** *bride*: Medea was supplanted by a new bride, Glauce or Creusa.

**504** The line is Golding's addition.

**518** *flintwort*: aconite or monkshood. The name is suggested by the elder Pliny's statement that it grows on bare rocks ('nudis cautibus'), *Naturalis Historia* 27. 2. 10.

**522–8** It was the last of Hercules' twelve labours to bring Cerberus up from the underworld.

**542–3** In Ovid Aegeus grieves that so dreadful a crime should nearly have been carried out.

**553** *For killing of the Cretish bull*: the story is mentioned in Apollodorus, *Epitome* 1. 5.

**556–6** The story of Vulcan's son is told in Apollodorus, *The Library* 3. 16. 17.

**583** *his son*: Minos' son, Androgeus, died fighting the bull of Marathon. Aeacus' involvement in his death seems to be Ovid's invention.

**596** *bear . . . the bell*: carry away the prize.

**614** *the hundred shires*: an anglicization of Ovid's 'populorum . . . centum' (a hundred peoples).

**622** *which shall infringed for me abide*: the meaning is clearly 'which shall remain unbroken', although this meaning is not recognized in *OED*. Compare 'infringible' (adj. obs.), 'unbreakable'.

**634** *This prince*: i.e. Cephalus.

**649** *country*: i.e. country's. The reading is retained in all editions.

**751** *when poles do scar their top*: expanding Ovid's 'agitata' (shaken).

**758** *the mother*: in Ovid, 'genitor' (father).

**775** *(O most wretched case!)*: Golding's addition.

**789–90** *whose . . . earth*: Golding's addition.

**801** *as bare of boughs . . . see*: apparently Golding takes 'rarissima' (very special) to mean 'very bare'.

**802** *(as all the rest of oaks)*: Golding's addition.

**819** *taunts*: branches, twigs. Golding's usage of this word is the only one recorded in OED.

**843** *Emmets*: i.e. ants. In Ovid they are 'Myrmidonas', falsely derived from the Greek μύρμηξ, ant.

**848** *way*: all editions up to 1603 give 'wy'. 1612 reads, 'Shall go a warfare and assone'.

**883** *His beauty*: Golding's addition, following Regius.

**891** *Orithyia*: see 6. 862 ff.

**898** *God*: for Ovid's 'diis' (gods).

**913** *op'nèd*: i.e. opened (with the sense 'declared, explained).

*what a holy thing was wedlock*: for Ovid's 'Sacra tori' (the rites of the wedding couch).

**915** *Which band . . . break*: perhaps a misunderstanding of Ovid's 'Primaque deserti . . . foedera lecti' (and the first bonds of the bed I had left behind). Golding's version presents a less reliable Cephalus.

**927** *wives*: in Ovid, an example of unfaithfulness, not specifically of women's wrongdoing.

**958** *I drave her to her shifts*: more damning than Ovid's 'dubitare coegi' (I forced her to hesitàte).

**987** Modern editions correct 'Naiades' (*brooknymphs*) to 'Laiades', i.e. Oedipus.

**988–90** It is the Sphinx who falls to the ground and Themis who avenges; Golding elides the two.

**1000** *Laelaps*: from the Greek λαῖλαψ, storm.

**1014** *like a wily fox*: for Ovid's 'callida' (cunning).

**1017** *as spinning wheel*: Golding's addition.

**1069** *like a hare-brained blab*: an idiomatic rendition of Ovid's 'temerarius index' (rash tell-tale).

**1078** *She wist not what to say or think*: in place of Ovid's 'Et dolet infelix veluti de pellice vera' (and she grieved, unhappy one, as if over a real mistress).

**1107** *the love*: in 1567, simply 'Love'. 1575 and later editions correct the metre to 'the love', except for 1612 which reads 'thy love'.

**1110** *I perceivèd by the same*: 1567 reads 'I received the same'. The line is changed in subsequent editions to correct the metre.

## THE EIGHTH BOOK

**18** *his golden viol*: for Ovid's 'lyram' (lyre). Phoebus laid down his instrument on a stone when he was helping to build the wall.

**20** *King Nisus' daughter*: Scylla.

**38** Golding omits Ovid 8. 34, shortening his description of Minos on horseback.

**54** *she*: i.e. Europa.

**69–70** *And as . . . prevail*: Golding's moral adaptation of Ovid's 'Et caussaque valet, caussamque tuentibus armis, / Ut puto, vincemur' (And he is strong both in his cause and in the arms that uphold his cause, so I think we shall be conquered).

**88–9** *and if their hearts . . . fearfulness*: Golding's addition.

**106–7** *(alas . . . pass!)*: enlarging on Ovid's 'heu facinus!' (Oh, what a crime!).

**111** This line is Golding's addition.

**159** *Syrts*: Syrtis, dangerous shallows on the coast of North Africa.

  *where none but serpents fostered be*: Golding's addition. Regius notes 'accolae nanque Syrtium feri sunt et peregrinis infestissimi' (for the people who live near Syrtis are wild and very dangerous to travellers).

**162** *thy mother was beguiled*: for Jove's deception of Europa, see 2. 1043–96.

**174** *she*: Pasiphae. Pasiphae was overcome by a passion for a bull and consummated her love by hiding inside a wooden (*of tree*) cow made for her by Daedalus. The story is told in Apollodorus, *The Library* 3. 1. 3–4.

**177** *Compel not . . . to glow?*: an idiomatic rendition of Ovid's 'ecquid ad aures / Perveniunt mea dicta tuas?' (do my words reach your ears at all?).

**191–2** *a hobby-hawk . . . wings of iron mail*: for Ovid's 'fulvis Haliaetus in alis' (osprey with tawny wings).

**199** *And for because . . . mark*: misunderstanding Ovid's 'a tonso . . . capillo' (from the shorn lock of hair). The name reflects Scylla's deed, not the bird's appearance.

**200** *The Greeks it 'ciris' call . . . a lark*: the bird's name is derived from the Greek κείρω, I cut. The second half of the line is, of course, Golding's addition. Unlike Golding, modern commentators have not established the identity of Ovid's bird; Golding is probably following Micyllus, who mentions that some commentators think the bird is the 'alaudam' (lark).

**206** *the monster*: the Minotaur.

**220** *as straight as any string*: Golding's addition.

**229–31** *Theseus . . . eldest daughter*: Golding introduces the characters to clarify Ovid's brief account. The names of Theseus and Ariadne are mentioned in Regius's marginal note.

**244** *the Kneeler-down*: the constellation of Hercules.

  *him that gripes the snake*: Ophiuchus.

**266–7** *blow the feathers . . . not long ago*: in place of Ovid's 'quas vaga moverat aura, / Captabat plumas' (tried to catch the feathers which the wandering breeze moved).

**347** *tribute*: see 8. 226–34 on the Minotaur.

**377–8** *as thick . . . by other stick*: i.e. as thick as possible. Golding's sentence introduces two meanings of Ovid's 'horrent' (to be dreadful, to stand up stiff).

**382** *shield*: Golding mistakes 'armos' (shoulders) for 'arma' (weapons, shields).

**401–2** 1567 indents these lines, but this appears to be a typesetting error.

**409** *Caeney*: for the story of the transformation, see 12. 211–35.

**414–15** *who with fire . . . to sear*: Golding's addition, drawing on Micyllus's note on Hercules and the Hydra.

**422** *father-in-law*: Laertes was the father of Odysseus.

**425** *Oecley's son*: the story is told in Apollodorus, *The Library* 3. 6. 2.

**463** *He rips their skins and splitteth them*: Golding's addition.

**480** *bullet*: for Ovid's 'moles' (huge rock).

**491** *took his rist*: literally, took his rise, i.e. vaulted. *OED* does not record this particular sense of 'rise', but since the reading is retained in all editions it is unlikely that there is an error here.

**499** *on goodly coursers*: 1567 reads 'on coursers'; subsequent editions correct the metre by the addition of 'goodly', except for 1603 which reverts to the 1567 reading.

**529** *this bragger*: more judgemental than Ovid's 'audentem' (daring).

**548** *Played hitty-missy*: an idiomatic rendition of Ovid's 'variat' (had varying luck).

**550** *did play the fiend*: for Ovid's 'saevit' (raged).

**557** *field of ground*: i.e. what a huge space.

**553** *shield*: see note to 8. 382.

**586** *church*: for Ovid's 'templis' (temple).

**624** *hellish*: for Ovid's 'sepulcrales' (sepulchral).

**625** *ye hellhounds three*: replacing Ovid's 'Eumenides'.

**643** *souls*: for Ovid's 'umbrae' (shades, ghosts).

**660** *pity*: for Ovid's 'pietas'.

**682** *The Lords and Commons*: Golding's phrase gives a parliamentary air to Ovid's 'vulgus, proceresque' (common people and nobles).

**695** *chest*: for Ovid's 'lecto' (bier).

**705** *birds*: the sisters of Meleager become guinea-fowl (in Greek, μελεάγριον).

**712** *evelong*: *OED* offers this quotation when defining 'evelong' as 'oblong' and cites the Latin to confirm it. But the Latin 'obliqua' (sideways, slanting) suggests rather the zigzag course that the stones take; there is no justification for translating it as 'oblong'. Golding's English would be more consistent with the Latin if 'evelong' could be understood as 'sidelong'. (John Baret's *Alveary* of 1580 offers 'sidelong' as a translation of 'obliquus': 'Sidelong or sidewise, *ex obliquo*'.)

**726** *down to table sat*: for Ovid's 'Discubuere toris' (reclined on couches).

**755** *Urchins*: i.e. sea-urchins, translated from Ovid's 'Echnidas'.

**767–8** *Be meek / And upright*: in Ovid, a comment about the father: 'si mitis, et aequus' (if he were gentle and fair).

**793** *God*: for Ovid's 'superi' (gods).

**800** *moorcocks, coots and cormorants*: an adaptation of Ovid's list of 'mergis, fulicisque' (gulls and coots).

**817** *cushions, homely gear*: for Ovid's 'textum rude' (a rough cloth).

**838** *sat down*: for Ovid's 'accubuere' (reclined).

**838–9** *right chare . . . bee*: for Ovid's 'succincta, tremensque' (girt up and trembling).

**863** *one poor goose*: a reminder, on a domestic scale, of the sacred geese which protected Rome (Livy, *Ab Urbe Condita* 5. 47).

**879** *church*: for Ovid's 'templum' (temple).

**889** *chaplains*: for Ovid's 'sacerdotes' (priests).

**908** *God*: for Ovid's 'dii' (gods).

**924** *Autolychus*: described at greater length at 11. 359–63.

**978** *fairy*: for Ovid's 'numinis' (deity).

**982** *white as clout*: Golding's addition.

**992** *the gap-toothed elf*: Golding's addition.

**1046** *brinkless*: Golding's use of the word is the only example offered in the *OED*.

**1094–5** *print . . . show*: i.e. scar.


## THE NINTH BOOK

**15** *him*: Oeneus.

**30** *Alcmena's son*: Jupiter came to Alcmena disguised as her husband, Amphitryon. Alcmena's account of Hercules' birth is given in 9. 332–90.

**45** *He caught up dust and sprinkled me*: wrestlers oiled themselves before a contest and then, to counteract the slipperiness of the oil, threw dust on each other.

**47** *crisp*: *OED* uncertainly proposes 'smooth', citing this example. The Latin is 'micantia' (fast moving).

**81–2** *the snake . . . Lerna*: the Hydra.

**90** *gripped*: 1567 and 1575 read 'graand'; all later editions change this to 'gripte' or 'gript'.

**103** *the treasury of plenteousness*: the horn of plenty or cornucopia is a common topos in both classical and Renaissance art.

**114** *his crab-tree face*: an idiomatic rendition of Ovid's 'vultus . . . agrestes' (rustic face).

**116–17** *this deformity . . . his comb*: an idiomatic rendition of Ovid's 'domuit iactura' (the loss humbled him).

**119** *fierce Ness*: Nessus, one of the Centaurs.

**121** *Jove's issue*: i.e. Hercules.

**143** *upon vain hope*: 1567 reads 'uppon a vaine hope'; subsequent editions omit the extra syllable except for 1603, which reverts to the 1567 reading.

**146** *thy father*: Ixion, who had attempted a similar outrage against Juno. In punishment he was bound to an endlessly turning wheel in Hades.

**169** *who . . . jealous over Hercules*: in Ovid, 'amans' (loving).

**178** *the filthy strumpet*: stronger than Ovid's 'altera' (another woman).

**182** *Meleager*: he killed the uncles who insulted him after the Calydonian boar-hunt. See 8. 560–85. Deianire was one of the two sisters not tranformed into birds after Meleager's death (8. 702).

**185** *What grief . . . to enterprise among*: what grief can make women try.

**216** *Saturn's daughter*: i.e. Juno, who hated Hercules because he was the product of Jove's seduction of Alcmene.

**223–44** This review of Hercules' achievements includes the twelve labours imposed by Eurystheus. These were: (i) the fight with the monstrous Nemean lion, which Hercules strangled (242); (ii) the fight with the nine-headed Lernean Hydra, which grew two heads where one had been cut off; with the help of his servant Iolaüs Hercules burnt off its heads, burying the last (immortal) one under a huge rock (236–7); (iii) the capture of the golden-hoofed deer of Diana (231); (iv) the destruction of the Erymanthian boar; while in pursuit of the boar, Hercules stopped at the cave of the Centaur Pholos, opened a cask of wine and the fragrance soon attracted the other Centaurs, against whom Hercules fought (235–6); (v) the cleansing of the stables of Augeas, which Hercules achieved in a day by turning the rivers Alpheus and Peneus through the stalls (229); (vi) the cleansing of the lake of Stymphalus of its man-eating birds (230); (vii) the capture of the Cretan bull (228); (viii) the capture of the mares of Diomedes, king of the Bistones in Thrace; Hercules killed Diomedes and, according to this version, the mares as well (238–41); (ix) the seizure of the girdle of Hippolyta, queen of the Amazons, who lived on the Thermodon River by the Black Sea (232–3); (x) the killing of the three-bodied monster Geryones (a mythical king in Spain), whose oxen Hercules captured (225–6); (xi) the fetching of the golden apples of the Hesperides; Hercules bore the weight of the heavens while Atlas fetched the apples which were guarded by the Hesperides and the dragon Ladon on Mount Atlas (233–4; 244); (xii) the bringing up of Cerberus from the underworld (227).

Hercules' list also mentions the killing of Busiris, who polluted the temples of Egypt with the blood of strangers until Hercules ended his blasphemous acts (223–4), and the destruction of the giant Antaeus, whom Hercules overcame by lifting him off the ground and so preventing him from touching the source of his strength, his mother Earth (224–5). Golding expands Ovid's very brief references to Augeus, the lake of Stymphalus and the deer of Diana, and adds the reference to the huge giant Cacus (Cake), son of Vulcan, who stole some of the oxen Hercules had taken from Geryones (243).

**247–8** *neither force of hand . . . art*: in Ovid, 'nec virtute . . . Nec telis armisque' (neither by valour nor by weapons and arms).

**250** *Eurysthey*: Eurystheus, who imposed the labours on Hercules.

**280** *Poean's son*: Philoctetes, friend and armour-bearer of Hercules, was the most celebrated archer in the Trojan War.

**329–31** Eurystheus continued to harass Hercules' children, who fled to Athens to secure help and then invaded Eurystheus' territory and killed him.

**335** *Hyll*: Hyllus was Hercules' eldest son by Deianira.

**352** *Lucina*: the Roman goddess of childbirth, corresponding to the Greek goddess Ilithyia.

**372–3** *some packing . . . Juno's part*: an idiomatic rendition of Ovid's 'iniqua / Nescio quid Iunone geri' (some injustice done by Juno).

**386** *stoutness*: for Ovid's 'Strenuitas' (activity).

**408** *fairies*: for Ovid's 'nymphis'.

**418** *foul Priap's filthy ware*: Priapus' genitals. Priapus tried to rape Lotis; the story is told in Ovid's *Fasti* 1. 415 ff.

**448** *God*: for Ovid's 'numina' (gods).

**479** *Iolay*: Iolaüs was the son of Iphicles, who was Hercules' half-brother. It is, though, in response to the request of Hercules, Hebe's husband, that the gift is granted, not, as Golding's text implies, to the request of Iolaüs himself.

**481–3** *whom . . . suffer*: i.e. Hebe was on the point of swearing that she would never again bestow such a gift, but Themis stopped her.

**485** *The brothers*: Polyneices and Eteocles, who took over the government of Thebes after the flight of their father Oedipus.

**486** *a prophet*: Amphiaraus, who was swallowed up alive in the earth.

**488** *The son*: Amphiaraus' son, Alcmaeon, carried out his father's last bidding by killing his mother, Eriphyle, who was responsible for Amphiaraus' death.

**492** *his wife*: Callirhoë.

*the fatal gold*: a necklace which became the cause of Alcmaeon's death.

**496** *Retire again to youthful years*: Golding assumes a parallel to Iolaüs' case; in Ovid, Callirhoë asks for years to be added to her children's lives so that they may attain manhood immediately.

**498** *his daughter-in-law*: Hebe.

**499** See note to 9. 496.

**503** *her husband*: Tithonus.

**515** See note to 9. 496.

**533** *The Goat Sea*: the Aegean Sea (incorrectly derived from αἴξ, αἰγός, goat).

**547** *The glittering gloss of godliness*: for Ovid's 'Mendaci . . . pietatis . . . umbra' (the false appearance of sisterly affection).

**569** *I awake*: 1567 reads 'I wake'; subsequent editions supply the extra syllable except for 1603 and 1612, which revert to the 1567 reading.

**571–2** *In sleep yet . . . awake*: for Ovid's 'nec abest imitata voluptas' (imagined pleasure is not absent).

**578** *O Lord*: for Ovid's 'O'.

**590** *The gods . . . than we*: following Regius and misunderstanding Ovid's 'dii melius!' (the gods forbid!).

**623** *the empty wax*: i.e. the wax tablet.

**626** *book*: modernizing Ovid's 'tabellas' (tablets).

**646** *God*: for Ovid's 'dii' (gods).

**681** *Now through chance . . . regard*: Golding's addition.

**699** This line is Golding's addition.

**749** *purpose of attempting*: 1567 reads 'purpose attempting'; subsequent editions supply the extra syllable except for 1603, which reverts to the 1567 reading.

**751** *and yet . . . to stay*: Golding's addition.

**766–7** *that same puck . . . goatish body*: Golding's additions to Ovid's description, following Regius's mention of the goat's body.

**786** *underneath a sugarchest*: in Ovid, 'nigra . . . sub ilice' (under a dark holm-oak). 'Sugarchest' is a term applied to various hardwood trees. OED cites John Higins, *The Nomenclator* (tr. 1585): 'the blacke alder: some take it to be that which is commonly called sugerchest'.

**791** *yeoman*: to indicate Ovid's 'Ingenua de plebe' (of free birth but of common stock).

**812–13** *Moreover . . . diadem*: for Ovid's 'regale decus' (regal splendour).

**814** *The barking bug Anubis*: an Egyptian divinity worshipped in the form of a human being with a dog's head. It is unlikely that 'bug' is a misprint for 'dog'; it is retained in all editions and Golding also uses 'bug' (a fantastical object of terror) to describe the dogs attached to Scylla's body at 14. 68.

*the saint of Bubast*: Bubastis, whom the Greeks identified with Artemis (Diana). Golding offers 'saint' for Ovid's 'Sancta' (sacred).

**815** *The pied-coat Apis*: the sacred bull of Memphis, worshipped as a god among the Egyptians.

*the god*: Harpocrates, who was depicted as a child with his finger to his lips.

**864** *the daughter of the sun*: Pasiphae, who, hidden in a wooden cow, coupled with a bull (868), see 8. 174–6.

**905** *kerchief*: for Ovid's 'vittam' (fillet).

**912** *relics*: for Ovid's 'insignia' (tokens). Another of Golding's details which (like the earlier 'bug' and 'saint') gives a slight Roman Catholic overtone to the episode.

**922** *raughtish*: OED uncertainly proposes 'harsh' and cites only Golding. There is no reason to suppose an error; all editions retain the word, as they do again at 14. 325.

**929** *mother*: although all the definitions given in the OED relate to the child-bearing nature of women, here the meaning must be simply 'girl'.

## THE TENTH BOOK

**7** *the bride*: Eurydice.

**13** *Limbo*: for Ovid's 'Styga' (Styx).

**14** *souls*: for Ovid's 'simulacra' (ghosts).

**16** *lordly tyrant*: for Ovid's 'dominum' (lord).

**22** *the foul three-headed cur*: i.e. Cerberus.

**34** *our pageants do prolong*: Golding's addition.

**44–8** For the meaning of these lines, see 4. 565–74.

**67** *Her last farewell she spake so soft*: for Ovid's 'Supremumque vale' (a last farewell). All early editions read 'oft', but this is surely a misprint since 'soft' is required to make sense of the line. A MS correction in the Bodleian Library's 1575 edition supplies the missing 's'.

**70** *him*: a man, otherwise unknown, who turned to stone at the sight of Cerberus.

**75–8** Lethaea was proud of her beauty and provoked a goddess's wrath with an invidious comparison. Olenus wanted to save her by taking her punishment upon herself, but the goddess punished both.

**80** *Charon*: the ferryman of the rivers of the underworld.

**91** *stews*: Golding's addition, offering a moral perspective not in Ovid. Neither Regius nor Micyllus offers a moral comment here, but the annotation of Coelius Rhodiginus, which is included in various of the Regius editions from the mid-sixteenth century, reads, 'Quoniam vero de cinedis facta mentio est, sunt qui scribant, Orpheum Thraca principem omnium tanti sceleris, et libidinis detestande repertorem fuisse' (Indeed, since mention is made of those who indulge in unnatural lust, there are those who write that Orpheus at Thrace was the first inventor of all of so great a crime and of accursed lust).

**95** *this poet born of gods*: Orpheus was the son of Calliope, the Muse of epic poetry.

**97** *Chaon's tree*: the oak.

**97–8** *the trees . . . turnèd were*: poplars.

**98** *Phaeton's sisters*: see 2. 429–58.

**98–113** Golding's list of trees is close, but not identical, to Ovid's.

**112** Attis was changed into a pine-tree ('pinus'), rather than a pineapple-tree, after Cybele discovered his infidelity.

**115** *the god*: Apollo.

**123** *of all one growth*: all of the same size.

**134** Golding omits Ovid 10. 128, which is his desription of the stag lying down and drinking in the shade.

**147** *and aye one in mourning thou shalt be*: an unclear translation of Ovid's 'aderisque dolentibus' (and you shall be with those who mourn).

**153** *O Muse*: see note to 10. 95.

**168** *Amyclae's son*: Hyacinthus.

**175** *My father*: Orpheus presents himself as the son of Apollo here.

**176** *the god*: i.e. Apollo.

**181** *a painful mate*: i.e. a companion in his work.

**183** *His flames*: i.e. the flames of his love.

**186** *a sledge*: a large heavy hammer, in place of Ovid's 'lati . . . disci' (broad discus).

**198** *he strives with herbs to stay*: being the god of healing.

**216** *viol*: for Ovid's 'lyra' (lyre).

**217** *letters*: αἰαἶ, Greek for 'alas!' At line 229 Golding gives only two letters – *αι* – but, as Regius's notes point out, four letters – *αιαι* – are needed to make sense.

**219** *a valiant prince*: Ajax, who committed suicide after failing to win Achilles' shield; '*αιαι*' can be read as the Greek vocative of Ajax.

**235** *Propoets*: the story of the Propoetides is given at 10. 255–60.

**236** *Yea, even as gladly*: i.e. it was unwilling to have bred either.

**237** *Cerasts*: the Cerastae (from the Greek κεραστής, horned), whose story follows immediately.

**257** *To make their bodies common*: i.e. to prostitute their bodies.

**300** *who was nought at all to seek*: i.e. who knew.

**343** *The god of love*: i.e. Cupid.

**354** *godliness*: for Ovid's 'pietas'.

**388** *those same sisters three*: the Furies.

**395** *the same to end to bring*: i.e. to consummate this love.

**411** *godly mind*: for Ovid's 'pia'.

**440** *Her nurse still at her lay*: her nurse continued to badger her.

**452** *God*: for Ovid's 'deum' (gods).

**512** *The driver . . . pight*: for Ovid's more condensed 'inter . . . Triones' (between the Bears).

**518** *Icar and Erigone*: Erigone hanged herself for grief at the murder of her father, Icarius.

**539** *great baggèd*: i.e. pregnant.

**545** *Then hanging . . . rapier bright*: i.e. he then drew a bright rapier which was hanging nearby.

**577** *The misbegotten child*: Adonis.

**578** *defiled*: Golding's addition.

**616–21** Golding's translation does not clearly express Ovid's contrast: Venus *usually* rested in the shade, but *now*, like Diana (Phoebe), she roved the hills.

**660** *words* two syllables; 1567 reads 'woordes'.

**673–4** *(for why . . . skin)*: Golding's addition.

**682** *And wherefore . . . put not I myself in press*: why do I not exert myself.

**690** *The wind . . . her socks*: for Ovid's 'Aura refert ablata citis talaria plantis' (the wind blew back the streaming wings of her swift feet).

**733** *Look thou to that*: for Ovid's 'viderit' (let him look to himself ).

**754** Golding omits Ovid 10. 642.

**759** *and of my church the glebeland wont to be*: a Christian rendition of Ovid's text. The Latin reads, 'templisque accedere dotem / Hanc iussere meis' (and they bade that my temples be enriched with this gift). Glebeland was a portion of land assigned to a clergyman as a part of his benefice.

**775** *O Lord*: in Ovid, simply 'O'.

**806** *the mother of the gods*: Cybele.

**807** *Echion*: one of the men born of the dragon seed which Cadmus sowed; he survived the fratricidal battle and helped Cadmus to build Thebes. See 3. 143.

**807** Golding omits most of Ovid 10. 688.

**809** *out of season*: at an inappropriate time (because he was in a sacred place).

**816** *with the towered tops*: a reference to Cybele's crown.

**820–21** *Their shoulders were . . . before*: in place of Ovid's 'ex humeris armi fiunt' (their upper arms became the shoulders of animals). Golding does not make the mistake with 'armi' which he made at 8. 382 and 553.

**830** Textually this is the most problematic line in the whole work. Most available copies of the 1567 edition read, 'A nemis least thy valeantnesse be hurtfull to us both' (text A). The meaning of 'A nemis' is unclear. However, one copy of 1567 in the Bodleian Library, Oxford (Douce O. 159) reads, 'Least that thyne overhardinesse bee hurtfull to us both' (text B). This implies that a correction was made during the printing of the 1567 edition. Since text A clearly needs some correction whereas text B does not, it seems likely that the latter is the corrected version. But whoever inserted text B appears not to have known what was intended in text A; the problematic phrase is not clarified but abandoned. It seems likely, therefore, that the correction was made by the printer rather than by Golding himself. There is, in any case, no sign that Golding objected to the correction, since 1575, 1584, 1587 and 1593 all follow text B. The 1603 edition, followed by 1612, offers a new reading: '(Adonis) least thy valiantnesse be hurtfull to us both'. This is clearly an attempt to clean up the problem of text A, and indicates that 1603, followed by 1612, is based on a 1567 (A) text rather than on the series of intervening editions. Its correction is ingenious but not convincing, since the interjection reads very clumsily at this point in Venus' speech. Ovid's text does not help here, since the only word which Golding leaves untranslated is 'mihi' in the phrase 'care mihi' ('dear to me' or 'dear one, for my sake'). The impression given here of the relationship between the editions – that those up to 1593 build on previous corrections, while 1603, followed by 1612, starts afresh from a 1567 edition – is consistent with other corrections throughout the text.

Rouse, in his 1904 edition, retains text A, but is unaware of the presence of text B in a 1567 edition; he notes the reading of text B but assumes that it first appears in the second edition. Nims (1965) chooses text B, which he knows from Rouse's note.

**852** *Persephone*: she transformed a favourite nymph, Menthe, into a mint.

**859** *whose fruit*: i.e. the pomegranate.

*tender*: Ovid has 'lento', which can mean 'tough' or 'supple'. Perhaps Golding had not encountered many pomegranates.

**862** *the winds*: the Greek word for wind, ἄνεμος, is related to the name of the flower, the anemone.

## THE ELEVENTH BOOK

**9** *The lance*: i.e. the thyrse.

**17** *blowing shawms*: for Ovid's 'inflato Berecynthia tibia cornu' (the Berecynthian flute and the blown horn). The shawm was a medieval relative of the oboe.

**27** *a stag*: Golding omits Ovid's 'theatro' (in the amphitheatre).

**39** *fiends*: for Ovid's 'ferae' (wild women).

**42** Golding omits part of Ovid 11. 39, Orpheus stretching out his hands to the women.

**43** *O Lord*: for Ovid's 'proh Iuppiter' (by Jupiter).

**52** *boats with sable sail*: both Regius and Micyllus take 'carbasa' to mean 'garments'; Golding opts for the alternative meaning 'sails'.

**59** 1567 reads, 'And lyghted on Methymnye shore in Lesbos land. There'; 1575 and subsequent editions correct the metre with 'And there'.

**76** *chaplain*: for Ovid's 'vate' (bard).

**78** *Thracian women*: i.e. the *wives of Cicony* (line 3).

**83** *fowler subtlely hath*: 1567 reads 'fowlers suttlelye hathe'. Subsequent editions offer various emendations: 1575, 1584, 1587 and 1593 read 'fowler sutt[l]ely hath[e]'; 1603 retains 'fowlers suttlely hath'; and 1612 amends to 'fowlers suttlely have'.

**87** *Aflighted sore, to fly away*: following the correction in 1575 and all subsequent editions. 1567 reads, 'Aflayghted for to fly away'.

**99** *woodwards*: for Ovid's 'Satyri' (satyrs).

**110** *foster-child*: since the satyr Silenus was Bacchus' constant companion.

**127** *the Hesperids*: the Hesperides guarded the golden apples which Hercules obtained as one of his labours.

**130** *Danae*: to whom Jove came in the form of a shower of gold.

**171** *the fairy elves . . . together*: for Ovid's 'teneris . . . nymphis' (the soft nymphs).

**179** *the god of neat*: i.e. Pan, the god of flocks and shepherds.

**185** *crown of bay*: Ovid's 'lauro Parnaside' (laurel of Parnassus) emphasizes Apollo's superiority more strongly, since Parnassus was also the home of the Muses.

**187** *viol*: for Ovid's 'lyram' (lyre).

**188** *bow*: for Ovid's 'plectrum'.

**204** *nightcap*: a homely rendition of Ovid's 'tiaris' (turban).

**226** *the god that rules the surges*: Neptune.

**237** *His daughter*: Hesione.

**242** *Telamon*: he had assisted Hercules in this enterprise.

**244** *Peleus*: he had also helped.

**245** The line is Golding's addition.

**268** *I cannot tell you*: the narrative 'I' is Golding's; Ovid's text reads 'Ambiguum' (it is unclear).

**284** *the prophet*: Proteus.

294 *Nerey's daughter*: i.e. Thetis, a Nereid.

302 Whereas Ovid's Thetis only acknowledges her situation ('confessam'), Golding insists that she is pleased: *to both their joys*.

305 *murdering Phocus*: Peleus and his brother Telamon together murdered their half-brother, Phocus.

307 *Trachin*: a city in Thessaly.

318 *A branch of olive*: in Ovid, more specifically, 'Velamenta' (olive branches which were wound round with wool, carried by suppliants).

332 *this bird that lives by prey*: the hawk.

336 *So was he of a constant mind*: for Ovid's generalization, 'tanta est animi constantia' (so fixed is character).

337 *that noble star*: Lucifer.

343 *Thisbe*: a town of Boeotia, not the lover of Pyramus.

348 *the son of Lady May*: Mercury (Hermes).

358 *Maia*: Lady May.

360 *Autolychus*: Shakespeare uses both the name and the characteristics in *The Winter's Tale*.

378 *O God!*: for Ovid's 'O pietas'.

409–34 Perhaps picking up on Ovid's later description of the herdsman as 'agrestis' (rustic), Golding has him speak with a Somerset accent, stereotypically indicating rusticity. He has already used the accent for Battus and Mercury in 2. 869–75. As in the case of Battus, he fails to introduce the accent in the herdsman's first speech.

414 *A church*: for Ovid's 'Templa'.

423 *daubaken*: not in *OED*. The meaning of the word is unclear, but, if it is a misprint, it is not one that early compositors were able to correct. 1567, 1587, 1603 and 1612 read 'daubaken'; 1575 and 1584 read 'danbaken', which is no clearer; and 1593 changes the text to 'With blood and baken', again unhelpfully. The word looks as if it is connected to 'daubed' (smeared, soiled) or to 'baken' (dried), both of which make some sense in the context, but what exactly Golding intended remains a mystery.

437 *Psamathe*: a Nereid and the mother of Peleus' half-brother, Phocus. Her son's death has left her childless.

463 *she*: i.e. Psamathe.

473 *spells*: for Ovid's 'sortes' (oracles).

473–4 *(which are but toys . . . good)*: a damning assessment, in place of Ovid's 'hominum oblectamina' (the comforts of men).

475 *the god of Claros*: Apollo.

492 *To think . . . quake*: in place of Ovid's 'et ponti tristis imago' (and the dismal appearance of the sea).

523 *God*: for Ovid's 'fata' (Fates).

527–8 *that neither mast . . . fail*: Golding's addition.

531 *with pale and piteous look*: Golding's addition.

**548** *the dear departed part*: her husband.

**568** *The pilot*: i.e. the captain or master.

**581** *and the depth of hell*: for Ovid's 'imumque Acheronta' (and the depths of Acheron).

**584** *from hell*: for Ovid's 'inferno . . . de gurgite' (from some pool of the underworld).

**587** *gun*: for Ovid's 'ballista'.

**605** *lightning*: 1567 reads 'lightnings'; subsequent editions amend to 'lightning'.

**662** *Lucifer*: being Ceyx's father.

**671** *the church*: for Ovid's 'Templa'.

**680** *Thou rainbow*: Golding elucidates where Ovid merely gives the name 'Iri' (Iris). In contrast to the sluggish nature of the house of Slumber, the rainbow was regarded as the swift messenger of the gods.

**693** *watchful bird*: i.e. the cockerel. Golding adds *with barbèd bill*.

**700** *The River of Forgetfulness*: Lethe, the river in the underworld from which the dead drank, so obtaining forgetfulness (Greek, λήθη) of their past.

**722** *though he knew for what she came*: for Ovid's 'cognovit enim' (for he recognized her).

**736** *Morph*: from the Greek μορφή, shape, figure.

**743** *Icelos*: from the Greek εἴκελος, resembling.

**744** *Phobetor*: from the Greek φόβος, terror, object of terror.

**745** *Phantasos*: from the Greek φαντάζεσθαί, to resemble.

**765** *The cloudy south*: i.e. Auster, the south wind.

**772** *Limbo*: for Ovid's 'inania Tartara' (the void of Tartarus).

**777** *Alcyone*: four syllables.

**791–2** *and I knew . . . hands*: Golding connects 'manus' (hands) to 'agnovi' (I recognized), rather than to 'tetendi' (I stretched out). The result is effective, but at odds with the Latin.

**805** *nor yet been forcèd twice to die*: in place of Ovid's 'nec mors discreta fuisset' (nor would my death have been separate [from yours]).

**852–3** *but surely . . . felt*: whereas Golding's tone is persuasive, Ovid's is assured: 'at ille / Senserat' (but he did feel it).

**860** The line is Golding's addition; Regius mentions that the sea is 'navigabili' (navigable).

**867** *cormorant*: for Ovid's 'mergum' (sea-bird, gull).

**875** *he*: i.e. Hector.

**880** *with spade and mattock*: Golding's anglicization of Ovid's 'gracili . . . bicorni' which Regius helpfully glosses: 'instrumentum . . . rusticum' (a rustic instrument).

**886** *Cebrius*: a river-god.

**918** Golding has perhaps forgotten that the story of Aesacus is told by 'an ancient father' who is himself a character in the narrative; the comment about *the Latins* is appropriate only to Golding's narrative voice. The Latin name in question is 'mergus' (diver), from 'mergere' (to dip or dive).

## THE TWELFTH BOOK

3 *brother*: the plural is implied. Ovid gives 'fratribus' (brothers).

5 *a lasting war*: the ten-year Trojan War, which was caused by Paris' abduction of Helen, wife of Menelaus, from Greece.

10 *At road*: in sheltered water.

13 *speckled*: for Ovid's 'caeruleum' (blue, dark).

18 *Calchas*: the wisest soothsayer among the Greeks at Troy, who advised them in their various difficulties.

28–9 *and never . . . in time*: for Ovid's 'neque . . . tacet' (nor was he silent).

30 *wrath conceivèd just*: Agamemnon had once killed a deer in the grove of Artemis (Phoebe); in her anger Phoebe produced the calm which prevented the Greeks from setting sail.

33 *Iphigen*: Iphigenia, daughter of Agamemnon.

49 The sense of this line is clear, although the phrasing is paradoxical.

60 *some coal-carriers' part do play*: Golding's idiomatic addition.

69 *he lays to understand*: i.e. he reckons to understand.

73 *bid them base*: i.e. challenged them.

74 *Protesilay*: Protesilaus was the leader of warriors from several Thessalian regions, and was the first to leap from the Greek ships upon the Trojan shore.

92 *Thou goddess' son*: Achilles was the son of Thetis (see 11. 301–2).

99–101 Whereas Achilles is a grandson of Nereus, Cygnet was the son of Neptune.

109 *list*: for Ovid's 'circo' (arena).

118 *Axaetion*: king of Thebe and father of Andromache, who married Hector.

121–2 Having been wounded by Achilles, Telephus learnt from an oracle that he would be cured only by the person who had wounded him. Since the Greeks had also learnt from an oracle that they would not reach Troy without Telephus' help, Achilles cured him with the rust of the spear with which he had been wounded.

143 *morion*: see note to 6. 96.

154 *bolt upright*: flat on his back.

156–7 *And leaning with his elbows . . . headpiece*: for Ovid's 'Tum clypeo, genibusque premens precordia duris, / Vincla trahit galeae' (pressing on his breast with his shield and hard knees, he pulled on his helmet-thongs).

162 *the fowl*: i.e. a swan.

173 *sitting down*: for Ovid's 'Discubuere toris' (reclined on couches).

217 *Thy father*: Peleus.

235 *feats of chivalry*: for Ovid's 'studiis . . . virilibus' (manly exercises).

238 *His cloud-bred brothers*: the Centaurs, part man and part horse, offspring of Ixion and a cloud.

268 *bolt upright*: see note to 12. 154.

271–2 *cups and cans . . . pots and trays*: a homely rendition of Ovid's 'pocula . . .

fragilesque cadi, curvique lebetes' (goblets and fragile flasks and curved basins).

**275** *bridehouse*: for Ovid's 'penetralia' (sanctuary).

**283** *knapped him in the necks*: for Ovid's 'Stravit humi' (hurled him to the ground). Golding's *necks* does not imply that the Lapith had more than one neck.

**286** *hell*: for Ovid's 'tartareas . . . umbras' (the shades of Tartarus).

**296** *a vowed hart's horn*: i.e. a hart's horn which had been hung up as a votive offering.

**339** *wizard*: for Ovid's 'augur' (seer).

**342** *of Herc'les' bow to die*: see 9. 119–59.

**344** *Sir Dryant's hand did all alike them spare*: i.e. Dryant killed them all.

**345** *Caenaeus*: not the Caen whose story Nestor is narrating.

**356** *bolt upright*: see note to 12. 154.

**358** *flushing like a spout*: Golding's addition.

**395** *squire*: for Ovid's 'Armiger' (armour-bearer).

**403** *wattling*: literally, boughs and twigs interlaced to make a wattle wall, fence, etc.; here used to refer to the framework of ribs.

**408** *burgonet*: anachronistic; a light sixteenth-century helmet with visor, for Ovid's 'galea' (helmet).

**438** *or little worse than it*: Golding's addition.

**440** *Castor*: one of the twin sons of Jupiter and Leda, later placed with Pollux among the stars as Gemini. Castor was famed for his skill in taming and managing horses.

**463** *dyèd swart*: became dark. 'Dye' can be understood intransitively as 'to take on a colour'. It is possible that '*dyèd*' should instead be read 'dièd', but this gives a very clumsy phrase. There is no reference to Cyllarus' body becoming dark in either Ovid's text or the Regius/Micyllus notes.

**478** *as cream is wont to do*: the reference is to the straining of curds in the process of cheese-making.

**489** *held him wag*: kept him at bay.

**505** *did make a wide and deadly gap*: Golding's addition.

**513** *auburn*: Golding's addition.

**518** *a mother*: as at 9. 929, the word indicates only that she is female, not that she has borne children.

**522** *for rape*: i.e. because of rape, as told at 12. 211–35.

**530** *ribs*: for Ovid's 'ora' (face).

**537** *sidling*: i.e. turning the sword sideways.

**556–7** *Or what avails . . . in one?*: for Ovid's 'et quid fortissima rerum / In nobis duplex natura animalia iunxit?' (and [what help is it] that a double nature has joined in us the strongest of living things?).

**580** *Limbo*: for Ovid's 'inania . . . Tartara' (the void of Tartarus).

**584** Golding omits Ovid 528, the noise of the bird's wings.

**607–8** *that most stout . . . of Troy*: Golding's addition.

**621** *practising*: i.e. acting like.

**631–2** *Lord Admiral . . . of Rhodes*: for Ovid's 'Rhodiae ductor . . . classis' (captain of the fleet of Rhodes). Rhodes had fallen to the Ottomans in 1522, and hence comprised part of the Ottoman Empire which was threatening Christian Europe at the time that Golding was writing.

**636** *his pleasant tales*: a somewhat inappropriate shift from Ovid's 'dulci . . . ore' (in a pleasant voice), influenced by Regius's gloss: 'suavi sermone. nam (ut ait Hom.) suavior melle ab ore Nestoris oratio profluebat' (sweet speech; for, as Homer says, speech sweeter than honey used to flow from the mouth of Nestor).

**637** *the table*: for Ovid's 'toris' (couches).

**655** *If ever he do come within my danger*: if he is ever within my power, at my mercy.

**673** *carpet-knight*: Golding's addition; a term for a stay-at-home soldier.

**677** *Queen Penthesilea*: queen of the Amazons. She came to the aid of the Trojans after Hector's death, but was killed by Achilles.

**680** *That same god*: i.e. Vulcan, god of fire.

**682** *coffin*: for Ovid's 'urnam' (urn).

**688** *Ajax Oiley* Ajax the son of Oileus, not Ajax the son of Telamon.

**689–90** *Atreus' younger son . . . his elder*: Menelaus and Agamemnon respectively.

**691** *the sons of Telamon and Laërt*: Ajax and Ulysses respectively.

**692** *bear the bell away*: win the prize.

## THE THIRTEENTH BOOK

**3** *The owner*: i.e. Ajax.

**13** *bears he the bell*: see note to 12. 692.

**21–3** *To think it mine . . . stands in hope*: for Ovid's 'Aiaci non est tenuisse superbum, / Sit licet hoc ingens, quidquid speravit Ulysses' (It is no honour for Ajax to have gained a prize, however great, to which Ulysses has aspired).

**24–5** *sit . . . cushion*: miss his mark, i.e. fail to win the shield. M. P. Tilley, *A Dictionary of the Proverbs in England in the Sixteenth and Seventeenth Centuries* (Ann Arbor: 1950) records 'miss the cushion' (C928) and 'set (one) beside the cushion' (C929). Compare John Skelton: 'And whan he weneth to sytte / Yet may he mysse the quysshon!', *Collyn Clout* 995–6.

**26–7** *yet should nobility . . . me*: i.e. my nobility should advantage me.

**30** For Aeacus, see 7. 605–850. Aeacus was renowned for his justice during his life and after his death became one of the three judges in Hades.

**31** Sisyphus was renowned for his greed and deceitfulness. His punishment in Hades was to roll a huge stone up a hill endlessly.

**35** *Achives*: Achaei, Greeks.

**37** *He was my brother*: more exactly, Achilles' cousin; Ajax' father, Telamon, and Achilles' father, Peleus, were brothers.

*that was*: i.e. that which was.

**40** *the Aeacids*: the family of Aeacus.

**48** *Escried the crafty fetches*: when Ulysses feigned madness, Palamedes detected his stratagem by placing his infant son in front of him while he was ploughing.

**56** *Poean's son*: Philoctetes. On the journey to Troy Philoctetes received a wound (either a snake-bite or from one of his poisoned arrows) which produced such an intolerable stench that, on Ulysses' advice, the Greeks left him in Lemnos.

**61** *he*: Philoctetes.

**76** The line is Golding's addition.

**88** *God*: for Ovid's 'superi' (gods).

**92** *He made a rod to beat himself*: for Ovid's 'legem sibi dixerat ipse' (he had established a precedent for himself).

**104–5** *and bringeth . . . gods*: specifically, Hector's part in the war provokes the involvement of Apollo. A separate tradition makes Hector the son of Apollo.

**114** *all the fiends*: for Ovid's 'Iovem' (Jove).

**122** *Dulichius*: Ulysses.

**122–4** *the horses white . . . by night*: exploits of Ulysses during the Trojan War. An oracle had declared that Troy would never be taken if Rhesus' white horses once drank of the water of the Xanthus and fed on the grass of the Trojan plain; Ulysses and Diomedes slew Rhesus by night and carried off his horses. Dolon was a spy of the Trojans; Helenus (*Helen*) a son of Priam who joined the Greeks, ensnared by Ulysses. The *stealth of Pallady* refers to Ulysses' theft of Pallas' holy image from Troy, which he speaks of later at 13. 408–12, and see also 13. 461–2.

**128** *Ithacus*: Ulysses.

**130** *who shoots . . . mark*: i.e. who always has his own goals in mind(?). Golding's addition, presumably proverbial.

**154** *Laërtes' son*: i.e. Ulysses.

**164** *he wiped his watery eyes*: as a skilful orator, Ulysses uses gesture as part of his persuasions.

**168** *a dolt and grosshead*: more striking than Ovid's 'hebes' (dull).

**176** *the fourth from Jove*: Ajax was the son of Telamon, son of Aeacus, son of Jupiter.

**192** *His father*: i.e. Achilles' father.

**194** *To Phthia or to Scyros Isle*: where Peleus and Pyrrhus lived.

**224** *the winds did fail*: see note to 12. 30.

**234** *his brother*: Menelaus, for whose wife Helen the war was fought.

**242** The line is an expansion of Ovid's 'viris' (men).

**288** *paid*: punished. Ulysses beat Thersites for railing against Agamemnon; see Homer, *Iliad* 2. 211–77.

**309** *and his horses which were white*: Golding's addition.

**311–13** *Deny you me . . . than you are*: If you deny me the shield of Achilles, whose horses the enemy demanded in return for his night's work, Ajax will be more generous to me than you (since Ajax had ironically proposed dividing the shield between Ulysses and Diomedes).

**336** *his brother*: for Ovid's 'ducis' (captain).

**349–50** *Thetis for her son . . . gift*: when Patroclus, who was wearing Achilles' armour, had been killed in the war, Achilles was overcome with grief. Thetis consoled him, promising him new armour to be made by Vulcan, and Iris exhorted him to retrieve his friend's body.

**401** *to the hellish pit*: Golding's addition.

**404–5** *(if that Fortune say / Amen)*: for Ovid's 'faveat Fortuna' (if Fortune favours me).

**405** *thee and eke thine arrows*: Ulysses had learnt from Helenus that Troy could not be taken without the presence of Philoctetes and the bow and arrows of Hercules which were in Philoctetes' possession.

**406** *the Trojan prophet*: Helenus. See note to 13. 122–4.

**408** *chapel*: for Ovid's 'penetrale' (shrine).

**409** *The Phrygian Pallad's image*: see note to 13. 122–4.

**418** *the idol from her chapel and her shrine*: a Christian rendition of Ovid's 'aede Deam raptam' (the goddess seized from her temple).

**431** *t'other Ajax*: Ajax, son of Oileus, known as 'the lesser' (Moderatior). Golding translates Ovid's 'moderatior' in the sense of 'more restrained', perhaps following Regius's suggestion that Ovid is punning at this point: '*Moderatior* Oilei filius, qui inter fortes ab Homero numeratur. Ex arte autem iudices conciliat Ulysses illos tum a modestia, tum a virtute laudando' (Moderatior, the son of Oileus, who is numbered among the strong by Homer. But through his skill Ulysses wins over those judges by praising [him] both for his restraint and for his valour).

**465** *He*: Ajax.

**478** *The selfsame letters*: see 10. 217–20 and notes.

**482** *Thoant's and Hypsiphyle's realm*: Lemnos, where the women killed all the men on the island.

**486** *the lord of them*: Philoctetes.

**489** *Lost . . . her woman's shape*: the transformation of Hecuba happens at 13. 680–82.

**490–91** *In the place . . . Hellespont*: it makes more sense to connect this phrase to the previous sentence, but Golding's phrasing, following the punctuation of his Latin text, requires that it be connected to the next words, *did Ilion burn in height*.

**494** *Phoebus' priestess*: Cassandra.

**495** *Grays*: Greeks. Golding anglicizes Ovid's 'Graii'. See also 14. 503.

**495–6** *most spitefully . . . ta'en*: for Ovid's 'Invidiosa . . . praemia' (an enviable booty).

**499** *Astyanax*: Hector's son.

**511** *void of care*: Golding's addition.

**516** *Biston men*: a people of Thrace.

**535** *Polyxene*: Polyxena, daughter of Priam and Hecuba (and beloved of Achilles according to some traditions).

**540–41** *and rather . . . woman*: because of her manly courage.

**558** *Limbo*: for Ovid's 'Stygios . . . manes' (the Stygian shades).

**614** *Penelope*: Ulysses' wife.

**683** *bears yet the name*: the place was called Cynossema, from the Greek κυνος σῆμα, sign of the dog.

**689** *the Morning*: Aurora had favoured the Trojans since her son Memnon, king of the Ethiopians, had come to the assistance of his uncle Priam towards the end of the war.

**706** *bringing to thee light*: the early editions offer various readings. 1567, 1575 and 1612 read 'bringing in thee light'; 1584 and 1603 read 'bringing to thee light'; 1587 and 1593 read 'bringing to the light'.

**726** Golding omits Ovid 13. 608.

**729** *one flew*: according to Ovid, all the birds fight (also at line 739).

**741** *Dymant's daughter*: Hecuba.

**747** *The son of Venus*: Aeneas.

**750** *godly*: for Ovid's 'pius'.

**755** *Apollo's town*: Delos.

**757** *church*: for Ovid's 'templo' (temple).

**760** *When she of childbirth travailèd*: see 6. 428–9.

**765** *unless I take my marks amiss*: unless I am mistaken.

**768** *mitre*: a Christian rendition of Ovid's 'vittis' (fillets).

**816** *what town . . . was meant*: i.e. Thebes, in Boeotia. It could be recognized by its seven gates.

**823–5** *of which the one . . . did also spend her life*: Golding's translation is a loose rendition of a passage of Ovid which is corrupt and makes little sense.

**829** *who died with such renown*: Golding's addition, in place of Ovid's 'quos fama Coronas / Nominat' (whom fame has named Coroni).

**836** In Ovid they also give him a sacrificial saucer ('pateram').

**840** *th'infection of the air*: following the main text of Regius's Latin, 'luem' (plague, contagion), rather than the marginal reading, '[loci] Iovem' (climate), which is the accepted reading in modern texts.

**844** *Aëllo*: one of the Harpies, see 7. 4.

**847** *Ambrace*: Apollo, Diana and Hercules quarrelled over Ambracia and appointed the judge Craguleus to judge between them. He awarded the city to Hercules and was therefore turned into stone by Apollo.

**850** *Dodon grove*: a grove in Dodona dedicated to Jupiter. The will of the god was declared by the wind rustling through the trees.

**851** *the sons of King Molossus*: Antonius Liberalis' *Metamorphoses* tells the story of Munichos, king of the Mollosians, whose sons were turned into birds by Zeus to escape being burnt to death when their fortress was attacked.

**855** *The Trojan prophet*: Helenus, see *Helen* (line 857), seer and one of Priam's sons.

**891** *beyond all God's forbode*: for Ovid's 'nullo cum fine' (endlessly).

904 *marquisotte*: to cut in Turkish fashion, all shaven away except for the moustache. Golding increases the Cyclops' affectation; Ovid gives only 'recidere' (cut).

920 *fiend*: for Ovid's 'Cyclops'.

929 *primrose leaf*: for Ovid's 'folio . . . ligustri' (privet leaves).

942 *warried*: full of knots. This is the only example cited in *OED*.

963 *fruits all sorts*: for Ovid's 'arbutei foetus' (the fertile arbute-tree).

1003 *my father*: Neptune.

1008 *Nerey*: here signifying Nereid or daughter of Nereus.

1012 *dwarf*: Golding's addition.

1022 Golding starts a new paragraph here, but it seems unhelpful to retain it.

1025 *fiend*: for Ovid's 'ferus' (fierce).

1032 *Simethus*: Ovid reads, 'Simethius heros' (the Symaethian hero). Golding has adapted the adjective (deriving from the names of Acis' mother and her father) into a new name for Acis himself.

1035 *The round-eyed devil*: for Ovid's 'Cyclops'.

1040 *the force his father had before*: i.e. Acis was also to be made a god.

1050 *grey*: for Ovid's 'caerulus' (blue, dark).

1105 *another nature*: i.e. another element, water instead of air.

1110 *Tethys*: all editions mistakenly read 'Thetis'. Thetis was the wife of Peleus, Tethys the wife of Oceanus.

1114 *breastbulk*: breast or trunk. Not in *OED*.

1123 *greyish*: for Ovid's 'caerula' (blue, dark).

1130 *court, which full of monsters lay*: for Ovid's 'Prodigiosa . . . atria' (wondrous house), following Regius's gloss: 'aedes monstrorum plenas' (house full of monstrous things).

## THE FOURTEENTH BOOK

1–2 *who lately . . . god of sea*: Golding's explanatory addition.

3 *which upon the face of Giant Typho lies*: Jove had punished the rebellious giants by imprisoning them under mountains.

6 *cracked*: Golding's addition, probably owing to Regius's discussion of Rhegium, a town in Calabria opposite Messina in Sicily; Regius mentions Sicily being broken off ('adrupta') from Italy.

32 *her father's deed*: when Apollo exposed Venus and Mars together; see 4. 206–28.

52 *russet*: for Ovid's 'caerula' (blue, dark).

63 *which . . . to frame*: Golding's explanatory addition, following Regius: 'portenta ac monstra facientibus' (which created monsters and wondrous things).

68 *bugs*: see note to 9. 814.

82 *She spoiled Ulysses of his mates*: Ulysses was the beloved of Circe.

89 *The Tyrian queen*: Dido, who fell in love with Aeneas and on his departure killed

herself on a pyre which she had built, pretending that she was going to cure herself of her love by the use of magic rites. The story is told in Virgil, *Aeneid* 4.

**100** *Juno's messenger*: Juno, hating the Trojans, sent Iris to burn Aeneas' ships. He managed to save all but four. See *Aeneid* 5. 604–99.

**103** *the mermaids*: i.e. the Sirens.

**106** *Ape Isle*: Golding's version of Ovid's 'Pythecusas', which is derived from the Greek πίθηκος, ape.

**118** This line is Golding's expansion of Ovid's 'rauco stridore' (hoarse jabbering).

**128** *godliness*: for Ovid's 'pietas'.

**137–8** *And saw . . . stout Anchises*: Aeneas' visit to the underworld is related at length in *Aeneid* 6.

**145** *God*: for Ovid's 'diis' (gods).

**183** *Limbo*: for Ovid's 'Sedibus . . . Stygiis' (Stygian realms).

**186** *his nurse*: Caieta. The town of Caieta stood in Latium on the borders of Campania.

**213** *the noise*: Ulysses taunted the blind Polyphemus as he departed.

**223** *He could not see*: Ulysses had contrived to make the giant drunk, and then burnt out his one eye with a flaming pole.

**232** *fiend*: for Ovid's 'ferox' (fierce).

**240** *a dozen of our fellows*: a misunderstanding of Ovid's 'vidi bina meorum / Ter, quater affligi sociorum corpora terrae' (I saw the bodies of two of my companions dashed to the ground three or four times), but probably prompted by Micyllus's discussion of possible readings.

**241** *or hunger-starvèd hound*: Golding's addition.

**245** *like an aspen leaf*: Golding's addition.

**249** *and I must also go to pot*: Golding's addition. In modern usage the phrase has lost its original implication of being cooked and eaten. Compare *Coriolanus* (I. iv), where Martius' entry into Corioli is described as going 'To th'pot, I warrant him.'

**256** *finding grace*: for Ovid's 'movi' (I moved them).

**269** *ancient Lamy's town*: where the Leastrygones, a race of cannibals, lived. They captured and ate some of Ulysses' crew and destroyed most of his ships.

**321** *the cursèd witch*: for Ovid's 'dea dira' (the cruel goddess).

**325** *raughtish*: see note to 9. 922.

**338** *moly*: a fabulous herb. The name was applied to various plants in Golding's day, in particular to wild garlic.

**362** *chancel*: for Ovid's 'Aede' (temple).

**364** *church*: for Ovid's 'aede' (temple).

**416** *like a witch*: Golding's addition.

**418** *her father's head*: i.e. the sun.

**452** Golding omits Ovid 14. 396. Ovid adds 'Nec quidquam antiquum Pico, nisi nomina restat' (and Picus kept nothing of his former self except his name).

**461** *fiends*: for Ovid's 'deos' (gods).

**475** *they sent their eyes*: misunderstanding the sense of 'lumina' in Ovid's 'obvia lumina portant' (they carried torches), despite Regius's explanation 'funalia, faces' (wax-torches, torches).

**502** *grace*: for Ovid's 'pietatis' (piety).

**512** *his wife*: Latinus' daughter, Lavinia, had been engaged to Turnus, but on Aeneas' arrival her father promised her to him.

**513** *the shire*: Golding's addition.

**531** *the Prince of Naryx*: Ajax, who carried off Cassandra from the temple of Pallas Athene. The goddess persecuted the Greek fleet on its voyage home in her anger at the sacrilege.

**542** *the wound I had her given*: Diomedes had wounded Venus in the Trojan War.

**576** *doubtful bird*: Ovid does not specify the bird, but Golding proposes the *elk*, a term for the wild swan or hooper and for the wild goose.

**586** *fairies*: for Ovid's 'nymphae' (nymphs).

**611** *Dame Cybel*: Golding's explanatory addition. The name appears in Regius's note here.

**612** *sound of bells and noise of shawms*: for Ovid's 'tinnitibus aethera pulsi / Aeris, et inflati . . . murmure buxi' (the clash of beaten cymbals and the noise of the boxwood flute).

**620** *The sons of Astrey*: i.e. the winds.

**632** *bred in mountains hard*: i.e. the trees from which the ships were made came from the mountains originally.

**641** *Alcinous' ships*: Alcinous had provided ships to carry Ulysses home to Ithaca. They were turned to stone by Neptune.

**659** *the city's name*: i.e Ardea, 'heron'.

**663** *(who . . . at odds)*: Golding's addition, following Regius's gloss: 'quae semper ei fuerat adversata' (who was always opposed to him).

**665** *July*: Ascanius Julus, son of Aeneas.

**677** *worthy is a saint in heaven to be*: for Ovid's 'caelesti numine dignus' (worthy of deity in heaven).

**693** *Ascanius with the double name*: Ascanius, Aeneas' son, was also known as Julus.

**713** *her name*: Pomona, derived from 'pomum' (fruit). Golding's marginal note offers a convincingly English equivalent.

**728** *fiend*: for Ovid's 'deus' (god). The god is Priapus, god of fruitfulness, whose symbol was the phallus.

**731** *sly*: Golding's addition.

**745** *wimple*: Golding's anachronistic rendition of Ovid's 'mitra' (headscarf).

**751** *in all the world this hour*: Golding's addition. Golding's language has Marian overtones.

**764–5** *Queen Helen . . . suitors*: Helen was sought in marriage by the noblest chiefs from all parts of Greece; they subsequently sailed to Troy and fought the Trojan War to avenge her abduction by Paris.

**765** *the lady*: Hippodame. See 12. 236 ff.

**766** *the wife*: Penelope.

**770** *fairies*: for Ovid's 'numina' (gods).

**788** *the firstlings are his right*: Vertumnus was particularly concerned with crops and gardens.

**818** *Kids*: or Haedi, a small double star in the hand of the Waggoner (Auriga).

**881** *the Lenten's cold*: for Ovid's 'vernum . . . frigus' (the cold of spring).

**893** *Numitor*: deposed by his brother Amulius, but later restored to the throne by his grandsons, Romulus and Remus.

**895** *Pale*: Pales, god of shepherds and cattle.

**897** *Tarpey*: Tarpeia promised to betray the Capitoline to the Sabines in return for what they wore on their left arms, meaning their bracelets and rings. When they had captured the citadel, the Sabines fulfilled their promise by instead piling their shields upon her and crushing her to death.

**902** *Ilia's son*: Romulus.

**909** *church*: Golding's addition. Regius refers to Janus' temple.

**923** *Mars's knight*: i.e. the Roman soldiery.

**933** *The god of battle*: Mars.

**956** *sacred shrine*: for Ovid's 'pulvinaribus altis' (high couches [of the gods]).

**957** *Quirin*: Quirinus was the name given to Romulus after his deification.

**964** *canonizèd*: Golding's addition.

**966** *holy*: Golding's addition.

**977** *Thaumant's imp*: i.e. Iris.

   *Quirin's hill*: one of the seven hills of Rome.


## THE FIFTEENTH BOOK

**6** *the Sabine rites*: Numa, the second king of Rome, was a native of Cures in the Sabine country.

**7** *his*: 1567 reads 'the'; all other editions correct to 'his' except 1603, which reverts to 'the'.

**10** *the town*: Crotona.

**11** *asking*: i.e as Numa asked.

**12** *well seen*: skilled, versed.

**14** *the Spanish kine*: oxen of Geryones. See note to 9. 223–44 (x).

**60** *fatal*: i.e. destined.

**89** *to content both mind and eye*: Golding's addition.

**101** *the Cyclops' guise*: see 14. 226–44.

**104** *clean void of all such rage*: Golding's addition.

**117** *godliness*: for Ovid's 'pietate'.

**125** *at Bacchus' altar*: Bacchus was the god of wine.

**145** *he . . . he*: i.e. the *sacrifice unblemishèd* (142), an ox.

**171** *Limbo*: Golding's addition. A jibe here against Roman Catholicism, since Limbo was not a part of Protestant belief.

**176–7** *Howbeit, they . . . live again in new*: a confused translation of Ovid's 'semperque priore relicta / Sede, novis domibus vivunt habitantque receptae' (and always, when they have left their former seat, they are received into new homes where they live and dwell).

**181** *church*: for Ovid's 'templo'.

**192** *godliness*: for Ovid's 'pietas'.

**211** *Pallant's daughter*: Aurora.

**234–5** *overcast . . . hair as white as snow*: an expansion of Ovid's 'quos habet, alba capillos' (what hair it has is white).

**242** *prison*: in place of Ovid's 'domo' (home).

**244** *four-footed*: four syllables. 1567 reads 'fowerfooted'.

**251** *Milo*: a celebrated athlete, six times victor in the Olympic games and six times in the Pythian games. There are many stories of his extraordinary feats of strength.

**255** *Helen*: carried off by Theseus with the help of Pirithoüs to Attica in her youth, later by Paris to Troy, precipitating the Trojan War.

**290** *and scales of seafish*: Golding's addition.

**310** *the Centaurs*: see note to 9. 223–44 (iv).

**324** *and steeples*: Golding's addition.

**358** *King Proetus' daughters*: Lysippe, Iphinoë and Iphianassa, who were stricken with madness on reaching maturity, either because they despised the worship of Bacchus or because they compared their beauty with Juno's.

**373–4** *Symplegads . . . unmovable*: see note to 7. 87. The Symplegads became rooted after Jason and the Argonauts had managed to pass between them safely.

**386** *Or brimstone . . . doth lightly fall*: for Ovid's 'Luteave exiguis ardescunt sulfura fumis' (or yellow sulphur burns with scanty flames).

**401–2** *kill an ox . . . bees*: compare the idea behind Samson's riddle, 'Out of the eater came forth meat, and out of the strong came forth sweetness', Judges 14. 14 and previous verses.

**411** *butterflies*: for Ovid's 'Ferali . . . papilione' (funereal butterfly).

**420** *Of such a size as . . . to conceive*: for Ovid's 'et in formam quantam capit ipsa reducit' (and brings it into such shape as she has herself).

**426** *Juno's bird*: the peacock.

**446** *godlily*: for Ovid's 'pius'.

**453** *The creature*: a chameleon.

**468** *which grass doth overgrow*: Golding's addition.

**501** *good*: in place of Ovid's 'penatigero' (carrying the Penates).

**515** *Thyestes-like*: Thyestes' brother, Atreus, killed Thyestes' two sons in revenge for the death of his own son Plisthenes, and he served their flesh up at a banquet before Thyestes, who (like Tereus) unwittingly ate his own offspring.

**519** *the lowing of the dam*: in Ovid, the lowing of the calf itself.

**527** *risp*: the most likely meaning here is 'twig', pre-empting *limetwigs* in the next line. Twigs were smeared with bird-lime, a sticky substance, to catch birds.

**529** *feared feathers*: feathers were hung on trees to frighten the deer towards the nets.

**536** *his wife*: Egeria.

**545–6** *Dian, whom Orestes ... had fet*: an explanatory expansion of Ovid's 'Oresteae ... Dianae' (Orestean Diana), based on Regius's commentary. Orestes fetched the statue of Diana from Tauric Chersonesus in order to cure his madness.

**549** *Theseus' son*: Hippolytus.

**556** *stepdame*: Phaedra, daughter of Pasiphae. Phaedra fell in love with Hippolytus and, when rejected, accused him of making an attempt on her honour.

**596** *bright Apollo's son*: Aesculapius, the god of medical art.

**600** *Cynthia*: Diana.

**621** *The lady of Amazon's son*: Hippolytus, son of Hippolyte, queen of the Amazons.

**628** *by searching bulks of beasts*: i.e. reading signs in the entrails of animals. Golding's addition.

**647** *wizard*: for Ovid's 'aruspex' (seer).

**657** *he*: i.e. Cipus.

**669** *wizard*: for Ovid's 'augur' (seer).

**695–6** *at which this Cipus ... entered Rome*: Golding's addition, based on Regius: 'portae illius per quam ingredi poterat Cippus' (that gate through which Cippus could have entered).

**701** *sacred saints*: for Ovid's 'sacris' (deities).

**707** *Amid the world*: compare 10. 178.

**712–13** *the table from the ... chancel*: a Christian rendition of Ovid's 'cortina ... imo ... adyto' (the tripod in the innermost shrine).

**720** *Epidaur*: Epidaurus was the chief seat of the worship of Aesculapius.

**728** *sith they ... in the end*: Golding's addition, probably influenced by Regius's gloss: 'suum auxilium, hoc est Aesculapium, ad quem in adversis confugiebant' (their own aid, this is Aesculapius, in whom they used to take refuge in times of misfortune).

**732** *the lord ambassador*: for Ovid's 'Romane' (Roman).

**734** *chapel*: for Ovid's 'aede' (temple).

**736** *meekly*: for Ovid's 'placido ... pectore' (calmly).

**737** *This serpent*: serpents, being symbols of renovation and reputed to have the power of discovering healing herbs, were sacred to Aesculapius.

**753** *church*: for Ovid's 'aede' (temple).

**756** *'tiz God, 'tiz God!*: Golding's priest, unlike Ovid's, speaks in rustic accent at the moment of revelation. See Introduction.

**761** *godly*: for Ovid's 'pium'.

**765** *of his church*: Golding's addition, following Regius's mention of the temple.

**773** *His train of chaplains*: for Ovid's 'agmen' (his train).

**784** *church*: for Ovid's 'templa'.

**817** *the nuns that*: for Ovid's 'quae' (those who). Regius refers to 'virgines ... Vestales'.

**832–3** *our city ... with us*: here Golding speaks with Ovid's narrative voice.

**839** *his progeny*: Caesar Augustus.

**841** *as Augustus is*: Ovid wrote the *Metamorphoses* under Caesar Augustus. It was completed while he was in exile (AD 8–c. 17), and Ovid's praise of Augustus, though conventional, also reflects his desire to regain favour and return to Rome.

**853–4** *the other ... for a god*: in Ovid, simply 'Ille deus faciendus erat' (he had to be made a god); *the other* is Julius Caesar.

**855** *bishop*: for Ovid's 'Pontifici' (high priest).

**873** *keep them from my throat*: in Ovid, simply 'Quos prohibete' (keep them away).

**875** *bishop*: for Ovid's 'sacerdotis' (priest).

**887** *sent from hell*: for Ovid's 'Stygius' (Stygian).

**890** *the chapels of the gods*: for Ovid's 'sanctis ... lucis' (sacred groves).

**894** *churches*: for Ovid's 'templa'.

**909** *the fatal sisters three*: the Fates or Parcae.

**921–2** *he ... is his heir and bears his name*: Augustus was recognized as Julius Caesar's adopted son under the name of Gaius Julius Caesar Octavius.

**927** *The great Pompeius' son*: Sextus Pompeius, youngest son of Pompey the Great.

**929** *the Queen of Egypt*: Cleopatra, who was Mark Antony's lover.

**931** *her canop*: in Ovid, the reference is to the Egyptian city Canopus, as Regius makes clear: 'est autem Campus urbs Aegypti' (Campus is an Egyptian town). Golding's 1567 compositor uses black-letter type here, indicating that he does not recognize the word as a proper name; his standard procedure is to use Roman type for proper names. This may be the compositor's error, or (though less likely) it may imply that Golding understood the word as 'canopy', synecdochically used to signify the throne of Egypt as a parallel to the Roman Capitol.

**940** *A holy wife shall bear to him a son*: a slight misunderstanding on Golding's part. Livia bore Tiberius by Tiberius Claudius Nero before she became Augustus' wife; Tiberius was later adopted by Augustus. Regius makes the relationships clear: 'ex Livia natus ab Aug. adoptatus' (born of Livia, adopted by Augustus).

**945** *cresset*: for Ovid's 'iubar' (star).

**969** *the triple-shapèd world*: earth, sea and sky.

**972–3** *ye gods ... canonizèd*: for Ovid's 'diique indigetes' (and native gods).

**978** *church*: for Ovid's 'arces' (citadel).

**997** *Laus & honor soli Deo*: Golding's addition (Praise and glory be to God alone).

# GLOSSARY

In cases where Golding uses a word in both a modern and an obsolete sense, only the latter is listed below. Problematic words are discussed in the notes rather than in the glossary. Phrases, except for the most brief and common ones, are also explained in the notes rather than below.

*abash* (v.) to lose confidence
*abashed* (adj.) confounded, discomfited
*ability* (n.) means (financial)
*abode* (n.) delay
*abroach, to set* (phr.) to broach, publish
*abroad* (adv.) widely, at large
*abye* (v.) to pay for, suffer for
*account, make* (phr.) to give an undertaking
*acknown* (adj.) acknowledged
*admit* (v.) to suppose
*adrad* (adj.) frightened
*adust* (adj.) burnt, scorched
*adventure* (n.) trial, hazardous enterprise
*advertise* (v.) to inform, notify
*advertisement* (n.) admonition
*advouterer* (n.) adulterer
*advoutery* (n.) adultery
*affection* (n.) passion, lust
*affeebled* (adj.) weakened, enfeebled
*affianced* (adj.) betrothed
*afford* (v.) to offer, give out
*affray* (v.) to frighten
*affright* (adj.) terrified
*aflight* (adj.) flying
*aflighted* (adj.) distressed

*against* (prep.) opposite, in front of; in preparation for
*aghast* (adj.) frightened
*ail* (n.) beard (of corn)
*alate* (adv.) recently
*algates* (adv.) always, everywhere
*allow* (v.) to praise
*alonely* (adv.) only
*aloof* (adv.) at a distance
*amain* (adv.) with great force, exceedingly
*ambassade* (n.) deputation
*ambrosy* (n.) ambrosia, fabled food of the gods
*amend* (v.) to surpass
*amomy* (n.) amomum (odoriferous plant)
*anon* (adv.) straight away, soon
*apaid* (adj.) pleased
*appair* (v.) to make worse, weaken
*appal* (v.) to damage, impair, make pale (with fear); to fail, decay
*appalled* (adj.) enfeebled
*appoint* (v.) to fix, make ready
*arrant* (adj.) good-for-nothing
*arras work* (n.) tapestries
*artificial* (adj.) skilfully made

*aslake* (v.) to calm
*asp* (n.) poplar
*astonied* (adj.) stunned
*astraught(ed)* (adj.) distraught, distracted
*attach* (v.) to attack
*attaint* (v.) to convict
*attaint* (adj.) infected
*attainted* (adj.) corrupted
*attent* (adj.) attentive
*augment* (v.) to add
*avaunce* (v.) to advance
*avaunt* (v.) to go away
*aver* (n.) beast
*avoid* (v.) to depart
*a-wallop* (phr.) boiling noisily
*awk* (adj.) reverse
*awkly* (adv.) in the wrong direction
*axle-tree* (n.) fixed bar or beam on
    which the opposite wheels of a
    carriage rotate
*ax-tree* (n.) axle-tree, axle, axis
*bain* (adj.) lithe, supple
*baken* (adj.) hardened
*bale* (n.) torment, woe, misery
*baleful* (adj.) evil
*balk* (n.) beam; isthmus
*ban* (v.) to curse
*bane* (n.) death, destruction, ruin, harm
*bare* (n.) bare skin
*battle* (v.) to nourish
*bawd* (n.) pimp
*bayard* (n.) bay horse, taken as a type of
    blindness or blind recklessness
*beak* (v.) to project, stick out
*beam* (n.) timber
*bear-breech* (n.) acanthus
*beck* (n.) nod, gesture
*beck* (v.) to nod
*bedlam* (n.) madman
*bedreint* (adj.) drenched, soaked
*behew* (v.) to hack down
*behight* (v.) to promise

*behoof* (n.) use, benefit, purpose
*beldame* (n.) old woman, nurse
*belike* (adv.) perhaps
*belive* (adv.) hastily, at once
*belk* (v.) to boil, throb; to belch
*bent* (adj.) determined
*beray* (v.) to disfigure, defile, bespatter
*beseem* (v.) to befit
*beseeming* (adj.) befitting, seemly
*beslubber* (v.) to soil, besmear
*besprent* (adj.) besprinkled
*bested* (v.) to assist
*bested* (p.p.) beset
*betake* (v.) to take leave of
*beteem* (v.) to think fit
*betide* (v.) to happen
*beweltered* (adj.) soaked, besmeared
*bewray* (v.) to reveal
*bill* (n.) weapon, broadsword, axe
*bit* (n.) bite
*blab* (n.) chatterer, tell-tale
*blame* (n.) culpability, fault
*blast* (n.) blight, disease
*blast* (v.) to blight
*blaze* (v.) to proclaim
*blin* (v.) to stop
*blo* (adj.) blackish-blue
*blow* (v.) to fume
*blush* (n.) glance
*board* (n.) table
*bob* (v.) to strike
*boin* (v.) to swell
*boisterously* (adv.) fiercely, violently
*bollen* (adj.) swollen
*boot* (v.) to help, be of use, profit
*bote* (v.) (past tense of) to bite
*bought* (n.) bend, curve, loop
*bourd* (n.) merry tale, joke
*bowels* (n.) entrails; offspring
*boxen* (adj.) of boxwood
*braid* (n.) sudden movement; attack
*brainpan* (n.) skull

*brake* (v.) (past tense of) to break
*bratch* (n.) bitch-hound
*brave* (adj.) grand, fine, handsome
*brawned* (adj.) muscular
*bray* (v.) to bruise or pound with
   mortar
*breme* (adj.) celebrated, famed
*brim* (n.) border
*bruit* (n.) rumour, noise, reputation
*bruit* (v.) to rumour, spread abroad
*brunt* (n.) blow, violent attack, shock,
   force
*brunt, at the* (phr.) suddenly
*brust* (v.) (past tense of) to burst
*buck* (n.) body of cart
*bug* (n.) object of terror
*bulchin* (n.) bull-calf
*bulk* (n.) belly
*burd* (n.) offspring
*burgeon* (n.) shoot, swelling bud
*burgonet* (n.) steel cap of infantry or
   helmet with visor
*buskin* (n.) boot reaching to the calf or
   knee
*buskle* (v.) to hurry
*buss* (v.) to kiss
*bustle* (v.) to stir
*buy* (v.) to pay the penalty for
*by-corner* (n.) out-of-the-way corner
*caddow* (n.) jackdaw
*caitiff* (n.) villain
*callet* (n.) lewd woman
*callow* (adj.) without feathers
*can* (v. irreg.) to know, have
   knowledge of
*cankered* (adj.) corrupt, wicked
*cannel-bone* (n.) neck-bone
*canvas* (v.) to discuss, scrutinize, toss
*caparison* (n.) ornamented covering
   spread over horse's saddle or
   harness
*car* (n.) chariot

*carf* (n.) cut
*cark* (n.) distress, care, toil
*carl* (n.) base fellow, boor
*carpet-knight* (n.) stay-at-home soldier
   (contemptuous)
*carrack* (n.) galleon
*cartware* (n.) team of horses
*casting* (n.) vomit
*cate* (n.) food
*cattle* (n.) livestock
*caul* (n.) close-fitting cap, hair-net,
   head-dress
*cense* (v.) to perfume
*certes* (adv.) assuredly
*chafe* (v.) to be angry
*chair* (n.) chariot
*challenge* (v.) to claim
*chamber-work* (n.) sexual indulgence
*champaign* (adj.) level and open
*chance* (n.) fortune
*chank* (v.) to champ, chew, crush
*chanted* (adj.) enchanted
*chare* (adj.) careful, caring
*charily* (adv.) carefully
*chase* (n.) tract of unenclosed land for
   hunting
*cheer* (n.) countenance, expression,
   mood; hospitality
*cheerly* (adj.) cheerful
*child* (v.) to give birth
*childer* (n.) children
*chink* (v.) to crack open
*choler* (n.) anger
*chop* (v.) to drop suddenly
*chrysolite* (n.) a name given to various
   gems of a green colour
*chuff* (n.) boor, rustic
*cinder* (n.) gritty soil
*cindery* (adj.) gritty
*circumstance* (n.) circumlocution
*clawback* (n.) toady, flatterer
*clean* (adv.) completely

*cleanly* (adj.) dexterous
*clee* (n.) claw, hoof
*clerkly* (adv.) learnedly
*clew* (n.) thread
*clift* (n.) cleft
*clift* (v.) to split
*clime* (n.) region
*clip* (v.) to embrace, surround
*clodded* (adj.) stuck together in clods
*closely* (adv.) secretly
*clottered* (adj.) coagulated
*clout* (n.) piece of cloth
*clowre* (n.) surface of ground, grassy ground, turf
*clubbish* (adj.) clownish, addicted to clubs
*clung* (adj.) shrivelled
*coal-carrier* (n.) one who does the dirty work for others
*coast* (v.) to skirt, go
*coat-plight* (n.) fold of coat
*cocker* (v.) to pamper
*cod* (n.) seed pod
*cods* (n.) testicles
*colewort* (n.) cabbage, greens
*coll* (v.) to embrace
*collop* (n.) offspring
*colly* (adj.) coal-black
*colour* (n.) outward appearance concealing the truth, rhetorical ornamentation
*comeliness* (n.) propriety, decency
*company* (v.) to consort
*compass* (n.) circumference, bound, curve
*compass* (v.) to obtain, achieve, contrive
*compassed* (adj.) arched
*compound* (v.) to settle
*comprehend* (v.) to include
*condescend* (v.) to agree
*conduit pipe* (n.) water pipe

*confection* (n.) medicinal preparation
*confound* (v.) to mix up, overthrow, destroy
*confusely* (adv.) confusedly
*consume* (v.) to waste away, perish
*convey* (v.) to sustain, keep; to transform
*cope* (n.) firmament
*cope* (v.) to contend, join battle, come to blows; to meet
*copemate* (n.) adversary, antagonist
*cornel* (n.) Cornelian cherry
*corse* (n.) corpse
*corsie* (n.) grievance
*cote* (n.) cottage
*cote* (v.) to outstrip
*cothe* (v.) to faint
*couch* (v.) to lie down
*countervail* (v.) to make up for
*couple* (n.) leash
*courage* (n.) mind, spirit, disposition
*courser* (n.) charger, stallion
*cousin-german* (n.) cousin
*covert* (n.) covering
*coy* (v.) to caress
*crabfish* (n.) crab
*crab-tree* (adj.) knotted, crooked
*crake* (v.) to grate, creak; to brag
*cranny* (n.) small hole, crack
*cranny* (v.) to crack open
*creak* (v.) to speak stridently or querulously
*cresset* (n.) iron basket holding wood, coal, etc., to be burnt for light
*crink* (n.) twist; intricate turn of thought or speech
*crisp* (adj.) clean
*crooked* (adj.) perverse
*crop* (n.) stomach
*crope* (v.) (past tense of) to creep
*crown* (n.) head
*cuckquean* (n.) female cuckold

*cull* (v.) to embrace

*cullis* (n.) strong broth

*culm* (n.) soot, smut

*cumbered* (adj.) troubled

*cunning* (adj.) skilful

*cunning* (n.) learning, cleverness, skill

*curat* (n.) piece of body armour, generally consisting of breast-plate and back-plate fastened together

*curbed* (adj.) bordered, curved, bowed

*curious* (adj.) inquiring, inquisitive, prying

*curiously* (adv.) skilfully, exquisitely

*curstly* (adv.) savagely

*customably* (adv.) habitually

*dam* (n.) mother

*dankish* (adj.) wet

*dare* (v.) to gaze stupidly, crouch

*dart* (n.) javelin, spear

*daunt* (v.) to subdue, dim

*daw* (n.) simpleton

*default* (n.) defect, fault, offence

*define* (v.) to conclude

*deluded* (adj.) beguiled, deceived

*delve* (v.) to dig up

*demean* (v.) to express

*depend* (v.) to be connected with

*descry* (v.) disclose

*desert* (n.) deserving

*despite* (n.) anger, scorn, vexation, insulting action, injury

*despiteful* (adj.) cruel, spiteful

*despoil* (v.) to deprive

*detect* (v.) to expose, lay open

*device* (n.) plan, scheme

*devise* (v.) to meditate, deliberate

*diffamed* (adj.) infamous

*dight* (v.) to arrange, equip, offer

*digress* (v.) to depart

*ding* (v.) to beat, dash

*dint* (n.) blow, force, thunderclap; impact; indentation

*disappoint* (v.) to prevent

*disbar* (v.) to prevent

*discomfortably* (adv.) inconsolably

*dismay* (v.) to be filled with dismay

*display* (v.) to spread out

*dispoint* (v.) to defeat, frustrate, prevent, disappoint

*dissever* (v.) to separate

*distribution* (n.) term for the rhetorical figure whereby an orderly division or enumeration is made of the principal qualities of a subject

*divorce* (n.) division, separation

*dole* (n.) distribution, delivery (of blows, death)

*doll* (n.) palm of hand

*doom* (n.) law, judgement

*doon* (v.) to do

*dop* (v.) to duck

*dosser* (n.) horn

*doubt* (v.) to fear, be uncertain

*dowel* (n.) bolt fastening together two pieces of wood, stone, etc. or plugs of wood driven into a wall to receive nails

*drave* (v.) (past tense of) to drive

*dreary* (adj.) melancholy

*dreep* (v.) to drip, droop, let fall in drops

*dreint* (adj.) overwhelmed, drowned

*drib* (v.) to shoot (arrow) so that it falls short

*drift* (n.) scheme

*drudge* (n.) servile creature

*drumslade* (n.) drum

*dug* (n.) breast

*dure* (v.) to endure, continue in existence

*ear* (v.) to plough

*eche* (v.) to increase

*eft* (adv.) afterwards, again

*eft . . . eft* first . . . then

*eftsoon* (adv.) again, a second time
*eftsoons* (adv.) soon afterwards
*egal* (adj.) equal
*eke* (adv.) also
*elf* (n.) child
*eme* (n.) uncle
*endue* (v.) to endow
*enforce* (v.) to drive, exert; to overcome by violence, rape
*engender* (v.) to copulate
*enhance* (v.) to lift up with pride
*ensue* (trans. v.) to follow
*ensure* (v.) to betroth
*entreat* (v.) to treat, handle, deal with
*environ* (v.) to encircle
*erewhile* (adv.) formerly
*erewhile . . . erewhile* at one time . . . at another
*erne* (n.) eagle
*erst* (adv.) before, first
*escry* (v.) to discover
*eschew* (v.) to abstain
*estate* (n.) condition
*esteem* (v.) to deem, think, judge
*everych one* (adj., pron.) every one
*exact* (v.) to extract
*exception* (n.) objection, cavil
*exempt* (v.) to remove
*fact* (n.) deed
*fail* (v.) to be lacking
*fain* (adj.) glad, eager, obliged
*fairy* (n.) the inhabitants of fairy-land collectively
*falchion* (n.) broad curved sword
*fancy* (n.) notion, whim, delusive imagination
*fardel* (v.) to furl
*fast* (adj.) obstinate, assured
*fat* (n.) vat
*fear* (v.) to frighten
*featly* (adv.) deftly
*fee* (n.) reward, wages, prize, spoil

*fell* (adj.) fierce, cruel
*felly* (n.) curved piece of wood jointed with others to form the rim of a wheel
*fence* (v.) to protect, shield
*fenny* (adj.) muddy
*fere* (n.) spouse
*fervent* (adj.) burning
*fet* (v.) to fetch
*fetch* (n.) contrivance, trick
*fierce* (v.) to inflame
*fillet* (n.) headband, ribbon
*filthy* (adj.) contemptible
*fine* (n.) end
*fine* (v.) to refine
*fine, in* (phr.) finally
*fisk* (v.) to frisk
*fistock* (n.) fist
*fistula* (n.) ulcer
*fitter* (n.) fragment
*flacker* (v.) to flap
*flag* (n.) rush, reed
*flare* (v.) to spread out
*flaring* (adj.) spread out
*flask* (v.) to flap; to cause to flutter
*flat* (adv.) entirely, directly
*flattering* (adj.) pleasing to the imagination
*flaw* (n.) sudden gust of wind
*fleck* (v.) to flutter
*flee* (v.) to fly
*fleet* (adj.) swift
*fleet* (adv.) shallowly
*fleet* (v.) to travel, sail, flow, drift, flit
*flicker* (v.) to flutter, flap
*flight* (adj.) frightened, set flying; swift
*flighted* (adj.) frightened, put to flight
*flight-shot* (n.) distance of the flight of an arrow
*fling* (v.) to kick and plunge violently (of a horse)
*flitch* (n.) side

*flood* (n.) sea, river

*flourish* (v.) to adorn

*fodder* (n.) food, grazing for cattle

*foil* (n.) defeat; track of hunted animal

*foil* (v.) to defile, pollute; to overthrow

*foil, take the* (phr.) to be defeated, take a fall

*foin* (n.) thrust, push

*fond* (adj.) foolish

*fondling* (n.) fond or foolish person

*food* (v.) to feed

*footing* (n.) footprint

*footmanship* (n.) skill in running

*forbear* (v.) to do without

*force* (n.) strength

*force* (v.) to impose; to care, be concerned

*forcement* (n.) compelling motive

*ford* (n.) sea

*fordead* (adj.) utterly still and speechless

*fordo* (v.) to kill

*forecast* (n.) planning

*foredoom* (n.) judgement made in advance, prophecy

*forehend* (v.) to seize beforehand

*forelaid* (adj.) overcome, overpowered

*fore-misgiving* (n.) foreboding

*forepast* (adj.) gone by (of time)

*foreseen* (adj.) aware of, having prior knowledge of

*forespeak* (v.) to predict

*forespeaking* (n.) prediction

*foretop* (n.) hair over the forehead

*forfend* (v.) to forbid

*forgo* (v.) to leave, lose

*forgrown* (adj.) grown to a huge size, overgrown, misshapen; covered with hair

*forladen* (adj.) encumbered

*forlorn* (adj.) morally lost

*formest* (adj.) first

*forpine* (v.) to pine away

*forslow* (v.) to be slow, dilatory

*forspent* (adj.) worn out

*forswollen* (adj.) hugely swollen

*forthink* (v.) to repent

*forwearied* (adj.) exhausted

*founder* (n.) originator

*frame* (v.) to prepare

*frank* (v.) to cram, feed greedily

*fraught* (v.) to load

*fray* (v.) to frighten, assault, deflower

*frayne* (v.) to demand

*freckled* (adj.) yellowish-brown

*freke* (n.) man

*frequent* (v.) to practise, use habitually

*fret* (v.) to adorn; to devour, destroy

*friend* (n.) relative

*frisk* (n.) dance

*frith* (n.) wood

*frizzled* (adj.) curly

*frizzle-topped* (adj.) curly-haired

*fro* (prep.) from

*frolic* (adj.) merry

*frosh* (n.) frog

*frow* (n.) priestess or female votary of Bacchus

*froward* (adj.) naughty, perverse

*frush* (v.) to smash

*fumble* (v.) to speak indistinctly

*fume* (n.) anger, passion

*fume* (v.) to burn

*furiousness* (n.) madness

*furniture* (n.) apparel, adjuncts, equipment

*furred* (adj.) coated with morbid matter

*gad* (n.) metal spike

*gad* (v.) to rove, wander

*gaincope* (v.) to intercept

*gall* (v.) to graze

*gat* (v.) (past tense of) to get

*gay* (n.) flower

*gear* (n.) talk, matter

*geat* (n.) goat

*gender* (v.) to beget, produce
*gest* (n.) tale
*ghastful* (adj.) dreadful
*gin* (v.) to begin
*gird* (v.) to jibe, sneer, strike; to rush, start, spring
*glad* (v.) to make glad
*glade* (n.) opening
*glance* (v.) to allude obliquely; to dart, flash
*glaster* (v.) to glitter
*glister* (v.) to glitter
*glory* (v.) to boast
*gloss* (n.) obscure words; superficial lustre
*gnar* (v.) to snarl, growl
*gon* (v.) to go
*goodman* (n.) husband
*goodwife* (n.) wife
*gorget* (n.) throat armour or clothing
*goshawk* (n.) a large, short-winged hawk
*gowl* (n.) front of neck
*grece* (n.) stair
*grew'nd* (n.) greyhound
*griffe* (v.) to graft
*grin* (n.) snare
*gripe* (n.) vulture
*gripe* (v.) to clench, grip, seize
*gripple* (adj.) niggardly
*groin* (n.) snout
*grudge* (v.) to grumble, complain
*guard* (n.) ornamental border
*guard* (v.) to trim
*guerdon* (n.) reward
*guise* (n.) custom
*gull* (n.) gullet; gully
*gull* (v.) to hollow out with running water
*gut* (n.) passage of water
*hain* (n.) pasture preserved from grazing

*hale* (v.) to drag
*halt* (v.) to walk unsteadily
*ham* (n.) thigh
*hand, out of* (phr.) straight away
*handsel* (n.) omen
*handsomeness* (n.) convenience
*handwarp* (n.) kind of cloth with warp prepared in a particular way
*hap* (n.) chance, fortune
*hap* (v.) to chance
*harbourless* (adj.) inhospitable
*hard* (adj.) unmanageable, unfeeling
*hard* (adv.) close
*hardly* (adv.) boldly
*hardy* (adj.) bold, presumptuous
*harness* (n.) armour
*harp* (v.) to guess, give voice to
*harry* (v.) to drag
*haught* (adj.) lofty, proud, arrogant
*head* (v.) to behead
*headily* (adv.) rashly, impetuously
*heady* (adj.) headstrong
*heap* (n.) multitude
*heavy* (adj.) angry, sorrowful
*hent* (v.) to lay hold of, seize
*herd* (n.) keeper of herd of animals
*heretoforn* (adv.) formerly, before now
*hernsew* (n.) heron
*hest* (n.) command, promise
*hie* (v.) to hasten, go quickly
*hight* (v.) to be called
*hill* (v.) to cover
*hind* (n.) servant
*hing* (v.) (past tense of) to hang
*hire* (n.) payment, reward
*hoar* (adj.) grey (-haired); keen, biting
*hobby-hawk* (n.) small falcon
*hoise* (v.) to hoist, rise
*hose* (n.) stockings or breeches
*host* (n.) battle
*host* (v.) to lodge
*hounce* (n.) ornament on collar of horse

*hove* (v.) to behove
*hover* (v.) to cover
*hudder-mudder* (n.) hugger-mugger, secrecy
*hugy* (adj.) huge
*hurdle* (n.) wattled frame
*hyen* (n.) hyena
*imbrue* (v.) to stain, soak
*imp* (n.) offspring
*impeach* (v.) to hurt
*impeachment* (n.) hindrance
*imply* (v.) to contain
*impugn* (v.) to fight against
*incontinent* (adv.) immediately
*indifferent* (adj.) impartial
*indifferently* (adv.) equally, impartially
*indite* (v.) to utter, dictate
*infamed* (adj.) infamous
*infamy* (n.) scandalous reputation
*infest* (adj.) hostile
*ingrate* (adj.) ungrateful
*intermit* (v.) to stop for a while
*intertalk* (v.) to speak to each other
*inwards* (n.) entrails
*ire* (n.) anger
*ivy-tod* (n.) ivy-bush
*iwis* (adv.) certainly, indeed
*jack* (n.) knave
*jade* (n.) horse (usually contemptuous)
*jamb* (n.) side post of doorway
*jennet* (n.) horse (specifically, a small Spanish horse)
*jet* (v.) to stroll
*job* (v.) to peck, stab
*joy* (v.) to enjoy
*juggling* (adj.) deceptive
*keep* (n.) care, notice
*kell* (n.) kiln
*kemb* (v.) to comb
*kenned* (adj.) known
*kenning* (n.) sight
*kie* (n.) cattle

*kind* (n.) nature
*kindle* (v.) to give birth
*kindly* (adv.) naturally, properly
*kine* (n.) cattle
*kirtle* (n.) gown
*knack* (n.) trick, device
*knap* (n.) summit
*knap* (v.) to strike
*knee-pan* (n.) knee-cap
*knit* (v.) to put together
*knop* (n.) lump
*knowledge* (v.) to acknowledge
*label* (n.) ribbon
*lance* (v.) to pierce
*lap* (n.) skirt
*large-flewed* (adj.) with large hanging chaps
*latch* (v.) to catch, receive
*late* (adv.) recently
*latter* (adj.) last
*lavish* (adj.) unrestrained
*lay* (v.) to strike
*leasing* (n.) lying, falsehood
*leechcraft* (n.) medicine, medicinal science
*leese* (v.) to lose
*leet* (n.) district under jurisdiction
*leman* (n.) lover
*lenger* (adj., adv.) longer
*let* (n.) cause of delay
*let* (v.) to hinder, obstruct, prevent, hold back
*level* (v.) to aim
*lever* (n.) pole, beam, crowbar, etc
*leveret* (n.) young hare
*lewd* (adj.) wicked
*lewdness* (n.) wickedness
*lief* (adj.) beloved
*liefer* (adv.) rather
*lightly* (adv.) easily, quickly
*lights* (n.) lungs
*like* (v.) to please

*list* (v.) to wish, like
*lither* (adj.) sluggish, withered, impotent; insubstantial; supple
*load* (adj.) laden
*loathsomeness* (n.) disgust, repugnance
*long* (v.) to belong
*lore* (n.) advice, instruction
*losel* (n.) good-for-nothing
*lote-tree* (n.) lotus-tree
*lotted* (adj.) allotted.
*lowering* (adj.) gloomy, threatening
*lure* (v.) to call loudly
*luskish* (adj.) sluggish
*maim* (n.) injury
*main* (adj.) huge, strong, solid
*mainly* (adv.) forcefully, violently
*make* (n.) spouse, mate
*malapertness* (n.) presumptuousness
*manchet* (n.) bread
*margent* (n.) margin
*marish* (n.) marsh
*masty* (n.) mastiff
*matron* (n.) wife
*maugre* (prep.) despite
*maund* (n.) wicker basket
*maw* (n.) stomach
*may* (n.) maid, virgin
*maze* (n.) state of bewilderment
*mazedness* (n.) stupor, bewilderment
*mazer* (n.) drinking-cup
*meacock* (n.) coward, weakling, effeminate person
*meddle* (v.) to mingle
*meed* (n.) wages, reward
*meet* (adj.) suitable
*mell* (v.) to interfere, speak
*meng* (v.) to mix
*ment* (v.) (past tense of ) to mix
*mention* (n.) evidence
*mere* (n.) pond
*mete* (v.) to measure

*mickle* (adj., adv.) much
*mind* (v.) to intend, remember, bear in mind
*minion* (n.) darling
*minion* (adj.) dainty
*miscontent* (adj.) displeased
*misdeem* (v.) to suspect, think evil of
*misdoubt* (v.) to fear
*misgive* (v.) to be apprehensive about, have forebodings about
*mistrust* (v.) to anticipate (something bad)
*mo* (adj., adv.) more
*moan* (v.) to lament
*moil* (v.) to worry, be restless
*mood* (n.) anger
*moorish* (adj.) of a moor
*mop* (v.) to grimace
*mops* (n.) young girl
*mought* (v.) (past tense of ) may
*mould* (n.) earth, ground
*mow* (v.) to grimace
*murrain* (n.) plague
*muster* (v.) to appear
*nat* (adv.) not
*natheless* (adv.) nevertheless
*naughtiness* (n.) wickedness
*naughty* (adj.) wicked
*nave* (n.) the central part of wheels into which the end of the axle-tree is inserted and from which the spokes radiate
*ne* (conj.) nor
*neat* (n.) cattle
*neatherd* (n.) cowherd
*neb* (n.) beak, mouth, bill
*nephew* (n.) grandson, descendant
*nether* (adj.) lower
*neuter* (adj.) neutral
*new-yeaned* (adj.) new-born
*nock* (n.) notched piece of horn in butt-end of arrow

*nocked* (adj.) fitted in notch of the
    bowstring, ready for shooting
*noddle* (n.) nape
*noddy* (n.) simpleton
*noint* (v.) to anoint
*nonce, for the* (phr.) for the particular
    purpose, for the occasion
*not* (v.) to cut (short hair or beard)
*nurture* (n.) education
*obit* (n.) funeral rites
*object* (v.) to bring forward; to express
    (disapproval)
*obsequy* (n.) funeral, ceremony
*open* (v.) to bring up (in conversation)
*original* (n.) origin
*orped* (adj.) valiant, bold, fierce,
    furious, strenuous
*osier* (n.) a species of willow
*ouch* (n.) brooch, necklace, etc.
*outrage* (v.) to rage furiously
*outrageous* (adj.) extreme
*outrageously* (adv.) excessively, with
    great force
*overcuriously* (adv.) overmeticulously
*overdreep* (v.) to droop over, overhang
*overdrip* (v.) to overhang
*overfell* (adj.) very fierce
*overlade* (v.) to overburden
*overseen* (adj.) rash, deluded
*overthwart* (adv., prep.) across
*packing* (n.) intrigue, plotting
*painful* (adj.) painstaking
*pall* (n.) cloak
*palmed* (adj.) flat with projecting points
*palsy* (n.) disease of nervous system
*panion* (n.) criminal
*pap* (n.) nipple
*parcel* (n.) part
*parget* (n.) plaster, roughcast
*pass* (v.) to care, regard, concern
    oneself; to neglect, omit
*passing* (adj.) enormous

*passing* (adv.) exceedingly
*pate* (n.) head
*paunch* (v.) to disembowel
*paynim* (n., adj.) pagan
*peakishly* (adv.) obscurely, remotely
*peevish* (adj.) mean
*peise* (v.) to balance
*pelf* (n.) property; riches (deprecatory),
    trash, worthless thing
*pelt* (n.) pelting of missiles
*pelting* (adj.) paltry
*pend* (n.) pen
*pent* (adj.) imprisoned, penned
*perbrake* (v.) to vomit
*perdie* (int.) indeed
*perilous* (adj.) terrible
*pestered* (adj.) clogged, thickly massed,
    troubled
*pight* (v.) to place, pitch
*pine* (v.) to afflict with suffering
*pipkin* (n.) small earthenware pot
*pismire* (n.) ant
*pitch-tree* (n.) resinous conifer
*plaint* (n.) complaint, lament
*plaintful* (adj.) mournful
*plash* (n.) pool
*plaster* (n.) medicine
*plat* (n.) plan, ground plan, outline
    (used both of land planning and of
    literary invention)
*platter-mouth* (n.) broad flat mouth
*plight* (n.) fashion, manner, state,
    (good) condition
*plight* (v.) to give as a pledge
*plump* (adv.) with a sudden drop
*poleaxe* (n.) battle-axe
*policy* (n.) cunning
*pommy* (n.) pumice
*pomp* (n.) ceremonial procession
*port* (n.) style of living, social position;
    bearing
*portly* (adj.) stately

*possess* (v.) to occupy
*post alone* (phr.) entirely alone
*postern gate* (n.) private or side gate
*pouldron* (n.) shoulder-plate
*prank* (v.) to dance, prance arrogantly
*prate* (v.) to chatter
*preaching* (n.) discourse, serious
    exhortation
*precinct* (n.) boundaries
*presently* (adv.) in person
*press* (v.) to push, drive, assail, harass,
    attack
*prest* (v.) to enlist
*pretend* (v.) to offer, profess
*pretensedly* (adv.) feignedly
*prew* (adj.) valiant
*prick* (n.) spike, thorn; apex, highest
    point
*prick* (v.) to make a track in running
*pritch* (n.) offence
*privity* (n.) secret thing
*privy* (adj.) secret
*process* (n.) narrative
*profess* (v.) to announce
*proof* (n.) trial, experiment
*proof, put in* (phr.) to test, assay
*protest* (v.) to call to witness
*prove* (v.) to try
*pulled* (adj.) shorn
*quail* (v.) to fade, fail, become weak
*queach* (n.) dense growth of bushes,
    thicket
*queachy* (adj.) boggy; paltry, feeble
*quean* (n.) strumpet
*quest* (n.) knights engaged in adventure
*quetch* (v.) to utter a sound, stir
*quick* (n.) skin
*quick* (adj.) alive, pregnant
*quire* (n.) gathering of leaves in a book
*quite* (v.) to requite
*quite* (adj.) free
*quook* (v.) (past tense of) to quake

*rage* (n.) (sexual) passion
*raise* (v.) to utter, speak loudly
*rake* (n.) track, groove
*rake* (v.) to draw together
*ramp* (v.) to tear
*ramping* (adj.) standing erect, showing
    fierceness
*rank* (adj.) abundant; wicked,
    rebellious
*rascal* (adj.) common
*raspis* (n.) raspberries
*rate* (n.) manner
*rate* (v.) to scold, chide
*rathe* (adv.) early
*raught* (v.) to catch hold of, reach at
*ray* (n.) array
*raze* (v.) to graze
*read* (v.) to interpret, explain; to
    foretell, declaim
*rear-roasted* (adj.) undercooked
*reave* (v.) to plunder
*rebated* (adj.) blunted
*reckless* (adj.) thoughtless, careless
*reckon* (v.) to go through (a list)
*recomfort* (v.) to soothe, console
*redoubted* (adj.) revered, feared
*redound* (v.) to echo, result, accrue
*reek* (n.) fume, vapour; water-plant,
    seaweed, wrack
*rejoiced* (adj.) delighted
*remorse* (n.) biting force
*require* (v.) to inquire (about)
*rere* (n.) noise, shout, voice
*residue* (n.) the others, the rest
*resolve* (v.) to melt, dissolve
*respect* (n.) regard
*respect, in* (phr.) in comparison
*resty* (adj.) rancid; restive
*revolt* (v.) to return
*ribald* (n.) rascal
*riched* (adj.) enriched
*riddle* (n.) coarse-meshed sieve

*ridge-bone* (n.) spine
*rig* (v.) to play the wanton
*rind* (n.) bark
*rist* (n.) rise
*rive* (v.) to pierce
*rivelled* (adj.) wrinkled, shrivelled
*roche* (n.) rock
*rock* (n.) distaff
*rod* (n.) stick, shoot (of plant)
*roil* (v.) to roam
*roister* (n.) swaggering bully
*room* (n.) place
*rope* (v.) to gush, fall in torrents
*rore* (v.) to stir up
*rosin* (n.) resin
*rother-beast* (n.) ox
*round* (adj.) clear
*rout* (n.) company, band
*rovers, at* (phr.) at random
*ruck* (v.) to squat, perch
*rudeness* (n.) roughness
*rudesby* (n.) uneducated person
*ruff* (n.) elation, pride
*runagate* (n.) fugitive
*ruth* (n.) pity
*ruthful* (adj.) pitiful
*sadly* (adv.) steadily, heavily
*sallow* (n.) willow
*sample* (n.) example
*sanguine* (adj.) blood-red, ruddy
*scale* (v.) to ascend
*scalt* (v.) to scald
*scalt* (adj.) enflamed, raw
*scantling* (n.) sample, rough sketch
*scape* (n.) transgression
*scape* (v.) to escape
*scar* (v.) to clip, trim (a tree or branch)
*scareful* (adj.) terrifying
*scathe* (n.) harm
*scud* (v.) to dart, run quickly
*sear* (adj.) dry

*sear* (v.) to dry up, blight, burn
*seld* (adv.) seldom
*servage* (n.) servitude
*set abroach* (phr.) to broach
*several* (adj.) separate
*shag-haired* (adj.) shaggy-haired
*shawm* (n.) medieval instrument of the oboe class
*sheen* (adj.) shining
*sheepish* (adj.) simple, silly
*sheer* (adj.) bright, shining, thin
*shent* (adj.) disgraced
*shift* (n.) subterfuge, contrivance, expedient
*shift* (v.) to change; to escape, slip away; to manage; to put people off with a subterfuge
*shirl* (adj.) shrill; rough (of hair)
*shirlly* (adv.) shrilly
*shirlness* (n.) shrillness
*shiver* (n.) fragment
*shiver* (v.) to splinter
*shock* (n.) crowd
*shoring* (n.) slope
*shoring* (adj.) sloping, bordering
*shoringness* (n.) slopingness
*shream* (v.) to scream
*sicker* (adj.) certain, firm
*side* (adj.) large
*sidle* (trans. v.) to turn sideways
*silly* (adj.) simple, pitiful
*simple* (n.) plant, herb
*sith* (adv., prep., conj.) since
*sithe* (n.) time
*skene* (n.) dagger, small sword
*skill* (n.) reason
*skill* (v.) to avail, help, matter
*slake* (v.) to diminish, loosen
*slaky* (adj.) muddy
*sledge* (n.) large heavy hammer
*sleight* (n.) trickery, skill, skilfulness
*slight* (adj.) insubstantial

*slighty* (adj.) light, insubstantial

*slobber* (v.) to blubber, cry

*slug* (n.) sluggard

*slug* (v.) to lie idly

*smally* (adv.) very little

*snarl* (v.) to ensnare, entangle

*snarled* (adj.) twisted

*snetched* (adj.) slaughtered

*snuff* (v.) to draw up through the nostrils

*sod* (v.) to soak

*sod* (adj.) boiled

*sometime* (adv.) occasionally, at a particular time in the past

*soot* (adj.) sweet

*soothfast* (adj.) truthful

*sorry* (adj.) paltry

*sort* (n.) crowd

*souse* (n.) heavy blow

*souse* (v.) to swoop

*spalt* (adj.) brittle

*sped* (v.) (past tense of) to succeed

*speed* (n.) success, good fortune

*speed* (v.) to succeed

*spill* (v.) to kill

*spindle-shank* (n.) long thin leg

*spire* (v.) to rise

*spirget* (n.) pin or peg for hanging things on

*spirk* (n.) sprout, shoot

*spite* (n.) harm, injury, outrage, malice, hatred

*spite* (at) (v.) to regard or treat spitefully, maliciously

*spitter* (n.) young deer

*splay* (v.) to spread out

*spoil* (v.) to deprive by force, strip, rob, despoil

*sprent* (adj.) sprinkled

*springe* (n.) snare

*sprite* (n.) spirit

*spurn* (v.) to kick

*square, out of* (phr.) not in the proper or normal way, out of order

*stablish* (v.) to establish, ratify

*stack* (v.) (past tense of) to stick

*stain* (v.) to put in the shade

*stale* (v.) (past tense of) to steal

*stale* (adj.) hackneyed, commonplace

*stalworth* (adj.) strong, courageous

*starched* (adj.) stiffened

*stark* (adj.) rigid

*state* (n.) high rank

*stateliness* (n.) haughtiness, arrogance, high estate

*stay* (n.) restraint; reliance, support

*stay* (v.) to restrain, hinder, delay; to support

*stead* (n.) place

*steal* (n.) shaft

*stew* (n.) pond

*stews* (n.) brothel

*stint* (v.) to stop

*stock* (n.) lifeless trunk

*stomach* (n.) the seat of passions; often expressive of pride, obstinacy, malice or spirit, courage

*stomach* (v.) to be angry, resent

*stoop* (n.) post, pillar

*stound* (n.) state of stupefaction; time

*stour* (adj.) violent, fierce

*stourness* (n.) roughness, greatness

*stout* (adj.) proud

*stoutness* (n.) arrogance, stubbornness, valour

*stover* (n.) winter food for cattle

*strain* (v.) to clasp

*strake* (v.) (past tense of) to strike

*straught* (adj.) distraught, out of one's mind

*strave* (v.) (past tense of) to strive

*stripe* (n.) blow, stroke; mark left by a lash

*stripling* (n.) youth

*stroy* (v.) to destroy
*stroy-good* (n.) destructive creature
*stub* (n.) tree stump
*sty* (v.) to rise, ascend
*subscribe* (v.) to write
*subtle* (adj.) finely powdered; thin (of air)
*subtleness* (n.) delicacy
*suchy* (adj., adv.) such
*sue* (v.) to follow, issue; to petition
*suffer* (v.) to submit to
*supply* (v.) to compensate for
*suppose* (v.) to consider
*surmise* (v.) to allege, feign
*surmised* (adj.) made up, imagined
*surmount* (v.) to mount, rise, surpass
*surprise* (v.) to overpower, capture
*swage* (v.) to assuage
*swale* (n.) shade
*swart* (adj.) dark, swarthy
*sweak* (v.) to swing
*swelt* (v.) to scorch, burn, swoon
*swelting* (adj.) sweltering
*swift* (n.) newt
*swing* (n.) authority
*swinge* (v.) to brandish
*swound* (v.) to faint
*table* (n.) tablet
*tackling* (n.) tackle
*target* (n.) light round shield
*tarriance* (n.) delay
*tattle* (v.) to chatter, gossip
*team-ware* (n.) team of horses
*teen* (n.) anger, rage, grief
*teil* (n.) lime or linden tree
*tenantry* (n.) estate
*tettish* (adj.) obstinate
*thereuntil* (adv.) thereunto
*thew* (n.) attribute, virtue
*thick* (n.) thicket
*thirl* (v.) to pierce, spin
*tho* (adv.) then

*thorough* (prep.) through
*three-tinéd* (adj.) three-pronged
*throat-boll* (n.) larynx, throat
*through(ly)* (adv.) thoroughly, completely
*thwart* (adv.) across
*thyrse* (n.) staff, sometimes wreathed with ivy or vine branches, borne by Bacchus and his votaries
*tide* (n.) time
*tile-sherd* (n.) broken piece of tile
*tillman* (n.) ploughman
*timbrel* (n.) tambourine or similar instrument
*timely* (adv.) early
*timpan* (n.) drum, tambourine
*tine* (n.) branch of deer's horn; one of various leguminous plants growing as weeds among corn, etc
*tinking* (adj.) clashing (of metal)
*tire* (v.) to tear, tug
*tod* (n.) bush
*toil* (n.) net set to enclose the space into which quarry is then driven
*toll* (v.) to draw, allure
*toot* (v.) to gaze
*tower* (v.) to soar
*toy* (n.) light caress; trick, curiosity
*toy* (v.) to caress
*toying* (adj.) trifling
*toze* (v.) to comb, unravel fibres of
*trace* (n.) the pair of chains or straps by which a horse's collar is connected to the splinter-bar of a chariot
*trade* (n.) method
*train* (n.) deceit, trickery, stratagem
*traverse* (n.) curtain, hanging
*treat* (v.) to negotiate
*trice* (v.) to pull
*trim* (adj.) fine, suitable
*trimly* (adv.) finely
*troll* (v.) to whirl, roll

*trot* (n.) old woman
*trouble* (v.) to interrupt
*troublous* (adj.) grievous
*trow* (v.) to trust, believe
*trull* (n.) girl, strumpet, prostitute
*try* (v.) to find out
*tubbish* (adj.) like a tub
*turmoil* (v.) to move restlessly
*turn* (n.) alteration
*turned* (adj.) altered
*tush* (n.) tusk
*tway* (adj.) two
*twibill* (n.) double-bladed axe
*unappalled* (adj.) undiminished
*unattainted* (adj.) unblemished
*unavoided* (adj.) unavoidable
*unbeware(s)* (adv.) unawares
*uncouth* (adj.) unknown
*uncouth* (n.) news
*uneath* (adv.) scarcely
*unhandsomely* (adv.) discourteously
*unkembed* (adj.) uncombed
*unleeful* (adj.) unlawful
*unnurtured* (adj.) undisciplined
*unpartial* (adj.) impartial
*unpend* (v.) to release
*unsurmised* (adj.) not feigned
*until* (prep.) unto
*unwares* (adv.) unexpectedly, without (his) being aware
*unweeting* (adj.) unwitting
*unwieldy* (adj.) lacking in strength
*unwonted* (adj.) unusual
*unwrought* (adj.) uncompleted, not done
*ure* (n.) use
*ure, out of* (phr.) obsolete
*use to* (v.) to be accustomed to
*usurp* (v.) to take possession of
*utter* (adj.) furthest
*utter* (adv.) utterly
*varlet* (n.) rogue

*vaunce* (v.) to advance
*vaunt* (n.) boast
*vaunt* (v.) to boast
*venge* (n.) revenge
*virtue* (n.) strength
*void* (v.) to dismiss
*wag* (n.) mischievous boy
*wain* (n.) wagon
*wale* (n.) wave, current
*wanze* (v.) to fade away, waste
*ward* (n.) shelter, protection
*ward* (v.) to guard
*ware* (adj.) aware, conscious
*ware* (n.) genitals
*warry* (adj.) gnarled
*waryish* (adj.) unwholesome-looking
*washing* (adj.) swashing
*waste* (v.) to ravage, spend
*watershoot* (n.) water carried off by drainage
*watershot* (n.) sudden flood
*wax* (v.) to grow, become
*weal* (n.) well-being
*weasand* (n.) throat, windpipe
*wedlock* (n.) wife
*weed* (n.) garment
*ween* (v.) to suppose, think, believe
*welkin* (n.) sky, heaven
*well-beseen* (adj.) good-looking
*welter* (v.) to writhe, be soaked
*whelked* (adj.) twisted, ridged (like a whelk)
*whelm* (v.) to cover over, crush
*whenas* (adv.) when
*whereas* (adv., conj.) where
*whether* (pron., adj.) which
*whewl* (v.) to cry plaintively, howl
*whiles* (conj.) while
*whipstock* (n.) handle of whip
*whist* (v.) to fall silent
*whist* (adj.) silent
*whizz* (v.) to rustle

*wight* (n.) person
*wight* (adj.) swift
*wind* (oneself) out (v.) to extricate
    (oneself)
*wind* (refl. v.) to go on one's way
*windlass* (n.) circuit
*windlass, fetch a* (phr.) to make a circuit
*wist* (v.) to know
*wistly* (adv.) intently
*wit* (n.) intellect, reason, sense,
    cleverness, wisdom
*wit* (v.) to know, find out
*witch* (n.) witch elm or mountain ash
*witching* (adj.) bewitching
*withal* (adv.) moreover, as well
*withe* (n.) halter made of twisted
    branches
*womb* (n.) belly, entrails
*wone* (v.) to dwell, inhabit
*wont* (n.) custom
*wonted* (adj.) usual, accustomed
*wood* (adj.) insane, furious
*woodness* (n.) madness, fury

*woodspeck* (n.) woodpecker
*woodward* (n.) forester
*woof* (n.) weft, thread going from side
    to side of web
*worm* (n.) any animal that creeps or
    crawls, reptile
*wot* (v.) to know
*wreak* (n.) revenge
*wreak* (v.) to revenge
*wreck* (n.) something cast ashore from a
    wrecked ship
*writhen* (adj.) coiled, twined
*wry* (v.) to conceal; to twist, contort
*yeaning-time* (n.) time of birth
*year-mind* (n.) anniversary requiem
    service
*yearn* (v.) to mourn, grieve
*yede, yode* (v.) (past tense of) to go
*yerk* (v.) to strike smartly
*yesk* (v.) to belch
*ygrow* (p.p.) grown
*youngling* (n.) youngster
*younker* (n.) youth

# INDEX

Only major figures are recorded in this index. Alternative names and variant spellings are given. The diaeresis is used to help with pronunciation.